THE
RIGHTS OF LAW ENFORCEMENT OFFICERS

6th Edition

by Will Aitchison

LRIS PUBLICATIONS
PORTLAND, OREGON

Published by Labor Relations Information System
3021 NE Broadway
Portland OR 97232
503.282.5440
www.LRIS.com

Aitchison, William Bruce, 1951 -

ISBN 978-1-880607-24-4

Cover design by Marc R. Fuller

ACKNOWLEDGMENTS

Writing a 534-page book with 1,815 footnotes referring to thousands of cases and statutes, and somehow producing something that remotely reads like it was written in English, requires a group effort and tremendous teamwork. Debbie Friels led our efforts, keeping the writing of the book on schedule, coordinating all aspects of the production of the book, and facing down the daunting task of formatting the final copy of the book and getting the book printed. My assistant Carol Green, who has run my law practice for more than 15 years, not only proofread the book but also held my professional life together while the book was being written.

Marc Fuller at LRIS was responsible for not only designing the cover of the book, but also coming up with the idea for and creating the book's CD, a task that meant organizing and formatting hundreds of cases. Mallory Maddox, weighing in from North Carolina, not only checked the hundreds of new citations in the book, but made editing changes that improved the flow of the text. Anya King of my law office and Tanja Olson of LRIS both proofread the book, and their careful eyes caught many things the rest of us missed. I never would have had the time to write this edition of the book without the immensely capable Breanne Sheetz, our law firm's associate attorney who gave me the breath of relief from my FLSA practice necessary to research this book.

My greatest thanks are to my clients. I've represented law enforcement officers and their labor organizations almost 30 years, and it's been a wonderful journey. I've had challenging cases in areas of law more varied than most lawyers ever see, cases that allow one to stretch the mind and use the imagination. It's one of those law practices – and I don't mean to overstate it – where when the day is done, you feel as if you've helped make someone's life a bit better.

But the best part has been the people. I look with the greatest respect at the job done by police officers, and often marvel how unsuited I would be for the work. The friendships I have gained over the years with officers across the country remain one of my greatest treasures. To Rob Heun, Mark O'Neill (the annual New Jersey bagels are a special treat), Steve James, Mike Mosco, Everett Robbins, Rick Weisman, Derek Hsieh, Todd Shanks, Mark Herron, Jay Pentheny, and Tenari Ma'afala; and to those who have enlivened LRIS seminars over the years, people like Joe Cornell, Kreg Muller, Bill Cornell, Terry McAllister, John Chrystal, Mark Whitley, and Cheryl Smith; to my law partners and co-counsel, including the indestructible Chris Vick, Jeff Julius, Hillary McClure, Derrick Isackson, Vlad Devens, Bob Kiesnowski, Gary Orseck, Damon Taaffe, Gary Messing, Jim Lane, Mike Napier, the gang at Rains, Lucia & Stern, and to others too numerous to mention (you know who you are), I am more than grateful for your acquaintance.

A special word of appreciation is in order for my wife, Valerie, once a labor lawyer in her own right and now a domestic relations mediator. She not only tolerated the hours spent writing the book, but she proofread every single word of this book, a task few would take on voluntarily. Her changes improved the book greatly.

ABOUT THE AUTHOR

Will Aitchison is a Portland, Oregon attorney who has, over the course of his career, represented over 100 law enforcement and firefighter labor organizations in five western states.

Aitchison graduated from the University of Oregon (Honors College) in 1973, and received his Doctor of Jurisprudence Degree from Georgetown University Law Center in Washington, D.C. in 1976. After two years of clerking for Chief Judge Herbert Schwab of the Oregon Court of Appeals, Aitchison entered private practice and has been representing labor organizations since that time. In addition to his private practice, Aitchison has served as both an arbitrator and a pro tem district court judge, and has contributed numerous articles to various periodicals.

Aitchison is the author of The FMLA: Understanding the Family & Medical Leave Act, Interest Arbitration (Second Edition), The FLSA – A User's Manual (Fourth Edition), The Rights of Firefighters (Third Edition), A Model Law Enforcement Contract: A Labor Perspective (Third Edition), and A Model Firefighter's Contact: A Labor Perspective, all published by Labor Relations Information System.

Aitchison has lectured on numerous occasions throughout the country on FLSA issues and topics concerning labor relations and personnel issues, and has served as an expert witness and consultant in a variety of employment matters.

Aitchison resides in Portland, Oregon with his wife Valerie. Aitchison is the father of four sons, Michael, age 23, Matthew, age 22, and Alex and Luke, seven-year old twins.

TABLE OF CONTENTS

CHAPTER 4
PROCEDURAL RIGHTS IN THE DISCIPLINARY PROCESS   191

CHAPTER 10
RELIGION AND THE LAW ENFORCEMENT WORKPLACE 373

CHAPTER 11
THE RIGHTS OF LAW ENFORCEMENT OFFICERS TO
BRING CIVIL LAWSUITS 385

CHAPTER 15
THE FAIR LABOR STANDARDS ACT

CHAPTER 1

INTRODUCTION

The last 30 years have seen a dramatic evolution of the law enforcement function in the United States. As our society becomes increasingly complex, so do the roles which must be filled by law enforcement officers.

Today's law enforcement officer is expected to be a master of many trades. Simplistically, the officer is expected to perform the traditional tasks of law enforcement and crime prevention. In actuality, in order to perform these tasks, a law enforcement officer today must possess a variety of skills. In the course of any given day, a law enforcement officer may be called upon to act as a social worker by intervening in a family dispute, use a variety of computer programs, wrestle with a combative suspect who resists being taken into custody, act as a prosecutor in traffic law cases, provide emergency medical treatment to the victims of an automobile accident, maneuver an unwieldy police car through the streets of a city at high speed in response to a burglary-in-progress call, reason with an individual who is threatening to commit suicide, draft affidavits of probable cause in preparation for obtaining and serving search warrants, or dismantle a laboratory recently used to manufacture methamphetamines or other dangerous drugs.

The complexity of the job does not end with the tasks the law enforcement officer is required to perform on the street. Increasingly, a law enforcement officer must almost be an attorney in order to follow rules of criminal procedure which seem to change at a dizzying pace, changes which create the following responsibilities or effects for a law enforcement officer:

- The need to keep abreast of changes in statutory procedural and substantive rules of criminal procedure and search and seizure, as well as following recent changes in the necessary elements of various crimes;

- The increasing job requirements placed upon officers by systems of community policing;

- The need to understand and apply the dictates of numerous courts on the constitutional rights of suspects. In some states, the local state court systems have interpreted state constitutional provisions differently from the way federal courts have interpreted identical provisions of the Federal Constitution, requiring the law enforcement officer to understand and apply two entirely different sets of constitutional rules;

- The exposure of the officer and the officer's family to civil lawsuits brought by those arrested or encountered by the officer.

Often lost in the focus on the rights possessed by criminal suspects has been the notion that law enforcement officers themselves possess rights. Those rights are often ill understood and sporadically applied. This book is designed to be a comprehensive review of the rights of law enforcement officers. The book is designed for the layperson, yet contains the supporting case law and statutory citations necessary to make it a reference tool for attorneys.

This book is different from other books governing labor relations in the public sector. Instead of taking a generalized approach to the subject, this book is directed specifically at the law enforcement environment. As a result, virtually all of the thousands of cases discussed in this book specifically arise out of the law enforcement setting.

This sixth edition of *The Rights of Law Enforcement Officers* contains numerous changes from previous versions of the book. It includes references to hundreds of new cases decided in the last five years. In addition, the new book contains a number of modifications from previous editions, including:

- The complete rewriting of the chapter on free speech, something that became necessary as decisions from the United States Supreme Court completely changed the legal landscape in the area;

- An expansion of the book's treatment of freedom of association, including new developments in the area of "association with criminals" rules and the ability of employers to monitor and regulate an officer's off-duty relationships;

- A restructuring and expansion of the book's discussion of the *Garrity* and *Weingarten* rules;

- A substantial revision of the book's treatment of the law of discrimination, including a discussion of trends in the law on "reverse discrimination" and hostile work environment;

- Discussions of developing law in areas as diverse as the legality of videotaping in the law enforcement workplace, an employer's right to monitor electronic communications systems, and how religious freedom issues have become part of the law enforcement employment setting;

- The substantial expansion of the book's tables describing disciplinary cases and the negotiability of wages, hours, and working conditions, and an expansion of the book's treatment of peace officer bills of rights.

This edition of the book chronicles two parallel developments in the law which have emerged over the last ten years. One development is the growing conservatism of the federal courts. This conservatism has made federal courts more inhospitable to constitutional and statutory claims lodged by law enforcement officers, particularly in the areas of due process, freedom of speech, and the right to privacy. The result has been that the vast majority of recent federal court lawsuits brought by law enforcement officers in areas such as freedom of speech and employment discrimination have been unsuccessful.

A concurrent development has been the increasing inclination of state courts to interpret state constitutions in a fashion more generous than the federal courts would interpret an identical provision in the United States Constitution. These twin developments have led to a confusing state of the law with respect to the rights of law enforcement officers. For example, in some states random drug testing of law enforcement officers is permissible, where in others it violates a privacy provision of a state constitution.

This book categorizes the rights of law enforcement officers under the following general headings:

- The collective bargaining rights of law enforcement officers, discussed in Chapter 2.

- The standards for disciplinary action against a law enforcement officer, discussed in Chapter 3.

- The constitutional right to certain procedures in the disciplinary process, including the *Garrity*, *Loudermill*, and *Weingarten* rules, discussed in Chapter 4.

- Bills of rights for law enforcement officers, discussed in Chapter 5.

- The constitutional right to privacy held by law enforcement officers, and how the right to privacy applies in the work environment, discussed in Chapter 6.

- A law enforcement officer's constitutional right to freedom of speech, discussed in Chapter 7.

- A law enforcement officer's constitutional right to freedom of association, discussed in Chapter 8.

- A law enforcement officer's right to engage in political activities, discussed in Chapter 9.

- A law enforcement officer's constitutional right to freedom of religion, discussed in Chapter 10.

- The rights of law enforcement officers to bring civil suits against suspects and others who injure them on the job, discussed in Chapter 11.

- The rights of law enforcement officers under workers' compensation and pension laws and to a safe working environment, discussed in Chapter 12.

- The rights of law enforcement officers under the Civil Rights Act of 1991 and to be free from employment discrimination, discussed in Chapter 13.

- The rights of law enforcement officers under the Americans With Disabilities Act and other laws governing the rights of disabled employees, discussed in Chapter 14.

- The rights of law enforcement officers under the Fair Labor Standards Act, discussed in Chapter 15.

- The remedies available to law enforcement officers through the court system, discussed in Chapter 16.

CHAPTER 2

LAW ENFORCEMENT OFFICERS AND COLLECTIVE BARGAINING

The History Behind Law Enforcement Collective Bargaining.

Initially, the traditional labor movement resisted including law enforcement personnel in its ranks. One of the first attempts by law enforcement officers to unionize came in 1897, when a group of police officers in Cleveland petitioned the American Federation of Labor (which has now merged with the Congress of Industrial Organizations to form the AFL-CIO) for membership. The AFL rejected the petition with not a bit of hostility, commenting:

> "It is not within the province of the trade union movement to especially organize policemen, no more than to organize militiamen, as both policemen and militiamen are often controlled by forces inimical to the labor movement."[1]

The AFL's initial resistance to law enforcement labor organizations softened over the years, and by 1919 the AFL had chartered 37 local police unions across the country. That same year brought the first major police strike when 1,200 Boston police officers walked off the job. When riots erupted, the governor of Massachusetts called in the state militia and all 1,200 striking officers were fired.[2]

The Boston police strike dealt a serious blow to the efforts to organize law enforcement labor organizations. The relationship between traditional organized labor and law enforcement again soured, and the public was openly opposed to the formation of law enforcement labor organizations. Though there were several abortive attempts to form law enforcement labor organizations in the intervening period,[3] it was not until the early 1960s that law enforcement labor organizations again began to form in any numbers.[4]

The history of the law enforcement labor movement since the 1960s has differed in several respects from that of the preceding era. First, the attitude of the public towards law enforcement labor organizations changed. Where in 1959 a public opinion poll showed 55% of those surveyed opposed police unions,[5] by 1967 more than 60% of the public favored police unions.[6] Second, when law enforcement officers have formed labor organizations in recent years, they have turned to independent labor organizations more often than they have to organizations affiliated with national bodies.[7] Third, law enforcement labor organizations have increasingly engaged in collective bargaining under the auspices of state and local collective bargaining laws.

The General Structure Of Laws Governing Collective Bargaining For Law Enforcement Officers.

Without question, the broadest grant of rights to law enforcement officers exists in collective bargaining agreements. Under collective bargaining agreements, the wages and benefits of law enforcement officers are guaranteed for the duration of the agreement, and, most significantly, officers who dispute a decision of their employer concerning working conditions usually have the right to appeal that decision through a grievance procedure which culminates with a final and binding decision by a neutral third party.

Under the terms of the federal National Labor Relations Act, state governmental bodies and their political subdivisions such as cities and counties are excluded from the definition of "employer," and are not brought within the scope of federal labor laws. As a result, laws regulating collective bargaining for state, county, and city law enforcement officers have developed on a state-by-state basis and, occasionally, on a local basis.

Though public employee collective bargaining laws in each state are different, the general thrust of laws can be summarized by three simplified models, the "Binding Arbitration" model, the "Meet and Confer" model, and the "Bargaining Not Required" model.

The "Binding Arbitration" Model. In states following the binding arbitration model, public employees are granted the right to select exclusive representatives for the purposes of bargaining with their employers. In such states, the public employer and the labor organization are required to bargain in good faith until impasse, and then to submit any unresolved disputes to a process known as "interest arbitration," where a neutral third party selected by the parties makes a final and binding resolution of those issues.

In binding arbitration, the neutral third party decides what the terms and conditions of the new collective bargaining agreement will be, usually using standards established by state statute. Michigan's collective bargaining law contains standard language governing the right of law enforcement labor organizations to binding arbitration, a right which is always accompanied by a ban on the right of law enforcement officers to strike:

> "It is the public policy of this state that in public police and fire departments, where the right of employees to strike is by law prohibited, it is requisite to the high morale of such employees and the efficient operation of such departments to afford an alternate, expeditious, effective and binding procedure for the resolution of disputes, and to that end the provisions of this act, providing for compulsory arbitration, shall be liberally construed."[8]

There are three general types of binding arbitration laws, reflecting differences in the latitude given arbitrators to render decisions. Under the first type, known as an "issue-by-issue" law, an arbitrator has the obligation to render a decision on each issue independently, and to craft an award on each issue that best accomplishes the purposes of the arbitration statute. Under the second type of law, known as "final offer, issue-by-issue," the arbitrator renders a decision on each issue independently, but must award the final offer made by one of the parties, and is not free to craft a compromise position which has not been specifically proposed by either party. The third type of law, known as "total package" arbitration, requires the arbitrator to select the most reasonable of the total packages submitted by

Laws regulating collective bargaining for state, county, and city law enforcement officers have developed on a state-by-state basis and, occasionally, on a local basis.

each party, even if selected elements of that party's total package might not have been awarded by the arbitrator on an issue-by-issue basis. All states with binding arbitration require an arbitrator to analyze a set of criteria established by statute, usually including factors such as the wages and benefits paid in comparable jurisdictions, the cost of living, and an employer's ability to pay.[9]

Employers have challenged binding arbitration laws under a variety of theories, including arguments that binding arbitration is an unconstitutional delegation of legislative authority and that binding arbitration inappropriately interferes with a city or county's home rule status. Almost uniformly, such challenges have not been successful, with courts upholding binding arbitration as a rational means to bring about the resolution of bargaining disputes involving law enforcement officers.[10]

The "Meet and Confer" Model. In states following the meet and confer model, law enforcement officers have the same rights to organize and select their collective bargaining representative as is the case with the binding arbitration model. However, in such states employers are only obliged to "meet and confer" with the collective bargaining representative, typically with no method of impasse resolution specified in the bargaining law.

When negotiations end in impasse in a meet and confer setting, the employer is allowed to unilaterally implement its last best offer, or at least that portion of the offer that contains mandatory subjects of bargaining.[11] This leaves the officers in the position of either accepting the employer's last offer of settlement, taking whatever form of job action is permissible under the laws of the state, or attempting political or other measures to resolve the collective bargaining dispute.

The bargaining obligations of an employer in a "meet and confer" state are (1) to meet with the labor organization promptly on request, personally, and for a reasonable period of time; and (2) to try to agree on matters within the scope of representation.[12] Good faith negotiations in a meet and confer setting have been characterized as a "subjective attitude" which requires a genuine effort to reach agreement, an effort which is "inconsistent with a predetermined position not to budge on particular issues."[13]

Both parties to the bargaining process are required to exchange information freely on matters pertaining to the bargaining relationship.

As is the case with states following the binding arbitration model, in meet and confer states both parties to the bargaining process are required to exchange information freely on matters pertaining to the bargaining relationship. The obligation to exchange information requires sharing information about bargaining issues such as the comparable jurisdictions used by each party in negotiations,[14] the approach taken by each in calculating changes in the cost of living, and how each evaluates the employer's ability to pay. The obligation to share bargaining information is also ongoing in nature, and requires an employer to provide information about its enforcement of its residency and drug testing requirements,[15] a justification of how it has made assignment decisions,[16] and even extends to sharing information about prior disciplinary cases, including the recommendations of line supervisors for discipline in a particular case.[17]

The "Bargaining Not Required" Model. The last model for public sector collective bargaining laws is found in those states that do not statutorily require or, in some cases, allow collective bargaining for law enforcement officers. In some of these states, bargaining laws have been enacted by the state legislature only to later be declared unconstitutional by the courts (Indiana, for example, has such a history). In the majority of such states, a statewide collective bargaining statute covering law enforcement officers has never been enacted. In some states where collective bargaining has not been granted on a statewide basis, certain cities and counties within the state have voluntarily chosen to bargain with their law enforcement officers.[18]

The following table summarizes the current status of collective bargaining laws governing law enforcement officers, and lists which of the three general models are followed in each state.[19] As can be quickly seen, the distribution of states with collective bargaining and those without such laws is quite geographically distinct. States without bargaining laws are centered in the South and the Southwest. States with bargaining laws are found in the Northeast, the Midwest, and on the West Coast.

COLLECTIVE BARGAINING LAWS GOVERNING LAW ENFORCEMENT OFFICERS

State	Binding Arbitration Model	Meet & Confer Model	Bargaining Not Required Model
Alabama			X
Alaska	X		
Arizona			X
Arkansas			X
California	X		
Colorado			X
Connecticut	X		
Delaware	X		
District of Columbia	X		
Florida		X	
Georgia			X
Hawaii	X		
Idaho			X
Illinois	X		
Indiana		X	
Iowa	X		
Kansas	X		
Kentucky		X	
Louisiana			X
Maine	X		
Maryland		X	
Massachusetts	X		
Michigan	X		
Minnesota	X		
Mississippi			X
Missouri		X	
Montana	X		
Nebraska		X	
Nevada	X		
New Hampshire	X		
New Jersey	X		
New Mexico		X	
New York	X		
North Carolina			X
North Dakota		X	
Ohio	X		
Oklahoma	X		
Oregon	X		
Pennsylvania	X		
Rhode Island	X		
South Carolina		X	
South Dakota		X	
Tennessee			X
Texas			X
Utah			X
Vermont	X		
Virginia			X
Washington	X		
West Virginia			X
Wisconsin	X		
Wyoming			X

The Exclusion Of Law Enforcement Officers From Collective Bargaining Laws.

As the foregoing table demonstrates, considerable diversity exists among state laws governing the rights of law enforcement officers to bargain collectively. The trend clearly is in the direction of the binding arbitration model, which not only is in place in a majority of states, but has also been fairly recently adopted by such populous states as California, Illinois and Ohio.

Even in the absence of state statutes, individual cities and counties are usually allowed to adopt a system of collective bargaining. Colorado, for example, has no statewide collective bargaining law governing police. However, Denver and other cities have adopted charter provisions providing for a comprehensive system of collective bargaining governing its police officers. In some states with a meet-and-confer model, individual jurisdictions have the ability to adopt a binding arbitration approach. Thus, though for years California's collective bargaining laws provided only a meet-and-confer approach, cities such as San Francisco, Oakland, and San Jose enacted laws requiring that binding arbitration be used as the last step in the bargaining process.

Absent a state statute or local law specifically permitting law enforcement officers to bargain collectively, a law enforcement labor organization has no right to compel an employer to bargain with it. Laws granting collective bargaining rights to firefighters and other public employees but denying such rights to law enforcement officers have been upheld as constitutional and do not violate the principle of equal protection of the laws.[20] Similarly, state laws granting police officers the right to bargain collectively but denying such rights to deputy sheriffs have been upheld,[21] as have laws allowing bargaining for larger law enforcement agencies but denying the right to bargain to smaller agencies.[22] As well, laws granting collective bargaining rights to law enforcement officers but denying such rights to other employees have been upheld.[23]

State laws governing the rights of law enforcement officers to bargain collectively regulate only the bargaining relationship between a labor organization and an employer, not actual membership in a labor organization. Neither a state nor a local governmental body can forbid an employee from joining a labor organization and participating in its activities, since the right to be a member of a labor union is protected by the First Amendment to the United States Constitution. As noted by the United States Supreme Court in 1945: "[T]he right * * * to discuss, and inform people concerning the advantages and disadvantages of unions and joining them is protected not only as part of free speech, but as part of free assembly."[24] However, while law enforcement officers may have the unfettered right to be members of a labor organization, that right does not compel an employer to bargain with the labor organization unless it is required to do so by state or local law.

Some jurisdictions allowing for collective bargaining by law enforcement officers have decreed that bargaining need only take place with labor organizations

While law enforcement officers have the unfettered right to be members of a labor organization; that right does not compel an employer to bargain with the labor organization unless it is required to do so by state or local law.

which are not affiliated with a national labor organization or with labor organizations which do not advocate the right to strike. For example, New York City's local collective bargaining law provides as follows:

> "No organization seeking or claiming to represent members of the police force of the police department shall be certified if such organization (i) admits to membership, or is affiliated directly or indirectly with an organization which admits to membership employees other than members of the police force of the police department, or (ii) advocates the right to strike."[25]

Laws confining the collective bargaining relationship to independent labor organizations have been upheld by the courts, which have reasoned that such laws do not prohibit <u>membership</u> in any labor organization, they simply regulate with whom a law enforcement employer must bargain. Courts upholding these laws have stressed the importance of the members of a law enforcement agency remaining neutral in all labor disputes:

> "The City's interest in maintaining the existence and appearance of police neutrality is fully as substantial as the interest advanced in support of [the collective bargaining law]. Police occupy a key role in our society by virtue of their responsibility for law enforcement, and their loyalties are clearly as important, if not more important, to the City than the loyalties of guards to their employers. This Court cannot, therefore, conclude that the City may not properly recognize and prevent the divided loyalties that could develop if police officers were called upon to police labor disputes involving labor groups with which they were affiliated."[26]

Eligibility For Inclusion In A Bargaining Unit Of Law Enforcement Officers.

Where collective bargaining exists for law enforcement officers, it is rare that all members of a law enforcement agency are eligible to be in a collective bargaining unit. Employees whose jobs are "supervisory," "managerial," or "confidential" may, depending upon the local law, be either excluded from collective bargaining[27] or be required to be in a bargaining unit separate from rank-and-file members.[28]

Supervisory Employees.

Supervisory employees may not be eligible for membership in a collective bargaining unit of law enforcement officers. The question of who is a "supervisor" under a collective bargaining law has been extensively litigated, primarily with respect to the positions of sergeant and lieutenant. The following definition of "supervisor," which parallels the definition in the National Labor Relations Act,[29] is taken from Oregon's collective bargaining laws:

> "'Supervisory employee' means any individual having authority in the interest of the employer to hire, transfer, suspend, lay off, recall, promote, discharge, assign, reward or discipline other employees, or having responsibility to direct the employees, or to adjust their grievances, or effectively to recommend such action, if in connection therewith, the exercise of such authority is not of a merely routine or clerical nature, but requires the use of independent judgment."[30]

Other states use similar definitions, but require as well that supervisors "normally [perform] different work" from their subordinates.[31]

Managerial Employees.

Managerial employees may also be ineligible for membership in a collective bargaining unit. Typically, managerial employees are high in the supervisory chain of a law enforcement agency and are usually appointed officials. They must meaningfully perform the following tasks in order to be excluded from a collective bargaining unit:

- The formulation of departmental policy;

- The development of programs used by the department, and the implementation and management of those programs;

- The conducting of public relations on behalf of the department;

- The formulation of the department's budget, and the presentation of and advocacy for the budget at higher levels;

- The making of purchasing decisions;

- The making of hiring recommendations; and/or

- The exercise of a significant role in the disciplinary process.[32]

Because the tests for managerial employees are so strict, it is possible that even a police chief or director of public safety in a smaller agency might not be considered managerial, and thus would be eligible for membership in a law enforcement labor organization's bargaining unit.[33] In larger agencies, lieutenants and captains may well have little enough of a role in the formulation of policy that they are eligible for collective bargaining.[34]

Confidential Employees.

Of the three general exclusions from membership in a collective bargaining unit, the confidential employee exclusion generally involves the fewest number of employees. As the Illinois statute illustrates, a confidential employee usually must be a direct assistant to an individual intimately involved with collective bargaining matters:

> "'Confidential employee' means an employee, who in the regular course of his or her duties, assists and acts in a confidential capacity to a person who formulates, determines and effectuates management policies with regard to labor relations or who in the regular course of his or her duties has authorized access to information relating to the effectuation or review of the employer's collective bargaining policies."[35]

Under the standard definition for confidential employees, an individual in charge of an internal affairs unit would not necessarily be considered a confidential employee unless the individual possesses knowledge pertinent to collective bargaining.[36]

Examples Of Exclusion/Inclusion In A Bargaining Unit.

What follows are brief position-by-position discussions of certain classifications of law enforcement employees and their exclusion or inclusion in law enforcement bargaining units:

Master Police Officer: With the move to community policing in the 1990s, many police departments have created a position known as "master police officer." Master police officers may have some quasi-supervisory duties as well as administrative responsibilities. Without exception, employment relations commissions have ruled that master police officers should be included in the same bargaining unit as rank-and-file police officers.[37]

Detectives: In almost every case, detectives are likely to be included in a bargaining unit with patrol officers. Even in cases where detectives have internal affairs responsibilities, it is still likely that they will be placed in the rank-and-file bargaining unit with patrol officers.[38]

Sergeants: Much of the litigation involving inclusion or exclusion from a law enforcement bargaining unit has involved the position of sergeant. While some cases support the exclusion of sergeants from either collective bargaining or from bargaining units containing rank-and-file law enforcement officers,[39] the vast body of cases overwhelmingly support the inclusion of sergeants in such bargaining units.[40]

Lieutenants: Most cases hold that lieutenants are "supervisors" who may not be included in a collective bargaining unit with rank-and-file police officers.[41]

However, a minority of cases, most notably from Florida, have held to the contrary.[42]

Captains: In several cases, courts and labor relations boards have held that police captains are supervisors or managers who should not be included in a bargaining unit with rank-and-file officers.[43] In some states supervisory employees such as captains or even undersheriffs have collective bargaining rights, but must be included in a different bargaining unit than rank-and-file officers.[44]

Majors: In the only reported case addressing the propriety of including majors in a bargaining unit, the Connecticut State Board of Labor Relations held that majors should not be excluded from the bargaining unit where the Board found that, even though the majors possessed substantial authority within divisions they headed, they did not exercise substantial department-wide command authority on a regular basis.[45]

Deputy Chiefs: In most cases, deputy chiefs are likely to be excluded from collective bargaining. However, in *Matter of City of Ann Arbor*, the Michigan Employment Relations Commission ruled that deputy chiefs were not "executives" who were barred from collective bargaining by law. The Commission held that even though the deputy chiefs acted as high level supervisors, policy matters were ultimately formulated and determined exclusively by the police chief. The Commission also held relevant the fact that the deputy chiefs did not have ultimate authority in contractual matters.[46]

Undersheriffs: In states where supervisory or executive personnel are entitled to participate in collective bargaining but may not be placed in the same bargaining unit as rank-and-file personnel, it is possible to have an undersheriff constitute a one-person collective bargaining unit.[47]

Dispatch Personnel: The law varies considerably across the country as to whether it is appropriate to include dispatch personnel in a rank-and-file law enforcement bargaining unit. In some states, a clear line is drawn between sworn law enforcement personnel and any non-sworn employees, including dispatchers, with the two sets of employees never mixed into the same bargaining unit. In other states, where dispatchers are considered emergency personnel who are banned from striking and are entitled to interest arbitration, dispatchers are routinely mixed into bargaining units with sworn personnel.[48] In yet a third model, a "mixed" bargaining unit of sworn and non-sworn personnel is allowed, but is not necessarily the favored form for the structure of representation.[49] Unless they have significant management responsibilities, first-level dispatch supervisors will likely be included in the rank-and-file bargaining unit.[50]

Clerical Personnel: As is the case with dispatch personnel, the practices with respect to whether clerical personnel can be included in a law enforcement bargaining unit vary from state to state. Some states, where the last step in the negotiations process for law enforcement officers is binding arbitration, forbid so-called "mixed" units of sworn and non-sworn personnel.[51] Other states, even some of those with binding arbitration, allow mixed units of sworn and clerical personnel.[52]

Corrections Officers/Jailers: In *Ingham County Board of Commissioners v. F.O.P.*, the Court held that jail security officers were not within the definition of "police officer" under a collective bargaining law and thus were not entitled to interest arbitration.[53] However, in *Webb County v. Webb County Deputies' Association*, the Court held that the term "policeman" is broad enough to include jailers and detention officers, reasoning that jailers are sworn, certified employees who regularly serve in a professional law enforcement capacity.[54]

Animal Control Officers: In one case where dog wardens were under the jurisdiction of the police department and performed investigatory duties with regard to animal control laws, a state labor board expanded a police officer bargaining unit to include the classification.[55]

Liquor Control Officers: Liquor control officers are generally not considered to be law enforcement officers under collective bargaining laws.[56]

Park Rangers: In an Iowa case, a public employment relations commission held that park rangers could not be excluded from an existing bargaining unit on the basis of either managerial or supervisory status. The park rangers had no disciplinary authority and were not involved in the formulation of policy on behalf of their employer.[57]

Child Support Investigators: Child support investigators are usually not considered to be police officers for the purpose of inclusion in a law enforcement labor organization.[58]

Unfair Labor Practices.

States with collective bargaining almost always have statutes that list a number of labor practices deemed to be "unfair." The usual list of unfair labor practices includes:

- A refusal to bargain in good faith over subjects that are mandatory for bargaining.[59]

- Interference, restraint, or coercion of employees because employees have exercised their collective bargaining rights.

- The "domination" of a labor organization by an employer.

- Failing to furnish information relevant to the collective bargaining process.

- Inappropriate "interference" by an employer with the internal activities of a labor organization.

- Discrimination against employees who have exercised their collective bargaining rights.[60]

- A refusal to reduce to writing an agreement reached in the bargaining process.

The usual form of challenging any of these practices is through the filing of an "unfair labor practice" or "prohibited practice" complaint with the state agency responsible for administering the collective bargaining laws. Most states have a relatively quick statute of limitations – on occasion as low as six weeks – for the filing of such complaints.[61]

Mandatory Subjects For Bargaining.

Where a law enforcement employer is obligated to bargain collectively, the bargaining topics over which bargaining may be conducted are generally classified under one of three categories – mandatory, permissive, or illegal topics of bargaining.[62] Mandatory subjects of bargaining – usually those described as topics pertaining to wages, hours, and terms and conditions of employment – must be bargained if raised by either side.[63] Permissive subjects of bargaining – usually falling under the general heading of "management rights" – are those over which bargaining may occur, but is not compelled.[64] Illegal subjects of bargaining are those over which the employer is forbidden by law from bargaining.[65] The distinction between the different categories of bargaining subjects is particularly important where interest arbitration is the last step in the bargaining process, since only mandatory subjects of bargaining may generally be referred to interest arbitration.[66]

Where the obligation to bargain exists, it has importance not only during the time when negotiations for an actual contract are being conducted, but also during the term of the contract and after the contract expires. The obligation to bargain is continuing in nature, a characteristic that may significantly limit an employer's flexibility in making certain decisions. If a matter is a mandatory subject for bargaining, an employer may not make changes in past practices affecting the matter without first negotiating with the labor organization representing its officers.[67] This restriction applies whenever a labor organization has been certified as the bargaining representative for employees. The continuing duty to bargain can even invalidate an employer's efforts to change its past practices through enacting a charter amendment.[68]

If a matter is a mandatory subject for bargaining, an employer may not make changes in past practices affecting the matter without first negotiating with the labor organization representing its officers.

Two cases from Washington provide a good example of this so-called "continuing duty to bargain." In one case, the collective bargaining agreement covering a city police department had expired when the employer decided to change from a fixed-shift system where shifts were selected by seniority to a system where shifts rotated every few months. In the second case, the employer made changes in the method of allocating standby assignments. Even though a contract was in effect at the time of the changes, the contract did not address the method of standby assignment allocation. In both cases, the employers were held to have committed unfair labor practices by making the changes without first negotiating with their respective unions. The Washington Public Employment Relations Commission held that, absent a clear waiver of the union's right to bargain, the continuing duty to bargain prohibited the implementation of any changes in such mandatorily negotiable hours of work issues.[69]

A labor organization can waive the right to bargain over changes in past practices in one of two ways: by "inaction" and by "contract." A "waiver by inaction" occurs when the labor organization has knowledge that the employer intends to make a change in past practice (or has actually made such a change), but does not timely demand to bargain over the change.[70] Even a six-week delay in demanding the right to bargain has been held to waive bargaining rights.[71] In order to have a labor organization's demand to bargain held untimely, the employer generally must establish that it provided actual and timely notice of its intended action.[72]

A "waiver by contract" exists where the labor organization has contractually given the right to the employer to make changes in mandatory subjects of bargaining. To be effective, "contract waivers" must be specific and clearly articulated. For example, a management rights clause that generally gives the employer the right to establish hours of work would likely not be specific enough to allow the employer the unilateral right to change work shifts, or to change from fixed to rotating shifts.

For bargaining rights to exist mid-contract, the labor organization must establish that the past practice the employer is intending to change has been consistent and long-standing.[73] The labor organization must also establish that there has been an actual <u>change</u> in past practices in order to demand bargaining during the term of the contract. For example, in one case, the police association in New York City was attempting to bargain over a Department directive that banned "hog-tying" of suspects. The Court ruled that the directive was not negotiable because the labor association failed to prove the existence of a past practice which allowed hog-tying, resting its decision on testimony that hog-tying was not taught during training and on the word of the supervisor of the patrol force that in 41 years of service he had never seen hog-tying used in the Department.[74]

In addition, an employer's right to make changes in mandatory subjects of bargaining can also be limited by a collective bargaining agreement. Contractual clauses typically labeled "Maintenance of Benefits" or "Existing Conditions" forbid an employer from changing wages, hours, or working conditions. The contract covering Buffalo, New York's police officers contains an example of such a clause:

> "All conditions or provisions beneficial to employees now in effect which are not specifically provided for in this Agreement or which have not been replaced by provisions of this Agreement shall remain in effect for the duration of this Agreement, unless mutually agreed otherwise between the Employer and the Association."[75]

"Maintenance of Benefits" clauses enhance a labor organization's ability to prevent changes in past practices.

"Maintenance of Benefits" clauses enhance a labor organization's ability to prevent changes in past practices. Where under the general continuing duty to bargain, a labor organization only has the ability to demand that an employer bargain to impasse over changes in past practices that are mandatorily negotiable, a maintenance of benefits clause allows a labor organization to simply refuse to agree to the change, no matter whether the employer is willing to bargain over the issue. This distinction is particularly important in states where the bargaining process does not culminate with binding arbitration, but instead allows an employer to unilaterally implement its last best offer on a bargaining issue.

Where a topic is mandatory for bargaining, the employer must negotiate about the topic with the labor organization, and not with individual union members. For example, since discipline is mandatorily negotiable, an employer would violate its bargaining obligation if it entered into a "last chance" agreement with a troubled employee unless the employee's labor organization also was a party to the agreement.[76] This ban on one-on-one contracts with individual union members is a strong one, and has invalidated a wide variety of employer agreements with individual union members, including the payment of a signing bonus,[77] a contract with newly-hired officers that they will repay the costs of their training if they quit to go to work for another law enforcement employer,[78] and an agreement with a probationary employee to extend the probationary period.[79]

The following table summarizes decisions of courts and employment relations boards or commissions on the status of certain bargaining topics for law enforcement officers.[80] Some variations exist among the different states as to whether particular topics are mandatorily negotiable. For example, where the establishment of a civilian review board has been held in Michigan, Maine, and Washington to be a mandatory subject of bargaining, California and Pennsylvania have deemed it permissive in nature. Accordingly, the following table should be used only as a general guide.

STATUS OF BARGAINING TOPICS FOR POLICE OFFICERS

CASE NAME	MANDATORY	DESCRIPTION
Ammunition		
Town of West Milford, 30 NJPER ¶77 (N.J. PERC 2004)	Yes	Union proposal that employer provide 60 rounds of reload ammunition per month. Held to be mandatorily negotiable because of the employee interest in having the employer supply and pay for ammunition necessary to maintain weapons training and certification.
Arbitration of Discipline		
Borough of River Edge, 13 NPER NJ-22001 (N.J. PERC 1990)	No	Proposal pre-empted by another state statute governing disciplinary appeals.
City of Castleberry v. Orange County PBA, 482 So.2d 336 (Fla. 1986)	Yes	Civil service system existed.
City of Decatur v. AFSCME, 522 N.E.2d 1219 (Ill. 1968)	Yes	Civil service system in state law.

CASE NAME	MANDATORY	DESCRIPTION
City of Mount Vernon, 32 NYPER P 3030 (N.Y. PERB 1999)	Yes	Proposal for interest arbitration of discipline and discharge. State statute creating alternative appeal system did not preempt bargaining over arbitration of discipline.
City of Pasco, Decision 3368-A (Wash. PERC 1990)	Yes	Statewide civil service system existed by statute.
Henshey v. Township of Lower Merion, 588 A.2d 83 (Pa.Cmwlth. 1991)	Yes	Binding arbitration of termination grievances; civil service system existed.
Parisi v. Jenkins, 603 N.E.2d 566 (Ill. App. 1992)	No	Under state law, police commission's power to impose discipline cannot be subject to outside review other than by appeals through courts.
Police Local v. Helsby, 404 N.Y.S.2d 396 (A.D. 1978)	Yes	Disciplinary sanctions and procedures.
Union Township v. FOP, 19 OPER 1017 (Ohio App. 2001)	Yes	Interest arbitration decision calling for binding arbitration of discipline.
Assignments/Classifications/Job Duties		
Borough of Avalon, 15 NPER NJ-24135 (N.J. PERC 1993)	Mixed	Employer had non-negotiable right to require police officers to obtain EMT certificates, but compensation to officers who received EMT training was negotiable.
Borough of Dumont, 24 NJPER ¶29008 (N.J. PERC 1998)	Yes	Employer refused to arbitrate grievance alleging that it reassigned a detective sergeant for disciplinary reasons. Sergeant's salary was reduced upon his assignment to non-investigatory duties.
City of Middletown, 17 NPER CT-26030 (Conn. SBLR 1995)	Mixed	Merger of traffic and patrol divisions of police department. City allowed to merge divisions but required to bargain over impact of merger.
City of Niagara Falls and Niagara Falls Police Captains and Lieutenants Assn., 33 NYPER P 4603 (N.Y. PERB ALJ 2000)	Mixed	Proposal to require job postings to contain "reasonable" requirements mandatory for bargaining; proposal requiring that job openings be filled within ten days impinged too much on management rights.
City of Perth Amboy, 17 NPER NJ-25171 (N.J. PERC 1994)	No	Cessation of 30-year practice of allowing on-duty officers to participate in charitable fundraising drive.
City of Rochester and Rochester Police Locust Club, U-22824 (N.Y. PERB 2003)	Mixed	Assignment of overtime is a managerial prerogative, although the procedures for the assignments of such overtime must be negotiated.
City of Worcester v. Labor Relations Commission, 799 N.E.2d 630 (Mass. 2002)	Mixed	City elected to have police officers enforce laws pertaining to school attendance and truancy. Decision non-negotiable to the extent it implicated City's ability to set its law enforcement priorities.

CASE NAME	MANDATORY	DESCRIPTION
Fraternal Order of Police v. City of Philadelphia, 29 PPER P 29142 (Pa. LRB 1998)	No	City unilaterally directed sergeants and lieutenants to review results of internal affairs investigations of police officers and to indicate their participation in the review in writing. Assignment found to be within management's right to direct workforce.
Hampton Police Association, Case No. P-0719-20 (N.H. PERB 2006)	Yes	Enactment of anti-nepotism policy barring employment of certain relatives.
International Union of Police Associations v. State of Florida, 26 FPER P 31224 (Fla. PERC Gen. Counsel 2000)	No	Employer issued directive ordering troopers to end past practice of not issuing traffic citations to on-duty law enforcement officers.
Milwaukie Police Employees Association, Case No. UP-63-05 (Or. ERB 2007)	No	Employer unilaterally reassigned two officers from detective positions which carried with them premium pay, to patrol duties. Board treated change in job status as an "assignment issue," which is not negotiable under Oregon law, rather than as a "promotion issue," which is negotiable.
New York State Correctional Officers and PBA, Inc., 33 NYPERB P 4598 (N.Y. PERB Dir. 2000)	No	Employer allowed non-uniformed supervisory personnel to supervise pat frisks of uniformed personnel.
Somerset County Sheriff's Office, PERC No. 2007-66 (N.J. PERC 2007)	No	Corrections union sought to arbitrate grievance challenging employer's refusal to consider a sergeant for a permanent assignment as a "kitchen officer." Under New Jersey law, job assignments are a non-negotiable topic.
State of Florida, 27 FPER ¶32015 (Fla. PERC 2000)	No	Employer discontinued practice of allowing state troopers to refrain from issuing traffic citations to on-duty police officers. Past practice was void against public policy.
Township of Cherry Hill, 18 NPER NJ-27061 (N.J. PERC ALJ 1996)	No	Unilateral implementation of master police officer program, not negotiable because no benefits paid to employees obtaining master police officer status.
Township of Woodbridge, 25 NJPER ¶30081 (N.J. PERC 1999)	No	Assignment of police captain to different division and work hours upon his return from disability leave; employer's decision was based upon managerial right to seek national accreditation.
Village of Bensenville, 19 PERI ¶119 (Ill. Labor Board 2003)	Yes	Employer unilaterally implemented program to cross-train its police officers as firefighters and EMTs and to assign them related duties. Neither a zipper clause or a management rights clause in the parties' bargaining agreement permitted the employer to carry out such a fundamental change without bargaining over the change.

CASE NAME	MANDATORY	DESCRIPTION
Wilkes-Barre PBA, 29 PPER P 29152 (Pa. LRB ALJ 1998)	No	Employer issued new rule permitting only one police officer to attend summary offense hearings. Employer's decision analogized a non-negotiable staffing issue.
York County Prison, LAIG 6438 (Brogan, 2006)	Mixed	Employer unilaterally eliminated canine unit. While employer allowed to make the decision to disband the unit, it was required to bargain over the impacts of doing so. Employer ordered to continue premium pay and reimbursement of medical expenses for the three years of the current contract even though the unit had been disbanded.

Bargaining

CASE NAME	MANDATORY	DESCRIPTION
City of Harper Woods, Case No. C06 D-087 (Mich. ERC 2007)	No	Employer proposed ground rule that all bargaining sessions be held at its facilities. Location of bargaining sessions not a mandatory subject of bargaining.

Callbacks

CASE NAME	MANDATORY	DESCRIPTION
Township of Middletown, Case No. CO-2005-226 (N.J. PERC 2006)	Yes	Employer changed past practice of allowing officers one hour of travel or "shape up" compensation upon receiving a callback. Practice negotiable because of monetary impacts.

Canine Program

CASE NAME	MANDATORY	DESCRIPTION
Kingston Police Benevolent Association, Inc., Case No. U-26553 (N.Y. PERB 2007)	Yes	Employer unilaterally discontinued past practice of defraying the costs of police officers for veterinary services and food for specially-trained police canines in their care after the canines have been taken out of service. The provision by the City of the veterinary care and food for out-of-service dogs is an economic benefit and thus a form of compensation for unit members.

Charter Amendments

CASE NAME	MANDATORY	DESCRIPTION
City of Chester v. FOP, 615 A.2d 893 (Pa.Cmwlth. 1992)	Yes	Court reversed charter amendment establishing residency requirements.
City of Fresno v. Fresno Fire Fighters Local 753 and Fresno Police Officers' Association, 32 Cal.Rptr.2d 449 (Cal. App. 1994)	Yes	Contractual agreement not to submit charter change to voters asking for repeal of charter's wage-setting formula.
People ex rel. Seal Beach POA v. City of Seal Beach, 36 Cal.3d 591 (1984)	Yes	If topic of charter amendment is mandatory, must be bargained before submitted to voters. Charter amendment required the termination of any employee who participated in strike.

Civilian Review Board

CASE NAME	MANDATORY	DESCRIPTION
Berkeley Police Association v. City of Berkeley, 76 Cal. App.3d 931 (1977)	No	Institution of civilian review board; held to be "organic decision" involving structure of government.

CASE NAME	MANDATORY	DESCRIPTION
City of Portland, http://www.state.me.us/mlrb/decisions/ppc/01-IR-01.htm (Me. LRB 2001)	Yes	Declaratory judgment on negotiability of different types of civilian oversight of internal affairs investigations. Employer's proposals found mandatorily negotiable because of impact on discipline, grievance procedures, and internal affairs investigations.
Pontiac Police Officers Association v. City of Pontiac, 246 N.W.2d 831 (Mich. 1976)	Yes	Institution of civilian review board; held to be part of disciplinary system.
Spokane Police Guild and City of Spokane, Decision 5054, PECB (Wash. PERC Hearing Examiner 1995)	Yes	Unilateral implementation of civilian review board with ability to review police department disciplinary files.

Compensatory Time Off

CASE NAME	MANDATORY	DESCRIPTION
Albany Police Officers Union Local 2841, AFSCME Council 82 and City of Albany, U-27333 (N.Y. PERB 2008)	Yes	Unilateral implementation of a 30-day limitation on when requests to use compensatory time off could be submitted and a 14-day rule on when supervisors can begin to act upon such requests. New rules impose new procedural restrictions on use of paid leave.
City of Pasco, Washington, Decision #9181-A (Wash. PECB 2008)	Yes	Employer unilaterally eliminated compensatory time off system and cashed out employees' accrued compensatory time off. Commission rejected the argument that recent change in case law surrounding the Fair Labor Standards Act necessitated the elimination of comp time.
Officers of the Upper Gwynedd Township Police Department, 31 PPER P 31126 (Pa. LRB ALJ 2000)	Yes	Employer issued order capping accrual of compensatory time off at 16 hours and eliminating the carryover of comp time from year to year.

Contracts with Union Members

CASE NAME	MANDATORY	DESCRIPTION
City of Grosse Pointe Park, 14 MPER ¶32051 (MERC 2001)	Yes	Employer offered signing bonuses to applicants for position of police officer.
City of Lewistown v. Lloyd, 143 P.3d 702 (Mont. 2006)	Yes	Pre-employment contract requiring officer to repay training costs if officer did not remain employed for 36 months.[81]
City of Mt. Vernon, 23 GERR 667 (New York) (BNA 1986)	Yes	Repayment of training costs if employee quits to take another law enforcement job. Provision may not be part of contract with individual employee; to be enforceable, must be negotiated with employee's union.
City of Newark, 29 NJPER ¶137 (N.J. PERC 2003)	Yes	Employer contended that releases signed by grievants prohibited labor organization from proceeding to arbitration over issue covered by release.
Howard County, 1 (9) Public Safety Labor News 5 (Fishgold, 1993)	Yes	Extension of probationary period for individual employee.

CASE NAME	MANDATORY	DESCRIPTION
Putnam County Sheriff's Department, 35 NYPER ¶4561 (N.Y. PERB ALJ 2002)	Yes	Employer unilaterally instituted stipend of $6,300 per year for aviation officer. Since matter was mandatory subject of bargaining, employer could not grant benefit to any employees without negotiating with Union. Delay of two months in filing unfair labor practice charge did not render charge untimely.
State of Connecticut, 15 NPER CT-23079 (Conn. SLRB 1992)	Yes	Unilateral decision to place two new hires above Step 1 on the salary grade.
Suffolk County, 34 NYPER ¶3,034 (N.Y. PERB 2001)	Yes	Employer preferentially exempted one employee from one-year service eligibility requirement for tuition reimbursement. Employer's decision to do so "inherently destructive" of Union's status as exclusive bargaining representative.
Town of Ludlow, http://www.state.ma.us/lrc/ Decisions/ Recent/MUP-2422.pdf (Mass. LRC 2002)	Yes	Employer required new hires to sign agreement to repay costs of training academy if they left work within five years of employment. Though employer contended agreements were signed pre-employment, Commission found that agreements had impacts on employee post-hire.
Town of West New York, 25 NJPER P 30046 (N.J. PERC ALJ 1999)	Yes	Employer placed newly-hired police officer at higher than the entry rate because of settlement agreement arising from police officer's civil lawsuit. Private settlement agreement did not obviate obligation to bargain with labor organization.
Town of Winchester, 19 NPER CT-27074 (Conn. SBLR 1996)	Yes	Agreement with individual police officer to promote officer to sergeant in exchange for officer foregoing legal action in connection with his prior demotion from rank of sergeant.
Washington County Police Officers Association, No. UP-12-02 (Or. ERB 2003)	Yes	Employer required new hires to sign contract agreeing to repay up to $10,000 in training costs if they left employment within 24 months after the conclusion of their probationary periods.
Washington State Patrol, 3 (8) Public Safety Labor News 7 (Wash. PERC 1995)	Yes	Last chance agreement with trooper who displayed alcohol-related performance difficulties.
Court Appearances		
City of Chester, 13 NPER PA-22006 (Pa. LRB 1990)	Yes	New requirement that officers testifying in court work out duration of overtime minimum.
City of Detroit, 18 NPER MI-26069 (Mich. App. 1995)	Yes	Transfer to retirement board of authority to decide whether disabilities were incurred in the line of duty.

CASE NAME	MANDATORY	DESCRIPTION
City of Newburgh, 19 NPER NY-14635 (N.Y. PERB Director 1996)	Yes	Proposal that employees be compensated for travel to court appearances.
County of Hudson, 16 NPER NJ-25041 (N.J. PERC 1994)	Yes	Proposal which would require minimum pay of four hours for court appearances.
Ellwood City Police Wage and Policy Unit, 30 PPER P 30135 (Pa.Cmwlth. 1999)	No	Police department provided court with police work schedules in order to avoid payment of overtime for court appearances.
South Park Township Police Association v. Pennsylvania Labor Relations Board, 33 PPER ¶33035 (Pa.Cmwlth. 2002)	No	New rule requiring on-duty officers who were required to testify in court to report back to the police station for duty at the conclusion of the court appearance. Policy did not apply to off-duty court appearances.

Deferred Compensation

CASE NAME	MANDATORY	DESCRIPTION
Snohomish County, Washington, 2005 WL 636212 (Wash. PERC 2005)	Yes	Employer refused to submit to arbitration on labor organization's proposal for deferred compensation matching contribution. Proposal was not preempted by state law establishing statewide retirement system for law enforcement officers.

Disability Benefits

CASE NAME	MANDATORY	DESCRIPTION
City of Detroit, 18 NPER MI-26069 (Mich. App. 1995)	Yes	Transfer to retirement board of authority to decide whether disabilities were incurred in the line of duty.
County of Greene, 14 NPER NY-13045 (N.Y. PERB 1992)	Yes	Unilateral establishment of hearing procedure to determine retroactive entitlement to disability benefits and termination of those benefits.
County of Westchester v. Westchester County Corrections Officers Benevolent Assn., 717 N.Y.S.2d 651 (A.D. 2000)	No	Employer refused to arbitrate grievance seeking the recovery of work-related disability benefits. Under New York law, issues of job-related disability are not mandatory for collective bargaining.
Dunmore Police Association v. Borough of Dunmore, 31 PPER P 31052 (Pa. LRB ALJ 2000)	Yes	Employer enacted ordinance reducing disability pension benefit to 50% of average of last three years of officer's salary.
Mass. Police Assoc. v. City of Newton, 484 N.E.2d 1326 (Mass. 1985)	Yes	Proposal for paid accidental disability leave.
Town of Orangetown, 16 NPER NY-14532 (N.Y. PERB ALJ 1994)	Yes	Proposals for vacation and sick leave benefits for disabled employees above those required by state workers' compensation laws.
Township of Lacey, 17 NPER NJ-25193 (N.J. PERC 1994)	Yes	Unilateral enrollment of police officers in state disability plan.

CASE NAME	MANDATORY	DESCRIPTION
Township of Riverside, 16 NPER NJ-25167 (N.J. PERC 1994)	Mixed	Change in past practice of paying disabled officers difference between salary and workers' compensation benefits. Union not untimely in waiting to file ULP until practice implemented.
Triborough Bridge and Tunnel Authority, 17 NPER NY-13076 (N.Y. PERB 1994)	Yes	Proposal to limit workers' compensation supplemental payment to an amount necessary to bring employee to regular salary.

Disciplinary Procedures and Standards

CASE NAME	MANDATORY	DESCRIPTION
AFSCME Council 31 and County of Williamson, 15 PERI P 2003 (Ill. SLRB 1999)	Yes	Sheriff refused to process grievances over disciplinary issues, and advised union that such matters would be resolved exclusively through newly-created merit commission. State merit system law held not to supercede right to collectively bargain over discipline.
Asotin County, Washington, Decision 9549-A (Wash. PERC 2007)	Yes	After expiration of contract, employer terminated an employee without just cause. Disciplinary standards were a mandatory subject of bargaining that continued after the contract expired.
City of Buffalo, 13 NPER NY-13050 (N.Y. PERB 1990)	Yes	New disciplinary work rules, including "association with criminals," "obey all laws," and "report all violations" rules.
City of Camden, PERC No. 2004-7 (N.J. PERC 2003)	Yes	Proposal for legal representation during internal affairs investigations.
City of Holyoke, www.state.ma.us/lrc/Decisions/Recent/ MUP-2475 (Mass. LRC 2002)	Yes	Employer deviated from contract's requirement that it complete non-criminal internal investigations within 15 days from receipt of complaint. Employer's action termed "repudiation" of contract.
City of Milwaukee, No. 32115 (Wis. PERC 2007)	Mixed	Police department was contemplating implementing "early warning system." Implementation of system mandatory for bargaining to the extent it impacted wages, hours, and mandatorily negotiable working conditions.
City of Mount Vernon v. Cuevas, 289 A.D.2d 674 (App.Div. 2001)	No	Proposal concerning disciplinary procedures; the City had established disciplinary procedures in its City Charter in 1922. New York state collective bargaining law specifically disallows bargaining over previously-established disciplinary procedures.
City of Pasco, Decision 3368-A (Wash. PERC 1990)	Yes	Representation during disciplinary interviews.
City of Passaic, 26 NJPER P 31027 (N.J. PERC 1999)	Yes	Arbitration award sustaining grievance alleging that employer violated contract by not providing officers facing discipline with a hearing before an employee hearing board established by ordinance.

CASE NAME	MANDATORY	DESCRIPTION
City of Philadelphia, 31 PPER P 31023 (Pa. LRB 1999)	No	Employer issued formal disciplinary policy governing the off-duty actions of police officers. Concerns about off-duty drinking and then taking police actions raised concerns of civil liability and safety which outweighed union's concerns.
City of Sherrill, 14 NPER NY-14532 (N.Y. PERB ALJ 1992)	Yes	Establishment of procedure for selection of hearings officers in disciplinary proceedings.
Cook County, 15 PERI P 3009 (Ill. LRB 1999)	No	Employer proposed that union waive its right to file challenges in arbitration to suspensions and discharges.
Cook County Sheriff, 13 NPER IL-21235 (Ill. LLRB 1990)	Yes	Unilateral implementation of lump-sum suspensions; change in past practice of allowing representatives to question witnesses and review files.
County of Passaic, 29 NJPER ¶91 (N.J. PERC 2003)	Yes	Proposal for bill of rights. Fact that proposal would mirror statewide statutory bill of rights did not make its inclusion in contract non-negotiable.
Deschutes County, Oregon, Case No. UP-32-04 (Or. ERB 2006)	Yes	After contract expired, employer issued dispatcher a reprimand without just cause. Standard of just cause determined to be part of "status quo" an employer must maintain during bargaining for new contract.
Fairview Township Police Association, 31 PPER P 31019 (Pa. LRB 1999)	Yes	Employer ended policy of two-year duration under which it purged disciplinary records from employees' files and reinstated prior policy of retaining records on permanent basis.
Fraternal Order of Police v. City of Reading, 29 PPER P 29146 (Pa. LRB 1998)	No	Adoption of work rule prohibiting conduct that creates a "hostile work environment" of a sexually or racially harassing nature.
IBPO Local 316 v. State of Connecticut, 1998 WL 234836 (Conn. Sup. 1998)	No	Use of surveillance camera in disciplinary investigation to determine source of official police documents that were being leaked to the press.
New Jersey Institute of Technology, 29 NJPER ¶139 (N.J. Super. 2003)	Yes	Employer refused to proceed to arbitration over issue of whether sergeant was entitled to representation by an attorney at a pre-disciplinary hearing.
New Jersey Transit Commission, #2008-31 (N.J. PERC 2007)	Yes	Employer refused to process to arbitration a grievance challenging police officer's five-day suspension. Under New Jersey law, "minor discipline" may be submitted to binding arbitration if the contract so provides.
New York State Law Enforcement Officers Union and City of Albany, U-27105 (N.Y. PERB Dir. 2008)	Yes	Employer unilaterally replaced portion of work rule prohibiting off-duty consumption of intoxicating beverages with a new rule prohibiting consumption of such beverages within eight hours of reporting to duty. Change negotiable because of impact on disciplinary process.

CASE NAME	MANDATORY	DESCRIPTION
Pennsylvania State Police v. Pennsylvania Labor Relations Board, 764 A.2d 92 (Pa. 2000)	No	Employer unilaterally ceased granting probationary employees pre-disciplinary hearings.
Police Benevolent Association of the New York State Troopers, Inc. and State of New York (Division of State Police), Case No. U-22830 (N.Y. PERB 2006)	No	Employer unilaterally changed procedures to be followed during the investigation of "critical incidents." Under New York law, the disciplinary procedures for members of the State Police is a prohibited subject of negotiations.
State of New Jersey v. State Troopers Fraternal Organization, 634 A.2d 478 (N.J. 1993)	No	New Jersey state law prohibits negotiations over disciplinary standards if civil service system exists.
Town of Wallkill, 14 NPER NY-14566 (N.Y. PERB ALJ 1991)	Yes	Proposal for representation during interrogations arising from disciplinary charges and providing for no more than a 24-hour delay to accommodate the employee's request for representation.
Upper Gwynedd Township v. Upper Gwynedd Township Police Association, 777 A.2d 1187 (Pa.Cmwlth. 2001)	Yes	Validity of interest arbitrator's award imposing grievance arbitration as the last step in the disciplinary appeal process.
Whatcom County, 2002 WL 359378 (Wash. PERC 2002)	Yes	Implementation of policy and procedures manual containing, among other things, disciplinary standards and a code of conduct.
Drug Testing/Workplace Searches		
AFSCME District Council 88 v. Valley Township, 1 NPER 3:5 (Pa. LRB 1997)	Mixed	Employer not obligated to bargain over mandatory drug testing for commercial driver's license holders; employers required to mandatorily bargain over implementation of drug and alcohol testing for employees who do not hold CDLs.
Borough of Hopatcong, 13 NPER NJ-22028 (N.J. PERC 1990)	Mixed	Reasonable suspicion standard negotiable; probable cause standard not negotiable.
City of Canton, 16 NPER OH-24540 (Ohio SERB Hearing Officer 1993)	Yes	Implementation of policy requiring drug testing for employees returning to work after participation in substance abuse program.
City of Gainesville, 19 NPER FL-27258 (Fla. PERC 1996)	Yes	Employer unilaterally imposed drug-free workplace program that permitted City to restrict or eliminate drug rehabilitation program and to establish new standards for declaring a position to be safety sensitive.
City of Newark, 13 NPER NJ-21186 (N.J. PERC 1990)	Yes	Procedural aspects of a drug screening policy.

CASE NAME	MANDATORY	DESCRIPTION
City of Newark, 27 NJPER ¶32078 (N.J. PERC ALJ 2001)	Yes	Employer enacted drug screening policy requiring police officers to disclose prescription and non-prescription medications and any type of steroids that "impair[ed] the ability to function effectively." Because officers would be compelled to disclose all their medications, at risk of incurring discipline for non-disclosure, even if they were unaware of any impairment or had been advised that risk of impairment was small, policy impermissibly intruded on officers' expectations of privacy and autonomy.
City of Warren, 15 NPER MI-24056 (Mich. ERC 1993)	Yes	Though City had no drug testing policy, it assigned officers to consolidate drug task force which required drug testing. Drug testing became condition of employment by virtue of City's participation in task force.
City of Yakima, Decision 9062-B (Wash. PERC 2008)	Yes	Employer failed to respond to Union's demand to bargain over whether a random drug testing program should be in existence; contract was silent on the issue, and Union opposed random testing.
County of Nassau, 17 NPER NY-13054 (N.Y. PERB 1994)	Yes	Implementation of drug testing policy for existing employees; broadly worded "zipper" clause did not constitute clear and unmistakable waiver by union of right to bargain over drug testing.
F.O.P. v. City of Miami, 131 LRRM 3171 (Fla. 1989)	Mixed	Reasonable suspicion testing of specific officers not negotiable; random testing negotiable.
Holliday v. City of Modesto, 280 Cal.Rptr. 206 (Cal. App. 1991)	Yes	Unilateral implementation of drug testing.
In the matter of Deputy Sheriffs' Benevolent Association of Onondaga County, Inc., 32 NYPERB P 4526 (N.Y. PERB ALJ 1999)	No	Search of deputy's backpack located on shelf in supply room. Employer had past practice of routine searches of all contents in supply room including items (such as deputies' backpacks) in which K-9 dogs expressed interest.
Law Enforcement Labor Services, Inc. 695 N.W.2d 630 (Minn. App. 2005)	Mixed	Minnesota state statute allowed employer to unilaterally establish a random drug-testing plan. However, process of implementation and effects of plan mandatory for bargaining.
Duration		
Milwaukee County, Decision No. 30431 (Wis. ERC 2002)	No	Proposal that contract remain in full force and effect until replaced by subsequent agreement. State law limited duration of contracts to three years.

CASE NAME	MANDATORY	DESCRIPTION
Education		
Beaverton Police Association v. City of Beaverton, 194 Or. App. 531 (Or. App. 2004)	Yes	City changed its past practice to require that sergeants have an associate degree in criminal justice or a closely-related field, and changed method of calculating "life experience" credits towards the educational requirement. City required to bargain over impacts of the change.
Employee Groups		
County of Fresno, California, 29 PERC ¶47 (Cal. PERB 2005)	No	Employer established a "working group" of employees to provide the Sheriff with recommendations in the area of shift selection, scheduling days off, vacation selection, and "swapping" time off. Labor organization which later protested "working group" actually had appointed some members to the group.
Employee Rights		
City of Paterson, New Jersey, PERC No. 2007-62 (N.J. PERC 2007)	No	Employer installed overt security cameras inside and outside its public safety complex without notice to or bargaining with the labor organizations representing public safety employees. Commission concluded that since cameras were part of an overall security system, and were overt rather than covert, management's rights to protect "people and property" overrode any employee privacy interest.
Township of Hillsborough, 30 NJPER ¶8 (N.J. PERC 2004)	No	Police Chief ordered a police officer not to file criminal charges against a civilian who had filed an internal affairs complaint against the officer. Case decided solely on whether the issue was a mandatory subject of bargaining, and did not deal with the officer's rights as a citizen to file such charges.
Employer Facilities		
Bergen County, 19 NPER NJ-27123 (N.J. PERC 1996)	Yes	Police union's proposal that it be allowed to use office within employer's facility.
City of Paterson, 19 NPER NJ-27138 (N.J. PERC 1996)	Yes	Employer terminated union president's ability to use photocopy and facsimile machines, city telephone, and rescinded practice of providing office facilities and equipment to Union.
City of Sepulpa, 102 LA 636 (Neas, 1994)	Yes	Increase in green fees charged employees at employer-owned golf course.
State of Illinois, 17 PERI ¶2014 (Ill. SLRB Gen. Coun. 2001)	Mixed	Employer not required to bargain over decision to relocate offices used by union; however, employer required to negotiate over location of new union office because the location involved a condition of employment, and the benefits concerning location of office outweighed minimal burden on Department's management authority.

CASE NAME	MANDATORY	DESCRIPTION
Town of Orangetown, 16 NPER NY-14532 (N.Y. PERB ALJ 1994)	Mixed	Proposal that police officers be allowed free use of City's recreational facilities. Proposal mandatory to the extent it applied to bargaining unit members.
Town of Windsor, 19 NPER CT-27079 (Conn. SBLR 1996)	No	Employer eliminated practice of allowing employees to work on or wash private vehicles at employer-owned facilities while off-duty. Not negotiable since use of public equipment for personal purposes was not directly or indirectly related to work.
Equipment		
City of Iowa City v. Iowa PERB, PEB ¶34,591 (Iowa) (CCH, 1985)	Yes	Proposal that employer provide bulletproof vests.
City of Newark, No. 2006-44 (N.J. PERC 2005)	Yes	Proposal that employer broadcast the wind chill factor and heat index twice a day. Adoption of proposal would not require the employer to purchase new equipment.
City of Okmulgee, Oklahoma, 124 LA 423 (Walker, 2007)	No	Employer unilaterally issued policy in handbook concerning use of the employer's computers and the Internet. Terms for use of computers were not "material, substantial and significantly affecting the terms and conditions of employment."
Dormont Borough Police Association, 32 PPER ¶32100 (Pa. LRB 2001)	Yes	City installed new lockers for police officers. Physical conditions of workspace, including size and construction of lockers, were mandatory for bargaining.
Snohomish County, Decision 9770-A (Wash. PECB 2008)	Yes	Installation of new roll-up doors in correctional facility. The new doors increased the inmate-deputy ratio when one deputy was on a break by allowing other on-duty deputies to supervise the absent deputy's area.
Town of Shawangunk, 34 PERB P 4510 (N.Y. PERB ALJ 2001)	Yes	Proposal that officers be provided with night sights and three magazines for their duty weapons.
Town of Wallingford, Decision No. 3902 (Conn. SLBR 2003)	No	Order barring police officers from carrying personal cell phones while on duty. Management rights clause in contract gave employer the right to determine the "equipment" officers could use.
Village of Blasdell, 6:1 NPER 9 (N.Y. PERB ALJ 1997)	Yes	Employer discontinued practice of allowing employees to carry personal cell phones while on duty. Management rights clause ruled to be nonspecific and not a waiver of bargaining rights; no evidence that carrying cell phones impaired performance of duty.
Family And Medical Leave Act		
City of Schenectady, 727 N.Y.S.2d 748 (App.Div. 2001)	Yes	Employer refused to arbitrate a grievance challenging the placement of an officer on family leave. The contract provided unlimited sick leave; employer contended it was simply implementing the FMLA.

CASE NAME	MANDATORY	DESCRIPTION
FOP, Lodge 10 v. City of Allentown, 32 PPER ¶32110 (Pa. LRB ALJ 2001)	Yes	Employer unilaterally enacted policy requiring officers to substitute paid leave for FMLA leave entitlement.

Financial Disclosure

City of Buffalo, 18 NPER NY-17008 (N.Y. PERB ALJ 1995)	Yes	Enforcement of financial disclosure requirement; City's ethics code and need to root out official corruption did not override obligation to bargain.

Fitness Standards

City of Cedar Rapids, 16 NPER IA-24002 (Iowa PERB 1993)	Yes	Implementation of physical performance test regulation.
City of Easton, 13 NPER PA-22033 (Pa. LRB ALJ 1990)	Yes	Implementation of mandatory physical fitness plan.
City of Grand Rapids, 17 NPER MI-26014 (Mich. ERC 1994)	No	Voluntary physical fitness program which was not a condition of employment. Program had no significant impact on wages, hours, or benefits.
City of Olympia, PEB ¶45, 799 (Wash. ERB) (CCH, 1989)	Yes	City must bargain over all aspects of mandatory physical fitness plan.
City of Oneonta, 15 NPER NY-14553 (N.Y. PERB ALJ 1993)	Yes	Minimum physical fitness standards, including run, bench press, body fat test, and stretch test. Union's time to file unfair labor practice charge began to run on date City unequivocally announced implementation of standards.

Grievance Procedures

City of Pittsburg, Decision 1563-M (Cal. PERB 2003)	No	City Council's use of a consultant to review and recommend what action to take in response to grievances is a matter of managerial prerogative that is not negotiable.
Communication Workers of America, Case No. CA-2003-017 (Fla. PERC 2003)	No	Employer took position in bargaining that only employees had the right to file grievances, not the labor organizations. Commission held that labor organizations have non-waivable right to process grievances in their own names.
Township of West Milford, 30 NJPER ¶77 (N.J. PERC 2004)	Yes	Union proposal to define as a grievance "any complaint, difference or dispute between the employer and any employee with respect to the interpretation, application, or violation of any provisions of the agreement or any applicable rule or regulation or policies, agreements, or administrative decisions affecting any employee covered by this agreement."

CASE NAME	MANDATORY	DESCRIPTION
Village of Saugerties Police Benevolent Association, 33 NYPER P 4531 (N.Y. PERB Dir. 2000)	Yes	Proposal sought to define the "grievance." Proposal did not extend the grievance beyond the four corners of the collective bargaining agreement.

Grooming and Dress Codes

CASE NAME	MANDATORY	DESCRIPTION
City of Chester, 13 NPER PA-22006 (Pa. LRB 1990)	No	New requirement that off-duty officers testify in uniform.
City of West Haven, 13 NPER CT-22010 (Conn. SBLR 1990)	Yes	Change in past practice of allowing weekend and evening employees to wear jeans to work.
County of Riverside, 27 GERR 1245 (Cal. 1989)	Yes	New dress code requiring detectives to wear suit and tie.
Fraternal Order of Police v. City of Fort Lauderdale, PEB ¶45,389 (Fla.) (CCH, 1988)	Yes	"No beards" policy.
Law Enforcement Labor Services v. Hennepin County, 449 N.W.2d 725 (Minn. 1990)	No	Length and style of hair, mustaches, and fingernails; decision rests on inherent power of sheriff.

Hiring Practices

CASE NAME	MANDATORY	DESCRIPTION
Kirkland Police Officers' Guild, 2000 WL 277929 (Wash. PERC 2000)	No	Unfair labor practice complaint alleging that employer unilaterally modified its practices regarding rehiring former employees.

Holidays

CASE NAME	MANDATORY	DESCRIPTION
County of Passaic, 29 NJPERC ¶91 (N.J. PERC 2003)	Yes	Proposal that holiday pay be included in base salary. Matter negotiable since it concerned wages; issues of whether holiday pay was pensionable to be decided by pension system.

Hours of Work

CASE NAME	MANDATORY	DESCRIPTION
Borough of Closter, PERC No. 2008-56 (N.J. PERC 2008)	Yes	Proposal to set work schedule in contract. Work schedules are mandatorily negotiable, except under circumstances where the employer proves a particularized need to preserve or change a work schedule to effectuate a specific governmental policy.
Borough of South River, PERC No. 2008-38 (N.J. PERC 2008)	No	Employer instituted new practice of requiring employees to use separate forms for requesting vacation leave and compensatory time off. Practice found not to "directly affect the work and welfare of officers."

CASE NAME	MANDATORY	DESCRIPTION
Insurance		
Borough of Woodcliff Lake, 29 NJPER ¶ 153 (N.J. PERC 2003)	Yes	Union sought arbitration of a grievance that Borough violated the parties' collective bargaining agreement by terminating its payment of health insurance premiums for the surviving spouse of a retired police officer. Commission concluded that health insurance issues are generally negotiable.
City of Edmonds, Decision 8798-A (Wash. PERC 2005)	No	Employer unilaterally raised prescription drug co-payments. Union waived right to bargain by failing to timely demand negotiations after learning of proposed change.
Borough of Emerson, 2005-68 (N.J. PERC 2005)	Yes	Labor organization proposed health insurance be provided current employees after they retire. Commission found that post-retirement health benefits mandatory for bargaining if not preempted by specific state statute.
City of Augusta, http://www.state.me.us/mlrb/decisions/ppc/01-09.htm (Me. LRB 2001)	Yes	Change in health carrier resulting in a change in the overall benefit structure. Fact that changed benefits were in the control of the health carrier did not eliminate the obligation to bargain.
City of Newark, 29 NJPER¶38 (N.J. PERC 2003)	Yes	Employer refused to proceed to arbitration over question of whether it was required to indemnify an officer against a $30,000 judgment awarded in a case where the officer was alleged to have assaulted a suspect.
City of Passaic, 29 NJPER ¶91 (N.J. PERC 2003)	Yes	Proposal would require employer to provide false arrest and indemnity insurance. Proposal mandatory even though it applied to off-duty conduct.
City of Schenectady, 17 NPER NY-17005 (N.Y. App. 1995)	Yes	New requirement that officer obtain authorization from City's physician for any surgical procedure recommended by the officer's personal physician.
Commonwealth of Pennsylvania, 917 A.2d 889 (Pa.Cmwlth. 2007)	Yes	After interest arbitrator required employees to participate in "mandatory generic" features of a prescription health plan, employer unilaterally implemented its own definition of the term "mandatory generic." The Court upheld subsequent grievance arbitrator's order that employer bargain over the meaning of the term "mandatory generic."
Delaware County, 16 NPER PA-24174 (Pa. LRB ALJ 1993)	Yes	Implementation of premium co-payment; existence of other plans without co-payment did not eliminate negotiability of change.
Detroit P.O.A. v. City of Detroit, PEB ¶34,500 (Michigan) (CCH, 1985)	Yes	Bargainable even though change made at insurer's request.

CASE NAME	MANDATORY	DESCRIPTION
Essex County Sheriff, PERC No. 2006-86 (N.J. PERC 2006)	Yes	Employer unilaterally changed health insurance specifications during bid process. Union was aware of change and requested bargaining, and employer did not have valid business necessity defense nor contractual waiver.
Fraternal Order of Police, Haas Memorial Lodge No. 7 v. City of Erie, 32 PPER ¶32147 (Pa. LRB ALJ 2001)	Yes	Employer unilaterally changed prescription benefits, including a smaller co-payment than what had been proposed by the Union Health and Welfare fund.
PBA of City of Mount Vernon v. PERB, PEB ¶34,818 (New York) (CCH, 1987)	Yes	Proposal that future employees would not be eligible for coverage if spouse had insurance.
Scott Township, 18 NPER PA-26189 (Pa. LRB ALJ 1995)	Yes	Decision to become self-insured for workers' compensation coverage; no change in level of benefits or manner of receiving benefits.
Skagit County Deputy Sheriffs Guild v. Skagit County, Decision 8886-A (Wash. PERC 2007)	Yes	Employer unilaterally implemented $50 annual deduction for dental insurance. Fact that employer sent all represented employees a benefit package two months before the change that reflected a $50 deductible for dental insurance did not suffice to meet the employer's bargaining obligations.
State Employment Relations Board v. State of Ohio, 645 N.E.2d 759 (Ohio App. 1994)	Yes	Increase in employees' premium rates and changes in coverage.
Township of Bridgewater, 16 NPER NJ-25109 (N.J. PERC ALJ 1994)	Yes	Imposition of co-payment requirement on employees covered by HMO plan.
Township of Nutley, 16 NPER NJ-25018 (N.J. PERC 1993)	No	Proposal would require City to utilize specific insurance carrier.
Triborough Bridge and Tunnel Authority, 17 NPER NY-13076 (N.Y. PERB 1994)	Yes	Proposal for health insurance cost-containment program.
West Caldwell Township, 19 NPER NJ-27226 (N.J. PERC 1996)	Yes	Proposal for maintenance of health benefits clause.
Yates County Deputy Sheriffs Association, PEB ¶45,511 (N.Y. PERB) (CCH, 1989)	Yes	Increase in prescription drug insurance co-payment from $2 to $5.

CASE NAME	MANDATORY	DESCRIPTION
Insurance for Retirees		
Borough of Matawan, 25 NJPER P 30140 (N.J. PERC 1999)	Yes	Proposal to include in contract past practice of paying health insurance premiums for retirees. Matter not preempted by state law requiring uniformity of benefits.
Borough of Upper Saddle River, Case No. 2008-22 (N.J. PERC 2007)	Yes	Retiree health care benefits negotiable under New Jersey law if provided on a uniform basis.
City of Linwood, 24 NJPER P 29068 (N.J. PERC ALJ 1997)	Yes	Unilateral cessation of health benefits for dependents of retirees.
City of Cohoes, 17 NPER NY-13058 (N.Y. PERB 1994)	Yes	Fact that payments would continue beyond term of agreement under which employee retired did not render proposal non-mandatory.
City of Peekskill, 15 NPER NY-14643 (N.Y. PERB ALJ 1992)	Yes	City unilaterally required retirees to pay portion of health insurance premium where City paid 100% of premium in the past.
County of Ulster and Ulster County Sheriff, Case No. U-25870 (N.Y. PERB 2005)	Yes	Proposal for health insurance for retirees and dependents.
Essex County Sheriff, 19 NPER NJ-27190 (N.J. PERC 1996)	Yes	Employer refused to comply with contract clause providing for post-retirement health insurance; employer contended the matter was preempted by state law.
Law Enforcement Labor Services v. Mower County, 29 GERR 622 (Minn. App. 1991)	Yes	Unilateral change after conclusion of bargaining.
Rhode Island v. Rhode Island State Police Lodge 25, PEB ¶45,374 (Rhode Island) (CCH, 1988)	Yes	Proposal for post-retirement insurance.
Town of Yorktown, 14 NPER NY-14557 (N.Y. PERB ALJ 1991)	No	Proposal for health insurance to cover already-retired former employees.
Yakima County, Decision 9338 (Wash. PERC 2006)	Yes	Proposal would provide employer-paid medical coverage to police officers who have retired because of job-related disabilities. Issue held not to be preempted by state statutory scheme for disability pensions.
Interest Arbitration		
Klauder v. San Juan County Deputy Sheriffs' Guild, PEB ¶34,808 (Wash.) (CCH, 1986)	No	Provision would require interest arbitration of future contracts.

CASE NAME	MANDATORY	DESCRIPTION
Village of Williams Bay, Decision #30385-A (Wis. ERC 2002)	No	Union not covered by state interest arbitration law proposed that future contract disputes be resolved through interest arbitration. Commission found that effect of clause on terms and conditions of employment "is at best remote."
Job Duties		
Madera County Deputy Sheriffs Association v. Madera County Civil Service Commission, 2005 WL 236513 (Cal. App. 2005)	Yes	County imposed new requirement that district attorney investigators maintain detailed time records of their daily activities.
Job Specifications		
State of Rhode Island Department of Corrections, ULP-5657 (R.I. LRB 2005)	Yes	Employer unilaterally changed job specifications for two represented positions. No defense that change in specifications was initiated as a result of requests from union members.
Layoffs		
City of Pasco, Decision 3368-A (Wash. PERC, 1990)	Yes	Proposal that layoffs be seniority-based.
Dept. of Corrections v. P.B.A. Local 105, 2008 WL 2050832 (N.J. Super. A.D. 2008)	No	Furloughs resulting from shutdown of non-essential services as a result of state budget impasse. Legislative history made clear that Legislature intended to exempt furlough decisions from bargaining.
IUOE, Local 571 v. City of Plattsmouth, 660 N.W.2d 480 (Neb. 2003)	Yes	City unilaterally eliminated department and laid off represented employee. Employer required to bargain over effects of layoff before laying off employee.
Schuykill Haven Borough v. Schuykill Haven POA, 914 A.2d 936 (Pa.Cmwlth. 2006)	No	Arbitrator ordered that new contract contain a "no layoffs" clause. Court found that the total number of police officers or firefighters that a municipality desires to employ is an inherent management right.
Leave of Absence		
Dineen v. City of Chicago, PEB ¶34,800 (Illinois) (CCH, 1987)	Yes	Provision required employee seeking political office to take leave of absence.
West Caldwell Township, 19 NPER NJ-27226 (N.J. PERC 1996)	Yes	Proposal for unpaid leave of absence so that at least one officer could attend funeral of officers in other agencies who are killed in the line of duty.
Legal Representation and Indemnification		
City of Newark, 24 NPER P 29035 (N.J. PERC 1998)	Yes	Employer refused to arbitrate grievance challenging failure by City to provide legal representation to officers who were defendants in civil lawsuits.

CASE NAME	MANDATORY	DESCRIPTION
City of Newark, 29 NJPER ¶38 (N.J. PERC 2003)	Yes	Employer refused to proceed to arbitration over question of whether it was required to indemnify an officer against a $30,000 judgment awarded in a case where the officer was alleged to have assaulted a suspect.
City of Waterviliet, 13 NPER NY-14514 (N.Y. PERB ALJ 1991)	Yes	Requirement that employer defend and indemnify employees.
County of Passaic, 29 NJPERC ¶91 (N.J. PERC 2003)	Yes	Proposal would require employer to provide false arrest and indemnity insurance. Proposal mandatory even though it applied to off-duty conduct.
Township of New Bergen, 16 NPER NJ-24261 (N.J. PERC 1993)	Yes	Proposal would require employer to provide automobile insurance for officers who use personal vehicles on employer's business.
Union County 25 NJPER P 30141 (N.J. PERC 1999)	Yes	Past practice of allowing corrections officers in non-disciplinary court cases to select a defense attorney from a list of attorneys or to select another attorney who agreed to bill at County-approved rates.
Waterloo Police Prot. Ass'n v. Public Empl. Rels. Bd., 497 N.W.2d 833 (Iowa 1993)	Yes	Proposal for general and punitive damage coverage.
Light Duty		
Bern Township Police Association v. Bern Township, 30 PPER P 30061 (Pa. LRB 1999)	Yes	Unilateral assignment of light duty to sergeant on day shift; employer required to negotiate the impacts of such an assignment on the work schedules of other officers.
Capitol City Lodge No. 141 v. Ingham County Board of Commissioners, 2003 WL 283811 (Mich. App. 2003)	Yes	Employer unilaterally implemented new policies restricting light-duty assignments to employees with job-related injuries. Clause in collective bargaining agreement giving Sheriff the exclusive right to "determine assignments" not a waiver by the Union of the right to bargain over the issue.
City of Englewood, 16 NPER NJ-25128 (N.J. PERC 1994)	Yes	Requirement that officer on disability leave exhaust sick leave before being placed on light-duty status.
City of Wenatchee, 1998 WL 928320 (Wash. PERC 1998)	Yes	Unilateral termination of past practice of making light duty available for temporarily disabled officers.
City of Westerfield v. Labor Relations Commission, 770 N.E.2d 558 (Mass. App. 2002)	Yes	Employer with past practice allowing employees to remain on workers' compensation leave ordered employee to perform light-duty work.
Town of Carmel, 667 N.Y.S.2d 789 (A.D. 1998)	Yes	Employer changed practices to require light-duty officers to work desk without assistance; in past, desk officers had assistance of full-duty uniformed officer. Union demanded to negotiate over eligibility of desk officers for safety stipend.

CASE NAME	MANDATORY	DESCRIPTION
Township of Cherry Hill, 16 NPER NJ-25071 (N.J. PERC 1994)	Yes	Method of allocation of light-duty assignments, and provision of medical benefits and reimbursement for medical expenses for employees on assignment.
Township of Mt. Olive, 19 NPER NJ-27216 (N.J. PERC 1996)	Yes	Assignment of non-police duties to light-duty police officer.
Longevity		
City of Tarpon Springs, 16 NPER FL-25162 (Fla. PERC 1994)	Yes	Termination of longevity increases following expiration of contract.
Township of Gallaway, 24 NJPER P 29125 (N.J. PERC 1998)	Yes	Proposal for 10% longevity allowance for individuals who have announced intent to retire.
Triborough Bridge and Tunnel Authority, 17 NPER NY-13076 (N.Y. PERB 1994)	Yes	Proposal to increase longevity payments and to include lump sum longevity allowance in rate of pay for pension purposes.
Management Rights		
City of Cocoa, 15 NPER FL-23235 (Fla. PERC 1992)	No	Clause would waive union's rights to bargain over changes in mandatory subjects of bargaining.
City of Vail, UP-14-02 (Or. ERB 2003)	Yes	Employer closed its police department. Though the decision to no longer provide police services was a management right, employer required to bargain over impacts of decision before implementing it. Employer required to reinstate employees, make them whole, and negotiate over impacts.
Town of Branchburg, PEB ¶45,422 (N.J.) (CCH, 1989)	Yes	Clause would reserve management rights not abridged by contract.
Meal Periods		
Chautauqua County Sheriff's Association, PEB ¶(N.Y. PERB) (CCH, 1989)	Yes	Implementation of new receipt requirements for employer-paid meals.
County of Elizabeth, 26 NJPER P 13007 (N.J. PERC 1999)	Yes	Grievance challenging unilateral change in negotiated meal period from 45 to 30 minutes.
City of Hazleton, 17 NPER 26018 (Pa. LRB ALJ 1994)	Yes	Order prohibiting police officers from taking meal periods at residences of friends.
County of Nassau, 14 NPER NY-13029 (N.Y. PERB 1991)	Yes	Unilateral reduction of length of the meal break from 40 to 30 minutes.

CASE NAME	MANDATORY	DESCRIPTION
City of Nassau, 35 NYPER ¶4544 (N.Y. PERB ALJ 2002)	Yes	Employer unilaterally discontinued practice of paying employees $15 in meal money on days they worked 10 hours on a regularly-scheduled day off. Practice had been in existence more than 20 years.
County of Nassau, 30 NYPER P 4704 (N.Y. PERB ALJ 1997)	Yes	Employer unilaterally discontinued food service operations and closed cafeteria area between 2:00 and 4:00 a.m. Substitution of vending machines for cafeteria a "clear change in employees' terms and conditions of employment."
Dormont Police Association, 32 PPER ¶31224 (Pa. LRB ALJ 2001)	No	Employer unilaterally ended practice of allowing officers to take joint meal periods. Officers' interests in promotion of morale and productivity resulting from shared meal periods outweighed by public safety implications of fact that joint meal periods resulted in no officers on patrol during certain times of the day.
Fraternal Order of Transfer Police v. Southeastern Pennsylvania Transportation Authority, Case No. PERA-C-05-201-E (Pa. LRB 2005)	No	Employer unilaterally enacted new rules requiring that all lunches be taken on the officer's assigned beat or within walking distance of the beat assignment. Designation of where meals could be eaten a matter of inherent managerial prerogative.
Town of Windsor Locks, 16 NPER CT-25015 (Conn. SBLR 1993)	Yes	Single meeting where Town and Union discussed Town's intended change in past practice of permitting civilian dispatchers to leave premises on meal breaks insufficient to fulfill Town's duty to bargain where meeting took place one day before change.
Village of Lancaster, 13 NPER NY-14606 (N.Y. PERB ALJ 1990)	No	Proposal would allow officers to select meal periods.

Medical Examinations

Orangetown Policemen's Benevolent Association, Case No. U-25717 (N.Y. PERB 2007)	Yes	Employer announced new policy that Union representatives would not be allowed to videotape or audiotape medical examinations to determine line-of-duty injuries. The video or audiotaping of the medical examination is a mandatory subject of negotiation because it is a procedure for accumulating evidence to be utilized in the review of the initial determination and is not excluded from bargaining.

Off-Duty Conduct

Fraternal Order of Police, Lodge #5 v. City of Philadelphia, 30 PPER P 30185 (Pa. LRB 1999)	Yes	Unilateral implementation of formal written policy prohibiting certain types of off-duty behavior.

CASE NAME	MANDATORY	DESCRIPTION
Off-Duty Employment		
AFSCME, Local 2413 v. Town of St. Johnsbury, 12 NPER VT-21060 (Vt. LB 1991)	Yes	Restriction on secondary employment.
Borough of Hopatcong, 13 NPER NJ-22028 (N.J. PERC 1990)	No	Proposal that employer require street contractors to use at least one police officer for security.
City of Highland Park, PEB ¶45,659 (Mich. ERC) (CCH, 1988)	Mixed	Requirement for advance permission for outside employment; union made untimely demand to bargain and failed to prove existence of past practice.
City of Paterson and Paterson PBA, PERC No. 2004-6 (N.J. PERC 2003)	No	City assumed responsibility for administration of off-duty work program, and instituted requirement for prior approval of any off-duty work. Decision to regulate off-duty work held to be management right.
City of Pullman, 1 Public Safety Labor News 3 (Williams, 1994)	Yes	Ban on all secondary employment in security positions.
City of Reading, 19 NPER PA-27259 (Pa. LRB 1996)	No	New requirement that officers desiring to engage in non-police off-duty work obtain prior approval before engaging in the work.
Elizabethtown Borough, 29 PPER P 29099 (Pa. LRB ALJ 1998)	Yes	Unilateral implementation of ban on all off-duty employment.
Somerset County Sheriff, 28 NJPER ¶33,077 (N.J. PERC 2002)	Yes	Rate pay for work performed for outside contractors.
State of Connecticut, 13 NPER CT-22006 (Conn. SBLR. 1990)	Yes	New requirement that officers not work two consecutive shifts.
Township of Hanover, 16 NPER NJ-25039 (N.J. PERC 1994)	Yes	Implementation of plan for distribution of off-duty employment opportunities.
Township of Union, 32 NJPER 53 (N.J. PERC Dir. 2006)	No	Unilateral termination of "Jobs in Blue" program under which off-duty work in uniform was administered. Under New Jersey law, employer has management right to control off-duty employment.
Ulster County Sheriff, 16 NPER NY-14665 (N.Y. PERB ALJ 1993)	Yes	Unilateral implementation of ban on off-duty employment with other law enforcement agencies.

CASE NAME	MANDATORY	DESCRIPTION
On-Call Practices		
Bensalem Township Police Benevolent Association, PF-C-03-150-E (Pa. LRB ALJ 2005)	Mixed	Employer initiated change in on-call practices for detectives. Decision to make the change not mandatory for bargaining, but employer required to bargain over effects of the decision.
Douglass Township, 34 PPER ¶131 (Pa. LRB ALJ 2003)	Yes	Unilateral implementation of requirement that sergeant or next ranking officer respond to a page within 15 minutes.
Overtime/Compensatory Time Off		
Borough of Roseland, 26 NJPER P 31077 (N.J. PERC 2000)	Yes	Employer issued memorandum announcing policy change requiring payment of overtime at end of year rather than continuing past practice of allowing officers to convert accumulated comp time at any time.
Brookline Police Association, PEB ¶45,749 (Mass. LRC) (CCH, 1989)	Yes	Unilateral change in practice of paying compensatory time for court appearances.
City of Beacon, 30 NYPER P 4695 (N.Y. PERB ALJ 1997)	Yes	Proposal to allow employees to elect compensatory time off in lieu of cash compensation for overtime. Proposal was not preempted by FLSA.
City of Newburgh, 19 NPER NY-14635 (N.Y. PERB Director 1996)	Yes	Proposal for four hours' minimum pay for employees who voluntarily accept extra work.
City of Pasco, Decision 9181 (Wash. PERC 2005)	Yes	Employer initiated change in past practice concerning use of compensatory time off. When Union filed unfair labor practice complaint in protest, employer eliminated compensatory time off.
City of Philadelphia, 18 NPER PA-27133 (Pa. LRB Hearing Examiner 1996)	Yes	City unilaterally rescinded practice of paying employees double time; contract specifically provided for payment of time and one-half.
City of Stamford, 14 NPER CT-23051 (Conn. SBLR 1992)	No	Cessation of mistaken practice of paying employees double time; contract specifically provided for payment of time and one-half.
Dunn County v. Wisconsin Employment Relations Commission, 718 N.W.2d 138 (Wis. App. 2006)	Yes	County challenged legality of contract clause that required Department overtime be offered to bargaining unit members first, and then to other qualified employees within the Department. Court found that clause related to wages, hours, and conditions of employment, and did not infringe upon County's constitutionally-protected prerogatives.
Kalama Police Guild, Decision 6773-A-PECB (Wash. PERC 2000)	No	Police Chief worked patrol shifts rather than assigning work on overtime basis to employees. Evidence showed Chief had history of working such shifts.

CASE NAME	MANDATORY	DESCRIPTION
Matter of Borough of Little Ferry, PEB ¶45,301 (N.J.) (CCH, 1988)	Yes	Proposal that seniority govern overtime assignments.
Town of Kearny, 25 NJPER P 30173 (N.J. PERC 1999)	Yes	Unilateral change in past practice of replacing absent police officers by initially offering overtime to off-duty supervisors of rank equal to that of absent officer.
Township of Lopatcong, 17 NPER NJ-26010 (N.J. PERC ALJ 1994)	Yes	Repudiation of contract's requirement that officers on duty alone after sunset receive double time. City's argument that premium pay interfered with management rights rejected.
Triborough Bridge and Tunnel Authority, 16 NPER NY-14595 (N.Y. PERB ALJ 1994)	Yes	Proposal that overtime be equalized among bargaining unit members.
Ventura County Professional Peace Officers' Association, No. J1910-M (Cal. PERB 2007)	No	Employer unilaterally implemented mandatory overtime policy. Contract specifically granted employer right to assign overtime.
Village of Lombard, 15 PERI P 2007 (Ill. SLRB General Counsel 1999)	Mixed	Decision whether or not to have mandatory overtime held not mandatory for bargaining; procedures for the assigning of overtime mandatory for negotiations.
Parity Clauses		
Association of Oregon Corrections Employees v. State Dept. of Corrections, 164 P.3d 291 (Or. App. 2007)	Yes	Police union attacked employer's alleged promise to other unions that no labor organization would receive a wage increase.
City of Barberton, 13 NPER OH-21914 (Ohio Court of Common Pleas 1990)	Yes	City entered into "me too" agreement with another union; upheld because police union won its wage proposal in arbitration and was unable to show harm from "me too" clause.
County of Sullivan, 18 NPER NY-14677 (N.Y. PERB ALJ 1995)	Prohibited	County signed collective bargaining agreement with other bargaining units tying wage increases to that received for County Sheriff's Union.
Town of Orangetown, 16 NPER NY-14532 (N.Y. PERB ALJ 1994)	Mixed	Proposal that police officers receive equal amount of holiday and "other special occasion" time off as received by employees in other bargaining units. Mandatory for negotiations, but subject to later nullification.
Town of Shrewsbury, PEB ¶45,438 (Mass. LRC) (CCH, 1988)	No	Clause in superior officers' contract tied wage rates to officers' contract.

CASE NAME	MANDATORY	DESCRIPTION
Whatcom County Deputy Sheriff's Guild, Decision 8512-A (Wash. PERC 2005)	Yes	Law enforcement organization challenged "parity" or "me too" clauses in employer's other labor contracts. Commission found parity clauses are not per se illegal, and can be enforced if they do not have a demonstrable impact on the bargaining process.

Parking Rates

CASE NAME	MANDATORY	DESCRIPTION
City of Jacksonville, 17 NPER FL-26178 (Fla. PERC 1995)	Yes	Imposition of paid parking upon bargaining unit members.
City of Milwaukee, Decision 31221-B (Wis. PERC 2005)	No	At request of private parking subcontractor, City discontinued practice of allowing motorcycle officers to park motorcycles in City parking facility. Contract contained language requiring City to reimburse employees for parking charges, and to give notice of available parking facilities. PERC concluded availability of alternate parking coupled with contract language indicated parties had "bargained to completion" over the issue, and allowed City to make the change.
Franklin County Sheriff, 20 OPER ¶130 (Ohio SERB 2003)	Yes	Employees working in new location who were formerly able to park for free in fenced lot were required to pay a monthly parking fee. Board found that parking fees were reasonably related to wages and terms and conditions of employment.
Los Angeles Police Prot. League v. Los Angeles, 212 Cal.Rptr. 251 (A.D. 1985)	Yes	Imposition of $5.00 per month charge for parking in city lots.
Omaha Police Union, Local 101, IUPA v. City of Omaha, Case No. 1121 (Neb. CIR 2007)	Yes	Employer eliminated 13 parking stalls that had been used on a first-come, first-serve basis by bargaining unit members. Management rights clause did not constitute waiver of right to bargain.

Pay Practices

CASE NAME	MANDATORY	DESCRIPTION
City of Beacon, 30 NYPER P 4695 (N.Y. PERB ALJ 1997)	Yes	Proposal to set rates for work out of classification.
City of Boston v. Labor Relations Commission, No. 97-P-1232 (Mass. App. 1999)	Yes	Employer attempted to discontinue 13-year practice of payment of pay differential to captains who were not entitled to receive differential under contract. Court held that "complete agreement" clause in contract not an enforceable waiver of bargaining rights.
City of Garfield, 26 NJPER P 31144 (N.J. PERC 2000)	Yes	City refused to arbitrate grievance over whether it violated contract when it compensated sergeant at sergeant's rate rather than lieutenant's salary rate for duties performed while he was assigned as shift commander.

CASE NAME	MANDATORY	DESCRIPTION
City of Jersey City, 17 NPER NJ-26105 (N.J. PERC 1995)	Yes	Unilateral implementation of new payroll system with a payroll lag time.
City of Newark, PERC No.2008-60 (N.J. PERC 2008)	Yes	Employer refused to arbitrate grievance challenging failure of employer to continue paying hazardous duty premiums to officers using sick leave. Topic mandatory for negotiations because of economic impact.
City of Newburgh, 19 NPER NY-14635 (N.Y. PERB Dir. 1996)	Yes	Proposal for tuition reimbursement for job-related classes.
City of Tarpon Springs, 16 NPER FL-25162 (Fla. PERC 1994)	Yes	Termination of merit steps following expiration of contract.
County of Bergen, 18 NPER NJ-27077 (N.J. PERC 1996)	No	Police organization sought to compel County to pay annual salary adjustments during negotiations of a new contract; past practice of County's doing so held to be a voluntary act, not binding in the future.
County of Bond, 16 NPER IL-25144 (Ill. SLRB 1994)	Yes	Implementation of wage scale different from that set forth in contract.
Local 2787 v. City of Montpelier, 643 A.2d 838 (Vt. 1993)	Yes	Change from weekly to bi-weekly pay periods; union did not demand to bargain over change for at least 13 months after employer announced intended change.
New York State Corrections Officers, No. U-23174 (N.Y. PERB ALJ 2005)	Yes	Employer enacted new policy authorizing the withholding of unit members' paychecks for the untimely submission of time cards, and requiring members to call in before the pre-shift briefing for each day they were absent.
Sheriff of Worcester County v. Labor Relations Commission, 808 N.E.2d 331 (Mass. App. 2004)	Yes	Employer unilaterally changed from weekly payroll system to monthly system.
Township of Cherry Hill, 19 NPER NJ-27199 (N.J. PERC 1996)	Yes	Change in payday from Thursday to Friday.
Township of Exeter, 17 NPER PA-26078 (Pa. LRB 1995)	No	Institution of time clock policy.
Township of Nutley, 16 NJPER P 31048 (N.J. PERC 2000)	Yes	Unilateral reduction of starting salaries of newly-hired police officers during pendency of interest arbitration hearings.
Wilkes-Barre Police Benevolent Association v. City of Wilkes-Barre, 29 PPER P 29041 (Pa. LRB ALJ 1998)	Yes	City unilaterally stopped 30-year old practice of handing out paychecks at roll call and began mailing checks to officers' homes.

CASE NAME	MANDATORY	DESCRIPTION
Pension Benefits		
Borough of Butler, 26 NJPER P 31051 (N.J. PERC 2000)	No	Proposal providing for flat payment of 20% of salary upon retirement of employee who had worked 25 years. Not negotiable because benefit was not paid to current employees as a reward for years of service.
Brotherhood of West Chester Police v. Borough of West Chester, 798 A.2d 797 (Pa. Cmwlth. 2002)	No	Borough's voters enacted a charter provision allowing higher pension benefits from those set by state law. The Court found state pension law legally pre-empted bargaining over higher pension benefits.
City of Carbon Borough, 18 NPER PA-27079 (Pa. LRB ALJ 1996)	Yes	Unilateral implementation of ordinance eliminating retired officers' ability to participate in an alternative formulation of pension benefits and increasing service requirement for police pension eligibility.
City of Erie Police Department, 18 NPER PA-27056 (Pa. LRB ALJ 1996)	Yes	City unilaterally discontinued COLA increases to pension benefits for retired police officers.
City of Flint, 18 MPER ¶15 (Mich. ERC 2005)	Yes	Employer enacted ordinance change to limit the number of pay periods used to compute the final average compensation for purposes of computing pension benefits.
City of New London, 16 NPER CT-25054 (Conn. SBLR 1994)	Mixed	Unilateral removal of some retirees from pension trust fund in order to pay them future pensions from general fund; no showing that action affected stability of trust fund, and retirees are not "employees" within scope of collective bargaining law.
City of Oak Park, 11 NPER P 29066 (Mich. ERC 1998)	Yes	City passed ordinance under which pension benefits of City employees who were convicted of certain crimes could be forfeited. Mere fact that ordinance was considered at two public council meetings did not indicate that Union had waived right to bargain over ordinance; City held to have failed to provide Union adequate notice of intended change.
County of LaCrosse, 508 N.W.2d 9 (Wis. 1993)	Yes	Proposal to grant jailers same pension benefits as police officers.
Detroit P.O.A. v. City of Detroit, 214 N.W.2d 803 (1974)	Yes	Level of pension benefits.
Fraternal Order of Police, Reading Lodge #9 v. City of Reading, 30 PPER P 30062 (Pa. LRB 1999)	No	City unilaterally increased pensions for retired officers. Even though increased benefits necessarily reduced funds for future retirement of bargaining unit members, City not required to negotiate over changes directly impacting only non-bargaining unit retirees.
Matter of Garden City, PEB ¶45,335 (N.Y.) (CCH, 1988)	No	Proposed reduction in existing retirement benefits.

CASE NAME	MANDATORY	DESCRIPTION
Prospect Park Borough, 18 NPER PA-27078 (Pa. LRB ALJ 1996)	Yes	Unilateral establishment of mandatory pension contribution from police employees who had not previously contributed to fund.
Town of Barrington, 1993 WL 65458 (R.I. 1993)	Yes	Reduction in retirement service requirement from 25 to 20 years.
Town of Stratford, 18 NPER CT-27048 (Conn. SBLR 1996)	Mixed	Unilateral implementation of requirement that present and future disability retirees complete questionnaire and/or submit to medical examination in order to retain disability pension benefits.
Upper St. Clair Township, 18 NPER PA-26159 (Pa. LRB ALJ 1995)	Yes	Unilateral change in level of pension benefits.
Wilkes-Barre Township, 878 A.2d 977 (Pa.Cmwlth. 2005)	Yes	Employer unilaterally enacted ordinance changing the computation of pension benefits so that vacation and sick leave cashout would not be considered in computing the monthly pension. The Court found that local ordinances "may not be used as a guise" to avoid bargaining obligations.
Pension Boards		
City of Detroit v. AFSCME Council 25, 118 Mich. App. 211 (1982)	Yes	Composition of police retirement board.
Performance Evaluations		
City of Rochester, 19 NPER-27076 (Mich. ERC 1996)	No	Continuation of informal, unstructured evaluations by Police Chief of Department employees' evaluations were not included in personnel file and had no impact on tenure, discipline, or promotions.
Personal Days Off		
Town of Greenburgh, 14 NPER NY-14559 (N.Y. PERB ALJ 1992)	No	Proposal for use of personal days off without regard to staffing.
Personnel Files		
AFSCME v. City of New Britain, 538 A.2d 1022 (Conn. 1988)	No	Purging of materials from files; bargaining law overridden by Public Records Act.
Borough of Hopatcong, 13 NPER NJ-22028 (N.J. PERC 1990)	Yes	Contract provision requiring employer to maintain confidential file; separate file maintained for Public Records Act purposes. Proposal to allow officer access and rebuttal rights to securely maintained personnel files.
Village of Lancaster, 13 NPER NY-14606 (N.Y. PERB ALJ 1990)	Yes	Proposal that reprimands be removed after one year.

CASE NAME	MANDATORY	DESCRIPTION
Physical Examinations		
Fraternal Order of Police, Fort Pitt Lodge No. 1 v. City of Pittsburgh, 33 PPER ¶33103 (Pa. LRB ALJ 2002)	No	Employer unilaterally implemented physical fitness and swimming tests for members of the SWAT Team. Testing found to be rationally related to duties of Team members, and thus were an extension of the selection process.
City of Schenectady, 15 NPER NY-17009 (N.Y. S.Ct. 1992)	Yes	New requirement that injured officers submit to physical examination on their own time after returning to work.
Law Enforcement Labor Services, 463 N.W.2d 546 (Minn. App. 1990)	Mixed	Establishment of physical examination policy; effects, not establishment, of policy negotiable.
Polygraph Examinations		
IBPO v. LRC, PEB ¶34,096 (Mass.) (CCH, 1984)	No	Polygraph examinations for officers suspected of criminal vandalism.
PBA v. City of White Plains, 12 NY PERB ¶3046 (1979)	Yes	Polygraph examinations relating to non-criminal employee discipline.
Premium Pay		
Borough of Upper Saddle River, #2008-22 (N.J. PERC 2007)	Yes	Proposal would allow the parties to agree on future premium pay positions.
Privacy		
Multnomah County, Oregon, Case No. UP-18-06 (Or. ERB 2008)	No	After receiving requests from the media, employer disclosed bargaining unit members' sick leave usage, overtime pay, and discipline. Since the employer had never before received such requests from the media, there was no "past practice" the employer changed in releasing the information.
Probationary Period		
New York State Troopers, Inc., 35 NYPER ¶3024 (N.Y. PERB 2002)	Inconclusive	Labor organization contended that employer made unilateral change in long-standing interpretation of word "probation" as used in disciplinary settlements. At unfair labor practice hearing, labor organization failed to demonstrate the practice in existence before the change.
Production Standards/Quotas		
City of Canton, 13 NPER OH-21907 (Ohio SERB ALJ 1990)	Yes	Implementation of "points" requirement for patrol officers.
Triborough Bridge and Tunnel Authority, 16 NPER NY-14595 (N.Y. PERB ALJ 1994)	Yes	Proposal concerning employee quotas.

CASE NAME	MANDATORY	DESCRIPTION
Promotions		
Broadnax v. City of New Haven, 932 A.2d 1063 (Conn. 2007)	No	Under Connecticut law, ultimate decisions with respect to promotion (as opposed to promotional procedures) are not mandatory for collective bargaining.
City of Allentown, 18 NPER PA-26209 (Pa. LRB ALJ 1995)	Yes	Consideration of employees for promotion who received scores lower than the minimum possible cutoff level under the collective bargaining agreement.
City of Buffalo, 18 NPER NY-13023 (N.Y. PERB 1996)	No	City varied from appointing individual placing first on a police civil service examination; the long-standing past practices allowed City to select from top three candidates.
City of Chester, 17 NPER PA-26145 (Pa. LRB 1995)	Yes	Creation of lieutenant's position.
City of Cleveland, 14 NPER OH-23388 (Ohio SERB 1992)	Yes	Decision to not make promotions to fill vacancies within department.
City of Detroit v. Detroit Police Lieutenants and Sergeants Association, 2007 WL 397146 (Mich. App. 2007)	Yes	Employer unilaterally changed the criteria for promotion to the rank of sergeant. Issue negotiable even though those taking the examination were not members of the bargaining unit.
City of Dubuque v. PERB, 444 N.W.2d 495 (Iowa 1989)	Yes	Change in evaluations used in promotional process.
Hamburg Police Officers Association, Case No. PF-C-06-54-E (Pa. LRB 2006)	No	Employer unilaterally changed promotional standards applying to the amount and proximity of recent discipline that would disqualify an applicant. Where promotional procedures are mandatory for bargaining, promotional standards are not.
City of Hartford, 17 NPER CT-26052 (Conn. SBLR 1995)	Mixed	Change in weighting from equal weighting of components to 80% weighting placed on oral examination; no duty to bargain with regard to study materials selected for examination.
City of Huber Heights, 13 NPER OH-21856 (Ohio SERB ALJ 1990)	Yes	Elimination of requirement that lieutenant serve as sergeant first.
City of Milwaukee, No. 32138 (Wis. PERC 2007)	No	Police supervisors' association submitted bargaining proposal requiring employer to grant hearing to employees passed over for promotions. Under Wisconsin law, a union has no right to bargain over the process the employer uses to identify and list who is eligible for promotion.

CASE NAME	MANDATORY	DESCRIPTION
FOP Rose of Sharon Lodge No. 3, 30 PPER P 30113 (Pa.Cmwlth. 1999)	No	Employer reduced length of service time required for promotion of police officers. Employers not obligated to bargain over job qualifications under Pennsylvania law.
Franklin Park and Illinois State Board of Labor Relations, 638 N.E.2d 1144 (Ill. App. 1994)	Yes	Wide-ranging decision on negotiability of promotional issue. Promotional criteria, weighting criteria, minimum eligibility requirements, order of promotions from eligibility list, and posting of examination scores found to be mandatorily negotiable; promotional standards to positions outside of bargaining unit found not to be mandatorily negotiable.
Fraternal Order of Police, Lodge #5, 30 PPER P 30039 (Pa. LRB ALJ 1999)	No	Union demanded access to City's policy regarding use of internal affairs complaints as criteria for promotions and transfers. City held to have managerial right to determine qualifications for promotion or transfer.
Glendale Prof. Policemen's Association v. City of Glendale, 264 N.W.2d 594 (Wis. 1978)	Yes	Clause restricted discretion of chief in making promotions.
Pennsylvania State Troopers Assn. v. Pennsylvania State Labor Relations Board, 809 A.2d 422 (Pa.Cmwlth. 2002)	No	Change in weights assigned oral and written portions of promotional examination. While promotional procedures mandatory for bargaining, weighting of test scores was not.
Policemen's Benevolent and Protective Association, #156, 15 PERI P 3010 (Ill. LLRB 1999)	No	Labor organization made bargaining proposal over promotional criteria for promotions to positions of sergeant and lieutenant. As promotional positions were outside of the rank-and-file bargaining unit, employer had no obligation to bargain over proposal.
Salisbury Township, 16 NPER PA-25041 (Pa. LRB Hearing Examiner 1994)	Yes	Implementation of new civil service rules and regulations concerning promotional procedures and standards.
SERB v. City of Cincinnati, 20 OPER ¶145 (Ohio SERB ALJ 2003)	Yes	Employer attempted to apply charter amendment to go outside Department to fill the promotional position of assistant police chief. Change in method of filling such vacancies was negotiable because it impacted the terms and conditions of bargaining unit members.
State of New Jersey, 26 NJPER P 31040 (N.J. PERC 2000)	No	Employer rescinded several promotions to the position of sergeant eight days after they were made, citing the fact that officers were subjects in an internal affairs investigation.
State of New Jersey and State Troopers Non-Commissioned Officers Association, 28 NJPER ¶33149 (N.J. PERC 2002)	No	Request for binding arbitration of group grievance challenging employer's decision not to promote bargaining unit members while internal investigations were pending. Employer's interest in knowing results of internal investigation before permanently promoting employees outweighed employee's interest in obtaining promotions.

CASE NAME	MANDATORY	DESCRIPTION
Town of Norwell, 14 NPER MA-23007 (Mass. LRC 1992)	Yes	Change in past practice of promoting individuals ranked first on civil service list.
Town of Piscataway, 30 NJPER ¶57 (N.J. PERC 2004)	Yes	While employer allowed the prerogative to set promotional criteria and to apply those criteria to its final promotional decisions, it was required to bargain over the order in which it would administer the components of the promotional system and whether to have the results of the written portion of the examination withheld until all other aspects of the promotional process were completed.
Township of Piscataway, 31 NJPER ¶17 (N.J. Sup. 2005)	Yes	Employer refused to bargain over proposals concerning the order in which the employer would administer various components of the promotional process and whether to withhold the results of one component – the numerical scores from the written examination – until all other aspects of the promotional process were completed. Court found proposals did not impinge upon managerial prerogative of determining criteria for promotions.
Town of Westfield, 16 NPER NJ-24184 (N.J. PERC 1993)	Mixed	Proposal to set minimum qualifications for promotional exams, including weights to be given to various promotional criteria.
Township of Wall, 28 NJPER 33005 (N.J. PERC 2001)	Yes	Union filed grievance challenging employer's decision to deviate from a rank-ordered promotional list.
Upper Southampton Township Police Benevolent Assn., 31 PPER P 31068 (Pa. LRB ALJ 2000)	No	Employer appointed sergeant to acting lieutenant position. Promotions to positions outside of bargaining unit not mandatory for negotiations.
Village of Elk Grove Village, 21 PERI ¶14 (Ill. LRB Gen. Counsel 2005)	No	Employer proposed that to the extent that negotiated promotional procedures conflicted with a recently-enacted statewide promotional law, the contract would control. Proposal not mandatory since the minimum guarantees in the promotional law were not waivable.

Psychological Testing

CASE NAME	MANDATORY	DESCRIPTION
City of Buffalo, 13 NPER NY-14569 (N.Y. PERB ALJ 1990)	Yes	Testing and counseling of officers involved in traumatic incidents or use of force.
City of Haverhill, 13 NPER MA-21032 (Mass. LRC 1990)	Yes	Results analogized to drug testing.
County of Allegan, 14 NPER MI-23024 (Mich. ERC 1992)	Yes	Requirement that employees submit to psychological testing as condition of employment.

CASE NAME	MANDATORY	DESCRIPTION
Hill v. City of Winona, 454 N.W.2d 659 (Minn. App. 1990)	Yes	Giving of a compulsory psychological examination.

Residency

CASE NAME	MANDATORY	DESCRIPTION
City of Bernard, 598 N.E.2d 15 (Ohio App. 1991)	Yes	Residency requirement must be bargained before it is imposed.
City of Hialeah, 13 NPER FL-21338 (Fla. PERC 1990)	Yes	Giving of bonus points on exams to City residents.
City of York, 17 NPER PA-25178 (Pa. LRB 1994)	Yes	Implementation of residency policy.
County of Cook v. Illinois LRB, 807 N.E.2d 613 (Ill. App. 2004)	Yes	Employer refused to bargain over proposals dealing with residency. Court held that residency is not a matter of inherent managerial authority.
Plains Township Police Bargaining Unit v. Plains Township, 33 PPER ¶33019 (Pa. LRB ALJ 2001)	Yes	Employer enacted new civil service rules requiring continued residency for duration of officers' employment. Argument that new language merely "clarification" of existing rules rejected.
Throop Borough, 16 NPER PA-25063 (Pa. LRB 1994)	No	Unilateral imposition of residency requirement on new police hires.
Township of Moon v. Police Officers of Township of Moon, 498 A.2d 1305 (Pa. 1985)	Yes	Residency requirement not an exclusive management right and is subject to bargaining and arbitration.
Watervliet Police Benevolent Association, 35 NYPER ¶4596 (N.Y. PERB ALJ 2002)	Yes	Unilateral imposition of residency requirement for police department.

Retention of Benefits

CASE NAME	MANDATORY	DESCRIPTION
City of Beacon, 30 NYPER P 4695 (N.Y. PERB ALJ 1997)	Yes	Employer's proposal to delete maintenance of benefits clause from contract
City of Camden, PERC No. 2004-7 (N.J. PERC 2003)	Yes	Proposal for retention of benefits clause. Held to be mandatory so long as it did not seek to regulate working conditions outside of bargaining unit.

Retirement

CASE NAME	MANDATORY	DESCRIPTION
Alaska Correctional Officers Association v. State of Alaska, Case No. 06-1481-ULP (Alaska Department of Labor 2007)	No	State enacted law prospectively changing retirement system from defined benefits to defined contribution program. Retirement not mandatory subject of bargaining under Alaska law.

CASE NAME	MANDATORY	DESCRIPTION
City of Detroit, Case No. C06 B-023 (Mich. ERC 2007)	No	Employer enacted ordinance changing amortization period for pension plan. State law completely delegated to the City the right to set the amortization period.
Snohomish County and Snohomish County Deputy Sheriffs' Association, Decision 8733-C (Wash. PERB 2006)	Yes	Proposal that employer make contribution to employee's deferred compensation account. Proposal not preempted by statewide police/fire retirement plan.
Village of Saugerties, Case U-25832 (N.Y. PERB 2005)	Yes	Police union referred to arbitration proposal that would convert unused sick leave to provide additional health insurance for retirees and dependents.

Ride-Along Policies

West St. Paul v. Law Enforcement Labor Services, 30 GERR. 343 (Minn. 1992)	Yes	Adoption of policy allowing explorer scouts to ride along; viewed as safety issue.

Right to Counsel in Shooting Situations

Long Beach POA v. City of Long Beach, 156 Cal. App.3d 996 (1984)	Yes	Unilateral change in past practice of allowing counsel in shooting cases.

Rules and Regulations

City of Newark, 32 NJPER ¶47 (NJ. PERC 2006)	Yes	Union proposed continuation of contract clause allowing it to file grievances concerning new rules and regulations. Under New Jersey law, clause could only apply to rules and regulations dealing with mandatorily negotiable subjects.
West Caldwell Township, 19 NPER NJ-27226 (N.J. PERC 1996)	Yes	Proposal that employer give union ten days' notice of changes in rules.

Safety Issues

Borough of Paterson, 26 NPER P 31041 (N.J. PERC 2000)	Yes	Employer refused to arbitrate grievance alleging that its failure to assign an additional police officer to a shift violated the safety provisions of the collective bargaining agreement.
California Correctional Peace Officers Association v. State of California, 23 PERC P 30069 (Cal. PERB ALJ 1999)	Yes	Reconfiguration of prison population without negotiating effects of plan, including impacts on training, safety, and performance reports.
City of Newark, Case No. SN-2006-026 (N.J. PERC 2006)	Yes	Proposal for institution of safety committee and accident review board. Ruled mandatory for bargaining because of impact on safety.

CASE NAME	MANDATORY	DESCRIPTION
City of New Haven, 16 NPER CT-25020 (Conn. SBLR 1993)	Yes	Union's request for access to a facility to bring industrial hygienist onto premises to test air quality.
State of California, 23 PERC P 30114 (Cal. PERB ALJ 1999)	Yes	Employer installed new entry-exit security monitoring system at juvenile detention facility. Bargaining issues included privacy of storage of employee fingerprints, possibility of discipline through use of machine as timekeeping device, and possible impact on work hours.
Seniority		
Capital City Lodge #12, Fraternal Order of Police v. City of Harrisburg, 30 PPER P 30042 (Pa. LRB ALJ 1999)	Yes	Unilateral change from seniority shift bidding to platoon system as a means of implementing community policing program.
Camden County Sheriff, 30 NJPER ¶10 (N.J. PERC 2004)	Yes	Proposal that if a sheriff's department absorbed or merged with any other law enforcement agency, the newly-acquired employees would not bring with them any seniority for job-bidding purposes.
Shift Scheduling		
Association of Oregon Corrections Employees, Case No. UP-33-3 (Or. ERB 2005)	Yes	Employer implemented new schedule that changed the start and stop times of days off for several shifts.
Atlantic Highlands v. PBA, 469 A.2d 80 (N.J. Super. 1983)	No	Shift schedules not negotiable in small towns.
Borough of Belmar, 17 NPER NJ-26107 (N.J. PERC ALJ 1995)	Yes	Alteration of frequency of shift rotation from one to three weeks and requiring that officers seeking to exchange days, hours and tours of duty provide reasons in writing.
Borough of Bernardsville, No. 2008-4 (N.J. PERC 2007)	Mixed	Employer discontinued an alleged practice of permitting officers assigned to full-day, off-site training to discontinue their workdays at the end of training, even if the training did not last the normal length of the 12-hour shift. While issue was mandatory for bargaining, Union unable to prove that employer had consistent practice of not charging compensatory time to account for difference between training day and normal shift.
Borough of Bogota, 24 NJPER P 29112 (N.J. PERC 1998)	Yes	Change in shift schedule of detectives designed to reduce overtime costs.
Borough of Highland Park, 17 NPER NJ-25196 (N.J. PERC 1994)	Mixed	Seniority shift selection that allows employer to take special skills of employees into consideration is mandatorily negotiable; strict seniority clauses are not mandatorily negotiable.

CASE NAME	MANDATORY	DESCRIPTION
Borough of Peacock, 28 NJPER ¶33081 (N.J. PERC 2002)	Yes	Proposal for advanced notice of changes in shift schedules. No evidence that proposal "impeded governmental policy."
Borough of Prospect Park, 14 NPER NJ-23129 (N.J. PERC 1992)	No	Proposal to replace 5-2 workweek with 4-2 workweek and create shifts that overlapped by 15 minutes; proposal interfered with Borough's right to determine staffing levels.
Borough of Ramsey, 15 NPER NJ-24144 (N.J. PERC 1992)	Yes	Change in shift rotation schedule to reduce overtime costs.
Borough of Sayreville, 13 NPER NJ-21244 (N.J. PERC 1990)	Yes	Establishment of new shift.
Borough of Taylor, 14 NPER PA-23067 (Pa. LRB Hearing Examiner 1992)	Yes	Change from fixed shift schedule to rotating schedule.
Borough of Union Beach, 14 NPER NJ-23160 (N.J. PERC 1992)	Yes	Proposal for 4-10s; Borough desired to maintain rotating five-day schedule because of lower overtime costs.
Camden County Sheriff, 25 NJPER P 30190 (N.J. PERC 1999)	Yes	Proposal that shifts be assigned by seniority and education; proposal contained exception for position demonstrated by employer to require special training, experience or other qualifications.
City of Bowling Green, LAIG 4872 (Mini, 1993)	Yes	Unilateral institution of a ten-hour shift.
City of Bremerton, PEB ¶45,352 (Wash. PERC) (CCH, 1987)	Yes	Change from fixed to rotating shift system.
City of Camden, 17 NPER NJ-26064 (N.J. PERC 1995)	Mixed	Rescission of 4-2 work schedule and implementation of 5-2 schedule with 17 fewer days off. Decision to change based on emergency need to deploy additional police officers in response to escalating murder rate during evening hours. City allowed to maintain new schedule for limited period prior to bargaining impact.
City of Plainfield, 26 NJPER 31071 (N.J. PERC 2000)	Yes	Proposal for fixed 4/10 shifts in police department.
City of Reading, 30 PPER P 30121 (Pa. LRB 1999)	No	City assigned sergeants to rotating shifts; employer's interest in enhancing sergeants' supervisory ability and increasing police visibility outweighed employees' interests.
City of Syracuse, 19 NPER NY-14642 (N.Y. PERB ALJ 1996)	Yes	Proposal to eliminate two-tiered shift schedule and to place all employees on same work schedule.

CASE NAME	MANDATORY	DESCRIPTION
City of York, 18 NPER P-26171 (Pa. LRB ALJ 1995)	Yes	Unilateral implementation of shift and reassignment of officers to other shifts; grant in management rights clause of right to determine schedules not sufficient to waive bargaining obligation.
County of Middlesex, 16 NPER NJ-24161 (N.J. PERC 1993)	Mixed	Elimination of weekend shift in order to save overtime costs.
County of Warren, 18 NPER NY-14624 (N.Y. PERB ALJ 1995)	Mixed	Change from fixed to rotating shift; contract's grant of right to establish shift schedule so long as 8-hour day maintained held to be waiver of right to bargain.
Detroit POA v. City of Detroit, PEB ¶34,318 (Michigan) (CCH, 1984)	Yes	Change to rotating shifts.
Hudson County, 19 NPER NJ-27167 (N.J. PERC 1996)	No	Proposal that shifts be assigned on basis of seniority; absence of language allowing right to deviate from seniority to meet operational needs rendered proposal not negotiable.
Huntington Beach POA v. Huntington Beach, 129 Cal. Rptr. 893 (Cal. App. 1976)	Yes	Change from 4-10 schedule.
Indiana Borough, 18 NPER PA-27068 (Pa. LRB ALJ 1996)	Yes	Unilateral change from rotating shifts to fixed shift system; employer's contention that management rights and zipper clauses gave it authority to make changes rejected on grounds that clauses were too broadly worded and didn't specifically address the issue of shifts.
Lacey Township, 13 NPER NJ-21263 (N.J. PERC 1990)	Yes	Shift selection by seniority; proposal allowed employer latitude where employees had special skills.
Mansfield v. Labor Relations Commission, 766 N.E.2d 128 (Mass. App. 2002)	Yes	Alteration of shift schedules of patrol officers to eliminate "split shift," consisting of two swing and two graveyard shifts per week. Court found that changes in the schedule directly affected "hours" mandatorily negotiable under the law.
Mt. Laurel Township. v. Mount Laurel PBA, 521 A.2d 369 (N.J. Super. 1987)	Yes	Shift schedules negotiable in larger towns.
New Jersey Transit Corporation, 18 NPER NJ-27106 (N.J. PERC 1996)	No	Decision to rotate police officers from road patrol to foot patrol every three, instead of every four, months; rotation did not involve change in shift or hours worked.
North Berks Regional Police Association, #PF-C-06-75-E (Pa. LRB 2006)	No	Employer changed shift schedule of one employee, requiring him to work weekends. Where shift schedules in general are a mandatory subject of bargaining, the change in schedule of one employee must be analyzed under contractual language, not under the general duty to bargain.

CASE NAME	MANDATORY	DESCRIPTION
Patrolman's Benevolent Association of the City of New York, 35 NYPER ¶33149 (N.Y. PERC 2002)	Yes	Union proposed that officers on patrol work same schedule as sergeants.
Rockland County Sheriff, 16 NPER NY-14629 (N.Y. PERB ALJ 1993)	Yes	Unilateral change in starting and quitting times of employees and addition of new shift to work schedule.
Selinsgrove Borough, 15 NPER PA-24102 (Pa. LRB 1993)	Yes	Unilateral change in shift schedule following interest arbitration decision; broadly-worded management rights clause did not constitute clear and unmistakable waiver of right to bargain.
Skagit County, 2001 WL 1509361 (Wash. PERC 2001)	Mixed	Employer changed days off of deputy to accommodate special event. While topic of days off mandatory for negotiations, employer showed it had routinely changed shift schedules for special events without either negotiating with Union or paying employees overtime.
Somerset County Sheriff, 27 NJPER ¶32127 (N.J. Super. 2001)	Yes	Grievance challenged Sheriff's decision to allow less senior male corrections officers to choose shifts before senior female officers. Grievance arbitrable to the extent it did not violate Sheriff's obligation under state law to have one female correction officer working each shift.
Town of Bellingham, 450 Mass. 1011 (Sup. 2007)	Yes	Interest arbitration panel ordered that work schedules be changed to 24-hour shifts.
Town of Branchburg, PEB ¶45,422 (N.J.) (CCH, 1989)	Yes	Proposal for rotating shifts.
Town of Greece, 18 NPER NY-13078 (N.Y. PERB 1995)	No	Creation of fourth police platoon with different hours of work. Union waived right to bargain by agreeing to management rights clause that reserved to employer right to "direct the workforce and to schedule work hours."
Town of McCanless v. McCanless Police Officers Association, 952 A.2d 1193 (Pa.Cmwlth. 2008)	No	Employer assigned officer split schedule to ensure coverage notwithstanding co-worker's military leave. The Court found that the new law "cannot be interpreted in a way to deprive the public employer of its ability to discharge its essential function as a public enterprise."
Town of Yorktown, 35 NYPER 3017 (N.Y. PERB 2002)	Yes	Union's proposal seeking to set the number of days worked per year, as well as hours of shifts.
Township of Union, New Jersey, PERC No. 2007-64 (N.J. PERC 2007)	No	Employer ordered all superior officers to attend meetings on computer statistics program without regard to whether meetings fell on managers' days off. PERC held employer had management right to organize computer statistics program training in a manner it deemed most effective.

CASE NAME	MANDATORY	DESCRIPTION
Township of Upper Saucon, 1993 WL 1018 (Pa. Cmwlth. 1993)	Yes	Change from 7-2, 7-2, 6-4 schedule to 5-8 schedule.
United Federation of Police v. Blooming Grove, PEB ¶45,316 (N.Y.) (CCH, 1988)	Yes	Change in shift schedules.
Village of Evergreen Park, 19 NPER IL-27137 (Ill. SLRB General Counsel 1996)	No	Proposal that patrol duties be assigned solely on the basis of seniority; no exception in proposal for public safety requirements.
Shift Trades		
Borough of Paramus, 28 NJPER ¶33,002 (N.J. PERC 2001)	No	Union filed grievance challenging denial of detective's request to temporarily trade assignments with detective in a different section.
County of Mercer, Case No. SN-2006-037 (N.J. PERC 2006)	Yes	Employer unilaterally implemented restrictions on shift exchanges. Under previous practice, matter ruled to be mandatory for bargaining.
Village of Lancaster, 13 NPER NY-14606 (N.Y. PERB ALJ 1990)	Yes	Proposal to allow shift trades with supervisory approval.
Sick Leave		
Borough of River Edge, 13 NPER NJ-22001 (N.J. PERC 1990)	Yes	Proposal that officers report any on-duty injury within eight hours.
Borough of Spring Lake, PEB ¶45,445 (N.J. PERC) (CCH, 1988)	No	Requirement that officer furnish doctor's slip for each future absence; on non-compliance, no withdrawal of sick leave benefit or out-of-pocket costs to officer.
City of Cedar Rapids, 16 NPER IA-24002 (Iowa PERB 1993)	Yes	Implementation of new sick leave regulation requiring employee to obtain doctor's certificate at employee's expense.
City of Linden, 14 NPER NJ-23143 (N.J. PERC Director 1992)	No	Directive barring police officers from using home answering machines to screen calls while sick.
City of Onondaga, 18 NPER NY-17010 (N.Y.S.C. 1996)	Yes	Imposition of new sick leave verification policy.
City of Orange Township, 27 NJPER ¶32046 (N.J. PERC 2001)	Yes	City unilaterally eliminated negative sick leave balance and required officers to choose between employer-selected options for accounting for a negative balance through forfeiture of compensatory time or vacation time or having current pay docked.

CASE NAME	MANDATORY	DESCRIPTION
City of Pasco, Decision 9337 (Wash. PERC 2006)	Yes	Employer submitted to interest arbitration a proposal limiting use of sick leave where injuries were covered by third-party employers. Union's failure during negotiations and mediation to give employer notice that it believed proposal was not mandatory is not necessarily fatal to Union's case.
Cleona Borough, 19 NPER PA-27239 (Pa. LRB ALJ 1996)	Yes	Unilateral implementation of policy requiring police officers to obtain doctor's slip after only one day of sick leave; prior policy required doctor's slip after three days of sick leave. Employer singled out Union president in applying new policy.
Kitsap County, Decision 8402-B (Wash. PERC 2007)	No	Employer unilaterally implemented an absence control tracking system (ACTS) which used software to monitor employee sick leave. PERC determined that implementation of the ACTS software was a managerial right, and was a technological change brought about to make the employer's operation more efficient without changing any existing employer sick leave policy.
New Hampshire Department of Safety, 921 A.2d 924 (N.H. 2007)	Yes	After contract expired, employer unilaterally changed method of calculation of sick leave and vacation, reducing some leave accruals by as much as three days a year.
New Jersey Transit Corporation, PERC No. 2006-91 (N.J. PERC 2006)	Yes	Employer refused to arbitrate grievance challenging change in "doctor slip" requirements under sick leave policy.
New Jersey Transit Corporation and P.S.A., Local 304, PERC No. 2006-89 (N.J. PERC 2006)	No	Employer refused to arbitrate grievance challenging failure by employer to return two officers to work from sick leave unless the officers re-qualified with their firearms. Commission held that employer had non-negotiable management prerogative to require fitness testing prior to returning officers to work.
New York State Correctional Officers Association, 35 NYPER ¶4541 (N.Y. PERB ALJ 2002)	Yes	Employer unilaterally discontinued longstanding practice of allowing employees to draw from accrued vacation leave credits for absences previously attributed to sick leave. Even though practice of "conversion of sick leave" was limited to employees on one shift, employer's detailed tracking of conversions was sufficient to establish reasonable expectation that practice of allowing all unit members to make such conversions would continue.
Patrolman's Benevolent Association of the City of New York, 35 NYPER, ¶603 (N.Y. PERB ALJ 2002)	Yes	Union proposal would limit the amount of time employees on sick leave would be restricted to home.

CASE NAME	MANDATORY	DESCRIPTION
Town of Wallkill, 14 NPER NY-14566 (N.Y. PERB ALJ 1991)	Yes	Proposal providing for doctor certification in case of employee on sick leave three or more consecutive days.
Vestal Police Benevolent Association, 35 NYPER ¶4600 (N.Y. PERB 2002)	Yes	Eight-year practice of compensating employees for low use of sick leave. Fact that City Council unaware of practice not dispositive in light of the fact that the practice was instituted by a police chief.
Wilkes-Barre Police Benevolent Association, 33 PER 33087 (Pa. LRB 2002)	Yes	Employer unilaterally discontinued practice of allowing officers to donate sick leave to another officer's account. LRB found two instances of donated sick leave over 15-year period is sufficient to demonstrate past practice.

Smoking Policy

CASE NAME	MANDATORY	DESCRIPTION
Borough of Ellwood City, 941 A.2d 728 (Pa.Cmwlth. 2008)	No	Employer enacted ordinance banning smoking in all City buildings, vehicles, or equipment. Not mandatory for bargaining because the rule applied not just to employees, but to citizens.
City of Seattle, 27 GERR 1538 (Wash. PERC 1989)	Yes	Unilateral implementation of smoking policy.
Commonwealth of Pennsylvania, 34 PPER ¶91 (Pa. LRB BLJ 2003)	No	Landlord of building leased by employer banned smoking throughout the building. Employer had no duty to bargain since lease granted landlord all rights to site management.
Lebanon County, 19 NPER PA-27260 (Pa. LRB 1996)	Yes	New work rule prohibiting detectives from smoking at desks.
Pennsylvania State Corrections Officers Association, 330 NJPER ¶33120 (Pa. LRB ALJ 2002)	Yes	Employer unilaterally imposed ban on smoking for corrections officers working at posts. Since no-smoking ban had an impact on employees' terms and conditions of employment, change in policy subject to bargaining.
Pennsylvania State Corrections Officers Association, 33 PPER ¶33179 (Pa.Cmwlth. 2002)	Yes	Employer issued order forbidding corrections officers from smoking while on duty. Board concluded that impact of policy on employees outweighed management rights of employer.

Staffing

CASE NAME	MANDATORY	DESCRIPTION
Borough of Montoursville, 16 NPER PA-25011 (Pa. Cmwlth. 1993)	No	Reversal of arbitrator's award requiring minimum number of police officers to be retained by employer.
Borough of Westwood, 89 GERR 24 (N.J. ERB 1981)	No	Minimum staffing clause in contract.
California State Employees Association, 24 PERC P 31008 (Cal. PERB ALJ 1999)	Yes	Elimination of corrections officer position from prison library. Union established that elimination of position greatly increased security risks for library staff.

CASE NAME	MANDATORY	DESCRIPTION
City of Boston v. PPA, 532 N.E.2d 640 (Mass. 1989)	No	Overturning of arbitrator's decision requiring two-person cars.
City of Mattoon, 13 PERI ¶2004 (Ill. SLRB 1997)	No	Proposal for minimum staffing levels in police department. Fact that minimum staffing clauses had appeared in prior contracts did not make subject negotiable.
City of Johnstown, 15 NPER NY-13085 (N.Y. PERB 1992)	No	Minimum staffing proposal.
City of Newark, 32 NJPER 47 (N.J. PERC 2006)	No	Union proposed continuation of contract clause requiring the City to "equalize tour personnel department-wide" in the event of sickness or vacation. Under New Jersey law, staffing levels are not mandatory for bargaining.
City of Quincy, 16 NPER FL-25192 (Fla. PERC General Counsel 1994)	No	Alteration of staffing levels following expiration of collective bargaining agreement.
City of Sault Ste. Marie v. FOP, 414 N.W.2d 168 (Mich. App. 1987)	No	Number of officers in patrol car and on shift.
City of Sea Isle, 19 NPER NJ-27125 (N.J. PERC 1996)	No	Police union's proposal specifying deployment of personnel and staffing levels.
City of Syracuse, 16 NPER NY-14527 (N.Y. PERB ALJ 1994)	Mixed	Proposal for premium pay for work performed when staffing at low levels and to assign specific officer to fill a vacancy.
City of Utica, 19 NPER NY-17507 (N.Y. S.Ct. 1996)	No	Discontinuance of staffing and apparatus requirement contained in terms of expired contract.
Crawford County, PEB ¶43,427 (Wis. 1972)	No	Number of officers on duty.
Ellwood City Police Wage and Policy Unit, No. PF-C-04-75-W (Pa. LRB 2005)	Yes	Employer enacted new policy reducing from two to one the number of officers used to transport male prisoners. Safety implications overrode management rights issue.
Oak Park Public Safety Officers Association v. City of Oak Park, 277 Mich.App. 317 (Mich. App. 2007)	No	Public safety officer union sought to refer to binding arbitration continuation of contract language containing the minimum staffing levels per platoon, shift, and patrol car. The Court concluded that Union failed to prove that contract language had a "significant impact on safety."
Police Bargaining Unit v. Borough of Montoursville, 634 A.2d 830 (Pa.Cmwlth. 1993)	No	Proposal for minimum number of officers per shift. Arbitrator's award reversed.

CASE NAME	MANDATORY	DESCRIPTION
Town of North Salem, 13 NPER NY-14511 (N.Y. PERB Dir. 1991)	No	Number of officers per patrol tour.
Town of Orangetown, 16 NPER NY-14532 (N.Y. PERB ALJ 1994)	Mixed	Proposal regarding number of officers per shift, rank of officers, and premium pay when staffing below certain level. Premium pay only mandatory aspect of proposal.
Town of Orchard Park, 16 NPER NY-14632 (N.Y. PERB ALJ 1993)	Mixed	Elimination of Sunday shift for detective unit and change in work schedules. Employer allowed to eliminate Sunday shift but required to bargain over changed work hours and schedules.
Township of Lopatcong, 18 NPER NJ-26184 (N.J. PERC 1995)	Yes	Contractual provision for double-time pay for officers working after dark; held not to be an illegal staffing proposal.
Township of West Milford, 26 NJPER P 31042 (N.J. PERC 2000)	No	Employer refused to arbitrate grievance alleging that employer violated contract by assigning more than three officers to a tactical police patrol shift. Staffing levels non-negotiable in New Jersey.
Village of Buchanan, 19 NPER NY-13061 (N.Y. PERB 1996)	No	Proposal that "floaters" be on duty for a minimum number of days; proposal held to interfere with employer's management right to deploy work force.
Subcontracting		
Albany Police Officer Union, 35 NYPER ¶ 4550 (N.Y. PERB ALJ 2002)	No	Sheriff elected to discontinue practice of using City police for prisoner transport functions. Since City had no control over Sheriff's decision, City not required to bargain over issue.
Allegheny County Deputy Sheriffs' Association, Case No. PERA-C-06-374-W (Pa. LRB 2006)	No	Employer began using videoconferencing to conduct certain prisoner hearings, resulting in a decrease in the need of bargaining unit members to transport prisoners. Under Pennsylvania law, employers not required to bargain over introduction of new technology.
Anacortes Police Guild, 2000 WL 1448857 (Wash. PERC 2000)	Mixed	Employer eliminated all dispatch positions in favor of participating in newly-formed county-wide dispatch center. Decision to participate non-negotiable as a core managerial right. While effects of decision were negotiable, union failed to make timely demand to bargain over effects.
Borough of Roseland, 26 NJPER P 31077 (N.J. PERC 2000)	Yes	Employer refused to arbitrate grievance challenging its decision to call in a civilian dispatcher to fill a temporary vacancy on a shift in lieu of police officer.
Burlington County, 24 NJPER P 29046 (N.J. PERC ALJ 1997)	Yes	Employer transferred corrections officer work performed by sworn officers to non-sworn personnel.

CASE NAME	MANDATORY	DESCRIPTION
California State Employees Association v. Department of Corrections, 23 PERC P 30105 (Cal. PERB ALJ 1999)	Yes	Unilateral assignment of non-bargaining unit corrections officers to run prison's satellite kitchens.
City of Akron, 16 OPER P 1489 (Ohio SERB 1999)	Yes	Transfer of call-taking supervisory duties from sergeants to civilian employees. No employees lost jobs as a result of the transfer.
City of Allentown v. Pennsylvania Labor Relations Board, 851 A.2d 988 (Pa. Cmwlth. 2003)	Yes	Employer unilaterally transferred work of court liaison officer to civilian personnel.
City of Bethlehem, 15 NPER PA-24045 (Pa. Cmwlth. 1993)	Yes	Civilianization of police dispatch functions.
City of Boston v. Labor Relations Commission, 787 N.E.2d 1184 (Mass. App. 2003)	Yes	Transfer of policing functions at housing projects from Police Department to non-bargaining unit police officers.
City of Boston, http://www.state,ma.us/lrc/Decisions/Recent/MUP-2267.pdf (Mass. LRC 2002)	Yes	Employer unilaterally assigned latent fingerprint collection work to non-bargaining unit personnel.
City of Bridgeport and City of New Haven, 16 NPER CT-24077 (Conn. SBLR 1993)	Yes	Request and use of state police officers to perform routine patrol duties.
City of Jeannette v. Pennsylvania Labor Relations Board, 890 A.2d 1154 (Pa. Cmwlth. 2006)	Yes	Employer assigned Police Chief to 8:00 p.m. to 4 a.m. patrol shift in place of a bargaining unit police officer. The Court concluded that "an unfair labor practice occurs when an employer unilaterally removes work that is exclusively performed by the bargaining unit without prior bargaining with the union."
City of Egg Harbor, 24 NJPER P 29108 (N.J. PERC 1998)	Yes	Grievance challenging transfer of work performed by police officers to non-bargaining unit part-time officers.
City of Harrisburg, 13 NPER PA-22039 (Pa. LRB ALJ 1991)	Yes	Assignment of citation duties to park rangers.
City of Jersey City, 713 A.2d 472 (N.J. 1998)	No	Reassignment of numerous clerical, administrative, and technical jobs held by police officers to civilians. The Court held that under New Jersey law, reorganization undertaken for other than purely economic reasons is a managerial prerogative.

CASE NAME	MANDATORY	DESCRIPTION
City of Jersey City, 18 NPER NJ-27003 (N.J. PERC ALJ 1995)	Yes	Replacement of sworn fiscal officer with civilian employee, hiring of retired police officers to work in property room, and substitution of civilians for officers assigned to pistol range.
City of Jersey City, 18 NPER NJ-27003 (N.J. PERC ALJ 1995)	No	Reassignment of mail delivery and motor pool work from sworn officers to civilian employees; City had history of assigning police clerical duties outside of bargaining unit.
City of New Bedford, PEB ¶45,693 (Mass. LRC) (CCH, 1989)	Yes	Transfer of dispatch and records functions to non-unit personnel.
City of Newburgh, 19 NPER NY-14635 (N.Y. PERB Director 1996)	Yes	Proposal to prohibit subcontracting.
City of New Haven v. New Haven Police Union, 557 A.2d 506 (Conn. 1989)	Yes	Ending of practice of using full-time officers performing extra duty to provide security at residences for the elderly.
City of Peekskill, 35 NYPER 4509 (N.Y. PERB ALJ 2002)	Yes	Unilateral change in past practice of offering overtime dispatching work to qualified police officers.
City of Philadelphia, 18 NPER PA-27161 (Pa. LRB 1996)	Yes	Employer entered into contract with private firm to provide security at Municipal Building; defense of economic justification did not eliminate right to bargain over issue.
City of Philadelphia, 13 NPER PA-22042 (Pa. LRB ALJ 1991)	Yes	Assignment of evidence duties to non-unit civilians.
City of Philadelphia, 18 NPER PA-27009 (Pa. LRB ALJ 1995)	Yes	Unilateral assignment of graphic artists' work to non-bargaining unit personnel.
City of Pittsburgh, 16 NPER PA-25020 (Pa. Cmwlth. 1994)	Yes	Assignment of non-bargaining unit commander to conduct roll call where task performed in past by bargaining unit sergeants.
City of Reading, 32 PPER ¶32158 (Pa. LRB ALJ 2001)	Yes	Transfer of work of administering security card system from bargaining unit sergeant to non-sworn, non-bargaining unit records personnel. Fact that transfer was made as part of technology upgrade not a defense to employer's obligation to bargain over change.
City of Rochester, 16 NPER NY-14670 (N.Y. PERB ALJ 1993)	Yes	Unilateral assignment of civilians to telephone reporting unit. Performance of work in past by interns did not establish past practice of using civilians to perform work.
City of Salem v. Salem Police Employee's Union, PEB ¶35,432 (Or. S.Ct.) (CCH, 1989)	Yes	Creation of reserve police force.

CASE NAME	MANDATORY	DESCRIPTION
City of Tonawanda, 16 NPER NY-14620 (N.Y. PERB ALJ 1993)	Yes	Assignment of civilians to work parade duty historically performed by bargaining unit members.
City of Tonawanda, 32 NYPER P 4634 (N.Y. PERB Dir. 1999)	No	Unilateral transfer of warrant service duties. While civilianization resulted in loss of bargaining unit work, there was no change in job qualifications or the level of services provided by the bargaining unit.
City of Yonkers, 15 NPER NY-14581 (N.Y. PERB ALJ 1993)	Mixed	Assignment of non-bargaining unit typists to perform work previously performed by police officers; City increased qualifications for job in question.
Commonwealth of Pennsylvania, 17 NPER PA-25150 (Pa. LRB ALJ 1994)	Mixed	Assignment of responsibility for evictions, investigation, seizures of property, and citations to non-bargaining unit personnel mandatory for bargaining. Assignment of responsibility for issuing parking tickets, courtesy notices, and incident reports non-negotiable where non-unit personnel had performed work in past.
Commonwealth of Pennsylvania, 18 NPER PA-27104 (Pa. LRB Hearing Examiner 1996)	Yes	Unilateral reassignment of tasks of checking employee identification and issuing visitor passes from capital police to non-bargaining unit personnel.
County of Grand Traverse, 13 NPER MI-21144 (Mich. ERC 1990)	Mixed	Use of non-bargaining unit aides to transport mental patients; work had never been performed by bargaining unit.
County of Hudson, 19 NPER NJ-27204 (N.J. PERC 1996)	No	Employer transferred all police functions to sheriff's office; employer had right in contract to abolish work force.
County of Ingham, 16 NPER MI-25020 (Mich. ERC (1994)	Mixed	Unilateral elimination of Emergency Services Coordinator position and assigning of duties to new position; no impact on bargaining unit because no employee was laid off, lost pay, or any other benefits.
County of Kalamazoo, 13 NPER MI-21143 (Mich. ERC 1990)	Yes	Subcontracting of in-state prisoner transportation.
County of Onandaga, 15 NPER NY-17015, 187 A.D.2d 1014 (N.Y. S.Ct. 1992)	Yes	Unilateral assignment of non-union corrections officers to guard pre-trial and pre-sentence individuals.
County of Suffolk, 18 NPER NY-13002 (N.Y. PERB 1996)	No	Transfer of care and custody of detainees to non-bargaining unit personnel; Association failed to establish that work in question had been performed exclusively by bargaining unit members.
County of Westchester, 16 NPER NY-14647 (N.Y. PERB ALJ 1993)	Yes	Unilateral assignment of non-bargaining unit personnel to issue court-enforced traffic tickets at community college.

CASE NAME	MANDATORY	DESCRIPTION
Dunn County v. Wisconsin Employment Relations Commission, 718 N.W.2d 138 (Wis. App. 2006)	Yes	The County sought declaration that contract clause was unenforceable because it provided that no one outside the bargaining unit should normally perform work done by employees within the bargaining unit. Court found that the clause was primarily related to wages, hours, and conditions of employment.
Erie County Sheriff's Police Benevolent Association, 34 NYPER 4592 (N.Y. PERB ALJ 2001)	Not Resolved	Employer assigned non-bargaining unit personnel to provide traffic and police services at football games. Complaint dismissed as untimely where Union waited to file complaint for more than four months after date work was assigned.
Fraternal Order of Police, Lodge #5 v. City of Philadelphia, 30 PPER P 30077 (Pa. LRB ALJ 1999)	Yes	Unilateral assignment of civilians to perform police work of producing maps and graphical representations of crime statistics. Defense that civilians had developed software to produce the work did not change the fact that the work previously had been performed exclusively by members of the bargaining unit.
Fraternal Order of Police v. City of Williamsport, 29 PPER P 29109 (Pa. LRB 1998)	Yes	Creation of new job positions of police captain and assistant chief, and transfer of work from bargaining unit members to the new positions. Although employer had managerial right to create positions, it was required to negotiate prior to the transfer of work or was required to obtain unit clarification removing the employees from the bargaining unit.
Fraternal Order of Police, Lodge 7, PEB ¶45,527 (Pa. LRB) (CCH, 1989)	Yes	Transfer of traffic court duties to non-unit personnel; defense of clerical nature of duties rejected.
Fraternal Order of Police, Lodge 9 v. City of Reading, 33 PPER 33064 (Pa. LRB ALJ 2002)	Yes	City police department used county detectives to staff mobile command unit. Consistent past practice existed of using City officers for the assignment.
Fraternal Order of Police, Lodge 19, PEB ¶45,671 (Pa. LRB) (CCH, 1989)	Yes	Hiring of part-time police officers.
Geistown Borough, 18 NPER PA-26206 (Pa. LRB 1995)	Yes	Subcontracting of entire police department.
In the matter of Borough of Bogota, 25 NJPER P 30058 (N.J. PERC 1999)	No	Transfer of police dispatch functions to civilian employees.
Jenkins Township, 14 NPER PA-23091 (Pa. LRB Hearing Examiner 1992)	Yes	Township unilaterally entered into mutual aid agreement under which neighboring borough provided police services previously performed by Township's officers.

CASE NAME	MANDATORY	DESCRIPTION
Los Angeles School Police Association, 30 PERC 85 (Cal. PERB 2006)	No	Employer had past practice of using non-sworn personnel, as well as school police officers, to patrol District high school football games. Employer did not violate its obligation to bargain merely by increasing the quantity of work performed by non-bargaining unit employees.
Michigan Law Enforcement Union v. City of Highland Park, PEB ¶34,400 (Michigan) (CCH, 1984)	Yes	Creation of auxiliary police force (reserves).
Milwaukie Police Employees Assoc. v. Milwaukie Police Department, UP-111-92 (Or. ERB 1992)	Yes	Transfer of duties of a vacant clerical position out of the bargaining unit.
Multnomah County Correction Deputies Association, Case No. UP-58-05 (Or. ERB 2008)	Yes	Corrections employer ended a "close street supervision" program and transferred the work performed by bargaining unit members to a different unit made up of members of a different bargaining unit. Board cited lost overtime opportunities as the basis for concluding that the transfer of work was mandatory for bargaining.
Onandaga County Sheriff, 13 NPER NY-14591 (N.Y. PERB ALJ 1990)	Yes	Assignment of non-unit corrections officers to guard prisoners.
Pennsylvania State Police, #PF-C-06-102-E (Pa. LRB 2007)	Yes	Employer assigned civilian employees to assist troopers in performing school bus safety inspections. Under past practice of 16 years' duration, troopers had performed inspections without assistance of civilians.
Pennsylvania State Troopers Association, 36 PPER ¶8 (Pa. LRB ALJ 2005)	Yes	Employer unilaterally implemented a technologically advanced incident information management system in its consolidated dispatch centers and unilaterally began assigning non-unit members to supervise police communications operators at its centers. Prior to the system's implementation, unit members supervised the operators.
Perry County, 91 PERI ¶124 (Ill. Labor Board 2003)	No	Employer eliminated captain's position, transferring work to lieutenants. Since lieutenants were within the bargaining unit, no impermissible subcontracting.
PBA of the Village of Buchanan, PEB ¶45,534 (N.Y. ERB) (CCH, 1989)	Yes	Transfer of patrol duties to non-unit personnel.
Port Authority of New York and New Jersey, 2006 WL 3524136 (N.J. Super. 2006)	Yes	Employer transferred work performed by police officers to non-bargaining unit employees. Language reserving to the employer the right to make decisions regarding its "mission and management," including its "organization, staffing, planning, operating, and financial policies," was not a waiver of the right to bargain over subcontracting.

CASE NAME	MANDATORY	DESCRIPTION
Rialto Police Benevolent Association, 66 Cal.Rptr.3d 714 (Cal. App. 2007)	Yes	City decided to enter into a contract with the County Sheriff to provide law enforcement services rather than continuing to maintain a police department. The permanent transfer of work away from the bargaining unit clearly had a significant effect on wages, hours, and working conditions of bargaining unit members.
Rochester Police Locust Club, PEB ¶45,396 (New York) (CCH, 1988)	Yes	Using civilian security guards to direct traffic.
Sacramento Police Officers Association v. City of Sacramento, 54 Cal.Rptr.3d 167 (Cal. App. 2007)	No	Employer implemented policy to hire retirees as temporary non-career employees to remedy a short-term staffing shortage in the Police Department. The Court concluded that the shortage of personnel was "beyond the power of the Union to remedy, other than through overtime to the limits of human endurance, a remedy itself fraught with danger to public safety."
State of Connecticut, 19 NPER CT-27057 (Conn. SBLR 1996)	No	Assignment of retired troopers to perform evening and weekend home duties. No evidence that bargaining unit members suffered job losses; no obligation to bargain over lost overtime opportunities. Contract specifically allowed for such subcontracting.
State of New York Correctional Services, 18 NPER NY-14559 (N.Y. PERB ALJ 1996)	Yes	Unilateral assignment of supervision of inmate utility work crew to non-bargaining unit civilians.
Suffolk County Sheriff, 15 NPER NY-14670 (N.Y. PERB ALJ 1992)	No	Removal of corrections officers from investigator positions and reassigning work to deputies.
Town of Burlington, Case No. MUP-04-4157 (Mass. ERB 2008)	Yes	Employer changed the "pecking order" in which non-sworn municipal employees would be assigned to paid police details.
Town of East Hartford, Decision 3853-A (Conn. SBLR 2004)	Yes	Employer joined regional SWAT-type team as well as regional traffic unit, causing members from other departments to perform work inside the city limits.
Town of Putnam Valley, 14 NPER NY-14622 (N.Y. PERB Director 1991)	Yes	Unilateral transfer to state police of investigative work previously performed exclusively by Town's detectives.
Township of North Bergen, 16 NPER NJ-24212 (N.J. PERC 1993)	Yes	Proposal requiring employer to provide non-regular personnel assigned to any quasi-law enforcement duties with distinct uniforms and vehicles, and to require employer to assign only bargaining unit members to patrol duty in regular marked police vehicles.
Village of Westchester, 92-2 FPPR 28 (Ill. SLRB 1991)	Yes	Use of auxiliary police force.

CASE NAME	MANDATORY	DESCRIPTION
Wallingford Police Union v. City of Wallingford, 1999 WL 786359 (Conn. 1999)	No	Use of special constables to perform traffic-control functions at concert facility. Bargaining unit personnel had not exclusively performed all traffic-control work in the past.
Westchester County Corrections Officers Benevolent Association, Inc., 33 PERB P 3057 (N.Y. PERB Chair. 2000)	No	Employer subcontracted prison ward guard duties to state corrections officers. Labor organization failed to establish that it had exclusively performed work in the past.
Wilkes-Barre Police Benevolent Association, 32 PPER ¶32096 (Pa. LRB ALJ 2001)	Yes	Assignment of parking enforcement to newly-created parking enforcement attendants. Work in question had been performed exclusively by members of police officers' bargaining unit.
Terminal Leave		
Borough of Hawthorne, PERC No. 2008-45 (N.J. PERB 2008)	Yes	Employer unilaterally changed policies with respect to the ability to use terminal leave prior to retirement. PERC found that argument concerning propriety of terminal leave "should be made to an arbitrator."
Township of Bridgewater, 2006-62 (N.J. PERC 2006)	Yes	Employer adopted ordinance discontinuing terminal leave benefit. Under the benefit, officers were allowed to stop working before their effective retirement date, using excess sick leave even though they were not actually sick.
Transfers		
City of Buffalo, 14 NPER NY-14537 (N.Y. PERB ALJ 1992)	Mixed	City violated its obligation to bargain over the impact of transfers and reassignments; no facts indicated that union had demanded to negotiate the impact.
City of Newark, 32 NJPER 47 (N.J. PERC 2006)	Mixed	Union proposed continuation in contract of clause requiring the employer to "consult with the union" concerning transfers, and requiring the employer to "give consideration to such factors as qualifications, seniority, and the good of the Department." Commission found that "consultation" requirement is mandatory for bargaining since procedures related to promotions are mandatory under New Jersey law. However, since the standards for transfer are not mandatory for negotiation, the remainder of the clause struck down.
City of Trenton and PBA, Local 11, 2004-54 (N.J. PERC 2004)	No	Superior Officers Association filed a grievance challenging the transfer of a captain from the Internal Affairs Unit to patrol. Under New Jersey law, police employees who believe they have been unjustly reassigned or transferred must challenge the decision in court, not through the grievance procedure.
City of Trenton, 2005-59 (N.J. PERC 2005)	No	Grievance challenging disciplinary transfer. Recently-enacted New Jersey state law that allows for grievance arbitration over "minor" disciplinary penalties does not extend to allowing arbitration of disciplinary transfers.

CASE NAME	MANDATORY	DESCRIPTION
Union County Sheriff, 28 NJPER ¶33113 (N.J. PERC 2002)	No	Union sought arbitration of grievance challenging transfer of police officer. Under New Jersey law challenges to transfer decisions are not subject to a grievance procedure but must be filed through a state court lawsuit.
Training		
Borough of Dunellen, 18 NPER NJ-26159 (N.J. PERC 1995)	No	Proposal requiring employer to determine which officers should receive training.
City of Highland Park, 18 NPER IL-27087 (Ill. SLRB General Counsel 1996)	No	Proposal that City maintain 15-minute in-service training at beginning of each workday; proposal inappropriately interfered with City's right to manage work force and determine manner in which services were provided.
Truthfulness		
Pennsylvania State Troopers' Association, 36 PPER ¶38 (Pa. LRB ALJ 2005)	No	State issued a new rule that required troopers to be "truthful and honest in the discharge of their duties." While no specific rule existed on the issue in the past, evidence showed that the mandate for truthfulness and honesty was inherent in the job of trooper before the enactment of the rule, and had, in fact, been the subject of a number of disciplinary charges against individual troopers.
Uniforms		
Borough of Bogota, 15 NPER NJ-24117 (N.J. PERC 1993)	Yes	City's new requirement that all officers wear bulletproof vests, causing officers to pay costs of altering or replacing dress blouses.
Burlington County, 27 NJPER ¶32093 (N.J. PERC 2001)	Yes	After contract expired and while negotiations for a new contract were pending, employer refused to pay annual uniform allowance under clause in expired agreement. Uniform allowance clause did not explicitly and specifically end benefit as of certain date.
City of Camden, 13 NPER NJ-21262 (N.J. PERC 1990)	No	Directive requiring officers to report in summer and winter uniform for semi-annual inspection.
Law Enforcement Labor Services v. City of Roseville, PEB ¶34, 707 (Minnesota) (CCH, 1986)	Yes	Issue of allowance versus quartermaster system.
Suffolk County Police Benevolent Assn., Inc. and County of Suffolk, Case No. U-26202 (N.Y. PERB ALJ 2006)	No	Employer ordered officers to wear nameplates on the outside of their uniforms at all times. Employer's right to control contents of uniform outweighs minimal safety considerations raised by the union.

CASE NAME	MANDATORY	DESCRIPTION
Village of Lancaster, 13 NPER NY-14606 (N.Y. PERB ALJ 1990)	No	Proposal that employer furnish off-duty badges.
Union Business		
Bergen County, 19 NPER NJ-27123 (N.J. PERC 1996)	Yes	Police union's proposal for leave to conduct union business.
City of Jersey City, 18 NPER NJ-27094 (N.J. PERC 1996)	Yes	Police union sought arbitration over failure of City to grant a union official leave time to conduct union business; no interference with managerial prerogative.
City of Jersey City, 19 NPER NJ-27150 (N.J. PERC 1996)	Yes	Employer refused to arbitrate grievance challenging denial of leave to second union representative to administer contract. Employer cited concerns over cost as justification for its position.
State of New Jersey, 19 NPER NJ-27134 (N.J. PERC 1996)	Yes	Police employer unilaterally terminated union leave which had been provided under terms of recently-expired contract.
State of Wisconsin (Department of Corrections), No. 31272-B (Wis. ERC 2007)	Yes	Employer repudiated past practice of relieving union representative's caseload so that he could attend to union duties during the course of the normal workday.
Town of North Attleboro v. Labor Relations Commission, 779 N.E.2d 654 (Mass. App. 2002)	No	Employer denied Union's request for dues deduction increase for members electing dental insurance plan. Union had increased dues deductions in the past upon Union's request, it had only done so on a bargaining unit-wide basis, not on an individual basis.
West Caldwell Township, 19 NPER NJ-27226 (N.J. PERC 1996)	Yes	Proposal that union officials be given release time.
Use of Force Policies		
Association for Los Angeles Deputy Sheriffs v. County of Los Angeles, 83 Cal.Rptr.3d 494 (Cal. App. 2008)	No	Ban on multiple employees involved in deadly force incident from consulting with the same attorney at the same time.
Caruso v. Board of Collective Bargaining, 555 N.Y.S.2d 133 (A.D. 1990)	No	Ban on hog-tying of prisoners; change in past practice not established.
City of Newburgh, 19 NPER NY-14635 (N.Y. PERB Director 1996)	Yes	Proposal for four days of paid leave for officers involved in the use of deadly force.
Pasco Police Officers' Association, 4 Washington LLD 6 (Wash. PERC 1994)	Yes	City unilaterally discontinued board of review for police-related accidents and discharges of firearms.

CASE NAME	MANDATORY	DESCRIPTION
San Jose POA v. City of San Jose, 144 Cal.Rptr. 648 (Cal. App. 1978)	No	Unilateral change in use-of-force policy.
Vacations		
Borough of Bradley Beach, PEB ¶45,806 (N.J. PERC) (CCH, 1989)	Yes	Must be bargained in absence of evidence of specific staffing shortages.
Borough of Dunellen, 18 NPER NJ-26159 (N.J. PERC 1995)	No	Proposal to require employer to backfill for officers using vacation time.
Borough of Lodi, 32 NJPER 33 (N.J. PERC 2006)	Yes	Employer unilaterally implemented policy restricting the number of officers allowed to take vacation on any one day, and imposing "blackout" dates when vacations could not be taken.
Borough of Rutherford, 19 NPER NJ-27163 (N.J. PERC 1996)	Yes	Employer refused to arbitrate grievance challenging new practice of refusing to grant vacation requests on Saturday. Additional overtime costs to fill in for employees on vacation did not render the topic non-negotiable.
City of Newburgh, 19 NPER NY-14635 (N.Y. PERB Director 1996)	Yes	Proposal for distribution of vacation times subject to employer's staffing needs.
City of Philadelphia, 18 NPER PA-27007 (Pa. LRB 1995)	Yes	Unilateral change in schedules to accommodate vacations; employer's need to reduce overtime costs and to ensure adequate coverage did not override bargaining obligation.
City of Reading, 16 NPER PA-24135 (Pa. LRB Hearing Examiner 1993)	Yes	Unilateral change in practice of barring police officers from using vacation time in single day "blocks" except in emergency, unless officers had first exhausted personal or compensatory time off.
City of Torrington, 17 NPER CT-26033 (Conn. SBLR 1995)	Yes	Implementation of 48-hour notice requirement for officers requesting vacation or compensatory time off.
Commonwealth of Pennsylvania, 29 PER P29076 (1998)	No	Unilateral decision to post vacation schedule in room to which non-police had access. Minimal impact on officer's rights outweighed by managerial prerogative.
County of Rockland, 15 NPER NY-14601 (N.Y. PERB ALJ 1992)	Yes	Unilaterally charging an employee's vacation in part against accrued holiday time; County changed its practice to conform with its executive policies that had existed for 11 years.
Galloway Township, 29 NJPER ¶35 (N.J. PERC 2003)	Yes	Grievance challenging employer's decision to limit the number of police officers who could be off duty on a given shift.

CASE NAME	MANDATORY	DESCRIPTION
Middletown Township, 19 NPER PA-27203 (Pa. LRB 1996)	Yes	New vacation policy limiting number of officers allowed to use vacation at any one time.
Town of Carmel, 19 NPER NY-13053 (N.Y. PERB 1996)	Yes	New work rule providing that vacation approvals would not be issued until 90 minutes prior to shift.
Town of Carmel, 19 NPER NY-14612 (N.Y. PERB ALJ 1996)	No	Discontinuance of past practice allowing police officers to overlap vacation times with other police officers; practice held to interfere with employer's staffing rights.
Town of Greenburgh, 14 NPER NY-14559 (N.Y. PERB ALJ 1992)	Yes	Proposal to permit officers employed for at least two years to split vacation times.
Town of Kearny, 17 NPER NJ-26120 (N.J. PERC 1995)	Yes	Alteration of number of employees permitted on vacations at same time.
Township of North Bergen, 16 NPER NJ-24212 (N.J. PERC 1993)	Yes	Proposal to require employees to take vacation in seven-day blocks.
Village of Lancaster, 13 NPER NY-14606 (N.Y. PERB ALJ 1990)	Mixed	Proposal that officers have discretion in using vacation negotiable; proposal governing number of clerks and officers who could be on vacation at any one time not negotiable.
Westchester County Correction Officers Benevolent Association, Inc. and County of Westchester, Case No. U-24784 (N.Y. PERB ALJ 2006)	No	Employer unilaterally changed the method by which it calculated the number of vacation slots made available to correction officers during the year. A change in the number of employees that can take vacation at any given time primarily affects staffing, and is not mandatorily negotiable, as long as the employer does not change the method by which vacation preferences are granted and the amount of vacation that employees may use is not diminished.
Vehicles		
Borough of Bradley Beach, PEB ¶45,806 (N.J. PERC) (CCH, 1989)	Yes	Air conditioning in patrol vehicles.
Borough of River Edge, 13 NPER NJ-22001 (N.J. PERC 1990)	Yes	Employer proposal that employees not be picked up at home in an employer-owned vehicle.
Borough of Taylor, 14 NPER PA-23067 (Pa. LRB Hearing Examiner 1992)	Yes	Termination of practice of allowing off-duty officers to use police vehicles to attend court.
City of Elizabeth, 26 NJPER P 31007 (N.J. PERC 1999)	Yes	Union grievance challenging change in policy limiting the number of take-home cars used by on-call employees.

CASE NAME	MANDATORY	DESCRIPTION
City of Hazleton, 17 NPER PA-26047 (Pa. LRB 1995)	Yes	Elimination of practice of permitting off-duty police officers to use police vehicles to drive to court appearances; defense that change necessary to comply with FLSA rejected.
City of Iowa City v. Iowa PERB, PEB ¶34,591 (Iowa) (CCH, 1985)	Yes	Proposals included requirement that cars be equipped with radio, siren, PA, spotlight, rechargeable flashlight, electronically operated shotgun rack and plastic shield.
City of Nassau, 35 NYPER ¶4556 (N.Y. PERB ALJ 2002)	Yes	Employer unilaterally discontinued seven-year practice of allowing commanding officers to have use of their vehicles on a 24/7 basis. Employer required to make officers whole for any expenses incurred when not allowed access to vehicles.
City of Newark, Case No. SN-2006-026 (N.J. PERC 2006)	Yes	Proposal for an annual stipend for the use of personal vehicles during the performance of the workday. Proposal ruled to "intimately and directly affect employee work and welfare."
City of Portland, 13 NPER OR-21046 (Or. ERB 1990)	Yes	Provision of off-duty vehicles to lieutenants and captains.
City of Stamford, 14 NPER CT-23050 (Conn. SBLR 1992)	Yes	Change in practice of permitting employees to use employer-owned vehicles to commute.
City of Tampa, PEB ¶45,436 (Florida) (CCH, 1988)	Yes	Take-home car policy.
County of Nassau, 626 N.Y.S.2d 235 (A.D. 1995)	Yes	Change in past practice of allowing take-home cars.
Los Angeles School Peace Officers Association, 27 PERC ¶34003 (Cal. PERB 2002)	Yes	Employer ended past practice of allowing detectives to use employer-owned vehicles to commute to and from work. Employer required to reimburse detectives for all losses incurred during period they were unable to use employer-owned vehicles.
Omaha Police Union, Local 101 IUPA v. Omaha, Case No. 1121 (Neb. CIR 2007)	Yes	Employer unilaterally reduced from 60 to 21 the number of take-home vehicles. Generalized management rights clause not a waiver of the right to bargain. Employer required to pay impacted employees at the normal mileage reimbursement rate, plus interest.
Plumstead Township, 1: NPER 10 (Pa.Cmwlth 1998)	Yes	Unilateral elimination of take-home car policy.
State of Illinois, 13 PERI ¶2014 (Ill. SLRB, 1997)	Yes	Issuance of new restrictions on take-home cars.
Township of New Bergen, 16 NPER NJ-24260 (N.J. PERC 1993)	No	Proposal to allocate individual personnel to patrol cars.

CASE NAME	MANDATORY	DESCRIPTION
Town of Secaucus, PEB ¶44,246 (N.J.) (CCH, 1984)	Yes	Condition of tires.
Town of Wallkill, 14 NPER NY-14566 (N.Y. PERB ALJ 1991)	No	Proposal prohibiting transport of prisoners in vehicles lacking a screen between front and back seats; demand would have interfered with the Town's governmental mission.

Wages

CASE NAME	MANDATORY	DESCRIPTION
Borough of Taylor, 14 NPER PA-23067 (Pa. LRB Hearing Examiner 1992)	No	Installation of time clocks; officers already required to sign log books.
City of Camden, PERC No. 2004-7 (N.J. PERC 2003)	Yes	Proposal to include longevity and holiday pay in base pay for compensation purposes.
City of Pittsburgh, 15 NPER PA-24073 (Pa. LRB Hearing Examiner 1993)	Yes	City unilaterally implemented resolution establishing a lower pay rate for recruits than that set forth in interest arbitration award. Police union's unfair labor practice charge was not untimely where filed six weeks after union became aware of resolution.
Cliff v. Blydenberg, 661 N.Y.S.2d 736 (Sup. 1997)	Yes	County enacted law imposing salary cap on County employees. Law held to violate obligation to bargain found in state collective bargaining law.
Levitt v. Board of Collective Bargaining of the City of New York, N.E.2d 1 (A.D. 1992)	Yes	Implementation of a policy requiring employees to disclose and repay tax owed to the City through payroll deduction.
Toms River Township, No. 2008-30 (N.J. PERC 2007)	Yes	Employer took the position that it had the unilateral right to place new employees anywhere in the salary structure. Commission held proposal dealt with compensation issue that "directly affects employee welfare."
West Caldwell Township, 19 NPER NJ-27226 (N.J. PERC 1996)	Yes	Proposal to increase base rate for officers reaching 20 years of service.

Weapons

CASE NAME	MANDATORY	DESCRIPTION
City of New Haven, PEB ¶45,434 (Conn.) (CCH, 1988)	Yes	Change in practice concerning size and use of take-home weapons.
City of Newark, 29 NJPER¶174 (N.J. PERC 2003)	No	After officer was involved in shooting and became the defendant in a civil lawsuit, City assigned him to a non-armed position. Requiring the City to "re-arm" the officer would substantially limit the City's policymaking power to determine the conditions under which it is proper for its officers to be armed.

CASE NAME	MANDATORY	DESCRIPTION
Rachel Park Township, 18 NPER NJ-27068 (N.J. PERC 1996)	No	Union grievance challenging City's refusal to allow retiring officers to retain their weapons; arbitration would permit employer's ability to decide whether it should provide weapons to private citizens.
Shillington Borough, 13 NPER PA-21195 (Pa. LRB ALJ 1990)	No	Placement of disabled officer on light duty without weapon.
Workers' Compensation		
Hazle Township, Case No. PERA-C-07-107-E (Pa. LRB 2007)	Yes	Employer refused to comply with arbitrator's award compelling it to make pension contributions for and make whole the sick leave of an employee with an on-the-job injury. Commission found that employer's arguments were an "impermissible collateral attack" on the finality of an arbitrator's opinion.
New Britain Township Police Benevolent Association v. New Britain Township, 33 PPER 33030 (Pa. LRB ALJ 2001)	Yes	Employer unilaterally established new procedures for hearings to consider Heart-Lung benefit applications. State law allowing employer to hold hearings did not eliminate obligation to bargain over charges.
Richland Township, 19 NPER PA-27215 (Pa. LRB ALJ 1996)	Yes	New policy that police officers injured on duty be examined by an employer-selected physician in order to receive medical benefits; officers were previously allowed to visit own doctors.
West Caldwell Township, 19 NPER NJ-27226 (N.J. PERC 1996)	Yes	Proposal that employer provide up to one year of paid leave for employees suffering from compensable injuries.
Workload		
Muhlenberg Township, 30 PPER P 30038 (Pa. LRB ALJ 1999)	No	Labor organization demanded to bargain over increase in workload following employer's agreement to provide police services in contiguous municipality. Employer's decision to provide additional service an inherent managerial right not subject to negotiations. Labor organization's additional claim that employer should have bargained over effects of change such as staffing, shift changes, and restricted leave usage, was barred by the fact that labor organization was late seven months in demanding to bargain over impact of changes.

The Duty Of Fair Representation Owed By A Labor Organization To Its Members.

By virtue of its status as the exclusive collective bargaining representative of a bargaining unit, a labor organization owes a single duty to its members – the "duty of fair representation."[82] The duty of fair representation does not require a labor organization to provide representation for its members in all cases,[83] nor does it require a labor organization to refer even a meritorious grievance to arbitration.[84]

Rather, the duty is fundamentally procedural in nature, and requires only that a union's conduct not be arbitrary, discriminatory, or in bad faith.[85] A union can even act negligently without violating the duty of fair representation.[86] In some states, the duty is even more limited, and requires only that a labor organization refrain from committing intentional misconduct against its members.[87]

Under the standard formulation of the duty of fair representation, a union has the right to make an honest mistake, to make good faith errors in judgment, or to reach an incorrect conclusion about the chances of prevailing in a particular case, all without violating its duty of fair representation.[88] As the General Counsel of Florida's Public Employment Relations Commission put it:

> "The union is the representative but not the servant of the employee. It not only may, but should, exercise judgment and discretion in its representative capacity. When a union's judgment is at issue, as it is here, the union's actions are reviewed to ascertain whether they fall within the wide range of reasonableness granted bargaining agents by the courts."[89]

A union has the right to make an honest mistake, to make good faith errors in judgment, or to reach an incorrect conclusion about the chances of prevailing in a particular case, all without violating its duty of fair representation.

What is important is that the labor organization use fair procedures in the way it processes member requests and that it apply those procedures consistently. The hallmark of a union meeting its duty of fair representation is an impartial, complete investigation of potential grievances.[90] The duty of fair representation allows a labor organization to freely make decisions as to the merits of a grievance,[91] extend the time limits in a grievance procedure to allow an employer more time to respond,[92] weigh the economic and other costs of the grievance against the likely outcomes,[93] accept a settlement that is in the best interests of all its members even though it displeases the officer filing the grievance,[94] and even recommend that an officer resign in lieu of termination based upon its evaluation of the situation.[95]

By way of example, many of a union's decisions, particularly in the area of seniority and choosing proposals for collective bargaining, will benefit some of its members and potentially harm others. In other cases, a union's urgings to the employer that it impose equal disciplinary sanctions on individuals charged with the same offense might adversely impact certain employees,[96] and a union challenging a promotional process will almost invariably be taking a position that will harm at least one of its members.[97] Under such circumstances, the union's decisions will not subject it to liability for a breach of the duty of fair representation, even if the union fails to notify or consult with the employees who were adversely affected by its decisions.[98] What the union cannot do in such cases is to take discriminatory positions, ignore meritorious grievances or process grievances in a perfunctory manner.[99] In the words of one court, "a union does not violate its duty of fair representation if it, in good faith, 'sacrifice[s] particular elements of the compensation package' to the detriment of some employees because the chosen elements would likely result in increased benefits for the employees in the bargaining unit as a whole."[100]

Even if a union official acts inappropriately in handling a grievance, there still may not be liability for breach of the duty of fair representation. For example, in one case a police union president tore up a handwritten grievance he believed was not only illegible, but unmeritorious as well. Though the Michigan Employment Relations Commission viewed the conduct as discourteous, it declined to find a breach of the duty of fair representation, noting that the union president later agreed to write the grievance and was successful in getting the discipline which the grievance was challenging reduced.[101] For an employee to prevail in a duty of fair representation claim arising out of a union's failure to process a grievance, the employee must not only show that the union acted inappropriately but also that the employee's grievance was meritorious.[102]

In most states, the duty of fair representation is owed to all employees in the union's collective bargaining unit, not just those employees who are members of the union. Accordingly, a union may be compelled under the law to provide representation to an employee who has never paid the union any dues, and it is inappropriate for the union to deny such representation on the grounds of the employee's non-membership in the union.[103]

The duty of fair representation applies only to matters which are within the scope of collective bargaining and over which the union is the exclusive representative of the employees.[104] Accordingly, a union has no obligation to provide representation to non-members such as retirees.[105] Similarly, there is no obligation to provide representation to employees in matters which are outside the scope of bargaining,[106] such as furnishing a lawyer to provide a defense against criminal charges,[107] or representing an employee in a private action before a personnel or civil service board,[108] or even with respect to internal union discipline matters.[109] As well, a union need not provide representation where others, and not just the union, have the opportunity to represent employees. As one court noted in a case where a law enforcement union was sued for failing to provide an officer with an attorney in a pre-disciplinary hearing:

> "[T]he Federation did not bargain to be the exclusive representative or advocate at the Departmental disciplinary hearings (as it is throughout the grievance process). It only bargained for certain procedures to be followed. The Federation claims its only duty is to ensure that the procedures bargained for were followed at the disciplinary hearing. We agree. The Federation did that much.

[The officer] had a right to be represented by his own attorney, and that attorney had the right to cross-examine and present evidence. The Federation fulfilled its limited duty when those procedural rights were present."[110]

As part of the duty of fair representation, a union has an obligation to provide bargaining unit members with requested information directly relevant to their employment.[111] If an employee's labor representative changes, the old representative retains the duty of fair representation to process a grievance filed before the change in representation.[112]

Depending upon local and state law, enforcement of the duty of fair representation may occur through the courts or exclusively with a state labor board.[113] In states where the "exclusive jurisdiction" to hear duty of fair representation claims lies with a labor board, employees who mistakenly bring duty of fair representation claims in court will find their lawsuits dismissed and, because of the relatively quick statutes of limitations before labor boards, may find themselves time-barred from filing any claim whatsoever.[114]

Under a federal law known as the Landrum-Griffin Act, there is extensive regulation of the internal activities of labor organizations to ensure that unions follow fair procedures and that the possibility of corruption is minimized. However, since most law enforcement labor organizations are not covered by the Landrum-Griffin Act, the internal workings of law enforcement labor organizations are usually completely unregulated by the law. For example, in a Florida case, a police officer filed an unfair labor practice charge against the Fraternal Order of Police, alleging that the FOP had improperly restricted eligibility for union office to members who had attended at least four meetings in the prior year. Florida's Public Employment Relations Commission dismissed the charge, finding that internal union matters were beyond the scope of the collective bargaining laws.[115] In a Connecticut case, a court held that a union's violation of its bylaws would not constitute a breach of the duty of fair representation unless the breach was accompanied by "malicious intent, hostility, discrimination, dishonesty, or fraud."[116]

A union has an obligation to provide bargaining unit members with requested information directly relevant to their employment.

The Right To Strike.

Law enforcement officers are generally forbidden by law from striking. These prohibitions may appear in state statutes or may be incorporated in the internal rules of a law enforcement agency. Some states have found a general common law prohibition on the right of police officers to strike even in the absence of a state statute prohibiting such strikes. Restrictions on the rights of law enforcement officers to strike have been uniformly upheld.[117]

Where the right to strike does not exist, a labor organization which engages in an illegal strike may be liable for civil damages. Some state legislatures have enacted statutes which allow public employers the right to bring civil lawsuits against labor organizations which engage in illegal strikes.[118] Courts in states without such liability statutes have split on whether a union which has engaged in an illegal strike may be sued. Some courts are willing to imply such a cause of action.[119] The majority of courts have held that the absence of a state law specifically authorizing such liability forbids implying it. Where civil suits are permitted against a labor organization, they can only be brought by the public employer, not by private citizens or businesses.[120]

The Right Not To Be A Member Of A Labor Organization.

In those states with statewide collective bargaining laws, the issue of whether an individual can be compelled to join a labor organization is handled in one of three ways: Through practices known as "**open shops**," "**closed shops**," and "**agency shops**."

Open shops exist in states with laws providing that no individual can be compelled to join any labor organization. Employees in those states can freely choose to join or not join the labor organization representing the bargaining unit of which the employee is a member. The labor organization still has the legal obligation to represent all eligible employees of its bargaining unit, whether the employee has joined the organization or not.

Closed shops involve union contracts which provide that an individual must become a member of a labor organization in order to remain an employee. Under a series of Supreme Court decisions, closed shops are illegal for public sector employees since they have the potential to force employees to engage in "speech" against their will through the use of a portion of their union dues for political activities.[121]

Agency shops are a middle ground between closed and open shops. Agency shop provisions require all employees to either be members of the labor organization or to pay to the labor organization their "fair share" of the costs of the negotiation and administration of the collective bargaining agreement. The rationale behind the agency shop approach is that since a labor organization may have a legal obligation to represent all eligible employees of its bargaining unit, whether actual union members or not, it is appropriate for employees who are not union members to pay for the benefits of a collective bargaining agreement.

The Supreme Court has held that agency shop requirements do not violate the constitutional rights of non-members provided the labor organization only assesses members charges that are "germane" to the collective bargaining process,[122] and that it follows certain mandated procedures.[123] Since fair share employees are not members of a labor organization, the organization has the right to deny them a vote in officer elections and contract ratification votes, the ability to attend union meetings, and the right to receive any benefits not related to the bargaining process, such as the ability to attend a union picnic or other function.

"Fair share" dues or fees are different than the "in lieu of" dues payments made by those with religious objections to membership in a labor organization. Where religious objectors are allowed to pay an amount equivalent to union dues to a non-religious charity, fair share dues are paid to the labor organization. Fair share dues, which must be calculated on an annual basis, represent that percentage of normal union dues expended on costs that are germane to the collective bargaining process.[124] Most reported cases describe fair share assessments in the range of 80-95% of normal union dues.[125]

The fair share procedures required by the courts include: (1) An obligation to provide adequate explanation of the basis for the agency fee, including the results of an audit showing which expenses are claimed as germane to the bargaining process, or, in other words, which expenses are chargeable to fair share employees;[126] (2) the provision of a reasonably prompt opportunity to challenge the amount of the fee before an impartial arbitrator; and (3) the establishment of an escrow for the amounts reasonably in dispute while such challenges are pending.[127] If these procedures for assessing, collecting, and accounting for fair share payments are not followed, a fair share provision in a collective bargaining agreement may be ruled unenforceable in whole or in part.[128]

Labor organizations affiliated with national groups have frequently been subject to litigation attacking the use of fair share fees to pay dues to the national groups.[129] Where a national affiliation exists, the local organization must inform fair share members of the percentage of dues paid to each parent affiliate. In addition, the notice given to fair share members must specify the purposes for which the national dues are spent, and must allocate the national dues based upon whether the dues are spent for collective bargaining related purposes.[130]

Courts hearing fair share cases are often placed in the middle of a heated dispute. As succinctly noted by one court:

> "The long and short of it is that no payment of funds to the union by the dissenting non-members would be wholly satisfactory to them however much benefit they might unwontedly receive as beneficiaries of the collective bargaining agreement. Equally, no fair share calculation which requires non-members to pay less than union members pay in dues can ever be wholly satisfactory to the unions. Such differentials are bound to be noticed by the union members and to be a disincentive to continued union membership."[131]

Discrimination Based On Union Activity.

Where collective bargaining is allowed, it is illegal for an employer to discriminate against an employee because of the employee's union activities. Adverse action an employer takes against an employee or a labor organization which is motivated by anti-union bias, hostility or animus is usually directly prohibited by collective bargaining statutes. Even in the absence of a statute directly forbidding anti-union discrimination, courts will imply an obligation on the part of an employer not to engage in such conduct. Illegal discrimination may involve disciplining an officer,[132] reprimanding an officer for not meeting a ticket quota,[133] laying off an officer[134] or even the entire police department,[135] the ending of release time for a union officer,[136] terminating the probationary status of an officer,[137] denying an officer a promotion,[138] lowering an officer's score on a promotional examination,[139] failing to assign an officer to work out of classification as a temporary supervisor,[140] transferring the officer,[141] removing the officer from a specialty position,[142] reducing the amount of hours of work given to an officer[143] or changing the officer's shift,[144] denying an officer's request for training,[145] or refusing to consider a part-time officer for a full-time job.[146] The normal remedy in such cases is to order the employer to take all the necessary action to undo the illegal discrimination and make the employee whole, whether that involves reinstating, promoting, or retransferring the officer.[147]

Since it is rare to find an employer who has admitted taking actions based upon its dislike of unions, most anti-union discrimination cases proceed on the basis of circumstantial evidence. It is common in such cases for labor organizations to establish that other similarly-situated employees have not been treated similarly, and that the only distinguishing characteristics are the employee's union activities.[148] Additionally, where there is a suspicion of anti-union discrimination, the absence of documentation or corroboration of an employer's allegations is viewed as evidence establishing anti-union bias.[149] Critical to any anti-union bias case, however, is proof that the employer actually knew of the employee's activities within the labor organization.[150]

Most states follow a three-part test in judging anti-union bias cases. Under the test, a union contending that a particular action is the product of anti-union bias must show: (1) That the employee engaged in protected activity; (2) that the employer was aware of that protected activity; and (3) that but for the protected activity the adverse action would not have been taken against the employee.[151] An employer's lack of adequate reason for the adverse action taken may be part of the union's *prima facie* case.[152] After the union proves this *prima facie* case, the burden of proof shifts to the employer to demonstrate that the same action would have been taken absent the protected activity.[153] Since different legal issues are involved, a finding by an arbitrator that an employer had just cause to discharge a law enforcement officer does not prevent a state labor relations board from concluding that the same discharge was the product of anti-union bias, and ordering the reinstatement of the officer.[154]

Illegal anti-union bias can be directed at a labor organization as well as at individual employees. An example of such a case involved the City of Troy, New York. When the Troy Police Benevolent Association (PBA) refused to agree to contract concessions made by other City unions, the City ended the PBA president's full-time release status, assigned him to previously nonexistent foot patrol duties, instituted new release time reporting requirements, ordered the PBA to vacate office space which it had occupied for 20 years, threatened to discipline the PBA president, and issued an order that the PBA president's personnel file be delivered to the City manager. Most of the City's actions were taken on the day after the PBA criticized the City in the local press and just as the City and the PBA were embroiled in a bitter battle over a grievance challenging several unilateral changes made by the City in the working conditions of police officers. New York's Public Employment Relations Board found that the City's actions established that the City had illegally retaliated against the PBA for the PBA's failure to agree to the contract concessions.[155]

An employer does not engage in anti-union bias if it merely applies its existing rules to union conduct in a non-discriminatory way. For example, an employer which bans the transport of civilians in police cars has the right to prevent a union official from using his police car to chauffer a union attorney to a meeting.[156]

Illegal Interference With A Union's Internal Matters.

A common feature of public sector collective bargaining laws is a prohibition on an employer injecting itself into the internal activities of a labor organization. An employer can run afoul of this prohibition in any of a number of ways:

- By interrogating union officials about their activities on behalf of the union, including conversations they have with union members.[157]

- By disciplining a union president for making public statements, even where the employer believes the statements are false.[158]

- By prohibiting a law enforcement labor organization from engaging in fund raising.[159]

- By interfering with the conducting of a no-confidence vote.[160]

- By making threatening remarks to officers and cadets about joining a particular labor organization.[161]

- By issuing press releases during negotiations which not only falsely described the union's bargaining position but which also threatened the use of part-time officers to control costs.[162]

NOTES

[1] Carl E. Heustis, *Police Unions*, 48 Journal of Criminal Law, Criminology and Police Science 643 (November, 1958).

[2] International Association of Chiefs of Police, *Police Unions and Other Police Organizations*, IACP Bulletin No. 4, Washington, D.C. (September, 1944).

[3] *See Fraternal Order of Police v. Harris*, 10 N.W.2d 310 (Mich. 1943)(Court upheld order forbidding membership in the Fraternal Order of Police); *City of Jackson v. McLeod*, 24 So.2d 319 (Miss. 1946)(Court sustained discharges of police officers for joining American Federation of State, County and Municipal Employees).

[4] M.W. Aussieker, Jr., *Police Collective Bargaining*, Public Employee Relations Library, No. 18 (1969); Burpo, Delord & Shannon, *Police Association Power, Politics and Confrontation: A Guide For The Successful Police Labor Leader* (Charles C. Thomas 1997).

[5] Edmund P. Murray, *Should the Police Unionize*, The Nation, June 13, 1959, p. 530.

[6] Gallup Poll on Police Unions, New York Times, January 12, 1967, p. 52.

[7] Virtually all state police labor organizations are non-affiliated independent organizations. Many of the larger city police unions, including those in New York, San Diego, Phoenix, Seattle, Portland and Detroit, are non-affiliated for the purposes of collective bargaining.

[8] *See* §423.231 et seq., Michigan Comp. Laws Annotated (West, 1994).

[9] *Hillsdale PBA v. Borough of Hillsdale*, 644 A.2d 564 (N.J. 1994).

[10] *Municipality of Anchorage v. Anchorage Police Department Employee's Association*, 839 P.2d 1080 (Alaska 1992); *City and County of San Francisco*, 43 Cal. Rptr.2d 421 (Cal. App. 1995); *City of Detroit v. Detroit Police Officers' Association*, 294 N.W.2d 68 (Mich. 1980); *City of Richfield v. Local 1215, International Ass'n of Fire Fighters*, 276 N.W.2d 42 (Minn. 1979); *Medford Firefighters' Association v. City of Medford*, 595 P.2d 1268 (Or. App. 1979). *But see County of Riverside v. Superior Court*, 30 Cal.4th 278 (Cal. 2003)(binding arbitration violates unique provision of California state constitution); *Salt Lake City v. Inter. Assn. of Fire Fighters*, 563 P.2d 786 (Utah 1977)(overturns binding arbitration as unconstitutional delegation of legislative authority).

[11] *City of Cocoa*, 15 NPER FL-23235 (Fla. PERC 1993)(employer may not unilaterally implement management rights clause).

[12] *Los Angeles County Civil Service Commission v. Superior Court*, 588 P.2d 249 (Cal. 1978).

[13] *Placentia Fire Fighters v. City of Placentia*, 129 Cal.Rptr. 126 (Cal. App. 1976).

[14] *City of Bellevue and IAFF, Local 1604*, 831 P.2d 738 (Wash. 1992).

[15] *City of Detroit*, 16 NPER MI-25066 (Mich. ERC 1994).

[16] *State of California*, 18 NPER CA-26117 (Cal. PERB ALJ 1995).

[17] *Washington State Patrol Troopers Association v. State of Washington*, Decision 4710 (Wash. PERC ALJ 1994).

[18] This "local option" has been adopted by such cities as Phoenix, Arizona, Boise, Idaho, Denver, Colorado, and San Antonio, Texas. In states following the

"meet and confer" model, there usually exists a "local option" to allow interest arbitration as the last step in the bargaining process. For example, even though for years California followed the meet and confer model, cities in California such as Oakland and San Jose had local laws providing for interest arbitration.

[19] This table is taken from *Interest Arbitration (Second Edition)*(Labor Relations Information System, Portland, OR, 2000).

[20] *Beverlin v. Board of Police Commissioners of Kansas City*, 722 F.2d 395 (8th Cir. 1983); *Vorbeck v. McNeal*, 407 F. Supp. 733 (E.D. Mo. 1976).

[21] *Fraternal Order of Police v. Brescher*, PEB ¶34,310 (S.D. Fla.)(CCH, 1984)(deputies are not public employees since they hold office by appointment from the sheriff rather than as employees); *Sikes v. Boone*, PEB ¶34,106 (N.D. Fla.)(CCH, 1983)(not unconstitutional to not give deputies bargaining rights but to give police officers such rights. Florida courts later ruled that the underlying collective bargaining statutes did grant deputies the right to bargain); *Allegheny County Deputy Sheriff's Association v. PLRB,* PEB ¶34,641 (Pa.Cmwlth.)(CCH, 1986).

[22] *Confederation of Police v. City of Chicago*, 529 F.2d 89 (7th Cir. 1976); *City of Enid v. Public Employees Relations Bd.*, 133 P.3d 281 (Okla. 2006)(different treatment of larger employers not unconstitutional); *Yakima County Deputy Sheriff's Association v. Board of Commissioners*, 601 P.2d 936 (Wash. 1979)(grant of binding arbitration only to larger counties and cities not unconstitutional).

[23] *American Federation of State, County and Municipal Employees v. Jefferson County*, 110 L.R.R.M. 2372 (W.D. Ky. 1982).

[24] *Thomas v. Collins*, 323 U.S. 516 (1945). *See Mescall v. Rochford*, 655 F.2d 111 (7th Cir. 1981); *Police Officers' Guild, Nat. Union of Police Officers v. Washington*, 369 F. Supp. 543 (D. D.C. 1973); *Melton v. City of Atlanta*, 324 F. Supp. 315 (N.D. Ga. 1971).

[25] New York City Collective Bargaining Law, New York City Administrative Code, §12-314(b).

[26] *International Brotherhood of Teamsters, Local 344 v. NLRB*, 568 F.2d 12 (7th Cir. 1977).

[27] *City of Santa Fe*, 2007 WL 5737341 (N.M. PELRB 2007).

[28] *See* Chapter 41.56, Revised Code of Washington; *Metropolitan Alliance of Police, Bellwood Command Chapter No. 339 v. Illinois Labor Relations Bd.*, 820 N.E.2d 1107 (Ill. App. 2004). Public employee bargaining laws which require supervisors to be in different bargaining units than rank-and-file members have been held to not violate the First Amendment's protections of freedom of association. *See Wilton v. Mayor and City Council of Baltimore*, 772 F.2d 88 (4th Cir. 1985); *York County Fire Fighters Association v. County of York, Virginia*, 589 F.2d 775 (4th Cir. 1978). Such laws generally permit supervisory units to be affiliated with a parent organization which numbers a rank-and-file unit as one of its affiliates. *Oak Park v. Illinois State Labor Rel. Bd.*, 522 N.E.2d 161 (Ill. App. 1988); *Hudson County,* 10 NJPER ¶15,153 (N.J. PERC 1984).

[29] *See* Title 29, §152 (11), United States Code.

[30] §243.650 (23), Oregon Revised Statutes.

[31] §75-4322 (b), Kansas Statutes.

[32] *See generally* §23.40.250(5), Alaska Statutes Annotated; Chapter 150(E), §1, Massachusetts Annotated Laws; §28-9.4-2(2), Rhode Island General Laws.

33 *Elizabeth Borough*, 18 NPER PA-26207 (Pa. LRB 1995)(police chief not a managerial employee and properly includable in police union's bargaining unit); *Homestead Borough*, 18 NPER PA-26203 (Pa. LRB 1995)(same); *Township of Chartiers v. P.L.R.B.*, PEB ¶34,753 (Pa. Cmwlth.)(CCH 1986)(sergeants and police chief not managerial and properly includable in police union's bargaining unit); *Lower Mount Bethel Township*, 13 NPER PA-21156 (Pa. LRB 1990)(public safety director not managerial employee).

34 *Connecticut Dept. of Public Safety v. State, Bd. of Labor Relations*, 2008 WL 2375390 (Conn. Super. 2008).

35 Chapter 5, §315/3(c), Illinois Annotated Statutes.

36 *City of Buffalo*, 14 NPER NY-14049 (N.Y. PERB Dir. 1991).

37 *City of Winter Park*, 16 NPER FL-25113 (Fla. PERC 1994).

38 *Village of Oak Park v. ISLRB*, 522 N.E.2d 161 (Ill. App. 1988); *Township of Pennsauken*, 16 NPER NJ-24191 (N.J. PERC Dir. 1993).

39 *See Fraternal Order of Police v. City of Dayton*, 396 N.E.2d 1045 (Ohio App. 1978); *Village of Midlothian*, 18 NPER IL-26116 (Ill. SLRB 1995); *Town of Hookset*, 2008 WL 5039185 (N.H. PELRB 2008); *Oregon State Police*, 2008 WL 5053546 (Or. ERB 2008).

40 *E.g. McLeod County v. Law Enforcement Labor Services, Inc.*, 499 N.W.2d 518 (Minn. App. 1993)(sergeants includable in rank-and-file bargaining unit); *AFSCME Local 490 and Town of Bennington*, 571 A.2d 63 (Vt. 1989)("working sergeants" should be placed in rank-and-file bargaining unit); *City of Wasilla*, 2008 WL 2595158 (Alaska 2008)(sergeants not supervisory); *FOP v. City of Coconut Creek*, 13 NPER FL-21355 (Fla. PERC 1990)(city police sergeants not supervisory); *Town of Mangonia Park*, 13 NPER FL-21316 (Fla. PERC 1990); *Central Florida PBA*, PEB ¶45,613 (Fla. PERC)(CCH, 1989)(city police sergeants not supervisory); *City of Pekin*, 23 PERI ¶174 (Ill. LB 2007)(sergeants not supervisory); *City of Dubuque*, PEB ¶45,644 (Iowa PERB)(CCH, 1989)(city police sergeants not supervisory); *Town of Litchfield*, 13 NPER NH-21015 (N.H. PERLRB 1990)(city police detective sergeants not supervisory); *State of New Hampshire*, 13 NPER NH-22000 (N.H. PELRB 1990)(New Hampshire State Police sergeants not supervisory); *In re Fraternal Order of Police*, SERB 89-016 (1989)(Ohio State Highway Patrol Sergeants not supervisory); *City of Tualatin*, 13 NPER OR-21045 (Or. ERB 1990)(city police sergeants not supervisory).

41 *Anchorage Police Dept. Command Officers' Ass'n v. Municipality of Anchorage*, 177 P.3d 839 (Alaska 2008); *City of Wasilla*, 2008 WL 2595158 (Alaska LRA 2008); *City of Cocoa Beach*, 18 NPER FL-26203 (Fla. PERC 1995); *City of Freeport v. Labor Relations Board*, 554 N.E.2d 155 (Ill. 1990); *AFSCME and Cook County*, PEB ¶45,627 (Ill. LLRB)(CCH, 1989); *Bristol County Sheriff*, 2009 WL 207328 (Mass. LRC 2009).

42 *In re: Petition of the City of Melbourne*, PEB ¶45,342 (Florida)(CCH, 1988). *See Town of Ponce Inlet*, 15 NPER FL-23229 (Fla. PERC 1992); *Town of Mangonia Park*, 13 NPER FL-21316 (Fla. PERC 1990); *Bristol County Sheriff*, 2009 WL 207328 (Mass. LRC 2009); *Hampton Fall*, 2009 WL 326581 (N.H. PLRB 2009); *County of Wayne*, 16 NPER NY-14021 (N.Y. PERB Director 1994); *In re Gahanna*, SERB 85-052 (Ohio 1985); *Port of Portland*, 13 NPER OR-22014 (Or. ERB 1991).

43 *AFSCME and Cook County*, PEB ¶45,627 (Ill. LRRB)(CCH, 1989); *Fraternal Order of Police v. Pennsylvania LRB*, 560 A.2d 145 (Pa. 1989).

[44] *Muskegon County Professional Command Association v. County of Muskegon*, 464 N.W.2d 908 (Mich. App. 1990).

[45] *City of New Haven*, 13 NPER CT-22058 (Conn. SBLR 1991).

[46] *Matter of City of Ann Arbor*, PEB ¶45,388 (CCH, 1988). *See also City of Saginaw*, PEB ¶45,659 (Mich. ERC)(CCH, 1988)(deputy chiefs can be included in supervisory bargaining unit).

[47] *Muskegon County Professional Command Association v. County of Muskegon*, 464 N.W.2d 908 (Mich. App. 1990).

[48] *Oregon State Department of Police*, 13 NPER OR-21034 (Or. ERB 1990).

[49] *Illinois Council of Police v. Illinois Labor Relations Bd.*, 899 N.E.2d 1199 (Ill. App. 2008); *Massachusetts Board of Higher Education*, 2008 WL 5395622 (Mass. 2008).

[50] *Illinois Dept. of Cent. Management Services v. Illinois Labor Relations Bd., State Panel*, 888 N.E.2d 562 (Ill. App. 2008).

[51] *See* Chapter 41.56, Revised Code of Washington.

[52] *City of Clearwater*, 13 NPER FL-22101 (Fla. PERC 1991).

[53] *Capitol City Lodge #141 of Fraternal Order of Police v. Ingham County Board of Com'rs*, 399 N.W.2d 463 (Mich. App. 1986).

[54] *Webb County v. Webb County Deputies' Association*, 768 S.W.2d 953 (Tex. App. 1989).

[55] *Town of Trumboll*, 13 NPER CT-22059 (Conn. SBLR 1991).

[56] *FOP v. Commonwealth of Pennsylvania*, PEB ¶34,021 (Pa.)(CCH, 1983).

[57] *State of Iowa*, 16 NPER IA-24003 (Iowa PERB 1993); *City of San Antonio v. San Antonio Park Rangers Association*, 850 S.W.2d 189 (Tex. App. 1992).

[58] *San Bernardino County Sheriffs Employees Benefit Association v. San Bernardino County Public Employees Association*, 8 Cal.Rptr.2d 658 (Cal. App. 1992).

[59] *E.g., Village of Dixmoor*, 16 PERI ¶2038 (Ill. SLRB Gen. Counsel 2000).

[60] *E.g., California Correctional Peace Officers Association v. State of California*, 25 PERC ¶32,015 (Cal. PERB ALJ 2000).

[61] *Borough v. Pennsylvania Labor Relations Board*, 794 A.2d 402 (Pa.Cmwlth. 2002).

[62] A good early discussion of bargaining topics can be found in Clark, *The Scope of the Duty to Bargain in Public Employment, in Labor Relations Law in the Public Sector* 81 (A. Knapp ed. 1977).

[63] *Portland Firefighters Association v. City of Portland,* 751 P.2d 770 (Or. 1988).

[64] If an employer chooses to agree to include a permissive subject of bargaining in a collective bargaining agreement and finds the provision to its distaste, it may simply refuse to include the provision in a subsequent agreement. *Paterson Police Local v. City of Paterson*, 432 A.2d 847 (N.J. 1981).

[65] *City of Portland*, 8 PECBR 8115 (Or. 1985).

[66] *City of Buffalo*, 13 NPER NY-13036 (N.Y. PERB 1990).

[67] *County of Perry*, 19 NPER IL-124 (Ill. LRB 2003).

[68] *Plains Township Police Bargaining Unit v. Plains Township*, 33 PPER ¶33,019 (Pa. LRB ALJ 2001).

[69] *City of Bremerton*, PEB ¶45,352 (Wash.)(CCH, 1987).

[70] *City of Iowa City*, 17 NPER IA-26005 (Iowa PERB ALJ 1995)(delay of 90 days in filing unfair labor practice charge); *County of Nassau*, 35 NYPER ¶4583 (N.Y. PERB ALJ 2002); *City of Reading*, 17 NPER PA-26132 (Pa. LRB ALJ 1995); *City of Philadelphia*, 13 NPER PA-22042 (Pa. LRB Hearing Examiner 1991)(six-week delay between filing of unfair labor practice charge and violation of duty to bargain did not render the charge untimely).

[71] *Throop Borough*, 16 NPER PA-25012 (Pa. LRB ALJ 1993).

[72] *Law Enforcement Labor Services, Inc. v. City of Luverne,* 463 N.W.2d 546 (Minn. App. 1990).

[73] *Peekskill Police Association*, 35 NYPER ¶3016 (N.Y. PERB 2002).

[74] *Caruso v. Board of Collective Bargaining of the City of New York*, 555 N.Y.S.2d 133 (A.D. 1990).

[75] Quoted in *Model Law Enforcement Contract, 1993 Edition* (Labor Relations Information System, Portland, OR, 1993).

[76] *Washington State Patrol*, 3 (8) Public Safety Labor News 7 (Wash. PERC 1995).

[77] *City of Grosse Pointe Park*, 14 MPER ¶32051 (Mich. ERC 2001).

[78] *City of Mt. Vernon*, 23 GERR 667 (New York) (BNA 1986).

[79] *Howard County*, 1 (9) Public Safety Labor News 5 (Fishgold, 1993).

[80] Most states draw guidance from private sector precedent developed under the National Labor Relations Act in making judgments about whether bargaining topics are mandatory, permissive or prohibited. *E.g., Detroit Police Officers Ass'n v. Detroit*, 214 N.W.2d 803 (Mich. 1974).

[81] Where collective bargaining considerations are not present, obligations that departing officers repay the costs of training are upheld to the extent they do not violate the FLSA's minimum wage requirements. *City of Oakland v. Hassey*, 78 Cal. Rptr.3d 621 (Cal. App. 2008).

[82] *Vaca v. Sipes*, 386 U.S. 171 (1967). See also *Steele v. Louisville & N.R.R.*, 323 U.S. 192 (1944); *Yavoroski v. American Federation of State, County and Mun. Employees*, 2006 WL 2345940 (Pa. Com.Pl. 2006).

[83] *State of New Jersey*, 29 NJPER ¶66 (N.J. PERC ALJ 2003).

[84] *In re Stefensmeier*, 2005 WL 6194746 (Iowa PERB 2005).

[85] *City of East Grand Rapids*, 20 MPER ¶10 (Mich. ERC 2007); *County of Erie*, 17 NPER NY-13081 (N.Y. PERB 1994); *Madachy v. FOP*, 23 OPER ¶504 (Ohio ERB 2006).

[86] *Wiese v. Multnomah County Corrections Deputies Association*, 2008 WL 2661932 (Or. ERB 2008).

[87] *Metropolitan Alliance of Police v. State Labor Relations Bd.*, 2003 WL 23018186 (Ill. App. 2003).

[88] *Pearn v. Fraternal Order of Police*, 28 FPER ¶33,236 (Fla. PERC Gen. Counsel 2002); *Police Benevolent Association*, 15 NPER FL-23266 (Fla. PERC Gen. Counsel 1992).

[89] *Bravo v. Dade County PBA*, 31 FPER ¶118 (Fla. PERC Gen. Counsel 2005).

90 *Yavoroski v. American Federation of State, County and Mun. Employees,* 2006 WL 2345940 (Pa. Com.Pl. 2006); *In re AFSCME,* 2008 WL 5395612 (Mass. LRC 2008).

91 *Dortch v. Metropolitan Alliance of Police,* 18 PERI ¶3032 (Ill. LRB 2002); *Covino v. Superior Officers Association,* 33 NPER ¶4615 (N.Y. PERB ALJ 2000).

92 *Boshell v. Association of Professional Police Officers,* 17 PERI ¶3025 (Ill. SLRB Gen. Counsel 2001).

93 *In re Sparks,* 2007 WL 5439798 (D.C. PERB 2007).

94 *Hood v. Policemen's Benevolent and Protective Association,* 17 PERI ¶2025 (Ill. SLRB 2001).

95 *Mehr v. FOP,* 28 FPER ¶33,227 (Fla. PERC Gen. Counsel 2002).

96 *City of Miami,* 16 NPER FL-25157 (Fla. PERC Gen. Counsel 1994).

97 *Rhames v. PBA,* 17 NPER FL-25265 (Fla. PERC Gen. Counsel 1994).

98 *Barton v. City of Bristol,* 294 F. Supp. 184 (D. Conn. 2003); *County of Mercer,* 14 NPER NJ-23126 (N.J. PERC Dir. 1992).

99 *Davis v. Fraternal Order of Police Lodge No. 8 of Douglas County,* 731 N.W.2d 901 (Neb. App. 2007); *City of New York,* 13 NPER NYC-21060 (N.Y. City Board of Collective Bargaining 1990).

100 *Labbe v. Hartford Pension Commission,* 682 A.2d 490 (Conn. 1996).

101 *City of Highland Park,* 13 NPER MI-22024 (Mich. ERC 1991).

102 *Michigan State University APA,* 21 MPER ¶60 (Mich. App. 2008).

103 *Galloway Twp. Board of Education v. Galloway Twp. Ass'n of Education Secretaries,* 393 A.2d 207 (N.J. 1978).

104 *Amalgamated Association of Street, Electric Railway & Motor Coach Employees of America v. Lockridge,* 403 U.S. 274 (1971).

105 *Grasso v. Fraternal Order of Police, Glassboro Lodge No. 108,* 2008 WL 4066430 (N.J. Super. A.D. 2008); *Hadley v. Multnomah County Deputy Sheriffs Association,* 2008 WL 1966712 (Or. ERB 2008).

106 *Police Benevolent Association (Mallow),* 17 NPER FL-26163 (Fla. PERC 1995)(request for union assistance to obtain materials from personnel file; personnel file access not covered by collective bargaining agreement).

107 *NAACP v. Detroit Police Officers Association,* 821 F.2d 328 (6th Cir. 1987); *Fraternal Order of Police,* 14 NPER NJ-23082 (N.J. PERC 1992).

108 *California State Employees Association (Fox),* 17 NPER CA-26091 (Cal. PERB 1995)(personnel board).

109 *Berich v. Ithaca Police Benev. Ass'n, Inc.,* 804 N.Y.S.2d 833 (A.D. 2005).

110 *Tchida v. Police Officers' Federation of Minneapolis,* 375 N.W.2d 856 (Minn. App. 1985)(emphasis in original); *see Magnuson v. Florida PBA,* 34 FPER ¶244 (Fla. PERC 2008)(no duty of fair representation in pre-disciplinary process). *But see Daniels v. Manatee Education Association,* 34 FPER ¶113 (Fla. PERC 2008)(fact that employee can be represented by private attorney does not necessarily mean that no *Weingarten* rights apply).

111 *Westchester County Department of Corrections Superior Officers' Association, Inc.,* 16 NPER NY-13077 (N.Y. PERB 1993).

112 *Police Officers Association of Michigan,* 17 NPER MI-25112 (Mich. ERC 1994).

[113] *Foley v. AFSCME, Council 31*, 556 N.E.2d 581 (Ill. App. 1990)(duty of fair representation claims cannot be brought in courts; must be brought before state labor relations board); *State ex. Rel. Ohio Dep't of Mental Health v. Nadel*, 786 N.E. 2d 49 (Ohio 2003)(same); *In re Ponton*, 39 PPER ¶162 (Pa. LRB 2008)(duty of fair representation claims only enforceable through the courts).

[114] *Allen v. Hennepin County*, 680 N.W.2d 560 (Minn. App. 2004); *Brondes v. IUPA*, 19 OPER ¶1848 (Ohio App. 2002); *Franklin City Law Enforcement Ass'n v. F.O.P. Lodge 9*, 59 Ohio St.3d 167 (1991); *see Rosequist v. International Association of Fire Fighters*, 49 P.3d 651 (Nev. 2002); *Huff v. Fraternal Order of Police*, 19 PERI ¶131 (Ill. SLRB 2003).

[115] *Moore v. Fraternal Order of Police*, 16 NPER FL-25032 (Fla. PERC General Counsel 1993).

[116] *Labbe v. Hartford Pension Commission*, 682 A.2d 490 (Conn. 1996).

[117] *Olshock v. Village of Skokie*, 541 F.2d 1254 (7th Cir. 1976)(assumes without analysis that participation in police strike would be cause for discharge); *Ex parte City of Florence*, 417 So.2d 191 (Ala. 1982)(rules that discharge is an automatic result of an illegal strike under local law).

[118] §§447.505 and 447.507, Florida Statutes Annotated (West 1981)(bans strike by public employee or employee organization and subjects the employee organization to liability for damages to the public employer for violation; §20-7.5-1-14(b), Indiana Code Annotated (Burns 1975)(same); §111.89(2)(c), Wisconsin Statutes Annotated (same).

[119] *City Firefighters State of Missouri v. Kansas Local 42*, PEB ¶34,181 (Mo. App.)(CCH, 1984).

[120] *Lamphere Schools v. Lamphere Federation of Teachers*, 252 N.W.2d 818 (Mich. 1977)(no civil remedy for damages against union engaged in illegal strike because of preemptive effect of state laws); *City of Fairmont v. Retail, Wholesale and Department Store Union*, 283 S.E.2d 589 (W.Va. 1980)(same).

[121] *Chicago Teachers Union, Local No.1 v. Hudson*, 475 U.S. 292 (1986).

[122] *Lehnert v. Ferris Faculty Association*, 500 U.S. 507 (1991).

[123] *Nashua Teachers Union v. Nashua School District*, 707 A.2d 448 (N.H. 1998); *Zorica v. AFSCME District Council 33*, 686 A.2d 461 (Pa.Cmwlth. 1996).

[124] *Sims v. Parkland College Support Staff*, 18 PERI ¶1090 (Ill. ELRB ALJ 2002).

[125] *E.g., Davidson v. IFT*, 17 PERI ¶1012 (Ill. ELRB ALJ 2001).

[126] *Robinson v. Pennsylvania State Corrections Officers Ass'n*, 363 F. Supp. 2d 751 (M.D. Pa. 2005); *Wynd v. HERE, Local 1*, 18 PERI ¶1154 (Ill. ELRB ALJ 2002).

[127] *Abood v. Detroit Board of Education*, 431 U.S. 209 (1977). *See generally Cummings v. Connell*, 177 F. Supp. 2d 1060 (E.D. Cal. 2001).

[128] *Tierney v. City of Toledo*, 824 F.2d 1497 (6th Cir. 1987); *In re Gibney*, SERB 89-004 (Ohio 1989).

[129] *E.g. Sims v. Parkland College Support Staff*, 18 PERI ¶1090 (Ill. ELRB ALJ 2002).

[130] *Malamud v. CFA*, 26 PERC ¶33,074 (Cal. PERB 2002); *Reece v. City of Columbus*, 826 F. Supp. 1115 (S.D. Ohio 1993), *rev'd on other grounds*, 71 F.3d 619 (6th Cir. 1995).

131 *Tierney v. City of Toledo*, 917 F.2d 927 (6th Cir. 1990).

132 *Reno Police Protective Association*, 715 P.2d 1321 (Nev. 1986)(demotion); *City of Hialeah Gardens*, LAIG 5107 (Sherman, 1994)(termination); *Florida PBA*, 22 FPER ¶27,049 (Fla. PERC 1996)(demotion); *Sheriff of Williamson County*, 14 PERI ¶2016 (Ill. SLRB 1998)(suspension and termination); *Borough of Sayreville*, 17 NPER NJ-26135 (N.J. PERC 1995)(discharge); *Borough of Bristol*, 15 NPER PA-13161 (Pa.Cmwlth. 1992)(discharge); *City of Philadelphia*, 17 NPER PA-26117 (Pa. LRB ALJ 1995).

133 *Fairview Township*, 28 PPER ¶28,124 (Pa. LRB ALJ 1997).

134 *Kiskiminetas Township,* 15 NPER PA-23182 (Pa. LRB ALJ 1992).

135 *Upper Mount Bethel Police Association v. Upper Mount Bethel Township*, 28 PPER ¶28,195 (Pa. LRB ALJ 1997); *Selinsgrove Borough*, 15 NPER PA-24102 (Pa. LRB 1993); *Emporium Borough*, 14 NPER PA-23136 (Pa. LRB 1992).

136 *City of Troy*, 17 NPER NY-14526 (N.Y. PERB ALJ 1995).

137 *Valley Township*, 13 NPER PA-22046 (Pa. LRB Hearing Examiner 1991).

138 *Sheriff of Jackson County v. Illinois State Labor Relations Board*, 15 PERI ¶4004 (Ill. App. 1999); *Borough of Sayreville*, 13 NPER NJ-21199 (N.J. PERC Hearing Examiner 1990).

139 *Bellefonte Police Officers Association*, 27 PPER ¶27,257 (Pa. LRB 1996); *Fraternal Order of Police, Queen City Lodge #10*, 27 PPER ¶27,250 (Pa. LRB 1996).

140 *Officers of the Upper Perk Police District*, 27 PPER ¶27,092 (Pa. LRB ALJ 1996).

141 *City of Philadelphia*, 17 NPER PA-26114 (Pa. LRB 1995)(deputy sheriff transferred in retaliation for conducting poll on behalf of Union to determine employees' view of new staffing policy); *Metropolitan Police Department*, 98 LA 1159 (Bowers, 1992)(sergeant transferred after expressing concern about new shift schedule).

142 *Borough of Stone Harbor*, 14 NPER NJ-23105 (N.J. PERC ALJ 1992).

143 *Derry Borough Police Association*, 29 PPER ¶29,237 (Pa. LRB 1997); *East Taylor Township*, 16 NPER PA-24107 (Pa. LRB ALJ 1993).

144 *City of Chicago*, 14 NPER IL-23067 (Ill. LLRB 1992); *Paxtang Borough Police Association*, 28 PPER ¶28,041 (Pa. LRB ALJ 1997).

145 *Ellwood City Police Wage & Policy Unit v. Ellwood City Borough,* 29 PPER ¶29,125 (Pa. LRB ALJ 1998).

146 *Windsor Locks Police Department*, 13 NPER CT-21069 (Conn. SBLR 1990).

147 *Metropolitan Alliance of Police*, 15 PERI ¶3002 (Ill. LLRB Gen. Counsel 1998).

148 *City of Chester*, 13 NPER PA-21182 (Pa. LRB Hearing Examiner 1990)(enforcement of residency rule only against union activist).

149 *Windsor Locks Police Department*, 13 NPER CT-21069 (Conn. SBLR 1990). For example, in one case an employer attempted to justify its threatened transfer of employees who were organizing a labor organization on the grounds that the police budget was running a deficit. When the employer was unable to prove that such a deficit in fact existed, an administrative law judge held that the justification

was pretextual in nature and that the true reason for the transfer was retaliation for the organizing efforts. *Manor Borough*, 18 NPER PA-26194 (Pa. LRB ALJ 1995).

[150] *City of Rye*, 17 NPER NY-14573 (N.Y. PERB Director 1995)(police commission had no knowledge that police union had initiated binding arbitration at the time he took unrelated disciplinary action against police union president); *PBA of County of Nassau*, 32 NYPER ¶4504 (N.Y. PERB ALJ 1999)(no proof that chief knew of inspector's protected activity of testifying at arbitration hearing); *Hemlock Township Police Officers Association v. Hemlock Township*, 30 PPER ¶30,056 (Pa. LRB ALJ 1999)(employer fired officers before they engaged in organization effort).

[151] *City of Reading v. PLRB*, 568 A.2d 715 (Pa.Cmwlth. 1998).

[152] *Illinois Fraternal Order of Police*, 14 PERI ¶2029 (Ill. SLRB 1998).

[153] *Upland Borough*, 25 PPER ¶25,195 (Pa. LRB 1974).

[154] *Sheriff of Adams County*, 15 PERI ¶2024 (Ill. SLRB 1999).

[155] *City of Troy*, 17 NPER NY-14526 (N.Y. PERB ALJ 1995).

[156] *Pennsylvania State Troopers Association v. Commonwealth of Pennsylvania*, 30 PPER ¶30,125 (Pa. LRB ALJ 1999).

[157] *Palm Beach County PBA v. City of Riviera Beach*, 25 FPER ¶30,190 (Fla. PERC 1999).

[158] *County of Macon*, 14 NPER IL-23081 (Ill. SLRB 1992).

[159] *Village of Depew*, 14 NPER NY-13009 (N.Y. PERB 1992).

[160] *City of Dunedin v. Local No. 2327*, 4 FPER ¶4258 (Fla. 1978).

[161] *Somerset County Sheriff*, 22 NJPER ¶27,149 (N.J. PERC 1996).

[162] *Wilkes-Barre Police Benevolent Association*, 29 PPER ¶29,040 (Pa. LRB ALJ 1998).

CHAPTER 3

DISCIPLINARY STANDARDS AND LAW ENFORCEMENT OFFICERS

Introduction.

Traditionally, law enforcement employers were termed "at-will employers," a status which allowed them to discipline and discharge employees without concern that the employee could successfully challenge the disciplinary action.[1] The only restriction placed on the disciplinary actions of at-will employers is that discipline cannot be imposed for reasons that either violate the federal or a state constitution, or for reasons that violate a statute.

Today, it is extremely rare to find a law enforcement employer who remains an at-will employer. Virtually all are subject to restrictions on their disciplinary authority, restrictions imposed by collective bargaining agreements, civil service rules, state laws, or their own internal rules and procedures. Though the level of job protection varies tremendously depending upon the type of restrictions placed upon the employer, virtually all law enforcement employees are entitled to some measure of substantive protection from inappropriate discipline.

Employees Not Covered By Collective Bargaining Agreements Or Civil Service Laws.

Absent a state law requiring the employer to meet certain disciplinary standards, law enforcement agencies may freely discipline their employees as long as they do so in compliance with the United States Constitution and federal law.

Police officers who are granted the least protections from improper discipline are those who work in law enforcement agencies which are not subject to collective bargaining agreements or civil service laws. Absent a state law requiring the employer to meet certain disciplinary standards, these law enforcement agencies may freely discipline their employees as long as they do so in compliance with the United States Constitution and federal law.[2] Employees working for these agencies are termed "at-will" employees because they are said to retain their jobs only at the will of the employer. A good expression of the definition of an "at-will" employee can be found in the California Labor Code:

> "An employment, having no specified term, may be terminated at the will of either party on notice to the other. Employment for a specified term means an employment for a period greater than one month."[3]

At-will employees can be fired for a good reason, a bad reason, or for no reason at all, so long as the employer's decision does not violate any federal or state laws. Not only do at-will employees not have any substantive protections for their jobs, they often are not subject to any procedural disciplinary protections such as peace officer bills of rights. It is perfectly permissible, for example, to discharge an at-will officer without investigating the complaint against the officer,[4] or to discharge an at-will officer who has only been charged, but not convicted, of a crime, where to do so to officers with some sort of job security would likely not be upheld.[5]

Some courts regard the rules and regulations of at-will employers as creating a binding contract with employees. Such a contract, though only implied by the law rather than expressly stated, can, in some circumstances, create substantive job protections an employer must follow.[6] For example, in one case a police dispatcher was discharged for a variety of performance problems. The dispatcher filed a lawsuit, contending that the procedures used in discharging her violated the staff policy manual of the police department. The Court held that, even in the absence of a collective bargaining agreement covering the dispatcher, the staff policy manual constituted a binding contract from which the employer was not free to deviate:

> "[O]nce an employer has promulgated a policy 'presumably with a view to obtaining the benefit of improved employee attitudes and behavior and improved quality of the work force, the employer may not treat its promise as illusory.' * * * A policy manual of the type here cannot be allowed to create rights for employees, including the right not to be arbitrarily discharged after notice and hearing, which disintegrate when an employee attempts to exercise them."[7]

The implied contract created by operations manuals and regulations can contain procedures that an employer must follow prior to disciplining an employee. If the employer's rules also list the grounds upon which employees may be disciplined, the employer may be required to justify its decision on both substantive as well as procedural grounds.[8]

Employees Covered By Civil Service Laws.

The majority of states have enacted civil service laws, which provide a good deal more in the way of job protection than is granted to at-will employees.[9] Civil service systems vary widely in the procedures they use and in the protections they give employees. Some civil service laws allow hearings to be conducted by hearing officers,[10] while others command that the civil service board itself conduct the hearing.[11] The majority of civil service laws make the decisions of civil service boards either completely unreviewable in court or extremely difficult to review,[12] while a minority freely allow appeals from civil service decisions.[13]

Given the deference shown in most states to the decisions of civil service boards, it is not uncommon for courts to apply a presumption that the findings of fact made by the board are "*prima facie* correct," without even examining the underlying basis for those findings.[14] In some cases, courts have held that they will only reverse a civil service board's disciplinary decision if an "abuse of discretion" or a "manifest error" is found.[15] In other cases, courts have held that in order to be reversed, discipline imposed by a civil service board must be "discriminatory,"[16] "clearly wrong,"[17] or "arbitrary and capricious."[18] Yet other courts have held that civil service boards have the authority to actually increase the punishment imposed by an employer, a prospect which makes appeals to such boards a chancy proposition.[19] Other courts have compelled law enforcement officers appealing

The majority of states have enacted civil service laws, which provide a good deal more in the way of job protection than is granted to at-will employees.

discipline through the civil service process to show that a particular conclusion was "against the manifest weight of the evidence."[20] One court has even held that if a civil service board determines that if charges relating to the employee's work performance are proven, the board has no authority to modify a disciplinary penalty,[21] while another court commented that it was constrained to uphold a termination decision even when it felt the penalty was "severe."[22]

The Appeal Of Discipline Where Employees Are Granted Job Protection Through A Collective Bargaining Agreement.

Law enforcement officers have had more favorable results appealing discipline through grievance arbitration procedures contained in collective bargaining agreements than those subject to civil service laws or internal departmental policies. Most certainly the reason for the difference in results is the structure of the proceedings in arbitration as opposed to the judicial and civil service systems. Not only is the standard of review of disciplinary decisions more liberal in arbitration than in civil service systems or court, but the burden of proof in arbitration lies with the employer to show that the discipline imposed met the contractual standards for discipline. In courts and in many civil service systems, the employee usually shoulders the burden of proving that the discipline imposed was unjust.

In addition, most arbitration clauses provide that an arbitrator's decision is "final and binding," meaning that arbitration is usually a faster and less expensive means of appealing discipline. Though courts are occasionally tempted to review the decision of arbitrators they perceive as wrongly decided, the standards for challenging arbitration decisions pose almost insurmountable hurdles. As phrased by the Supreme Court, an arbitrator's decision will only be overturned in "rare instances" and only where the arbitrator's award does not "draw its essence" from the collective bargaining agreement. Moreover, "as long as an honest arbitrator is even arguably construing or applying the contract and acting within the scope of his authority, the fact that a court is convinced he committed serious error does not suffice to overturn his decision."[23] Put another way, an arbitrator can be wrong on the facts and wrong on the law and a court will not overturn the arbitrator's opinion.[24] Only in rare instances where the arbitrator's decision violates a public policy clearly established by statute does one usually find a court overturning an arbitrator's decision.[25]

Most collective bargaining agreements provide that discipline imposed must be supported by "just cause." Under a "just cause" standard, the basic question is whether the employer's disciplinary decision is fair under all of the circumstances in the case. Such a standard involves a review not only of whether the officer engaged in misconduct which warrants discipline, but also of whether the level of discipline imposed was fair given the officer's offense.

An arbitrator's decision will only be overturned in "rare instances" and only where the arbitrator's award does not "draw its essence" from the collective bargaining agreement.

The just cause standard carries with it a significantly broader scope of review than that customarily applied by courts reviewing the discipline of police officers. Where in court the legal issue may be whether the employer was "arbitrary or capricious," and the factual inquiry limited to whether there is any evidence to support the employer's disciplinary decision,[26] in arbitration under a just cause standard, the issue will be whether the employer's decision was supported by proven facts and whether the particular discipline imposed was fair considering those facts.

Just Cause For Discipline.

The "just cause" standard is at once seemingly simple and yet quite complex. At its most basic, just cause for discipline means that the discipline is fair and appropriate under all of the circumstances. Winnowed apart, the just cause standard actually has twelve different components, all of which are separate inquiries:

The just cause standard actually has twelve different components, all of which are separate inquiries.

1. Have the charges against the officer been factually proven? Courts, civil service boards, police commissions, and arbitrators all require that the employer bear the burden of proving that discipline is justified. However, a variety of thresholds for the burden of proof have been applied.[27]

In general, the burden of proof in any disciplinary cases in court or before a civil service board or police commission, or in discipline cases in arbitration involving short suspensions or other low-level discipline, is proof by a preponderance of the evidence.[28] If the appeal is to an arbitrator, and the sanction is a demotion, termination, or other serious discipline, the arbitrator is likely to impose the stricter burden of proof of "clear and convincing evidence."[29] A minority of arbitrators have held in cases where the alleged conduct of the employee, if proven, would constitute evidence of criminal wrongdoing, that an employer must prove its disciplinary case beyond a reasonable doubt – the same burden of proof applied in criminal trials.[30]

Where an employer lodges specific factual charges against an officer, it must prove all of the elements of the charges it brings. For example, in one case an employer fired an officer for six reasons: (1) Being involved in a verbal and physical confrontation with a private citizen; (2) exposing his buttocks in public; (3) engaging in lewd and suggestive dancing; (4) interfering with the arrest of a personal acquaintance; (5) engaging in recreational gambling while on duty; and (6) appearing in public while intoxicated. When the City only met its burden of proof as to Charges 5 and 6, a court overturned the discharge, imposing a 90-day suspension in lieu of the termination.[31]

2. Was the punishment imposed by the employer disproportionately severe under all the circumstances? This element of just cause is a statement of the rough justice principle that the punishment should fit the crime. The notion of proportionality of punishment takes into account factors such as harm to the department resulting from the officer's conduct, the officer's work record, and the underlying seriousness of the conduct.[32]

3. Did the employer conduct a thorough investigation into the incident?
Particularly in cases involving discipline of law enforcement officers, courts and arbitrators tend to require that an employer's investigation of misconduct be just as thorough and complete as would the employer's investigation in a criminal case.[33] Such an investigation should, at a minimum, include examining all investigatory leads and conducting personal interviews with witnesses.[34]

4. Were other employees who engaged in conduct similar or identical to that of the officer treated as harshly by the employer? Commonly referred to as the "disparate treatment" defense, this question focuses on the employer's pre-existing pattern of discipline imposed in identical or similar cases. If an employer substantially varies from prior sanctions in similar cases where there is no significant difference in the work records of the officers involved, the harsher discipline is likely to be set aside or modified.[35] At the heart of the defense is the notion that an employer's pattern of discipline puts employees on notice as to the sanctions the employer believes are appropriate in a given case, and that to vary from such a pattern of discipline without prior notice to employees is inherently unfair.[36]

5. Was the officer's misconduct the product of action or inaction by the employer? The fifth of the just cause inquiries encompasses an increasingly wide variety of theories, all of which have the common theme that the employer has either done or not done something that contributed in part to the incident giving rise to the discipline. For example, where an employee commits misconduct but had not been adequately trained by the employer as to how to handle the particular situation, discipline is likely to be reduced or completely reversed.[37] Similarly, if supervisors contributed to the atmosphere which led to the officer's misconduct, discipline will likely be modified.[38]

6. Did the employer take into consideration the officer's good or exemplary work history? This concept focuses on the notion that an employer is obligated not just to consider the nature of the employee's conduct, but also the character of the employee as demonstrated through the employee's work history.[39]

7. Did the employer take into consideration mitigating circumstances?
Mitigating circumstances an employer is required to take into account prior to imposing discipline include the officer's state of mind at the time of the alleged misconduct,[40] the officer's physical condition,[41] and whether the officer was provoked into the misconduct.[42] At the core of the concept of the consideration of mitigating circumstances is the determination of whether the employee's conduct was more on the order of a mistake brought about by a chain of events or whether, on the other hand, the employee's conduct exemplified a deep-rooted inability to perform the functions of the job.

8. Was the officer subjected to progressive or corrective discipline? The principle of progressive or corrective discipline mandates that punishment be meted out in increasingly severe doses in an effort to correct (as opposed to punish) the behavioral problems of an employee.[43] The idea behind progressive discipline is that the imposition of lower levels of discipline will get the employee's attention, encouraging him to correct his behavior patterns.[44] While progressive discipline is generally the rule in disciplinary cases, it need not be followed if the employee's misconduct is so severe that it warrants the immediate imposition of a high level of discipline.

9. Was the employer motivated by anti-union bias? As discussed in greater length in Chapter 2 of this book, an employer's decision to impose discipline cannot be based on the improper motive of bias against a labor organization.[45] This issue commonly arises where the target of discipline is a union officer or activist, where there is a pattern of more lenient discipline for similar offenses in the past, and where the relationship between the labor organization and the employer is a difficult one.[46]

10. Are the employer's rules clear and understandable? Before an employer may apply its rules to discipline employees, it must establish that its rules are understandable by the average police officer. If a rule is reasonably capable of more than one interpretation, discipline imposed under the rule will likely be overturned.[47] However, even broadly-written rules such as a rule forbidding the use of "excessive force" or "obscene language" are enforceable if they are readily understandable by the average officer.[48]

11. Is the officer likely to engage in similar misconduct in the future? Usually only in cases of termination, courts and arbitrators will inquire as to whether the officer is or can be rehabilitated,[49] or whether the conduct was an aberration from the type of conduct normally displayed by the officer.[50]

12. Was the officer accorded procedural due process in the disciplinary investigation? In this context, due process means not only constitutional due process,[51] but also what is termed "industrial due process." Industrial due process is a broader notion than constitutional due process, and includes not only concepts such as fair pre-disciplinary hearings,[52] but also a ban on basing a disciplinary decision solely on hearsay in cases where complaining witnesses are not called to testify,[53] a requirement that employees be allowed representation during disciplinary interviews,[54] and a prohibition against punishing an officer twice for the same offense.[55] The difference between constitutional and industrial due process is best seen in cases where the employer's investigation has been delayed. While even as much as a five-year delay in completing an investigation may not be enough to violate constitutional due process,[56] delays of one year or less violate industrial due process and often result in the reversal of discipline.[57]

Any of the above components of just cause may be used as a defense to a disciplinary charge and, if proven, may be sufficient to cause an arbitrator, civil service board, or a court to reverse or mitigate disciplinary sanctions meted out by a law enforcement employer.

Particular Types Of Discipline And Discharge Cases.

Law enforcement officer discipline cases arise in a wide variety of circumstances. The policies and procedures manuals of a law enforcement agency typically are voluminous, with officers employed by the agency subject to discipline if they fail to conform to all of the policies. Given that such manuals may run the gamut from correct arrest procedures to rules about uniform attire, and particularly given the ever-creative nature of some off-duty behavior, it is not surprising that law enforcement discipline cases are varied and involve widely different factual circumstances.

A common theme one hears is that law enforcement officers are subject to a "higher standard" than other employees. This higher standard is often described in two ways. First, the notion is that conduct which might not be punishable if the individual were employed as a carpenter, an accountant, or in any other position, would be punishable if engaged in by a law enforcement officer. Second, the belief is that if misconduct has been proven, law enforcement officers are subject to a higher degree of discipline than other types of employees.

In compiling this book, the author reviewed over 2,500 disciplinary cases involving law enforcement officers. This review has led to the conclusion that if the "higher standard" ever truly existed, it is seriously diminished today and is limited to a very narrow set of facts. Overall, courts and arbitrators considering discipline cases involving law enforcement officers apply the same general principles relevant to discipline cases involving other types of employees. The concepts of progressive discipline, procedural due process, and the fairness of the disciplinary sanction have just as firm a foundation in law enforcement cases as they do in non-law enforcement cases.

Where the "higher standards" can be said to exist are in the limited areas where the employee has been convicted of a crime or has engaged in an act of dishonesty. In such cases, law enforcement officers are generally treated more harshly than general employees, though the strength of the old rule that a criminal conviction or a finding of untruthfulness meant the automatic forfeiture of a law enforcement officer's job has now waned.

Four of the most litigated areas in the discipline of law enforcement officers have been discipline under "conduct unbecoming" regulations, discipline resulting from an officer's off-duty conduct, insubordination incidents, and discipline for refusal to submit to a polygraph examination. Each of the areas will be discussed below.

Conduct Unbecoming An Officer.

By far the largest number of law enforcement disciplinary cases arise under rules prohibiting "conduct unbecoming" a law enforcement officer. Derived from similar rules in the military service, "conduct unbecoming" regulations have been applied in a wide variety of cases to punish misconduct that warrants disciplinary charges but does not squarely fall within other specific rules of an agency.

On many occasions, "conduct unbecoming" regulations have been challenged as being unconstitutionally vague. The basis of the vagueness doctrine is that to be enforceable, a governmental regulation which is applied to deny a public employee a benefit must reasonably advise the employee of what conduct is forbidden and

Courts and arbitrators considering discipline cases involving law enforcement officers apply the same general principles relevant to discipline cases involving other types of employees.

"Conduct unbecoming" regulations have been applied in a wide variety of cases to punish misconduct that warrants disciplinary charges but does not squarely fall within other specific rules of an agency.

what is permitted.[58] In other words, the regulation must have a "rough idea of fairness" in order to be consistent with the requirements of the due process clause of the Fifth Amendment.[59]

A few courts have accepted vagueness challenges to "conduct unbecoming rules" and have refused to enforce "conduct unbecoming" regulations. As explained by one court:

> "In determining whether the rule 'conduct unbecoming a member and detrimental to the service' conforms with the constitutionally-mandated 'rough idea of fairness,' it is necessary to examine whether the rule creates a standard of conduct which is capable of objective interpretation by those policemen who must abide by it, by those Departmental Officials who must enforce it, and by any administrative or judicial tribunal which might review any disciplinary proceeding. On its face, the rule proscribes only conduct which is both 'unbecoming' and 'detrimental to the service.'

> "It is obvious, however, that any apparent limitation on the prohibited conduct through the use of these qualifying terms is illusory, for 'unbecoming' and 'detrimental to the service' have no inherent, objective content from which ascertainable standards defining the proscribed conduct could be fashioned. Like beauty, their content exists only in the eye of the beholder. The subjectivity implicit in the language of the rule permits police officials to enforce the rule with unfettered discretion, and it is precisely this potential for arbitrary enforcement which is abhorrent to the Due Process Clause. Further, where, as here, a rule contains no ascertainable standards for enforcement, administrative and judicial review can only be a meaningless gesture."[60]

The vast majority of courts, however, have ruled that "conduct unbecoming" regulations are not necessarily void for vagueness, and do not violate the principles of due process.[61] For example, in *Arnett v. Kennedy*, the United States Supreme Court sustained a "conduct unbecoming" regulation, holding that the regulation was necessary to the employer's operation:

> "[I]t is not feasible or necessary for the Government to spell out in detail all that conduct which will result in retaliation. The most conscientious of codes that define prohibited conduct of employees includes 'catch-all' clauses prohibiting employee 'misconduct,' 'immorality,' or 'conduct unbecoming.'"[62]

Whether a "conduct unbecoming" regulation can be constitutionally applied in a given situation will depend almost entirely on the facts of the incident giving rise to the discipline. As noted by the California Supreme Court in one of the leading cases in the area, the permissible application of a "conduct unbecoming" regulation will turn on whether the officer could reasonably anticipate that his or her conduct would be the subject of discipline:

The vast majority of courts have ruled that "conduct unbecoming" regulations are not necessarily void for vagueness, and do not violate the principles of due process.

"[W]e construe 'conduct unbecoming' a city police officer to refer only to conduct which indicates a lack of fitness to perform the functions of a police officer. Thus construed, [the rule] provides a sufficiently specific standard against which the conduct of a police officer in a particular case can be judged. Police officers, like teachers and veterinarians, will normally be able to determine what kind of conduct indicates unfitness to perform the functions of a police officer."[63]

The overwhelming majority of courts have followed this narrow approach by upholding "conduct unbecoming" regulations in law enforcement agencies, but only in circumstances where the conduct in question would clearly be viewed as punishable by a reasonable law enforcement officer.[64]

In order to discipline an officer for unbecoming conduct, the employer must have a rule in place which specifically prohibits "conduct unbecoming."[65] A wide variety of conduct has been held to appropriately fall within the scope of "conduct unbecoming" regulations. What follows is a general summary of the types of conduct that may be regulated by "conduct unbecoming" regulations, assuming that the conduct is not otherwise constitutionally protected:

In order to discipline an officer for unbecoming conduct, the employer must have a rule in place which specifically prohibits "conduct unbecoming."

- Association with crime figures.[66]

- Bigotry.[67]

- Criminal conduct,[68] even where the officer has not been convicted of the crime.[69]

- Dishonesty.[70]

- Driving crimes committed while off duty.[71]

- Fighting.[72]

- Insubordination.[73]

- Mishandling of property belonging either to the law enforcement agency or to others.[74]

- Sexual misconduct,[75] particularly if on duty.[76]

- Substance abuse, including use of alcohol and drugs.[77]

- Use of force outside of department guidelines.[78]

- Verbal tantrums.[79]

In order to be the basis for discipline, a "conduct unbecoming" regulation must be applied to actions that have a provable adverse relationship on the officer's performance. In other words, a "conduct unbecoming" rule can only regulate "any conduct which has a tendency to destroy public respect for municipal employees and confidence in the operation of municipal services."[80] While private conduct can be the basis for a "conduct unbecoming" charge, there must be an adverse impact on the public employer before the charge can be the basis for discipline.[81]

Off-Duty Conduct.

The off-duty conduct of law enforcement officers can be regulated by their employers, but only to the extent that there is a direct relationship between the off-duty conduct and a provable impact on the job performance or the effective functioning of the agency.[82] A classic example of the distinction between off-duty conduct which is subject to the employer's control and that which is not is provided by cases involving an employee's off-duty membership in the Ku Klux Klan. In one case where the employee was merely a passive member of the Ku Klux Klan, and drew no relationship between his membership and his job, a court held that an employer had no right to discipline the officer for such membership.[83] However, in a case where the officer publicized the fact that he, as a law enforcement officer, is a member of the group, and has participated in the group's activities while identifying himself as a law enforcement officer, a court held that there is a sufficient relationship between the officer's off-duty conduct and his job so as to make the discipline of the officer permissible.[84]

Insubordination Incidents.

In addition to the general rules governing the validity of discipline, insubordination incidents have generated a well-developed body of law requiring an employer to take certain steps before an officer can be disciplined for insubordination. That body of law can be summarized in the form of the following questions, all of which are likely to be asked by an arbitrator, court, or hearings board considering the appropriateness of discipline for insubordination:

- Was the officer given a direct order by a supervisor to perform or not perform a certain deed?

- If the officer was not given a direct order, was the officer subject to specific and clear rules which had been distributed to the officer which compelled the officer to perform the deed?[85]

- Was the officer specifically advised that the failure to comply with the order or the applicable rules would subject the officer to the degree of discipline which was eventually imposed?[86]

- Did the officer in fact disobey the order or the rules? If there was no outright disobedience, was the conduct not merely an "expression of frustration" as opposed to a "defiant attitude"?[87]

- Was the order one which did not require the officer to violate the law or unduly jeopardize his safety?[88]

- Was the employer free from fault in provoking or contributing to the incident of insubordination?[89]

If the answer to any of these questions is "no," then it is likely that the discipline imposed upon the officer will be at least reduced, if not overturned entirely. If the answer to all of the questions is "yes," then it is likely that the discipline imposed by the employer, no matter how severe, will be sustained.

Polygraph Examinations.

The giving of polygraph examinations in the investigatory process is often regulated by statute. An increasing number of states have now enacted laws forbidding a law enforcement agency from conditioning continued employment on an officer's willingness to submit to a polygraph examination.

Where there are no state statutes forbidding the use of polygraphs, the majority approach allows a law enforcement employer to compel the taking of a polygraph examination, providing that the questions on the examination are specifically and narrowly tailored to the performance of the officer's duties and are not used in a subsequent criminal prosecution.[90] The remainder of courts, however, will not allow a law enforcement employer to discharge an officer because of a refusal to submit to a polygraph examination, holding that the same unreliability which prevents the polygraph's admissibility in court should preclude the dismissal of a police officer for failure to take a test.[91]

Some states have enacted polygraph statutes which forbid the giving of polygraph examinations to any employees except those involved in law enforcement. Currently the courts are split on whether such statutes unconstitutionally discriminate against law enforcement officers. The courts upholding such statutes rely on the public trust which is placed with law enforcement officers.[92] Courts finding such statutes to be a denial of equal protection of the laws focus on the singling out of law enforcement employees for adverse treatment under the laws:

> "We cannot doubt that police officers occupy a position of public trust in our society, but this fact does not breathe life into an ambiguous statute whose enforcement is sought exclusively against police officers. By the clear wording of the statute, secretaries, clerks, dispatchers, meter maids and dogcatchers are as much employees of public law enforcement agencies as are police officers, but they do not occupy the same position of power and concomitant trust that must reside in our police forces. To hold that all 'public law enforcement agencies' can be compelled, under the statute, to take a polygraph examination, would be to stamp them all as second class citizens. And an interpretation restricting the classification to police officers would stamp an even smaller class as second class citizens."[93]

Whatever the status may be of the use of polygraph examinations as a condition of employment, it is clear that an employer can require a polygraph examination as a precondition to assignment to a specialty unit. For example, the City of

Los Angeles is forbidden by the California Peace Officer Bill of Rights from compelling any employee to take a polygraph examination. In spite of that prohibition, a court upheld the use of a polygraph to screen employees requesting transfer into an organized crime unit, reasoning that the ban on the polygraph did not prohibit the Department from using the polygraph "in sifting through applicants to find the best possible officers for its most sensitive assignments."[94]

Some state statutes forbidding polygraph examinations have exceptions that allow polygraph examinations if they are given in the course of a criminal investigation. With such a statutory scheme, it may be possible for a law enforcement agency to discipline an officer based upon the results of a polygraph examination given during a criminal investigation even though no criminal charges actually resulted against the officer.[95]

Summary Of Disciplinary Cases Involving Law Enforcement Officers.

What follows is a table reviewing decisions involving the discipline of law enforcement officers. For convenience, the cases are grouped alphabetically into general subject headings, though one case may discuss a variety of different topics.

Since the cases listed below involve decisions of both arbitrators and the courts, the standards of review of the discipline vary significantly from case to case. Accordingly, the case summaries must be used with a good deal of care; a defense which would mandate the reversal of discipline in arbitration might be ruled irrelevant in a court challenge to the same discipline, and vice versa.[96]

POLICE DISCIPLINARY CASES

CASE NAME	INITIAL SANCTION	RESULT ON APPEAL	DESCRIPTION
Absenteeism			
Auglaize County Sheriff, 121 LA 311 (Goldberg, 2005)	Termination	Termination	Corrections officer walked off job during discussion with management and union about her use of sick leave. Defense of "constructive discharge" rejected where there was no reasonable basis to conclude that she was being fired or discharge was imminent.
City of Okmulgee, Oklahoma and Fraternal Order of Police, Lodge 96, 119 LA 1227 (Robinson, 2004)	1-Day Suspension	No Discipline	Employer failed to follow own policy of allowing an employee the opportunity to explain her absence from work before disciplining her.

CASE NAME	INITIAL SANCTION	RESULT ON APPEAL	DESCRIPTION
City of Palestine v. Ramirez, 925 S.W.2d 250 (Tex. App. 1996)	Termination	Termination	Dispatcher abandoned work during middle of shift and subsequently refused to comply with orders to report to supervisor's office; numerous prior disciplinary actions.
Graves v. Office of Employee Appeals, 805 A.2d 245 (D.C. App. 2002)	Termination	Termination	Corrections employee was absent from work without leave for ten consecutive days.
Haney v. City of Los Angeles, 134 Cal. Rptr.2d 411 (Cal. App. 2003)	Termination	Termination	Officer absented himself from a duty post without authorization and submitted false daily activity report as to his location. In fact, the officer was holding a private Memorial Day barbeque celebration with other officers instead of engaging in patrol duties.
Metropolitan Police Department, 1:8 NPER 16 (Fishgold, 1997)	Termination	28-Day Suspension	Police officer was absent without leave. Evidence established that City did not routinely terminate officers "even for extensive periods of AWOL."
Perry County v. PLRB, 634 A.2d 808 (Pa.Cmwlth. 1993)	Termination	Reinstatement	Sergeant involved in union organizational campaign was absent from work site for twenty seconds; decided on the basis of anti-union bias.
Sheriff of Stark County, Ohio, 27 LAIS (2009)	30-Day Suspension	15-Day Suspension	Corrections officer failed to report for overtime. Though employee had prior disciplinary record, Arbitrator ruled suspension too harsh.
Siwek v. Police Bd. of City of Chicago, 872 N.E.2d 87 (Ill. App. 2007)	Termination	Termination	Officer with poor disciplinary record violated Department's rules forbidding outside employment when on paid medical leave status. Civil service board rejected officer's defense of lack of knowledge of rule.
Town of Barnstable v. Personnel Administrator, 56 Mass.App.Ct. 1106 (Mass. App. 2002)	Termination	Reinstatement	Officer terminated for being absent without leave. Court concluded that employer was aware that officer was absent because a restraining order prohibited him from carrying a firearm, and that officer properly communicated with employer about reason for absence.
Township of Flint, LAIG 6463 (Braverman, 2007)	Reduction Of Work Schedule From 40 to 24 Hours	Restoration Of Work Schedule	Employer contended that reduction in work schedule based on a dispatcher's absenteeism was not disciplinary in nature, and that the schedule reduction was made to avoid paying overtime resulting from backfilling for dispatcher when she was absent. The Arbitrator concluded that schedule reduction was disciplinary in nature, that the dispatcher had violated no work rule, and that the employer had not placed her on notice that her work shift could be reduced unless her absenteeism problems were corrected.

CASE NAME	INITIAL SANCTION	RESULT ON APPEAL	DESCRIPTION
Velazuez v. Village of Bratenahl, 2003 WL 549967 (Ohio App. 2003)	Termination	Termination	Officer who had antagonistic relationship with Chief (who was also his father-in-law) verbally resigned his job, turned in his equipment, and stopped coming to work. Failure of officer to sign formal resignation documents did not mean he had not, in fact, abandoned his job.

Conduct Unbecoming, Off Duty

CASE NAME	INITIAL SANCTION	RESULT ON APPEAL	DESCRIPTION
Allman v. Police Board of Chicago, 489 N.E.2d 929 (Ill. App. 1986)	Termination	Termination	Waving of unregistered gun at bar while intoxicated; drunk while at police station.
Balinton v. City and County of San Francisco, 2003 WL 21363360 (Cal. App. 2003)	Order That Officer Work In Support Position Without Gun	Order That Officer Work In Support Position Without Gun	While off duty, officer was arrested and charged with various criminal offenses, including burglary and false imprisonment, as a result of an incident in which he entered his then-girlfriend's apartment without her consent and took a jewelry box. Officer pled no contest to two misdemeanor counts, received suspended sentence and subsequently violated terms of probation by calling the complaining witness at least 30 times.
Campbell v. Hamilton County, NPER 10:9 (2000)	Termination	Termination	Probation officer cautioned a female probationer about appearing before a judge, commenting: "Whatever you do, don't dress up in court. Judge Mallory strokes pretty white women." Case decided on free speech grounds.
City of Cincinnati, LAIG 6138 (Duff, 2004)	Indefinite Suspension	Reinstatement With Back Pay	City suspended lieutenant without pay pending outcome of criminal proceedings relating to the submission of time sheets and vouchers concerning the Boy Scouts. Arbitrator concluded that suspension pending court proceedings should not be without pay unless employer is capable of proving wrongdoing independent of simply the lodging of criminal charges.
City of Conroe, Texas, LAIG 6207 (Greer, 2005)	Indefinite Suspension	15-Day Suspension	Off-duty altercation with the employer's Purchasing Director over whether a police officer's dogs defecated in a neighbor's yard. Employer rushed its investigation because the officer was scheduled for military service and the Purchasing Director received no discipline in the fracas.
City of El Paso, 76 LA 595 (Carr, 1981)	3-Day Suspension	2-Day Suspension	Incident involving screaming at, handcuffing, and citing of neighbor who threw rock at officer's dog.

CASE NAME	INITIAL SANCTION	RESULT ON APPEAL	DESCRIPTION
City of Fort Worth, Texas, 2001 WL 1479992 (Jennings, 2001)	3-Day Suspension	3-Day Suspension	While working off duty in a department store, officer used inappropriate force in detaining an individual to issue a criminal trespass warning. Officer also conducted an illegal search of individual's purse. While the Arbitrator found officer was a good employee, concluded that he did not have the authority to overturn the employer's decision unless the decision was arbitrary and capricious.
City of Houston, LAIG 5195 (Eisenmenger, 1996)	4-Day Suspension	4-Day Suspension	Arrest of third cousin; officer used uniform and profanity to attempt to "scare straight" cousin.
City of Lowell v. Civil Service Commission, 856 N.E.2d 918 (Mass. App. 2006)	30-Day Suspension	No Discipline	Officer suspended for conduct unbecoming on a chartered bus following an evening spent in a restaurant and a bar. Employer failed to prove that officer was the one who made improper statements to the bus driver and another officer.
City of Philadelphia, Pennsylvania and Fraternal Order of Police, Lodge 5, LAIG 5613 (Gershenfeld, 2000)	10-Day Suspension	5-Day Suspension	Officer became involved in an off-duty altercation with a neighbor. Though officer guilty of charges, City failed to comply with procedural requirement that officer be given a copy of the charges against him in a timely fashion.
Conley v. City of Akron, Unpublished opinion (Ohio App. 1993)	Termination	Termination	Intoxicated officer at bar called waitress a "cunt," invited her to "give him head," pointed a gun at a bouncer, and struck the bouncer with the magazine from the gun; officer never identified himself as police officer.
County of Blair, 118 LA 238 (Miller, 2003)	10-Day Suspension	10-Day Suspension	Corrections officer screamed profanity at inmate. Officer had previously been disciplined for insubordination, making sexual remarks to an inmate about his wife, and making sexual gestures behind a nurse's back.
Cranston v. City of Richmond, 710 P.2d 845 (Cal. 1986)	Termination	Termination	Driving sports car at 95 m.p.h. on wet streets during chase by police; officer had received many prior disciplinary actions.
DeClara v. Metropolitan Transit Authority, 748 F. Supp. 92 (S.D. N.Y. 1990), *aff'd* 930 F.2d 911 (2d Cir. 1991)	Termination	Termination	Officer appeared on videotape shot by other officers titled "Bubba On Patrol"; tape showed officer patrolling Grand Central Station partially nude (officer was wearing gun, tie, socks, shoes and hat); officer also shown questioning whether black interviewee ate a lot of watermelon and tap-danced.

CASE NAME	INITIAL SANCTION	RESULT ON APPEAL	DESCRIPTION
Federal Bureau of Prisons, 114 LA 475 (Cohen, 2000)	14-Day Suspension	14-Day Suspension	Corrections officer got into violent bar fight with a fellow officer. Fact that suspended officer had already been discharged and had pending appeal of discharge (in which he later prevailed) irrelevant as to whether employer had just cause to impose discipline for bar fight.
Greater Cleveland Regional Transit Authority, 26 LAIS 2029 (Duff, 1999)	Termination	Reinstatement Without Back Pay	Police officer at retirement party threatened other officers while brandishing his personal firearm when they took his car keys, believing him too drunk to drive. Arbitrator found that termination was excessive because evidence did not clearly establish that the officer threatened to start shooting if his keys were not returned, nor did it show that the officer pointed the firearm at others.
Kelly v. Salt Lake City Civil Service Commission, 8 P.3d 1048 (Utah App. 2000)	Termination	Termination	Police officer became intoxicated after taking prescription sleep medication, called dispatch center and threatened to blow up building in which dispatch center was located. Court found that officer's intoxication was voluntary.
Lensey v. City of Shreveport Municipal Fire and Police Service Board, 839 So.2d 1032 (La. App. 2003)	Termination	Termination	Officer became embroiled in off-duty dispute between her fiancé and bus driver, resulting in officers from another department arresting her. No finding of detrimental impact on officer's department.
Mahadio v. Kerik, 748 N.Y.S.2d 494 (App. Div. 2002)	25-Day Vacation Forfeiture	25-Day Vacation Forfeiture	Off-duty officer, while shopping, made threatening remark to employee, addressed persons in the store in an ethnically offensive manner, and inappropriately waved his service weapon.
Metropolitan Police Dept. v. Baker, 564 A.2d 1155 (D.C. App. 1989)	Termination	Termination	Court held officer should have known of wife's embezzlement, since family purchased two new vehicles, added deck to house, and kept up payments on two other cars, all on a joint income of $1,724 monthly, which remained constant over time period.
Sheehan v. Kelly, 626 N.Y.S.2d 129 (A.D. 1995)	10-Day Vacation Forfeiture	10-Day Vacation Forfeiture	Officers obstructed traffic on Brooklyn Bridge during demonstration on behalf of police association.
Shepack v. New Orleans Police Department, 791 So.2d 733 (La. App. 2001)	3-Day Suspension	3-Day Suspension	Off-duty officer made traffic stop while in civilian clothing. Department's rules specifically prohibit such stops.

CASE NAME	INITIAL SANCTION	RESULT ON APPEAL	DESCRIPTION
Velasques v. Kerik, 742 N.Y.S.2d 277 (A.D. 2002)	Termination	Termination	While off duty, officer "savagely beat a civilian." Administrative law judge rejected officer's claim of self defense against his much smaller victim.
Walck v. City of Albuquerque, 828 P.2d 966 (N.M. App. 1992)	Termination	Reinstatement	Intentionally ramming car into wife's automobile while wife leaving residence of another man; no evidence that incident resulted in discredit to Department.

Conduct Unbecoming, On Duty

CASE NAME	INITIAL SANCTION	RESULT ON APPEAL	DESCRIPTION
Anderson v. City of Blue Earth, 1999 WL 639201 (Minn. App. 1999)	Termination	Termination	Police Chief failed to address deficiencies cited in a performance review, made personal calls on City's cellular phone, requested that a police officer and dispatcher convey false information to his wife as to his whereabouts when he was with his girlfriend.
Broward County, 110 LA 581 (Hoffman, 1998)	Termination	Termination	Sergeant gave two new deputies fake drug tests as a prank. Sergeant carried prank into "realm of abuse and insult" by taking recruits' photographs with urine specimens, and insistence that one recruit drink two cans of soda and then standing directly behind the recruit while he attempted to urinate "suggests of perversion."
Casanova v. State Personnel Board, 2004 WL 161467 (Cal. App. 2004)	Termination	Termination	Highway Patrol trooper became involved in off-duty "road rage" incident with citizen. While on duty on two subsequent occasions, trooper inappropriately stopped the same citizen, issued citations, was profane, and inappropriately placed citizen in custody.
City of Cuyahoga Falls, Ohio, 116 LA 545 (Coine, 2001)	Termination	Termination	Officer brought alcohol to a home of an 18-year old girl he had ticketed earlier in the evening for driving under the influence. Officer also had numerous driver-to-driver meetings with female officer while on duty at times when he was needed for patrol applications.
City of Dayton v. Fraternal Order of Police, 2000 WL 706829 (Ohio App. 2000)	Termination	Suspension	Officer became involved in dispute with fast-food cashier over correct amount of change given officer at drive-through window; dispute culminated with officer using pepper spray. Court upheld Arbitrator's decision, which reinstated the officer based on good work record and the fact that officer only engaged in a single act of misconduct.

CASE NAME	INITIAL SANCTION	RESULT ON APPEAL	DESCRIPTION
City of Fort Worth, Texas, LAIG 5648 (Goodman, 2000)	1-Day Suspension	No Discipline	Police officer disciplined for commenting to motorist that motorist's truck was not worth defending against a carjacking, asking the motorist why he possessed a concealed handgun license, and emptying the motorist's gun before giving it and the bullets to the motorist separately. Arbitrator concluded that motorist was agitated and argumentative, and that "officer safety indicates a prudent officer would not return a loaded weapon to a nervous, agitated, argumentative citizen."
City of Houston, LAIG 6130 (Goodman, 2004)	9-Day Suspension	5-Day Suspension	Police officer became embroiled in verbal confrontation with employee of a fast-food concession located at an airport, was disrespectful to the employee, and used improper language during the confrontation. The City did not summon the fast-food employee to the arbitration hearing, denying the officer the opportunity for cross examination. As such, Arbitrator reversed portion of suspension dealing with use of profanity.
City of Hurst, Texas, LAIG 6522 (Moore, 2007)	3-Day Suspension	No Discipline	Officer suspended for using profane language at juveniles under arrest for the beating of a teenager. Contrary to Texas law, the complaint against the officer was not in writing and signed by the individual making the complaint. Arbitrator declined to consider the officer the "complainant" because he reported the incident to his supervisor.
City of Inglewood, LAIG 5200 (Tamoush, 1996)	2-Day Suspension And Removal From Overtime Duty	2-Day Suspension	While on overtime detail at a basketball stadium, officer threatened to shoot belligerent suspect who took martial arts stance and referred to suspect as a "bitch." Arbitrator rejected defense that officer's comments were "future-oriented and not dealing with suspect's present behavior." No justification for additional sanction of removal from overtime work.
City of Inglewood, LAIG 5548 (Roberts, 1999)	10-Day Suspension	10-Day Suspension	Police officer engaged in a verbal exchange with a desk officer which escalated into a physical confrontation in which the officer slapped the desk officer, cutting her lower lip. Officer had previously been suspended for making inappropriate comments.

CASE NAME	INITIAL SANCTION	RESULT ON APPEAL	DESCRIPTION
City of Inglewood, LAIG 5558 (Tamoush, 1999)	3-Day Suspension	Written Reprimand	Officer with 17 years of experience failed to report other officers' misuse of MDTs to heckle each other about the results of a Raiders-Cowboys football game. Arbitrator found suspension an excessive penalty.
City of Irving, Texas, LAIG 5286 (Larsen, 1997)	Indefinite Suspension	Reinstatement Without Back Pay	Detective made threats against superior officers, implying that she would be calling in favors owed by mobsters and that her supervisors would be found dead. Arbitrator concluded that detective was "simply popping off."
City of Pasadena, LAIG 6242 (Campos, 2005)	Termination	Reinstatement With Back Pay	In an incident that started out as horseplay, officer drew his firearm and pointed it at other officer who had just drawn his firearm and pointed it at the officer. The City failed to introduce charging letter at hearing, leading to conclusion that burden of proof was not met.
City of Plano, Texas, LAIG 5313 (Hays, 1997)	Indefinite Suspension	Indefinite Suspension	Three-year police officer served alcohol to underage minors at Explorer Scout meeting. Conduct was a violation of state law.
City of Port Arthur, Texas, LAIG 6590 (Williams, 2008)	3-Day Suspension	No Discipline	Officer made unnecessary and inappropriate statements about internal Police Department issues in an incident report. The City did not follow its own rules in the evaluation of the report or in the imposition of discipline.
City of Portland, (Hanlon, 1985)	Termination	Reinstatement	Selling of T-shirts which read "smoke 'em, don't choke 'em" after Chief banned use of carotid hold following accidental death of citizen.
City of Portland, 77 LA 820 (Axon, 1981)	Termination	Reinstatement	Killing of opossums, and leaving carcasses on sidewalk in front of restaurant owned by family with crime connections.
City of Sacramento, 26 LAIS 2087 (Riker, 1999)	Termination	10-Day Suspension	Employee permitted a member of a youth gang to drive the vehicle and used a departmental computer for personal business. Employer took 14 months to complete the investigation and another 13 months to make a disciplinary decision.
City of San Antonio, LAIG 4814 (Wolitz, 1993)	5-Day Suspension	Oral Reprimand	Officer remarked to court coordinator that judge's ruling on motion to suppress was "a chicken-shit decision." No other member of Department had ever been disciplined for profanity.

CASE NAME	INITIAL SANCTION	RESULT ON APPEAL	DESCRIPTION
City of Warren, 120 LA 1332 (Adamson, 2004)	10-Day Suspension	5-Day Suspension	Officer shut off video recorder while giving a citizen a traffic ticket for running a red light. Penalty mitigated because of officer's almost ten years of service with a clean disciplinary record, the fact that the officer committed no misconduct during the unrecorded portion of the traffic stop, and the stresses of the job associated with the officer's assignment to an area known for drug dealing in which citizens acted in a hostile manner toward the officer.
Cleveland Metropolitan Housing Authority, LAIG 5369 (Richard, 1998)	3-Day Suspension	3-Day Suspension	Male officer conducted a strip search of a female suspected of completing a drug transaction. Though officer contended he only had the woman pull her shirt and bra away from her body and shake them, officer's partner corroborated the complainant's account.
Hamilton County, 96 LA 331 (Klein, 1991)	30-Day Suspension	7-Day Suspension	Spreading rumors that senior officer fixed a case and was having an affair with a female deputy; similarly-situated employee had not received as severe discipline and employee had good work record, though was "bullheaded."
Hammond v. City of Amsterdam, 586 N.Y.S.2d 364 (A.D. 1992)	Termination	Termination	D.A.R.E. officer placed D.A.R.E. bumper stickers on Department's patrol cars; when another officer then placed 20 D.A.R.E. bumper stickers on D.A.R.E. officer's personal vehicle, D.A.R.E. officer punched other officer in jaw.
Hanford v. City of Arnold, 49 S.W.3d 707 (Mo. App. 2001)	Termination	Termination	Officer and person at site that officer and other officer were executing a warrant were "getting in each other's faces" and on several occasions officer challenged the person to fight. Officer failed to tape record his conversation with the person as required by Department rules, and removed his gun and badge and placed it in police car in which arrestee had been placed.
Illinois Institute of Technology Police Dept., 96-1 ARB 6140 (McGury, 1996)	5-Day Suspension	1-Day Suspension	Involvement in a physical altercation with two maintenance workers. Officer had good work record and did not institute altercation, though he was responsible in small part for its escalation.
Kannisto v. City and County of San Francisco, 541 F.2d 841 (9th Cir. 1976)	15-Day Suspension	15-Day Suspension	Calling supervisor "unreasonable, contrary, vindictive, belligerent, and unpleasant."

CASE NAME	INITIAL SANCTION	RESULT ON APPEAL	DESCRIPTION
Kline v. City of Grinnell Civil Service Commission, 671 N.W.2d 532 (Iowa App. 2003)	Termination	90-Day Suspension	Officer terminated for (1) being involved in a verbal and physical confrontation with a private citizen; (2) exposing his buttocks in public; (3) engaging in lewd and suggestive dancing; (4) interfering with the arrest of a personal acquaintance; (5) engaging in recreational gambling while on duty; and (6) appearing in public while intoxicated. City only proved charges 5 and 6.
Maciariello v. Sumner, 973 F.2d 295 (4th Cir. 1992)	Demotion	Demotion	Conducting of secret investigation of supervisor.
Massachusetts Bay Transportation Authority, LAIG 6308 (Brynie, 2005)	Demotion	20-Day Suspension	Lieutenant told subordinate that he would "rather be considered a racist than a chicken," and was sharply critical of the Department, its policies, and its personnel in a telephone conversation with a subordinate that was tape-recorded. Arbitrator unpersuaded that lieutenant was incapable of performing in a supervisory position, and ruled that the lieutenant's "ill advised and flip remark" did not go to the heart of his supervisory responsibilities.
Michigan Department of Corrections, LAIG 5653 (Wolkinson, 2000)	Termination	Termination	Corrections officer made disparaging comments about a hospital to an inmate while the inmate was receiving medical treatment. Additionally, officer discussed her personal medical situation and her finances with the inmate.
Milwaukee County Deputy Sheriffs' Association v. Milwaukee County, Case #553 (Wis. PERC 2004)	1-Day Suspension	No Discipline	When deputy complained to sergeant about an inspector, sergeant replied that the inspector "only thought women were good for f___ing." The sergeant's discipline overturned because County failed to prove adverse impact on its operations. The Arbitrator observed: "It is recognized that deputies and supervisors among themselves sometimes swear and say things that are not politically correct."
Murray v. U.S. Dept. of Justice, 821 F. Supp. 94 (E.D. N.Y. 1993)	Termination	Termination	FBI agent smashed the windows of a car improperly parked in his parking space; defense of racial discrimination not proven.
Nye County, LAIG 4904 (Staudohar, 1993)	Termination	Termination	Deputy sheriff played cards with inmate with cell door open, negligently allowed inmate to escape, and otherwise had a "cavalier approach to the handling of inmates."

CASE NAME	INITIAL SANCTION	RESULT ON APPEAL	DESCRIPTION
Pruitt v. Howard County Sheriff's Department, 623 A.2d 696 (Md. App. 1993)	Termination	Termination	"Nazi-like" behavior, including hand salutes, heel clicks, and use of exaggerated German accents, and terms such as "achtung" and "sieg heil."
Reno Police Prot. Ass'n v. City of Reno, 715 P.2d 1321 (Nev. 1986)	Demotion	Reinstatement	Sergeant (union president) canceled complaint number assigned to investigation of another officer's off-duty conduct; decided on anti-union discrimination grounds.
Rounds v. Town of Vestal, 790 N.Y.S.2d 561 (N.Y. A.D. 2005)	Termination	Termination	Police Chief terminated for directing a sergeant to advise patrol officers that their handguns could be withdrawn from use unless they voted for a change of leadership in their union. Court rejected argument that complaining officers were not credible, reasoning that credibility determinations were best left to the original hearing officer.
San Francisco Police Department, 94-1 ARB ¶4001 (Riker, 1993)	Termination	2½-Month Suspension	Dispatcher used coarse and profane language against co-worker; employer had done nothing to resolve friction between the two, which had been brewing for several months.
Scioto County Sheriff, 115 LA 532 (Feldman, 2001)	30-Day Suspension	No Discipline	Deputy sheriff who was not responding to an emergency drove at 120 m.p.h., and physically assaulted another deputy. Employer inappropriately asked employee to waive contractual right to a pre-disciplinary hearing without involving the union in the matter.
Stark County Sheriff, 118 LA 407 (Feldman, 2003)	Termination	Reinstatement With Back Pay	Employer failed to provide deputy with notice prior to disciplinary hearing against him. Arbitrator concluded "specific notice of wrongdoing must be given. It simply is not enough to say 'he did it and he knows what he did.'"
State of Michigan, LAIG 5557 (VanAuken-Haight, 1999)	5-Day Suspension	1-Day Suspension	Corrections officer participated in practical joke in which officer tricked inmate into drinking vinegar in an attempt to negate the effects of a urinalysis test for drugs. Inmate became ill as a result. Penalty mitigated by officer's 10-year discipline-free record and the fact that the prisoner did not require medical treatment.
Teamsters and Grant County, 88-2 ARB ¶8392 (Lacy, 1988)	4-Day Suspension	Reinstatement	Derogatory comments about Sheriff. Arbitrator required that progressive discipline be followed.

CASE NAME	INITIAL SANCTION	RESULT ON APPEAL	DESCRIPTION
Williams v. Department of Police, 996 So.2d 1142 (La. App. 2008)	2-Day Suspension	2-Day Suspension	Sergeant commented to an officer about a female officer wearing a thong. The Court found that comment "bore a real and substantial relationship to the efficient operation of the Department."

Confidentiality

CASE NAME	INITIAL SANCTION	RESULT ON APPEAL	DESCRIPTION
Herzog v. Township of Fairfield, 2002 WL 537500 (Cal. App. 2002)	Termination	Termination	Officer read confidential affairs document and disseminated it to a newspaper.

Conflict of Interest

CASE NAME	INITIAL SANCTION	RESULT ON APPEAL	DESCRIPTION
City of Chester, 114 LA 912 (Feldman, 2000)	Termination	Termination	Officer had 63 hours of phone conversations over a four-month period with an officer in a nearby town who was the subject of criminal charges. Conversations included discussing personalities of arresting officers, reviewing evidence against other officer, and discussing investigatory file.
City of Sacramento v. Superior Court, 2003 WL 1875801 (Cal. App. 2003)	Termination	Termination	After giving a 21-year old woman a traffic ticket, officer later appeared in court to state that he had no independent recollection or notes about the matter, resulting in the dismissal of the citation. Officer subsequently told suspect he wanted further contact with her in return for getting the ticket dismissed. Officer obtained her work and home telephone numbers and called her at both places against her wishes, subsequently lying to Internal Affairs about whether he made the phone calls.
Michigan Department of Consumer and Industry Services, LAIG 5696 (Korney, 2000)	3-Day Suspension	3-Day Suspension	Investigator sold a computer to a business he had recently investigated for possible code violations. Arbitrator found investigator "should not have business dealings with employers who are the subject of an ongoing investigation or one that has recently concluded."
Sircher v. Police Board, 382 N.E.2d 325 (Ill. App. 1978)	Termination	Termination	Recommending attorney to accident victims.
United States v. Jackson, 55 FEP Cases 86 (E.D. Va. 1991)	Termination	Reinstatement	Deputy terminated for trying to induce motorist to buy tires from shop owned by deputy; complaining citizen was convicted felon with poor reputation for truth; deputy had just filed EEOC complaint against Sheriff.

CASE NAME	INITIAL SANCTION	RESULT ON APPEAL	DESCRIPTION
Courtesy			
City of Fort Worth, LAIG 5400 (Pelhan, 1998)	1-Day Suspension	Letter Of Reprimand	Officer approached one of two female combatants in a women's shelter and said: "Hey girl, come over here. I need to talk to you." Arbitrator concluded that officer did not intend to be disrespectful, demeaning or discourteous, and was not "truly cognizant" that the use of the term "girl" could be perceived as insulting or offensive.
Town of Groton, LAIG 4342 (Celentano, 1990)	2-Week Suspension	2-Day Suspension	Alteration of liability waiver forms used by City with citizens who had locked themselves out of cars to contain choices such as "behaved like an asshole"; no intent by 16-year officer to publicly embarrass Department.
Criminal Charges			
Immigration and Naturalization Service, 114 LA 872 (Neas, 2000)	Indefinite Suspension	Reinstatement With Back Pay	Employer indefinitely suspended Border Patrol officer who was indicted for off-duty assault arising out of an altercation starting outside a nightclub. Officer was not guilty of committing the assault, acted in self-defense, and employer made no effort to conduct an independent investigation by interviewing available witnesses.
Criminal Conduct			
Bailey v. LSU Healthcare Services Division, 767 So.2d 946 (La. App. 2000)	Termination	Termination	Police officer pled guilty to felony which resulted in loss of state police certification. Court found possession of certification an essential requirement of the job of police officer.
Barrett v. Sanders, 584 S.E.2d 676 (Ga. App. 2003)	Termination	Termination	Deputy sheriff was involved in high-profile series of home invasions and burglaries made by three individuals in sheriff's uniforms who entered homes on pretense of serving what ultimately proved to be fake warrants.
Berry v. Department of Public Safety and Corrections, 835 So.2d 606 (La. App. 2002)	Demotion	Demotion	State trooper failed to report on federal income tax form wages earned from off-duty traffic details. Trooper also engaged in secondary employment without permission as required by Department's rules.
Borschel v. City of Perry, 512 N.W.2d 565 (Iowa 1994)	Termination	Termination	Criminal charges (though no conviction) that officer sexually abused minor daughter; officer was at-will employee.

CASE NAME	INITIAL SANCTION	RESULT ON APPEAL	DESCRIPTION
Broward County, 112 LA 609 (1999)	Termination	Termination	Corrections officer permitted husband to physically abuse their children and prevented police officer from investigating the crime. Arbitrator rejected defense that employee should not be terminated because of good work record.
Burke v. City of Anderson, 612 N.E.2d 559 (Ind. App. 1993)	Termination	Termination	Participation in shooting which arose out of gambling debt; officer was paid $500 to participate in shooting.
California Highway Patrol v. California State Personnel Board, 2005 WL 1358949 (Cal. App. 2005)	Termination	Reinstatement With Back Pay	Trooper alleged to have converted to personal use a handgun seized as evidence. Charges dismissed because employer failed to lodge them within the time limit of a three-year statute of limitations provided by State law.
Cittadino v. Department of Police, 558 So.2d 1311 (La. App. 1990)	120-Day Suspension	120-Day Suspension	Selling of video poker machines in state where gambling was then illegal.
City of Inglewood, LAIG 5407 (Perea, 1998)	Termination	Termination	Officer pled guilty to illegally obtaining hunting license in another state. Arbitrator concluded that crime involved "moral turpitude" and that discovery of conviction by criminal defense counsel could potentially be offered into evidence in criminal cases in which officer was involved.
City of Irving, Texas, LAIG 6658 (Bennett, 2008)	Termination	Termination	Officer with prior off-duty DWI incident terminated after being arrested for a second DWI charge. Fact that officer was found not guilty in criminal court not dispositive of disciplinary proceedings.
City of Irving, 106 LA 1057 (Moore, 1996)	Termination	Termination	Captain convicted of Class A misdemeanor for tampering with governmental records by submitting falsified doctor's slips to use sick leave.
City of Leominster v. Stratton, 792 N.E.2d 711 (Mass. App. 2003)	Termination	Reinstatement With Back Pay	Allegation that police officer had sexually abused his daughter and stepdaughter, and physically abused his wife. Daughter recanted her allegations, testifying she made them at the instigation of officer's wife. Stepdaughter did not testify at hearing. Hearings officer found wife to be not credible and officer testified in a believable manner.

CASE NAME	INITIAL SANCTION	RESULT ON APPEAL	DESCRIPTION
City of New Haven v. AFSCME, 544 A.2d 186 (Conn. 1988)	Termination	Termination	Court upheld Arbitrator's opinion reinstating officer who had been criminally convicted of bribery.
City of Oklahoma City, 123 LA 24 (Walker, 2006)	Termination	Reinstatement With Back Pay	Officer accused of having sex with prostitutes. Arbitrator found lack of clear and convincing evidence that conduct occurred, particularly where prostitute's reputation for dishonesty discounted her testimony, and where officer testified in a credible manner. Arbitrator also held inadmissible captain's recitation of prostitute's statements, finding that hearsay should not be admissible in termination cases except in the most extreme circumstances.
City of Orlando, 1 NPER 2:8 (Sergent, 1997)	Unspecified Suspension	Reinstatement With Back Pay	Officer stopped while off duty for DWI. Though deputy testified officer's car weaved at 70 mph from shoulder to middle of lane and though officer's breathalyzer tests were "borderline," Arbitrator held that employer did not establish by clear and convincing evidence that officer was driving under the influence.
City of Philadelphia, LAIG 4158 (1988)	Termination	Reinstatement	Off-duty accident resulting in conviction of vehicular homicide.
City of Rogers City, Michigan, 110 LA 92 (Daniel, 1997)	Termination	Termination	Officer convicted of misdemeanor of providing alcoholic beverage to fiancée who was a minor.
Cortez v. Safir, 717 N.Y.S.2d 138 (N.Y. A.D. 2000)	Termination	Termination	Officer brandished firearm during off-duty traffic dispute and was subsequently found to have violated Department rules regarding resisting arrest, failing to follow instructions, making false and misleading statements, failing to safeguard his weapon, and failing to maintain an adequate log entry.
Costa v. City of New York, 715 N.Y.S.2d 65 (A.D. 2000)	Termination	Termination	Officer operated an unregistered, uninspected and uninsured motor vehicle with a suspended driver's license and stole registration and inspection stickers from abandoned cars to replace his own expired stickers.
Davis v. City of Evanston, 629 N.E.2d 125 (Ill. App. 1993)	Termination	Termination	Willful failure to file state tax returns; officer had committed 29 separate violations of departmental rules and had received 16 reprimands and 13 suspensions in the past.
El Paso County, 93-2 ARB ¶3404 (Moore, 1993)	Termination	Termination	Detective engaged in solicitation of prostitution; detective contended he was investigating 2½-year-old murder case.

CASE NAME	INITIAL SANCTION	RESULT ON APPEAL	DESCRIPTION
Feltri v. Kelaher, 2008 WL 1874427 (N.J. Super. A.D. 2008)	Termination	Termination	Off-duty driving while intoxicated, followed by threats to "get" the jobs of the arresting officers and use of derogatory language towards officers.
Holycross v. Indiana State Police Board, 502 N.E.2d 923 (Ind. App. 1987)	Termination	Termination	Eavesdropping on conversation in supervisor's office in violation of state law.
James v. City of New York, 2008 WL 2885320 (S.D. N.Y. 2008)	Termination	Termination	Corrections officer terminated following his plea of guilty to a tax fraud charge relating to an inflated claim of exemptions. Claim of race discrimination rejected.
Lawson v. Shelby County Sheriff's Office, 961 So.2d 158 (Ala. Civ. App. 2007)	Termination	60-Day Suspension	Corrections officer used Department intercom system to eavesdrop on conversation between her sergeant and lieutenant. Criminal nature of employee's conduct mitigated by employee's good work record.
Lombas v. Police Department, 467 So.2d 1273 (La. App. 1985)	Termination	Reinstatement	Presence at illegal poker game while off duty and out of uniform.
McKeaman v. Safir, 739 N.Y.S.2d 380 (A.D. 2002)	Termination	Termination	Sergeant provided confidential license plate ownership information to a person known to be involved in crime. Sergeant had prior disciplinary record and failed to safeguard his firearm while off duty.
Schexnayder v. New Orleans Police Dept., 474 So.2d 461 (La. App. 1985)	Termination	Termination	Attempt to cash check of another police officer without authorization, and by forging signature.
Segars v. City of Buffalo, 654 N.Y.S.2d 919 (A.D. 1997)	Termination	Termination	Criminal conviction for menacing.
State of Maine, LAIG 5261 (O'Brien, 1996)	Termination	Termination	Conviction for off-duty trespassing on neighbor's property, which had been posted "no trespassing" and "no hunting." Trooper shot decoy doe on property four times, and then threatened to arrest game warden and to impound warden's vehicle.
State of Nebraska, 108 LA 1163 (Caffera, 1997)	Termination	Termination	Two-year employee did not report arrest for passing bad checks. Employee was warned of consequences of disobeying rule, and had inconsistent performance history.

CASE NAME	INITIAL SANCTION	RESULT ON APPEAL	DESCRIPTION
Thomas v. Police Board, 414 N.E.2d 11 (Ill. App. 1980)	Termination	Reinstatement	Accumulation of 201 unpaid parking tickets.

Criticism of Employer

CASE NAME	INITIAL SANCTION	RESULT ON APPEAL	DESCRIPTION
City of Balch Springs, LAIG 5339 (Williams, 1997)	3-Day Suspension	3-Day Suspension	Officer falsely alleged that ability of 400-pound applicant to pass physical agility test even at an unusual time of day was based upon applicant's relationship with the Chief. Arbitrator concluded officer should have investigated allegations before making them.
Village of Scotia, 13 PERB P 7008 (N.Y. A.D. 1998)	Demotion	Reinstatement	Demotion of sergeant for writing letter criticizing Police Chief's motivation for supporting mayor's dispatch plan. Letter was written in sergeant's capacity as a Union official, and therefore was protected activity.

Discipline

CASE NAME	INITIAL SANCTION	RESULT ON APPEAL	DESCRIPTION
City of Laurel v. Brewer, 919 So.2d 217 (Miss. App. 2005)	Termination	Reinstatement Without Back Pay	Officer terminated for releasing K-9 dog on a suspect who was handcuffed. Civil Service Board determined that a videotape of an officer claiming to have handcuffed the suspect was coerced, and that eyewitnesses corroborated the fact that the suspect was not handcuffed. Back pay denied because of Civil Service proceedings continued at officer's request pending resolution of criminal charges.

Dishonesty, During Testimony, In Reports, and On Applications

CASE NAME	INITIAL SANCTION	RESULT ON APPEAL	DESCRIPTION
Adolf v. Civil Service Commission of the County of Ventura, 2003 WL 549967 (Ohio App. 2003)	Termination	Termination	Sexual assault investigator prepared reports in six cases that contained a large number of inaccuracies, misrepresentations, misinterpretations, and demonstrated a pattern of deception. Investigator admitted that errors and omissions in his reports had harmed the district attorney's office, the public, the victims of the crimes he had investigated, and the persons were arrested and then released because the cases were not prosecutable.
Angelopoulos v. New York Civil Service Commission, 574 N.Y.S.2d 44 (A.D. 1995)	Termination	Termination	Failure to indicate on employment application that officer had been arrested for desertion while serving in army under assumed name; falsification discovered five years after officer began career.

CASE NAME	INITIAL SANCTION	RESULT ON APPEAL	DESCRIPTION
City of El Paso, LAIG 6408 (Britton, 2006)	Termination	Reinstatement Without Back Pay	Officer terminated for falsely claiming his lights were on at the time of an intersection accident. While the Arbitrator sustained driving charge, truthfulness charge reversed on the grounds that automatic vehicle locator system could not pinpoint precisely whether officer's lights were on at the time of the collision.
City of El Paso, LAIG 6514 (Detwiler, 2007)	Termination	Termination	Officer stopped and falsely arrested a minor female for driving while intoxicated and was dishonest during the subsequent investigation of the minor's complaint. Complainant passed a polygraph examination; officer failed test. While the Arbitrator did not believe that polygraphs are scientifically foolproof, he held there was sufficient independent evidence of the officer's untruthfulness.
City of Fort Worth, LAIG 6131 (Goodman, 2004)	Termination	90-Day Suspension And Demotion	Sergeant terminated for falsely stating in personnel investigation that he had formally interviewed certain witnesses, and for misattributing statements to members of the Sheriff's Office. Personnel commission found that sergeant's report was "admittedly abysmal" and "showed significant carelessness," but was not intentionally untruthful.
City of Meriden, Decision 3908 (Conn. SBLR 2003)	5-Day Suspension	5-Day Suspension	Police officer gave dishonest testimony in grievance arbitration hearing. Board rejected argument that since the City did not prosecute officer for perjury, it was prohibited from disciplining her.
City of Pawtucket v. Ricci, 692 A.2d 678 (R.I. 1997)	Termination	Reinstatement With Back Pay	Applicant omitted reference to arrest for indecent exposure and possession of marijuana when filling out employment application. Information concerning the arrest was in employer's possession.
City of Pomona, CSMCS Case No. 84-3-440 (Perea, 1985)	Termination	5-Day Suspension	Filing of incorrect crime reports indicating officer had performed work which had not been performed.
Civil Service Commission of Coralville v. Johnson, 653 N.W.2d 533 (Iowa 2002).	Termination	Termination	Officer was untruthful when he made reports and gave his testimony concerning his interrogation and investigation of a robbery suspect. Officer had 30 years of experience with the Department and six prior disciplinary offenses.

CASE NAME	INITIAL SANCTION	RESULT ON APPEAL	DESCRIPTION
Commonwealth Dept. of State Police v. Commonwealth Civil Service Com'n, 24 Mass.L.Rptr. 35 (Mass. Super. 2008)	13-Month Suspension	8-Month Suspension	Trooper charged with five instances of untruthfulness. Civil Service Commission determined that two of the charges were unproven.
Curry County Sheriff's Dept., PEB ¶45,593 (CCH, 1983)	Termination	Termination	Untruthfulness at arbitration hearing.
Department of Law Enforcement v. Stanley, 566 So.2d 20 (Fla. App. 1990)	30-Day Suspension	No Discipline	Untruthfulness during internal affairs interview. Court noted that though answers were "indirect," they were not dishonest. Court criticized vague, ambiguous and inartfully phrased questions by internal affairs interviewer.
Gray v. Department of Personnel, 592 N.Y.S.2d 376 (A.D. 1993)	Termination	Termination	Untruthfulness on employment application discovered three years after employment.
Jacobo v. Board of Trustees, 788 So.2d 362 (Fla. App. 2001)	Forfeiture Of Pension Benefits	Forfeiture Of Pension Benefits	Officer convicted of official misconduct for falsely reporting on an arrest affidavit that a suspect who was shot by another officer was carrying a gun. Under state law, pension benefits forfeited if employee convicted of a felony involving breach of public trust.
McDaniel v. City of Evansville, 604 N.E.2d 1223 (Ind. App. 1992)	20-Month Suspension Plus Demotion	20-Month Suspension Plus Demotion	Falsification of affidavit; additionally, officer committed off-duty battery.
Ponto v. County of Riverside, 2007 WL 1509572 (Cal. App. 2007)	Termination	Termination	At the request of defense attorney, probation officer changed recommendation made by other probation officer without disclosing what she had done. First officer and attorney had formerly had a romantic relationship, which officer did not disclose in internal affairs interview.
State of Ohio, 125 LA 428 (Feldman, 2008)	Termination	Reinstatement Without Back Pay	Trooper lied to officer investigating traffic stop, contending that he had checked his audio-visual equipment as required by employer's rules. Trooper subsequently voluntarily admitted he had lied, had nine years of good performance, and was undergoing significant stress in his home life at the time of the incident.

CASE NAME	INITIAL SANCTION	RESULT ON APPEAL	DESCRIPTION
Town of Lady Luck, 26 LAIS 2045 (1999)	Termination	5-Day Suspension	Officer allegedly brandished service firearm in a public place, waved it at a tow truck operator, and lied about incident during investigation. Arbitrator found that complaining witness – a rookie officer – had a record for spreading gossip and lying about federal officers, and that charge of untruthfulness could not be sustained.
Town of Magnolia Park, 98-1 ARB ¶5097 (Hoffman, 1998)	Termination	Termination	Omission in initial job application of fact that officer had been fired from previous job. Omission discovered seven years later; officer also provided false information in internal affairs and *Loudermill* hearings.
Vazquez v. Kelly, 852 N.Y.S.2d 72 (A.D. 2008)	Termination	Termination	Officer was absent without leave, submitted false leave reports in connection with her absence, forged documents, and failed to qualify with her handgun. Mitigating circumstances did not override nature of offenses.
Winnebago County, Illinois Sheriff's Department, LAIG 6192 (Briggs, 2004)	Termination	Termination	Corrections officer was repeatedly dishonest with employer about reasons for use of sick leave. Arbitrator rejected defense that alcoholism led to the offense, and noted that officer was dishonest during the arbitration hearing.
Wyatt v. Harahan Municipal Fire and Police Civil Service Board, 935 So.2d 849 (La. App. 2006)	Termination	Termination	Officer made false report about his police car being vandalized. Criminal investigation occurred at the same time. The statue of limitation in state law for disciplinary investigations does not begin to run until the criminal investigation is concluded.

Dishonesty, General

CASE NAME	INITIAL SANCTION	RESULT ON APPEAL	DESCRIPTION
Ansbro v. McGuire, 414 N.Y.S.2d 334 (A.D. 1979)	Termination	Reinstatement	Falsification of overtime to increase salary for retirement. Twenty-three-year employee.
Border Patrol, 106 LA 1175 (Rezler, 1996)	Termination	Reinstatement With Back Pay	U.S. Attorney sent letter that she would not allow Border Patrol officer to testify in agency cases in the future; U.S. Attorney refused to substantiate her allegations, and Border Patrol officer was never provided the opportunity to determine the underlying basis of her charges against him.
Borrero v. Safir, 712 N.Y.S.2d 230 (App. Div. 2001)	Termination	Termination	Officer refused to comply with an order to return to work and made false and misleading statements regarding her injuries in order to obtain a disability retirement.

CASE NAME	INITIAL SANCTION	RESULT ON APPEAL	DESCRIPTION
Castagna v. City of Seal Beach, 2008 WL 2445546 (Cal. App. 2008)	Termination	Reinstatement With Back Pay	Twenty-seven-year police officer terminated when Probate Court concluded he committed perjury about whether he witnessed the signing of an agreement to transfer property to himself. Appeals Court found more credible the testimony of document examiners that there was no method of determining whether agreement was forged, and concluded employer had not met its burden of proof.
City of Centralia, 102 LA 520 (Stuteville, 1994)	30-Day Suspension	30-Day Suspension	Officer read and photocopied confidential memorandum on his lieutenant's desk.
City of Cincinnati, #52-390-00606-07 (Colvin, 2008)	Termination	Termination	One-year officer neglected to serve citations on citizens, which could have resulted in the citizens being arrested, lied to her sergeant about the issue, and maintained her untruthful story for seven months. Arbitrator found no basis for mitigation of penalty.
City of Cincinnati, LAIG 6273 (Newman, 2005)	Termination	10-Day Suspension	Lieutenant terminated for improperly using pepper spray at the scene of a domestic violence call and dishonesty in not reporting the incident. The Arbitrator upheld use of force charge since there was no evidence of threatening behavior on the part of any individual, but concluded that the City failed to meet its burden of proving the lieutenant was deliberately dishonest in his "draft report."
City of Hialeah, LAIG 5316 (Lambert, 1997)	20-Hour Suspension	20-Hour Suspension	Officer falsely claimed to have stopped an intoxicated individual when in fact he was en route to his mother's house to take a bathroom break.
City of Houston, Texas, 96-2 ARB ¶6310 (Moore, 1996)	10-Day Suspension	10-Day Suspension	Off-duty officer called dispatch to report a break-in at his home. Officer neglected to mention that "suspect" was his wife, who was also a police officer. Officer also escalated the dispute when he held his wife by the neck and made her go into a parking lot with him.
City of Isanti, Minnesota, 120 LA 461 (Daly, 2004)	Termination	68-Day Suspension	Officer terminated for lying to Chief about nature of his physical condition, which involved a narcotic dependency, and for not providing fitness-for-duty evaluation to the City. In fact, officer participated in evaluation, but doctor mistakenly sent results to County instead of City. As a result, termination was mitigated to suspension.

CASE NAME	INITIAL SANCTION	RESULT ON APPEAL	DESCRIPTION
City of Lawton, Oklahoma, 2001WL 574317 (Prlogdky, 2001)	1-Day Suspension	No Discipline	Officer responding to suicide scene moved the victim's gun, unloaded it, and placed it on an egg carton on top of an automobile hood, all before the crime scene personnel arrived. Officer charged with not accurately reporting the order of events. Applying a clear and convincing burden of proof, the Arbitrator concluded that the officer was not intentionally untruthful, though officer's accounts were "at times contradictory, confusing, and did not provide a complete picture of the events that transpired."
City of Milwaukee, 112 LA 682 (Dichter, 1999)	5-Day Suspension	No Discipline	Sergeant agreed to officer's request to post inaccurate statement about settlement of non-police related litigation. Arbitrator concluded that sergeant merely was careless in her reading of the document and was not dishonest.
City of Pearland, Texas, LAIG 6493 (Campos, 2007)	Indefinite Suspension	Reinstatement With Back Pay	Twenty-year detective indefinitely suspended for untruthfulness regarding an off-duty incident involving an argument with a security guard. Videotapes that captured the incident supported detective's version of events.
City of Reno, LAIG 4281 (Staudohar, 1989)	Termination	45-Day Suspension	Sergeant falsely gave impression to deputy city attorney that Department wanted charges against reporter dismissed; sergeant's 17 years of service warranted mitigation.
City of Stamford, 97 LA 261 (Pittocco, 1991)	Termination	Termination	Officer fraudulently made insurance claim; officer made no restitution, had personnel file "replete" with reprimands, and invoked Fifth Amendment during arbitration.
City of Tallahassee v. Big Bend Police Benevolent Association, 710 So.2d 214 (Fla. App. 1998)	Termination	4-Month Suspension	Lieutenant accused of sexual misconduct on duty and giving false statements to Police Chief. Applying clear and convincing standard of proof, Arbitrator sustained only dishonesty charge.
City of Youngstown, 107 LA 588 (Skulina, 1996)	Termination	Termination	Officer received City pay for five days of National Guard training but did not attend the training. The Arbitrator concluded that officer had no legitimate excuse for being absent from National Guard duty.
Coletti v. Civil Service Commission, 790 N.E.2d 242 (Mass. App. 2003).	Termination	Termination	Officer wrote a letter to a newspaper about a confidential police matter, lied about it to his employer, and made an unauthorized record check.

CASE NAME	INITIAL SANCTION	RESULT ON APPEAL	DESCRIPTION
Correia v. City of Rochester, 749 N.Y.2d 449 (A.D. 2002)	Termination	Termination	Officer intentionally struck civilian with a flashlight and then denied having done so in a subsequent report and statement.
County of Los Angeles, 108 LA 622 (Richman, 1997)	Removal From Multi-Jurisdictional Task Force	Removal From Multi-Jurisdictional Task Force	Deputy lied during investigation into alleged misuse of County gas privileges.
District of Columbia Metropolitan Police Department, 901 A.2d 784 (D.C. 2006)	Termination	Reinstatement With Back Pay	Termination for dishonesty and off-duty misconduct reversed because employer failed to comply with contract's requirement that disciplinary proceedings be concluded within 55 days. The investigation took roughly 600 days.
Fisch v. Allsop, 4 P.3d 204 (Wyo. 2000)	Termination	Termination	Police officer was absent without leave and then misled supervisors about reasons for absence.
Franklin v. California State Personnel Board, 2003 WL 22457060 (Cal. App. 2003)	Termination	Termination	Youth correctional counselor failed to document misconduct on the part of inmates, left inmates unsupervised, retaliated against an inmate, and made false statements to an investigating officer.
Green Bay Police Protective Association, Wis. PERC No. 64974 (Shaw, 2006).	Temporary Suspension	No Discipline	Officer was temporarily suspended pending investigation into fraudulent travel claims. Employer agreed that suspension was inappropriate. Arbitrator ordered make-whole remedy, to include payment for lost overtime opportunities.
Hadfield v. City Council of the City of Fullerton, 2005 WL 1244214 (Cal. App. 2005)	Termination	Termination	Officer provided inaccurate and misleading verbal descriptions of calls, and made two false statements during the internal affairs investigation into the matter. The City Council had the authority to overturn an advisory arbitrator's opinion, which found that the statements were merely "misleading" and not dishonest.
Huemiller v. Ogden Civil Service Commission, 101 P.3d 394 (Utah App. 2004)	Termination	Termination	Officer directed disabled motorist to towing company in which he had an interest and lied about the matter in an internal affairs investigation. Court upheld employer's automatic termination policy for officers who have been dishonest, even where the officer had a lengthy unblemished career.
In re Radlinger, 782 N.E.2d 1215 (Ohio App. 2002)	240-Hour Suspension	240-Hour Suspension	Officer failed to appear in court, later giving the excuse that he was conducting a homicide investigation. In fact, officer was taking his father to a doctor's appointment.

CASE NAME	INITIAL SANCTION	RESULT ON APPEAL	DESCRIPTION
Johnson v. City of Long Beach, 2002 WL 1760888 (Cal. App. 2002)	Termination	Termination	Officer falsified his employee time records for five dates, failed to turn in his employee time records in a timely fashion on eight occasions, carried an unauthorized "ride-along" passenger, and failed to file crime reports in a timely fashion.
Macklin v. City of New Orleans, 300 F.3d 552 (5th Cir. 2002)	Termination	Termination	Off-duty police officer struck a man over the head with his police baton then lied to investigators about it.
McGeehee v. City/ Parish of East Baton Rouge, 809 So.2d 258 (La. App. 2001)	1-Day Suspension	1-Day Suspension	Sergeant gave innocuous and non-credible account of sexually offensive joke he told to a female corporal. Joke could be characterized as sexual harassment.
Meraz v. City of Sacramento Civil Service Board, 2001 WL 1353636 (Cal. App. 2001)	Termination	Termination	Officer issued traffic ticket to young woman and then began pursuing a social relationship with her. Officer lied about events when questioned by his employer, and failed to raise due process and other procedural rights claims in a timely manner.
Metropolitan Police Department, District of Columbia, LAIG 5392 (Donegan, 1997)	Termination	30-Day Suspension	Officer who misrepresented to sergeant that watch commander had granted leave request discharged for untruthfulness and inefficiency. Arbitrator upheld untruthfulness charge, but found that employer did not establish inefficiency.
Michigan Department of Corrections, LAIG 5394 (Scales, 1997)	Termination	7-Day Suspension	Corrections officer failed to report that she received 11 cards and letters from an inmate over three-year period, and initially lied about receiving the correspondence when first confronted. Warden initially recommended seven-day suspension, but recommendation was overturned by his supervisors. Arbitrator concluded that other employees received less severe discipline for "far more serious violations of the rules."
Michigan Department of Corrections, LAIG 5638 (Brown, 2000)	Termination	Termination	Corrections officer discharged for permitting inmates to be outside the facility in the presence of a drunk female. Arbitrator rejected charges that Department's disciplinary investigation was intimidating and concluded that the corrections officer "prepared a cover story, and he and the inmates all told the same story to avoid discipline."

CASE NAME	INITIAL SANCTION	RESULT ON APPEAL	DESCRIPTION
Mieles v. Safir, 706 N.Y.S.2d 437 (S.Ct. 2000)	Termination	Termination	Police officer used false pretenses to trick the owner of a broken-down vehicle into giving the officer the title to the car. The officer then removed the vehicle from the street and sold it to a salvage company.
Rozek v. Bristol Borough, 613 A.2d 165 (Pa.Cmwlth. 1992)	Termination	Reinstatement	Alleged untruthfulness concerning cashing of check while officer on sick leave; decided on basis of anti-union bias.
Scaturico v. Ward, 552 N.Y.S.2d 24 (A.D. 1990)	Termination	Termination	Failure to report officers who stole food stamps and coins.
State of Rhode Island v. Rhode Island Brotherhood of Correctional Officers, 725 A.2d 296 (R.I. 1999)	Termination	Termination	Corrections officer concealed her arrest and conviction from her employer. Court overruled Arbitrator's decision, finding that Rhode Island law does not allow an arbitrator to substitute lower disciplinary sanction once finding of just cause has been made.
Sweeney v. City of Ladue, 64 FEP Cases 1633 (8th Cir. 1994)	Termination	Termination	Untruthfulness concerning sexual relationship with other police officer.
Tuttle v. Department of Justice, 167 P.3d 864 (Mont. 2007)	Termination	Termination	Supervisor of Highway Patrol cadets misappropriated state funds, lied to investigators and cadets, and sexually harassed at least one female trooper. Supervisor's conduct was not "minor" requiring imposition of progressive discipline.
Tippery v. Montgomery County Police Department, 685 A.2d 788 (Md. App. 1996)	Termination	Termination	Officer struck a suspect in the face and later lied about his actions. Officer's performance evaluations indicated a pattern of use of excessive force.
Wilburn v. Mississippi Highway Safety Patrol, 17 IER Cases 1666 (Miss. App. 2001)	Termination	Termination	Officer issued tickets for offenses he had not in fact witnessed, and indicated on traffic citations that he had seen the violations.
Williams v. City of Bakersfield, 2002 WL 537500 (Cal. App. 2002)	Termination	Termination	Officer was dishonest about his activities while on a dispatch in an area in which a murder had been committed two days before. The officer denied being given the potential murder weapon by witness; murder case subsequently could not be prosecuted because of the loss of weapon.

CASE NAME	INITIAL SANCTION	RESULT ON APPEAL	DESCRIPTION
Domestic Violence			
Border Patrol and AFGE Local 2366, 115 LA 661 (Goodman, 2001)	5-Day Suspension	No Discipline	Accusations of officer's wife that he harassed her on duty in uniform were not credible; officer was on light duty at the time. Employer did not establish misuse of authority when officer requested welfare check on his two sons, since he was acting as any citizen could under the circumstances.
Chicago Housing Authority, LAIG 4978 (Cohen, 1994)	Termination	18-Month Suspension	Series of domestic violence charges; progressive discipline not followed.
City of Cleveland, 108 LA 912 (Skulina, 1997)	Termination	Reinstatement Without Back Pay	Police officer was convicted of criminal assault after hitting 13-year-old child of woman with whom he was living. Employer had not uniformly discharged officers who committed off-duty crimes, and officer, who believed child had hit his mother, did not really intend to injure the child.
City of Kalamazoo, LAIG 5376 (Grissom, 1998)	Termination	Reinstatement With Back Pay	Officer discharged for violating a bond which stipulated that he stay away from girlfriend. Arbitrator concluded City's investigator "adopted an arms-length, heavy-handed approach on a criminal track that left the officer bereft of dignity, money and a place to live." City produced no witnesses at arbitration hearing. Arbitrator also concluded that City treated another similarly-situated employee much more leniently.
City of Memphis v. Civil Service Commission, 239 S.W.3d 202 (Tenn. App. 2007)	Termination	Reinstatement With Back Pay	Off-duty officer hit both boyfriend-officer and on-duty officer who had intervened in dispute, and later drove her car into boyfriend-officer, causing him to fall to the ground. Court upheld civil service decision that City relied on incomplete investigative report, and failed to consider officer's state of mind and overall good work record.
City of Philadelphia, LAIG 5336 (Skonier, 1997)	Termination	Reinstatement Without Back Pay	Officer discharged his weapon during an argument with his ex-wife. Additional allegations relied on by employer that officer physically abused ex-wife and surreptitiously videotaped step-daughter in her bedroom not proven by employer.

CASE NAME	INITIAL SANCTION	RESULT ON APPEAL	DESCRIPTION
Clough v. Civil Service Commission, 797 N.E.2d 1223 (Mass. App. 2003)	Termination	Termination	Officer threatened to assault his wife and burn down their house, caused significant damage to property in the home, and falsely claimed that his wife had kidnapped their daughters. Defense rejected that officer's emotional condition was product of his earlier responding to an on-duty call involving the murder of an infant.
Dash v. Brown, 604 N.Y.S.2d 108 (A.D. 1993)	Termination	Termination	Off-duty use of excessive corporal punishment on children in probationary officer's care.
Dronet v. Department of Police, 613 So.2d 735 (La. App. 1993)	Termination	Termination	During domestic dispute, officer broke into girlfriend's house, threw food around apartment, and pushed over some furniture.
Ehler v. Missouri State Highway Patrol, 254 S.W.3d 99 (Mo. App. 2008)	Termination	Termination	Police were repeatedly called to house of highway patrol trooper for domestic incidents and frequently found him in an intoxicated state.
Floyd v. Department of Police, 787 So.2d 1138 (La. App. 2001)	Termination	Termination	Officer discharged her firearm (twice) at her ex-boyfriend, failed to report recovery of stolen weapon to NCIC (even though she was assigned to NCIC at the time), and failed to disclose during mitigation hearing that medication may have made her act irrationally.
FOP v. City of Philadelphia, 29 PPER P 29120 (Pa. Cmwlth. 1998)	Termination	Termination	Domestic violence incident resulting in police officer's wife requiring medical treatment for a broken thumb and contusions to the ribs and knee. Officer was arrested and charged with aggravated assault.
Grant v. Department of Police, 750 So.2d 382 (La. App. 4th Cir. 2000)	Termination	Termination	Officer struck acquaintance in mouth, causing cut to bridge of nose, threw television set at her, and locked her in closet. Court found that "the act of domestic violence at the hands of a commissioned police officer under any circumstances is particularly reprehensible and obviously prejudicial to the efficient operation of the police department."
Mahan v. Department of Treasury, 89 M.S.P.R. 140 (M.S.P.B. 2001)	Termination	Termination	Officer fired her government-issue firearm in the "general direction" of her husband during domestic dispute. Officer failed to establish claim of self defense.
McCloud v. Rodriguez, 710 N.E.2d 37 (Ill. App. 1999)	Termination	Termination	Officer beat his wife about the head and shot her with his service revolver, carried out eight-hour standoff with police, and threatened to shoot himself and anyone entering his house.

CASE NAME	INITIAL SANCTION	RESULT ON APPEAL	DESCRIPTION
Morrison v. Summit County Sheriff's Department, 2001 WL 688895 (Ohio App. 2001)	Termination	Termination	Officer struck his wife and, on a separate occasion, threw her to the ground. Under TRO, officer forbidden to possess handguns.
Opp v. City of Huntington Beach Personnel Commission, 2003 WL 192478 (Cal. App. 2003)	Termination	Termination	Detention officer discovered his estranged wife in bed with another man. After sending her nude lover fleeing for his life, officer attacked his wife, and "in a scene rather too reminiscent of the last act in Othello, almost strangled her."
Pennsylvania State Police, 6:1 NPER 10-11 (1997)	Termination	8½-Month Suspension	Trooper pled guilty to driving while intoxicated and making "terroristic threats" to former girlfriend. Mitigating factors included 13-year excellent work record, lack of prior similar cases.
Rayes v. Bratton, 651 N.Y.S.2d 521 (A.D. 1997)	Termination	Termination	Striking of estranged wife with handgun and handcuffing her against her will.
State of Nebraska, 110 LA 129 (Caffera, 1998)	Termination	Termination	Corrections officer convicted of misdemeanor crime of domestic violence. Since federal law prohibited officer from possessing firearm, termination ruled not to be excessive.
Van Baale v. City of Des Moines, 550 N.W.2d 153 (Iowa 1996)	Termination	Termination	Convictions for domestic violence and obstruction of justice (officer brandished a gun when he was arrested).
Vance v. City of Los Angeles, 2003 WL 1795643 (Cal. App. 2003)	Termination	Termination	While off duty, officer had long-standing affairs with two women, neither of whom knew of the other's existence. When women eventually encountered each other at officer's house, officer assaulted one of the women. Subsequent investigation revealed a pattern of psychological and physical abuse of both women on the part of the officer.

Driving

Appeal of Leis, 455 A.2d 1277 (Pa. Cmwlth. 1983)	3-Day Suspension	Reinstatement	Failure to use siren, resulting in accident; siren use discretionary under rules.
Bickl v. Smith, 23 S.W.3d 865 (Mo. App. 2000)	10-Day Suspension	10-Day Suspension	Primary officer in pursuit of motorist failed to report police pursuit to dispatch.

CASE NAME	INITIAL SANCTION	RESULT ON APPEAL	DESCRIPTION
Borough of Dormont, Pennsylvania, 115 LA 106 (Dean, 2000)	5-Day Suspension	3-Day Suspension	Police officer was "extraordinarily negligent" in backing his car across an intersection, colliding with another car. Officer's actions did not constitute "conduct unbecoming" as charged because of no showing that actions "undermined the morale or efficiency" of the employer.
Brooks v. Civil Service Commission, Shaler Township, 4 NPER 4:5 (Pa.Cmwlth. 2000)	Termination	Termination	Officer had been progressively disciplined for driving problems, and had also served a 60-day suspension for engaging in sexual activity in patrol car.
Charlevoix County, LAIG 4309 (Chiesa, 1989)	Written Reprimand	No Discipline	Nine accidents in nine years; police report did not indicate that most recent accident, a slide on black ice, was the officer's fault.
City of Cincinnati, 106 LA 492 (Braverman, 1995)	24-Hour Suspension	Written Reprimand	Officer involved in third negligent accident in three years when he did not use lights and siren in responding to code call; other driver, who made illegal left turn and was driving under the influence, was proximate cause of accident. Other officers with worse driving records were treated less severely.
City of Clairmont, LAIG 4845 (Cooper, 1993)	Termination	30-Day Suspension	On-duty motor vehicle accident by officer who had previously been demoted for using excessive force. Arbitrator found negligence, but no gross negligence since other officers responding to calls traveled at excessive rates of speed.
City of Englewood, Ohio, LAIG 5270 (Keenan, 1997)	Reprimand	Counseling	Minor accident resulting in $500 in damages to a vehicle and a fence. Employer's rules required progressive discipline beginning with counseling, and employee had no prior disciplinary record.
City of Fort Worth, Texas, LAIG 5615 (Pelhan, 2000)	3-Day Suspension	3-Day Suspension	Officer drove car into guide wire between telephone pole and retaining wall. Officer was not responding to an emergency, and was driving on an off-road sidewalk area between two parking lots.

CASE NAME	INITIAL SANCTION	RESULT ON APPEAL	DESCRIPTION
City of Fort Worth, Texas, LAIG 5637 (Sherman, 2000)	3-Day Suspension	1-Day Suspension	Sergeant involved in chargeable motor vehicle accident while responding to fight at nightclub. Contrary to employer's assessment, officer's driving record was "perfect" until time of incident, leading arbitrator to conclude that the employer's "reasoning was faulty." Additionally, the three-day suspension "was longer than 90 percent of the other suspension issued for accidents and three times the median level of suspensions for accidents."
City of Houston, 117 LA 408 (Moore, 2002).	Termination	Termination	Officer had seven preventable motor vehicle accidents in six years and was working under terms of last-chance agreement at time of final accident.
City of Lufkin, LAIG 5101 (Sherman, 1995)	Termination	Reinstatement Without Back Pay	Four chargeable accidents in one-year period; last accident occurred when officer failed to place vehicle in "park" when initiating foot pursuit and car rolled 50 feet, destroying a bush. Termination ruled too harsh.
City of Mayfield Heights, LAIG 5002 (Duda, 1994)	Termination	Reinstatement	Collision while responding to suicide; accident reconstructionists disproved employer's claim about officer's speed, and Department erred in using member of accident review board as hearing officer.
City of Oceanside, 92-2 ARB ¶6333 (Thompson, 1996)	Suspension Of Unspecified Length	No Discipline	Police officer was rear-ended after activating overhead lights to question suspects. Police Chief and investigating captain differed on whether situation constituted an "emergency" under Department rules and thus differed on disciplinary conclusions. Officer had been involved in four prior preventable accidents.
City of Oklahoma City, 100 LA 1183 (Woolf, 1993)	Non-Removable Written Reprimand	Removable Written Reprimand	On-duty accident at 75 m.p.h.; accident review board did not conduct fair and sufficient investigation.
City of Richmond Heights, 123 LA 232 (Lalka, 2006)	5-day Suspension	5-day Suspension	Officer backed into mailbox. While such an offense ordinarily would not have warranted a suspension, officer had ten accidents in last four years, six of which occurred after he went to remedial driver's training.
City of San Antonio, LAIG 4680 (Baldovin, 1992)	10-Day Suspension	3-Day Suspension	Without authorization, officer allowed off-duty officer to ride with him on patrol to videotape activities.

CASE NAME	INITIAL SANCTION	RESULT ON APPEAL	DESCRIPTION
City of Wichita Falls, Texas, LAIG 5393 (Larson, 1998)	1-Day Suspension	1-Day Suspension	Officer ran red light and collided with another automobile. Arbitrator rejected defense that collision could have been avoided if brakes on the other vehicle were in better condition.
Civil Service Commission v. Vargo, 553 A.2d 103 (Ill. App. 1988)	5-Day Suspension	5-Day Suspension	Leaving of keys in patrol car, which was subsequently stolen and totally destroyed.
Dwyer v. City of White Plains, 613 N.Y.S.2d 45 (A.D. 1994)	5-Day Suspension	5-Day Suspension	Failure to exercise due care at an intersection; driving at an excessive rate of speed.
Ramsey County, 100 LA 209 (Gallagher, 1992)	3-Day Suspension	3-Day Suspension	Deputy who had previously received suspension for on-duty accident ran over post in parking lot.
Schwartz v. Brown, 857 F. Supp. 291 (S.D. N.Y. 1994)	Termination	Termination	Two separate incidents where officer struck and killed pedestrian; numerous speeding and other traffic violations; officer had vanity plate "MY T QUICK."
Scioto County, Ohio Sheriff, 115 LA 532 (Feldman, 2001)	30-Day Suspension	No Discipline	Deputy with serious prior disciplinary record drove at 120 m.p.h. without justification and physically assaulted fellow deputy. Though employee waived pre-disciplinary hearing, employer failed to obtain Union's acceptance of waiver of hearing.
State of Ohio Highway Patrol, 96-2 ARB ¶6281 (Bowers, 1996)	2-Day Suspension	2-Day Suspension	State trooper failed to terminate high-speed pursuit which continued through a school zone, on the wrong side of the road, and around traffic, until the suspect collided with another vehicle, severely injuring the driver. Department policy required high-speed pursuits to be terminated when the danger to the public and the trooper were outweighed by the need to apprehend the suspect; trooper radioed description and license number of fleeing vehicle.
Town of Newington, 98 LA 886 (Stewart, 1992)	2-Day Suspension	2-Day Suspension	Intersection collision involving five vehicles; officer did not use due care before proceeding through intersection while on code call.

Evidence Handling

CASE NAME	INITIAL SANCTION	RESULT ON APPEAL	DESCRIPTION
Goins v. Village of New Boston, 2000 WL 1800519 (Ohio App. 2000)	Termination	Reinstatement	Lieutenant maintained evidence in his personal locker. Employer did not meet burden of proving that lieutenant intended to use the evidence, including drugs and money, for his own personal use.

CASE NAME	INITIAL SANCTION	RESULT ON APPEAL	DESCRIPTION
Excessive Force			
Boston Police Department v. Dean, 779 N.E.2d 165 (Mass. App. 2002)	9-Month Suspension	9-Month Suspension	Officer encountered suspect who had assaulted her earlier in the evening in a booking room. When suspect kicked officer, officer responded by striking suspect in face, breaking her nose.
Broward County, 98 LA 219 (Frost, 1991)	15-Day Suspension	15-Day Suspension	Striking of handcuffed citizen with riot baton during altercation where citizen objected to deputies' breaking up campsites of homeless individuals.
Brown v. Bossier City, 887 So.2d 731 (La. App. 2004)	Termination	Termination	Although reasonable persons could disagree with conclusion that videotape of incident showed officer used excessive force, in a non-union environment, a court is without authority to substitute its judgment for that of a civil service board as to either the officer's culpability or punishment.
Chelf v. Civil Service Commission, 515 N.W.2d 353 (Iowa App. 1994)	Termination	Termination	Striking of suspect with flashlight three to six times in legs; evidence of sanctions in other excessive force cases inadmissible under Iowa law.
City of Austin, LAIG 5614 (McKee, 2000)	10-Day Suspension	10-Day Suspension	Officer struck suspect approximately seven times with a baton; suspect's actions only constituted "passive resistance." Arbitrator noted that officer "wielded The Asp with the power of an experienced ballplayer swinging an aluminum baseball bat. For many, such a beating would cause permanent physical damage, if not death."
City of Bloomington, PEB ¶45,564 (CCH, 1983)	10-Day Suspension	Reinstatement	Striking of teenage girl in mouth with flashlight.
City of Boulder, PEB ¶45,033 (CCH, 1978)	Termination	Reinstatement	Excessive force used against prisoner in holding cell.
City of Cincinnati, LAIG 5256 (Bill, 1996)	5-Day Suspension	No Discipline	Officer sprayed pepper mace into face of detainee who was struggling to break free from officers who were trying to handcuff him. Arbitrator rejected finding of citizen's panel convened by City Manager and concluded that officer followed training and used mace appropriately.

CASE NAME	INITIAL SANCTION	RESULT ON APPEAL	DESCRIPTION
City of El Paso, 91-4 ARB ¶4205 (Stephens, 1993)	10-Day Suspension	Reversal Of Suspension	During struggle, officer kicked suspect in jaw. Other officer who hit suspect with flashlight not disciplined. Civilian review board recommended written reprimand, and Chief did not impose discipline until five months after he announced his disciplinary decision at a press conference.
City of Harrisburg v. Pickles, 492 A.2d 90 (Pa.Cmwlth. 1985)	Termination	Reinstatement	Shooting of unarmed suspect after long chase.
City of Houston, PEB ¶49,068 (CCH, 1986)	5-Day Suspension	Reprimand	Arbitrator found prisoner who complained of force not credible, but found "unnecessary roughness."
City of Houston, 107 LA 328 (Moore, 1996)	5-Day Suspension	No Discipline	Officer working extra employment at high school allegedly slapped a student who had been called into a vice-principal's office because of misconduct. Arbitrator concluded officer's recounting of events more credible than that of the student and student's mother.
City of Huber Heights, 102 LA 1060 (Bittel, 1994)	9-Month Suspension	9-Month Suspension	Officer punched a prisoner several times, then was dishonest about what he had done.
City of Lebanon, LAIG 4754 (DiLauro, 1993)	5-Day Suspension	No Discipline	During arrest with combative suspect, officer placed hand on suspect's head and pushed him to ground, causing injury to suspect's forehead. City failed to interview officer and inappropriately focused on possible legal ramifications against it.
City of Pasadena, PEB ¶45,260 (CCH, 1980)	20-Day Suspension	20-Day Suspension	Excessive force used in subduing jaywalker.
City of Philadelphia, LAIG 5411 (Laskin, 1998)	10-Day Suspension	No Discipline	Two officers allegedly assaulted concert attendee following a concert by the rock group Phish. Arbitrator questioned victim's recollection of events, and disbelieved victim's statement that out of several individuals in his group, he was the only person not smoking marijuana or drinking alcohol at the concert. Arbitrator concluded that "there is not a scintilla of evidence that either officer touched the civilian."
City of Portland, 104 LA 647 (Henner, 1995)	Termination	Reinstatement	Firing of 22 shots at fleeing suspect; shots fired in response to articulable threats posed by suspect, and employer failed to adequately consider impact of post-traumatic stress on officer.

CASE NAME	INITIAL SANCTION	RESULT ON APPEAL	DESCRIPTION
City of Redwood City, 98 LA 306 (Riker, 1991)	30-Day Suspension	No Discipline	Officer struck suspect in face in holding cell; suspect had been verbally abusive, had spat in officer's face once, and was preparing to spit in officer's face again.
City of Toledo, 99-ARB ¶5452 (Ellmann, 1998)	Termination	Reinstatement With Back Pay	Alleged excessive force in racially-tinged incident. Photographs of suspect did not establish that excessive force was used, and suspect gave "critical" inconsistencies in relating various accounts of the incident.
City of Tulsa, Oklahoma, 99-2 ARB Para. 3205 (Chlumley, 1999)	2-Day Suspension, Written Reprimand	No Discipline	Officer given a suspension for excessive force in bumping suspect with a police car, and reprimand for pursuit policy violation. Employer unable to prove how officer violated pursuit policy, and lack of evidence of excessive force was so significant as to be "arbitrary."
Colon v. McGuire, 470 N.Y.S.2d 156 (A.D. 1984)	Termination	Reinstatement	Newly-hired officer pointed gun at head of citizen who was rude to officer's partner.
Dickens v. Ohio Department of Public Safety, 2006 WL 2972674 (N.D. Ohio 2006)	Termination	Termination	Trooper discharged service weapon at unarmed suspect, whom he believed was making an aggressive movement at trooper's partner. Arbitrator concluded that deadly force not appropriate under circumstances.
Douglas County, Nevada, LAIG 5317 (Rappaport, 1997)	Termination	2-Day Suspension	Deputy took suspect to ground and placed knee in back of suspect whom employer believed was non-belligerent. Though videotape corroborated that the employee used force, Arbitrator held that "subjective considerations must also come into play and specifically what the deputy's perceptions were at the time of the incident and why he took the actions which were clearly visible on the tape." Though deputy's conduct inappropriate, termination ruled too severe a penalty.
Franklin Co. Sheriff v. Frazier, 881 N.E.2d 345 (Ohio App. 2007)	Termination	90-Day Suspension	Deputy terminated for excessive force and untruthfulness; hearings board determined that untruthfulness charge was not proven.
Klee v. Board of Fire and Police Commissioners, 574 N.E.2d 241 (Ill. App. 1991)	10-Day Suspension	10-Day Suspension	Shoving of citation down the shirt of a traffic violator.

CASE NAME	INITIAL SANCTION	RESULT ON APPEAL	DESCRIPTION
Michigan Department of Corrections, 24 LAIS 3794 (House, 1997)	Termination	Reinstatement With Back Pay	Corrections officer struck inmate around shoulders. Arbitrator accepted self-defense claim, noting inmate struck the officer from behind. Although officer had other options instead of striking the inmate, the actions taken were within the Department's rule that employees "may use all necessary and suitable means, including the use of physical force."
Peterson v. Civil Service Commission of Cedar Rapids, Iowa, 697 N.W.2d 127 (Iowa App. 2005)	Termination	Termination	Though Court concluded that videotape of car stop was ambiguous on issue of whether officer used excessive force in kneeing suspect, the Court determined that testimony of two other officers on the scene that officer used excessive force sufficed to sustain charge. Termination justified in part by prior sustained discipline for overreaction to situation where driver refused to obey order.
Port Authority of New York and New Jersey, LAIG 5365 (Scheiman, 1998)	10-Day Suspension	No Discipline	Relying on testimony of lieutenant at scene, employer suspended officer for allegedly twice stomping with foot on forearm of wife involved in domestic dispute. Arbitrator accepted version of officer, supported by Secret Service agent who was at the scene, that he was simply pushing wife away with his foot so he could better control husband.
Potter v. Saffir, 728 N.Y.S.2d 428 (A.D. 2001)	Forfeiture Of 20 Vacation Days	Forfeiture Of 20 Vacation Days	Without provocation or justification, officer struck individual with nightstick during the course of an arrest.
Rodriguez v. Ward, 564 N.Y.S.2d 356 (A.D. 1991)	1-Year Probation	1-Year Probation	Off-duty officer placed barrel of gun to motorist's neck, and threatened to blow head off.
Sacramento Police Association, 1 MHMC Labor Bulletin 3:4-5 (August, 1996)	160-Hour Suspension	No Discipline	Witness overlooked by internal affairs investigations supported conclusion that use of force was reasonable.
San Francisco County, 2001 WL 1152561 (Riker, 2001)	Termination	Termination	Corrections officer punched inmate twice in stomach and omitted fact from his report of the incident. Inmate was handcuffed with his hands behind his back. Arbitrator rejected defense of deputy's good work record.
Serpas v. New Orleans, 483 So.2d 1259 (La. App. 1986)	Termination	Reinstatement	Beating of parking control attendant who was vulgar to officer.

CASE NAME	INITIAL SANCTION	RESULT ON APPEAL	DESCRIPTION
Wagner v. City of Omaha, 464 N.W.2d 175 (Neb. 1991)	15-Day Suspension	4-Day Suspension	Officer struck unarmed non-resisting suspect in abdomen with baton after suspect failed to obey instructions; two other officers saw no reason for use of baton.
Esparza v. Bexar County, 2003 WL 23005015 (Tex. App. 2003)	Termination	Termination	Three corrections officers assaulted an inmate in retaliation for an earlier incident in which the inmate attempted to bite one of the officer's ears.
Financial Matters			
City of North Vernon v. Brading, 479 N.E.2d 619 (Ind. App. 1985)	Termination	Reinstatement	Writing of a bad check.
Davis v. City of Evanston, 629 N.E.2d 125 (Ill. App. 1993)	Termination	Termination	Officer with bad work record willfully failed to file state income tax returns.
Detz v. Hanover, 539 F. Supp. 532 (E.D. Pa. 1982)	Termination	Reinstatement	Police chief filed bankruptcy; without greater indication of misconduct, termination inappropriate.
Marhold v. Brown, 592 N.Y.S.2d 28 (A.D. 1993)	Termination	Termination	Issuance of a number of bad checks.
Pennsylvania State Police v. Pennsylvania State Troopers Ass'n, 633 A.2d 1330 (Pa. Cmwlth. 1993)	Termination	Reinstatement Without Back Pay	Issuance of a series of bad checks; Department failed to take disciplinary action for more than a year. Delay "totally unacceptable from a progressive disciplinary point of view."
Firearms Offenses			
Benton Harbor and Fraternal Order of Police, 103 LA 816 (Allen, 1994)	Termination	Suspension	Failure to register handgun; employer's progressive discipline schedule mandated suspension for first offense.
City of Florida City, 24 LAIS 3793 (Vause, 1997)	Termination	Termination	Sergeant accidentally shot gun into a neighbor's bedroom without checking to see if anyone had been harmed. Sergeant had poor disciplinary record.
County of Washington, Ohio, 122 LA 725 (Befort, 2006)	Termination	30-Day Suspension	Deputy engaged in eight instances of horseplay with guns, including "tracking" other officers with gun and pulling gun at roll call. Deputy's supervisors were aware of the conduct and did nothing to warn the deputy or advise him of the consequences of repetition of misconduct.

CASE NAME	INITIAL SANCTION	RESULT ON APPEAL	DESCRIPTION
Detroit Transportation Corp. and Police Officers Association of Michigan, LAIG 6378 (Cousens, 2006)	Termination	10-Day Suspension	While walking through employees' parking lot, security officer was attacked by a vagrant, whom she shot with her personal weapon. Termination for violation of employer's rule banning personal weapons at the workplace overturned because of widespread disregard for rule, disregard that amounted to a "waiver" of the rule.
Hankla v. Long Beach Civil Service Commission, 40 Cal. Rptr.2d 583 (Cal. App. 1995)	Termination	Termination	Off-duty officer became involved in argument with another motorist; in course of argument, officer accidentally shot the motorist.
Homa v. Civil Service, 650 P.2d 1323 (Colo. App. 1982)	Termination	Termination	Possession of grenades.
Immigration and Naturalization Service, 114 LA 1284 (Harkless, 2000)	Demotion	Conditional Reinstatement	Demotion of immigration inspector who had two accidental discharges of her weapon. Employer ignored a firearms policy requiring that remedial training be given to all employees who had accidental discharges. Reinstatement conditional on medical documentation that employee was physically able to use handgun where she had automobile accident in which she had lost vision in one eye.
Kappel v. Police Board of Chicago, 580 N.E.2d 1314 (Ill. App. 1991)	Termination	Termination	Off-duty sale of handgun with obliterated serial number; ownership of unregistered weapons.
Michigan Department of Corrections, LAIG 5695 (Jason, 2000)	Termination	Reinstatement With Back Pay	Corrections officer fired for off-duty carrying of concealed weapon without a permit. Internal affairs investigator relied on police reports rather than conducting independent investigation; Arbitrator concluded that weapon belonged to officer's wife.
O'Connor v. Kelly, 627 N.Y.S.2d 1 (A.D. 1995)	25-Day Suspension	25-Day Suspension	Officer leaned over his partner to fire his weapon from inside the patrol car.
Rinando v. Ward, 552 N.Y.S.2d 581 (A.D. 1990)	3-Year Suspension	3-Year Suspension	Off-duty officer left revolver on bedstead; gun later used in shooting which left individual paraplegic. Penalty did not "shock court's sense of fairness."

CASE NAME	INITIAL SANCTION	RESULT ON APPEAL	DESCRIPTION
Fraternization			
AFSCME District Council 88 v. County of Lehigh, 798 A.2d 804 (Pa.Cmwith. 2002)	Termination	Reinstatement	Corrections officer alleged to have engaged in sexual relationship with former inmate. Sole issue in challenge to Arbitrator's opinion reinstating corrections officer was whether Arbitrator improperly refused to admit the videotape was not properly authenticated.
Bowden v. Bayside State Prison, 633 A.2d 577 (N.J. A.D. 1993)	Termination	Termination	Corrections officer played cards with inmates and paid gambling debts by bringing 65 packs of cigarettes into prison.
County of San Benito, California, 113 LA 231 (Poole, 1999)	Termination	3-Week Suspension	Corrections officer charged with smuggling cigarettes and assorted other misconduct. Though Arbitrator sustained charges of gambling with inmates and other inappropriate conduct, Arbitrator held that charge of assisting with smuggling not proven and reversed discharge.
El Paso County Sheriff's Department, 117 LA 1304 (Moore, 2002)	Termination	Termination	Corrections officer escorted friend and former officer, who had been incarcerated, from jail upon his release. Officer had been ordered by his supervisors not to associate with former officer/inmate.
Flosi v. Board of Fire & Police Commissioners, 582 N.E.2d 185 (Ill. App. 1991)	Termination	No Discipline	Assistant chief's association with female heroin addict whom he was trying to develop as informant; City believed there was no legitimate law enforcement purpose for the relationship. No departmental guidelines on fraternization or development of informants.
Graham v. San Diego County Civil Service Commission, 2007 WL 2600672 (Cal. App. 2007)	Termination	Termination	While visiting her brother, who was incarcerated in a state prison, a booking clerk at a county correctional facility met her brother's cell mate, and later married him. No discussion of constitutionality of employer's fraternization rules.
Holt v. Washington Dept. of Corrections, 6 Wash. LLD 2 (1996)	Termination	Termination	Fourteen-year corrections officer cashed a money order for an inmate, escorted the inmate to the Department of Licensing, and bought car repair parts for the inmate.
Leek v. New Jersey Dept. of Corrections, 2008 WL 2026428 (N.J. Super. A.D. 2008)	30-Day Suspension	30-Day Suspension	Corrections sergeant who was also a minister testified on behalf of a parishioner at a sentencing hearing, discussing during his testimony his perspective as a corrections employee.

CASE NAME	INITIAL SANCTION	RESULT ON APPEAL	DESCRIPTION
Van Slyke v. Onondaga County, 688 N.Y.S.2d 312 (A.D. 1999)	Removal From Layoff List (Equivalent Of Termination)	Removal From Layoff List (Equivalent Of Termination)	Corrections officer accepted gifts and gratuities from inmates in exchange for favors.
Village of Romeo, LAIG 4838 (Glendon, 1993)	15-Day Suspension	Written Reprimand	Use of City computer for personal purposes and copying of Departmental computer files onto a floppy disk and taken to residence. No evidence that contents of disk divulged to third party, and employee had previously unblemished work record.
Williamson County, IL, PERI ¶2016 (Ill. SLRB 1998)	Termination	Reinstatement With Back Pay	Charge that corrections officer gambled with inmate. Fact that employer treated officer, who was union president, much more harshly than other similarly-situated employees indicated that true motive for discharge was anti-union bias.

Freedom of Speech

CASE NAME	INITIAL SANCTION	RESULT ON APPEAL	DESCRIPTION
Jefferson v. Ambroz, 11 IER Cases 1675 (7th Cir. 1996)	Termination	Termination	Probation officer criticized Police Department and court system while falsely identifying self on radio call-in show as a gang member; First Amendment free speech guarantees no defense to discharge.

Insubordination

CASE NAME	INITIAL SANCTION	RESULT ON APPEAL	DESCRIPTION
Allegan County Sheriff's Office, LAIG 4382 (Patton, 1990)	3-Day Suspension	Reprimand	Dispatcher refused to obey sergeant's order to enter cards into computer; sergeant told dispatcher that failure to obey orders would result in reprimand.
Ben v. Housing Authority of New Orleans, 879 So.2d 803 (La. App. 2004)	Termination	Termination	While on duty, officer specifically refused to obey a lieutenant's direct order to turn over a portable radio, became visibly angry toward his lieutenant, used inappropriate and disrespectful language, and may have drawn his handgun with the intent to point it at the lieutenant.
Borough of Edgeworth v. Blosser, 672 A.2d 854 (Pa.Cmwlth. 1996).	Termination	Termination	Police officer who found item in police station he suspected was a listening device called in outside officer to assist in the investigation because he distrusted his own department.
Boston Police Department v. Collins, 721 N.E.2d 928 (Mass. App. 2000)	5-Day Suspension	5-Day Suspension	Officer engaged in a heated conversation with and swore at a superior officer.

CASE NAME	INITIAL SANCTION	RESULT ON APPEAL	DESCRIPTION
Boston Police Patrolmen's Association v. City of Boston, 805 N.E.2d 80 (Mass. App. 2004)	3-Day Suspension	Written Reprimand	Officer disciplined for failure to write parking tickets as instructed by supervisor. City failed to prove all charges made against officer.
Broward County Sheriff's Office, 122 LA 56 (Cocalis, 2005)	10-Day Suspension	5-Day Suspension	Deputy refused to sign his performance evaluation, left his post without permission, and refused lieutenant's order to return. Arbitrator concluded events were related in time and substance so as to constitute one offense, and five-day suspension was the next logical progression on the progressive discipline scale from a three-day suspension the deputy had previously received.
City of Cleburne, LAIG 5067 (Detwiler, 1994)	Indefinite Suspension	Indefinite Suspension	Officer refused to provide Department with name of informant who told him that officer's ex-brother-in-law had been driving while intoxicated with officer's three-year old niece on board.
City of Dayton, 15 NPER OH-24051 (Ohio SERB Hearing Officer 1992)	Transfer And Written Reprimand	No Discipline	Making of critical and profane remarks to Police Chief; remarks occurred during grievance meeting in which officer acted as union representative.
City of Galveston, LAIG 6627 (Molina, 2008)	2-Day Suspension	No Discipline	Officer suspended for failing to obey a directive to operate his mobile video/motor vehicle recorder and for loudly swearing at two sergeants. Suspension overturned because employer's notice of discipline failed to specifically list the supporting basis for the charge of insubordination, and officer merely "adjusted" his voice to "match" or "beat" his sergeant's loud voice level.
City of Galveston, LAIG 4824 (Youngblood, 1993)	Indefinite Suspension	Reversal Of Discipline	Refusal to take drug test; order to take test under reasonable suspicion drug policy based on statement of individual with known mental difficulties.
City of Green Forest v. Morse, 873 S.W.2d 155 (Ark. 1994)	Termination	Termination	Disobeying of instructions to terminate high-speed chase.
City of Middletown, 1:5 NPER 8 (1997)	Written Reprimand	Verbal Warning	Officer did not comply with instructions of lieutenant to move his car from parking lot that was to be plowed. Order was inadequately communicated (yelled across parking lot), officer had good work record, and the Department failed to complete an independent investigation as required by the collective bargaining agreement.

CASE NAME	INITIAL SANCTION	RESULT ON APPEAL	DESCRIPTION
City of Philadelphia, LAIG 4254 (Ryan, 1989)	1-Day Suspension	Reversed	Refusal to transport prisoner with AIDS; City failed in its obligation to train officers on dangers of AIDS.
City of Philadelphia, 1:5 NPER 8 (1997)	10-Day Suspension	10-Day Suspension	Officer refused to write traffic ticket to operator of motor vehicle that an off-duty detective witnessed driving recklessly.
City of Piqua, 107 LA 1158 (Heekin, 1997)	1-Day Suspension	1-Day Suspension	School liaison officer met privately with a high school girl who had previously expressed intimate intentions towards him; Police Chief had issued officer an order never to meet alone with the girl. Officer's defense that order was not written rejected by Arbitrator.
City of Plano, Texas, LAIG 6377 (Bartman, 2006)	1-Day Suspension	Letter of Reprimand	Twenty-two-year officer refused to comply with sergeant's direction to handle a shoplifting call. Penalty reduced because of officer's long, discipline-free record.
Corpion v. Jenne, 869 So.2d 660 (Fla. App. 2004)	Demotion	Reinstatement Without Back Pay	Sergeant made comments in the workplace which were critical of the employer and violated the Department's policy. Arbitrator concluded that a temporary demotion and retraining were warranted in lieu of a permanent demotion.
Delaware County, LAIG 4897 (Aronin, 1993)	Termination	Reinstatement	Despite order to do so, deputy refused to attend interview with detective at district attorney's office in absence of labor representation. Arbitrator applied decision in *Weingarten v. NLRB.*
Department of Corrections v. State Civil Service Commission, 837 A.2d 1273 (Pa. Cmwlth. 2003)	Termination	5-Day Suspension	Corrections officer refused direct order to work overtime, using profanity in the process. Officer's babysitter was not available after officer's regular shift, officer's refusal was his first refusal to obey his superior's order in his 12-year employment with Department, and termination exceeded normal range of sanctions on a disciplinary matrix.
Department of Corrections v. Unemployment Compensation Bd. of Review, 943 A.2d 1011 (Pa.Cmwlth. 2008).	Termination	Termination	Corrections officer's fear of retaliation from fellow employees did not justify violation of department rules that he report illegal conduct on part of other employees.

CASE NAME	INITIAL SANCTION	RESULT ON APPEAL	DESCRIPTION
Guy v. City of Steubenville, 768 N.E.2d 1243 (Ohio App. 2002)	Termination	Termination	Officer refused to sign a release authorizing EAP counselor to disclose Police Department events transpiring in counseling session. EAP counseling and disclosure of information was mandatory under consent decree under which City was operating. Officer had prior discipline for insubordination.
Hamilton County, LAIG 4164 (1988)	5-Day Suspension	5-Day Suspension	Refusal to cut hair after being ordered to comply with grooming code.
IBPO v. Town of Windsor, 483 A.2d 626 (Conn. Sup. 1984)	2-Day Suspension	No Discipline	Refusal to sign warrant which officer had not served.
Immigration and Naturalization Service, U.S. Boarder Patrol, 115 LA 1546 (Goodstein, 2001)	5-Day Suspension	No Discipline	Union president engaged in heated discussion at job site with supervisor about Union issues. Supervisor provoked the angry discussion, and Union president had contractual right to be at the job site and address the job issues.
Jefferson County Sheriff, 122 LA 1101 (Pelt, 2006)	Termination	Termination	Deputy refused end-of-shift assignment to handle traffic accident. Arbitrator disbelieved deputy's proffered reason – a headache – where deputy never raised the headache defense before, and at the time responded to the request that he work with threats and swearing.
Kalamazoo County Sheriff's Deputies Association, 1 (12) Public Safety Labor News 10 (Chiesa, 1993)	Termination	Reinstatement With Full Back Pay	Dispute between deputy and lieutenant over reprimand; Arbitrator found lieutenant overreacted, and that discipline based on "insolent" tone of voice must be proven by overwhelming evidence.
Lugo v. City of Newburgh, 618 N.Y.S.2d 421 (A.D. 1994)	Termination	Termination	Engaging in outside employment contrary to specific orders; office\r had been warned on 20 occasions that he was not to engage in outside employment because of his sick leave abuse.
Mahaffey v. Winston County Sheriff's Department, 96 Fed. Appx. 191 (5th Cir. 2004)	Termination	Termination	At-will deputy sheriff accused Sheriff of engaging in illegal conduct. Court rejected argument that deputy's firing was an impermissible "political patronage" dismissal.
Metropolitan Washington Airports Authority, 114 LA 589 (Moore, 2000)	30-Day Suspension	30-Day Suspension	Police officer refused to take beat on airport grounds, incorrectly believing that operating use of vehicle with defective siren violated state law. Officer also directly called his sergeant a "f__king moron."

CASE NAME	INITIAL SANCTION	RESULT ON APPEAL	DESCRIPTION
Michigan Department of Corrections, LAIG 5624 (Long, 2000)	3-Day Suspension	No Discipline	Corrections officer suspended for insubordination for telling an acting-sergeant to "quit f__ing with people." Arbitrator criticized employer's lack of specific responses throughout grievance procedure and held that the only statement proven to be made by the officer was "this is pathetic," which did not amount to insubordination.
Municipality of Anchorage, (Beck, 1989)	Termination	2-Week Suspension	Refusal to answer questions in internal investigation; employee not told of consequences of failure to respond to questions.
National Park Service, PEB ¶45,178 (CCH, 1979)	10-Day Suspension	10-Day Suspension	Refusal to enter crowd without riot helmet.
O'Keefe v. Safir, 713 N.Y.2d 525 (A.D. 2000)	Termination	Termination	Officer failed to comply with orders on five separate occasions in eight months, associated with a person reasonably believed to be a criminal, and failed to properly safeguard his weapon.
Pinkney v. Civil Service Commission, 688 A.2d 1252 (Pa. Cmwlth. 1997)	Termination	Termination	Corrections officer refused to obey direct order to divulge the name of an inmate informant who provided information about prison gangs.
Port Authority of New York and New Jersey, LAIG 5076 (Nicolau, 1995)	10-Day Suspension	10-Day Suspension	Officer refused direct order to process suspect who had been arrested during previous shift; officer incorrectly believed that there was no probable cause for the arrest.
Richardson v. Board of Supervisors, 250 Cal. Rptr. 1 (1988)	Termination	Reinstatement	Insubordination provoked by attitude of supervisor.
Sambo v. City of Mitchell, 427 N.W.2d 379 (S.D. 1988)	Termination	Reinstatement	Direct refusal to obey order; employer relied on prior discipline outside of purging period.
Sickler v. Town of Hunter, 769 N.Y.S.2d 662 (N.Y. A.D. 2004)	Termination	60-Day Suspension	Police officer failed to comply with Chief's instructions to submit four written incident reports by a specific time. Officer had no discipline in prior 25 years of service.

CASE NAME	INITIAL SANCTION	RESULT ON APPEAL	DESCRIPTION
Town of Hooksett, LAIG 6481 (Daly, 2006)	1-Day Suspension	1-Day Suspension	After Chief issued memo directing officers not to leave their vehicles idling, a sergeant gave a direct order to an officer to leave his car's engine running whenever his emergency lights were flashing. The officer's refusal to comply with the sergeant's order was not justified by reliance on the Chief's previous directive. Officer should have obeyed the order and then filed a report questioning the order.
White v. Municipal Fire and Police Civil Service Board of the City of Shreveport, 882 So.2d 1217 (La. App. 2004)	Termination	Reinstatement With Back Pay	Officer terminated for taking newer (but still used) badge cover from desk in area containing used equipment, where Department intended that new badge covers be given to new recruits. Officers were welcome to take badge covers from the desk without accountability, and there was no indication that the officer was ever told that the particular badge cover she took was one that had been earmarked for a new recruit.
Yanis v. McGuire, 469 N.Y.S.2d 736 (A.D. 1983)	6-Day Suspension	6-Day Suspension	Failure to act as interpreter when ordered to do so.

Job Performance

CASE NAME	INITIAL SANCTION	RESULT ON APPEAL	DESCRIPTION
City of Terrell, Texas, LAIG 6239 (Fox, 2005)	3-Day Suspension	No Discipline	Officer issued three-day suspension when an assault rifle he had confiscated from a suspect discharged through the ceiling and roof of the police dispatch center. Suspension overturned because it was not issued by the "Department head," as specifically required by state law.
Lewis County, Washington, 03-2 ARB ¶3491 (CCH)(Abels, 2003)	10-Day Suspension	No Discipline	Employee suspended for five separate instances of misconduct, including showing up late for work, receiving personal phone calls, failing to do a security check, and routinely going to the front office to fill her water bottle and say hello to the staff after arriving at work. Arbitrator concluded investigation not fair since complainant was not contacted, that the employee was not given adequate notice that her conduct would lead to discipline, and that other employees had engaged in similar conduct without being disciplined.

Military Service

CASE NAME	INITIAL SANCTION	RESULT ON APPEAL	DESCRIPTION
City of West Haven, PEB ¶45,151 (CCH, 1979)	6-Day Suspension	Reinstatement	Enlistment in National Guard contrary to Department's rules.

CASE NAME	INITIAL SANCTION	RESULT ON APPEAL	DESCRIPTION
Reopplle v. Massachusetts, 133 LRRM 2055 (D. Mass. 1989)	30-Day Suspension	Reinstatement	Enlistment in army reserve unit contrary to Department's rules.

Misconduct of Fellow Employees

CASE NAME	INITIAL SANCTION	RESULT ON APPEAL	DESCRIPTION
City of Austin, Texas, LAIG 5338 (Greer, 1997)	Indefinite Suspension	45-Day Suspension	Police officer did not report that fellow officer working off-duty job at music festival received a portion of stolen gate proceeds. Officer received none of the stolen money and had no supervisory responsibilities over second officer. At least one other officer knew of the incident, did not report it, and was not disciplined.
State of Delaware, LAIG 5617 (Light, 1999)	30-Day Suspension	No Discipline	Corrections officer suspended for failing to report the abuse of an inmate by other corrections officers. Arbitrator concluded that employer failed to meet burden of proving that officer was present at the incident. Log books did not note the officer's attendance, and the main witness against the officer was a convicted rapist. Arbitrator commented that "there is a real difference between belief and proof, and the leap from the former to the latter is impermissible unless linked by competent evidence."
City of Owosso, 115 LA 971 (Goodstein, 2001)	Termination	Reinstatement With Back Pay	Officer fired for not stopping another officer from using excessive force against prisoners. Arbitrator concluded officer's responsibilities under the circumstances would have been to report to supervisor and not to intervene. In fact, officer (and another arbitrator) did not believe that excess force had been used.

Neglect of Duty

CASE NAME	INITIAL SANCTION	RESULT ON APPEAL	DESCRIPTION
Bruggemand v. State Civil Service Commission, 4 NPER 12:8 (April, 2001)	5-day Suspension	5-day Suspension	Corrections officers neglected to appropriately conduct inmate count, failing to discover an inmate's escape. Evidence showed that officers were properly trained by their employer to "see flesh" during inmate counts, and not merely rely on seeing hair sticking out from under blankets.
Christian County, Illinois, Sheriff's Department, 2001 WL 738480 (Winton, 2001)	Termination	Reinstatement Without Back Pay	Corrections officer repeatedly failed to complete required cell checks. Employer erroneously believed that officer was a probationary employee not entitled to union representation and denied the employee representation at a disciplinary hearing.

CASE NAME	INITIAL SANCTION	RESULT ON APPEAL	DESCRIPTION
City of Chicago, PEB ¶49,017 (CCH, 1985)	Suspension	Reinstatement	Failure of canine officer to control dog which bit seven-year-old boy.
City of Cincinnati, LAIG 5225 (Florman, 1996)	2-Day Suspension	2-Day Suspension	Four-year police officer failed to attend assigned firearms training, choosing to fill out paperwork instead. Officer had history of not obeying orders, and did not consult superiors as to whether attending training or completing paperwork had higher priority.
City of Hialeah, 121 LA 745 (Hoffman, 2005)	40-Hour Suspension	No Discipline	Officer failed to respond to pages, and did not respond during hurricane. Officer called Department as soon as he realized his pager was defective and that there was a possible emergency, though by that time the emergency had ended. Employer did not discipline similarly-situated sergeant.
City of Houston, LAIG 5257 (Greer, 1996)	4-Day Suspension	2-Day Suspension	While working off-duty, two officers broke up a domestic altercation, but did not arrest either combatant and did not file an incident report. Arbitrator concluded that officers had no reason to believe that woman combatant was injured, and thus were not obligated to make an arrest. Discipline partially upheld for failing to write incident report and failing to obtain off-duty work permits.
City of Inkster, Michigan, LAIG 6591 (Glendon, 2008)	Termination	Reinstatement With Back Pay	Officer terminated for various acts of neglect of duty, including an ongoing failure to abide by Department's rules. Arbitrator concluded employer failed to establish the underlying policies which the officer was alleged to have violated, and the employer did not prove that the officer's conduct had gotten steadily worse.
City of Miami Beach, 98-1 ARB ¶5160 (Kravit, 1998)	Transfer To Uniform Patrol	Reinstatement With Back Pay	Detective alleged to spend inappropriate amount of time at vacant house. City did not accord officer disciplinary hearing called for in Department's manual.
City of Opa-Locka, LAIG 5273 (Humphries, 1997)	Termination	Reinstatement	Officer disciplined for taking more than 30 minutes to respond to a call involving threats to an unarmed City employee during the performance of his duties. Officer advised dispatcher of location waiting to fuel vehicle at pump and dispatcher held call. Arbitrator found common practice of holding calls, and numerous similar incidents of holding such calls had gone undisciplined.

CASE NAME	INITIAL SANCTION	RESULT ON APPEAL	DESCRIPTION
City of Philadelphia, LAIG 4413 (Price, 1990)	5-Day Suspension	Reinstatement	Decision to transport intoxicated citizen (who later died) to station rather than to hospital; employer unable to define word "semiconscious" in own rules.
City of Reading, LAIG 5360 (DiLauro, 1998)	2-Day Suspension	Oral Warning	En route to the scene of domestic violence call as back up, officer stopped to check out an unrelated stop of a motorist. Though officer took only four minutes in all to respond to call, primary officer was injured by suspect. Case decided on progressive discipline grounds and on officer's minor deviation from policy.
City of Reno, 93 LA 19 (1989)	1-Day Suspension	Reinstatement	Failure to incarcerate intoxicated woman, who was later raped; employer's rules gave officer discretion in incarcerating or releasing intoxicated individuals.
City of Sumner, Washington, 115 LA 580 (Calhoun, 2001)	2-Day And 4-Day Suspensions	No Discipline	Officers did not respond to fellow officer's radio call that he was investigating "suspicious activity." Department failed to discipline sergeant who was also in the area and failed to respond. Additionally, officers were involved in a prolonged visit with their lieutenant, who was working part-time at an automobile dealership and who permitted lengthy visits from on-duty officers.
Cuyahoga Co. Sheriff's Dept. v. Ohio Patrolmen's Benevolent Assn., 2006 WL 3095684 (Ohio App. 2006)	5-Day Suspension	2-Day Suspension	Corrections officer left post without permission. Arbitrator concluded that employer invoked the wrong rule in disciplining the officer.
Gladwin County, 25 LAIS 2009 (Brown, 1997)	1-Day Suspension	1-Day Suspension	Detective left 9mm handgun on the seat of an unlocked four-wheel drive vehicle. Arbitrator based his decision on the fact that detective was the Department's firearms instructor.
Hong v. Brown, 577 N.Y.S.2d 817 (A.D. 1992)	30-Day Suspension	30-Day Suspension	Off-duty officer in a bar failed to call 911 when a patron who left the premises was shot outside. Officer did nothing to aid the victim, and failed to assist arriving officers in their investigation.

CASE NAME	INITIAL SANCTION	RESULT ON APPEAL	DESCRIPTION
Jefferson County Sheriff's Department, 117 LA 732 (Duff, 2002)	Demotion From Deputy To Corrections Officer	Demotion From Deputy To Corrections Officer	Deputy assigned to court security spent inappropriate amount of time chatting with girlfriends while off his post and was not courteous enough with elderly visitors. Arbitrator concluded "recreational activities indulged in while being paid to work are highly improper."
Kaminsky v. Board of Fire & Police Commissioners, 559 N.E.2d 87 (Ill. 1990)	Termination	30-Day Suspension	Officer failed to respond as backup, spent 68 and 77 minutes on half-hour lunch, and failed to respond to fire.
Launius v. Des Plaines Fire & Police Comm'n., 603 N.E.2d 477 (Ill. 1992)	Termination	Termination	Officer left work during emergency to respond to wife's call about flooding in basement.
Montgomery Co. Sheriff's Office and FOP, LAIG 6459 (Dell, 2007)	Demotion	Reinstatement Without Back Pay	Transportation deputy demoted to position of corrections officer for allegedly failing to supervise inmates in community service program. Arbitrator concluded that the "overwhelming and undisputed testimony is that it is almost impossible to watch all of the inmates on these low-risk inmate work programs all of the time." Grievant did not request back pay.
Rouse v. Brown, 575 N.Y.S.2d 57 (A.D. 1991)	Termination	Termination	In homicide case, officer failed to question witnesses at the scene or otherwise investigate incident, failed to secure murder weapon, and led supervisors to believe another precinct was handling case. Officer had substantial prior disciplinary record.

Obesity

CASE NAME	INITIAL SANCTION	RESULT ON APPEAL	DESCRIPTION
City of Richland, (Axon, 1988)	Indefinite Suspension	Reinstatement	Officer failed to comply with order to lose 50 pounds in six months.
Smaw v. Virginia State Police, 862 F. Supp. 1469 (N.D. Va. 1994)	Demotion	Demotion	Female dispatcher did not comply with hiring requirement that she lose three pounds per month; decided on handicap discrimination basis.

Off-Duty Conduct

CASE NAME	INITIAL SANCTION	RESULT ON APPEAL	DESCRIPTION
Township of Jackson, Ohio, 112 LA 811 (Graham, 1999)	2-Day Suspension	No Discipline	Officer involved in off-duty altercation while participating in softball game. Arbitrator concluded that officer was not the antagonist, tried to avoid the altercation, and that no adverse impact on the Department was established.

CASE NAME	INITIAL SANCTION	RESULT ON APPEAL	DESCRIPTION
Off-Duty Employment			
Borlin v. Civil Service Comm. of Council Bluffs, 338 N.W.2d 146 (Iowa 1983)	Termination	Termination	Violation of ban on all second jobs by engaging in business of voice stress analysis.
City of Laredo, LAIG 6309 (Moore, 2005)	30-Day Suspension	No Discipline	Officer charged with working off duty without permission. Employer failed to comply with provision of local government code that required specific notice be given of appeal rights when discipline is issued.
City of Lubbock, 125 LA 454 (Moore, 2008)	Indefinite Suspension	No Discipline	Officer on long-term medical leave engaged in secondary employment without permission. Employer failed to follow state law requiring officer to be given a signed complaint at the time of the incident.
City of Marshall, Texas, LAIG 5621 (Hayes, 2000)	10-Day Suspension	5-Day Suspension	Officer received payment for off-duty detail which he did not work. Arbitrator found "there appeared to be no clear pattern between a particular departmental rule violation and the discipline imposed," and held that "justness required a more moderate punishment."
Dalton v. Russelville, 720 S.W.2d 918 (Ark. 1986)	Termination	Termination	Work as private detective without permission.
Hatzgionidis v. Department of Police, 580 So.2d 471 (La. App. 1991)	Termination	Reinstatement	While on limited duty, worked as security guard in drug store. Employer did not establish "impairment of the efficiency of the service."
Lawrence County Sheriff, 125 LA 304 (Harlan, 2008)	8-Day Suspension	Written Warning	Deputy working in off-duty job at grocery pursued customer who drove off without paying. Customer subsequently rammed deputy's car and deputy fired three shots into the customer's vehicle. Though employer's policy prohibited off-duty arrests for misdemeanors, in light of the customer's erratic behavior, deputy acted out of legitimate concern for public safety rather than in response to the theft.
Roper v. Versailles, 436 A.2d 1058 (Pa. Cmwlth. 1981)	Termination	Termination	Work as part-time police officer for another jurisdiction.
Rudnick v. City of Jamestown, 463 N.W.2d 632 (N.D. 1990)	Demotion	Demotion	Sergeant engaged in snow removal business while on duty; carried portable radio.

CASE NAME	INITIAL SANCTION	RESULT ON APPEAL	DESCRIPTION
Shields v. City of Shreveport, 565 So.2d 473 (La. App. 1990)	Termination	Termination	Drinking while in uniform while working as off-duty private security at a party.
Siwek v. Police Board of the City of Chicago, 872 N.E.2d 87 (Ill. App. 2007)	Termination	Termination	Officer on paid medical disability due to back and foot injuries worked as a security guard while on disability. While on disability, officer presented employer with numerous doctor slips indicating she could not work.
Viator v. City of New Iberia, 428 So.2d 1329 (La. App. 1983)	Termination	Termination	Engaging in second business of collecting bad checks while in uniform.

Overtime Abuse

CASE NAME	INITIAL SANCTION	RESULT ON APPEAL	DESCRIPTION
City of Hialeah and Dade County Police Benevolent Ass'n, 4:1 NPER 5 (Wolfson, 2000)	Suspension	Reinstatement	Police officer shopped on duty during an overtime holiday task force assignment. Arbitrator concluded that officer's shopping was consistent with aims of task force to "maintain a high profile to deter holiday-type crime."
City of Newark, 122 LA 242 (Smith, 2006)	Counseling	No Discipline	Employer counseled officer that his submission of overtime slip for a doctor's visit should not have been made to his precinct but instead to medical services department. Counseling constituted grievable discipline since the counseling advised officer that he would be charged with disobedience to orders if he committed the same offense again. Arbitrator concluded that officer substantially complied with City's overtime submission policy.

Performance Of Duty

CASE NAME	INITIAL SANCTION	RESULT ON APPEAL	DESCRIPTION
Chippewa County, No. 59586 (Houlihan, Wis. ERC 2002)	3-Week Suspension	Written Reprimand	Failure to follow arrest procedures, and making an arrest without probable cause. Suspension held too severe given deputy's unblemished ten-year career, and County failed to follow contract's requirement to issue discipline within 30 days of the complaint.
City of Atlantic Beach, 121 LA 105 (Hoffman, 2005)	Termination	Reinstatement With Back Pay	Officer discharged for making improper warrantless entry of house of individual who was suspected of domestic violence. Employer did not interview occupants of house or any witnesses besides sergeant who was with grievant, and did not call sergeant (who ordered grievant to enter the house) as a witness in arbitration hearing.

CASE NAME	INITIAL SANCTION	RESULT ON APPEAL	DESCRIPTION
City of DeSoto, Texas, LAIG 6343 (Fragnoli, 2006)	Termination	Reinstatement With Full Back Pay	Sixteen-year officer terminated for making an unlawful arrest. Arbitrator noted a "general disagreement" among witnesses as to whether the arrest was justified, and the City had never before terminated an officer because of a false arrest.
City of Portland, (Truesdale, 2006)(Unreported decision; copies available from LRIS).	900-Hour Suspension	No Discipline	Officer disciplined for inappropriate tactics leading up to use of deadly force that resulted in death of unarmed African-American woman. Arbitrator concluded that officer's tactics were within the scope of his training, and that the City's failure to conduct an internal affairs investigation was a "rush to judgment" that deprived it of adequate factual basis for its decision-making.
City of Portland, Maine, LAIG 6206 (Irvings, 2005)	Transfer	Reversal Of Transfer	Because transfer was "personally-focused response to the conclusion that a lieutenant was unable to meet performance standards," it was disciplinary in nature and required just cause. Fact that lieutenant lost no pay in transfer did not change disciplinary nature of transfer.
City of Raymond, Washington, 121 LA 1168 (Romero, 2005)	Termination	Written Reprimand	Officer discharged for failing to submit evidence to a laboratory, failing to execute a search warrant for four days, and failing to acquire a witness statement. Employer's investigation failed to notify officer of the charges, an unfair pre-disciplinary hearing was conducted, and the employer wrongly failed to make an effort to determine both inculpatory and exculpatory facts.
City of Vallejo, California, 121 LA 1659 (Silver, 2005)	Termination	Termination	Eighteen-year officer with two prior suspensions on record was involved in three performance incidents: (1) Failure to call an interpreter in an altercation involving Spanish-speaking civilian and English-speaking civilian; (2) taking 18½ minutes to make a 2½ minute drive to another incident; and (3) failing to conduct a thorough investigation of a stolen car incident. Arbitrator concluded that officers' "work habits fluctuate from year to year without any particular consistency."
Clermont County Sheriff, 125 LA 592 (Bordone, 2008)	60-Day Suspension	No Discipline	Corrections officer allegedly lost his temper and struck a security camera. Discipline was impermissibly based on prior discipline for lack of control of temper. Prior discipline was more than two years old, was followed by training and counseling, and there was no direct evidence that the officer struck the camera out of anger.

CASE NAME	INITIAL SANCTION	RESULT ON APPEAL	DESCRIPTION
Milwaukee Deputy Sheriffs Association, Case 533 (Wis. ERC 2004)	5-Day Suspension	Written Reprimand	Prisoner escaped after slipping out of a handcuff used to secure her to a chair while in court. The disciplined deputy, who had loosened the handcuff in response to the prisoner's complaint of discomfort, had not been told by another deputy on the scene that sometime earlier the prisoner had previously slipped out of the handcuff. Decided on disparate treatment basis and because of Arbitrator's doubts about enforceability of employer's rule that deputies keep their eyes on their prisoners at all times.
Montgomery County Sheriff's Office, LAIG 6139 (Bell, 2004)	5-Day Suspension	5-Day Suspension	Employee failed to follow proper "lockdown" procedures and left three doors unlocked in correctional facility. Applying "clear and convincing" burden of proof, Arbitrator concluded that circumstantial evidence established that locking the doors was the employee's responsibility.
State of Montana, 122 LA 923 (Calhoun, 2006)	3-Day Suspension	No Discipline	Employer failed to interview employee suspended for failure to perform duties, and based disciplinary decision on reports from supervisors who did not speak to employee.
State of Ohio, 122 LA 897 (Graham, 2006)	10-Day Suspension	No Discipline	Detective disciplined for providing erroneous name of suspect, resulting in negative publicity of incorrect arrest and subsequent civil damages of $50,000. Detective had reasonable belief that he had provided the correct name, and some corroborating evidence supported the detective's belief.
Town of Salem, New Hampshire, LAIG 6322 (Altman, 2006)	Termination	3-Month Suspension	Sergeant with 19 years of service left work on three different occasions during the midnight shift (when he was the only supervisor on duty) to visit his girlfriend's house for several hours. Punishment mitigated based on disparate treatment of similarly-situated employees, and Arbitrator concluded that "at worst, the sergeant was guilty of committing an error of judgment."

CASE NAME	INITIAL SANCTION	RESULT ON APPEAL	DESCRIPTION
Town of Tyngsborough, LAIG 6391 (Brown, 2006)	Written Reprimand	No Discipline	Officer issued reprimand for failing to submit a report concerning the issuance of speeding ticket in the parking lot of a bar and his status as a witness to the bar owner's delivery of a no trespass order to the driver. Fact that employer issued order reminding employees to write reports under such circumstances after discipline had been imposed implied that inadequate notice of rules was given by the employer.
Village of Twin Lakes, Wis. PERC No. 65248 (Gallagher, 2006)	Written Reprimand	No Discipline	Officer reprimanded for serving an arrest warrant at an inconvenient (for the suspect) time of day. Arbitrator concluded that officers in the past had served similar warrants at all times of the day and night without being disciplined.
Physical/Emotional Condition			
Borough of East Comemaugh, Pennsylvania, 121 LA 1693 (Frankiewicz, 2005)	Termination	Reinstatement With Back Pay	Police officer discharged for being unable to perform his duties for medical reasons. Contract allowed employer to terminate after two-year period of layoff or failure to work, and officer was willing to submit to independent medical examination.
Childress v. Dept. of Police, 487 So.2d 590 (La. App. 1986)	Termination	Reinstatement	On-the-job injuries, including being shot, ejected through window of car after chase, and having ear almost severed; officer fired when doctor recommended one month's therapy before return to work.
City of Allentown, 100 LA 592 (DiLauro, 1992)	Termination	Reinstatement Without Back Pay	Psychologist diagnosed officer as exhibiting "strong anti-social behavior and a level of depression, agitation, and rage posing a threat to the safety of himself and others." Officer had seen psychologist through employee assistance program.
Detroit Transportation Corp., LAIG 4781 (Glazer, 1993)	Termination	Reinstatement	Psychiatrist for officer who was victim of sexual harassment recommended extension of leave of absence for six to eight weeks. Employer relied on earlier evaluation by its own doctor in ordering officer to report for work immediately.
In re Del Valle, 2007 WL 412827 (N.J. Sup. A.D. 2007)	Termination	Termination	Psychologist diagnosed officer as suffering from depression, anxiety, alcohol dependence, and delusional thinking, concluding that the officer was unable to "benefit from alcohol abuse therapy because of his declination to use medications."

CASE NAME	INITIAL SANCTION	RESULT ON APPEAL	DESCRIPTION
Morgan County Sheriff, 98 LA 975 (Cohen, 1992)	5-Day Suspension	No Discipline	Officer ordered to give medical release for psychological history wrote "signed under duress" on release; officer did not refuse to comply with request for independent psychological examination.
Norman v. Board of Fire and Police Commissioners, 614 N.E.2d 499 (Ill. App. 1993)	Termination	Reinstatement	Unexcused absence from work; officer had received advice from doctor that he was unable to return to work after on-duty injury.
Town of Harwich, 116 LA 1461 (Alleyne, 2002)	Termination	Reinstatement	Town discharged officer with back injury for refusing to return to work after one medical panel determined she was fit for duty, and Town and labor organization had not completed bargaining over relationship between job-related injuries and light-duty work.

Political Activities

CASE NAME	INITIAL SANCTION	RESULT ON APPEAL	DESCRIPTION
Eau Claire County, LAIG 4228 (1989)	5-Day Suspension	5-Day Suspension	Deputy assigned to remove all roadside political signs removed only signs belonging to Republican candidates.

Polygraph Examination

CASE NAME	INITIAL SANCTION	RESULT ON APPEAL	DESCRIPTION
Kelley v. Sheriff's Merit Commission of Kane County, 866 N.E.2d 702 (Ill. App. 2007)	120-Day Suspension	Reinstatement With Back Pay	Even though state legislature did not exempt corrections officers from polygraph examinations as it did police officers, polygraphs not reliable enough to base any disciplinary decision upon. Corrections officer could not be disciplined for insubordination for refusing to take a polygraph examination.

Productivity/Performance/Rules Violations

CASE NAME	INITIAL SANCTION	RESULT ON APPEAL	DESCRIPTION
Bureau of Special Investigation v. Coalition of Public Safety, 722 N.E.2d 441 (Mass. 2000)	Termination	3-Month Suspension	Investigator accessed confidential tax records for inappropriate purposes. Actions of investigator violated state law.
City of Benton Harbor, 103 LA 817 (Allen, 1994)	Termination	5-Day Suspension	City "bunched" nine disciplinary charges including driving while intoxicated, speeding, and mooning the police station; progressive discipline not followed.
City of Fort Lauderdale, PEB ¶49,205 (CCH, 1988)	15-Day Suspension	14-Day Suspension	Firing five shots at an undercover officer who should have been recognized.

CASE NAME	INITIAL SANCTION	RESULT ON APPEAL	DESCRIPTION
City of San Antonio, LAIG 4349 (Massey, 1990)	1-Day Suspension	No Discipline	Officer failed to notify radio he was making stop while en route to stolen car call; other officers not disciplined for same conduct.
Clisham v. Board of Police, 613 A.2d 254 (Conn. 1992)	Termination	Reinstatement	Termination of Chief reversed because member of hearing board made public statements in support of Chief's discharge prior to hearing.
Dept. of Public Safety v. Mayfield, 563 So.2d 1230 (La. App. 1990)	Termination	Reinstatement	Failure to separate two fighting inmates, one of whom later stabbed the other; Department failed to provide employee with training where separation of inmates was taught.
North Carolina Department of Corrections v. McNeely, 3 NPER 10:16 (N.C. App. 2000)	Termination	Termination	Corrections officer left control room post without being relieved. Officer was standing in a corridor adjacent to the control room, smoking a cigarette and reading a novel.
Putnam County Sheriff's Department, 92-2 ARB ¶6306 (Nelson, 1996)	Demotion	Demotion	Demotion from deputy sheriff to corrections officer. Deputy failed to sign out of service for meal periods, disobeyed an order not to visit a friend during work hours, and appeared on television to criticize the Department's pending discipline against him. Deputy had been progressively disciplined, including receiving a seven-day suspension two months before his demotion.
Valley Township, 13 NPER PA-22046 (Pa. LRB Hearing Examiner 1990)	Termination	Reinstatement	Termination of 18-year and 6-month officers for tardiness reversed on grounds of anti-union bias; one officer had previously received written reprimand for same incident.

Racially, Sexually and Religiously Directed Conduct

CASE NAME	INITIAL SANCTION	RESULT ON APPEAL	DESCRIPTION
Blase v. Washington Dept. of Corrections, 6 Wash. LLD 2 (1996)	Termination	Termination	Corrections lieutenant videotaped a "look alike" contest aimed at a corrections officer who named him as a respondent in a successful suit, joked about shooting her if she were a hostage, placed gift-wrapped manure in her Christmas stocking, called her a "c---," had intercourse with a female subordinate while on duty, and allowed the main control booth door to be blocked open.
Bureau of Maine State Police, 568 N.E.2d 1363 (Me. 1989)	Termination	Reinstatement	Sergeant fired for having sex with informant during investigation. When sergeant filed grievance challenging termination, lieutenant granted the grievance. Lieutenant's grant of grievance subsequently upheld in arbitration and in court.

CASE NAME	INITIAL SANCTION	RESULT ON APPEAL	DESCRIPTION
City of Ada, Oklahoma, 27 LAIS 2006 (1999)	Demotion	Reinstatement With Back Pay	Demotion of sergeant to police officer for allegedly sexually harassing female dispatcher by walking past her and snapping her bra strap. Department's Board of Inquiry recommended a reprimand. Arbitrator concluded that single incident did not create an "intimidating, offensive or hostile work environment" and did not constitute sexual harassment.
City of Ansonia, 100 LA 123 (Stewart, 1992)	Non-Removable Written Reprimand	Removable Written Reprimand	Black officer reported location by saying "I am in the first jungle" in reference to a housing complex. Officer did not intend racial connotation to remark.
City of East Providence v. McLaughlin, 593 A.2d 1345 (R.I. 1991)	Demotion And 6-Month Suspension	No Discipline	Use of racially-oriented language in undercover operation; language was type which could be expected to be used to successfully negotiate drug buys. Inappropriate use of language could have been handled by verbal reprimand.
City of Fort Worth, Texas, 99-2 ARB Para. 3141 (Jennings, 1999)	2-Day Suspension	Written Reprimand	African-American police officer used the term "boy" to his African-American suspect. Applying principles of progressive discipline, Arbitrator reduced suspension, commenting that the officer was attempting to serve as a "peacemaker" in a dispute.
City of Killeen, Texas, 26 LAIS 3193 (Greer, 1999)	Termination	15-Day Suspension	Nineteen-year police officer called fellow officer a "faggot" and commented that the officer preferred a smaller gun because it would be easier to "stick it in." Employer had not punished employees committing similar offenses as harshly (or at all), and assigned a hostile sergeant to investigate the incident.
City of Palm Beach Gardens, 117 LA 929 (Abrams, 2002)	10-Day Suspension	No Discipline	Officer accused of making racial slurs against Haitians. City did not transcribe internal affairs interview, as required by statewide bill of rights. Officer testified he provided exculpatory account during interview, and other witnesses to the incident were not credible.
City of Philadelphia, Pennsylvania, LAIG 5647 (Jaffe, 2000)	48-Hour Suspension	No Discipline	Paramedic allegedly insulted a male transvestite by referring to him as "Honey," and questioning his gender during a trip to the hospital. Arbitrator found no intent to belittle or embarrass patient and that the paramedic's language, while not politically correct, was not rude or insulting. Arbitrator relied on paramedic's history of having transported a number of AIDS patients without showing that he treated gay persons and/or transvestites rudely.

CASE NAME	INITIAL SANCTION	RESULT ON APPEAL	DESCRIPTION
City of Stephenville, LAIG 4777 (Hughes, 1993)	1-Day Suspension	1-Day Suspension	Sergeant described officer he suspected of using sick leave as a "f---ing bitch."
City of Youngstown, 19 NPER OH-27448 (Ohio App. 1996)	Termination	Termination	Police officer broadcast music and shouted racial epithets from his police car before dawn.
County of Ramsey, 114 LA 993 (Neigh, 2000)	2-Day Suspension	2-Day Suspension	Corrections officer distributed a newsletter to 11 individuals entitled "Where Are The Balls" with a theme that women are inferior to men. The newsletter listed the officer as the editor, and was eventually widely distributed within the correctional facility.
East Bay Region Parks District, Published in *Labor Beat,* June, 1997 by Carroll, Burdick & McDonough.	Termination	4-Week Suspension	Officer asked three dispatchers out for dates; officer used his patrol car and emergency lights to stop one of the dispatchers at night to ask her out. Arbitrator concluded that while conduct did not amount to sexual harassment, officer's use of the emergency equipment to stop dispatcher showed extremely poor judgment.
Jurgens v. City of North Pole, 153 P.3d 321 (Alaska 2007)	Termination	Termination	Sergeant made several personal phone calls to dispatchers, both while sober and while under the influence, while they were working and at home. Sergeant stopped the dispatchers in his patrol unit, verbally compared the dispatchers' breasts and body parts, and described how he wanted to have sex with them.
Knight v. Department of Police, 619 So.2d 1116 (La. App. 1993)	Termination	Reinstatement	In telephone conversation with desk officer, captain used racially derogatory term to describe black female officer. Though comments may have been racially oriented, captain did not discriminate in his treatment of officer.
Macoupin County, Illinois, 120 LA 1308 (Klauss, 2005)	Termination	Reinstatement With Back Pay	Corrections officer discharged for describing fellow officer with a German background and "kraut lips," and for sleeping on the job. Arbitrator concluded that "kraut lips" is not an ethnic slur, but simply was "boorish, stupid, and childish," reciting the dictionary definition of "kraut" as referring to "a thinly sliced, compressed and fermented cabbage." The sleeping charge not sustained where testimony of witnesses was vague and based on brief observations, and one instance was not credible where witness claimed to see grievant sleeping every day on hundreds of occasions, which no one else saw.

CASE NAME	INITIAL SANCTION	RESULT ON APPEAL	DESCRIPTION
Orange County, New York, LAIG 5050 (Simons, 1994)	Termination	Termination	Corrections officer lit a cross fashioned from broom handle and presented it to black employee. Defense that officer did not understand significance of burning cross rejected.
Stark County Sheriff and Fraternal Order of Police, 9602 ARB 6215 (Heekin, 1996)	Termination	Termination	Corrections officer made crude comments to female coworkers, grabbing one in the crotch, and threatened, intimidated and coerced several other coworkers. Defense that employer had no sexual harassment policy rejected because of extreme nature of conduct.
State ex rel Rice v. Bishop, 858 S.W.2d 734 (Mo. App. 1993)	5-Day Suspension	5-Day Suspension	Sergeant told female worker with cold that she needed a chest rub; complaint filed by male officer who overheard comment.
State Law Enforcement Bargaining Council and State of Nebraska (Caffera, 2006)	Termination	Reinstatement With Back Pay	Trooper joined Ku Klux Klan, and posted racially-oriented comments on a website. Trooper never acted on his beliefs, either on or off the job, and employer failed to prove that the trooper's comments caused actual disruption in the workplace.
Talmo v. Civil Service, 282 Cal. Rptr. 240 (Cal. App. 1991)	Termination	Termination	Deputy committed batteries on and made racial slurs against a fellow employee, placed a dead gopher in the pocket of a prisoner, and later lied about doing so. Progressive discipline argument rejected by Court.
Willmann v. Nebraska Department of Correctional Services, 2003 WL 21397834 (Neb. App. 2003)	Termination	Termination	Corrections lieutenant frequently discussed with unwilling female subordinate computer sex, his sexual exploits, how lonely he was, and how he and his wife were having difficulties, and sent messages through a third employee that he thought subordinate "has nice tits," "wants to get in your pants," and "has the hots for you."

Radio Procedures

CASE NAME	INITIAL SANCTION	RESULT ON APPEAL	DESCRIPTION
City of Wixom, PEB ¶45,258 (CCH, 1980)	Termination	Termination	Use of CB radio while on duty to solicit women.
Moore v. Borough of Ridley Park, 581 A.2d 711 (Pa. Cmwlth. 1990)	3-Day Suspension	3-Day Suspension	Officer remained out of radio contact for 32 minutes during the graveyard shift.

CASE NAME	INITIAL SANCTION	RESULT ON APPEAL	DESCRIPTION
Residency Rules			
City of Philadelphia, Pennsylvania, 4 NPER 10:12 (February, 2001)	Termination	Termination	Though 17-year police officer held driver's license and voter registration card within the city limits, his true residence was with his family in the suburbs. Employer's evidence was based upon a 39-day surveillance of the officer.
Ferguson v. Board of Police Commissioners, 782 S.W.2d 814 (Mo. App. 1990)	Unspecified Discipline	Discipline Upheld	Officer obtained legal separation to comply with residency rule; was later spotted sleeping, painting, and hanging Christmas lights on wife's house.
Fritzhall v. Board of Police Commissioners, 886 S.W.2d 20 (Mo. App. 1994)	Termination	Termination	Officer evaded residency requirement by using uncle's address while actually living with wife in suburbs.
Tomayko v. Bethel Park Municipality, 687 A.2d 423 (Pa. Cmwlth. 1997)	8-Day Suspension	8-Day Suspension	Officer did not comply with rule requiring residence within five air miles of police station. Court held that lack of intent to violate ordinance and mistake as to actual distance from police station were irrelevant in considering whether officer should be disciplined.
Town of Cicero, 115 LA 8 (Winton, 2000)	Termination	Reinstatement With Back Pay	Officer maintained home with wife outside of town, staying in the basement apartment of relatives for several days during the week. Police Chief told union membership "that he did not care where their families lived, but that officers had to have a place in town to live on days they were working."
Town of Cicero, 115 LA 741 (Nathan, 2001)	Termination	Reinstatement With Back Pay	Officer lived in basement of sister's house in city while co-owning house with estranged wife out of city.
Town of Cicero, 16 LA 1322 (Goldstein, 2002)	Termination	Termination	Cicero police officer filed tax return that listed Chicago house as his place of residence, maintained that he lived in Chicago when applying to become a foster parent, and paid mortgage and utilities on Chicago house. Officer never paid for allegedly living in basement of house in Cicero and purchased none of the furniture in the basement.
Sexual Misconduct			
Barker v. Kattelman, 634 N.E.2d 241 (Ohio App. 1993)	Termination	Termination	"Affair of the heart" with a dispatcher which involved illegal entry into dispatcher's home and illegal access to law enforcement data system to determine owner of car in dispatcher's driveway.

CASE NAME	INITIAL SANCTION	RESULT ON APPEAL	DESCRIPTION
Bexar County Sheriff's Department v. Sanchez, 131 S.W.3d 1 (Tex. App. 2003)	Termination	Termination	Sexual misconduct with inmate.
Borges v. McGuire, 487 N.Y.S.2d 737 (A.D. 1985)	Termination	Reinstatement	Pre-employment posing for adult magazines.
Bowling v. Los Angeles County Civil Service Commission, 93 Fire & Police Reporter 40 (1993)	15-Day Suspension	Termination	Bailiff masturbated in front of one court reporter and repeatedly had sex with another court reporter in the courtroom; Civil Service Commission rejected recommended suspension and imposed termination.
Boyce v. Ward, 551 N.Y.S.2d 7 (A.D. 1990)	Termination	Termination	Off-duty officer used position to solicit oral sex at massage parlor, then when services were denied, damaged walls, doors and light fixtures, and urinated on a table full of food.
Broward County Sheriff's Office, 115 LA 709 (Richard, 2001)	Termination	Termination	Off-duty officer caught in prostitution sting operation. Employer uniformly imposed penalty of discharge in response to similar offenses.
City of Bremerton, Washington, 121 LA 915 (Reeves, 2005)	10-Day Suspension	Oral Reprimand	Officer had a consensual affair with a 19-year old Explorer Scout. Employer did not adequately communicate its non-fraternization policy to employees.
City of Fort Worth, 114 LA 440 (Moore, 2000)	5-Day Suspension	5-Day Suspension	Female police officer falsely accused male officer of kissing her on the neck. Male officer took and passed a polygraph examination and three nearby eye witnesses did not see the encounter.
City of Key West, Florida, 96-2 ARB ¶6304 (Wolfson, 1996)	Demotion	30-Day Suspension	When officer asked captain for shift change to allow her to spend Christmas Eve with family, captain replied that the officer "should have had an abortion." When the same officer requested days off to attend college, captain responded that officer should "bring in knee pads if you want something around here." While conduct warranted discipline, demotion inappropriate because conduct did not demonstrate an inability to perform work of a police captain.

CASE NAME	INITIAL SANCTION	RESULT ON APPEAL	DESCRIPTION
City of Memphis v. Civil service Commission, 216 S.W.3d 311 (Tenn. 2007)	Termination	Termination	After making contact with 17-year-old girl through Internet chat room, officer began an on-line relationship that culminated with girl masturbating on web cam. Officer's acceptance of girl's offer to live with him in exchange for cleaning and laundry services never consummated because of intervention of Department.
City of Mobile v. Trott, 596 So.2d 921 (Ala. App. 1991)	Termination	Termination	Off-duty photography of 19-year-old nude model and improper use of police information system to verify model's age.
City of St. Paul, BMS 93-PA-1650 (Neigh, 1993)	Termination	Reinstatement With Back Pay, Conditioned On Treatment	Off-duty conviction of criminal sexual misconduct involving 14-year-old babysitter, plus criminal charge of harassing and making obscene phone calls to a woman. Mitigating circumstance of officer's own sexual abuse as child, good work record, and lack of likelihood of repetition of events.
City of Port Arthur, Texas, 117 LA 760 (Moore, 2002)	Termination	10-Day Suspension	City failed to prove that off-duty sexual encounter was non-consensual. However, lengthy suspension appropriate because encounter occurred in City park in officer's patrol district, and where officer engaged in littering by throwing used condom on ground after incident.
City of Riverside Police Dept. v. Adler, 2008 WL 2123757 (Cal. App. 2008)	Termination	Reinstatement With Back Pay	Arbitrator reversed termination of officer for child molestation on burden of proof grounds. Department overrode conclusion of its own investigation that the molestation charges could not be proven.
Collier v. Long Beach Civil Service Commission, 2002 WL 31087774 (Cal. App. 2002)	Demotion	Reinstatement Without Back Pay	Charge that sergeant, while on duty, started and maintained an inappropriate personal relationship with a minor and allegation that sergeant engaged in sexual misconduct. Court concluded that minor was an individual "given to extremely capricious and erratic behavior," and that evidence supported the conclusion that the sergeant was doing his job and not conducting an inappropriate personal relationship.
Cook v. South Carolina Department of Highways, 420 S.E.2d 847 (S.C. 1992)	Termination	Termination	Married officer had an affair with a married woman; Court emphasized that affair occurred in a small community.

CASE NAME	INITIAL SANCTION	RESULT ON APPEAL	DESCRIPTION
County of Santa Clara, 106 LA 1092 (Levy, 1996)	30-Day Suspension	No Discipline	Two male corrections officers were alleged to have positioned themselves to look at a female inmate during a strip search. Physical evidence and testimony of female corrections officer did not establish by clear and convincing evidence that male officers had acted inappropriately.
County of Shasta, California, 120 LA 377 (Pool, 2004)	Termination	Reinstatement	"Brief sexual act" between on-duty deputy and civilian ride-along. Arbitrator disregarded testimony from local DA that District Attorney's office could not work with deputy in the future, and instead relied on testimony from Sheriff's Department employees that deputy could continue to function in job. Arbitrator ordered make-whole remedy, but remanded case to parties to agree upon an appropriate remedy.
Fabio v. Civil Service Commission, 414 A.2d 82 (Pa. 1980)	Termination	Termination	Officer encouraged wife to have affair with another officer; officer himself had affair with wife's 18-year-old sister.
Fugate v. Civil Service, 791 F.2d 736 (9th Cir. 1986)	Termination	Termination	On-the-job sexual relations with prostitutes.
Hamilton v. City of Mesa, 916 P.2d 1136 (Ariz. App. 1995)	Termination	Termination	Police officer had affair with subordinate's wife.
Hopkins v. San Diego Port District, 2002 WL 1824964 (Cal. App. 2002)	Termination	Termination	After responding to a disturbance at a restaurant between a highly intoxicated, emotionally upset woman and her boyfriend, officer checked woman into her own hotel room to separate the warring parties. Officer later returned to the hotel room and had sex with the woman.
Hess v. Bennett, 554 S.W.2d 503 (Mo. App. 1977)	Termination	Termination	Eight officers had on-duty and off-duty affair with young woman.
Jackson v. Howell, 577 F. Supp 47 (W.D. Mich. 1983)	15-Day Suspension	15-Day Suspension	Sexual relationship with criminal complainant begun during investigation of complaint.
Jefferson County, Ohio, 114 LA 1508 (Klein, 2000)	Termination	Reinstatement With Back Pay	Corrections officer accused of sexual misconduct with female inmates. Since case involved potential crime, Arbitrator applied burden of proof beyond reasonable doubt. Arbitrator rejected polygraph examiner's testimony in part because examination was not recorded.

CASE NAME	INITIAL SANCTION	RESULT ON APPEAL	DESCRIPTION
Jones v. City of Hialeah, 294 So.2d 686 (Fla. App. 1974)	Termination	Termination	Engaging in sex while on duty, and developing obscene photographs at police station.
Kohlmeier v. University of California, Riverside, 2004 WL 1283999 (Cal. App. 2004)	Termination	Termination	Sergeant had an affair with subordinate officer's wife, who was also employed by the same department. Officer's daughter walked in on her mother performing oral sex on sergeant.
Major v. Hampton, 413 F. Supp. 66 (E.D. La. 1976)	Termination	Reinstatement	Renting of apartment with three other males for the purposes of off-duty sexual relationships.
Oliverson v. West Valley City, 875 F. Supp. 1465 (Utah 1995)	30-Day Suspension	30-Day Suspension	Adultery; state statute prohibiting adultery held not to violate right to privacy.
Oregon Department of Corrections, 113 LA 374 (Skratek, 1999)	Termination	30-Day Suspension	Corrections officer was initially untruthful about and failed to report another corrections officer who had indecently exposed himself at work. Employer had failed to punish other offenders as severely for similar past behavior.
Oregon State Police Officers Association, 1 (6) Public Safety Labor News 8 (1993)	Termination	24-Day Suspension	Sex on duty with ride-along; similar acts by management had not been punished by termination.
Owens v. City of Jennings, 454 So.2d 426 (La. App. 1984)	Termination	Reinstatement	Becoming unwed mother.
Pennsylvania State Police v. Pennsylvania State Troopers' Association, 17 NPER PA-26077 (Pa. 1995)	Termination	Reinstatement	So-called "jolly pecker" case, where trooper exposed himself in presence of fellow troopers; Court affirmed Arbitrator's opinion which found trooper's actions did not constitute conduct unbecoming under employer's rules.
Police Officers Labor Council v. City of Wyoming, 2006 WL 2000136 (Mich. App. 2006)	Termination	Termination	Officer contacted 15-year-old boy on the Internet, encouraged him to go to a bar, and stayed with the boy overnight. Officer's defense that he was unaware of the boy's age rejected in light of state law making ignorance of age no defense to charges of criminal sexual misconduct.
Potter v. Murray City, 760 F.2d 1065 (10th Cir. 1985)	Termination	Termination	Practice of polygamy.

CASE NAME	INITIAL SANCTION	RESULT ON APPEAL	DESCRIPTION
Puzick v. City of Colorado Springs, 680 P.2d 1238 (Colo. App. 1984)	30-Day Suspension	30-Day Suspension	Sergeant engaged in affair with probationary police officer.
Shuman v. Philadelphia, 470 F. Supp. 449 (E.D. Pa. 1979)	Termination	Reinstatement	Adultery; decided on right to privacy grounds.
Smith v. City of Jacksonville, 31 GERR 320 (1993)	Termination	Reinstatement Plus $149,500 In Damages	Transsexual lieutenant fired after discovered by another officer trying to change tire dressed in a woman's burgundy, French-cut bikini bathing suit with false breasts; decided on grounds that transsexualism is handicap under Florida's discrimination law.
State ex rel. Laux v. Gallagher, 527 N.W.2d 158 (Minn. App. 1995)	Termination	90-Day Suspension	Conviction of misdemeanor sexual assault on fellow member of National Guard; hearing board took employee's work record and employer's disciplinary history for officers convicted of misdemeanors into account.
Taylor v. Division of State Police, 2004 WL 1368847 (D. Del. 2004)	Termination	Termination	State trooper reportedly asked young women he had stopped for traffic violations to date him, often dismissing the charges if they agreed to do so. Two of the women were 16 years old at the time of the interaction with the trooper. Case decided on grounds of lack of racial discrimination.
Taylor v. New York State Division of State Police, 813 N.Y.S.2d 572 (N.Y. A.D. 2006)	Termination	Termination	State trooper purchased subscriptions to numerous child pornography web sites.
Terrusa v. Los Angeles County Civil Service Commission, 2004 WL 2828936 (Cal. App. 2004)	Termination	Termination	Deputy sheriff engaged in unwanted on-duty sexually-explicit conversation with security guard, and made false "and/or" incomplete statements during internal affairs investigation. Court concluded that deputy's conduct was at a minimum unprofessional, and as the conversation with the security guard lasted 35-40 minutes, "demonstrated a profound lack of judgment."
Tovey v. City of Jacksonville, 808 S.W.2d 740 (Ark. 1991)	10-Day Suspension	30-Day Suspension	Sexual intercourse while on duty; Civil Service Commission increased discipline from ten-day suspension.
Town of Silver City v. Garcia, 857 P.2d 28 (N.M. 1993)	Termination	Reinstatement	Corporal charged with having sex with 17-year old girl while on duty; Arbitrator concluded sexual contact occurred off duty.

CASE NAME	INITIAL SANCTION	RESULT ON APPEAL	DESCRIPTION
Washington State Patrol, 2 (9) Public Safety Labor News 9 (Lankford, 1994)	Termination	Reinstatement Without Back Pay	On- and off-duty affair with Explorer Scout. Employer erroneously believed affair began when Scout was under the age of consent. Fact that trooper was "sex addict" not a basis to further mitigate the punishment.

Sick Leave Abuse

CASE NAME	INITIAL SANCTION	RESULT ON APPEAL	DESCRIPTION
Bruno v. Police Dept., 451 So.2d 1082 (La. App. 1983)	Termination	Termination	Fifteen violations of sick leave policy.
Chattman v. City of Woonsocket, 2003 WL 21018396 (R.I. Super. 2003)	Termination	Termination	Officer missed 117 days of work in one year and 18 days of the first two months of the following year due to alleged ailments. On numerous occasions, officer called in sick for his graveyard shift assignments but attended classes the next morning at a local massage and/or karate school.
City of Auburn Hills, LAIG 4089 (1988)	1-Day Suspension	Reinstatement	Taking promotional examination while on sick leave; abuse not proven.
City of Peabody, LAIG 4236 (Golick, 1989)	5-Day Suspension	Reinstatement	City led officer who had exhausted sick leave to believe he could use vacation time for illness, then disciplined him for doing so.
City of Seven Hills, 100 LA 1080 (Weisheit, 1993)	Placement On Probation	Removal From Probationary Status	Inaccurate written report of another officer's alleged sick leave abuse; placement on probationary status illegal under Ohio law.
City of Solon, 114 LA 321 (Oberdank, 2000)	3-Day Suspension	3-Day Suspension	Over two-year period, officer on rotating shifts only used sick leave when working graveyard. Arbitrator observed that "ill health only seems to have plagued officer when he was supposed to work the graveyard shift."
Cottongim v. Onondaga, 524 N.E.2d 123 (1988)	Termination	Reinstatement	Similarly-situated male employee given only two-day suspension; female employee terminated.
Dobson v. City of Gallatin, 2006 WL 3805659 (M.D. Tenn. 2006)	Termination	Termination	After being suspended for missing court 21 times in two years, officer used sick leave on the same day he participated in physical agility testing in the hiring process for another agency.
Dwyer v. County of Suffolk, 816 N.Y.S.2d 151 (A.D. 2006)	Termination	Termination	After being put on disciplinary probation for sick leave abuse, corrections officer used excessive sick leave days and failed to submit medical information when requested.
Klickitat County Sheriff's Office, 6 Wash. LLD 2 (1996)	15-Day Suspension	15-Day Suspension	Corrections officer used sick leave, reporting he was too incapacitated to perform light-duty work, and then took a secondary job with a city police department.

CASE NAME	INITIAL SANCTION	RESULT ON APPEAL	DESCRIPTION
Krute v. Kelly, 853 N.Y.S.2d 52 (A.D. 2008)	Termination	Termination	Officer left the county and city while on sick leave without approval, exaggerated his illness over a one-year period, and engaged in off-duty employment without permission.
Lugo v. City of Newburgh, 618 N.Y.S.2d 421 (A.D. 1994)	Termination	Termination	Engaging in outside employment contrary to specific orders not to do so; officer had been warned on 20 occasions that he was prohibited from engaging in outside employment because of his excessive use of sick leave.
Miller v. North Little Rock Police Department, 2007 WL 2156404 (E.D. Ark. 2007)	3-Day Suspension	3-Day Suspension	While on sick leave, officer worked in local canine training academy. Officer's defense that ban on secondary employment while on sick leave only applied to security jobs rejected by Court.
Montana Public Employees Association, 04-1 ARB ¶3809 (Richard, 2004)	Termination	Termination	Diabetic correctional officer with marital problems often extended his days off through the use of sick leave, even after repeated counseling and warnings. Arbitrator concluded that "enough is enough."
Stark County, Ohio, 2001 WL 1013730 (Fully, 2001)	30-Day Suspension	No Discipline	Employee disciplined for using sick leave in conjunction with regular days off and vacation. Arbitrator found no pattern for abuse even though 55% of sick days were taken in conjunction with days off and vacation, where the employee's schedule called for 40% of workdays to be adjacent to days off.
Town of Johnston, LAIG 6240 (O'Brien, 2005)	Termination	Termination	For nine years in a row, dispatcher not only used entire 18 days of accrued sick leave, but was forced to go on unpaid leave for other absences. Employer was required to fill in for dispatcher with other employees on overtime basis.
Town of Walpole, LAIG 4395 (Walsh, 1990)	3-Day Suspension	Written Reprimand	Failure to provide doctor's slip as required by contract; first sick leave offense for 13-year officer.

Sleeping on Duty

CASE NAME	INITIAL SANCTION	RESULT ON APPEAL	DESCRIPTION
Brown v. Ward, 559 N.Y.S.2d 512 (A.D. 1990)	15-Day Vacation Forfeiture	15-Day Vacation Forfeiture	Failure to "remain alert" at post, absence from duty at United Nations security post for 10 and 12 minutes at a time.
Massachusetts Bay Transit Authority, LAIG 4295 (Bloodsworth, 1989)	1-Day Suspension	No Discipline	Officer allegedly asleep in car; Arbitrator convinced that radio in car did not work because of dead battery and that officer was "taking five," not sleeping.

CASE NAME	INITIAL SANCTION	RESULT ON APPEAL	DESCRIPTION
Michigan State University, LAIG 4156 (Kanner, 1988)	3-Day Suspension	Reinstatement	Arbitrator accepted defense that officer was meditating.
Moore v. Borough of Ridley Park, 581 A.2d 711 (Pa. Cmwlth. 1990)	3-Day Suspension	3-Day Suspension	Officer remained out of radio contact for 32 minutes while on graveyard shift.
Nebraska Dept. of Correctional Services v. Hansen, 470 N.W.2d 170 (Neb. 1991)	Termination	Termination	Corrections officer sleeping on duty; defense of sleepiness due to pain medication rejected.
Shortess v. Department of Public Safety & Corrections, 991 So.2d 1067 (La. App. 2008)	Termination	Four-Step Pay Reduction	Corrections officer sleeping on the job. Civil Service Commission took into account the officer's medical condition and medication in deciding to reduce the penalty.
Stapelton v. La Paglia, 616 N.Y.S.2d 679 (A.D. 1994)	Demotion	Reinstatement	Corrections officer found asleep on duty on two occasions; demotion too severe a penalty.
Ulster County Sheriff, 16 NPER NY-17511 (N.Y. S.Ct. 1993)	Demotion	Reinstatement	Sleeping on duty; supervisor consistently condoned and accepted sleeping by other employees.
University of Michigan, 94-1 ARB ¶4113 (Ellmann, 1993)	Termination	Termination	Dispatcher sleeping on duty; defense of stress resulting from high number of voluntary overtime assignments rejected.

Substance Abuse

CASE NAME	INITIAL SANCTION	RESULT ON APPEAL	DESCRIPTION
Baretto v. New York, 555 N.Y.S.2d 382 (A.D. 1990)	Termination	Termination	Refusal to provide sample for valid drug test.
Barreras v. New Mexico Dept. of Corrections, 838 P.2d 983 (N.M. 1992)	Termination	Termination	Drug-sniffing dog pointed to three corrections officers during random sniff of prison; officers were then submitted to drug testing and tested positive for marijuana.
Berenhaus v. Ward, 504 N.Y.S.2d 412 (A.D. 1986)	Termination	Reinstatement	Possession of marijuana.
Bettis v. Bratton, 641 N.Y.S.2d 631 (A.D. 1996).	Termination	Termination	Court rejected as "incredible" officer's claim that he tested positive for cocaine due to his ingestion of prescription medication that had been tampered with either in the manufacturing process or by the pharmacy that dispensed it.

CASE NAME	INITIAL SANCTION	RESULT ON APPEAL	DESCRIPTION
Butler v. Thornburgh, 900 F.2d 871 (5th Cir. 1990)	Termination	Termination	Four alcohol-related incidents involving FBI agent who had failed rehabilitation; last incident involved instigating fight with disabled gas station attendant and running employer's car into wall.
Caesar v. Department of Police, 609 S.W.2d 881 (La. App. 1992)	3-Day Suspension	No Discipline	Off-duty officer had three drinks and argued with bouncer at nightclub. No adverse impact on Department from incident.
Chippewa County, No. 60038 (Wis. ERC 2002)	1-Day Suspension	No Discipline	On-call detective responded to a scene of a suicide with alcohol on his breath and tested at 0.04 blood alcohol. Detective competently performed all crime duties and Arbitrator concluded that the detective was not under the "influence" of alcohol, as prohibited by the County's rules.
City of Detroit, 106 LA 1131 (Brown, 1996)	Termination	Termination	In violation of last chance agreement, police officer used alcohol and was involved in an automobile collision. Officer told investigators at scene: "I know I'm finished." Arbitrator upheld automatic discharge provisions of last chance agreement.
City of El Paso, 110 LA 411 (Moore, 1998)	Termination	Reinstatement With Back Pay	Police officer involved in off-duty one-car accident after drinking in bar. Officer was not arrested for off-duty DWI, no departmental rule prohibited drinking alcohol off duty, and officer had no alcohol-related offenses in ten years of employment.
City of Fort Worth, LAIG 6131 (Goodman, 2004)	Termination	Reinstatement Without Back Pay	After sergeant was placed on restrictive duty following attempts made by employer to convince him to enter an alcohol treatment facility, sergeant engaged in off-duty belligerent and verbally abusive behavior that led to his arrest by law enforcement officers from another jurisdiction. Arbitrator cited employee's good work record and failure of supervisory training on the need to be alert for symptoms of alcohol abuse or stress.
City of Houston, LAIG 4834 (Ruiz, 1993)	Termination	Termination	Off-duty alcohol-related vehicular accident. Officer had history of problems with behavior and alcohol, and had been provided therapy and counseling by the Department.
City of Lawrence, LAIG 4353 (Bornstein, 1990)	Termination	Reinstatement	Use of cocaine while on duty on two occasions; offense occurred five years previously; City failed to consider officer's good work record or potential for rehabilitation.

CASE NAME	INITIAL SANCTION	RESULT ON APPEAL	DESCRIPTION
City of Minneapolis v. Johnson, 450 N.W.2d 156 (Minn. App. 1990)	Termination	Termination	Use of cocaine; disparate treatment defense rejected even though City did not discharge users of marijuana.
City of Philadelphia v. FOP, 29 PPER ¶29121 (Pa.Cmwlth. 1998)	Termination	Reinstatement	Blood and urine of officer involved in on-duty accident found to have presence of cocaine and alcohol. Court's decision solely on issue of whether arbitrator who reinstated officer exceeded his jurisdiction.
City of Pittsburgh and Fraternal Order of Police, 27 LAIS 2025	Denial of Application For Reinstatement	Grant of Application For Reinstatement	Department rejected officer's application for reinstatement (per terms of a prior arbitration decision) after the officer submitted evidence of his drug rehabilitation efforts. Arbitrator relied heavily upon testimony of officer's counselor concerning officer's compliance with drug rehabilitation program.
Connecticut State Police Union v. Department of Public Safety, 862 A.2d 344 (Conn. App. 2004)	Termination	Termination	State Police trooper violated last-chance agreement that he not consume any alcohol on duty or off duty. Court upheld Arbitrator's finding that Intoxilizer was a reliable instrument in determining blood-alcohol level.
Corpus Christi Police Department, LAIG 4344 (Sisk, 1990)	Termination	30-Day Suspension	Abuse of Valium; 20-year officer cooperated with Department's investigation.
Cuyahoga County Sheriff's Department, 110 LA 307 (Richard, 1998)	Termination	Termination	Civilian correctional officer criminally convicted for purchasing crack cocaine. Noting that offense was a felony, Arbitrator rejected argument that other officers convicted of misdemeanors had not been discharged.
Ellerbee-Pryer v. State Civil Service Commission, 33 PPER ¶33131 (Pa. Cmwlth. 2002).	Termination	Termination	After testing positive for alcohol while at work, corrections officer failed to comply with terms of "last chance" agreement requiring her to complete treatment program.
Grubb v. Borough of Hightstown, 802 A.2d 596 (N.J. Sup. 2002).	Termination	Termination	Possession of anabolic steroids with intent to distribute.
Harmon v. New York City Police Dept., 591 N.Y.S.2d 411 (A.D. 1992)	Termination	Termination	Positive test for cocaine; defense that officer accidentally ingested cocaine rejected.
Heron v. McGuire, 803 F.2d 67 (2d Cir. 1986)	Termination	Termination	Addiction to heroin.

CASE NAME	INITIAL SANCTION	RESULT ON APPEAL	DESCRIPTION
Hughes v. Ward, 551 N.Y.S.2d 217 (A.D. 1990)	Termination	Termination	Alcoholic officer failed to report for work and missed compulsory medical examination.
In re Parkman, 2006 WL 2381925 (N.J. Super. A.D. 2006)	Termination	Termination	Police officer tested positive for cocaine. Court rejected defense that cocaine had been placed in officer's Kool-Aid without his knowledge.
In re: Phillips, 569 A.2d 807 (N.J. 1990)	Demotion	Demotion	Demotion from chief to officer for consuming three drinks, then driving with gun in possession; City had approached Chief before about alcohol problem.
Kerins v. City of Niagara Falls, 561 N.Y.S.2d 953 (A.D. 1990)	Termination	Reinstatement	Use of police influence to purchase liquor after hours; punishment ruled disproportionate.
Kirsch v. New Orleans Police Department, 859 So.2d 965 (La. App. 2003)	Termination	Termination	Employer met burden of proof through circumstantial evidence that police officer had consumed Ecstasy. Prescription bottle in which four pills of Ecstasy were found was retrieved from the officer's car after he was found unconscious at an intersection, and Department appropriately followed chain of custody procedures with respect to prescription bottle. The Court rejected the officer's claim that an unknown woman drugged him while he was in a bar and placed the Ecstasy pills in the prescription bottle.
Kloss v. Board of Comm'rs, 449 N.E.2d 845 (Ill. 1983)	Termination	Reinstatement	Off-duty threatening of other officer with gun while under influence of alcohol; Court found discipline unrelated to needs of police force or citizens.
Laborde v. Alexandria Mun. Fire and Police Board, 566 So.2d 426 (La. App. 1990)	Termination	Reinstatement	Off-duty DWI; City failed to prove substantial relationship between conduct and efficient operation of the Police Department. Officer was off duty from assignment as anti-drunk driving task force officer; incident involved chase with a captain from another agency.
Lamarr v. City of Memphis, 2004 WL 370298 (Tenn. App. 2004)	Termination	Termination	Officer involved in alcohol-related single vehicle accident while off duty. Officer claimed he had not been drinking during a 3.5-hour stretch while dancing at a nightclub, and falsely claimed to have been forced off road by an 18-wheel truck. The Department had "no tolerance" policy for alcohol-related offenses.

CASE NAME	INITIAL SANCTION	RESULT ON APPEAL	DESCRIPTION
Louisville And Jefferson County Metro Government ex rel. White v. Louisville Metro Police Merit Bd., 2008 WL 612337 (Ky. App. 2008)	Termination	27-Day Suspension	Officer smoked marijuana on at least two occasions in the past year. Civil service board rejected police chief's "zero tolerance" policy about drug use, and reinstated officer based on officer's record at attempts to control drug use.
Maher v. New Orleans Police Department, 788 So.2d 1250 (La. App. 2001)	Termination	Termination	Officer tested positive for cocaine during drug test administered after officer filed claim for on-the-job injury. Court rejected argument that test result was a false positive caused by dentist's administration of Lidocaine less than 48 hours prior to the drug test.
Norfolk County Sheriff's Department, LAIG 6606 (Altman, 2008)	14-Day Suspension Plus Random Drug Testing	No Discipline And No Random Drug Testing	Corrections officer refused to submit to drug test after returning from FMLA leave. Employer's drug test was outside the "window period" allowed by the contract for drug testing after the conclusion of FMLA leave. As such, employee not insubordinate because drug testing was not lawful.
Ohio State Patrol, 96 LA 613 (Bittel, 1990)	Termination	90-Day Suspension	Off-duty driving while intoxicated; employer failed to consider trooper's efforts at rehabilitation and likelihood of success.
Pennsylvania State Police v. Pennsylvania State Troopers Association, 634 A.2d 634 (Pa.Cmwlth. 1993)	Termination	Termination	State trooper failed to report wife's drug use to his superior.
Ray v. Denver, 677 P.2d 399 (Colo. App. 1984)	Termination	Reinstatement	Use of cocaine while on unpaid suspension.
Roy v. City of New York, 685 N.Y.S.2d 68 (A.D. 1999)	Termination	Termination	Officer refused to take drug test ordered after employer gained reasonable suspicion that officer was involved in use of drugs.
Sharkey v. Police Department, 578 N.Y.S.2d 599 (A.D. 1992)	Termination	Reinstatement	DWI conviction for off-duty driving; incident resulted in a fatal accident.
Shlumbohm v. City of Sioux Falls, 630 N.W.2d 93 (S.D. 2001)	Termination	6-Month Suspension	Officer drove while intoxicated, getting into one-car accident. The case decided on progressive discipline grounds. Court rejected the employer's argument that prior discipline involving other employees was irrelevant.

CASE NAME	INITIAL SANCTION	RESULT ON APPEAL	DESCRIPTION
Taylor v. Port Authority of State of New York, 643 N.Y.S.2d 103 (A.D. 1996)	Termination	Termination	Probationary police officer was stopped on two successive days for drunk driving while he was on vacation; second stop resulted in his arrest.
Thibodeaux v. City of Opelousas, 717 So.2d 254 (La. App. 1998)	Termination	Termination	Off-duty police officer ran off the road due to drunk driving, left scene of accident, entered nearby home without consent of owners, lied to owners when he was asked what he was doing in their home and in general created situation where multiple off-duty officers were called in to locate the officer and to deal with his vehicle which was wrecked and abandoned with his revolver on the seat.
Town of Enfield v. AFSCME, Council 4, Local 1029, 918 A.2d 934 (Conn. App. 2007)	Termination	5-Day Suspension	Police dispatcher used marijuana on an occasional basis. Dispatcher subsequently entered and successfully completed a pre-trial drug education program sponsored by a department of mental health. Arbitration panel held the "the gravity of the dispatcher's offense, when balanced against his flawless work record, did not support termination."

Supervisory Failure

CASE NAME	INITIAL SANCTION	RESULT ON APPEAL	DESCRIPTION
Austin v. Department of Police, 981 So.2d 42 (La. App. 2008)	Demotion and Suspension	No Discipline	Lieutenant demoted after prisoner escaped from officers under his supervision. Civil service board held that mistakes of subordinates should not be imputed to lieutenant in the absence of any failure of supervision on his part.
City of Baytown, Texas, LAIG 6400 (Bennett, 2006)	3-Day Suspension	3-Day Suspension	Sergeant failed to handcuff a prisoner in his custody; prisoner subsequently stole an ambulance and was shot by the police. The Arbitrator concluded that based on the prisoner's resistance to arrest and her vow that she would not go to jail, the sergeant should have ensured that the prisoner was handcuffed prior to placement in an ambulance, which she apparently used to manage her escape.
City of Richmond Heights, 123 LA 232 (Lalka, 2006)	Demotion	Demotion	Sergeant demoted to police officer because of inadequate report writing and failure to perform supervisory responsibilities. The entire Police Department combined did not have as bad a disciplinary record as the sergeant.

CASE NAME	INITIAL SANCTION	RESULT ON APPEAL	DESCRIPTION
City of Tyler, 24 LAIS 3901 (Moore, 1997)	10-Day Suspension	No Discipline	Lieutenant ordered a fellow officer to shoot tires of an automobile involved in a chase. Arbitrator concluded that lieutenant "had exhausted all other possibilities available to stop the vehicle." Department rules did not prohibit shooting tires of vehicles involved in chase.
Kennedy v. Marian Correctional Institution, 64 FEP Cases 1436 (Ohio 1994)	Demotion	Demotion	Captain engaged in several instances of sexual harassment; demotion to sergeant.
McAllister v. Priest, 442 S.W.2d 650 (Mo. 1968)	Termination	Demotion	General incompetence of supervisor; no evidence that employee could not perform at lesser rank.
Neidig v. Department of Corrections, 642 A.2d 538 (Pa. Cmwlth. 1994)	Demotion	Demotion	Lieutenant ordered an officer to transport an unruly prisoner without any assistance; prisoner escaped during transport.
Nye County, 102 LA 1133 (McCurdy, 1994)	Permanent Demotion	Temporary Demotion	Off-duty sergeant told youth to "get the fuck out" of gambling area; permanent demotion ruled too harsh.
Patterson v. City of Biloxi, 965 So.2d 765 (Miss. App. 2007)	Demotion	Demotion	Captain demoted to lieutenant following refusal to comply with readiness inspection. Captain had history of reprimands and discipline stemming from conflicts with supervisors and subordinates.
Portage County Sheriff, 110 LA 789 (Adamson, 1998)	2-Day Suspension	2-Day Suspension	Failure to properly supervise subordinate corrections officers after receiving performance evaluation criticizing lack of supervisory skills.
Siler v. Yuba County Sheriff's Department, 27 PORAC Law Enf. News 17 (Cohn, 1995)	Demotion	20-Day Suspension	Profanity and failure to supervise subordinates; use of profanity widespread in Department, and employer failed to follow own progressive discipline schedule.
Smith v. Municipal Fire & Police Civil Service Board of Eunice, 649 So.2d 566 (La. App. 1994)	Demotion From Assistant Chief To Sergeant	Reinstatement	After consuming two to three beers at a Monday night football gathering, assistant chief drove assigned police car while off duty and was speeding in residential zone; practices found to be "common for supervisory officers."
Southern California Rapid Transit District, 100 LA 701 (Brisco, 1992)	Demotion	Unpaid Suspension Of Unspecified Length	Detective used profanity in exchange with lieutenant; offense not inconsistent with responsibilities of detectives' job.

CASE NAME	INITIAL SANCTION	RESULT ON APPEAL	DESCRIPTION
Township of Clay v. Montville, 2004 WL 1366063 (Mich. App. 2004)	Demotion	1-Day Suspension	Township demoted corporal for multiple violations of the same policy. Demotion reversed because Department did not strictly apply the policy to all officers, and did not notify the corporal after the first violation that his conduct would likely lead to demotion in the future.
Warren County Ohio Sheriff, 4 NPER 12:8 (April, 2001)	Demotion	Demotion	Demotion of lieutenant to deputy sheriff for "secret and conspiratorial" conduct. Lieutenant discussed personnel issues at special township meeting and then attempted to cover up his attendance at the meeting, instructing deputies to keep quiet about the matter.
Wyckoff v. City of Phoenix, 2008 WL 2656103 (Ariz. App. 2008)	Demotion	Demotion	Sergeant was demoted after failing to adequately investigate a "missed court" incident involving one of his subordinates. Sergeant's substandard investigation, which included "incompetent and incomplete reports," coupled with his failure to follow a reasonable instruction given to him by his lieutenant, justified his demotion.
Theft			
Burgdorf v. Board of Police Commissioners, 936 S.W.2d 227 (Mo. App. 1996)	Termination	Termination	Theft from retail store that employed officer part-time as security guard.
Cain v. Eastern Michigan University, 2003 WL 22902845 (Mich. App. 2003)	Termination	Termination	Sergeant indiscriminately gave out her employer-issued private personal identification number to her subordinates to use for long distance calling at the employer's expense.
City of Galion, 112 LA 771 (1999)	Termination	Termination	Officer with 24 years of service was convicted of shoplifting. Arbitrator refused to mitigate penalty based on officer's length of service, finding that employer's concern about its image and the officer's credibility were valid.
City of Philadelphia, LAIG 4221 (1989)	Termination	Reinstatement	Officer left store without paying for several items; Arbitrator accepted defense of work-related "panic attack."
City of Philadelphia, LAIG 5048 (Stone, 1994)	Termination	Reinstatement Without Back Pay	Officer later cashed money order seized during execution of search warrant. While officer violated departmental procedures in handling of money order, good work record and lack of untruthfulness mitigated discharge.
Department of Public Safety, 461 A.2d 98 (N.H. 1983)	Termination	Reinstatement With Treatment	After working 15-hour shift, officer stole two tires; defense of work-related stress.

CASE NAME	INITIAL SANCTION	RESULT ON APPEAL	DESCRIPTION
Eberhart v. Ward, 555 N.Y.S.2d 329 (A.D. 1990)	Termination	Termination	Theft of money found during search of apartment used for drug dealing.
Greiner v. Greene County, 576 N.Y.S.2d 665 (A.D. 1991)	Termination	Termination	Misappropriation of handgun found at scene of suspicious fire; defense of stress produced by working three jobs rejected.
Habe v. South Euclid Civil Service Commission, Unpublished opinion (Ohio App. 1993)	Termination	Termination	Theft of money from church bingo operation for which officer was providing security.
Kujawa v. City of Williamsport, 445 A.2d 1348 (Pa. 1982)	Termination	Termination	Use of city gasoline in personal vehicle.
Miami Township v. FOP, 15 OPER P 1293 (Ohio S.Ct. 1998)	Termination	30-Day Suspension	Two occasions of theft of $100 bills found at crime scenes; officer expressed remorse for acts and had prior excellent work record. Court's decision limited to whether Arbitrator exceeded authority in reinstating officer.
Moore v. Constantine, 574 N.Y.W.2d 507 (1991)	Termination	Termination	Trooper misappropriated funds and sent money to family of corrections officer injured in accident.
New York State Department of Correctional Services, LAIG 5361 (Denson, 1998)	Termination	Reinstatement With Back Pay	Corrections counselor discharged for stealing plants that were supposed to be planted at employer's facility. Officer and his supervisor were told by supplier of flowers that they could take extra flowers for their personal use. Case decided on basis of grievant's state of mind.
O'Connell v. City of New York, 653 N.Y.S.2d 575 (A.D. 1997)	Termination	Termination	Off-duty police officer attempted to shoplift lawnmower.
Pennsylvania State Police, 6:1 NPER 10 (Pa.Cmwlth. 1997)	Termination	Reinstatement	Arrest for shoplifting resolved by civil compromise. Numerous other troopers had committed more serious offenses without being discharged.
Pennsylvania State Police v. Fraternal Order of Police, 656 A.2d 83 (Pa. 1995)	Termination	15-Day Suspension	Use of employer's credit card to purchase gas for personal vehicle where trooper convicted of crime for the offense; upheld Arbitrator's decision that punishment too severe.
Perez v. Ward, 550 N.Y.S.2d 629 (A.D. 1990)	Termination	Termination	Narcotics officer stole $20 in buy money.

CASE NAME	INITIAL SANCTION	RESULT ON APPEAL	DESCRIPTION
Philadelphia Housing Authority v. Fraternal Order of Police, 33 PPER ¶33,181 (Pa. Cmnwlth. 2002)	Termination	90-Day Suspension	Officer terminated for "theft of court crime" by appearing in court without a subpoena. Arbitrator concluded that officer made a mistake, but was intentionally dishonest.
State of Ohio, 108 LA 1109 (Feldman, 1997)	Termination	Leave Without Pay Pending Further Consideration	State trooper shoplifted seven compact disks. Trooper's fourth-degree felony conviction was expunged from his record, and his behavior was due in part to a difficult divorce. Discharge converted into reevaluation of case following consideration of further psychiatric examinations.
Town of Melbourne Beach, 91 LA 280 (Frost, 1988)	Termination	Reinstatement	Theft of cassette tape made of previous disciplinary hearing.

Ticket Quotas

CASE NAME	INITIAL SANCTION	RESULT ON APPEAL	DESCRIPTION
Begg v. Park Ridge, 459 N.E.2d 925 (Ill. 1984)	3-Day Suspension	3-Day Suspension	Failure to meet four-tickets-per-week quota.
Town of Westborough, LAIG 4310 (Pinkus, 1990)	7-Day Suspension	No Discipline	Alleged disclosure to newspaper of Department memorandum detailing quota system; evidence circumstantial and Arbitrator convinced document officer observed copying from bulletin board was a work schedule.

Unauthorized Flying

CASE NAME	INITIAL SANCTION	RESULT ON APPEAL	DESCRIPTION
City of El Paso, 118 LA 855 (Allen, 2003)	Transfer	No Transfer	Two officers took unauthorized training flight in Department plane, eventually having to make an emergency landing in another state. Chief, who was embarrassed by publicity over the incident, immediately transferred officers back to patrol. Contract forbids the use of transfers as method of discipline.

Use of Force

CASE NAME	INITIAL SANCTION	RESULT ON APPEAL	DESCRIPTION
City of Boca Raton, 25 LAIS 2010 (Richard, 1997)	Termination	Termination	Off-duty police officer involved in criminal justice courses unholstered his weapon in a classroom and pointed it at noisy students so they would be quiet while he studied for a quiz. Previously, officer was standing on a bridge between classrooms and removed his weapon, and "tracked" an unpopular "nerd" as the student walked across his field of view. Arbitrator rejected defense of officer's good work record and officer's remorse for his actions.

CASE NAME	INITIAL SANCTION	RESULT ON APPEAL	DESCRIPTION
Use of Property			
City of Jacksonville, 108 LA 799 (Welch, 1997)	Written Reprimand	No Discipline	Lieutenant used mobile data terminal to send message urging officers to vote against 12-hour workdays; lieutenant was union board member and communication to members was police business. No evidence that lieutenant intended to "destroy rather than promote high morale and discipline" as charged by employer.
Vehicles and Equipment			
City of Dayton, FOP Lodge 44, LAIG 6133 (Murphy, 2004)	8-Hour Suspension	No Discipline	Sergeant was suspended for improperly engaging in the pursuit of a suspect vehicle. Arbitrator credited sergeant's testimony that he was not involved in a pursuit, but was merely attempting to determine which direction the suspect vehicle traveled in order to possibly recover the vehicle or alert dispatch.
City of Englewood, Ohio, LAIG 5270 (Keenan, 1997)	Written Reprimand	Counseling	Immediate supervisor believed only counseling as a result of officer's accident during a pursuit (which resulted in over $500 in damages to her vehicle and a fence) was necessary; collective bargaining agreement required progressive discipline and officer had no record of prior discipline.
City of Houston, 125 LA 134 (Moore, 2008)	3-Day Suspension	3-Day Suspension	Officer who was third car in chase was involved in intersection collision with unrelated vehicle when the officer disregarded a traffic light. Officer was traveling at high speed and failed to use appropriate caution.
City of Lancaster, Texas, LAIG 6252 (Fragnoli, 2005)	Indefinite Suspension	Reinstatement Without Back Pay	Officer with history of driving at excessive speeds was involved in a collision while responding to a non-emergency complaint. While the officer was at fault in causing the collision, there was no evidence that he was counseled or trained following his earlier disciplinary incidents.
City of Livonia, Michigan, 1:5 NPER 8 (Kruger, 1997)	Payment For Lost Canister And Holster	Payment For Lost Canister And Holster	Police officer lost tear gas canister and holster from his belt; City had well publicized and enforced rule that loss of such equipment would require officer to reimburse for cost of equipment.
City of Mobile v. Boone, 640 So.2d 975 (Ala. App. 1994)	10-Day Suspension	5-Day Suspension	Briefcase left by lieutenant in vehicle stolen; lieutenant did not report theft for three days, and briefcase contained notebook with information on a sting operation as well as his pistol and a cash box.

CASE NAME	INITIAL SANCTION	RESULT ON APPEAL	DESCRIPTION
City of Warwick, LAIG 6432 (Cooper, 2006)	1-Day Suspension	1-Day Suspension	While pursuing a rape suspect, officer turned directly into the path of oncoming traffic. Officer's assumption that the oncoming traffic would turn left in order to avoid him was not a reasonable one.
City of Wichita Falls, 25 LAIS 3016 (1997)	1-Day Suspension	No Discipline	Officer drove patrol car over curb in response to burglary in process, causing several hundred dollars in damages. Department had no policies or guidelines for handling the type of incident, and no policies concerning how Accident Review Board's point system impacted discipline.
Darke County Sheriff's Office, 108 LA 848 (Dissem, 1997)	Termination	15-Day Suspension	Police officer who was driving recklessly hit another police car in front of him in a funeral procession. Though officer had prior discipline for driving violations, discharge unwarranted where performance evaluations rated officer as excellent, indicating officer responded to poor performance ratings and prior discipline by making improvements on the job.
Dunn v. New Orleans Police Department, 938 So.2d 217 (La. App. 2006)	Termination	Reinstatement With Back Pay	Police officer and his wife, who was not employed by the City, took two Department vehicles on a personal vacation trip to Florida. The internal affairs investigation exceeded the 60-day cap specified by state law.
Metropolitan Dade County, LAIG 5074 (Hoffman, 1995)	1-Day Suspension	No Discipline	Unauthorized personal use of patrol vehicle; since officer had already lost "home car" privileges for one month for same incident, suspension violated double jeopardy.
Sheriff of Williamson County, 14 PERI ¶2016 (Ill. SLRB 1998)	Termination	Reinstatement With Back Pay	Personal use of Sheriff's Department's computer database. Employee was Union president; decided on basis of anti-union bias where employee had "relatively clean" disciplinary record and where other employees who engaged in similar offenses were not treated as harshly.
Warren County Sheriff's Office, 122 LA 1451 (Wren, 2006)	5-Day Suspension	5-Day Suspension	Suspension appropriate for deputy who shot and wounded Labrador retriever where other options, including kicks and impact weapons, were available. Defense of disparate treatment rejected where other incident cited by deputy involved the justifiable shooting of a raccoon, even though the shots in the other case were negligently fired and punctured an above-ground pool.

NOTES

[1] *Johnson v. City of Buckner*, 610 S.W.2d 406 (Mo. App. 1980).

[2] Even in the case of employers who are truly "at-will" employers, discipline cannot either violate the constitutional rights of the employee or be in retaliation for the employee's exercise of constitutional rights. *Gray v. City of Gustine*, 273 Cal.Rptr. 730 (Cal. App. 1990); *Morris v. City of Kokomo*, 381 N.E.2d 510 (Ind. App. 1978).

[3] §2922, California Labor Code.

[4] *Gause v. Doe*, 451 S.E.2d 408 (S.C. App. 1994).

[5] *Borschel v. City of Perry*, 514 N.W.2d 565 (Iowa 1994).

[6] *Harkness v. City of Burley*, 715 P.2d 1283 (Idaho 1986).

[7] *Kaiser v. Dixon,* 468 N.E.2d 822 (Ill. App. 1984), *quoting Toussaint v. Blue Cross and Blue Shield of Michigan*, 292 N.W.2d 880 (Mich. 1980).

[8] *Harkness v. City of Burley*, 715 P.2d 1283 (Idaho 1986).

[9] *See generally* State Employee Grievances and Due Process: An Analysis of Contract Arbitration and Civil Service Review Systems, 29 So. Car. L. Rev. 305 (1978).

[10] §76-47, Hawai'i Revised Statutes.

[11] Title 29, §5949, Delaware Code.

[12] §18.272(5), Kentucky Revised Statutes.

[13] Chapter 240, §563, Oregon Revised Statutes.

[14] *Burns v. Police Board of City of Chicago*, 432 N.E.2d 1300 (Ill. App. 1982).

[15] *Wagner v. City of Omaha*, 464 N.W.2d 175 (Neb. 1991); *Herrmann v. Civil Service Commission of the Borough of Jenkintown*, 478 A.2d 961 (Pa.Cmwlth. 1984).

[16] *Borough of Jenkintown v. Civil Service Commission of Jenkintown*, 478 A.2d 941 (Pa.Cmwlth. 1984).

[17] *Johnson v. City of Welch*, 388 S.E.2d 284 (W.Va. 1989).

[18] *Dwyer v. Smith*, 867 F.2d 184 (4th Cir. 1989); *Antoine v. Department of Public Safety*, 681 So.2d 1282 (La. App. 1996); *Pierce County Sheriff v. Civil Service Commission*, 658 P.2d 648 (Wash. 1983).

[19] *Tovey v. City of Jacksonville*, 808 S.W.2d 740 (Ark. 1991); *Dickens v. La Tourette*, 663 S.W.2d 250 (Mo. App. 1983). *But see Freese v. County of Douglas*, 315 N.W.2d 638 (Neb. 1982)(civil service board has no authority to increase punishment beyond that imposed by the employer).

[20] *Collins v. Board of Fire and Police Commissioners of the City of Genoa*, 405 N.E.2d 877 (Ill. App. 1980).

[21] *Coon v. Civil Service Commission for Allegheny County*, 654 A.2d 241 (Pa.Cmwlth. 1995)(decided under peculiar wording of Pennsylvania's civil service statutes for sheriffs' office employees).

[22] *Tew v. Town Council of Town of Slocomb*, 621 So.2d 293 (Ala. App. 1992).

[23] *Eastern Associated Coal Corporation v. United Mine Workers of America, District 17*, 531 U.S. 57 (2000).

[24] *E.g., AFSCME, Council 4, Local 1565 v. Department of Correction*, 945 A.2d 494 (Conn. App. 2008); *County of Mercer v. Teamsters Local 250*, 946 A.2d 174 (Pa. Cmwlth. 2008).

[25] *State v. Connecticut State Employees Ass'n*, 947 A.2d 928 (Conn. 2008); *City of Highland Park v. Teamster Local Union No. 714*, 828 N.E.2d 311 (Ill. App. 2005)(public policy not violated by reinstatement of officer convicted of criminal trespass); *City of Minneapolis v. Police Officers' Federation*, 566 N.W.2d 83 (Minn. Ct. App. 1997)(no public policy prevented reinstatement of officer who had judgment entered against him in federal civil rights lawsuit); *Washington County Police Officers' Ass'n v. Washington County*, 63 P.3d 1167 (2003)(decision reversing termination of corrections officer for using marijuana does not violate public policy).

[26] Some courts do require a higher standard of proof – that of substantial evidence – in order to sustain an employer's disciplinary decision. *See Graham v. Wilkes*, 373 S.E.2d 90 (Ga. App. 1988).

[27] *Johnson v. Department of Police*, 575 So.2d 440 (La. App. 1991); *Grief Brothers Cooperage*, 42 LA 555 (Daugherty, 1964).

[28] *Clark v. Bd. of Fire and Police Comm'rs*, 613 N.E.2d 826 (Ill. App. 1993); *Burke v. City of Anderson*, 612 N.E.2d 559 (Ind. App. 1993); *Meyers v. Montgomery County Police Dept.*, 626 A.2d 1010 (Md. App. 1993); *Coleman v. Anne Arundel County Police Department*, 797 A.2d 770 (Md. App. 2002); *Romeo v. Dep't of Employment and Training*, 556 A.2d 93 (1988); *City of Milwaukee*, 78 LA 89 (Yaffe, 1982). *See also Chemical Leaman Tank Lines, Inc.*, 55 LA 435 (Rohman, 1970).

[29] *City of Oklahoma City*, 123 LA 24 (Walker, 2006); *Montgomery County Sheriff's Office*, LAIG 6139 (Bell, 2004); *City of Orlando*, 1 NPER 2:8 (Sergent, 1997); *City of Lawton, Oklahoma*, 2001 WL 574317 (Prlogdky, 2001); *Kroger Co.*, 25 LA 906 (Smith, 1955); *see City of Tallahassee v. Big Bend Police Benevolent Association*, 710 So.2d 214 (Fla. App. 1998)(upholding Arbitrator's opinion applying clear and convincing evidence standard).

[30] *Jefferson County, Ohio*, 114 LA 1508 (Klein, 2000). *See generally* cases cited in F. Elkouri & E. Elkouri, *How Arbitration Works* (6th Ed. 2003).

[31] *Kline v. City of Grinnell Civil Service Commission*, 2003 WL 22087588 (Iowa 2003); *see Caesar v. Department of Police*, 609 So.2d 881 (La. App. 1992).

[32] *Kerins v. City of Niagara Falls*, 561 N.Y.S.2d 953 (A.D. 1990); *Immigration and Naturalization Service*, 114 LA 872 (Neas, 2000); *City of Inglewood*, LAIG 5558 (Tamoush, 1999); *City of Ann Arbor, Michigan*, 59 LA 714 (Ellman, 1972).

[33] *Aerosol Techniques, Inc.*, 48 LA 1278 (Arbitration Board, 1967). A good discussion of the requirement for an adequate investigation in a case involving a challenge to the termination of a police officer can be found in *Municipality of Anchorage* (Beck, 1989)(reversal of termination for failure to obey order to answer questions in internal investigation setting)(unreported decision; copies available from LRIS).

[34] *Immigration and Naturalization Service*, 114 LA 872 (Neas, 2000); *Sacramento Police Association*, 1 MHMC Labor Bulletin 3:4-5 (August, 1996); *City of Oklahoma City*, 100 LA 1183 (Woolf, 1993).

[35] *City of Binghampton*, 65 LA 663 (Doner, 1975).

[36] *City of Kalamazoo*, LAIG 5376 (Grissom, 1998).

[37] *Department of Public Safety & Corrections v. Mayfield*, 563 So.2d 1230 (La. App. 1990)(discipline overturned; Department failed to adequately train sergeant in separation of fighting inmates); *Immigration and Naturalization Service*, 114 LA 1284 (Harkless, 2000)(demotion for second accidental discharge reversed; employer failed to follow own remedial training program for employees who had an accidental discharge).

[38] *Richardson v. Board of Supervisors*, 250 Cal.Rptr. 1 (1988)(discipline overturned; supervisor deliberately provoked confrontation with deputy); *San Francisco Police Department*, 94-1 ARB ¶4001 (Riker, 1993)(termination for workplace profanity reversed where employer had done nothing to resolve tensions that had persisted for several months between employees).

[39] *City of Stamford, Connecticut*, LAIG 4797 (Pittocco, 1993); *City of Boulder, Colorado*, 69 LA 1173 (Yarowsky, 1977)(excessive force incident).

[40] *New York State Department of Correctional Services*, 69 LA 344 (Kornblum, 1977).

[41] *Childress v. Department of Police*, 487 So.2d 590 (La. App. 1986).

[42] *San Francisco Police Department*, 94-1 ARB ¶4001 (Riker, 1993).

[43] *Tinner v. Police Board of the City of Chicago*, 378 N.E.2d 1166 (Ill. App. 1978); *Shlumbohm v. City of Sioux Falls*, 630 N.W.2d 93 (S.D. 2001); *Broward County Sheriff's Office,* 122 LA 56 (Cocalis, 2005).

[44] *Chicago Housing Authority*, LAIG 4978 (Cohen, 1994); *City of Fort Worth, Texas*, 99-2 ARB ¶3141 (Jennings, 1999).

[45] *Sheriff of Williamson County,* 14 PERI ¶2016 (Ill. SLRB 1998); *Borough of Sayreville*, 19 NPER NJ-21199 (N.J. PERC Hearing Examiner 1990); *City of Chester*, 13 NPER PA-21182 (Pa. LRB Hearing Examiner 1990).

[46] *Perry County v. PLRB*, 634 A.2d 808 (Pa.Cmwlth. 1993).

[47] *Lodderhose v. City of Ferguson*, 837 S.W.2d 361 (Mo. App. 1992).

[48] *Alston v. New York City Transit Authority*, 588 N.Y.S.2d 418 (A.D. 1992).

[49] *City of Portland*, 77 LA 820 (Axon, 1981).

[50] *County of Erie*, LAIG 2630 (1988).

[51] *Town of Plainville*, 67 LA 442 (McKane, 1976). *See generally* F. Elkouri & E. Elkouri, *How Arbitration Works* 673 (6th Ed. 2003).

[52] *City of Benton Harbor*, 103 LA 816 (Allen, 1994). *See City of Mayfield Heights*, LAIG 5002 (Duda, 1994)(principles of industrial due process violated when member of accident review board served as hearing officer in subsequent *Loudermill* hearing on discipline resulting from accident).

[53] *Mendoza v. Julian*, 2007 WL 3227437 (Cal. App. 2007); *McLean v. Mecklenburg County*, 448 S.E.2d 137 (N.C. 1994); *Garrett v. North Babylon Volunteer Fire Dept.*, 433 N.Y.S.2d 218 (A.D. 1980). A New York court has reached the opposite result, holding that under New York's statewide civil service system, disciplinary decisions can be based on uncorroborated hearsay. *Ayala v. Ward*, 565 N.Y.S.2d 114 (A.D. 1991).

[54] *Delaware County*, LAIG 4897 (Aronin, 1993).

[55] *Branza v. Martin*, 570 N.E.2d 411 (Ill. App. 1991); *Metropolitan Dade County*, LAIG 5074 (Hoffman, 1995).

[56] *Van Milligan v. Board of Fire and Police Commissioners*, 630 N.E.2d 830 (Ill. 1994)(five-year delay); *Berry v. Dinkins*, 576 N.Y.S.2d 107 (A.D. 1991)(two-year delay); *City of Atlanta v. Bell*, 425 S.E.2d 325 (Ga. App. 1992)(15-month delay). *But see Hunt v. Shettle*, 452 N.E.2d 1045 (Ind. App. 1983)(14-month delay in hearing violated due process).

[57] *Pennsylvania State Police v. Pennsylvania State Troopers Association*, 633 A.2d 1330 (Pa.Cmwlth. 1993)(termination of trooper who issued bad checks overturned where discipline was delayed by as much as a year). *See also City of*

Sacramento, 26 LAIS 2087 (Riker, 1999)(delay of 14 months); *City of Houston, Texas,* 105 LA 120 (Moore, 1995)(discipline overturned when imposed 250 days after employer became aware of incident; state law required discipline to be imposed within 180 days); *Chicago Housing Authority and Fraternal Order of Police, Illinois Labor Council,* LAIG 4978 (Cohen, 1994)(arbitrator found four-month delay in initiation of investigation "puzzling," but reversed discharge on other grounds).

[58] *Meehan v. Macy,* 392 F.2d 822 (1968), *modified,* 425 F.2d 469, *aff'd en banc,* 425 F.2d 472 (1969).

[59] *Colten v. Kentucky,* 407 U.S. 104 (1972).

[60] *Bence v. Breier,* 501 F.2d 1185 (7th Cir. 1974). *See also Davis v. Williams,* 598 F.2d 916 (5th Cir. 1979).

[61] *E.g., Piscottano v. Murphy,* 511 F.3d 247 (2d Cir. 2007); *Flanagan v. Munger,* 890 F.2d 1557 (10th Cir. 1989); *Rodriguez v. Personnel Bd. of City of Santa Ana,* 2006 WL 302414 (Cal. App. 2006); *Harper v. Crockett,* 868 F. Supp. 1557 (E.D. Ark. 1994); *McIsaac v. Civil Service Commission,* 648 N.E.2d 1312 (Mass. App. 1995).

[62] *Arnett v. Kennedy,* 416 U.S. 134 (1974). *See Parker v. Levy,* 417 U.S. 733 (1974).

[63] *Cranston v. City of Richmond,* 710 P.2d 845 (Cal. 1985)(emphasis in original). *See also Herzbrun v. Milwaukee County,* 504 F.2d 1189 (7th Cir. 1974); *Aiello v. City of Wilmington,* 623 F.2d 845 (3d Cir. 1980).

[64] *E.g., Kannisto v. City and County of San Francisco,* 541 F.2d 841 (9th Cir. 1976); *City of St. Petersburg v. Pinellas Co. Police Benevolent Association,* 414 So.2d 293 (Fla. App. 1982).

[65] *Fuqua v. City Council of Ozark,* 567 So.2d 354 (Ala. Civ. App. 1990).

[66] *Richter v. Civil Service Commission of Philadelphia,* 387 A.2d 131 (Pa. Cmwlth. 1978).

[67] *McMullen v. Carson,* 754 F.2d 936 (11th Cir. 1985); *Balinton v. City and County of San Francisco,* 2003 WL 21363360 (Cal. App. 2003).

[68] *Civil Service Commission of Philadelphia v. Wojtuski,* 525 A.2d 1255 (Pa. Cmwlth. 1987).

[69] *Aiudi v. Baillargeon,* 399 A.2d 1240 (R.I. 1979).

[70] *Thomas v. Board of Public Safety of the City of Chicago,* 414 N.E.2d 11 (Ill. 1980); *Winhorst v. Mayor of Jersey City,* 127 A. 586 (N.J. 1921).

[71] *Cranston v. City of Richmond,* 710 P.2d 845 (Cal. 1985); *Harris v. City of Colorado Springs,* 867 P.2d 217 (Colo. App. 1993).

[72] *Redo v. West Goshen Township,* 401 A.2d 394 (Pa.Cmwlth. 1979); *Federal Bureau of Prisons,* 114 LA 475 (Cohen, 2000).

[73] *Kannisto v. City and County of San Francisco,* 541 F.2d 841 (9th Cir. 1976).

[74] *Briley v. Little Rock Civil Service Commission,* 583 S.W.2d 78 (Ark. 1979).

[75] *Jackson v. Howell,* 577 F. Supp. 47 (W.D. Mich. 1983).

[76] *Police Commissioner v. Civil Service Commission,* 494 N.E.2d 27 (Mass. 1986).

[77] *Allman v. Police Board of Chicago,* 489 N.E.2d 929 (Ill. App. 1986); *Kelly v. Salt Lake City Civil Service Commission,* 8 P.3d 1048 (Utah App. 2000).

[78] *City of Fort Worth, Texas,* 2001 WL 1479992 (Jennings, 2001).

[79] *Kannisto v. City and County of San Francisco*, 541 F.2d 841 (9th Cir. 1976); *Miller v. City of York*, 415 A.2d 1280 (Pa.Cmwlth. 1980).

[80] *In re: Zeber's Appeal*, 156 A.2d 821 (Pa. 1959).

[81] *Tomkiel v. Tredyffrin Township Board of Supervisors*, 440 A.2d 690 (Pa. Cmwlth. 1982).

[82] M. Marmo, *Off-Duty Behavior by Police: Arbitrators Determine if On-The-Job Discipline is Appropriate*, 14 J. Police Sci. & Admin. 102 (1986).

[83] *Murray v. Jamison,* 333 F. Supp. 1379 (W.D. N.C. 1971).

[84] *McMullen v. Carson*, 754 F.2d 936 (11th Cir. 1985).

[85] *Hamilton County Sheriff's Department*, LAIG 4164 (Bittel, 1988)(five-day suspension upheld; failure to comply with grooming code after repeated orders to do so).

[86] *Allegan County Sheriff's Department*, LAIG 4382 (Patton, 1990)(reversal of three-day suspension after employer warned employee that continued conduct would result in a written reprimand); *Municipality of Anchorage*, (Beck, 1988)(discharge for failure to answer questions in internal investigations interview overturned; employer failed to convey that failure to respond to questions would result in discharge)(unreported decision; copies may be obtained from LRIS).

[87] *Fuqua v. City Council of Ozark*, 567 So.2d 354 (Ala. App. 1990).

[88] *IBPO v. Town of Windsor*, 483 A.2d 626 (Conn. Sup. 1984)(Court overturned discipline of officer who received suspension for refusing to sign a warrant he had not served).

[89] *Richardson v. Board of Supervisors*, 250 Cal.Rptr. 1 (1988)(discipline overturned; supervisor deliberately provoked confrontation with deputy).

[90] *See Wiley v. Mayor of Baltimore,* 48 F.3d 773 (4th Cir. 1995); *Introini v. Richland County*, 9 IER Cases 1143 (D. S.C. 1993); *Ex Parte Bostick*, 642 So.2d 472 (Ala. 1994); *Rivera v. City of Douglas*, 644 P.2d 271 (Ariz. App. 1982); *Harris v. City of Colorado Springs*, 867 P.2d 217 (Colo. App. 1993); *Jones v. Department of Public Safety and Corrections*, 923 So.2d 699 (La. App. 2005); *Furtado v. Town of Plymouth*, 867 N.E.2d 801 (Mass. App. 2007); *Warren v. City of Asheville*, 328 S.E.2d 859 (N.C. App. 1985); *In re Waterman*, 910 A.2d 1175 (N.H. 2006); *Soto v. City of Laredo*, 764 F. Supp. 448 (S.D. Tex. 1991).

[91] *Farmer v. City of Fort Lauderdale,* 427 So.2d 187 (Fla. 1983). *See Kelley v. Sheriff's Merit Com'n of Kane County*, 866 N.E.2d 702 (Ill. App. 2007); *Meadow v. Civil Service Board*, 781 P.2d 772 (Nev. 1989); *Stape v. Civil Service Commission*, 172 A.2d 161 (Pa. 1961). *See also City of Zanesville v. Sheets*, 525 N.E.2d 842 (Ohio App. 1987)(polygraph results inadmissible in police disciplinary proceedings); *City of Spokane, Washington and Spokane Police Officers' Guild,* (Gaunt, 1993)(unreported decision; copies available from LRIS).

[92] *Seattle Police Officers' Guild v. City of Seattle*, 494 P.2d 485 (Wash. 1972). *See also Eshelman v. Blubaum,* 560 P.2d 1283 (Ariz. App. 1977); *Baker v. City of Lawrence*, 409 N.E.2d 710 (Mass. 1979).

[93] *Oberg v. City of Billings*, 674 P.2d 494 (Mont. 1983).

[94] *Los Angeles Police Protective League v. City of Los Angeles*, 10 IER Cases 1192 (Cal. App. 1995). *See Fraternal Order of Police v. City of Philadelphia*, 546 A.2d 137 (Pa.Cmwlth. 1988)(no prohibition on using polygraph to screen applicants for special investigations unit).

95 *Furtado v. Town of Plymouth*, 888 N.E.2d 357 (Mass. 2008).

96 Occasionally, state laws will prohibit the issuance of certain types of disciplinary sanctions. Maryland, for example, has enacted a statute prohibiting a law enforcement agency from requiring its officers to work extra duty as a form of discipline.

CHAPTER 4

PROCEDURAL RIGHTS IN THE DISCIPLINARY PROCESS

Introduction.

A delicate balance exists in the investigation of complaints of misconduct lodged against law enforcement officers. Law enforcement agencies usually desire to investigate complaints of misconduct as quickly and as thoroughly as possible, so that the complaining party, the officer, and the public feel that appropriate attention has been paid to the complaint. Similarly, if evidence of misconduct is established, law enforcement agencies usually want to make swift disciplinary decisions to ensure that the disciplinary problem is rectified. Since law enforcement agencies are generally organized along quasi-military lines, officers who are the subject of complaints are usually ordered to cooperate fully in the investigation of the complaint, and are informed that if they fail to do so, their jobs may be at risk.

> *These constitutional rights, particularly the right to be free from compulsory self-incrimination and the right to procedural due process, often arise in the law enforcement workplace.*

At the same time that a law enforcement agency may have these needs to quickly investigate and adjudicate complaints of misconduct, an individual does not forfeit constitutional rights possessed by all citizens simply by accepting a job as a law enforcement officer. These constitutional rights, particularly the right to be free from compulsory self-incrimination and the right to procedural due process, often arise in the law enforcement workplace.

The result of this tension has been hundreds of court decisions balancing the rights and obligations of law enforcement employers and their employees. Yet even today, 30 and 40 years after some of the key decisions in the area have been issued by the United States Supreme Court, uncertainty exists in many important aspects of the procedural obligations of an employer in processing disciplinary and related issues. Who could guess, for example, that no case has ever directly addressed whether an officer involved in the use of deadly force has the right to counsel before giving a statement?

This chapter lays out the basic procedural rights held by officers in the disciplinary process. Necessarily, the chapter focuses most on the three core rules of disciplinary procedure – the *Garrity*, *Weingarten*, and *Loudermill* rules. However, the chapter also deals with emerging rules on procedural issues such as concepts of substantive due process, the exclusionary rule, and how entrapment principles apply in disciplinary settings.

A Law Enforcement Officer's Right To Be Free From Compulsory Self-Incrimination — The *Garrity* Rule.

In 1966, in a case known as *Garrity v. New Jersey*, the United States Supreme Court faced the issue of how the Fifth Amendment's protections against compulsory self-incrimination applied in a law enforcement disciplinary setting.[1] In *Garrity*, police officers were questioned during the course of a state investigation concerning alleged ticket fixing. The officers were ordered to respond to the investigator's questions, and were informed that a refusal to respond to the questions would result in their discharge from employment. The officers answered the questions, and their answers were used to convict them in subsequent criminal prosecutions.

The Supreme Court ruled that the use of the officers' statements in criminal proceedings violated the Fifth Amendment's guarantee that citizens cannot be compelled to be witnesses against themselves. The Court held that "the choice imposed on [the officers] was one between self-incrimination or job forfeiture," a choice the Court termed "coercion." In particularly strong language, the Court held that "policemen, like teachers and lawyers, are not relegated to a watered-down version of constitutional rights," and ruled that statements which a law enforcement officer is compelled to make under threat of possible forfeiture of his or her job could not subsequently be used against the officer in a criminal prosecution. As the Supreme Court later described, "the Fifth Amendment not only protects the individual against being involuntarily called as a witness against himself in a criminal prosecution but also privileges him not to answer official questions put to him in any other proceeding, civil or criminal, formal or informal, where the answers might incriminate him in future criminal proceedings."[2]

The Supreme Court addressed the flip side of the *Garrity* case the following year. In *Gardner v. Broderick*, a police officer being questioned about alleged bribery and corruption was discharged after refusing to sign a waiver of immunity which would have allowed the use of his statements in a subsequent criminal prosecution. The Court reversed the officer's discharge, holding that the officer was discharged solely for his refusal to waive a constitutional right. In language which has since become a guidepost for disciplinary investigations of law enforcement officers, the Court ruled that while a law enforcement agency can conduct an administrative investigation of an officer, it cannot in the course of that investigation compel the officer to waive the immunity necessary under *Garrity*:

> "If appellant, a policeman, had refused to answer questions specifically, directly, and narrowly relating to the performance of his official duties, without being required to waive his immunity with respect to the use of his answers or the fruits thereof in a criminal prosecution of himself, *Garrity v. New Jersey, supra,* the privilege against self-incrimination would not have been a bar to his dismissal. The facts of this case, however, do not present this issue. * * * He was dismissed solely for his refusal to waive the immunity to which he is entitled if he is required to testify despite his constitutional privilege."[3]

Gardner thus created two separate rules. First, if an employee lawfully invokes the self-incrimination privilege under the Fifth Amendment, the employee may not be disciplined for doing so without a grant of immunity from the use of the answers in a subsequent criminal proceeding.[4] Second, there exist affirmative limitations on an employer's ability to require answers to questions asked during an investigation of an employee – in the words of *Gardner*, the questions must be "specifically, narrowly, and directly" tailored to the employee's job.

The Supreme Court ruled that the use of the officers' statements in criminal proceedings violated the Fifth Amendment's guarantee that citizens cannot be compelled to be witnesses against themselves.

The Basic Requirements Of The *Garrity* Rule.

As it has been interpreted over the years, *Garrity* requires that before a law enforcement agency questioning one of its officers can discipline the officer for refusing to answer questions, the agency must:

- Order the officer to answer the questions under threat of disciplinary action,[5]

- Ask questions which are specifically, directly and narrowly related to the officer's duties or the officer's fitness for duty, and

- Advise the officer that the answers to the questions will not be used against the officer in criminal proceedings.[6]

If the officer then refuses to answer appropriate questions, the officer may be disciplined for insubordination.[7] Since the officer's answers cannot be used against the officer in a subsequent criminal proceeding, discipline for refusing to answer appropriate questions is permissible even if the officer is the subject of an active criminal investigation.[8] As an officer who has been ordered to give a statement is given immunity from the use of the statements in a criminal proceeding, the officer has no right to insist on the presence of an attorney before providing the statement.[9] However, under the *Weingarten* rule, as discussed in greater depth later in this chapter, the officer may be entitled to the presence of a union representative before the questioning begins.

If there is a sufficient relationship between an officer's off-duty conduct and on-the-job performance, a law enforcement agency has the right to question an officer about the off-duty conduct.[10] In such circumstances, the protections of *Garrity* fully apply to the questioning.[11]

These basic principles were applied in a case involving the citizen review board in Denver, Colorado. The ordinance authorizing the review board granted the board subpoena authority, which it used to try to compel officers to give statements. An appeals court quashed the subpoenas, reasoning as follows:

(1) The review board did not have the authority to discipline officers who refused to answer questions in testimony before the board; therefore

(2) The review board's lack of disciplinary authority meant it could not "compel" employees to give statements within the framework of the Fifth Amendment; therefore

(3) The review board could not grant officers testifying before it the necessary immunity under *Garrity*; thus

(4) The review board lacked the authority to compel the officers to testify.[12]

Simply because an officer can be ordered to answer questions in an administrative setting does not mean that a law enforcement agency has the right to insist that all of its questions be answered. As indicated by *Gardner v. Broderick*, in order to be valid, questions must have a direct bearing upon the officer's job. If the questions are not so limited, and especially if the questions go into areas of personal concerns, the agency may not insist on answers to the questions without violating the officer's right to privacy.[13]

The Scope Of The *Garrity* Rule — When Does It Apply?

Critical to the operation of the *Garrity* rule is that the employer actually require the employee to respond to questions, and that the employee be compelled by threat of possible discharge to respond. Absent such an order, not only does the employee have no obligation to respond to the questions (and the Department consequently has no right to discipline the employee for refusing to answer the questions),[14] but no immunity is given to the use of the employee's answers in a subsequent criminal prosecution.[15] It is not enough if the employee simply subjectively believes he is required to answer questions; rather, the employer must actually *do something* to make that belief reasonable.[16]

An "order" to answer questions can be written or oral. In some cases, the order or the "compulsion" to make a statement may even be implied. Most courts follow a two-part test, often referred to as the objective/subjective test, to determine if an employee's statements were voluntary or compelled. An employee is considered "ordered" or, in the parlance of the Fifth Amendment, "compelled" to answer questions if (1) the employee subjectively believes that he/she is compelled to give a statement upon threat of loss of job; and (2) the employee's belief is objectively reasonable at the time the statement was made.[17] Thus, it might be objectively reasonable for an officer to believe that statements made in an internal affairs setting, or as part of a criminal investigation conducted by the officer's employer, or in a polygraph examination, would be required as a condition of employment. On the other hand, it would not be reasonable for an officer to believe that testimony given in a job-related civil case (without invoking the Fifth Amendment) would be required.[18]

The protections of *Garrity* apply automatically whenever an officer or any public employee is required by a supervisor to answer questions as a condition of employment.[19] A statutory grant of immunity or a signed immunity agreement with a prosecutor is not necessary to give rise to the immunity envisioned by *Garrity* since the immunity envisioned by *Garrity* is self-executing.[20] As one court described it, "when an employee is confronted with the threat of an adverse employment action for refusal to answer questions, the very act of telling the witness that he would be subject to removal if he refused to answer was held to have conferred such immunity. Under these circumstances, no specific grant of immunity is necessary: It is the very fact that the testimony was compelled which prevents its use in subsequent proceedings, not any affirmative tender of immunity."[21] To trigger *Garrity* rights, the level of discipline imposed for not answering

> An "order" to answer questions can be written or oral.

> The protections of Garrity apply automatically whenever an officer or any public employee is required by a supervisor to answer questions as a condition of employment.

the questions must constitute a "substantial economic penalty" such as discharge; merely threatening the employee with a transfer or a short suspension may not be sufficient to invoke the *Garrity* rule.[22] At present, the law is unsettled as to how or if the *Garrity* rule applies when an officer is merely writing a required report as opposed to facing questioning.[23]

Reverse *Garrity* Warnings.

There is a split of opinion on whether an employer must actually give the employee an affirmative guarantee of immunity before the employer can demand answers. The majority of courts hold that whenever questioning could possibly lead to criminal charges, an employer must give an affirmative guarantee of immunity and warn the officer that failure to respond to questioning could lead to disciplinary action for insubordination.[24] Courts following this rule reason that law enforcement officers are not expected to be experts on the guarantees of the Fifth Amendment, and should not be required to guess whether they have criminal immunity for their statements. As noted by one court adhering to this latter view:

> "[M]erely to relieve a police officer, after the fact, of the possibility of prosecution, does not solve the dilemma with which he is faced while undergoing interrogation. The exclusion of the statement in a criminal proceeding is nothing more than the exclusion of a coerced statement. In the first place, the employee may not know of his rights to remain silent and to avoid self-incrimination; and, even if he is aware of that right, he almost certainly does not know that, under *Garrity*, as a matter of law, his response cannot be used against him in a criminal case. Absent the advice that [the officers] could not be prosecuted on the basis of the statement given, their statement was the product of a coercive choice. They were truly between Scylla and Charybdis. If they did not speak, they knew that they would be fired. If they spoke, what they said could lead to prosecution, and most likely, in any event, to conviction and dismissal from their jobs."[25]

A minority of courts hold that since *Garrity* rights automatically attach whenever an employee is required to answer questions as a condition of employment, there is no need for an employer to give such guarantees.[26] One court following the minority approach stressed the nature of a law enforcement officer's job, noting that "these deputies had at least five years' experience each, testified to familiarity with Department policy and criminal law, and were versed in the Department's procedures for placing suspects under arrest."[27]

The affirmative guarantees of immunity required by most courts are now usually referred to as "reverse-*Garrity* warnings." Reverse *Garrity* warnings should have these components:

- An order that the employee is required to answer the questions;

Courts following this rule reason that law enforcement officers are not expected to be experts on the guarantees of the Fifth Amendment, and should not be required to guess whether they have criminal immunity for their statements.

- A warning that if the employee refuses to answer the questions, significant discipline, up to and including termination of employment, may result; and

- A guarantee that the employee's statements and the fruits of those statements will not be used in the criminal prosecution of the employee.

The Scope Of Immunity Under *Garrity*.

A compelled statement under *Garrity* gains immunity only in a subsequent criminal proceeding. That means that a compelled statement under *Garrity* can be used for a wide variety of other purposes:

- To discipline the officer;[28]

- In a civil lawsuit brought against the employer and/or the officer;[29] and

- In criminal prosecutions of persons other than the officer.[30]

Under some circumstances, compelled statements can even be subpoenaed by a grand jury investigating police officers, so long as the statements are not inappropriately used by the grand jury (as described in greater detail below).[31] The mere release of internal affairs files to a prosecutor, without more, is not prohibited by the *Garrity* rule.[32] As the Supreme Court has commented in an analogous context, "mere coercion does not violate the Self-Incrimination Clause absent use of the compelled statements in a criminal case."[33]

An issue swirling around in state court cases interpreting the *Garrity* doctrine has been whether use and derivative use or transactional immunity results from an administrative interrogation under state constitutional law. Use and derivative use immunity is the narrower form of immunity; it provides an officer immunity from the use in a subsequent criminal proceeding of his statements and the fruits of his statements made in an administrative interrogation. Transactional immunity is much broader, and prohibits any prosecution over the entire transaction which is the subject of the questioning.

In *Garrity*, the Supreme Court held that only use and derivative use immunity was required under the federal constitution.[34] However, state courts are free to interpret their own constitutions more broadly than the federal constitution, and state legislatures are free to enact broader protections than those that exist at the federal level. In one case, the Massachusetts Supreme Court squarely held that whenever an officer is required to submit to a disciplinary interrogation, the officer is entitled to a complete grant of immunity from criminal prosecution for the entire transaction which is the subject of the interview – a grant of immunity which is much broader than that resulting under the federal constitution's *Garrity* rule.[35] A variety of other states, including Alaska, California, Hawai'i, Michigan, Mississippi, Ohio, Oregon, Rhode Island, South Carolina, and Washington have generally adopted transactional immunity rules, either by statute or through a state constitutional provision.[36]

Even in states following use and derivative use immunity rules, there is a good deal of controversy about precisely what the limitations are on the use of the statement or the fruits of the statement. For example, a federal court of appeals in the case involving the prosecution of Oliver North held that a prosecutor has an affirmative burden of proving that all testimony must be free of any taint from the immunized statement. In the words of the Court:

> "The District Court must hold a full hearing that will inquire into the content as well as the sources of the grand jury and trial witnesses' testimony. That inquiry must proceed witness by witness, line by line and item by item. For each grand jury and trial witness, the [prosecution] must show by a preponderance of the evidence that no use whatsoever was made of any of the immunized testimony either by the witness or by the prosecutor in questioning the witness. If [the prosecution] has in fact introduced trial evidence that fails this analysis, then the defendant is entitled to a new trial. If the same is true as to grand jury evidence, then the indictment must be dismissed."[37]

A similar result was produced in a case involving grand jury subpoenas for investigative files compiled by the Albuquerque Police Department, where a federal appeals court held that *Garrity*'s "total prohibition on use provides a comprehensive safeguard, barring the use of compelled testimony as an 'investigatory lead,' and also barring the use of any evidence obtained by focusing investigation on a witness as a result of his compelled disclosures."[38]

Reaching a different result in the prosecution of Los Angeles police officers Stacy Koon and Lawrence Powell arising out of the Rodney King case, a federal court held that all the prosecution need prove is that the substance of the testimony of any witness exposed to a compelled statement is based on a legitimate source independent of the immunized testimony. The Court was particularly concerned that the grant of immunity under *Garrity* is automatic, and flows directly from the order compelling a statement:

> "Immunity attaches in the *Garrity* context when a threat of the loss of employment forces a public employee to respond to questioning by another public employee. In this context, the individuals who question the employee are concerned about potential misconduct, and their goal is generally to learn the facts of a situation as quickly as possible. They do not necessarily act with the care and precision of a prosecutor weighing the benefits of compelling testimony against the risks to future prosecutions; indeed, they may not even have the prospect of prosecution and the requirements of the Fifth Amendment in mind."[39]

Following a similar analysis, one California court has held that a prosecutor could see an officer's compelled statement and use the compelled statement to persuade the victim to testify without violating *Garrity* (in California, *Garrity* rights are often referred to as *Lybarger* rights, a reference to a case decided under California's statutory Peace Officer Bill of Rights).[40]

Controversy also exists over whether a compelled statement under *Garrity* can be used either for impeachment or to prosecute the officer for perjury if the officer later testifies in a way contrary to the compelled statement. The general rule is that the Fifth Amendment permits the government to use compelled statements obtained during an investigation if the use is limited to a prosecution for collateral crimes such as perjury or obstruction of justice.[41] For example, in *United States v. Veal,* Miami police officers under investigation by the police department and the FBI for murdering a suspect and covering it up were prosecuted for the crime of making false statements during interviews conducted pursuant to the departmental investigation. A federal appeals court rejected the officers' contention that *Garrity* prohibited use of their statements at the trial for these collateral crimes, and rejected the argument that "statements protected by *Garrity* are forever barred from use in any prosecution, including one for perjury, false statements, or obstruction of justice."[42]

At least one state has enacted a statute that effectively gives *Garrity* protections to the use of statements in subsequent civil proceedings against an officer. In 1994, California added Section 3303(f) to its statutory Peace Officer Bill of Rights, which prohibits the use of compelled statements in most civil cases:

> "No statement made during interrogation by a public safety officer under duress, coercion, or threat of punitive action shall be admissible in any subsequent civil proceeding. This subdivision is subject to the following qualifications:
>
> "(1) This subdivision shall not limit the use of statements made by a public safety officer when the employing public safety department is seeking civil sanctions against any public safety officer, including disciplinary action.
>
> "(2) This subdivision shall not prevent the admissibility of statements made by the public safety officer under interrogation in any civil action, including administrative actions brought by that public safety officer, or that officer's exclusive representative, arising out of a disciplinary action.
>
> "(3) This subdivision shall not prevent statements made by a public safety officer under interrogation from being used to impeach the testimony of that officer after an in camera review to determine whether the statements serve to impeach the testimony of the officer.
>
> "(4) This subdivision shall not otherwise prevent the admissibility of statements made by a public safety officer under interrogation if that officer subsequently is deceased."[43]

There are few cases interpreting Section 3303(f),[44] and a very real question exists as to whether a California statute could, consistent with principles of federalism, bind a federal court with respect to the admissibility of evidence.

Concerned about the potential use of compelled statements, many law enforcement labor organizations have developed "advice of rights" cards for their members. The card used in San Antonio, Texas, suggests that officers preface all police reports with the following statement:

> "It is my understanding that this report is made for administrative, internal police department purposes only and will not be used as part of an official investigation. This report is made by me after being ordered to do so by lawful supervisory officers. It is my understanding that by refusing to obey an order to write this report that I can be disciplined for insubordination, and that punishment for insubordination can be up to and including termination of employment. This report is made only pursuant to such orders and the potential punishment/discipline that can result for failure to obey that order."[45]

The Right To Representation During A Disciplinary Interview — *Weingarten* Rights.

In settings where a labor organization has collective bargaining rights, the employee is entitled to representation by his collective bargaining representative under the so-called *Weingarten* rule. The 1975 case of *National Labor Relations Board v. J. Weingarten* arose under Section 7 of the National Labor Relations Act, which provides that employees have the right to join labor organizations "and to engage in other concerted activities for the purpose of collective bargaining."[46] In *Weingarten*, a private employer denied an employee's request for union representation during a disciplinary interview. The Supreme Court ruled the denial of representation a violation of Section 7, holding that the right to representation in disciplinary interviews was a necessary part of the collective bargaining process:

> "Requiring a lone employee to attend an investigatory interview which he reasonably believes may result in the imposition of discipline perpetuates the inequality the [National Labor Relations] Act was designed to eliminate, and bars recourse to the safeguards the Act provided 'to redress the perceived imbalance of economic power between labor and management.'"[46]

Because *Weingarten* was decided under the National Labor Relations Act (NLRA), the decision was not automatically binding on state and local governments. However, virtually all state collective bargaining laws contain provisions either identical or substantially similar to Section 7 of the NLRA. Thus, state courts and public employment relations commissions were quick to adopt the *Weingarten* rule under state public employee bargaining laws. Since not all the decisions of such administrative agencies are reported on a nationwide basis, it is difficult to determine if all states which have considered the issue have adopted the *Weingarten* rule.

What can be said is that, with two exceptions, every published decision of a state employment relations commission or court considering the adoption of the *Weingarten* rule has held that employees have the right to representation during disciplinary interviews.[48] The exceptions are New York and Rhode Island, where state courts have held that the right to representation exists under other than the *Weingarten* rule.[49] Since the *Weingarten* rule is a creature of collective bargaining, a labor organization can waive *Weingarten* rights through the collective bargaining process.[50] Moreover, it is illegal for an employer to discriminate against an employee for the exercise of *Weingarten* rights.[51]

In *Weingarten*, the Supreme Court established broad basic principles for representation in disciplinary interviews. As they have been interpreted by the courts over the years since the *Weingarten* decision, these principles provide:

- **The employee must reasonably believe that the interview will result in disciplinary action for the right to representation to exist.** It is the reasonable belief of the <u>employee</u>, not the <u>employer</u>, which dictates whether an employee is entitled to representation.[52] If the employee reasonably believes that discipline may result from the interview, the employee is entitled to representation even if the employer had no intention whatsoever to impose discipline.[53] The right to representation by a labor organization applies even when the interview is being conducted as part of a criminal investigation, and even when the interview is being conducted by an outside agency such as a district attorney's office.[54] However, if the employer assures the employee that no discipline will result from the interview and does not violate that pledge, no right to representation exists,[55] and mere "general anxiety" over whether discipline could possibly result is not enough to trigger the right to representation.[56] Also, if a collective bargaining agreement mandates that an employer give notice that an interview will be disciplinary in nature, and the employer gives no such notice, then it would be unreasonable for the employee to believe that discipline could result from the interview, and *Weingarten* representation would not be required.[57] Absent a reasonable belief that discipline could result, routine supervisor-employee interactions do not trigger the *Weingarten* rule.[58]

The last few years have seen a good deal of litigation over whether someone who the employer believes is merely a witness to misconduct has the right to representation under *Weingarten*. Because *Weingarten* rights turn on the <u>employee's</u> reasonable belief that discipline could result from an interview, the employer's designation of an employee as a "witness" will not necessarily eliminate *Weingarten* rights. Two cases, one from New Jersey and one from Oregon, illustrate these principles. In the New Jersey case, the New Jersey Public Employment Relations Commission held that supervisors interviewed as "witnesses" in an investigation into sexual harassment among their subordinates had the right to representation since they reasonably believed that they could be disciplined for failing to properly supervise the employees in their charge.[59] In the Oregon case, Oregon's

Key: Disciplinary Action

Employment Relations Board held that corrections officers interviewed as witnesses in an excessive force case had *Weingarten* representation rights because they reasonably could believe they would be subject to discipline for failing to either report or stop the use of force by another officer.[60]

- **The right to representation only exists where the employer is eliciting information from the employee.**[61] For example, if the employer is merely reprimanding the employee,[62] is requiring the employee to participate in a fitness for duty examination,[63] is interviewing the employee as part of a performance evaluation process,[64] or is discussing a non-disciplinary matter with the employee but is not conducting a disciplinary interview,[65] no right to representation exists. However, the right to representation does apply to an interview that turns into an investigatory session, even if it was originally convened to advise the employee of previously determined discipline.[66]

- **The right to representation exists even where the employer is eliciting information in written form.** Several cases stand for the proposition that *Weingarten* rights apply even when the employer is not actually questioning the employee, but is using other means to elicit information from the employee. For example, the majority rule is that *Weingarten* rights apply when the employer is compelling an employee to prepare a report that will be used in a disciplinary investigation.[67] A case decided by the Pennsylvania Labor Relations Board has even held that *Weingarten* rights apply when an employer is requesting that an employee submit to drug testing as part of a disciplinary investigation. Relying on similar cases decided by the National Labor Relations Board, the Pennsylvania Board held that "the purpose of the blood and urine tests at issue was to aid in the Employer's determination of whether discipline should be imposed. Thus we find that the Employer's request for testing occurred in this context as an investigatory interview (essentially consisting of a request to submit to blood and urine tests) and therefore, that the employee was entitled to the assistance of a union representative."[68]

- **The employee must request such representation.** Unlike the protections of the *Garrity* rule, *Weingarten* rights are not automatic; they must be invoked by the employee.[69] Most states hold that once an employee makes a request for union representation, the employer has three options: (1) grant the request; (2) dispense with or discontinue the interview; or (3) offer the employee the choice of continuing the interview unaccompanied by a union representative or having no interview at all and thereby dispensing with any benefits that the interview might have conferred on the employee.[70]

- **The employer does not select the *Weingarten* representative.** The employer does not have the right to select the representative who assists the employee during the disciplinary interview. Though there is some conflict among states on the issue, the usual rule is that the employee, not the labor organization, is entitled to pick the particular representative.[72] While there is no right under *Weingarten* to representation by a private attorney (though such a right may exist under a statutory bill of rights),[73] if it chooses, the labor organization has the right to select an attorney as its representative for the disciplinary interview.[73]

• **The right to representation exists regardless of rank, so long as the employee is represented by a labor organization for collective bargaining purposes.** In some states, police chiefs have the right to be part of a collective bargaining unit. Since *Weingarten* rights turn on whether the employee is part of a collective bargaining unit, in those states even police chiefs have *Weingarten* rights.[74]

• **The exercise of the right to representation cannot unduly interfere with legitimate needs of the employer. In order to establish undue interference with its operations, the employer must prove that a delay in the interview would be unreasonable under all of the circumstances or endanger the investigation.**[75] To establish that a delay in the investigation would interfere with its legitimate needs, an employer must prove that it has a need for an "efficient and timely investigatory process" that would be undermined by the requested delay in the interview.[76] An employer is clearly on shaky ground in demanding that the employee immediately find a union representative, and then insisting on proceeding with the interview when no representative can be immediately located. For example, in one police case, a labor relations board found a *Weingarten* violation where a police union representative's job duties required him to leave an interview and the police chief gave the employee "two minutes" to find another representative.[77]

The Role Of The Representative In Disciplinary Interviews.

The *Weingarten* rule is still evolving, particularly in the area of the role the union representative can play during the disciplinary interview. A few early cases imply that the representative has the right to counsel the employee prior to, but not during, the interview, and to otherwise be no more than a "fly on the wall," a passive observer of the interview. As the law has matured, however, courts and labor boards have taken a broader view of the role of the union representative. Today, the notion that an employer has the right to order a labor representative to be simply silent during a disciplinary interview has long been discarded.[78] The broad approach is strongly buttressed by the Supreme Court's opinion in *Weingarten*, where the Court described in generalities the role of the labor organization representative:

> "A single employee confronted by an employer investigating whether certain conduct deserves discipline may be too fearful or inarticulate to relate accurately the incident being investigated, or too ignorant to raise extenuating factors. A knowledgeable union representative could assist the employer by eliciting favorable facts, and save the employer production time by getting to the bottom of the incident occasioning the interview."[79]

The notion that an employer has the right to order a labor representative to be simply silent during a disciplinary interview has long been discarded.

What follows is a list of the type of activities in which a union representative could possible engage during a *Weingarten* interview, and whether those activities are generally thought to be within the scope of *Weingarten* rights:

- **The right to consult with the employee prior to the interview.** The Supreme Court's *Weingarten* decision indicates that the right to representation includes the ability of the representative to consult with the employee prior to the interview, and no court or labor board has ever held to the contrary under state law.[80]

- **The right to determine what the charges are prior to the interview.** Again, the Supreme Court's *Weingarten* decision itself supports the notion that the representative has the right to determine the charges against the employee prior to the interview. State labor boards have repeatedly supported this notion. However, the right to notice of charges does not extend so far as to allow a labor organization access to witness statements in advance of an interview.[81]

- **The right to privately consult with the employee during the interview.** Most states hold that *Weingarten* rights include the right of the representative to privately consult with the employee during the interview, so long as the consultation does not unduly disrupt the interview.[82]

- **The right to offer investigatory leads at the conclusion of the interview.** The Supreme Court's *Weingarten* decision also envisions the representative offering investigatory leads at the conclusion of a disciplinary interview. State labor boards have uniformly accepted this construction of the right to representation.

- **The right to offer mitigating circumstances at the conclusion of the interview.** Again, *Weingarten* itself describes the role of the union representatives as including the ability to offer mitigating circumstances at the conclusion of the interview, a concept accepted by state labor boards.[83]

- **The right to object to inappropriate questions during an interview.** Apparently only one state – Ohio – has found that the right to representation under *Weingarten* includes the right to object to inappropriate questions.[84]

Remedies For *Weingarten* Violations.

Labor boards have wrestled with the appropriate remedy when an interview violates *Weingarten* rights. One approach has been to reverse any discipline when the employer relies in any way upon the interview in making its disciplinary decision.[85] A similar approach is that if an employer violates a labor organization's *Weingarten* rights, any underlying disciplinary decision it imposes will be overturned unless the employer establishes that it would have reached the same decision without relying on information gathered during an interview which violated the *Weingarten* rule.[86]

A Law Enforcement Officer's Procedural Due Process Rights.

The Fifth Amendment to the United States Constitution contains a "due process" clause which provides as follows:

> "No person shall be * * * deprived of life, liberty, or property, without due process of law."

The Fifth Amendment thus requires that if the government acts to deprive any person of a "property" or "liberty" right, it must act with due process in doing so. Since law enforcement employers are, by definition, governmental agencies subject to the strictures of the Fifth Amendment, whenever they make employment decisions affecting property or liberty interests, they must do so in accord with the requirements of the Fifth Amendment.[87]

Under these general guidelines, two questions arise whenever a law enforcement officer has been disciplined:

- Does the officer have a property or liberty interest in the job which has been affected by the disciplinary action? and

- If so, did the employer accord the officer the necessary procedural due process prior to depriving the officer of the property or liberty interest?

How A Property Interest In A Law Enforcement Officer's Job Or A Benefit Associated With The Job Is Created.

There are seven common ways in which a law enforcement officer can gain a property interest in the job or a particular benefit associated with the job. In each case, the property interest is created through a continuing expectation of either employment or a particular benefit, an expectation which is secured by state or local law, or by other guarantees binding the employer. The seven ways through which a property interest may arise are as follows:

- A collective bargaining agreement between the officer's labor organization and the employer can contain a clause requiring the employer to have just cause or some other articulable reason to discipline the officer.[88]

- In the absence of a collective bargaining agreement, provisions in the employer's ordinances or charter can grant employees job protection or tenured status.[89]

- The operations or personnel manuals of the employer can grant protections against unjust disciplinary action,[90] but usually only if

The Fifth Amendment thus requires that if the government acts to deprive any person of a "property" or "liberty" right, it must act with due process in doing so.

A property interest is created through a continuing expectation of either employment or a particular benefit, an expectation which is secured by state or local law, or by other guarantees binding the employer.

they are written in specific language which provides some guarantees of future employment.[91] The mere fact that the employer's rules establish certain disciplinary procedures is likely not enough to create a property right unless it also includes a substantive grant of job protection.[92] Similarly, a reference to "full-time" employees does not create a property interest since it does not promise any protections from discipline.[93] However, a statement that employees can only be terminated for "cause" is sufficient to create a property right to the job.[94]

- Civil service rules or ordinances can grant employees some job protection against indiscriminate disciplinary action.[95]

- A state[96] or federal[97] statute can impose standards that a law enforcement employer must meet before imposing discipline.

- Even in the absence of any written guarantees of job security, the oral comments or promises of an employer may be enough to create a reasonable expectation of a right to continuing employment, assuming that the individual making the promise has the authority to bind the employer to a contract.[98] The appearance of authority to make such promises is not always legally binding; in one case, a probationary officer received assurances of continuing employment from a sergeant who subsequently became a chief, a former chief, and a village trustee, none of which actually had the authority to bind the employer.[99]

- A contract, ordinance, or statute can give rise to an expectation that the employee will continue to receive a particular benefit in the future without possibility of modification.[100]

If any of these seven conditions exist, the employee has a property right in the job. Since some sort of protection against arbitrary discipline exists in most law enforcement agencies today, only a minority of law enforcement officers do not have a property right to their jobs. Those who are generally thought to have no reasonable expectation of a continuing interest in employment and thus no property right to the job include police chiefs,[101] deputy sheriffs in states where all sheriff's office employees are considered "at-will" employees,[102] officers who are hired for a fixed term and then remain on the job after the term expires,[103] town marshals,[104] part-time officers,[105] reserve officers,[106] and officers in states where there is a presumption[107] or even a statute[108] that officers are at-will employees.

One of the most frequent areas of litigation on the question of whether property rights to the job exist concerns probationary employees. With only the most exceedingly rare exceptions, courts find that probationary employees have no property right to the job.[109] As one court observed, "probationary employees are treated as at-will employees who can be fired for any reason so long as it is not an unlawful one."[110] Along the same lines, probationary supervisors do not have a property interest in their promotional rank.[111] In those rare cases where a probationary employee is thought to have a property right, it is because there is a state statute or other set of applicable rules that prescribe the procedures an employer must use in terminating probation. If an employer violates those procedures, it will be held to have violated the due process rights of the probationary employee.[112]

Once an employee has a property right to the job, the employer may not act unilaterally to deprive the employee of the property right. For example, if an employee has gained permanent status, the employer may not convert the employee to probationary status, thereby depriving the employee of the right to due process.[113]

How Property Rights Are Affected By Employment Decisions.

Procedural due process rights apply whenever there is an interruption in the right to the continuing flow of benefits provided by the property right in the job. Thus, procedural due process applies in cases of:

- Discharge from employment.[114] However, if the employer is simply shutting down all operations – for example, if a City decides to abolish its police department – there is no property right to continuing employment.[115]

- Most temporary suspensions without pay.[116]

- Demotions.[117] However, in some cases where employees are unprotected by a collective bargaining or civil service process, a supervisor may have a property right to a job, but may not necessarily have a property right to the promoted position.[118]

- Where employees are involuntarily retired for a disability[119] or are placed on an unpaid leave of absence for medical[120] or psychological reasons.[121]

- Where the employee has been involuntarily removed from a layoff list[122] or from receiving disability benefits.[123]

- Where employees are denied sick leave when injured in the line of duty.[124]

- Where the employee has been reduced in pay grade for disciplinary reasons.[125]

- Where state statute establishes the employer's obligation to pay such costs and the employer has refused to pay an officer's criminal defense costs for a charge arising out of the officer's duties.[126]

Due process is required even in cases where the nature of the employee's offense – e.g., the conviction of a crime — makes certain that the employer's final

Procedural due process rights apply whenever there is an interruption in the right to the continuing flow of benefits provided by the property right in the job.

disciplinary decision will be discharge.[127] Most courts hold that due process need not precede the issuance of a written reprimand.[128]

Procedural due process generally need not be followed in the following circumstances:

- The reclassification of an employee to another job for non-disciplinary reasons.[129]

- Where an officer has merely been subjected to a disciplinary investigation without any discipline being imposed.[130]

- The denial of the right to engage in off-duty employment,[131] the right to work out of classification,[132] or of a transfer request.[133]

- Where a police officer has been given an administrative assignment, even if the assignment results in the loss of overtime opportunities.[134]

- The denial of step increases where no collective bargaining agreement covers the officer.[135]

- A demotion where no salary loss results.[136]

- Requiring an employee to attend a compulsory physical or psychological evaluation.[137]

- Where a temporary position is discontinued, even if the officer was working out of classification at a higher rate of pay in the position.[138]

- A change in the employee's days off[139] or the denial of the employee's request to use vacation time.[140]

- Denying an officer a disability retirement where the underlying retirement statute gave the employer the ability to transfer the officer to a non-line position.[141]

- Giving an employee an unfavorable performance evaluation.[142]

- Turning down an applicant for a job as a police officer.[143]

In most instances where an employee has been denied a promotion, no procedural due process rights are implicated.[144] As noted by a federal court of appeals with respect to promotions:

"Plaintiffs also cannot seriously contend state law grants them a protected property interest in a promotion, transfer, or any of the other benefits sought in connection with their employment. Plaintiffs have pointed to no state statute or regulation that so restricts the government employer's discretion in making these employment decisions as to grant public employees a legitimate claim of entitlement to these benefits. In fact, the Colorado Court of Appeals has expressly held that because Colorado law grants the appointing authority discretion to choose among the three highest-ranking applicants for a position, a public employee has no due process right to be selected for promotion. Accordingly, to the extent Plaintiffs' due process claim rests on the denial of the promotions, transfers, and other benefits themselves, they have demonstrated no entitlement to any particular decision and, as such, their claims must fail."[145]

However, if promotions are based on the fact of the employee meeting known criteria rather than discretionary judgment of the employer, procedural due process requirements may apply. In *Drogan v. Ward*, the Court interpreted New York's civil service laws as expressly creating a right to be considered for promotion limited only by the requirement that the officer successfully pass an examination. Under such circumstances, the Court held, the laws "invest one who has successfully completed an examination with a 'legitimate claim of entitlement' to the right to be considered for a promotion," a fact which required the employer to follow procedural due process before failing to consider a candidate who had successfully been placed on the promotional list.[146]

The most troublesome property right cases occur with respect to transfers and removal from specialty assignments, particularly those in county sheriff and state police agencies where the employee may be required to relocate significant distances. Where a transfer or reassignment is not accompanied by a loss of pay, there is no right to a hearing under general due process law, even if the transfer results in a loss of overtime opportunities.[147] Courts are split on the issue of whether due process requires a hearing if a transfer is accompanied by a loss of pay. A majority of courts hold that even in such cases, there is no right to a hearing before the transfer unless the employee has been given definite and permanent guarantees to the previous assignment.[148] However, if there are statutory or collective bargaining agreement protections against transfer being used as a form of discipline, or if the employer's rules forbid disciplinary transfers, an employee facing a disciplinary transfer would be entitled to a due process hearing.[149]

Where a transfer or reassignment is not accompanied by a loss of pay, there is no right to a hearing under general due process law.

How Liberty Interests Are Affected By Employment Decisions.

Cases involving a Fifth Amendment liberty interest in the job are much less common than cases dealing with property rights. The concept of a liberty interest focuses on the freedom to follow a trade, profession, or other calling.[150] If a governmental body acts in such a way that effectively excludes an officer from his profession, it is depriving the employee of a liberty interest, which it may not do without due process of law. More particularly, where an employer disciplines an officer for stated reasons, and where those reasons, if publicized, are likely to make the officer all but unemployable as a law enforcement officer in the future, the law insists that due process be followed.

The concept of a liberty interest focuses on the freedom to follow a trade, profession, or other calling.

At the heart of a liberty interest claim is that the employer's disciplinary charges or statements made in conjunction with those charges must be false and defamatory,[151] and impose on the employee "a stigma that foreclosed his freedom to take advantage of other employment opportunities."[152] To invoke due process, the charges need not be elaborate statements of the employee's wrongdoing, but must allege that the employee has engaged in some sort of misconduct.[153] Disciplinary charges that merely cause an employee a loss of prestige are not sufficient to impact a liberty right; what is necessary is that the charges impact the employee's future in law enforcement as a career.[154] Similarly, simply terminating an employee's employment without any other comment is not sufficiently stigmatizing to impair the employee's liberty rights,[155] nor is announcing that a police chief has been fired for making an error in judgment,[156] nor is announcing that a probationary employee does not meet departmental standards.[157]

Since a property interest in a job is more easily created and protected than a liberty interest, cases involving liberty interests generally only occur when an employee such as a probationary employee has no identifiable property interest in the job.[158] As described by one court, "although a probationary employee has no protected property interest in his employment, a public employer cannot deprive a probationary employee of his freedom to take advantage of other employment opportunities."[159]

Examples of employer actions and statements which have been held to implicate liberty interests include the following:

- Where a deputy sheriff in Texas was discharged for his suspected role in a series of thefts of saddles and cattle.[160]

- Where a dispatcher was fired because of her husband's suspected role in a car theft ring.[161]

- Where an officer was fired for being rude with citizens, insubordinate, and taking too long on coffee breaks.[162]

- Where an officer was discharged for untruthfulness.[163]

- Where a police chief disclosed to the public the details of an officer's request for medical retirement.[164]

- Where the accusations against the officer included charges that he had failed to keep a daily log, that there were "gross discrepancies" in the number of hours reflected on his time sheets, and that he was guilty of insubordination.[165]

- Where an officer was fired for allegedly having an affair.[166]

- Where a police chief was discharged for mismanagement and an abrasive personality style.[167]

- Where a corrections officer was fired for allegedly having sex with an inmate.[168]

- Where a chief's televised comments indicated that an officer committed a crime.[169]

The courts are currently split on whether an officer bringing a liberty claim must show that the stigmatizing information was actually disclosed, or need only show a likelihood that the information would be disclosed. Some courts have held that all that need be shown is the likelihood of disclosure, reasoning that the employee might not ever be aware of the actual disclosure of the information.[170] Other courts reach the contrary result, however, reasoning that an officer never suffers a tangible loss until the stigmatizing information is actually released to a third party.[171] In courts following the latter line of reasoning, the officer is also required to show that he has been denied employment opportunities based upon the release of the stigmatizing information.[172]

If an employer merely places the stigmatizing information in a non-public record, the employee's liberty rights are not implicated since there has been no "publication" of the information to third parties.[173] However, if the information is placed in a public record, the employee's liberty rights are impacted if some sort of public records or freedom of information law allows third parties the right to access to the information or if the employer does not have a confidentiality policy forbidding the disclosure of the information.[174] As explained by one court:

> "The officer's rights to live and work where he will, to pursue any livelihood or avocation, and to engage in the common occupations of life have been limited by placing his personnel file and the internal affairs report into the public record. The file and report have stigmatized the officer in the eyes of potential law enforcement employers and in the minds of citizens. We hold that the presence of stigmatizing information placed in the public record by a state entity, pursuant to a state statute or otherwise, constitutes sufficient publication to implicate the liberty interest under the Due Process Clause."[175]

In order to invoke an employee's liberty rights, the stigmatizing information must be released concurrently with the disciplinary action taken against the employee.[176] Most courts hold that liberty rights exist only if the employee is being terminated,[177] while a minority of courts find that liberty rights can be implicated even by a demotion.[178] No liberty rights exist if the employee is merely being transferred without any loss of pay.[179] If the information is released sometime after the termination of the employee, the release does not violate the employee's liberty rights even if it is false and defamatory.[180] In all cases, the officer must show that the stigmatizing information has had an actual impact on her employability as an officer.[181]

A liberty interest can even be involved in a rare type of case where the officer is not suing his employer, but instead another governmental body. In one case, a district attorney made disparaging out-of-court statements about a police chief. The chief's employer then decided not to renew his contract. A court found that the district attorney's comments did impact the chief's liberty rights, observing that "a jury could reasonably infer from the district attorney's public statements about not prosecuting cases investigated by the chief that the district attorney set in motion a series of events that he knew or should reasonably have known would cause the employer to deprive the chief of his constitutional rights. Also, the jury could infer that the district attorney knew that the employer would not provide the chief with a hearing after he made his statements and that, as a result, the employer's actions would violate the chief's constitutional right to due process."[182]

The Process Which Is Due Once A Liberty Or Property Right Is Created.

Once an employee establishes that a property or liberty interest has been affected by an employer's actions, the next question is what procedures the employer must follow in order to observe the officer's rights to procedural due process. In evaluating an employer's procedures, courts look to five factors:

- How likely it is that the procedures will prevent an erroneous deprivation of the officer's property or liberty rights to the job;

- Whether additional or other procedures would be more likely to prevent such error;

- The degree to which the employee's property or liberty rights are affected by the employer's decision. In other words, more "process" may be due with terminations than with short suspensions;[183]

- The burden which would be imposed on the employer if additional procedures were required; and

- The extent to which the procedures which exist post-discipline will not only correct any pre-discipline error, but would function to make an erroneously deprived employee whole again.[184]

The procedures required by due process fall into two categories, "pre-deprivation" and "post-deprivation" procedures.

The procedures required by due process fall into two categories – "pre-deprivation" and "post-deprivation" procedures. "Pre-deprivation" procedures are those procedures which must be followed before the property or liberty right of the employee is affected (e.g., before discipline is imposed). "Post-deprivation" procedures are those that must be observed after a property right is affected. Though the matter is not without some controversy, it seems clear that the principles of procedural due process require both "pre-deprivation" and "post-deprivation" procedures where property rights are affected,[185] and "pre-deprivation" procedures where liberty rights may be affected.[186]

There are no set constitutional rules as to how speedily an employer must act in either a disciplinary investigation or in holding pre-deprivation or post-deprivation hearings. In general, courts conclude that even fairly lengthy delays in completing an investigation or holding a hearing may not violate due process.[187]

For example, in one case, an officer was suspended without pay for ten months before a hearing was held. While a court found the delay "troublesome," it found no due process violation. The Court reasoned that while the officer "possessed a substantial private interest in his employment as a police officer, the government, however, maintained a strong interest in ensuring the suitability of those entrusted to enforce the laws as police officers." The Court cited the facts that (1) there had been a criminal finding of probable cause against the officer and, although he eventually was acquitted of those charges, that finding formed the basis for the administrative charge of conduct unbecoming, which was sustained by the hearings officer, albeit under a lesser burden of proof; (2) the officer did not press for an expedited hearing; and (3) the delay, in part, was caused by the grievance proceedings.[188]

As noted in Chapter 3, while lengthy delays in an investigation and/or a hearing might not violate the principles of due process, they may run afoul of a contract's requirement that an employer have "just cause" to discipline employees.

'Pre-Deprivation' And 'Pre-Disciplinary' Procedures Where Property Rights Exist.

Regardless of the existence of any post-discipline remedies the officer may have, the principles of procedural due process require, at a minimum, that except in extraordinary circumstances the officer be given notice of the employer's intention to impose discipline as well as some kind of hearing prior to being disciplined.[189] In addition, though an employer's rules are not necessarily binding in a constitutional sense,[190] the disciplinary procedures established by an employer's rules do provide a framework for assessing the "process that is due."[191]

Pre-Disciplinary Notice. The notice which an employer must provide an employee prior to a pre-termination hearing is currently a matter of considerable debate. The rule which seems to be emerging is that the notice must recite the general charges against the employee, the rules which the employee is alleged to have violated, and provide the employee with information as to how to respond to the charges.[192] The charges in the notice must either specifically inform the employee of the potential disciplinary sanction, or provide the officer with the "gist" of the allegations and possible sanction.[193] In the words of one court, the employee must be provided with "knowledge of the basis of those charges either by explanation or by reviewing the file containing the report of the internal affairs investigation conducted."[194] In some states, the notice must include a copy of all materials upon which the proposed discipline is based,[195] including the complete investigatory file.[196]

Once the notice has been given, additional charges cannot be added later without giving the employee a new right to respond to the charges.[197] The notice should provide enough time for the officer to be able to reasonably reply to the charges; while no absolute minimum amount of time is required between the

The notice must recite the general charges against the employee, the rules which the employee is alleged to have violated, and provide the employee with information as to how to respond to the charges.

notice and the hearing, one court has ordered the reinstatement of an officer with seven years of back pay because the officer only received four days' notice of the hearing.[198] At the other extreme, a court found no violation of procedural due process where an officer was given only 30 minutes to review an internal affairs file, reasoning that there were only nine pages in the file that the officer had not seen before, and that the officer had not shown he was disadvantaged by the limited time to review the file.[199]

Some courts buck the general trend of requiring specific notice of the charges against an officer. *Buckner v. City of Highland* is probably the best example of the outer limits to which an employer can go in not providing formal pre-disciplinary notice. The case involved an officer who was alleged to have sexually assaulted a woman and was provided verbal notice of the charges against him during a hospital visit by his union representative and a lieutenant. The Court approved of this exceedingly informal notice, noting that "an elaborate system of post-termination hearings, culminating in a formal arbitration proceeding, was provided to the [officer] under the collective bargaining agreement."[200] In another case, a court found no due process violation where the employee was provided with written notice of the "general reasons" for an investigation, reasons that were later orally more fully explained.[201]

Pre-Disciplinary Hearing. As has been noted repeatedly by the courts, "the chance to be heard, to present one's own side of the story, is a fundamental requirement of any fair procedural system."[202] The hearing need not be a formal, adversarial-type hearing, and the officer need not be allowed to have an attorney present during the hearing.[203] Usually, there exists no constitutional right to either call[204] or cross-examine witnesses,[205] though if the hearing board receives evidence, it must do so in the presence of the officer.[206] The hearing must, however, provide the officer with a reasonable opportunity to make a defense, and to make that defense to individuals who are in a position of authority with respect to the officer's discipline. Today, such hearings are commonly called *Loudermill* hearings, a name derived from a leading Supreme Court case describing the right to a hearing.[207]

Most courts agree that in cases of termination, the employee is entitled to an in-person hearing as part of due process, and that the charges against the employee cannot change after the hearing is conducted.[208] The grant of a hearing is not automatic; instead, the employee must affirmatively request the hearing to be entitled to one.[209] The hearing should be conducted either by the final decision-maker on the discipline, or by a person in the chain of command who has the authority to effectively recommend disciplinary action.[210] With very large agencies, even a captain who serves as the officer's commanding officer may have sufficient decision-making capabilities to conduct the necessary hearing.[211] Due process does not require that the deliberations of a hearings board be held in public,[212] nor does it require that a hearings board notify the officer of the right to appeal its decision.[213] A union contract cannot waive the officer's right to a pre-disciplinary hearing before the appropriate individual.[214]

The grant of a hearing is not automatic; instead, the employee must affirmatively request the hearing to be entitled to one.

There is a conflict between courts as to whether an in-person hearing is necessary in cases of suspensions, or whether due process is satisfied by merely allowing the employee an opportunity to present a written defense to the charges. The majority of courts hold that an in-person hearing is required, reasoning that only an opportunity to directly speak with the disciplinary decision-maker will provide the necessary "opportunity to be heard" under *Loudermill*.[215] Other courts find that in cases of minor discipline such as short suspensions, the opportunity to respond in writing to charges is sufficient to meet the requirements of due process.[216] An in-person hearing may not be necessary when the employer is acting to modify or terminate a benefit associated with the job (such as retirement benefits or light-duty status), with the employee's opportunity to present the employee's side of the issue in writing sufficing in lieu of a hearing.[217] So long as the employee is given a reasonable chance to tell his side of the story at the hearing, there are no constitutionally-mandated procedures that necessarily must be followed. For example, there is no constitutional requirement that the person or entity holding the hearing make detailed findings at the conclusion of the hearing.[218] Courts will also not second-guess the decision of an employer whether to grant a hearing date continuance requested by an employee.[219]

There are limited types of cases in which courts find that pre-disciplinary hearings are not constitutionally necessary so long as there is a thorough post-disciplinary review of the disciplinary action. The most notable exception to the general rule was described by the United States Supreme Court in *Gilbert v. Homar*, where the Court rejected the due process claim of a police officer who had been temporarily suspended without pay without a hearing after he was arrested on drug charges. Pointing to the serious nature of the public concern about an arrested police officer still working, the Court commented that "unlike in the case of a termination, where we have recognized that the only meaningful opportunity to invoke the discretion of the decision maker is likely to be before the termination takes effect, in the case of a suspension there will be ample opportunity to invoke discretion later – and a short delay actually benefits the employee by allowing state officials to obtain more accurate information about the arrest and charges."[220] Thus far, it appears courts are confining the rules espoused in *Gilbert* to the particular facts of the case (an arrested police officer), and are not reading the case as standing for the broad proposition that due process is unnecessary before the issuance of any suspension.

Another exception to the general rule mandating pre-disciplinary hearings occurs where it would be impractical or impossible to hold such a hearing. Such a situation might arise when an officer claims after the fact that she was coerced into resigning from employment, and that what appears to be a voluntary resignation was really an involuntary discharge.[221]

Bias And The Pre-Disciplinary Hearing Process. The law varies from state to state as to whether the official before whom the hearing is held may permissibly have a prior bias or prejudice about the matter. Some courts will grant wide latitude towards law enforcement agencies in this regard, even allowing the official before whom the hearing is held to draft the charges against the officer,[222] or holding that so long as the post-discipline decision-maker is unbiased, the pre-disciplinary process need not be quite so free of bias.[223] Courts following this more lenient approach to the bias rule allow the same hearing board to reconsider the case of an officer who has successfully challenged a disciplinary decision in the courts on the grounds that the hearing board did not follow due process in the first place.[224]

Most courts strictly require that the individual conducting the hearing be unbiased.[225] For example, in one case a court found a violation of due process where the only evidence of bias was that one member of a three-person hearing board was a part-time police officer under the command of the police chief who had instituted the disciplinary action.[226] In another case, a court overturned a discharge where two members of the hearing board testified as witnesses for the employer.[227] In a third case, a court found a due process violation where a board member was not only the alleged victim of the misconduct, but also appointed the board's investigator.[228] No matter how strongly the officer may believe the official is biased, if the officer chooses not to participate in the hearing, the officer may be held to have waived his rights to the hearing if his objections are purely speculative in nature.[229]

Apart from the issue of whether the individual conducting the hearing is biased is the question of whether the result of the hearing is pre-determined. If the employer has firmly and resolutely made up its mind to fire an employee without regard to the evidence, even an otherwise procedurally appropriate pre-disciplinary hearing may be constitutionally deficient. For example, in *Wagner v. City of Memphis*, a white lieutenant was charged with violating a variety of procedures in an incident in which he pepper sprayed two undercover African-American officers whom he did not recognize. The mayor ordered the Police Chief to terminate the lieutenant without regard to the evidence, telling the Chief that "black people elected me" and that the Chief's processing of the investigation in accordance with normal departmental practices "was killing me." The Court referred to the lieutenant's pre-disciplinary hearing as a "sham proceeding" that did not fill its constitutional function.[230]

Enhanced Procedural Due Process Rights.

The necessary procedures which must be followed once a property interest is involved, procedures known as that "process which is due," can be higher than the minimum levels involved in a *Loudermill* hearing if the employer is required to follow certain procedures in disciplining employees. For example, if the employer has promulgated regulations which require it to follow specific steps in the disciplinary process, it must strictly adhere to those procedures. If those procedures allow for an appeal, review or reconsideration of disciplinary actions, employees must be permitted to exercise such appeal rights.[231]

The "process which is due" can also involve more than the basic *Loudermill* hearing if specific disciplinary procedures are established by statute or by the rules of a law enforcement agency. Under this rationale, if a state has enacted a peace officer bill of rights, the bill of rights may establish the minimum procedural due process necessary in all disciplinary cases.

'Post-Deprivation' Or 'Post-Disciplinary' Procedures Where Property Rights Exist.

In addition to "pre-deprivation" procedures, the principles of due process also require that an employer follow certain procedures after implementing a decision that affects an employee's property rights.[232] The degree of "post-deprivation" or "post-disciplinary" procedures can be viewed as somewhat inversely proportional to the degree of "pre-deprivation" procedures the employer has followed – the less specific and thorough the pre-disciplinary notice and hearing, the more specific and thorough the "post-deprivation" procedures must be.[233] Somewhere in the process, whether "pre-deprivation" or "post-deprivation," the employee must be provided with a full evidentiary hearing which allows the employee to contest the accuracy of the charges.[234] And, as explained by one judge, where certain procedures may not be mandatory "pre-deprivation," they may be constitutionally required "post-deprivation":

> "By deciding that pre-termination procedures 'though necessary, need not be elaborate' when a prompt post-termination hearing is available, the Supreme Court recognized a continuum of rights and interests. At the beginning, during the pre-termination stage, the employer has much more latitude since its interests in avoiding workplace disruption are usually more significant. At the end – after termination – the interest of employees in a full and fair resolution of charges against them is paramount; any interest of the employer in secrecy can rarely be justified."[235]

The degree of "post-deprivation" or "post-disciplinary" procedures can be viewed as somewhat inversely proportional to the degree of "pre-deprivation" procedures the employer has followed.

At a minimum, the post-disciplinary appeal must involve a hearing before a different decision-maker than the individual who originally imposed the discipline.[236] Further, the employer must preserve the evidence it gathered in its disciplinary investigation and make that evidence available to the officer during the post-termination hearing.[237] In addition, where virtually all courts would hold that furnishing the employee with the names of witnesses is not a necessary "pre-deprivation" procedure, most courts hold that an employee must be furnished the names of witnesses prior to a "post-deprivation" hearing:

> "Regardless of whether pre-termination proceedings are adequate, the equivalent of a full evidentiary hearing is necessary either pre- or post-termination in order to meet the demands of due process. * * * At a minimum, to support the termination of a governmental employee who possesses a property interest, the

employer must provide to the employee * * * notice of both the names of those who have made allegations and the specific nature and factual basis for the charges."[2389]

If an employer creates a post-disciplinary appeal process that has the means to correct any problems with the employer's pre-disciplinary appeals, the fact that the employee failed to lodge a post-disciplinary appeal will likely be fatal to the employee later contending in court that a procedural due process violation occurred.[239] Also, the fact that a labor organization may be in control of a post-termination remedy such as a grievance procedure and does not file a grievance does not in any way mean that the post-termination remedy is unavailable (though the labor organization's decisions may implicate the duty of fair representation).[240]

Procedures Necessary Where Liberty Rights Exist.

The due process necessary where only liberty rights exist is far less extensive than the process required when a property right is involved. An employee facing termination who has a liberty interest in the job is entitled to a "name-clearing" hearing – a chance to tell his or her side of the story and correct any factual errors made by the employer. The employee must request a name-clearing hearing in order to be entitled to the hearing.[241]

The courts have identified few rules which apply to name-clearing hearings. It seems certain that some notice of the charges must be provided to the employee, who must then be given a meaningful opportunity to correct any factual mistakes made by the employer. Simply interviewing the employee in an internal affairs setting does not suffice as an adequate name-clearing hearing.[242] Courts have also held that the name-clearing hearing need not take place before the employee's termination or the publication of the damaging information.[243]

Substantive Due Process.

Where procedural due process rights mandate the procedures that must be followed when a property or liberty right is affected, substantive due process rights protect against grossly inappropriate conduct by governmental officials.

Where procedural due process rights mandate the procedures that must be followed when a property or liberty right is affected, substantive due process rights protect against grossly inappropriate conduct by governmental officials. Occasionally, governmental actions used by a law enforcement employer can be so coercive or inappropriate that regardless as to whether the officer has been granted a pre-disciplinary hearing, a court will conclude that the officer's so-called "substantive" due process rights have been violated. Substantive due process rights do not involve any underlying right to the job or the procedures used by the employer in impacting the employee's job, but rather deal with the processes unrelated to the notice/hearing process used by the employer in connection with a disciplinary case.

Though no firm legal standard defining substantive due process exists, courts tend to find violations of the principle when an employer's actions are so unreasonable as to be shocking to the court's conscience,[244] or are "truly irrational."[245] In some states, courts have allowed substantive due process claims to proceed only if the employee can show that the employer's actions were arbitrary and capricious.[246]

Most often, courts are reluctant to entertain substantive due process claims. As noted by one court in rejecting the substantive due process claim of an employee removed from a SWAT team assignment, "the protections of substantive due process are available only against egregious conduct which goes beyond merely offending some fastidious squeamishness or private sentimentalism and can fairly be viewed as so brutal and offensive to human dignity as to shock the conscience."[247]

A good example of a substantive due process case stemmed from two off-duty officers sleeping together one night. The female officer's estranged husband found out and made an "officer needs assistance" call to the Police Department, resulting in the prompt arrival on the scene of 20 officers. The Department questioned the officers for 14 hours, giving them no food. During the questioning, one of the officers vomited blood but was denied access to either a doctor or to counsel.[248]

The Court's condemnation of these procedures was blunt:

> "Clearly, the detention and interrogation was offensive to canons of decency and fairness. It is shocking to the conscience of this Court, and it is shocking and almost inconceivable that a police department would assume that it could maltreat its own employees in a manner which it knows would not be tolerated or approved by the courts, even were the object of the interrogation a person accused of a heinous crime. Due process, of course, is required, not merely for the protection of the unfortunate victim of coercive police tactics, but it is necessary to the integrity of the judicial process. Due process is violated by coerced confessions, because they are unreliable, and should not be allowed to contribute to a finding of guilt in a court of law which attempts to base its judgments on trustworthy and reliable evidence. Moreover, where the tactics used are offensive and outrage the public's sense of decency, it is society and society's standards of fundamental fairness that are offended."

The Court found that the procedures clearly violated the officers' right to due process:

> "We find in respect to each of them that the circumstances of their interrogation, when considered in their totality, were coercive and rendered the statements unreliable, untrustworthy, and involuntary, and, above all, the products of the denial of due process. * * * Giving full credence to the statements of the interrogators, it is apparent that the expressed attitude of the interrogating police officers and their conduct in light of the circumstances demonstrate beyond a reasonable doubt that the statements were of such a nature that to permit their use in the denial of a property right would contravene the constitutional protections of the Fourteenth Amendment. * * *

Moreover, the questioning that ensued was not confined narrowly, directly, and specifically to matters within the scope of the specific duties of the officers. Questions directed to whether the parties used contraception, whether pregnancy was likely to ensue, or how the sexual acts were performed are not the questions that can be asked by a public employer."

Another case involved a police officer who was suspended when criminal charges alleging the sexual abuse of children were lodged against him. When the criminal charges were not pursued because of questions about the credibility of the victims, the officer's employer conditioned his reinstatement upon completion of a psychological examination which included the use of the penile plethysmograph. The penile plethysmograph examination involved the measurement of the flow of blood to the officer's penis, and therefore his sexual arousal, when the officer was to be shown a variety of photographs or movies of unclothed individuals, including children, some of whom were posed in sexual situations. The Court upheld the officer's refusal to take the examination. While the Court held that the employer had the right to inquire into the officer's fitness for duty, it ruled that the specific means chosen for that inquiry – the penile plethysmograph — was far too intrusive and debasing and was consequently a violation of the officer's substantive due process rights.[249]

The following cases illustrate how the courts have applied the rule of substantive due process in the assessment of disciplinary procedures or decisions. As can be seen, the courts only sparingly apply substantive due process rules, holding in general that "the Due Process Clause of the Fourteenth Amendment is not a guarantee against incorrect or ill-advised personnel decisions."[250]

Situations Where Courts Have Found Violation of Substantive Due Process

Termination of officer based solely upon his wife's conversation with his daughter.[251]

A City Council deliberately evading a public meetings law to organize an effort to terminate a police chief they wanted to "get rid of."[252]

A City that publicly announced an officer was guilty of wrongdoing before doing any investigation of his culpability, at the same time basing its decisions in part on his race.[253]

One officer intentionally shooting and killing another during a methamphetamine raid.[254]

Substantive due process rights will only be found by a court where no more easily articulated constitutional right provides clear guidance in the area. However, where another constitutional amendment "provides an explicit textual source of constitutional protection" against the conduct about which an officer complains, "that Amendment, not the more generalized notion of 'substantive due process,' guides the analysis of the claim."[264]

The Exclusionary Rule In Disciplinary Cases.

The law varies from state to state as to whether the violation of an officer's constitutional right to be free from an illegal search and seizure forbids the introduction of illegally seized evidence in an internal investigation. The majority of courts have refused to apply the exclusionary rule to bar the use of illegally-seized evidence in a disciplinary proceeding, holding that the exclusionary rule applies exclusively in criminal cases.[265] A minority of courts, however, reason that discharge proceedings "have a sufficient quasi-criminal nature to warrant application of the exclusionary rule in order to protect Fourth Amendment rights" in the disciplinary process.[266] One court has even held that the exclusionary rule bars the introduction of illegally seized evidence in disciplinary proceedings, even if an agency other than the employer seized the evidence, reasoning as follows:

> "The primary purpose, if not the sole purpose, of the exclusionary rule is to deter future unlawful police conduct. To give effect to this deterrence function, we cannot allow one government agency to use the fruits of unlawful conduct by another branch of the same agency to obtain an employee's dismissal. Furthermore, the loss of a job is a very severe sanction which warrants special consideration."[267]

Use Of Entrapment To Gain Evidence In Disciplinary Matters.

If the law enforcement agency engages in entrapment in order to prove its disciplinary case, it is very likely that the resulting discipline will be overturned.

If the law enforcement agency engages in entrapment in order to prove its disciplinary case, it is very likely that the resulting discipline will be overturned. The leading case on point is *Maumus v. Department of Police, New Orleans*, arising out of an internal investigation performed by the City of New Orleans Office of Municipal Investigation into possible cocaine distribution. In the course of its investigation, the investigators lured an on-duty officer to a hotel room by using a skimpily-dressed, slightly intoxicated, and apparently very attractive acquaintance of the officer on the premise that the acquaintance knew the whereabouts of the officer's service revolver. Sometime after the officer entered the room, the investigators burst into the room, finding the officer "buck naked." The officer was fired for, among other things, neglect of duty and consumption of alcohol while on duty.

The Court reversed the officer's discipline, finding that "this governmental agency orchestrated the entire scenario which resulted in Officer Maumus' succumbing to a sexual enticement which was in violation of his police duties." The Court held that the conduct of the investigators violated the basic precepts of decency and fairness implicit in the due process clause:

> "In the instant case the Office of Municipal Investigation did in fact exceed the bounds of legal propriety. Their tactics of inducement were so pervasive as to constitute governmental misconduct. Fundamental fairness does not permit us to countenance such egregious conduct within the framework of criminal investigations, nor shall we do so within the framework of municipal disciplinary actions. It would be a denial of due process to allow an individual to be disciplined (and thereby forfeit his livelihood) as a result of such governmentally created violations of employment regulations."[268]

The Constitutional Rights Of Officers Who Have Been Involved In The Use Of Deadly Force.

An officer involved in the use of force is often placed in an untenable position. On one hand, the officer has an obligation to report the details of the incident promptly and completely to his or her department. On the other hand, by the very nature of the use of force, the officer's statements may form the basis for departmental discipline, civil liability and, even if not admissible in a criminal proceeding themselves, may have an impact on the officer's career. In other words, it is at least possible that the interests of an officer involved in the use of force may be adverse to those of the department to which the officer is required to give a statement.

Some law enforcement agencies recognize this inherent conflict and allow officers who have been involved in the use of force the right to consult with counsel prior to making an oral or written statement about the incident. Others have adopted similar policies not so much out of a concern for their officers, but out of a recognition that an officer who speaks without the advice of counsel may make statements which subject the employer to civil liability.

The law is becoming more settled that officers have the right to counsel after being involved in the use of deadly force before making a statement about the incident. The first case to address the issue, *Ward v. City of Portland*, involved two officers who were involved in a shooting who were conferring with counsel prior to giving a statement about the shooting. A supervisor in the police department ejected the attorney.[269] The case ended up being decided on procedural grounds, with the Court not addressing the underlying question of the right to counsel.

Recently, a California federal court decided a significant case arising out of a televised encounter between members of the Riverside County Sheriff's Office and several illegal aliens. When one of the involved deputies returned to his station, he was met by his lieutenant, who had already determined from the televised accounts that both an internal and criminal investigation of the deputy were likely. The lieutenant ordered the deputy to write a report about the incident. After the deputy began to write the report, his attorney arrived at the station. The lieutenant then ordered the attorney to leave.

The Court found that lieutenant's denial of the officer's right to be represented by an attorney to be a violation of due process. Describing the case as a "conundrum," the Court commented that a "police officer's duty to provide a report concerning his official actions is an essential element in the administration of our criminal justice system, and crucial to the maintenance of public confidence in it." However, the Court nonetheless found that the officer's rights to due process overrode these institutional interests:

> "If the deputy had been allowed the continued representation of his counsel at the time she was ordered from the report writing room, which was before he began to write the report, she might have advised

The law is becoming more settled that officers have the right to counsel after being involved in the use of deadly force before making a statement about the incident.

him that he could choose not to write the report with the possible consequence of termination of his employment for refusal to write the report. Another alternative would be to write the report with two possible consequences resulting there from. He could be impliedly waiving his Fifth Amendment right against self incrimination and the contents of the report could be used in a state and/or federal prosecution against him based in whole or in part on the statements in the report. In addition, the contents of such report also could be used punitively against him by his employer in an administrative employment disciplinary proceeding due to his involvement in the arrest. Further, his attorney could have advised him that before writing the report, he might seek immunity or at least transactional immunity from the state and federal criminal prosecutorial authorities precluding any criminal prosecution against him for his conduct during the subject events. Additionally, if he chose to write the report, counsel could have advised him respecting anything he wrote possibly incriminating him for potential criminal prosecution and/or being used against him in an employee disciplinary proceeding. Without such advice of counsel, there is a substantial risk of Watson's being deprived erroneously of his interest in not being fired from his employment and not being prosecuted for criminal offenses. Defendants provided no additional or substitute procedural safeguard against such a deprivation."[270]

If a department has a policy of allowing access to counsel, it may not be able to change that practice without first bargaining with the labor organization representing rank-and-file members of the department. Because the right to counsel affects a "working condition," it is a mandatorily negotiable item, and may not be changed without prior negotiations with the affected labor organization.[271]

It is also unsettled whether an officer who has been involved in the use of force has the right to representation by the officer's labor organization prior to being required to make oral or written statements about the incident. An officer who is about to be questioned about the recent use of force would appear to meet all of the criteria of the *Weingarten* case; that is, the officer is being required to submit to questioning from which the officer could reasonably assume that discipline might result. However, no reported case has addressed the issue.

A Police Officer's *Miranda* Rights.

Occasionally questions arise about when a police officer is entitled to the rights outlined by the Supreme Court's decision in *Miranda v. Arizona*.[272] The case of *People v. Probasco* illustrates the operation of the *Miranda* rule in a use-of-force setting. In the case, a deputy sheriff shot and killed a person he had stopped for a traffic violation. Another deputy arriving at the scene and sitting in the car with the deputy asked the deputy "how his baton and radio wound up on the porch." The first deputy responded by relaying an account of the incident that involved a foot chase, followed by the suspect's striking the end of the deputy's drawn gun, causing the gun to discharge. When the deputy was criminally charged with negligent homicide, he sought to suppress the statements made to the second deputy.

The Court rejected the motion to suppress. Though the Court found that the question about the baton and radio was an "interrogation" covered by the *Miranda* rule, it held that *Miranda* rights only apply in custodial interrogations. Defining custody as circumstances where a "reasonable person would consider himself deprived of his freedom of action in a significant way," the Court held that the deputy was not in custody at the time of the statement, and refused to suppress the statement:

> "There is simply nothing in the record, beyond normal employment obligations tied to [his] service as a deputy sheriff, that would support a finding that [the deputy] was in custody. A reasonable civilian sitting in that police car might have believed that he was in custody, but the reasonable police officer, while on duty, sitting in his police car with fellow officers that were also his friends, would not be likely to believe that his freedom of action was limited in a significant way."273

NOTES

[1] *Garrity v. New Jersey*, 385 U.S. 493 (1967).

[2] *Lefkowitz v. Turley*, 414 U.S. 70 (1973).

[3] *Gardner v. Broderick*, 392 U.S. 273 (1968). See also *Uniformed Sanitation Men Ass'n v. Commissioner of Sanitation of New York*, 392 U.S. 280 (1968).

[4] See *Hancock v. Baker*, 263 Fed.Appx. 416 (5th Cir. 2008).

[5] *In re Carroll*, 772 A.2d 45 (N.J. Super. 2001).

[6] See *Lefkowitz v. Turley*, 414 U.S. 70 (1973); *Confederation of Police v. Conlisk*, 489 F.2d 891 (7th Cir. 1973)(officer cannot be disciplined for invoking Fifth Amendment at grand jury proceedings).

[7] *Uniformed Sanitation Men Ass'n v. Commissioner of Sanitation of New York*, 392 U.S. 280 (1968); *Hanna v. Department of Labor*, 2001 WL 615292 (Fed. Cir. 2001); *Lybarger v. City of Los Angeles*, 710 P.2d 329 (Cal. 1985); *Eck v. County of Delaware*, 828 N.Y.S.2d 682 (A.D. 2007).

[8] *Gniotek v. City of Philadelphia*, 808 F.2d 241 (3d Cir. 1986).

[9] *St. Charles County Department of Corrections v. Tipton*, 2003 WL 21738871 (Mo. App. 2003); *Brougham v. City of Normandy*, 812 S.W.2d 919 (Mo. App. 1991).

[10] *Broderick v. Police Commissioner of Boston*, 330 N.E.2d 199 (Mass. 1975).

[11] *Michigan State Police Troopers Association v. Hough*, 872 F.2d 1026 (6th Cir. 1989)(unpublished opinion; text reproduced in Westlaw)(*Garrity* applied in case of off-duty criminal misconduct. The Court noted that an officer's off-duty criminal conduct may well affect the performance of his official duties: "Not only does criminal conduct jeopardize an officer's credibility as a witness and affiant by opening him up to impeachment, it threatens the morale of other officers."); *Department of Public Safety and Correctional Services v. Shockley*, 790 A.2d 73 (Md. App. 2002).

[12] *City and County of Denver v. Powell*, 969 P.2d 776 (Colo. App. 1998).

[13] *Shuman v. City of Philadelphia*, 470 F. Supp. 449 (E.D. Pa. 1979).

[14] *Department of Public Safety and Correctional Services v. Shockley*, 790 A.2d 73 (Md. App. 2002).

[15] *Singer v. State of Maine*, 10 IER Cases 811 (1st Cir. 1995); *Fraternal Order of Police v. Philadelphia*, 859 F.2d 276 (3d Cir. 1988); *Benjamin v. City of Montgomery*, 785 F.2d 959 (11th Cir. 1986); *United States v. Indorato*, 628 F.2d 711 (1st Cir. 1980); *Orozco v. County of Monterey*, 941 F. Supp. 930 (N.D. Cal. 1996); *National Union of Law Enforcement Officers v. Lucas*, 263 N.W.2d 7 (Mich. App. 1977).

[16] *U.S. v. Foley*, 2009 WL 243011 (D. Mass. 2009); *Wood v. Summit County*, 579 F. Supp. 2d 935 (N.D. Ohio 2008); *U.S. v. Ferguson*, 2007 WL 4240782 (D. Conn. 2007).

[17] *United States v. Camacho*, 739 F. Supp. 1504 (S.D. Fla. 1990)(interrogation of officers at residences and at police station covered by *Garrity* rule; officers advised by their attorney that their statements were compelled by departmental rules); *State v. Connor*, 861 P.2d 1212 (Idaho 1993)(officer did not have reasonable belief that his statements were compelled where supervisor told him he was not required to answer questions). See generally *United States v. Najarian*, 915 F. Supp. 1460 (D. Minn. 1996); *People v. Sapp*, 934 P.2d 1367 (Colo. App. 1997). Though the majority of cases follow the two-part objective/subjective test to determine if a statement

is compelled, *People v. Sapp*, 934 P.2d 1367 (Colo. 1997); *State v. Aiken*, 636 S.E.2d 156 (Ga. App. 2006); *State v. Connor*, 861 P.2d 1212 (Idaho 1993); *State v. Lacaillade*, 630 A.2d 328 (N.J. Super. 1993), *adopting the analysis in United States v. Friedrick*, 842 F.2d 382 (D.C. Cir. 1988); *see U.S. v. Bartlett*, 2007 WL 1830726 (E.D. Wis. 2007), two courts take a different approach. *United States v. Indorato*, 628 F.2d 711 (1st Cir. 1980)(stating implied threat, with no statute or ordinance mandating dismissal for refusal to answer questions, falls outside the *Garrity* "coerced testimony doctrine"); *People v. Coutu*, 599 N.W.2d 556 (1999)(holding that because there was no overt, actual threat of dismissal, *Garrity* did not apply).

[18] *Compare United States v. Camacho*, 739 F. Supp. 1504 (S.D. Fla. 1990)(statements made at police station) and *State v. Chavarria*, 33 P.3d 922 (N.M. App. 2001)(statements made to criminal investigator employed by same agency) and *Evans v. DeRidder*, 815 So.2d 61 (La. 2002)(polygraph examination) with *United States v. Vangates*, 287 F.3d 1315 (11th Cir. 2002)(statements made in civil trial).

[19] *Gilbert v. Nix*, 990 F.2d 1044 (8th Cir. 1993)(*Garrity* applies automatically whenever an employee is compelled to answer the employer's questions); *Weston v. H.U.D.*, 724 F.2d 943 (Fed. Cir. 1983)(*Garrity* applies to non-sworn personnel as well as to law enforcement officers).

[20] *Erwin v. Price*, 778 F.2d 668 (11th Cir. 1985); *Spielbauer v. County of Santa Clara*, 199 P.3d 1125 (Cal. 2009).

[21] *Sher v. U.S. Dept. of Veterans Affairs*, 488 F.3d 489 (1st Cir. 2007).

[22] *Chan v. Wodnicki*, 123 F.3d 1005 (7th Cir. 1997); *Fraternal Order of Police, Lodge No. 5 v. City of Philadelphia*, 859 F.2d 276 (3d Cir. 1988).

[23] *State v. Lacaillade*, 630 A.2d 328 (N.J. App. 1993); *People v. Kleeman*, 501 N.Y.S.2d 576 (Sup. Ct. 1986). Several courts, without analyzing the *Camacho* two-part test, have concluded that officers making statements because a departmental manual required the making of the statements were not entitled to *Garrity* protections. *See United States v. Indorato*, 628 F.2d 711 (1st Cir. 1980); *Watson v. County of Riverside*, 976 F. Supp. 951 (C.D. Cal. 1997); *People v. Coutu*, 599 N.W.2d 556 (Mich. App. 1999); *People v. Marchetta*, 676 N.Y.S.2d 791 (Crim. Ct. 1998).

[24] *See Modrowski v. Dep't of Veterans Affairs*, 252 F.3d 1344 (Fed. Cir. 2001); *Benjamin v. City of Montgomery*, 785 F.2d 959 (11th Cir. 1986); *United States v. Devitt*, 499 F.2d 135 (7th Cir. 1974); *Confederation of Police v. Conlisk*, 489 F.2d 891 (7th Cir. 1973); *Kalkines v. U.S.*, 473 F.2d 1391 (Ct. Cl. 1973); *Uniformed Sanitation Men Ass'n v. Commissioner of Sanitation of New York*, 426 F.2d 619 (2d Cir. 1970); *D'Acquisto v. Washington*, 640 F. Supp. 594 (N.D. Ill. 1986); *McLean v. Rochford*, 404 F. Supp. 191 (N.D. Ill. 1975); *Spielbauer v. County of Santa Clara*, 199 P.3d 1125 (Cal. 2009); *Debnam v. North Carolina Dept. of Corrections*, 421 S.E.2d 389 (N.C. 1992); *Oddsen v. Board of Fire and Police Commissioners*, 321 N.W.2d 161 (Wis. 1982); *see In re Grand Jury Subpoenas Dated December 7 and 8 v. United States*, 40 F.3d 1096 (10th Cir. 1994)(suggests such a rule would apply); *cf. Brougham v. City of Normandy*, 812 S.W.2d 919 (Mo. App. 1991)(warnings need only be given when there exists a possibility of a criminal prosecution). *See also Lybarger v. City of Los Angeles*, 710 P.2d 329 (1985)(decided under California's statutory Peace Officer Bill of Rights).

[25] *Oddsen v. Board of Fire and Police Commissioners*, 321 N.W.2d 161 (Wis. 1982).

[26] See Hill v. Johnson, 14 IER Cases 985 (8th Cir. 1998); Harrison v. Wille, 132 F.3d 679 (11th Cir. 1998); Hester v. City of Milledgeville, 777 F.2d 1492 (11th Cir. 1985); Gulden v. McCorkle, 680 F.2d 1070 (5th Cir. 1982); Debnam v. North Carolina Department of Corrections, 432 S.E.2d 324 (N.C. 1993).

[27] Aguilera v. Baca, 510 F.3d 1161 (9th Cir. 2007).

[28] See Hill v. Johnson, 160 F.3d 469 (8th Cir. 1998); Evans v. DeRidder, 815 So.2d 61 (La. 2002); Harmon v. Ogden City Civil Service Com'n, 171 P.3d 474 (Utah App. 2007).

[29] Frierson v. City of Terrell, 2003 WL 21955863 (N.D. Tex. 2003); Piercy v. Federal Reserve Bank of New York, 2003 WL 115230 (S.D. N.Y. 2003); Chism v. County of San Bernardino, 159 F.R.D. 531 (C.D. Cal. 1994).

[30] In re Denisewich, 643 A.2d 1194 (R.I. 1994).

[31] In re Grand Jury Subpoenas v. United States, 40 F.3d 1096 (10th Cir. 1994). But see In re Grand Jury Subpoenas Issued to Custodian of Records, St. Louis Metropolitan Police Department, No. 89 Misc. 492 (E.D. Mo. 1990).

[32] Pirozzi v. City of New York, 950 F. Supp. 90 (S.D. N.Y. 1996).

[33] Chavez v. Martinez, 538 U.S. 760 (2003).

[34] See Sher v. U.S. Dept. of Veterans Affairs, 488 F.3d 489 (1st Cir. 2007); Brown v. City of North Kansas City, 779 S.W.2d 596 (Mo. App. 1989).

[35] Carney v. City of Springfield, 532 N.E.2d 631 (Mass. 1989). See also Furtado v. Town of Plymouth, 888 N.E.2d 357 (Mass. 2008); Commonwealth v. Dormady, 667 N.E.2d 832 (Mass. 1996); Baglioni v. Chief of Police of Salem, 656 N.E.2d 1223 (Mass. 1995).

[36] See State v. Gonzalez, 853 P.2d 526 (Alaska 1993)(holding Alaska constitution requires transactional immunity); Griego v. Superior Court, 95 Cal.Rptr.2d 351 (Cal. App. 2000)(describing complicated California scheme of immunity); State v. Miyasaki, 614 P.2d 915 (Haw. 1980); State v. McKissic, 2002 WL 408930 (Mich. App. 2002)(describing Michigan state statute); Wright v. McAdory, 536 So.2d 897 (Miss. 1988)(holding Mississippi constitution requires transactional immunity); State v. Adams, 791 N.E.2d 1045 (Ohio App. 2003)(describing Ohio state statute); State v. Soriano, 684 P.2d 1220 (Or. App. 1984), aff'd, 693 P.2d 26 (1984)(holding Oregon constitution requires transactional immunity); State v. Price, 820 A.2d 956 (R.I. 2003)(describing Rhode Island state statute); State v. Thrift, 440 S.E.2d 341 (S.C. 1994)(holding South Carolina constitution requires transactional immunity); State v. Bryant, 983 P.2d 1181 (Wash. App. 1999)(describing Washington state statute).

[37] United States v. North, 910 F.2d 843 (D.C. Cir. 1990).

[38] In re Grand Jury Subpoena Dated December 7 and 8, Issued to Bob Stover, Chief of Albuquerque Police Dep't v. United States, 40 F.3d 1096 (10th Cir. 1994).

[39] United States v. Koon, 34 F.3d 1416 (9th Cir. 1994); see United States v. Daniels, 281 F.3d 168 (5th Cir. 2002).

[40] People v. Gwillim, 274 Cal.Rptr. 415 (Cal. App. 1990)(case decided under California's equivalent of Garrity – Lybarger v. City of Los Angeles, 710 P.2d 829 (Cal. 1985).

[41] McKinley v. City of Mansfield, 404 F.3d 418 (6th Cir. 2005); see United States v. Wong, 431 U.S. 174 (1977).

[42] United States v. Veal, 153 F.3d 1233 (11th Cir.1998).

[43] Gov't Code of California, §3303(f).

[44] *J.W. v. City of Oxnard*, 2008 WL 4810298 (C.D. Cal. 2008)(interprets portion of Section 3303(f) dealing with exception for impeachment).

[45] The San Antonio advice of rights card is described in an *amicus curiae* brief filed by Richard Williams, Corporation Counsel for the Village of Hoffman Estates, Illinois, in *United States v. Koon*, 34 F.3d 1416 (9th Cir. 1994), referred to in the text.

[46] *National Labor Relations Board v. J. Weingarten, Inc.*, 420 U.S. 251 (1975); *see* 29 U.S.C. §157.

[47] *Quoting American Ship Building Co. v. NLRB*, 380 U.S. 300 (1965). *See also International Ladies Garment Workers' Union, Upper South Department, AFL-CIO v. Quality Manufacturing Company*, 419 U.S. 816 (1975).

[48] **Arizona**, *City of Phoenix v. Phoenix Employment Relations Board*, 86 P.3d 917 (Ariz. App. 2004)(decided under local ordinance); **California**, *Civil Service Association v. San Francisco*, 150 Cal.Rptr. 129 (Cal. 1978); **Florida**, *City of Clearwater v. Lewis*, 404 So.2d 1156 (Fla. App. 1981); **Iowa**, *City of Marion v. Weitenhagen*, 361 N.W.2d 323 (Iowa App. 1984); **Massachusetts**, *Commonwealth of Massachusetts, Department of Public Welfare*, Case Number SVP-2062 (Mass. LRC, 1977); **Michigan**, *Wayne-Westland Educ. Assn. v. Wayne-Westland Comm. Schools*, 439 N.W.2d 372 (Mich. App. 1989); **Oregon**, *Amalgamated Transit Union v. Tri-County Metropolitan Transportation District,* 11 PECBR 480 (1989); **Pennsylvania**, *Conneaut School District*, 10 PPER Section 10092 (Nisi Order, 1979), 12 PPER Section 12155 (Final Order, 1981); **Washington**, *Teamsters v. Okanogan County*, 3 WPLLR 860 (PECD, 1985). *See also Madison School District*, 89 SERB-012 (Ohio)(1989)(right to representation exists under collective bargaining laws, but under different theory than *Weingarten*).

[49] *New York City Transit Authority v. New York State Public Employment Relations Bd.*, 864 N.E.2d 56 (N.Y. 2007); *Town of North Kingstown v. Local 473, IBPO*, 819 A.2d 1274 (R.I. 2003).

[50] *Ehlers v. Jackson County Merit Commission*, 697 N.E.2d 717 (Ill. 1998).

[51] *City of Highland Park*, 15 IPER 2004 (Ill. LLRB 1999).

[52] *City of Allen Park*, 16 MPER ¶39 (Mich. ERC 2003); *Puyallup Police Officers Association*, 1999 WL 739676 (Wash. PERC 1999).

[53] *City of Chicago*, 13 IPER ¶3014 (Ill. LLRB 1997); *City of Manchester*, 95 Fire & Police Reporter 21-2 (Greenbaum, 1994).

[54] *Delaware County*, LAIG 4897 (Aronin, 1993).

[55] *New Jersey State Police*, 15 NPER NJ-23212 (N.J. PERC 1992); *Pennsylvania State Corrections Officers Association*, 34 PPER ¶78 (Pa. LRB ALJ 2003).

[56] *SERB v. City of Cleveland*, 15 PERO ¶1037 (Ohio SERB 1997).

[57] *In re Grievance of Vermont State Employees' Ass'n, Inc.*, 893 A.2d 333 (Vt. 2005).

[58] *Loney v. Social Sec. Admin.*, 266 Fed.Appx. 912 (Fed. Cir. 2008).

[59] *State of New Jersey*, 27 NJPER ¶32,119 (N.J. PERC 2001); *see AFGE, Local 2544 v. FLRA,* 779 F.2d 719 (D.C. Cir. 1985); *IRS v. FLRA*, 671 F.2d 560 (D.C. Cir. 1982)(decided under National Labor Relations Act).

[60] *Oregon AFSCME Council 75 v. State of Oregon*, UP-9-01 (Or. ERB 2002).

[61] *PEMA v. Pennsylvania Labor Relations Board*, 768 A.2d 1201 (Pa.Cmwlth. 2001).

62 *California State Employees Association*, 21 PERC ¶28,137 (Cal. PERB ALJ 1997); *City of Flatrock*, 19 NPER MI-27095 (Mich. ERC 1996); *County of Atlantic*, 22 NJPER ¶27,169 (N.J. PERC ULP Dir. 1997); *Commonwealth of Pennsylvania*, 34 PPER ¶110 (Pa. LRB ALJ 2003).

63 *Snohomish County Deputy Sheriff's Association v. Snohomish County*, 1996 WL 260757 (Wash. PERC 1996).

64 *Seattle Police Officers Guild v. City of Seattle*, 1998 WL 823595 (Wash. PERC 1998).

65 *Metro-Dade Police Dept.*, 24 FPER ¶29,053 (Fla. PERC 1998); *Pennsylvania State Corrections Officers Association*, 34 PPER ¶134 (Pa. LRB 2003); *Falls Township*, 30 PPER ¶30,007 (Pa. LRB ALJ 1998).

66 *Cowlitz County*, 1999 WL 909589 (Wash. PERC ALJ 1999).

67 *New York City Transit Authority*, 36 NYPER ¶7009 (N.Y. S.Ct. 2003); *City of Reading*, 689 A.2d 990 (Pa.Cmwlth. 1997).

68 *Fraternal Order of Police v. Commonwealth of Pennsylvania*, 28 PPER ¶28,203 (Pa. LRB 1997). *See Safeway Stores, Inc.*, 303 NLRB 989 (1991).

69 *In re Exeter Police Ass'n*, 904 A.2d 614 (N.J. 2006); *Jackson v. State of Illinois*, 14 IPER ¶2035 (Ill. SLRB Gen. Coun. 1998); *City of Marine City Police Department*, 15 MPER ¶33,052 (Mich. ERC 2002); *South Jersey Port Authority*, 23 NJPER ¶28,277 (N.J. PERC ALJ 1997); *Ohio State University*, 20 OPER ¶216 (Ohio ERB 2003).

70 *Town of Hudson v. Labor Relations Com'n*, 870 N.E.2d 618 (Mass. App. 2007); *City of Chicago*, 3 PERI ¶3028 (Ill. LLRB 1987).

71 *National Labor Relations Board v. J. Weingarten, Inc.*, 420 U.S. 251 (1975)(right to representation is an individual right that benefits the group as a whole); *Anheuser-Busch, Inc. and International Brotherhood of Teamsters, Local Union No. 1149*, 337 NLRB 3 (2001), *aff'd*, 338 F.3d 267 (4th Cir. 2003)(employee can choose representative); *Com. Office of Admin v. Pennsylvania Labor Relations Board*, 916 A.2d 541 (Pa. 2007)(employee can choose representative).

72 Many of the "bills of rights" adopted by state statute or collective bargaining agreement allow for representation by counsel during disciplinary interviews. *See* discussion in Chapter 5.

The courts have reasoned that since the right to counsel provisions of the Sixth Amendment to the United States Constitution only apply once criminal, not administrative, proceedings have begun, an officer facing an internal investigation is not entitled to be represented by an attorney in the internal investigatory process unless the union representative happens to be the union's attorney. *Los Angeles Police Protective League v. Gates*, 579 F. Supp. 36 (C.D. Cal. 1984).

73 *Town of Hudson v. Labor Relations Com'n*, 870 N.E.2d 618 (Mass. App. 2007); *Cheltenham Township Police Association v. Cheltenham Township*, 846 A.2d 173 (Pa.Cmwlth 2004).

74 *Duryea Borough Police Department*, 34 PPER ¶158 (Pa. LRB ALJ 2003).

75 *City of Fraser, Michigan*, 15 NPER MI-24053 (Mich. ERC 1993).

76 *State of California*, 23 PERC ¶30,102 (Cal. PERB ALJ 1999).

77 *Millersville Borough*, 17 NPER PA-26100 (Pa. LRB ALJ 1995).

78 *King County Police Officers' Guild v. King County*, Decision 4299 (Wash. PERC 1993)(reverses discharge of employee when labor representative told

by employer to not participate in any way in the interview of the employee); *Commonwealth of Pennsylvania*, 32 PPER ¶32,095 (Pa. LRB ALJ 2001).

[79] *National Labor Relations Board v. J. Weingarten, Inc.*, 420 U.S. 251 (1975).

[80] *Pennsylvania State Corrections Officers Association*, 33 PPER ¶33,177 (Pa. LRB 2002).

[81] *Pennsylvania State Corrections Officers Association*, 34 PPER ¶52 (Pa. LRB 2003).

[82] *Commonwealth of Pennsylvania*, 34 PPER ¶83 (Pa.Cmwlth. 2003); *see System 99 and Walter Manning*, 289 N.L.R.B. 723, 131 L.R.R.M. 1226 (1988)(decided under National Labor Relations Act).

[83] *Pennsylvania State Corrections Officers Association*, 34 PPER ¶140 (Pa. LRB ALJ 2003).

[84] *See State Employee Relations Board v. City of Cleveland*, 14 OPER 1419 (Ohio PERB ALJ 1997).

[85] *Montour County*, 34 PPER ¶136 (Pa. LRB ALJ 2003).

[86] *Monroe County*, 34 PPER ¶55 (Pa. LRB ALJ 2003).

[87] *See Board of Regents v. Roth*, 408 U.S. 564 (1972).

[88] *Moffit v. Town of Brookfield*, 950 F.2d 880 (2d Cir. 1991)(just cause provision in collective bargaining agreement creates property right); *See also Kivett v. Marion County Sheriff's Dept.*, 2007 WL 906470 (S.D. Ind. 2007); *Smith v. Milwaukee County*, 954 F. Supp. 1314 (E.D. Wis. 1997); *In re Gregoire*, 689 A.2d 431 (Vt. 1996).

[89] *See Bolton v. City of Dallas, Tex.*, 472 F.3d 261 (5th Cir. 2006)(ordinance gave police chief property right to job); *Wilson v. Robinson*, 668 F.2d 380 (8th Cir. 1981); *Umholtz v. City of Tulsa*, 515 P.2d 15 (Okla. 1977). The mere listing of prohibited conduct, without an affirmative grant of job protection, may not be enough to give rise to a property interest. *See Ogletree v. Chester*, 682 F.2d 1366 (11th Cir. 1982); *Glenn v. Newman*, 614 F.2d 467 (5th Cir. 1980); *Harrison v. City of Adairsville*, 560 F. Supp. 445 (N.D. Ga. 1983).

[90] *Golem v. Village of Put-In-Bay*, 222 F. Supp. 2d 924 (N.D. Ohio 2002); *Maxey v. Smith*, 823 F. Supp. 1321 (N.D. Miss. 1993); *Ness v. Glasscock*, 781 P.2d 137 (Colo. App. 1989); *Maxwell v. City of Savannah, Georgia*, 487 S.E.2d 478 (Ga. App. 1999); *Harkness v. City of Burley*, 715 P.2d 1283 (Idaho 1986); *Hunt v. Shettle*, 452 N.E.2d 1045 (Ind. App. 1983). *But see Graham v. City of Oklahoma City*, 679 F. Supp. 1017 (W.D. Okla. 1986); *Johnson v. City of Welch*, 388 S.E.2d 284 (W.Va. 1989)(civil service commission not bound by police department rules which established progressive discipline system).

[91] *County of Dallas v. Wiland*, 124 S.W.3d 390 (Tex. App. 2003)(manual requiring "just cause" for discipline creates property right); *Semerau v. Village of Shiller Park*, 569 N.E.2d 183 (Ill. App. 1990)(personnel manual written in vague terms did not give rise to property right to job); *Pesek v. City of Brunswick*, 794 F. Supp. 768 (N.D. Ohio 1992); *Maxwell v. City of Savannah*, 487 S.E.2d 478 (Ga. App. 1997).

[92] *Whatley v. City of Bartlesville, Oklahoma*, 932 F. Supp. 1300 (N.D. Okla. 1996).

[93] *Darr v. Town of Telluride, Colo.*, 495 F.3d 1243 (10th Cir. 2007).

[94] *Poleo-Keefe v. Bergeron*, 2008 WL 3992636 (D. Vt. 2008).

[95] *Shawgo v. Spradlin*, 701 F.2d 470 (5th Cir. 1983); *City of Philadelphia v. FOP, Lodge No. 5*, 572 A.2d 1298 (Pa.Cmwlth. 1990).

96 *See Olshock v. Village of Skokie*, 541 F.2d 1254 (7th Cir. 1976); *Penland v. Long*, 922 F. Supp. 1085 (W.D. N.C. 1996); *Clisham v. Board of Police Commissioners*, 613 A.2d 254 (Conn. 1992); *Mondt v. Cheyenne Police Department*, 924 P.2d 70 (Wyo. 1996). For example, the Illinois Revised Statutes contain provisions establishing a just cause standard for the discharge or lengthy suspension of law enforcement officers. *See* Illinois Revised Statutes, Chapter 24, Paragraph 10-1-18.1 (covering cities greater than 500,000 in population); Illinois Revised Statutes, Chapter 24, Paragraph 10-1-18(b)(covering smaller cities). A statute can also require that procedural due process be followed even though no property right to the job exists. *See Hogarth v. Sheriff of Suffolk County*, 564 N.E.2d 397 (Mass. App. 1990).

97 *Richardson v. Felix*, 856 F.2d 505 (3d Cir. 1988).

98 *Schultea v. Wood*, 47 F.3d 1427 (5th Cir. 1995)(city manager did not have the authority to orally promise a chief that he would only be discharged for just cause); *Crowell v. City of Eastman*, 859 F.2d 875 (11th Cir. 1988); *see Garcia v. Reeves County*, 32 F.3d 200 (5th Cir. 1994)(Texas county commissioners have no authority to bind sheriff's disciplinary decisions through issuance of a personnel manual); *Hadley v. County of DuPage*, 715 F.2d 1238 (7th Cir. 1983)(verbal assurances from chief that officers would not be terminated except for just cause did not create property right because chief lacked authority to bind the City).

99 *Erickson v. Village of Willow Springs*, 876 F. Supp. 951 (N.D. Ill. 1995).

100 *Flannelly v. Board of Trustees of the New York City Pension Fund*, 6 F. Supp. 2d 266 (S.D. N.Y. 1998).

101 *Campbell v. Mercer*, 926 F.2d 990 (10th Cir. 1991); *Bowers v. Town of Smithsburg, Md.*, 990 F. Supp. 396 (D. Md. 1997); *Lane v. Town of Dover*, 761 F. Supp. 768 (W.D. Okla. 1991); *Harrington v. City of Portland*, 708 F. Supp. 1561 (D. Or. 1988).

102 *Whims v. Harbaugh*, 139 F.3d 897 (4th Cir. 1998); *Jackson v. Long*, 102 F.3d 722 (4th Cir. 1996); *Bumstead v. Jasper County, Texas*, 931 F. Supp. 1323 (E.D. Tex. 1996); *Brett v. Jefferson County, Georgia*, 925 F. Supp. 786 (S.D. Ga. 1996); *Brown v. Wheeler*, 669 So.2d 318 (Fla. App. 1996); *Seeley v. Board of County Commissioners*, 791 P.2d 696 (Colo. 1990). In *Williams v. Bagley*, 875 S.W.2d 808 (Tex. App. 1994), the Court upheld the right of a Texas sheriff to fire his entire department without granting a due process hearing.

103 *Vanderploeg v. Village of Merrionette Park*, 2008 WL 623622 (N.D. Ill. 2008).

104 *Olejniczak v. Town of Kouts*, 651 N.E.2d 1197 (Ind. App. 1995).

105 *Harris v. City of Auburn*, 27 F.3d 1284 (7th Cir. 1994).

106 *Murden v. County of Sacramento*, 160 Cal.App.3d 302 (1984)(reserves); *Waters v. Buckner*, 699 F. Supp. 900 (Ga. 1988)(reserves); *Garcia v. Garcia*, 751 S.W.2d 274 (Tex. App. 1988)(probationary employees).

107 *Foxx v. Town of Fletcher*, 2008 WL 927543 (W.D. N.C. 2008); *Bash v. City of Galena, Kansas*, 42 F. Supp. 2d 1171 (D. Kan. 1999).

108 *McNeill v. City of Canton, Miss.*, 2008 WL 249437 (S.D. Miss. 2008).

109 *Dennison v. City Of Phoenix*, 2009 WL 117986 (9th Cir. 2009); *Walsh v. Suffolk County Police Dept.*, 2008 WL 1991118 (E.D. N.Y. 2008); *Bartal v. Borough of Laureldale*, 515 F. Supp. 2d 556 (E.D. Pa. 2007); *Sagendorf-Tolteal v. County of Rensselaer*, 904 F. Supp. 95 (N.D. N.Y. 1995); *Gomez v. City of Sheridan by and Through Herring*, 611 F. Supp. 230 (D. Colo. 1985); *Elmer v. Board of*

Commissioners of Wilkins Township, 552 A.2d 745 (Pa.Cmwlth. 1989); *Williams v. Bagley,* 875 S.W.2d 808 (Tex. App. 1994). In an unusual case, a New York appellate court appears to have held that even a probationary employee is entitled to a pre-termination hearing if the employer's asserted justification is so lacking in merit as to be implausible. *Garrison v. Koehler,* 555 N.Y.S.2d 87 (A.D. 1990).

[110] *Yates v. Hall,* 508 F. Supp. 2d 1088 (N.D. Fla. 2007).

[111] *Ross v. Clayton County, Georgia,* 173 F.3d 1305 (11th Cir. 1999).

[112] *State ex rel. Dickerson v. City Of Logan,* 650 S.E.2d 100 (W.Va. 2006).

[113] *Eng v. New York City Police Dept.,* 977 F. Supp. 668 (S.D. N.Y. 1997).

[114] Procedural due process requires a hearing even when the officer who is discharged is already on an unpaid leave of absence. *Prue v. Hunt,* 558 N.Y.S.2d 1016 (A.D. 1990).

[115] *Wanless v. Village of South Lebanon,* 118 Fed.Appx. 967 (6th Cir. 2005); *Chaney v. Village of Potsdam,* 105 Fed.Appx. 18 (6th Cir. 2004).

[116] *See Ashton v. City of Indianapolis,* 88 Fed.Appx. 948 (7th Cir. 2004)(suspension of one day); *Bailey v. Kirk,* 777 F.2d 567 (10th Cir. 1985)(suspension of chief of police for four days); *Thomas v. Zaharek,* 289 F. Supp. 2d 167 (D. Conn. 2003)(suspension of 45 days); *Kennedy v. New York City,* 10 IER Cases 1174 (S.D. N.Y. 1995)(indefinite suspension); *D'Acquisto v. Washington,* 640 F. Supp. 594 (N.D. Ill. 1986)(indefinite suspension); *Hopkins v. Mayor & Council of City of Wilmington,* 600 F. Supp. 542 (D. Del. 1984)(suspension of police officer for 25 days); *Mondt v. Cheyenne Police Department,* 924 P.2d 70 (Wyo. 1996)(suspension for 40 hours).

[117] *Greene v. Barrett,* 174 F.3d 1136 (10th Cir. 1999); *Hennigh v. City of Shawnee,* 155 F.3d 1249 (10th Cir. 1998); *Shawgo v. Spradlin,* 701 F.2d 470 (5th Cir. 1983); *Fonville v. District of Columbia,* 448 F. Supp. 2d 21 (D. D.C. 2006); *Gray v. City of Gustine,* 273 Cal.Rptr. 730 (Cal. App. 1990); *Faught v. City of Alexandria,* 560 So.2d 671 (La. App. 1990).

[118] *Muncy v. City of Dallas, Texas,* 335 F.3d 394 (5th Cir. 2003).

[119] *Coffran v. Board of Trustees of New York City Pension Fund,* 842 F. Supp. 723 (S.D. N.Y. 1994); *Wydra v. Swatara Township,* 582 A.2d 710 (Pa.Cmwlth. 1990).

[120] *Ganley v. County of San Mateo,* 2007 WL 4554318 (N.D. Cal. 2007); *Ceko v. Martin,* 753 F. Supp. 1418 (N.D. Ill. 1990).

[121] *Bauschard v. Martin,* 1993 WL 79259 (N.D. Ill. 1993).

[122] *Delahoussaye v. City of New Iberia,* 937 F.2d 144 (5th Cir. 1991).

[123] *Kempkes v. Downey,* 861 N.Y.S.2d 415 (A.D. 2008).

[124] *Cholewin v. City of Evanston,* 899 F.2d 687 (7th Cir. 1990); *Hairston v. District of Columbia,* 638 F. Supp. 198 (D. D.C. 1986). *But see Swick v. City of Chicago,* 11 F.3d 85 (7th Cir. 1993).

[125] *Brown v. City of Los Angeles,* 125 Cal.Rptr.2d 474 (Cal. App. 2002).

[126] *Alejado v. City and County of Honolulu,* 971 P.2d 310 (Haw. App. 1998).

[127] *Dell v. City of Tipton,* 618 N.E.2d 1338 (Ind. App. 1993).

[128] *Compare Byrd v. Gain,* 558 F.2d 553 (9th Cir. 1977)(written reprimand can trigger due process) with *Miller v. Lovell,* 14 F.3d 20 (8th Cir. 1994)(no need for due process prior to issuance of written reprimand); *Lowe v. Kansas City Board of Police Commissioners,* 841 F.2d 857 (8th Cir. 1988)(written reprimand does not trigger due

process); *Hoffman v. Village of Sidney*, 652 N.Y.S.2d 346 (A.D. 1997); *Stanton v. City of West Sacramento,* 277 Cal.Rptr. 478 (Cal. App. 1991); *Cameron v. Dept. of State Police*, 361 N.W.2d 765 (Mich. App. 1984).

[129] *Coday v. City of Springfield*, 939 F.2d 666 (8th Cir. 1991)(reclassification of detectives to corporals).

[130] *Karchnak v. Swatara Township*, 540 F. Supp. 2d 540 (M.D. Pa. 2008).

[131] *Edwards v. City of Goldsboro*, 981 F. Supp. 406 (E.D. N.C. 1997); *Cybulski v. Cooper*, 891 F. Supp. 68 (D. Conn. 1995); *Wilmarth v. Town of Georgetown*, 555 N.E.2d 597 (Mass. App. 1990).

[132] *Ferros v. Georgia State Patrol*, 438 S.E.2d 163 (Ga. App. 1993); *Haskins v. City of Chattanooga*, 877 S.W.2d 267 (Tenn. App. 1993).

[133] *Knoblauch v. City of Warren*, 268 F. Supp. 2d 775 (E.D. Mich. 2003).

[134] *Izquierdo v. Sills,* 68 F. Supp. 2d 392 (D. Del. 1999).

[135] *City Council of Laramie v. Kreiling*, 911 P.2d 1037 (Wyo. 1996).

[136] *Rosado-Quinones v. Toledo*, 528 F.3d 1 (1st Cir. 2008).

[137] *Flynn v. Sandahl*, 58 F.3d 283 (7th Cir. 1995); *Hoover v. County of Broome*, 2008 WL 1777444 (N.D. N.Y. 2008).

[138] *Pina v. Lantz*, 495 F. Supp. 2d 290 (D. Conn. 2007).

[139] *Dill v. City of Edmond, Oklahoma*, 155 F.3d 1193 (10th Cir. 1998).

[140] *Hughes v. Alabama Department of Public Safety*, 994 F. Supp. 1395 (M.D. Ala. 1998).

[141] *Tripp v. City of Winston-Salem*, 655 S.E.2d 890 (N.C. App. 2008).

[142] *Turturici v. City of Redwood City*, 236 Cal.Rptr. 53 (Cal. App. 1993).

[143] *O'Brien v. City of Philadelphia*, 837 F. Supp. 692 (E.D. Pa. 1993); *Rinard v. Polk County*, 516 N.W.2d 822 (Iowa 1994). Reaching a contrary result, the Court in *Kovalchik v. Pennsylvania State Police*, 613 A.2d 150 (Pa.Cmwlth. 1992), held that the elaborate hiring selection procedures required by a consent decree gave a candidate for a police job a due process right to a hearing before being disqualified.

[144] *Garden v. Hawley*, 104 Fed.Appx. 2 (9th Cir. 2004); *Donovan v. Incorporated Village of Malverne*, 547 F. Supp. 2d 210 (E.D. N.Y. 2008); *Violissi v. City of Middletown*, 990 F. Supp. 93 (D. Conn. 1998); *Pollock v. Ocean City*, 968 F. Supp. 187 (D. N.J. 1997); *Olive v. City of Scottsdale*, 969 F. Supp. 564 (D. Ariz. 1996); *Hunter v. City of Warner Robbins,* 842 F. Supp. 1460 (M.D. Ga. 1994)(no property interest in promotion); *Ellison v. DeKalb County,* 511 S.E.2d 284 (Ga. App. 1999); *Schlicher v. Board of Fire and Police Com'rs of Village of Westmont*, 845 N.E.2d 55 (Ill. App. 2006); *Bielawski v. Personnel Administrator*, 663 N.E.2d 821 (Mass. 1996); *Virden v. Roper*, 788 S.W.2d 470 (Ark. 1990)(captain had no protected property interest in an assistant chief's job).

[145] *Teigen v. Renfrow*, 511 F.3d 1072 (10th Cir. 2007); *see United States v. City of Chicago*, 869 F.2d 1033 (7th Cir. 1989); *Bigby v. City of Chicago*, 766 F.2d 1053 (7th Cir. 1985), *quoting McCoy v. Board of Fire and Police Commissioners*, 398 N.E.2d 1020 (Ill. App. 1979) and *Board of Regents v. Roth*, 408 U.S. 564 (1972); *Aldridge v. City of Memphis*, 2007 WL 4570881 (W.D. Tenn. 2007).

[146] *Drogan v. Ward*, 675 F. Supp. 832 (S.D. N.Y. 1987); *see Sottiley v. New York City Police Department*, 595 N.Y.S. 822 (A.D. 1993).

[147] *Martinez v. City of New York*, 2003 WL 22879401 (2d Cir. 2003); *Gustafson v. Jones*, 117 F.3d 1015 (7th Cir. 1997); *Stiesveig v. State of California*, 80 F.3d 253

(9th Cir. 1996); *Clark v. Township of Falls*, 890 F.2d 611 (3d Cir. 1989)(reassignment of lieutenant without loss of pay); *Barton v. City of Bristol*, 294 F. Supp. 2d 184 (D. Conn. 2003); *Johnson v. City of Tarpon Springs*, 758 F. Supp. 1473 (M.D. Fla. 1991); *Abreu v. City of Chicago*, 1990 WL 103626 (N.D. Ill. 1990)(transfer of assignments). *See also Confederation of Police v. City of Chicago*, 547 F.2d 375 (7th Cir. 1977)(general discussion of due process in a transfer setting); *Mosrie v. Barry*, 718 F.2d 1151 (D.C. Cir. 1983)(discussion of meaning of "reduction of rank" and relationship to transfer and reassignment).

[148] *Potts v. Davis County*, 551 F.3d 1188 (10th Cir. 2009); *Izquierdo v. Sills*, 68 F. Supp. 2d 392 (D. Del. 1999); *Prudhomme v. Department of Police*, 568 So.2d 595 (La. App. 1990)(transfer from transit patrol unit accompanied by loss of pay supplement provided by transit authority not sufficient to trigger due process). *But see White v. County of Sacramento*, 646 P.2d 191 (Cal. 1982)(transfer accompanied by loss of pay requires procedural due process); *McManigal v. City of Seal Beach*, 212 Cal.Rptr. 733 (Cal. App. 1985)(transfer accompanied by loss of pay requires procedural due process). *See generally Hummel v. McCotter,* 28 F. Supp. 2d 1322 (D. Utah 1998)(assumes without deciding that transfer accompanied by loss of pay requires due process).

[149] *Ruhlman v. Barger*, 435 F. Supp. 447 (W.D. Pa. 1977).

[150] *Lawson v. Sheriff of Tippecanoe County, Indiana*, 725 F.2d 1136 (7th Cir. 1984).

[151] *Poolman v. City of Grafton, N.D.,* 487 F.3d 1098 (8th Cir. 2007); *Fleisher v. City of Signal Hill*, 829 F.2d 1491 (9th Cir. 1987); *see generally Smith v. Borough of Pottstown*, 1997 WL 597909 (E.D. Pa. 1997).

[152] *Formica v. Galantino*, 1989 WL 100836 (E.D. Pa. 1989)(police officers fired for spurning mayor's sexual advances), *quoting Board of Regents v. Roth*, 408 U.S. 564 (1972).

[153] *Goldbeck v. City of Chicago*, 782 F. Supp. 381 (N.D. Ill. 1992).

[154] *Roley v. Pierce County*, 869 F.2d 491 (9th Cir. 1989). *See Kennedy v. McCarty*, 778 F. Supp. 1465 (S.D. Ind. 1991)(liberty rights of reserve officer could not be affected by discharge since reserve had regular job and livelihood was not impaired).

[155] *Darr v. Town of Telluride, Colo.,* 495 F.3d 1243 (10th Cir. 2007)(department merely announced officer was no longer an employee); *Bazemore v. Koehler*, 564 N.Y.S.2d 428 (A.D. 1991)(probationary corrections officer who had been indicted for murder terminated for no stated reason; liberty rights not affected); *Lane v. Town of Dover*, 761 F. Supp. 768 (W.D. Okla. 1991)(stating that police chief terminated for the good of the service not sufficiently stigmatizing to invoke liberty rights); *see Melton v. Oklahoma City*, 928 F.2d 920 (10th Cir. 1991)(statement by public information officer that investigation underway not enough to impact liberty right).

[156] *Esposito v. Metro-North Commuter Railroad Co.*, 856 F. Supp. 799 (S.D. N.Y. 1994).

[157] *Mercer v. City of Cedar Rapids*, 308 F.3d 840 (8th Cir. 2002).

[158] *Hoffman v. City of Willimantic,* 680 F. Supp. 504 (D. Conn. 1988); *Fontana v. Commissioner*, 606 N.E.2d 1343 (Mass. App. 1993).

[159] *Sciolino v. City of Newport News, Va.,* 480 F.3d 642 (4th Cir. 2007), *quoting Bd. of Regents of State Colls. v. Roth,* 408 U.S. 564 (1972).

[160] *Wellbanks v. Smith County*, 661 F. Supp. 212 (E.D. Tex. 1987).

161 *Lawson v. Sheriff of Tippecanoe County, Indiana*, 725 F.2d 1136 (7th Cir. 1984).

162 *Heger v. City of Costa Mesa,* 282 Cal.Rptr. 341 (Cal. App. 1991). *But see Brito v. Diamond*, 796 F. Supp. 754 (S.D. N.Y. 1992)(allegations that probationary officer failed to respond to a call during lunch and falsely contended that he had responded to an emergency call are not sufficiently stigmatizing to invoke liberty rights).

163 *Fontana v. Commissioner of Metropolitan District Commission*, 606 N.E.2d 1343 (Mass. App. 1993).

164 *Barberic v. City of Hawthorne*, 699 F. Supp. 985 (C.D. Cal. 1987).

165 *Truhe v. East Penn Tp.*, 2007 WL 184890 (M.D. Pa. 2007).

166 *Zueck v. City of Nokomis*, 513 N.E.2d 125 (Ill. App. 1987); *see Hoffman v. McNamara*, 630 F. Supp. 1257 (D. Conn. 1986)(allegation that recruit had sex with another recruit while at academy sufficient to trigger need for name-clearing hearing).

167 *Binkley v. City of Long Beach*, 20 Cal.Rptr.2d 903 (Cal. 1993). C*ontra Carroll v. Town of University Park*, 12 F. Supp. 2d 475 (D. Md. 1997)(allegation of incompetence not enough to implicate liberty right).

168 *Penland v. Long*, 922 F. Supp. 1085 (W.D. N.C. 1996).

169 *Maxwell v. City of Savannah, Georgia*, 487 S.E.2d 478 (Ga. App. 1999).

170 *Brandt v. Board of Cooperative Educational Services*, 820 F.2d 41 (2d Cir. 1987); *Harrell v. City of Gastonia*, 2008 WL 2139619 (W.D. N.C. 2008).

171 *Johnson v. Martin*, 943 F.2d 15 (7th Cir. 1991); *Olivieri v. Rodriguez*, 944 F. Supp. 686 (N.D. Ill. 1996); *Roehrborn v. Lambert*, 11 IER Cases 668 (Ill. App. 1995).

172 *Clark v. Township of Falls*, 890 F.2d 611 (3d Cir. 1990).

173 *Johnson v. Martin*, 943 F.2d 15 (9th Cir. 1991)(no dissemination outside of police department of fact that probationary officer fired for drug use); *Walsh v. Suffolk County Police Dept.*, 2008 WL 1991118 (E.D. N.Y. 2008)(termination documents not actually placed in employee's file).

174 *Watson v. Sexton*, 755 F. Supp. 583 (S.D. N.Y. 1991).

175 *Buxton v. Plant City*, 871 F.2d 1037 (11th Cir. 1989). In a seemingly conflicting result, a lower federal court has held that the intergovernmental distribution of disciplinary information is not a "publication" of defamatory information. *Harrison v. Board of County Commissioners of Adams County*, 775 F. Supp. 365 (Colo. 1991); *see Hughes v. Alabama Department of Public Safety*, 994 F. Supp. 1395 (M.D. Ala. 1998).

176 *Pirela v. Village of North Aurora*, 966 F. Supp. 661 (N.D. Ill. 1997); *Waynick v. County of Dallas*, 1993 WL 52453 (Tex. App. 1993).

177 *Schultea v. Wood*, 29 F.3d 1112 (5th Cir. 1994); *Moore v. Otero*, 557 F.2d 435 (5th Cir. 1977); *Williams v. Perry*, 960 F. Supp. 534 (D. Conn. 1996); *see Christian v. City of Dallas*, 45 F. Supp. 2d 1353 (N.D. Tex. 1999)(release of stigmatizing information concurrent with suspension with pay does not invoke liberty rights).

178 *Gray v. City of Gustine*, 273 Cal.Rptr. 730 (Cal. App. 1990)(liberty rights triggered by demotion).

179 *Oladeinde v. City of Birmingham*, 963 F.2d 1481 (11th Cir. 1992).

180 *Siegert v. Gilley,* 500 U.S. 226 (1991); *see Haight v. City of San Diego*, 278 Cal.Rptr. 334 (1991)(former employee has no liberty rights).

181 *Vanderploeg v. Village of Merrionette Park*, 2008 WL 623622 (N.D. Ill. 2008).

182 *Hoffman v. Kelz*, 443 F. Supp. 2d 1007 (W.D. Wis. 2006).

183 *Ashton v. City of Indianapolis*, 88 Fed.Appx. 948 (7th Cir. 2004).

184 *See Cleveland Board of Education v. Loudermill*, 470 U.S. 532 (1985); *Mathews v. Eldridge*, 424 U.S. 319 (1976); *Buckner v. City of Highland Park*, 901 F.2d 491 (6th Cir. 1990).

185 *Peacock v. City of Elba*, 1997 WL 1068632 (M.D. Ala. 1997). *See also Carey v. Piphus,* 435 U.S. 247 (1978). *But see Verri v. Nanna*, 20 F. Supp. 2d 616 (S.D. N.Y. 1998); *Burleson v. Hancock County Sheriff's Department Civil Service Commission*, 872 So.2d 43 (Miss. App. 2003).

186 *See Davis v. Bexar County*, 775 S.W.2d 807 (Tex. App. 1989)(reversed on other grounds) 6 IER Cases 276 (Tex. 1990).

187 *Cronin v. Town of Amesbury*, 81 F.3d 257 (1st Cir. 1996)(three-year delay in post-disciplinary hearing did not violate due process since hearing could result in employee being made whole).

188 *Santana v. City of Hartford*, 894 A.2d 307 (Conn. App. 2006); *see Arredondo v. City of Billings Dept. of Police*, 143 P.3d 702 (Mt. 2006)(delay caused in part by officer's actions).

189 *See Cleveland Board of Education v. Loudermill*, 470 U.S. 532 (1985). *See also Soto v. City of Laredo*, 764 F. Supp. 448 (S.D. Tex. 1991); *Prue v. Hunt*, 558 N.Y.S.2d 1016 (A.D. 1990). There exists a minority view which argues that, in very limited circumstances, the existence of a post-disciplinary remedy can eliminate the need for a pre-disciplinary hearing. *See Muscare v. Quinn*, 520 F.2d 1212 (7th Cir. 1975); *Reed v. Dept. of Police,* 967 So.2d 606 (La. App. 2007)(in wake of Hurricane Katrina chaos, no need for pre-termination hearing if complete post-termination remedy in place). Even those courts adhering to this minority rule, however, demand extremely prompt post-disciplinary remedies. *See D'Acquisto v. Washington*, 640 F. Supp. 594 (N.D. Ill. 1986)(four-month delay from time of discipline to post-discipline hearing too lengthy).

190 *Beary v. Johnson*, 872 So.2d 943 (Fla. App. 2004).

191 *Fowler v. Johnson*, 961 So.2d 122 (Ala. 2006).

192 *Bass v. City of Albany*, 968 F.2d 1067 (11th Cir. 1992)(termination violated due process where notice did not include reference to psychological evaluation which was a basis for the termination); *Roorda v. City of Arnold*, 142 S.W.3d 786 (Mo. App. 2004)(notice must include statement of charges and supporting facts); *Bigando v. Heitzman*, 590 N.Y.S.2d 553 (A.D. 1992)(termination violated due process when employer failed to list rules and regulations employee was accused of violating); *see Sanders v. District of Columbia*, 522 F. Supp. 2d 83 (D. D.C. 2007).

193 *San Francisco Police Commission v. Police Commission of the City and County of San Francisco*, 1996 WL 75309 (N.D. Cal. 1996); *Reeves v. Thigpen*, 879 F. Supp. 1153 (M.D. Ala. 1995); *Formica v. Galantino*, 1989 WL 100836 (E.D. Pa. 1989).

194 *Mondt v. Cheyenne Police Department*, 924 P.2d 70 (Wyo. 1996).

195 *Martinez v. Personnel Board of the City of Loma Linda*, 2003 WL 429505 (Cal. App. 2003).

196 *Hrbek v. City of Bellevue Civil Service Com'n*, 2005 WL 1949498 (Neb. App. 2005).

197 *Buckner v. City of Highland Park*, 901 F.2d 491 (6th Cir. 1990); *see Humphrey v. Scott County Fiscal Court*, 211 Fed.Appx. 390 (6th Cir. 2006)(oral notice of pre-disciplinary hearing met due process requirements).

198 *Civil Service Commission v. Goldman*, 621 A.2d 1142 (Pa.Cmwlth. 1993); *see City of Mitchell v. Graves,* 612 N.E.2d 149 (Ind. App. 1993)(eight days not adequate notice for pre-termination hearing).

199 *Saltarella v. Town of Enfield*, 427 F. Supp. 2d 62 (D. Conn. 2006).

200 *Buckner v. City of Highland Park*, 901 F.2d 491 (6th Cir. 1990). *See also Austin v. Neal*, 933 F. Supp. 444 (E.D. Pa. 1996).

201 *In re Galatas*, 982 So.2d 972 (La. App. 2008).

202 *See D'Acquisto v. Washington*, 640 F. Supp. 594 (N.D. Ill. 1986).

203 *Panozzo v. Rhoads*, 905 F.2d 135 (7th Cir. 1990); *Balcerzak v. City of Milwaukee*, 980 F. Supp. 983 (E.D. Wis. 1997); *Williams v. Pima County*, 791 P.2d 1053 (Ariz. App. 1989). *But see Crimi v. Droskoski*, 630 N.Y.S.2d 337 (A.D. 1995).

204 *Angle v. Dow*, 822 F. Supp. 1530 (S.D. Ala. 1993); *In re Boespflug*, 845 P.2d 865 (N.M. App. 1992).

205 *Gordon v. Brown*, 620 N.Y.S.2d 749 (N.Y. 1994); *Town of Harrison Police Department*, LAIG 5268 (Scheinman, 1996).

206 *Neal v. Pike Township*, 530 N.E.2d 103 (Ind. App. 1988). One court has held that an officer does not have the right during a pre-disciplinary hearing to disclosure of the names of confidential informants involved in the case against the officer. *Coleman v. Kramer*, 603 N.Y.S.2d 140 (A.D. 1993).

207 *Cleveland Board of Education v. Loudermill*, 470 U.S. 532 (1985).

208 *Parker v. City of Fountain Valley*, 179 Cal.Rptr. 351 (Cal. App. 1981).

209 *Johnson v. City of Welch*, 388 S.E.2d 284 (W.V. 1989).

210 *Heger v. City of Costa Mesa*, 282 Cal.Rptr. 341 (Cal. App. 1991)(meeting with superior officer not sufficient to satisfy due process requirements).

211 *Los Angeles Police Protective League v. Gates*, 907 F.2d 879 (9th Cir. 1990).

212 *Bolliger v. San Diego Civil Service Commission*, 84 Cal.Rptr.2d 27 (Cal. App. 1999).

213 *Carver v. Nall*, 714 N.E.2d 486 (Ill. 1999).

214 *Guilford v. City of Buffalo*, 571 N.Y.S.2d 183 (N.Y. Sup. 1991).

215 *Click v. Board of Police Commissioners*, 609 F. Supp. 1199 (W.D. Mo. 1985).

216 *Gillard v. Norris*, 857 F.2d 1095 (6th Cir. 1988).

217 *Ganley v. County of San Mateo*, 2007 WL 4554318 (N.D. Cal. 2007); *Flannelly v. Board of Trustees of the New York City Pension Fund*, 6 F. Supp. 2d 266 (S.D. N.Y. 1998).

218 *Verri v. Nanna*, 20 F. Supp. 2d 616 (S.D. N.Y. 1998).

219 *State ex rel. Wilhoit v. Seay*, 248 S.W.3d 135 (Mo. App. 2008).

220 *Gilbert v. Homar*, 520 U.S. 924 (1997); *see Hummel v. McCotter*, 28 F. Supp. 2d 1322 (D. Utah 1998)(officer who had been convicted and was imprisoned at time of suspension had adequate post-disciplinary remedy); *Cole v. Delio*, 946 F. Supp. 283 (S.D. N.Y. 1996)(decided under local ordinance providing that any officer

suspended pending a criminal investigation is entitled to full back pay if the officer is not criminally convicted).

221 *Monroe v. Schenectady County*, 1 F. Supp. 2d 168 (N.D. N.Y. 1997).

222 *Panozzo v. Rhoads*, 905 F.2d 135 (7th Cir. 1990); *see Duchesne v. Williams*, 849 F.2d 1004 (6th Cir. 1988)(city manager who conducted pre-termination hearing later testified against employee); *Geberth v. Augustine*, 553 N.Y.S.2d 504 (1988)(chief stated prior to hearing that he intended to "make an example" of the accused officers; no due process violation found); *Rudnick v. City of Jamestown*, 463 N.W.2d 632 (N.D. 1990)(witness in disciplinary proceedings was also a member of the board which conducted a pre-demotion hearing).

223 *Vanderwalker v. King County*, 91 Fed.Appx. 545 (9th Cir. 2004).

224 *Dell v. City of Tipton*, 618 N.E.2d 1338 (Ind. App. 1993).

225 *Riggins v. City of Louisville*, 2008 WL 220730 (D. Colo. 2008); *Gray v. City of Gustine*, 372 Cal.Rptr. 730 (Cal. App. 1990); *Clisham v. Board of Police Commissioners*, 613 A.2d 254 (Conn. 1992). In *Ulster County Sheriff*, 16 NPER NY-17511 (N.Y. Sup.Ct. 1993), the Court found a violation of procedural due process where the sheriff both initiated the charges and acted as the final decision maker on the charges). *See generally Hadad v. Croucher*, 970 F. Supp. 1227 (N.D. Ohio 1997).

226 *Bender v. Board of Fire and Police Commissioners*, 627 N.E.2d 49 (Ill. App. 1993).

227 *Ferrara v. Magee*, 594 N.Y.S.2d 506 (A.D. 1993).

228 *Christ v. Battle Run*, 663 N.E.2d 722 (Ohio App. 1995).

229 *D'Acquisto v. Washington*, 750 F. Supp. 342 (N.D. Ill. 1990).

230 *Wagner v. City of Memphis*, 971 F. Supp. 308 (W.D. Tenn. 1997); *see Bettio v. Village of Northfield*, 775 F. Supp. 1545 (N.D. Ohio 1991)(officer suspended on charges known by employer to be false).

231 *Ness v. Glasscock*, 781 P.2d 137 (Colo. App. 1989).

232 *Cleveland Board of Education v. Loudermill*, 470 U.S. 532 (1985); *see Sutherland v. Tooele City Corporation*, 91 Fed.Appx. 632 (10th Cir. 2004); *Graning v. Sherburne County*, 172 F.3d 611 (8th Cir. 1999); *Hrbek v. City of Bellevue Civil Service Com'n*, 2005 WL 1949498 (Neb. App. 2005).

233 *See Sutherland v. Tooele City Corp.*, 91 Fed.Appx. 632 (10th Cir. 2004).

234 *Tolson v. Sheridan School District*, 703 F. Supp. 766 (E.D. Ark. 1988).

235 *Bexar County v. Davis*, 6 IER Cases 276 (Tex. 1990)(Doggett, dissenting).

236 *Sanchez v. City of Los Angeles*, 43 Cal.Rptr.3d 695 (Cal. App. 2006).

237 *DiCaprio v. Trzaskos*, 610 N.Y.S.2d 395 (App. Div. 1994)(discharge reversed when employer accidentally erased videotape of incident which was the basis for discipline).

238 *Tolson v. Sheridan School District*, 703 F. Supp. 766 (E.D. Ark. 1988). *See Hatcher v. Board of Public Education and Orphanage*, 809 F.2d 1546 (11th Cir. 1987); *Levitt v. University of Texas,* 759 F.2d 1224 (5th Cir. 1985); *Brouillette v. Board of Directors*, 519 F.2d 126 (8th Cir. 1975). *See also Agarwal v. Regents of University of Minnesota*, 788 F.2d 504 (8th Cir. 1986). *Contra Bexar County v. Davis*, 6 IER Cases 276 (Tex. 1990).

239 *Moreland v. Miami-Dade County*, 255 F. Supp. 2d 1304 (S.D. Fla. 2002); *Hunt v. City of Mulberry*, 173 F. Supp. 2d 1288 (M.D. Fla. 2001).

240 *Hudson v. City of Chicago*, 374 F.3d 554 (7th Cir. 2004).

241 *Winskowski v. City of Stephen*, 442 F.3d 1107 (8th Cir. 2006); *Vines v. City of Dallas*, 851 F. Supp. 254 (N.D. Tex. 1994).

242 *Fontana v. Commissioner*, 606 N.E.2d 1343 (Mass. App. 1993).

243 *Bell v. Town of Port Royal, South Carolina*, 586 F. Supp. 2d 498 (D. S.C. 2008).

244 *Tonkovich v. Kan. Bd. of Regents*, 159 F.3d 504 (10th Cir. 1998).

245 *Graning v. Sherburne County*, 172 F.3d 611 (8th Cir. 1999).

246 *Tregre v. Harris County Sheriff's Dept.*, 2008 WL 1998870 (S.D. Tex. 2008); *Schwartz v. Brown*, 857 F. Supp. 291 (S.D. N.Y. 1994).

247 *Barton v. City of Bristol*, 294 F. Supp. 2d 184 (D. Conn. 2003).

248 *Oddsen v. Board of Fire and Police Commissioners*, 321 N.W.2d 161 (Wis. 1982).

249 *Harrington v. Almy*, 977 F.2d 37 (1st Cir. 1992). *See Ware v. Curlay*, 934 F. Supp. 259 (E.D. Mich. 1996)(allegation that prison officials attempted to frame corrections officer for drug offense because he was black stated a claim for violation of substantive due process).

250 *Homar v. Gilbert*, 1999 WL 705140 (M.D. Pa. 1999).

251 *Singleton v. Cecil*, 155 F.3d 983 (8th Cir. 1998).

252 *Maxey v. Smith*, 823 F. Supp. 1321 (N.D. Miss. 1993).

253 *Moran v. Clarke*, 359 F.3d 1058 (8th Cir. 2004).

254 *Yancey v. Carson*, 2008 WL 687510 (E.D. Tenn. 2008).

255 *Zappola v. Hennig*, 20 F. Supp. 2d 1150 (N.D. Ohio 1998).

256 *Higgins v. City of Johnstown, New York*, 20 F. Supp. 2d 422 (N.D. N.Y. 1998).

257 *Williams v. Perry*, 960 F. Supp. 534 (D. Conn. 1996).

258 *Perry v. Taser Intern. Inc.*, 2008 WL 961559 (D. Colo. 2008); *Ryder v. Freeman*, 918 F. Supp. 157 (W.D. N.C. 1996).

259 *City of Lauderhill v. Rhames*, 864 So.2d 432 (Fla. App. 2003).

260 *Kaucher v. County of Bucks*, 455 F.3d 418 (3d Cir. 2006).

261 *Feirson v. District of Columbia*, 506 F.3d 1063 (D. D.C. 2007).

262 *Hart v. City of Little Rock*, 432 F.3d 801 (8th Cir. 2005).

263 *Washington v. City of North Las Vegas*, 161 Fed.Appx. 637 (9th Cir. 2005).

264 *Graham v. Connor*, 490 U.S. 386 (1989).

265 *Finkelstein v. State Personnel Board*, 267 Cal.Rptr. 133 (Cal. App. 1990); *Ahart v. Colorado Department of Corrections*, 964 P.2d 517 (Colo. 1998); *Grames v. Illinois State Police*, 625 N.E.2d 945 (Ill. App. 1993); *Charles Q v. Constantine*, 613 N.E.2d 511 (N.Y. 1993). *See also Williams v. City of Los Angeles*, 763 P.2d 480 (Cal. 1988).

266 *Rinderknecht v. Maricopa County*, 520 P.2d 332 (Ariz. App. 1974). Other cases to the same general effect are *Dept. of Law Enforcement v. Allen*, 400 So.2d 777 (Fla. App. 1981); *Board of Selectmen of Framingham v. Municipal Ct. of City of Boston*, 369 N.E.2d 1145 (Mass. 1977); *Conwell v. City of Albuquerque*, 637 P.2d 567 (N.M. 1981); *City of Brunswick v. Speights*, 384 A.2d 225 (N.J. Super. 1978);

and *Turner v. City of Lawton*, 733 P.2d 375 (Okla. 1986). An Ohio court ducked the issue in *Slough v. Lucas Cty. Sheriff*, 882 N.E.2d 952 (Ohio App. 2008), finding that even if the exclusionary rule applied in disciplinary cases, admitting the seized evidence in the particular case before it wouldn't violate the rule. At least one arbitrator has applied the exclusionary rule in a case where the bill of rights in a collective bargaining agreement was violated by the method of questioning during a disciplinary interview. *Metropolitan Police Department and Fraternal Order of Police*, LAIG 4241 (Johnson, 1989).

[267] *Minnesota Troopers v. Dept. of Public Safety*, 132 LRRM 2370 (Minn. App. 1989).

[268] *Maumus v. Department of Police*, 457 So.2d 37 (La. App. 1984).

[269] *Ward v. City of Portland*, 857 F.2d 1373 (9th Cir. 1988).

[270] *Watson v. County of Riverside*, 976 F. Supp. 951 (C.D. Cal. 1997). *See generally Arrington v. City of Dallas*, 970 F.2d 1441 (5th Cir. 1992)(relying on notion that Sixth Amendment right to counsel only applies to "critical phases" of a prosecution).

[271] *Long Beach Police Officers Association v. City of Long Beach*, 156 Cal. App.2d 996 (1984).

[272] *Miranda v. Arizona*, 384 U.S. 436 (1966).

[273] *People v. Probasco*, 795 P.2d 1330 (Colo. 1990); *see People v. Marchetta*, 676 N.Y.S.2d 791 (Crim. Ct. 1998). *See also State v. Connor*, 861 P.2d 1212 (Idaho 1993)(*Miranda* applies where interrogation of police officer is custodial).

CHAPTER 5

LAW ENFORCEMENT OFFICER BILLS OF RIGHTS

Introduction.

A perception that the rights of law enforcement officers are not always observed in the internal investigations process has led to the adoption of many statewide comprehensive procedural protections granted to law enforcement officers in the complaint investigation process, protections usually known by the name of law enforcement officer "bills of rights."[1] In at least 17 states, law enforcement officers have been granted these rights by statute.[2] Some statutory bills of rights are comprehensive, while in other states they are only partial.[3] In states that have not adopted statutory bills of rights, such provisions regularly appear in collective bargaining agreements between law enforcement employers and law enforcement labor organizations. In virtually all cases, the rights granted under a bill of rights are more expansive than those required under the constitution.[4]

Statutory Bills Of Rights.

Comprehensive statutory bills of rights exist in states such as California, Delaware, Florida, Illinois, Louisiana, Maryland, Minnesota, Nevada, New Mexico, Rhode Island, and Wisconsin. A good example of a statutory bill of rights is the statute in place in California, which can be found in the Government Code of California.[5] The California Bill of Rights is one of the nation's longest-standing and far more litigation occurs under it than under the bills of rights in all other states combined. For this reason, this chapter will use the California Bill of Rights to illustrate the principles normally covered by law enforcement officer bills of rights. The discussion that follows integrates not only California cases, but court decisions from around the country interpreting other states' statutory bills of rights.

The California Bill of Rights begins with a statutory declaration that the procedural protections of such a bill are necessary for the stable employer-employee relations critical for effective law enforcement:

> "The Legislature hereby finds and declares that the rights and protection provided to peace officers under this chapter constitute a matter of statewide concern. The Legislature further finds and declares that effective law enforcement depends upon the maintenance of stable employer-employee relations, between public safety employees and their employers. In order to assure that stable relations are continued throughout the state and to further assure that effective services are provided to all people of the state, it is necessary that this chapter be applicable to all public safety officers, as defined in this section, wherever situated within the State of California."[6]

Other statutory bills of rights have similar purpose statements. The Rhode Island Bill of Rights, for example, is designed "to protect the rights of policemen threatened with disciplinary action."[7]

The procedural protections of such a bill are necessary for the stable employer-employee relations critical for effective law enforcement.

The California Bill of Rights specifies that the law is applicable whenever a law enforcement officer is interrogated about a matter which "could" lead to punitive disciplinary action, and defines punitive disciplinary action as including dismissal, demotion, suspension, reduction in salary or pay grade, written reprimand, or transfer for purposes of punishment.[8] One court has even suggested that the Bill of Rights applies to involuntary disability retirements.[9] The Bill of Rights does not apply to non-disciplinary transfers that involve no reduction in pay.[10]

The Bill of Rights operates to bar disciplinary action taken in violation of its terms despite whether the disciplinary sanctions are accorded to the chief of police or probationary employees,[11] or when an officer is being discharged for medical reasons.[12] The Bill of Rights applies to probation officers,[13] but does not apply to coroners,[14] temporary employees or civilian police recruits, nor does it apply to firefighters who may have some ancillary law enforcement authority,[15] including fire marshals who may have criminal enforcement authority over fire code violations.[16] Also, if internal administrative processes result in the reversal of discipline, a claim for violation of the Bill of Rights is made moot.[17]

Procedural Rights Under A Bill Of Rights.

The California Bill of Rights contains a comprehensive set of procedural requirements which must be followed in the complaint investigation process involving a public safety officer.

Notice Of The Nature Of The Interview.

Under the California Bill of Rights, an employer must provide certain notifications to the employee about the nature of the investigation, and limit the number of individuals who may ask questions in the interview:

> "The public safety officer under investigation shall be informed prior to such interrogation of the rank, name and command of the officer in charge of the interrogation, the interrogating officers, and all other persons to be present during the interrogation. All questions directed to the public safety officer under interrogation shall be asked by and through no more than two interrogators at one time. The public safety officer under investigation shall be informed of the nature of the investigation prior to any interrogation."[18]

There are two broad exceptions to the "notice" and other guarantees found in the Bill of Rights concerning interrogations. First, the Bill of Rights does not apply to any interrogation occurring "in the normal course of duty, counseling, instruction, or informal verbal admonishment by, or other routine or unplanned contact with, a supervisor or any other public safety officer."[19] Courts have made it clear that the Bill of Rights is designed "to avoid claims that almost any communication is elevated to 'an investigation.'"[20] Second, the Bill of Rights does not apply "to an investigation concerned solely and directly with alleged criminal

The Bill of Rights does not apply to any interrogation occurring "in the normal course of duty, counseling, instruction, or informal verbal admonishment by, or other routine or unplanned contact with, a supervisor or any other public safety officer."

activities,"[21] though there is some controversy over whether this exception applies to all criminal investigation or just those criminal investigations performed by outside agencies.[22]

A frequent area of debate is what constitutes adequate notice of the "nature of the investigation." A Maryland court has probably answered that question best, holding that the Maryland Bill of Rights "does not necessarily require that all known detail or the exact charges be disclosed, but it must advise the officer as to the nature of the investigation, not just the existence of an investigation."[23] However, the notice must include at least some information about all of the charges contemplated against the officer.[24] In addition, the notice need not be "formal notice," and an informal notice that discipline would be imposed by a formal disciplinary letter meets the requirements of the Bill of Rights.[25]

Occasionally, questions have arisen as to whether a particular investigatory technique constitutes an "interrogation" for purposes of the Bill of Rights. The general rule appears to be that supervisory-subordinate exchanges are "interrogations" if the supervisor has any reason to believe that the employee committed misconduct.[26] However, polygraph examinations routinely given to drug enforcement officers are not an "interrogation" within the meaning of a bill of rights, even when the employer used the results of the polygraph examination to transfer employees out of the drug unit.[27] Moreover, the limit in the California Bill of Rights that only two investigators may ask questions is not violated if a third employer representative is in the room and does not ask questions, even if that third person adopts an "intimidating" attitude.[28]

A basic element of an interrogation is that, to be covered by a bill of rights, questioning must be conducted by an officer's own agency.[29] Thus, one court held that questions asked of an officer during a deposition taken as part of the officer's workers' compensation claim did not constitute an "interrogation," since the questions were being asked by the employer's workers' compensation attorney.[30] However, if the agency or individual conducting the questioning is acting "in concert" with the officer's employer, the bill of rights would apply to the questioning.[31]

Procedures For Disciplinary Interviews.

The California Bill of Rights regulates when an internal investigation interview may be conducted as well as the on-duty status of the officer during the interview:

> "The interrogation shall be conducted at a reasonable hour, preferably at a time when the public safety officer is on duty, or during the normal waking hours for the public safety officer, unless the seriousness of the investigation requires otherwise. If such interrogation does occur during off-duty time of the public safety officer being interrogated, the public safety officer shall be compensated for such

Polygraph examinations routinely given to drug enforcement officers are not an "interrogation" within the meaning of a bill of rights.

off-duty time in accordance with regular department procedures, and the public safety officer shall not be released from employment for any work missed."[32]

There are few cases interpreting what a "reasonable" time of day may be to conduct an interview. The prevailing line of thought is that the interview is conducted at a reasonable time if it is held during the officer's normal waking hours, even if the interview is on the officer's day off.[33]

Length Of Disciplinary Interviews.

The California Bill of Rights also regulates the length of the interrogation session, and mandates that an officer be provided with reasonable breaks during the session:

"The interrogating session shall be for a reasonable period taking into consideration the gravity and complexity of the issue being investigated. The person under interrogation shall be allowed to attend to his own personal physical necessities."[34]

How Interviews Are Conducted.

The California Bill of Rights ensures that interviews are conducted in a professional manner and that the personal privacy of the officer is protected:

"The public safety officer under interrogation shall not be subjected to offensive language or threatened with punitive action, except that an officer refusing to respond to questions or submit to interrogations shall be informed that failure to answer questions directly related to the investigation or interrogation may result in punitive action. No promise of reward shall be made as an inducement to answering any question. The employer shall not cause the public safety officer under interrogation to be subjected to visits by the press or news media without his express consent nor shall his home address or photograph be given to the press or news media without his express consent."[35]

Privacy In Lockers And Other Storage Spaces.

The California Bill of Rights requires that certain procedures be followed whenever an employer wants to search a "locker or other space for storage":

"[N]o public safety officer shall have his locker, or other space for storage that may be assigned to him, searched except in his presence, or with his consent, or unless a valid search warrant has been obtained or where he has been notified that a search will be conducted. This section shall apply only to lockers or other space for storage that are owned or leased by the employing agency."[36]

The Bill of Rights is not an absolute guarantee of privacy rights; rather, it requires an employer to either obtain a warrant for or consent to the search, or to search the locker or storage space in the officer's presence. A court has construed "other space for storage" to include desks, even if officers occasionally open the desk drawers of each other.[37]

Access To Materials Developed In Disciplinary Interrogations.

The California Bill of Rights grants law enforcement officers the right to access recordings and notes made of the interrogation:

> "The complete interrogation of a public safety officer may be recorded. If a tape recording is made of the interrogation, the public safety officer shall have access to the tape if any further proceedings are contemplated or prior to any further interrogation at a subsequent time. The public safety officer shall be entitled to a transcribed copy of any notes made by a stenographer or to any reports or complaints made by investigators or other persons, except those which are deemed by the investigating agency to be confidential. No notes or reports which are deemed to be confidential may be entered in the officer's personnel file. The public safety officer being interrogated shall have the right to bring his own recording device and record any and all aspects of the interrogation."[38]

There is presently an unresolved debate as to how much in the way of reports must be disclosed by the employer. One line of thought was described by a court in a case involving the San Diego Police Department. The Court found the Bill of Rights to implicitly contain a broad disclosure requirement:

> "[A prior decision of the California Supreme Court found that] some of the rights that the Act affords peace officers resemble those available in a criminal investigation, and concluded that because the Act appeared to borrow from the criminal law procedural rules, the criminal law approach to the timing of discovery (which gives no right to discovery until after the charges have been filed) was a persuasive reason for concluding that an accused officer was not entitled to discovery until after he or she was interrogated. A criminal defendant would be entitled to raw notes or tape-recorded statements of witnesses preserved by the police. Because the Act provides an officer with protections similar to those provided criminal defendants by criminal law procedural and discovery rules, an officer is entitled to protections similar to those enjoyed by criminal defendants, including the rights to raw notes and tape-recorded statements of witnesses preserved by City."[39]

A more limited view was taken by a court in a case involving the City of Sunnyvale, where the Court observed:

"It is unreasonable to suppose that the Legislature intended section 3303, subdivision (g), to afford an officer under investigation far-reaching disclosure rights, akin to the statutory discovery rights in criminal prosecutions, following an administrative interrogation of the officer when the Act does not expressly so provide but rather gives the investigating agency power to deem reports confidential, excludes such confidential items from the duty to disclose, and provides no mechanism for challenging such designation. The more reasonable interpretation, in light of the other features of section 3303 and other provisions of the Bill of Rights Act, is that the minimal rights of disclosure included in subdivision (g) were intended to prevent grossly abusive interrogation tactics and protect an officer's personnel file."[40]

The unresolved debate as to the scope of disclosure aside, some other rules are clear. Recordings and notes made of an interrogation must be disclosed in a reasonable period of time.[41] The right to review reports and other materials in an internal investigatory file arises only after the officer has been interrogated.[42] The right to review investigatory material does not extend to allow an officer the right to take the deposition of the police chief or other individual who imposed discipline.[43]

Changes From Disciplinary To Criminal Investigations.

The California Bill of Rights requires that if the focus of an investigation changes from administrative to criminal in nature, the officer under interrogation must be immediately apprised of the change:

"If, prior to or during the interrogation of a public safety officer, it is deemed that he may be charged with a criminal offense, he shall be immediately informed of his constitutional rights."[44]

This section of the Bill of Rights has been construed by the California Supreme Court to require a law enforcement agency to affirmatively warn an officer prior to an interrogation that the officer has the right to counsel during the interview, and that although the officer has the right to remain silent and not incriminate himself, his silence may be deemed insubordination that could result in discipline. The agency must also inform the officer that any statement made by the officer cannot be used against the officer in a subsequent criminal proceeding.[45]

Right To Representation In Interviews.

The California Bill of Rights also contains a grant of rights to representation similar to those described in the *Weingarten* case (discussed in Chapter 4), and limits the applicability of the Bill of Rights to more serious types of investigations:

"Upon the filing of a formal written statement of charges or whenever an interrogation focuses on matters which are likely to result in punitive action against any public safety officer, that officer, at his request, shall have the right to be represented by a representative of his choice who may be present at all times during such interrogation. The representative shall not be a person subject to the same investigation. The representative shall not be required to disclose, nor be subject to any punitive action for refusing to disclose, any information received from the officer under investigation for non-criminal matters.

"This section shall not apply to any interrogation of a public safety officer in the normal course of duty, counseling, instruction, or informal verbal admonishment by, or other routine or unplanned contact with, a supervisor or any other public safety officer, nor shall this section apply to an investigation concerned solely and directly with alleged criminal activities."[46]

The right to representation only exists where it is likely that punitive action could result against an officer. If the interaction between a supervisor and an officer is merely a routine discussion, no right to representation exists.[47]

The employee's right to select a representative is not absolute. If the employee's chosen representative is not reasonably available, the employee must either select another representative or participate in the interview without a representative.[48] In addition, an employer has some rights to place reasonable limits on the right to choose a particular representative. In one case, a court found reasonable an employer's rule forbidding officers involved in critical incidents from meeting with the same attorney at one time.[49] One state, Rhode Island, has held that the grant of the right to representation from an attorney by the Bill of Rights entirely replaces the right to representation in disciplinary interviews by a labor organization under the *Weingarten* rule.[50]

The right to representation only exists where it is likely that punitive action could result against an officer.

Time Limits On Investigations And Notice Of Proposed Disciplinary Action.

The California Bill of Rights has a strict statute of limitations requiring that "no punitive action" may be imposed upon any public safety officer for alleged misconduct unless the employer "completes its investigation and notifies the public safety officer of its proposed disciplinary action" within one year of discovering the alleged misconduct.[51] The discovery of the alleged misconduct must be "by a person authorized to initiate an investigation of the allegation of an act, omission, or other misconduct."[52] The overriding public policy purposes behind a statewide bill of rights are so strong that such a statute of limitations overrides a more lenient rule established by a local agency, even if the longer statute of limitations is in the employer's charter.[53]

The notice "of proposed disciplinary action" need not specify the precise penalty upon which the employer has initially decided. It is enough if the notice simply indicates that the employer has decided to impose discipline. One court has found that requiring more specific notice would run counter to officers' interests, reasoning that a requirement of specific notice "could have the practical effect of always leading the public agency to propose the maximum punishment in order to ensure it retained the full range of options in the subsequent disciplinary proceedings."[54]

Administrative Appeals Of Punitive Action.

The California Bill of Rights requires that a law enforcement agency provide officers the right to an administrative appeal of "punitive actions."[55] While the Bill of Rights leaves the specific detail of the administrative appeal to the local police agency,[56] the law is clear that a non-probationary officer may not be discharged without cause, after having received a full administrative hearing.[57] The minimum requirements of the administrative appeal include an independent re-examination of the decision conducted by someone not involved in the initial determination.[58] This independent examiner "cannot simply rely on the determination of the individual or agency that has initiated punitive action against a peace officer. Rather, the independent fact-finding implicit in the concept of an administrative appeal requires at a minimum that the hearing be treated as a *de novo* proceeding at which no facts are taken as established and the proponent of any given fact bears the burden of establishing it."[59] For this reason, the burden of proof lies with the employer during any such appeal.[60] The Bill of Rights gives no appeal rights to probationary employees.[61]

While the term "punitive actions" includes such standard forms of discipline as discharge, suspension, and demotion,[62] it also includes "any action that may lead to" such a standard form of discipline. A negative report by a citizen review board can well be a "punitive action" which triggers the appeal processes of the Bill of Rights.[63] Even a report of a review board that concludes that an officer acted within policy, but still criticizes the officer, is sufficiently punitive to trigger the right to appeal.[64]

Where a hearing requirement is part of a bill of rights, administrative hearings are mandatory prior to the imposition of discipline even though there may be criminal charges pending against the officer.[65] The bills of rights in some states provide that the appeals process of the bill of rights "shall supersede any State, county or municipal law, ordinance, or regulation."[66] In such states, the disciplinary appeal processes created by statutory bills of rights may pre-empt any other means of appealing discipline.[67]

Advance Notice Of Material Placed In Personnel File.

The California Bill of Rights contains extensive provisions regulating what may be placed in the personnel file of a law enforcement officer. Under the Bill of Rights, before any document containing an adverse comment may be placed in the personnel file of a law enforcement officer, the officer must first be given the opportunity to read and sign the document:

> "No public safety officer shall have any comment adverse to his interest entered in his personnel file, or any other file used for any personnel purposes by his employer, without the public safety officer having first read and signed the instrument containing the adverse comment indicating he is aware of such comment, except that such entry may be made if after reading such instrument the public safety officer refuses to sign; that fact shall be noted on that document, and signed or initialed by such officer."[68]

Response To Materials In Personnel Files.

The Bill of Rights gives the law enforcement officer the right to respond to any adverse comments placed in the officer's personnel file, a right which is so broadly construed that it applies even in cases where the officer wishes to respond to citizen complaints:[69]

> "A public safety officer shall have 30 days within which to file a written response to any adverse comment entered in his personnel file. Such written response shall be attached to, and shall accompany, the adverse comment."[70]

The courts give a broad reading to the term "personnel file." For example, a court found that an officer had a right to read and respond to notes made on index cards maintained by the Sacramento Police Department's internal affairs investigators.[71] The right to respond to materials placed in personnel files applies even after an officer's employment has been terminated or the officer has resigned.[72]

Interpreting a personnel file provision similar to that in the California Bill of Rights, Maryland's courts have taken a different approach, holding that unless negative materials are developed in conjunction with a disciplinary investigation, the materials are not protected by the personnel file provisions of a bill of rights. Applying this rationale, Maryland courts have held that reports of excessive use of sick leave[73] and even the writing of memoranda critical of an officer's performance which were placed in a file separate from the officer's personnel file are not covered by a bill of rights.[74]

Materials placed in a law enforcement officer's personnel file are not subject to disclosure except in unusual circumstances.

Confidentiality Of Personnel Files.

Through an interweaving of provisions found in different parts of California's statutes, materials placed in a law enforcement officer's personnel file are not subject to disclosure except in unusual circumstances.[75] Though a district attorney might have the right to access the materials in an officer's personnel file if the file is relevant to an investigation of the officer, once the district attorney gains possession of the materials he or she is subject to the same confidentiality requirements with respect to the file imposed on the officer's employer.[76] The prohibitions in the Bill of Rights against disclosure of personnel files are so strong that they prohibit disclosure of personnel files to the media,[77] even in public disciplinary appeals.[78]

Polygraph Examinations.

The California Bill of Rights grants law enforcement officers the unqualified right to refuse to take polygraph examinations given as a condition of employment:

> "No public safety officer shall be compelled to submit to a polygraph examination against his will. No disciplinary action or other recrimination shall be taken against a public safety officer refusing to submit to a polygraph examination, nor shall any comment be entered anywhere in the investigator's notes or anywhere else that the public safety officer refused to take a polygraph examination, nor shall any testimony or evidence be admissible at a subsequent hearing, trial, or proceeding, judicial or administrative, to the effect that the public safety officer refused to take a polygraph examination."[79]

If the polygraph examination is given for reasons other than as a condition of employment, it need not be prohibited. For example, a court of appeals in California has upheld the giving of polygraph examinations to all police officers seeking assignments in organized crime and other specialized units, reasoning that the polygraph examination was not, in the words of the Bill of Rights, "compelled."[80]

Remedies For Violations Of The Bill Of Rights.

An officer who believes that the statutory bill of rights has been violated ordinarily need not exhaust available administrative remedies prior to seeking relief in court; however, if the officer does start the administrative process, he must raise in those proceedings all relevant claims of violations of the bill of rights.[81] The remedies available in court include back pay and, in many cases, an award of attorney fees.[82] Interest is usually not recoverable on the back pay.[83] Officers seeking to recover damages under the California Bill of Rights must comply with a statute requiring claimants against governmental bodies to present their claims in writing prior to filing any lawsuit.[84]

Most statewide bills of rights also prohibit retaliation against an officer who asserts a claim under a bill of rights.[85] Some statewide bills of rights – for example, New Mexico's – do not provide a private cause of action in court for officers contending a breach of a bill of rights, leaving officers to administrative remedies.[86]

Most statewide bills of rights also prohibit retaliation against an officer who asserts a claim under a bill of rights.

NOTES

[1] *Abbott v. Administrative Hearing Board*, 366 A.2d 756 (Md. App. 1976).

[2] Bills of rights exist in the following states: **Arkansas**: Ark. Code Ann. §14-52-301; **California**: Cal. Gov't Code §3300; **Delaware**: Del. Code Ann., Title 11, §9200; **Florida**: Fla. Stat. Ann.§112.531; **Illinois**: Ill. Rev. Stat., Chapter 50, ¶725/1; **Kentucky**: Ky. Rev. Stat. Ann. §15.520; **Louisiana**: La. Rev. Stat. Ann. §40:2531; **Maryland**: Md. Ann. Code §3-101; **Minnesota**: Minn. Stat. Ann. §626.89; **Nevada**: Nev. Rev. Stat. §289; **New Mexico**: N.M. Stat. Ann. §29-14-1; **Rhode Island**: R.I. Gen. Laws §42-28.6-1; **Tennessee**: Tenn. Code Ann. §38-8-301; **Texas**: Tex. Rev. Civ. Stat. Ann. §143.123; **Virginia**: Va. Code Ann. §52-11; **West Virginia**: W.V. Code §8-14A-1; **Wisconsin**: Wis. Stat. §164.

[3] For example, Oregon, which has no bill of rights, has enacted a law which requires a public employer to have "cause" to discipline law enforcement officers. *See* Oregon Revised Statutes, Chapter 236.360. The Oregon statute is inapplicable to law enforcement officers covered by collective bargaining agreements, since those officers are presumably covered by the procedural and substantive disciplinary provisions in a contract.

[4] *Knox v. City of Elsmere*, 1995 WL 339096 (Del. Sup. 1995).

[5] The constitutionality of the California Bill of Rights was upheld in *Baggett v. Gates*, 649 P.2d 874 (Cal. 1982); *see City of Oroville v. Oroville Police Officers Ass'n*, 2008 WL 626047 (Cal. App. 2008). *See also Mesa v. Rodriguez*, 357 So.2d 711 (Fla. 1978)(upholds constitutionality of Florida's Bill of Rights); *Lynch v. King*, 391 A.2d 117 (R.I. 1978)(upholds constitutionality of Rhode Island Bill of Rights).

[6] Cal. Gov't Code §3301. In the words of a federal court, a law enforcement officer bill of rights is designed to protect officers from any impairment of their rights when their conduct is questioned. *Coalition of Black Leadership v. Cianci*, 570 F.2d 12 (1st Cir. 1978).

[7] *Hornoff v. City of Warwick Police Department*, 2004 WL 144115 (R.I. Super. 2004).

[8] *Los Angeles Police Protective League v. City of Los Angeles*, 124 Cal.Rptr.2d 911 (Cal. App. 2002)(reduction in pay grade); *Giuffre v. Sparks*, 91 Cal.Rptr.2d 171 (Cal. App. 1999)(disciplinary reassignment); *Gray v. City of Gustine*, 273 Cal.Rptr. 730 (Cal. App. 1990)(demotion of police chief subject to bill of rights); *see Loera v. Imperial County Sheriff's Department*, 2003 WL 22925257 (Cal. App. 2003).

[9] *Jordan v. Kirkman*, 2008 WL 4601297 (C.D. Cal. 2008).

[10] *Keeve v. City and County of San Francisco*, 2007 WL 81910 (N.D. Cal. 2007); *Benach v. County of Los Angeles*, 57 Cal.Rptr.3d 363 (Cal. App. 2007).

[11] *Hanna v. City of Los Angeles*, 260 Cal.Rptr. 782 (Cal. App. 1989); *Doyle v. City of Chino*, 172 Cal.Rptr. 844 (Cal. App. 1981). Some statutory bills of rights, such as that in Maryland, do not apply to probationary employees. *Mohan v. Norris*, 854 A.2d 259 (Md. App. 2004).

[12] *Bagby v. Civil Service Board of City of Oakland*, 271 Cal.Rptr. 343 (Cal. App. 1990).

[13] *Ponto v. County of Riverside*, 2007 WL 1509572 (Cal. App. 2007).

[14] *County of Riverside v. Steinberg*, 2003 WL 21061318 (Cal. App. 2003).

15 *Gauthier v. City of Red Bluff*, 41 Cal.Rptr.2d 35 (Cal. App. 1995); *Burden v. Snowden*, 828 P.2d 672 (Cal. 1992)(temporary employees); *Bell v. Duffy*, 168 Cal. Rptr. 753 (Cal. App. 1980)(recruits).

16 *White v. City of Vallejo*, 2004 WL 68796 (Cal. App. 2004).

17 *Nowotny v. Johnson*, 226 Fed. Appx. 705 (9th Cir. 2007).

18 Cal. Gov't Code §3303(b).

19 *Steinert v. City of Covina*, 53 Cal.Rptr.3d 1 (Cal. App. 2006).

20 *City of Los Angeles v. Superior Court*, 67 Cal.Rptr.2d 775 (Cal. App. 1997); *see Correa v. County of Riverside*, 2005 WL 3307396 (Cal. App. 2005).

21 Cal. Gov't Code §3303(i); *see Van Winkle v. County of Ventura*, 69 Cal.Rptr. 3d 809 (Cal. App. 2007).

22 In *Van Winkle v. County of Ventura*, 69 Cal.Rptr.3d 809 (Cal. App. 2007), the Court found that the exception applied to all purely criminal investigations. Another court within the California Court of Appeals has concluded that the exception applies only to criminal investigations conducted by outside agencies. *California Correctional Peace Officers Association v. State of California*, 98 Cal.Rptr.2d 302 (Cal. App. 2000).

23 *Ocean City Police Dept. v. Marshall*, 854 A.2d 299 (Md. App. 2004); *see Hinrichs v. County of Orange*, 125 Cal.App.4th 921 (2004).

24 *Pierce v. Kiesewetter*, 2007 WL 4427445 (Cal. App. 2007).

25 *Sulier v. State Personnel Bd.*, 22 Cal.Rptr.3d 615 (Cal. App. 2004).

26 *Wideen v. City of Fontana*, 2003 WL 22810464 (Cal. App. 2003); *City of Los Angeles v. Superior Court (Labio)*, 67 Cal.Rptr.2d 775 (Cal. App. 1997).

27 *Calhoun v. Commissioner, Baltimore City Police Dept.*, 654 A.2d 905 (Md. App. 1995).

28 *Correa v. City of Inglewood*, 2008 WL 4816653 (Cal. App. 2008).

29 *People v. Velez*, 192 Cal.Rptr. 686 (Cal. App. 1983).

30 *Shafer v. Los Angeles County Sheriff's Department*, 131 Cal.Rptr.2d 670 (Cal. App. 2003).

31 *California Correctional Peace Officers Assn. v. State of California*, 98 Cal. Rptr.2d 302 (Cal. App. 2000).

32 Cal. Gov't Code §3303(a).

33 *Eriksen v. Baca*, 2005 WL 3359755 (Cal. App. 2005).

34 Cal. Gov't Code §3303(d).

35 Cal. Gov't Code §3303(e).

36 Cal. Gov't Code §3309.

37 *Mullican v. City of Ontario*, 2004 WL 858721 (Cal. App. 2004).

38 Cal. Gov't Code §3303(f). A court has held that these provisions do not prohibit the use by a use-of-force review board of a report made by an officer about the shooting, reasoning that the confidentiality requirement applies only in connection with an interrogation of an officer. *Crupi v. City of Los Angeles*, 268 Cal.Rptr. 875 (Cal. App. 1990).

39 *San Diego Police Officers Assn. v. City of San Diego,* 120 Cal.Rptr.2d 609 (2002).

40 *Gilbert v. City of Sunnyvale*, 31 Cal.Rptr.3d 297 (Cal. App. 2005).

[41] *Pierce v. Kiesewetter*, 2007 WL 4427445 (Cal. App. 2007).

[42] *Pierce v. Kiesewetter*, 2007 WL 4427445 (Cal. App. 2007); *Pasadena Police Officers Association v. City of Pasadena*, 273 Cal.Rptr. 584 (Cal. 1990)(rejects argument that Bill of Rights requires pre-interrogation disclosure of notes, reports, or complaints).

[43] *Montgomery Co. v. Stevens*, 654 A.2d 877 (Md. App. 1995).

[44] Cal. Gov't Code §3303(g).

[45] *Lybarger v. City of Los Angeles*, 710 P.2d 329 (Cal. 1985). The failure to give such warnings can result in a variety of remedies, and in appropriate cases could possibly result in the disciplinary action taken against the officer being reversed or the statement given by the officer being suppressed. *Williams v. City of Los Angeles*, 252 Cal.Rptr. 817 (Cal. 1988).

[46] Cal. Gov't Code §3303(g). Under statutory bills of rights, the employee's representative may be entitled to object to inappropriate questions as well as observe the questioning of the employee. *See Nichols v. Baltimore Police Department*, 455 A.2d 446 (Md. App. 1983).

[47] *Steinert v. City of Covina*, 53 Cal.Rptr.3d 1 (Cal. App. 2006).

[48] *Upland Police Officers Association v. City of Upland*, 4 Cal.Rptr.3d 629 (Cal. App. 2003).

[49] *Association for Los Angeles Deputy Sheriffs v. County of Los Angeles*, 83 Cal.Rptr.3d 494 (Cal. App. 2008).

[50] *Town of North Kingstown v. Local 473, IBPO*, 819 A.2d 1274 (R.I. 2003).

[51] Cal. Gov't Code §3304(d).

[52] *Benefield v. California Dept. of Corrections and Rehabilitation*, 2009 WL 154573 (Cal. App. 2009).

[53] *Jackson v. City of Los Angeles*, 4 Cal.Rptr.3d 325 (Cal. 2003).

[54] *Mays v. City of Los Angeles*, 2008 WL 1745210 (Cal. 2008).

[55] Cal. Gov't Code §3304.

[56] *Howell v. County of San Bernardino*, 196 Cal.Rptr. 746 (A.D. 1983).

[57] *Zeron v. City of Los Angeles*, 79 Cal.Rptr.2d 130 (Cal. App. 1998); *Currieri v. City of Roseville*, 84 Cal.Rptr. 615 (A.D. 1970).

[58] *Chow v. San Diego County Civil Service Com'n*, 2004 WL 2244127 (Cal. App. 2004).

[59] *City of Oroville v. Oroville Police Officers Ass'n*, 2008 WL 626047 (Cal. App. 2008).

[60] *Caloca v. County of San Diego*, 126 Cal.Rptr.2d 3 (Cal. App. 2002).

[61] *Madrigal v. County of Riverside*, 2005 WL 2669400 (Cal. App. 2005); *Corcoran v. City of Huntington Beach*, 2001 WL 1193914 (Cal. App. 2001); *see Mohan v. Norris*, 871 A.2d 575 (Md. 2005).

[62] *See Gordon v. Horsley*, 102 Cal.Rptr.2d 910 (Cal. App. 2001).

[63] *Caloca v. County of San Diego*, 85 Cal.Rptr.2d 660 (Cal. App. 1999); *Hopson v. City of Los Angeles*, 188 Cal.Rptr. 689 (A.D. 1983). However, in other cases, courts have held that neither the placement of negative comments in a performance evaluation, *Turturici v. City of Redwood City*, 236 Cal.Rptr. 53 (Cal. App. 1987), nor the placement of negative comments in a "separation report" following an officer's resignation, *Haight v. City of San Diego*, 278 Cal.Rptr. 334 (Cal. App. 1991), nor

the denial of a merit increase due to poor work performance, *Howitt v. County of Imperial*, 258 Cal.Rptr. 384 (Cal. App. 1989), constituted punitive action. Under Rhode Island's Bill of Rights, a court found that a transfer from a detective position because of an officer's divulging confidential departmental information was not punitive in nature so as to invoke the Bill of Rights but was intended "to serve the Department's best interests." *Morgan v. City of Warwick*, 510 A.2d 1297 (R.I. 1986); *see Calhoun v. Commissioner, Baltimore City Police Department*, 654 A.2d 905 (Md. App. 1995)(same result under Maryland Bill of Rights).

[64] *Keating v. San Diego Civil Service Commission*, 2002 WL 472649 (Cal. App. 2002).

[65] *Artrip v. City of Hopkinsville*, 2008 WL 77715 (W.D. Ky. 2008).

[66] Md. Ann. Code, Art. 27 §728.

[67] *City of Pawtucket v. Ricci*, 692 A.2d 678 (R.I. 1997); *City of East Providence v. McLaughlin,* 593 A.2d 1345 (R.I. 1991).

[68] Cal. Gov't Code §3305.

[69] *Aguilar v. Johnson*, 247 Cal.Rptr. 909 (Cal. App. 1988).

[70] Cal. Gov't Code §3306.

[71] *Sacramento Police Officers Association v. Venegas*, 124 Cal.Rptr.2d 666 (Cal. App. 2002).

[72] *Haight v. City of San Diego,* 278 Cal.Rptr. 334 (Cal. App. 1991).

[73] *Leibe v. Police Department of the City of Annapolis*, 469 A.2d 1287 (Md. App. 1984).

[74] *Anastasi v. Montgomery County*, 719 A.2d 980 (Md. App. 1998).

[75] *See* California Penal Code, § 832.7; Cal. Gov't Code §6254(f).

[76] *Fagan v. Superior Court*, 4 Cal.Rptr.3d 239 (Cal. App. 2003).

[77] *City of Hemet v. Superior Court*, 44 Cal.Rptr.2d 532 (Cal. App. 1995); *City of Richmond v. Superior Court*, 38 Cal.Rptr.2d 632 (Cal. App. 1995).

[78] *San Diego Police Officers Association v. City of San Diego Civil Service Commission*, 128 Cal.Rptr.2d 248 (Cal. App. 2002).

[79] Cal. Gov't Code §3307.

[80] *Los Angeles Police Protective League v. City of Los Angeles*, 42 Cal.Rptr.2d 23 (Cal. App. 1995).

[81] *Moore v. City of Los Angeles*, 67 Cal.Rptr.3d 218 (Cal. App. 2007); *see Mounger v. Gates*, 193 Cal.App.2d 1248 (1987).

[82] *Baggett v. Gates*, 185 Cal.Rptr. 232 (Sup. 1982); *Otto v. Los Angeles Unified School District*, 130 Cal.Rptr.2d 512 (Cal. App. 2003)(attorney fees); *Henneberque v. City of Culver City,* 172 Cal.App.3d 837 (1985). *See also Sylvester v. City of Delray Beach*, 584 So.2d 214 (Fla. App. 1991)(court only has authority to award injunction for violation of anti-retaliation provisions of bill of rights; no authority to award money damages).

[83] *Hornoff v. City of Warwick Police Department*, 2004 WL 603487 (R.I. Super. 2004).

[84] *Lozada v. City and County of San Francisco*, 52 Cal.Rptr.3d 209 (Cal. App. 2006).

[85] In *Holcomb v. City of Los Angeles*, 259 Cal.Rptr. 1 (Cal. App. 1989), the Court held that the fact that a disciplinary hearing panel increased the Chief's

recommended discipline from five to fifteen days off did not constitute illegal retaliation for the officer's exercise of his right to appeal.

86 *Sedillo v. N.M. Dept. of Public Safety*, 149 P.3d 955 (N.M. App. 2006).

CHAPTER 6

THE RIGHT TO PRIVACY AND THE REGULATION OF OFF-DUTY CONDUCT

The Sources Of The Right To Privacy.

The United States Constitution contains no explicit right to privacy. In a series of cases primarily involving reproductive and abortion rights, the Supreme Court has inferred a right to privacy into the provisions of a combination of the First, Third, Fourth, Fifth, and Ninth Amendments. As it has been interpreted, the constitutional right to privacy provides protections in two areas:

- The individual's interest in avoiding disclosure of personal matters, and

- The individual's interest in being "let alone" – an interest in making certain decisions concerning personal matters such as marriage, procreation, contraception, family relationships, child rearing, and other off-duty activities free from any interference from government.[1]

Since law enforcement agencies have historically sought some degree of control over their employees in each of these areas, it is not surprising that a good deal of litigation has ensued over the years concerning a law enforcement officer's right to privacy. Initially, many of the privacy lawsuits filed by law enforcement officers met with success. However, few areas concerning the rights of law enforcement officers have seen as significant a change in recent years as the right to privacy. The growing conservatism of the federal courts has brought with it an unquestionable erosion in the job-related privacy rights of law enforcement officers, in areas ranging from drug testing to grooming codes.

Law enforcement officers have responded in three ways to the change in federal constitutional law concerning the right to privacy. Law enforcement officers have proposed, and occasionally obtained, legislative changes at the state level aimed at enhancing privacy rights, and have begun to aim privacy-related lawsuits at state rather than federal constitutional principles. At the same time, their labor organizations have increasingly focused on privacy issues in the collective bargaining process. As these developments have occurred, a variety of federal and state statutes have also been enacted giving employees privacy rights, particularly with respect to medical information.

The Right Not To Disclose Personal Matters.

In order for a law enforcement employer to require its officers to disclose personal matters, the employer must show that its interest in the disclosure outweighs the officer's privacy interest.[2] Put another way, an employer may not use its governmental authority to inquire into matters in which it does not have a legitimate interest.[3] The greater the degree of intrusion on an officer's privacy, the more significant the employer's need to know the information must be to override the officer's interests.[4] Conversely, where the officer's privacy interest is minimal, the officer may be forced to disclose the information in the face of a less strong governmental interest.

This balance has usually been phrased in terms of the legitimacy of the employer's need to know certain information about an employee. For example, if the information is relevant to an officer's on-the-job performance, it is more likely that the officer will be required to disclose the information. If there is no such relationship to on-the-job performance, disclosure of the information is not likely to be mandatory. As stated by one court in overturning the firing of a police officer for refusing to answer questions about an off-duty affair:

> "In the absence of a showing that a policeman's private, off-duty personal activities have an impact upon his on-the-job performance, we believe that inquiry into those activities violates the constitutionally protected right of privacy. The Police Department simply cannot have a carte blanche to investigate all aspects of a police officer's personal life."

Along these lines, even where an employer can make a legitimate inquiry into the private life of an employee, the inquiry must be made as narrowly as possible. Broad, sweeping requests for information are not likely to be valid. Thus, where an order to disclose all of an officer's personal medical records would likely be struck down, a request for particular medical information with a direct relationship to job performance might be acceptable.[5]

Applicants for law enforcement jobs have a difficult time bringing privacy claims challenging background investigations because virtually all law enforcement employers require applicants to sign waivers of privacy claims as a condition of considering their applications. Such waivers have been upheld as valid.[6]

Disclosure Of Financial Matters.

The compelled disclosure of financial information has been the subject of much litigation under the "disclosure of personal information" prong of the right to privacy. Usually, such cases arise when a news organization has made a request for salary information from a governmental employer, often for the names of and compensation paid to the top earners among employees. Courts routinely find that the disclosure of salary information does not violate the privacy rights of officers.[7] As one court held, this principle of disclosure extends even to retirees:

> "Given the fact that the retirees' identities alone are not expressly exempted from disclosure, there is only a negligible increase in the possibility that defendants' speculative litany of various calamities would actually befall a retired police officer merely because the officer's corresponding pension income is also known."[8]

Even more sweepingly, some public sector jurisdictions require their employees, including law enforcement officers, to regularly disclose a list of their assets, liabilities, and income. The basis for the compelled disclosure of financial information is the notion that the disclosure of financial information will deter corruption and dishonesty among public employees.

If the information is relevant to an officer's on-the-job performance, it is more likely that the officer will be required to disclose the information.

The leading case in the area is *Barry v. City of New York*, which upheld the City of New York's financial disclosure law. The financial disclosure law, which is applicable to employees with salaries greater than $25,000 per year, requires employees to divulge the following information:

- The source of all income over $1,000 per year received by the employee or the employee's spouse;

- All creditors to whom the employee or the employee's spouse owed more than $5,000; and

- The identity of all property owned by the employee valued at more than $20,000.

In upholding the financial disclosure ordinance, the Court recognized the interests of employees in keeping such financial information private, but held that the City's interest in a corruption-free work place overrode the employees' privacy concerns:

> "We think the statute as a whole plainly furthers a substantial, possibly even a compelling state interest. The purpose of the statute is to deter corruption and conflicts of interest among City officers and employees, and to enhance public confidence in the integrity of its government. * * * Whatever one may think of the intrusiveness of financial disclosure laws, they are widespread * * * and reflect the not unreasonable judgment of many legislatures that disclosure will help reveal and deter corruption and conflicts of interest."[9]

The Court stressed that it placed great importance on a portion of the ordinance which created a procedure for employees to make claims of privacy as to certain financial records and to have those claims heard by a neutral body.[10]

Where there is evidence of past corruption in the law enforcement agency, financial disclosure laws are even more likely to be upheld. For example, in *O'Brien v. DiGrazia*, certain officers of the Boston, Massachusetts Police Department who were suspected of corruption were required to complete a financial questionnaire listing all sources of income for themselves and their spouses, all significant assets held by them and any members of their households, to provide the previous five years' tax returns, and to make estimates of their expenses. The Court relied heavily on the existence of a mechanism to ensure that the financial records were to be held in confidence by the employer:

> "[The officers] do not claim that their financial affairs will be broadcast to the public, or even to other governmental agencies. * * * Assuming for argument's sake that this sort of privacy deserves a special constitutional solicitude, the interests on the Commissioner's side outbalances a patrolman's right to withhold financial information."[11]

Quite apart from the constitutional right to privacy, some states have enacted statutes which limit the circumstances under which a law enforcement officer may be required to disclose financial information. For example, California's Peace Officers Bill of Rights puts direct limits on the disclosure of financial information:

> "A law enforcement officer may not be required or requested to disclose any item of his property, income, assets, source of income, debts, or personal or domestic expenditures (including those of any member of his family or household) unless that information is necessary in investigating a possible conflict of interest with respect to the performance of his official duties, or unless such disclosure is required by State or federal law."[12]

Other protections in the area exist in collective bargaining states. Since financial disclosure requirements are mandatory subjects of bargaining, any changes in past practice in the area must be negotiated with the labor organization before they are implemented.[13]

Disclosure Of And Access To Medical Information.

When a law enforcement agency is seeking to have an employee disclose medical information, it must comply with not only constitutional privacy guarantees, but also specific statutes protecting privacy rights. Officers have had little success arguing that medical disclosure requirements violate the federal constitution. As long as an employer can show a reasonably direct relationship between the information and the employee's physical or emotional ability to perform the job, and if the examination bears on the officer's fitness for duty or ability to perform the job, the agency will have the authority to either obtain the officer's medical information[14] or to compel the officer to submit to a medical examination[15] or substance abuse evaluation.[16] Only absent such a relationship, would an employer's attempt to obtain medical information about an officer violate the officer's constitutional right to privacy. Similarly, an employer's decision to disclose medical information about an officer to the media – including the results of drug tests – would violate the right to privacy unless justified by business necessity (i.e., a law compelling the disclosure).[17]

For example, in one case where an officer threatened co-workers with physical harm, a court had no difficulty finding that the requested psychological examination was permissible.[18] In another case, a police officer who was acting irrationally was compelled by her employer to submit to an examination by a psychologist. The employee later sued the Department for violation of her right to privacy, claiming that she was compelled by the employer's order to disclose personal medical information to the psychologist. The Court rejected the officer's privacy claims by noting that the examination was carefully and narrowly conducted:

> "Furthermore, there is no evidence that the Department or the psychologists that it hired delved into any personal matters regarding the plaintiff which were unrelated to their legitimate interest in determining the plaintiff's psychological fitness for her position. The Court wishes to emphasize that this is not a case where the Police

When a law enforcement agency is seeking to have an employee disclose medical information, it must comply with not only constitutional privacy guarantees, but also specific statutes protecting privacy rights.

Department attempted to question or discharge the plaintiff because of her private, off-duty activities."[19]

A far reaching "compelled disclosure" case involving the disclosure of medical information arose out of a questionnaire the Philadelphia Police Department required all officers who were interested in a special investigations unit to complete.[20] Officers were required to provide the following information on the questionnaire:

- Any details on physical defects or disabilities from which the officer suffered.

- A list of prescription drugs used by the officer.

- A detailed history of any treatment the officer received for mental illness or a psychiatric condition.

- A list of each loan or debt over $1,000, and a listing of all income together with the sources of the income.

- A list of all property owned by the officer.

- A recitation of the criminal histories of all family members.

- A disclosure of the officer's personal habits with respect to gambling and the use of alcoholic beverages.

The Court held that with respect to each of these areas, the officers' right to privacy was outweighed by the governmental interest in a corruption-free and capable special investigations unit. In so ruling, the Court specifically noted that the unit had been created in response to a "wave of graft and other corruption" in which 31 police officers, including the Department's second in command, had been convicted on federal corruption charges. The Court also specifically required the employer to enact safeguards to prevent the unauthorized release of the information contained in the questionnaire.[21]

A similar result was reached in a case involving compulsory medical examinations required of all police officers working for New Jersey Transit. In upholding the requirement in the face of a constitutional challenge, a court ruled:

> "The Fourth Amendment does not require individualized reasonable suspicion for conducting the medical examination program. A federal court has held that conducting such tests pursuant to a uniform, non-discretionary policy satisfies the Fourth Amendment's purpose of safe-guarding the privacy and security of individuals against arbitrary invasions by governmental officials. Here, the privacy interest of the police officer is not as significant as the government's interest present in the random drug or alcohol testing. In the latter instance, the officer faces disciplinary, perhaps criminal sanctions. Here, the consequence is a determination of fitness to perform the functions of the position. Although we are mindful that an adverse determination

may result in termination, no officer has the right to hide his or her lack of fitness by asserting a privacy interest as a barrier to a physical examination. More importantly, no officer who is unfit for the position has the right to remain in the position."[22]

More protections against the disclosure of medical information can be found in statutes providing privacy protections. Foremost amongst these statutes is the Americans With Disabilities Act (ADA), which prohibits an employer from compelling an employee to produce medical or psychological information or forcing participation in a fitness-for-duty evaluation unless the employer has reasons that are "job related and consistent with business necessity."[23] Even where the employer legitimately obtains medical or psychological information under the ADA, the information must be limited to whether the employee can perform the essential functions of the job, and the employer must maintain that information confidentially in a limited-access file.[24] Employer inquiries under the ADA about an employee's medical condition must be quite specific. For example, a broad-based request that employees disclose to their employer all prescription drugs they are taking violates the ADA.[25]

Several cases have recently applied the ADA to hold illegal employer requirements that employees produce doctor's notes justifying the routine use of sick leave. A court's opinion in a case involving the Pennsylvania State Police does a good job of describing why courts find broad "doctor's notes" requirements violate the ADA:

> "[Prior cases] set forth the parameters of the business necessity defense when applied to employers such as a department of corrections and the Pennsylvania State Police, which serve law enforcement and public safety functions and whose employees must be prepared to respond definitively to unexpected emergencies. First, the employer must demonstrate that the medical inquiry at issue is vital to the employers' business and is narrowly formulated to prevent unnecessary intrusion into employees' medical information. The ADA forbids overbroad inquiries or those supported by mere convenience. Second, the employer must show that the medical inquiry serves the asserted business necessity when the employer chooses to make the inquiry. An employer may implement a broad inquiry after several weeks' leave if the length of absence gives the employer a reasonable basis to question the employee's ability to perform his or her job duties. A broad inquiry, however, is inappropriate at the outset of illness when the employer has little reason to doubt the employee's fitness. Finally, the employer must demonstrate that it has applied the inquiry to a class of employees whose job duties could be impaired by the illnesses it requires employees to report."[26]

The ADA's medical privacy provisions are bolstered by a smorgasbord of other federal laws. The Family and Medical Leave Act (FMLA), for example, limits the inquiries an employer can make in the "certification" process as to the reasons the employee is using family and medical leave.[27] The Health Insurance Portability and Accountability Act (HIPAA) has privacy provisions with particular implications for public safety employers who are self-insured. Additionally, collective bargaining agreements and/or state peace officer bills of rights can create privacy rights in the area of medical information beyond the rights protected by the federal constitution.

Officers sometimes contend that when they are required by their employer to participate in a fitness-for-duty evaluation, a doctor-patient relationship is formed between the officer and the examining physician or psychologist. The law is to the contrary. Courts routinely hold that "a physician who is retained by a third party to conduct an examination of another person and report the results to the third party does not enter in a physician-patient relationship with the examinee and is not liable to the examinee for any losses he suffers as a result of the conclusions the physician reaches or reports."[28]

The Disclosure Of Disciplinary Matters.

In virtually all states, the private or public nature of disciplinary records is governed by public record acts or freedom of information laws. To the extent that these laws forbid disclosure of certain disciplinary records, an officer's privacy rights will be violated if the records are disclosed.[29] On the other hand, if the laws make it clear that disciplinary records are open to public disclosure, an officer has no privacy interest in preventing disclosure.[30]

These principles were outlined by a court rejecting an officer's challenge to the release of the transcript of his disciplinary hearing:

> "To recover for an invasion of the right to privacy, there must be as a preliminary requirement 'an objectively reasonable expectation of privacy and improper government disclosure.' * * * It is well settled that the constitutional right to privacy is not implicated by the dissemination of information already in the public domain. The information, which plaintiff complains was improperly disseminated, was already in the public domain. Quasi-judicial administrative proceedings, such as Board of Rights hearings, are presumptively open to the public, and the final decision of a Board of Rights is considered a 'public record.'"[31]

Most public records laws today provide little protection from the disclosure of disciplinary records and internal affairs files.

Most public records laws today provide little protection from the disclosure of disciplinary records and internal affairs files. On several occasions, officers have claimed that such records are exempt from disclosure under a "law enforcement exception" found in most public records laws. Courts have regularly rejected such claims and ordered the disclosure of the records, reasoning that the law enforcement exception to public records laws applies only to criminal investigatory files.[32]

Courts have also found that privacy exceptions in public records acts do not protect against the disclosure of disciplinary or other personnel files, even where the employer has made specific promises of confidentiality to the officer.[33]

Internal affairs, disciplinary, and other personnel files may also be subject to disclosure in civil litigation instituted against the officer or the officer's employer,[34] in criminal cases where the defendant is claiming that he or she acted in self-defense, or in grand jury proceedings.[35] An officer's testimony in a grand jury proceeding can be disclosed by a prosecutor without violating the officer's right to privacy.[36]

Courts have also upheld the disclosure to the public of the name of an officer involved in a deadly force incident, even where the disclosure resulted in associates of the suspect later calling the officer's house and threatening his family.[37] In addition, provisions of a collective bargaining agreement which attempt to make confidential disciplinary documents which must be disclosed under a public records law are not enforceable and do not justify the failure to disclose the documents.[38]

The Right To Keep Confidential Personal Information Such As Addresses And Telephone Numbers.

Most police officers strenuously guard their privacy off the job, and resist any attempts to compel their employer to disclose their photographs, addresses, telephone numbers, or other personal information. Courts have been receptive to arguments that home addresses and telephone numbers of officers are protected by the right to privacy.

In one case, two local unions representing employees in federal agencies petitioned the agencies to provide them with the names and home addresses of the agency employees in the bargaining units represented by the unions. The Supreme Court upheld the agency's refusal to disclose the home addresses. The Court found that the exemption under the Freedom of Information Act which allows the non-disclosure of information which would constitute an unwarranted invasion of privacy applied to home addresses, commenting that "many people simply do not want to be disturbed at home by work-related matters."[39]

State courts interpreting state freedom of information laws have also held protected from disclosure information such as addresses and telephone numbers of law enforcement officers.[40] However, photographs are viewed on a different plane, with courts finding that non-undercover law enforcement officers have no expectation of privacy in their images since their faces are exposed to the public every day they work.[41]

Undercover officers have heightened privacy interests in personal information. In one case, a Columbus, Ohio lawyer defending members of the "North Posse" gang on drug charges obtained the personnel file of an undercover police officer from the City of Columbus by filing a public records act request with the City. The lawyer promptly forwarded the file, which contained the officer's home address, phone number, social security number, and other identifying information, to the gang members. The officer then sued, claiming the City's actions violated

Courts have been receptive to arguments that home addresses and telephone numbers of officers are protected by the right to privacy.

her right to privacy. Basing its decision more on the Fourteenth Amendment's freedom of liberty than upon traditional privacy analysis, a federal court of appeals ruled that though the public's right to know information about public employees was a significant one, the City's blanket release of the information to any member of the public violated the officer's right to privacy:

> "While there may be situations in which the release of this type of personal information might further the public's understanding of the workings of its law enforcement agencies, the facts as presented here do not support such a conclusion. The City released the information at issue to defense counsel in a large drug conspiracy case, who is asserted to have passed the information on to his clients. We simply fail to see how placing this personal information into the hands of the defendants in any way increases public understanding of the City's law enforcement agency where the defendants and their attorney make no claim that they sought this personal information about the officers in order to shed light on the internal workings of the Columbus Police Department. We therefore cannot conclude that the disclosure narrowly serves the state's interest in ensuring accountable governance. Accordingly, we hold that the City's actions in automatically disclosing this information to any member of the public requesting it are not narrowly tailored to serve this important public interest."[42]

Attempts to expand upon the Columbus case have been largely unsuccessful. Most notably, the same court that decided the Columbus case ruled against a group of corrections officers who claimed their privacy rights had been violated when their Social Security numbers were accidentally released to inmates. The Court clearly focused on the fact that the information that might be provided by Social Security numbers was readily available elsewhere:

> "First, scary though it may be, the diligent miscreant who wishes to exact vengeance can locate a person with limited information. The officers' names, general whereabouts, and approximate ages were already known to these prisoners. While the social security numbers and birth dates might have pinpointed the residence of a particular plaintiff, there are other methods of learning where persons reside; several hours in a car or several telephone calls might well provide the very same information. Voter registration records, county property records, and a plethora of other publically available sources exist through which persons can discover the residency of an individual and prisoners' accomplices have as ready access to them as any other citizen. The officers do not allege that this information allowed the prisoners to discover information that they would have been unable to otherwise."[43]

Of course, if an officer takes steps to publish information such as his home address, his reasonable expectation of privacy in the information will be destroyed. One case involved a San Francisco police officer who was disciplined after making a videotape parodying the work of police officers working in the City. The officer sued his employer, claiming, among other things, that the employer had failed to take adequate steps to safeguard his home address. A federal court dismissed the lawsuit, finding that the officer himself had published his home address on a web page on which he posted the videotape.[44]

Also, if personal information is properly disclosed by an employer but the subsequent distribution of the information by others involves inappropriate disclosure, there may be no liability for breach of the right to privacy. For example, one case began when an inmate threw an unidentified liquid substance from his cell, hitting the bodies and faces of three corrections officers. Following the incident, the three officers completed workers' compensation forms. The information provided on the forms included the officers' home addresses and telephone numbers, marital status, birthdates and social security numbers. A prosecutor subsequently filed charges against the inmate, and in the course of the criminal proceedings, forwarded the unredacted workers' compensation forms to the inmate's public defender, who in turn gave the forms to his client, who in turn disseminated the personal information in the forms to other inmates. In dismissing the officers' privacy claims, the Court ruled:

> "The parties who received copies of the unredacted forms were all entitled to the information. Only the inmates who received the private information from the public defender were not entitled to the information. The Department of Corrections was entitled to collect identifying information because workers' compensation claims were being filed. In turn, the Sheriff's Office and the Prosecutor were entitled to have the identifying information for investigatory and prosecutorial purposes. Likewise, the Public Defender and the defendant were entitled to the unredacted forms in order to authenticate them and defend against any restitution claim. Therefore, none of the Department of Corrections defendants publicly disclosed private information and the corrections officer's claims for invasion of privacy must fail since they cannot establish a *prima facie* element of that tort."[45]

Drug Testing And Law Enforcement Officers.

Three general principles have emerged from the dozens of drug-testing cases decided by the courts over the last five years. First, the drug testing of law enforcement officers, either on a random or a reasonable suspicion basis, does not violate the federal constitution. Second, random drug testing which might be constitutional under the federal constitution will not necessarily withstand challenge under state constitutional provisions. Third, without regard to whether random drug testing is constitutional, it is a subject that must be collectively bargained before it is implemented if the employer is subject to collective bargaining laws.

The drug testing of law enforcement officers, either on a random or a reasonable suspicion basis, does not violate the federal constitution.

The leading United States Supreme Court case, *National Treasury Employees Union v. Von Raab*, involved a challenge to the drug testing program of the United States Customs Service.[46] Under the program, employees who sought promotions or transfers to positions having a direct involvement in the Service's drug interdiction program or to positions which required the employee to carry firearms or to handle "classified" material were required to submit to drug testing. The Customs Service plan did not have an element of random testing. The Court approved of the drug-testing program, reasoning as follows:

> "Detecting drug impairment on the part of employees can be a difficult task, especially where, as here, it is not feasible to subject employees and their work-product to the kind of day-to-day scrutiny that is the norm in more traditional office environments. Indeed, the almost unique mission of the Service gives the Government a compelling interest in ensuring that many of these covered employees do not use drugs even off duty, for such use creates risks of bribery and blackmail against which the Government is entitled to guard. In light of the extraordinary safety and national security hazards that would attend the promotion of drug users to positions that require the carrying of firearms or the interdiction of controlled substances, the Service's policy of deterring drug users from seeking such promotions cannot be deemed unreasonable."

Every lower court decision under the federal Constitution since National Treasury Employees Union has held that purely random testing of law enforcement employees is constitutional.

Every lower court decision under the federal Constitution since *National Treasury Employees Union* has held that purely random testing of law enforcement employees is constitutional.[47] These courts have reasoned that if customs officers in the National Treasury Employees Union could be subject to drug testing simply because they carried a firearm, there is nothing unconstitutional about subjecting any law enforcement officer to random drug testing. Some courts have expanded the reach of random testing to civilian employees of law enforcement agencies who merely have access to non-confidential databases which the courts believe could be of assistance to drug smugglers or work in some sort of quasi-law enforcement capacity.[48]

If the employer wishes to use random drug testing, the selection of officers for drug testing must be purely random and pursuant to an established drug-testing program.[49] An employer may not, under the guise of a random drug-testing program, single out individual employees for drug testing.[50] Random testing can occur on an extremely frequent basis – one court has approved of a random testing program which subjected 10% of the sworn officers in an agency to drug testing each month.[51]

Where the employer has not adopted a formal random testing program and attempts to test employees on a case-by-case basis, courts require the employer to establish that it had reasonable suspicion for requiring the drug testing.[52] Courts have given an extremely broad reading to what constitutes reasonable suspicion that an officer is engaging in drug use, in many cases seemingly finding reasonable suspicion where they may not conclude that the same reasonable suspicion existed in a criminal case. Factors considered in determining whether reasonable suspicion exists generally include: (1) The nature of the tip or information; (2) the reliability of the information and, if one is involved, the informant; (3) the degree of corroboration of the suspicion; and (4) other factors such as physical evidence, recordings, and documentary evidence.[53]

Examples of facts which courts have found constitute reasonable suspicion justifying a drug test have included the following:

- Finding the identification of a detective at a known drug location;[54]

- The unsubstantiated allegation of a fellow officer[55] or a former girlfriend;[56]

- Accusations by suspects that the officer seized drugs from them which were subsequently not placed into evidence;[57]

- An officer's glassy-eyed appearance and unusual behavior[58] or "mood swings;"[59]

- An officer's high use of sick leave where the officer had previously been involved with drug use;[60]

- The finding of a crack cocaine vial next to the car of an officer who had been acting erratically for six months;[61] and

- Relying upon the response displayed by a drug-sniffing dog who passed through a locker room.[62]

Only where the chance that the officer has used drugs is very attenuated have courts found reasonable suspicion for a drug test lacking. For example, a court found that the mere fact that an officer was seen off duty with another officer who was later discovered to be involved in drug sales did not constitute reasonable suspicion for a drug test, upholding a jury verdict of $154,747 in favor of the officer.[63] In another case, a court found insufficient to establish reasonable suspicion that an officer had an attenuated relationship with a drug dealer (the officer was acquainted with the roommate of the dealer) and made a phone call to the department asking what was going on with a raid of the dealer's apartment.[64]

In all cases where drug testing is permissible, certain procedures must be followed to minimize the intrusion on the officer's privacy. For example, most courts have held that the employer's observation of the act of urination is an invasion of the officer's privacy absent reasonable suspicion that an officer will tamper with the urine sample.[65] In addition, the employer must take care to ensure that careful collection techniques are used to prevent contamination of the sample.[66] If the employee requests the presence of an attorney or a union representative during the drug testing process, the request must be honored by the employer.[67]

The decisions of the federal courts have not ended the controversy over whether random drug testing is permissible. As noted in the introduction to this book, state courts are now less reluctant than in the past to interpret state constitutions as providing more protection for personal rights than does the federal Constitution. The area of drug testing provides a good example of this trend.

In the mid-1980s, the Boston Police Department adopted a random drug-testing program. Following the *National Treasury Employees Union* opinion, the federal courts upheld the constitutionality of the program in 1989. However, in 1991, the Massachusetts Supreme Court struck down the program as violating the privacy provisions of the Massachusetts State Constitution. The Court reasoned that before police officers should be stripped of the privacy rights possessed by other citizens, the employer must prove that the need to invade privacy is documented by an overriding and factually-provable government concern. As the Court held, the absence of a significant drug problem among police officers forbids the imposition of random testing:

> "There is nothing in the record to indicate that there has been any problem, or any public perception of a problem, arising from the illicit use of drugs by Boston police officers. Indeed, there is nothing in the record to indicate that Boston police officers have unlawfully used controlled substances on or off duty. Moreover, there is no showing of how random drug testing by urinalysis will provide information that is needed to identify officers whose on-duty performance was affected by illicit drug use. * * * There is also no fact in the record, or otherwise established, to which the Commissioner points to show that a substantial public purpose requires and justifies random testing of the urine of Boston police officers * * * Constitutional safeguards should not be abandoned simply because there is a drug problem in this country. * * * It is at times when pressures on constitutional rights are greatest that courts must be especially vigilant in the protection of those rights."[68]

Since the decision of the Massachusetts Supreme Court, state supreme courts in Alaska and Arizona have held that random drug testing violates the state privacy rights of public safety employees.[69]

An Officer's Right To Be Free From Illegal Searches.

On occasion, a law enforcement agency that suspects that an officer has engaged in misconduct would like to search the officer's person or residence. If these searches are based upon probable cause and authorized by a warrant, they do not violate an officer's rights under the Fourth Amendment to be free from unreasonable searches and seizures.[70] Most of the law in the area, though, deals with searches that have been supported by neither probable cause nor a warrant.

Courts analyze the constitutionality of a warrantless search of an officer's person or residence using a variety of sliding scales.

- If the search is conducted away from the workplace, the search will likely be impermissible absent probable cause and a warrant, with the normal exceptions to the warrant requirement such as exigent circumstances.[71]

- If the search is conducted at the workplace, the search may be permissible if it is based upon reasonable suspicion that the officer has engaged in misconduct. [72]

- Administrative searches based upon reasonable suspicion that the officer has engaged in misconduct may be invalid if they are conducted in an unreasonably intrusive manner.[73]

- If a workplace search is based on less than reasonable suspicion, it will only be valid if the search is of an area where the officer has no reasonable expectation of privacy.[74]

Several cases illustrate these principles. *Los Angeles Police Protective League v. Gates* involved a sergeant suspected of involvement in a burglary ring. When the sergeant refused to allow the Department's investigators to conduct a search of a garage attached to his home without an appropriate warrant, the Department fired him for insubordination. In upholding the underlying basis of a $1,500,000 verdict for the sergeant against the City, the Court expressly rejected the City's arguments that the search could be based only upon reasonable suspicion that the sergeant was guilty of wrongdoing:

> "If a police officer were required to open up his home whenever there was a reasonable suspicion that evidence may be found there, then officers truly would have watered-down constitutional rights. They, like the rest of the people, must be able to retreat to a safe place free from the prying eyes of even the most well-intentioned employer. While there are numerous times when citizens find themselves in public places and subject to the reasonableness standard, * * * that does not mean that the historic integrity of the home should be so easily invaded. We hold that even a police officer's home cannot be invaded upon facts that would not permit the invasion of the home of persons who are not police officers."[75]

If the warrantless search is conducted of the officer's person while the officer is at the workplace and is conducted in a reasonable manner, the search may be based upon reasonable suspicion that the officer has engaged in wrongdoing. For example, in one case a court decided that an agency has the right to order its officers to appear in a lineup designed to allow a citizen complainant to identify which officer was involved in a particular incident.[76] Similarly, in another Los Angeles case, an officer who was suspected of being involved in burglaries who had his hands, uniform and wallet "blacklighted" by his Department was held not to have privacy rights sufficient to overcome the Department's interest in conducting the search.[77]

The last set of cases stands for the proposition that the more intrusive the search, the less likely it is to be approved, even if it is supported by reasonable suspicion and is conducted at the workplace. In *Kirkpatrick v. City of Los Angeles*, police officers who were accused of stealing $600 from a suspect were forced to submit to strip searches. The Court acknowledged that the government has an interest in police integrity that must be considered in evaluating the reasonableness of investigative searches of police officers. The Court balanced this government interest in the integrity of a police force against the officers' interest in not being subjected to highly intrusive searches of their persons. The Court concluded that this balance favored a finding that the strip search was illegal.[78] Along the same lines, body cavity searches of an officer must be justified by probable cause, and are subject to the same warrant requirements as any criminal searches.[79]

On the other hand, less intrusive workplace searches may not need reasonable suspicion or probable case. In one case, for example, the Louisiana Department of Public Safety and Corrections instituted a program of random "general searches" of employees, searches consisting of any combination of pat searches, searches of belongings, metal detector, and vehicle searches. A court upheld the constitutionality of the searches, citing a serious drug problem in the prison and the lack of disrobing and body cavity searches as part of the program.[80] In an Omaha case, a court upheld a department's order that an officer submit his bank records for two specific days. The order was given during an internal affairs investigation of a citizen complaint that the officer took money from him and wagered it at a casino the next day. Given the officer's assertion that he usually withdrew money from his bank account before wagering, the Court found the department's order reasonable even though it amounted to a warrantless search.[81] In a similar case, a court upheld the searches of the automobiles of corrections officers where the officers had signed consent forms allowing the searches.[82]

An Officer's Right To Be Free From Seizures.

When is an officer "seized" for purposes of Fourth Amendment analysis? It is clear that mere threat of possible job loss if an officer does not comply with a supervisor's order to go or remain somewhere is not enough to constitute a seizure.[83] A complicated case involving the Milwaukee, Wisconsin Police Department illustrates how the Fourth Amendment right to be free from an unreasonable "seizure" applies when an employer wishes to detain an officer pending an initial investigation.[84]

In the *Milwaukee* case, the Department conducted a sting operation on two officers it believed were illegally obtaining "street guns" by coercing suspected criminals. On the night of the sting operation, the two officers were working with a third officer. At the conclusion of the sting operation, the Department detained all three officers, even though it had no reason to believe that the third officer had committed a crime. None of the three officers were ever charged with a crime.

In a complex opinion dismissing the lawsuit of the first two officers, but allowing the third officer's lawsuit to proceed, a federal appeals court established the following principles:

- A seizure occurs when, in view of all the circumstances surrounding the incident, a reasonable person would have believed that he was not free to leave.[85]

- A Department may direct its officers to remain on duty or to accompany detectives to headquarters and either answer questions from supervisory officers as part of a criminal investigation about their alleged misconduct or invoke their Fifth Amendment rights against self-incrimination. An order to remain on the premises or accompany detectives, even if accompanied by a threat of discipline, is not a "seizure" implicating the officer's privacy rights since the Fourth Amendment does not protect against the threat of job loss.

- A Department may not seize an officer without probable cause who refuses to obey a command to remain on duty or report to a particular location in order to answer questions as part of a criminal investigation.[86] In such a circumstance, the Department only has the right to (1) institute investigative proceedings that could result in discipline; and (2) briefly stop, frisk, and question the officer if it has reasonable suspicion to do so under the *Terry* rule. [87]

In a subsequent case involving Los Angeles County deputy sheriffs, a court described the *Milwaukee* case as calling for the evaluation of the following factors in determining whether an order that an officer remain on site or at a precinct is a seizure for purposes of the Fourth Amendment:

- The experience level of the officer.

- Whether the treatment was consistent with that allowed by department guidelines or general policy.

- The occurrence of physical contact or threats of physical restraint.

- Whether the officer was explicitly refused permission to depart.

- Whether the officer was physically isolated.

- Whether the officer was given permission to use the restroom without accompaniment.

- Whether the officer was informed that he was the subject of a criminal investigation.

- Whether the officer was spoken to in a menacing or threatening manner.

- Whether the officer was under constant surveillance.

- Whether superior officers denied a request to contact an attorney or union representative.

- Whether the officer was allowed to retain law enforcement equipment, including weapons and badges.

- The duration of detention.

- The officer's receipt of overtime pay.[88]

Even minor physical interactions may not constitute a seizure within the scope of the Fourth Amendment. For example, one court held that a sergeant's momentary act in grabbing an officer's elbow was not tantamount to a seizure. The Court quoted from the Supreme Court's leading use-of-force case, *Graham v. Connor*, in holding that "not every push or shove, even it if may later seem unnecessary in the peace of a judge's chambers, violates the Fourth Amendment."[89]

An Officer's Privacy In Offices, Lockers And Desks.

The privacy rights officers have in their offices, lockers and desks depends upon the "legitimate expectation of privacy" the officers have in such areas.[90] As the Supreme Court has explained, the "expectation of privacy" (or lack of it) is almost always derived from promises the employer has made (or not made) that the areas are off-limits to other than the officer, and are not subject to random search. A reasonable expectation of privacy in a locker, desk, or office can be created either by the express promises of the employer or by implication.[91]

In one case, an agent for the Drug Enforcement Administration was provided with an office with a locking door, that was not open to the public, and that was not subject to regular visits by the employer. Since the employer never informed the agent that the office would be subject to search, the Court held that the agent reasonably believed that he had privacy rights to his office.[92]

In other cases, courts have approved warrantless searches of lockers in cases where the employer has not taken any action which could reasonably be construed as giving employees a reasonable expectation of privacy in their lockers.[93] For example, in one case, a court found that there was no reasonable expectation of privacy in a trooper's locker where supervisors routinely obtained access to the work-related contents of the locker.[94] In another case, a court found no reasonable expectation of privacy in lockers where a supervisor had an additional key to the lockers, and where the officers signed documents allowing "a search of their person, or automobile, or place of assignment on government property."[95]

If an officer has a reasonable expectation of privacy in an office, locker, or desk, the Fourth Amendment requires at a minimum that the employer establish reasonable suspicion for the search. Courts have struggled with precisely how much of a reason there must be for a search.[96] For example, in one case a court noted that a warrantless search of an officer's locker based only upon unidentified reports of the officer's possible criminal activity "may present a problem" because of the "thin" basis for the search.[97] In another case, a court expressly disapproved of a warrantless reasonable suspicion search of an officer's office, desk, and gym bag as part of an ongoing criminal investigation, reasoning that whenever a search is conducted pursuant to a criminal investigation it must be accompanied by a warrant (absent exigent circumstances) and probable cause.[98]

In some states, an officer's right to privacy in offices, lockers, and desks is guaranteed by statute. For example, California requires a warrant or prior notification for the search of a law enforcement officer's locker, providing that "no public safety officer shall have his locker, or other space for storage that may be assigned to him searched except in his presence, or with his consent, or unless a valid search warrant has been obtained or where he has been notified that a search will be conducted."[99] Interpreting the statute, a California court has held that an officer's desk drawer was within the definition of "other space for storage" protected by law.[100]

Privacy In Electronic Communications Systems And Computers.

As with physical areas such as a desk or locker, an officer's privacy rights in electronic communications to which he is a party will depend upon whether the officer has a reasonable expectation of privacy in the communications.[101] Three contrasting cases illustrate this principle.

In the first case, *PBA Local No. 38 v. Woodbridge Police Department*, officers sued their employer for electronically listening and using taping devices in various parts of the police headquarters and on the building's phone lines. All but two lines in the building were subject to recording, and the recording was signified by a beep every five seconds. It was general knowledge among officers that the beeps signified that the lines were being recorded. The Court noted that it was "clear that officers did not have a reasonable expectation of privacy in conversations which took place over the beeped lines."[102]

The second case, *Abbott v. Village of Winthrop Harbor*, also involved taped telephone lines. Prior to recording the conversations, the Police Chief explicitly issued a memorandum stating that one of the lines would not be recorded. Without issuing contrary notice, the Chief then recorded the line. The Court held that "it is a violation to wiretap or otherwise monitor the private communications of another without authorization, notice or consent." Though the employer argued that the officers had impliedly consented to the taping, the Court found that "knowledge of the capability of monitoring alone cannot be considered implied consent," and held that the officers stated a claim for violation of their privacy rights.[103]

In the third case, *Quon v. Arch Wireless Operating Company, Inc.*, two sergeants sued the Ontario, California Police Department after the Department reviewed text messages the sergeants sent and received on their Department-issued text messaging system. Though the Department's official written policy was that there was no expectation of privacy in text messages or other forms of Department

> An officer's privacy rights in electronic communications to which he is a party will depend upon whether the officer has a reasonable expectation of privacy in the communications.

communication, the lieutenant in charge of the wireless program told the sergeants and others that the Department would not audit or review their text messages if they agreed to pay for any overages above the allotted minutes on the system. In finding that the sergeants' privacy rights had been violated, the Court held:

> "The lieutenant was the one in charge of administering the use of the City-owned pagers, [and] his statements carry a great deal of weight. That the lieutenant was not the official policymaker, or even the final policymaker, does not diminish the chain of command. He was in charge of the pagers, and it was reasonable for the sergeants to rely on the policy – formal or informal – that the lieutenant established and enforced."[104]

In an analogous area, an officer's privacy rights in the contents of a work computer will depend upon what degree of confidentiality the employer has promised in the computer system. If the employer has rules that affirmatively state there is no expectation of privacy in computer data, then the employee will have no privacy rights in work computers.[105] Similarly, privacy interests in mobile data transmissions (MDTs) are governed by whether the officer has a reasonable expectation that the communications will be private. If the employer has announced that all MDT messages may be monitored or reviewed, the employee does not have a reasonable expectation of privacy with respect to communications made over such systems.[106]

Video Cameras In The Law Enforcement Workplace.

The law is still emerging as to the constitutionality of the use of video cameras in the workplace. The most important case in the area is *Bernhard v. City of Ontario*, a lawsuit filed by police officers who discovered their employer, in the course of investigating a flashlight theft, had conducted covert, warrantless video surveillance of their locker room. A court found that the officers had a reasonable expectation of privacy in their locker room:

> "Plaintiffs clearly expected that they would not be secretly videotaped in their locker room. There were no signs in the locker room, or anywhere else in the building, announcing that the locker room was subject to video, audio, or photographic surveillance. Plaintiffs were never informed by management, either orally or in writing, that they might be subject to such surveillance. They engaged in private activities in the locker room, such as changing clothes, using the bathroom, and showering. Finally, each Plaintiff submitted a declaration stating that he had a subjective expectation of privacy against the covert video surveillance of the locker room."

The Court also found that "no reasonable police officer" would have believed the surveillance was constitutional. Noting that "secret video surveillance is especially intrusive on the privacy interests protected by the Fourth Amendment," the

Court cited from a body of case law establishing the proposition that "it is clear that silent video surveillance results in a very serious, some say Orwellian, invasion of privacy."[107] Along the same lines, a court found that a police chief violated a dispatcher's right to privacy by placing an audio recorder in the women's restroom.[108]

Using similar rationale, a different federal court found that officers had a reasonable expectation of privacy that they would not be videotaped in a locker-break room,[109] while another court upheld a warrantless search of the office of a drug agent, but struck down the use of a hidden video camera in the same office as being too intrusive.[110] In another case, a court disallowed the use of video cameras to record the conduct of two narcotics investigators because the video cameras were installed as part of a criminal investigation into the officers' conduct.[111]

The 'Right To Be Let Alone' Aspect Of The Right To Privacy.

The second half of the right to privacy – the "right to be let alone" – applies to protecting the personal relationships of law enforcement officers.[112] The right to privacy provides protections both in marital and non-marital relationships,[113] and in cases where the conduct is protected simply because it is private. In the words of one court, such matters should be beyond the control of law enforcement employers because they do "not adversely affect persons beyond the actor, and hence are none of their business."[114]

The Right To Be Let Alone And Intimate Relationships.

In numerous cases, courts have held that the right to privacy prohibits a law enforcement agency from disciplining employees on the basis of off-duty personal or sexual relationships. In several cases, police departments have been held to have violated officers' rights to privacy when they disciplined them for off-duty affairs.[115] In another case, a police department was held to have violated a married officer's right to privacy when disciplining him for having an affair with an 18-year old,[116] while another department was held to have violated the right to privacy of a candidate for the job of police officer by rejecting her, in part, for having an affair with a married police officer.[117] The right to privacy has also been extended to protect an officer who has cohabited with a person who was not his spouse,[118] while another case resulted in the reversal of the discharge of an officer for maintaining an apartment with three other officers for the purpose of engaging in sexual relationships with consenting females.[119]

Among the cases stressing the need for a law enforcement agency to prove a relationship between the officer's off-duty conduct and job performance is one where a court held that a police applicant's privacy rights were violated when she was required to answer questions about her sexual relationship with a married police officer. The affair was conducted off duty, did not interfere with the job performance of either participant, and had not become a source of scandal in the department.[120] In another case, the Court held that a nudist could not be denied employment as a law enforcement officer simply because he was a nudist, noting that "what a policeman does in his private life, as with other public employees, should not be his employer's concern unless it can be shown to affect in some degree his efficiency in the performance of his job."[121] Using similar rationale, a court overturned the termination of a black officer who was fired after he and his wife permitted two white single women to board with them, holding that there was no showing that the officer's "conduct would materially and substantially impair his usefulness as a police officer."[122]

Only a few cases have run counter to this trend. One court upheld the termination of a Utah police officer for adultery, reasoning that "adultery is a transgression against the marriage relation which the law endeavors to protect."[123] A second case involved an unusual set of facts in which an at-will officer was fired for statements his wife made that she wanted to "frame" the police chief. The Court found that the discipline did not violate the officer's right to privacy, concluding that the employer "did not directly or substantially interfere with the officer's right to be married when they terminated him on the basis of his wife's recorded statement threatening to frame the police chief. The officer presented no evidence that his termination significantly discouraged, let alone made practically impossible, his marriage to his wife."[124] A third case upheld the decision of a civil service commission that a police officer's affair with the wife of another officer was a sufficient reason to deny him a promotion.[125]

This minority line of cases to the contrary, in order for a law enforcement agency to constitutionally discipline an officer for his or her personal relationships, there must be a direct correlation between the officer's activities and poor job performance.[126] As noted by one court, the burden of proof in this area is very strict:

> "Here the plaintiff police officer was required by the defendant officials to tell of his private, off-duty marital misconduct which in no way had affected the performance of his duties and which had not publicly reflected adversely upon the public image of the plaintiff as a police officer or of the Police Department as a public body. Given the opportunity to do so, the defendant police and city officials offered no evidence that shows marital misconduct engaged in privately and while off duty has any effect upon a police officer's duty performance. They disapprove, as most citizens do, of police officers running around on their wives. They do not even suggest that this disapproved-of conduct generally impairs the performance of a police officer's duty or specifically impaired this police officer's duty performance. There is no justification for these police officials requiring this police officer to cease running around on his wife as a condition of being an employee of the Athens Police Department. Constitutionally when off duty and out of uniform he can do privately what he wishes to do until such

time as it materially and substantially impairs his usefulness as a police officer."[127]

The clearest case of a nexus between an officer's sexual activity and on-the-job performance occurs when the sexual activities are themselves illegal.[128] Other examples of a nexus with job performance might be if the officer has an affair with a subordinate,[129] if the affair is with a crime victim,[130] or if the affair is with a person with a felony record.[131] As noted by one court, however, these limited exceptions to the general protection afforded by the right to privacy must be narrowly construed:

> "Even though activities such as those engaged in by plaintiff may be within the protected 'zone of privacy,' this protection is by no means absolute. For example, if the sexual activities of a public employee were open and notorious, or if such activities took place in a small town, the public employer might very well have an interest in investigating such activities and possibly terminating an employee. In such a case, the actions of the public employee with respect to his or her private life could be deemed to have a substantial impact upon his or her ability to perform on the job. We may concede, then, at least for the purposes of argument, that the Police Department has an interest and may legitimately investigate some areas of personal, sexual activities engaged in by its employees where those activities impact upon job performance. However, we are compelled to conclude that there are many areas of a police officer's private life and sexual behavior which are simply beyond the scope of any reasonable investigation by the Department because of the tenuous relationship between such activity and the officer's performance on the job. In the absence of a showing that a policeman's private, off-duty personal activities have an impact upon his on-the-job performance, we believe that inquiry into those activities violates the constitutionally-protected right of privacy. The Police Department simply cannot have a carte blanche to investigate all aspects of a police officer's personal life * * * We therefore hold that the widely acknowledged policy of the Police Department whereby police officers are required upon penalty of losing their jobs, to answer all questions propounded in an 'official investigation,' even though the questions have no bearing upon an officer's job performance, is unconstitutional."[132]

Homosexuality.

There is tremendous flux in the law with respect to whether a law enforcement officer can be disciplined or discharged for homosexuality. In 1986, the Supreme Court ruled that state laws could make homosexual sodomy a criminal violation.[133] Cases decided in the ensuing years often held that, if state law criminalized homosexual behavior, officers could be discharged simply for their homosexuality on the theory that the officer failed to comply with the law. As one court

The clearest case of a nexus between an officer's sexual activity and on-the-job performance occurs when the sexual activities are themselves illegal.

There is tremendous flux in the law with respect to whether a law enforcement officer can be disciplined or discharged for homosexuality.

noted, the illegality of underlying sexual behavior creates a "substantial barrier" to successfully asserting a privacy claim.[134]

Following this rationale, a court upheld a police department's refusal to hire an individual as a property room clerk because of his homosexuality. The Court expressed the concern that the clerk's job "entailed the handling of evidence in offenses involving homosexual conduct." The Court found particularly relevant the fact that the clerk did not attempt to conceal his homosexuality, and had "publicly flaunted" it.[135]

In a similar vein, a federal court of appeals upheld the FBI's former policy of not hiring homosexuals. The Court found critical the fact that FBI agents must be able to work in any state in the country, over half of which at the time had criminal laws forbidding homosexual sodomy. The Court was also clearly concerned about the possibility of the blackmail of homosexual agents:

> "FBI agents perform counterintelligence duties that involve highly classified matters relating to national security. It is not irrational for the Bureau to conclude that the criminalization of homosexual conduct coupled with the general public opprobrium toward homosexuality exposes many homosexuals, even 'open' homosexuals, to the risk of possible blackmail to protect their partners, if not themselves."[136]

Along the same lines, another court held that a police department had a right to ask employees whether they had engaged in sexual relations with a member of the same sex, commenting that the question did not seek information which the applicant had "a right to keep private."[137] A similar result was reached in a South Carolina case upholding the discharge of a police officer after he and a co-worker's husband masturbated in the same room, with a court concluding that there was no constitutional protection for homosexual behavior.[138]

A huge change in the law came in 2003, when the Supreme Court reversed itself, and in *Lawrence v. Texas* held that the Fifth Amendment granted individuals the right to engage in private, consensual homosexual acts and struck down a Texas statute criminalizing such conduct.[139] The logical extension of the Court's opinion is that state laws criminalizing homosexual behavior are unconstitutional and law enforcement agencies will not be able to discipline or discharge employees solely because of their homosexuality. This means that the cases that once stood in the minority in holding that homosexuals had constitutional job protections are now likely to become the majority rule.

These courts, which once held the minority opinion (now likely to be the prevailing opinion after *Lawrence*), held that a person cannot be dismissed from public employment solely because he or she is a homosexual.[140] As one court noted, while homosexual conduct "may be deemed immoral by the majority of our society, this alone does not justify denying * * * government employment."[141] Following this rationale, a court found that the Dallas Police Department's refusal to hire homosexual applicants violated the right to privacy of the applicants.[142] In another case, an officer was discharged for refusing to submit to a polygraph examination on the question of whether he had engaged in homosexual relations.

The Court reversed the discharge, and held in essence that the officer's sexual orientation was none of the employer's business:

> "[The officer] learned through counsel that the Department planned to inquire during his polygraph examination whether he was a homosexual and whether he had ever had a homosexual encounter in the Asheville area. Neither of these questions related specifically and narrowly to plaintiff's official duties and the charge which was being investigated. As a matter of law, plaintiff was justified in refusing to take a polygraph examination which included those questions."[143]

The Right To Be Let Alone And Other Off-Duty Conduct.

As might be inferred from the line of cases involving the right to be let alone and an officer's off-duty relationships, the right to privacy provides protections in other areas of an officer's off-duty life provided there is no demonstrable negative effect caused by the off-duty activities on the officer's job. For example, in one case a captain criticized the police chief while having drinks with a friend while off duty and out of the jurisdiction.[144] In overturning the captain's discipline, the Court held that the right to privacy protected the captain's statements:

> "We think it quite reasonable that he assumed he could vent a little steam over drinks, and we think that [the Captain], like everyone, has a legitimate interest in maintaining a zone of privacy where he can speak about work without fear of censure. It must be remembered that we are talking about off-duty shoptalk, which, although regrettably indiscreet and tactless, is nonetheless basically idle barroom chatter. Such conversation generally is not subject to sanction. We do not doubt that the Department may restrict the actions of its off-duty officers in many ways, but it does not follow that these off-duty restrictions may unnecessarily impinge upon private, social conversation."

Courts have also repeatedly cautioned law enforcement employers that intrusions in an employee's off-duty life must be undertaken carefully and only with specific justification. Courts have reversed discipline for off-duty activities where the employer's justification was "nebulous and ill-defined,"[145] or was based solely upon a general disapproval in the community of the type of conduct forming the basis for the discipline.[146] As phrased by one court: "The government must tread lightly when it investigates and regulates the private activities of its employees. Public employers must be careful not to transform anachronistic notions of unacceptable social conduct into law."[147]

Courts have reversed discipline for off-duty activities where the employer's justification was "nebulous and ill-defined."

The Right To Be Let Alone And Restrictions On Activities While An Officer Is On Sick Leave.

The right to privacy provides only limited protections to law enforcement officers when their employer attempts to limit their activities while they are on sick leave. It is clear that an employer has the legitimate right to ensure that sick leave is not abused.

The right to privacy provides only limited protections to law enforcement officers when their employer attempts to limit their activities while they are on sick leave. It is clear that an employer has the legitimate right to ensure that sick leave is not abused. Permissible regulations in pursuit of this goal include limiting the ability of officers on sick leave to travel out of town,[148] and even requiring employees on sick leave to remain at their homes except to make trips for purposes such as voting, attending church, and visiting a physician.[149] Most certainly the farthest-reaching case in the area is *Crain v. Board of Police Commissioners*, which upheld rules of the St. Louis Police Department forbidding officers on sick leave from leaving their residence except to obtain medical treatment, and reasoned as follows:

> "The Police Board [states] that the restrictive sick leave policy is necessary and serves the interests of safety and morale by expediting the recovery of sick officers, minimizing the burden on officers who may have to work longer hours while other officers are out sick, and assuring that officers on sick leave are not malingering and that the sick leave policy is not abused. The legitimacy of the Police Board's interests is obvious."[150]

If an employer wishes to regulate the activities of its officers while on sick leave, it must do so through clearly written regulations which leave little room for differing interpretations.[151] In addition, it is possible for an employer to go so far in controlling sick leave abuse so as to violate the employee's right to be let alone. For example, in *Pienta v. Village of Schaumburg, Illinois*, a departmental rule required officers on sick leave to remain in their homes. Officers on sick leave and their families were also subjected to surveillance inside and outside their homes, frequent telephone calls and unannounced visits by Police Department personnel. The Court, which referred to the regulations as "morale chilling," held the regulations governing the use of sick leave unconstitutional:

> "In effect, these regulations put plaintiffs under house arrest until their return to work. Their rights to vote, to exercise freely their religion by such attendance, to go to court, to attend political or family gatherings, and to travel were infringed."[152]

The Court held that the reasons advanced by the Department for the regulations – that of avoiding abuse of sick leave and efficiently allocating manpower – were not compelling enough to override the right to privacy in such an overreaching manner.

The Right To Be Let Alone And Personal Appearance: Grooming Codes And Tattoos.

The leading grooming code case is *Kelley v. Johnson*, in which the Supreme Court considered First Amendment freedom of speech and Fourteenth Amendment liberty challenges (but not a privacy challenge) to a police department grooming code covering the style and length of hair, sideburns, and mustaches and prohibiting beards and goatees except for medical reasons.[153] While the Court's opinion necessarily addressed only the constitutional issues raised in the case, the clear implication of the opinion, which upheld the grooming code, is that grooming codes do not violate the right to privacy. The Court found that grooming code rules must be "arbitrary" in order to be a deprivation of free speech or liberty rights, and in clear language upheld a broad right of law enforcement agencies to regulate such matters:

> "The overwhelming majority of state and local police of the present day are uniformed. This fact itself testifies to the recognition by those who direct those operations, and by the people of the States and localities who directly or indirectly choose such persons, that similarity in appearance of police officers is desirable. This choice may be based on a desire to make police officers readily recognizable to the members of the public, or a desire for the *esprit de corps* which such similarity is felt to inculcate within the police force itself. Either one is a sufficiently rational justification for regulations so as to defeat respondent's claim based on the liberty guarantee of the Fourteenth Amendment."[154]

Grooming code rules must be "arbitrary" in order to be a deprivation of free speech or liberty rights.

Showing the breadth of an employer's latitude to regulate grooming under the Constitution, one case dealt with a police department's ban on male officers wearing ear studs whether off or on duty. Stressing that the employer was a small town where officers were well known to the public, the Court upheld the ban. The Court noted that members of the public, family members, fellow officers, and supervisors all objected to the officers wearing ear studs, and, using language that seems disproportionate to the issue before it, held that the wearing of ear studs "caused an adverse impact on police discipline, *esprit de corps* and uniformity...and great public dissatisfaction as well."[155] In a similar case, a court upheld a rule of the Massachusetts State Police Department forbidding the wearing of mustaches, reasoning that the rule was necessary to assist the public in recognizing police officers or to promote a sense of "*esprit de corps.*"[156]

Officers have fared no better in filing constitutional challenges to tattoo regulations. The most important case in the area arose out of new rule in the Hartford Police Department that officers were required to cover all tattoos that were deemed by the Department to be unprofessional or offensive. In upholding the rule, a federal appeals court ruled that "the First Amendment rights of public employees are significantly more limited than those of the general public. A governmental employer may subject its employees to such special restrictions on free expression as are reasonably necessary to promote effective government. A police department has a reasonable interest in not offending, or appearing unprofessional before, the public it serves."[157]

A 2007 case involving firefighters and paramedics for the District of Columbia Fire Department injected uncertainty into the area of grooming codes. In 1993, Congress passed what was known as the Religious Freedom Restoration Act, or RFRA, a statute which provided some protection for religious expression. The Supreme Court later held that the RFRA could not constitutionally apply the Act to state and local governments.[158] However, since the District of Columbia is governed under federal as opposed to state law, the RFRA still applies to employment issues for the District. The firefighters and paramedics challenged the Fire Department's ban on beards, arguing that their beards were a form of religious expression protected by the RFRA. The Court agreed, and found as well that the Department had to consider "less restrictive means" of accomplishing its goals than banning beards on those with such religious beliefs.[159] Since the RFRA roughly adopted standards of reasonable accommodation that exist under the First Amendment's religious freedom guarantees, it may well be that a new theory of challenging bans on beards may be emerging.

Without regard to the constitutionality of grooming codes, the implementation of a grooming code clearly concerns a mandatory subject of bargaining.

Without regard to the constitutionality of grooming codes, the implementation of a grooming code clearly concerns a mandatory subject of bargaining in those states with collective bargaining for law enforcement officers. As was noted in one case, grooming codes not only affect an employee's comfort, convenience, appearance and self expression both on and off the job, but also subject an employee to discipline should the employee violate the code. All of these factors require the conclusion that, in states with collective bargaining, the imposition of a grooming code or a change in rules concerning tattoos must be preceded by collective bargaining.[160]

At least two arbitrators have overturned regulations concerning grooming. In one case, a change of chiefs brought a new rule which ended the practice of officers being allowed to wear beards. The evidence before the arbitrator indicated that the primary reason for the ban on beards was the personal preference of the chief and there was no evidence of an adverse reaction of the public to officers wearing beards. The arbitrator ordered the new rule withdrawn, holding that beards are essentially a matter of style and fashion and employees should be able to conform reasonably to such matters. The arbitrator noted that rules regulating beards impinge on an officer's private life and thus need to be within the bounds of reason and acceptability. In order to be upheld, the arbitrator found, a rule regulating grooming would have to be linked to on-the-job performance.[161]

In the second case, the arbitrator rejected a city's ban on "corn-row" hair styles. The City had imposed the ban because it considered the style to be a fad and too extreme for an officer to wear for a proper public image. The arbitrator concluded that the style was not "inappropriate for mainline police duty" nor was it "unkempt or extreme." The arbitrator ordered the Department to allow the affected female officer to wear the style, required the Department to pay her $100 for her hair stylist's expense, and to credit her with the personal day off she would be forced to use to have her hair restyled.[162]

Grooming codes occasionally implicate the religious freedom rights of law enforcement officers. In one case, a correctional facility ordered two correctional officers to cut their dreadlocks, a hair style which the Rastafarian officers believe to be an expression of their religious beliefs. A Court refused to grant judgment in favor of the correctional facility, commenting that the facility "clearly has failed to demonstrate that the directive is the least restrictive means of advancing the state's asserted interests in safety, discipline and *esprit de corps*. [The facility has] not offered evidence of even a single incident during the period of time the officers wore their modified dreadlocks – approximately one year – to support the argument that the officers' hairstyle posed any security risk because their hair could be grabbed by an inmate."[163]

The Right To Engage In Off-Duty Employment.

From time to time, law enforcement officers have argued that the "right to be let alone" component of the right to privacy should allow them to engage in second jobs without first obtaining the permission of their employers. With four exceptions, courts have regularly held that a law enforcement employer has a right to regulate the off-duty uniformed and non-uniformed employment of its officers.[164] The rationale for such decisions is that the emergency nature of law enforcement, the need to ensure that officers report for work in good physical and mental condition, and the need to prevent conflicts of interests, all work together to allow a law enforcement employer broad latitude in regulating off-duty employment.

The first of the four exceptions to the general rule occurs where the employer has failed to enact specific regulations banning certain types of off-duty work and has instead reserved to itself the right to approve or deny permission for off-duty work on a case-by-case basis. In such a case, the prohibition of off-duty work may fail because of the lack of standards under which the employer would exercise its discretion. As noted in one case, the lack of standards creates the possibility of "discrimination between members of the same police force inasmuch as the ordinance fails to fix any standard whatsoever to guide the applications for exemptions" under the rule.[165]

Second, if the employer has banned only some off-duty work, it has a burden of proving that it has a rational basis for distinguishing between the banned work and the work that is permitted. As noted by one court in a case where the employer banned off-duty security work:

> "In New Jersey, a police officer has an inherent duty to obey the law and to enforce it, and to use all reasonable means to enforce the laws applicable in his jurisdiction, and to apprehend violators. In addition, a municipal police officer [has] the full power of arrest for any crime committed in [the officer's] presence and committed anywhere in the

With four exceptions, courts have regularly held that a law enforcement employer has a right to regulate the off-duty uniformed and non-uniformed employment of its officers.

[state]. Because of these statutory duties, it is conceivable that an off-duty officer employed as a cabdriver would face more public exposure than an officer moonlighting as a security guard in a closed department store or school. A police officer working as a cabdriver who witnesses an assault or theft and responds to it could present a greater insurance risk to the Township than an off-duty security officer. This illustration is only one example, but it clearly demonstrates the problem of the Resolution's classification."[166]

The third exception to the general rule exists where the ban on off-duty work somehow impacts the officer's free speech rights. For example, the Supreme Court has struck down as unconstitutional a ban on employees receiving honoraria for delivering speeches and, following a similar rationale, a federal court of appeals has struck down a ban on employees serving as expert witnesses against the employer.[167]

Fourth, employers are usually not allowed to condition off-duty work on the requirement that the third-party employer assume all of the costs of workers' compensation and tort claim insurance for the officer. Courts have struck down these regulations on the theory that the law enforcement agency benefits whenever the officer takes true law enforcement action on behalf of the third-party employer. As noted by one court, "the public has benefited when an off-duty member of the police force responds to a serious police matter regardless of whether the officer's actions also benefit a paid detail employer."[168]

Some states have enacted statutes governing the circumstances under which an officer can engage in off-duty employment. California's statute is an example of such a law:

"[A] local agency officer or employee shall not engage in any employment, activity, or enterprise for compensation which is inconsistent, incompatible, in conflict with, or inimical to his or her duties as a local agency officer or employee or with the duties, functions, or responsibilities of his or her appointing power or the agency by which he or she is employed.

"An employee's outside employment, activity, or enterprise may be prohibited if it: (1) involves the use for private gain or advantage of his or her local agency time, facilities, equipment and supplies; or the badge, uniform, prestige, or influence of his or her local agency office or employment, or (2) involves receipt or acceptance by the officer or employee of any money or other consideration from anyone other than his or her local agency for the performance of an act which the officer or employee, if not performing such act, would be required or expected to render in the regular course or hours of his or her local agency employment or as a part of his or her duties as a local agency officer or employee, or (3) involves the performance of an act in other than his or her capacity as a local agency officer or employee which act may later be subject directly or indirectly to the control, inspection, review, audit, or enforcement of any other officer or employee or the agency by which he or she is employed, or (4) involves such time demands as would render performance of his or her duties as a local agency officer or employee less efficient."[169]

Anti-Nepotism Rules.

Many agencies have nepotism rules barring two employees who are either related to each other or living together from working together. Some anti-nepotism rules bar these individuals from working for the same department or even the same employer (so-called "exogamy" rules).[170] Narrower anti-nepotism rules prohibit supervisor-subordinate relationships between relatives or couples or bar them from working the same shift. Though courts recognize that an element of the right to privacy includes the right to marry, they have uniformly upheld the constitutionality of anti-nepotism rules, reasoning that the employer's interest in avoiding potential personnel and officer safety problems outweighs any impact on the officers' right to marry.[171] Rules that bar dating between employees of different rank have also been upheld on the rationale that an employer's interest in minimizing sexual harassment lawsuits satisfies constitutional standards.[172]

A form of anti-nepotism rule forbidding marital relationships between an inmate and a corrections officer has also been upheld. While courts acknowledge rules requiring a corrections officer to choose between the job and a marriage, they hold that the need of the correctional facility for security outweighs any impairment of the right to marry an individual of one's choice.[173]

The Constitutionality Of Residency Rules.

The validity of rules requiring public employees to reside in a particular location as a condition of continued employment has been a considerable subject of legal debate over the years. Initially, it was thought that residency rules impinged on an employee's constitutionally-guaranteed right to travel or right to privacy.[174] By now, however, it seems well settled that a public employer can constitutionally require its law enforcement officers to reside within its jurisdictional limits, so long as it has some "rational" reason for doing so.[175]

The most frequently advanced arguments for residency rules is that an employer has a legitimate interest in having law enforcement officers participate in and pay taxes to the community, improving community attitudes and cooperation, increasing loyalty to the community, reducing absenteeism, and ensuring that the employee is quickly available for the emergencies inherent in police work.[176] Seemingly putting the matter to rest, the Supreme Court commented in 1976 in its last pronouncement on public employee continuing residency requirements, "[T]his kind of ordinance is not irrational."[177]

It seems well settled that a public employer can constitutionally require its law enforcement officers to reside within its jurisdictional limits, so long as it has some "rational" reason for doing so.

Only two types of residency requirements are regularly called into question today. The first are "durational" residency requirements, which require that an individual have resided in a community for a specified duration in order to be eligible for employment in the first place. Durational residency requirements are considered suspect, both because of the impact they have on the right to travel and because of concerns of the perpetuation of racial segregation.[178] An impermissible durational residency requirement can be established by the informal practices of the employer, as in one case where a court ruled that an applicant for a police officer job who was told that he was not being hired because he was not a "local" and that the city "took care of its own" had stated a cause of action for the violation of his constitutional rights.[179]

The second type of disputed residency clause is one which requires city police officers to live within the confines of the county within which the city is located, not the city itself. Because the traditional justifications for residency ordinances – the notions of paying taxes to the employer, living in the juris-dictional limits of the law enforcement agency, and the need for prompt response times – residency requirements that city police officers live within a county are likely not to be upheld.[180]

Simply because most residency requirements are constitutional does not nec-essarily mean that an employer is unilaterally free to enact and impose them. In some states, local residency rules have been outlawed by state statutes.[181] In addi-tion, in those states where law enforcement officers have the right to collectively bargain, residency requirements have been uniformly held to be mandatorily nego-tiable.[182] As a result, an employer acting in a collective bargaining environment must first negotiate the residency requirement with the pertinent law enforcement labor organization before it may be imposed. In states where interest arbitration is the last step in the bargaining process, this may mean submitting a residency requirement to arbitration.

Also, it is clear that, whatever their legality, courts and arbitrators simply do not like residency rules, and will occasionally stretch the law to find that an officer has complied with a residency rule. A good example of this tendency is a case involving a Cleveland police officer, who claimed to live with his brother in the Cleveland city limits as required by a Cleveland ordinance. The officer actu-ally owned a home in a suburb of Cleveland, where his wife and children lived. The officer's children went to school in the suburb. Distressed about the officer's residence, the City assigned an investigator to monitor the officer's actions. On eight different days over a period of three months, the officer's car was seen parked at the home in the suburbs, and on two of those occasions, the officer was seen departing the home with his children. The Ohio Court of Appeals bluntly con-cluded that "the officer's presence at the home in the suburbs does not establish proof that he lived there or that he made that home his residence."[183]

NOTES

[1] *See Whalen v. Roe,* 429 U.S. 589 (1977); *Paul v. Davis,* 424 U.S. 693 (1976). While there is no specific provision of the Constitution creating a right to privacy, courts have inferred a right to privacy within the "penumbra" of a number of the original Bill of Rights, including the First, Third, Fourth, and Ninth Amendments. In a number of states, state constitutional provisions directly create a right to privacy. E.g. Constitution, State of Alaska, Article I, Section 22 ("the right of the people to privacy is recognized and shall not be infringed"); Constitution, State of California, Article I, Section 1 (defines "pursuing and obtaining privacy" as an "inalienable right").

[2] *See Fraternal Order of Police v. City of Philadelphia,* 812 F.2d 105 (3d Cir. 1987).

[3] *Eastwood v. Department of Corrections of the State of Oklahoma,* 846 F.2d 627 (10th Cir. 1988).

[4] A minority of courts require a "compelling" governmental interest in all cases where the right to privacy is implicated, rather than just in cases where the intrusion on the officer's privacy is high. *See Mangels v. Pena,* 789 F.2d 836 (10th Cir. 1986).

[5] *Shuman v. City of Philadelphia,* 470 F. Supp. 449 (E.D. Pa. 1979).

[6] *Aceto v. Town of Bloomfield,* 2006 WL 1405579 (D. Conn. 2006).

[7] *International Federation of Professional and Technical Engineers, Local 21, AFL-CIO v. Superior Court,* 165 P.3d 488 (Cal. 2007).

[8] *E.g., Detroit Free Press, Inc. v. City of Southfield,* 713 N.W.2d 28 (Mich. App. 2005).

[9] *Barry v. City of New York,* 712 F.2d 1554 (2d Cir. 1983). *See also Walls v. City of Petersburg,* 895 F.2d 188 (4th Cir. 1990)(Court upholds requirement that employees list all debts on form used for background investigation); *IAFF, Local 1264 v. Municipality of Anchorage,* 973 P.2d 1132 (Alaska 1999)(upholds public disclosure of wages and benefits paid individual firefighters); *State ex rel. Jones v. Myers,* 581 N.E.2d 629 (1991)(upholds disclosure of earnings of public employees). On at least three separate occasions, the United States Supreme Court has rejected appeals of decisions upholding financial disclosure laws similar to those in New York City. *Montgomery County v. Walsh,* 336 A.2d 97 (Md. App. 1975), *appeal dismissed,* 424 U.S. 901 (1976); *Fritz v. Gorton,* 517 P.2d 911 (Wash. 1974)(en banc), *appeal dismissed,* 417 U.S. 902 (1974); *Stein v. Howlett,* 289 N.E.2d 409 (Ill. 1972), *appeal dismissed,* 412 U.S. 925 (1973). At the time of these decisions, the rejection of an appeal by the Supreme Court had the legal effect of a decision on the merits affirming the judgment of the lower court.

[10] Laws requiring police officers to disclose property owned within city limits have also been upheld. *Evangelista v. City of Rochester,* 580 F. Supp. 1556 (W.D. N.Y. 1984). *See also Illinois State Employees Association v. Walker,* 315 N.E.2d 9 (Ill. 1974).

[11] *O'Brien v. DiGrazia,* 544 F.2d 543 (1st Cir. 1976).

[12] §3308, Government Code of California; Article 27, Section 729, Maryland Code Annotated. Under California's law, the employer is allowed to inquire into an officer's personal finances where the information sought might indicate a conflict of interest. *Ass'n for Los Angeles Deputy Sheriffs v. County of Los Angeles,* 236 Cal. Rptr. 495 (Cal. App. 1987).

[13] *City of Auburn,* 13 NPER NY-13044 (N.Y. PERB 1990).

[14] *Pyrcz v. Branford College*, 1999 WL 706882 (Mass. Sup. 1999).

[15] *Thomas v. Kansas City, Missouri Police Dept.*, 2006 WL 27117 (W.D. Mo. 2006); *Nolan v. Police Commissioner of Boston*, 420 N.E.2d 335 (Mass. 1981).

[16] *Davis v. City of New York*, 2007 WL 2973695 (E.D. N.Y. 2007).

[17] *Mason v. Stock*, 869 F. Supp. 828 (D. Kan. 1994); *Landrum v. Board of Commissioners*, 685 So.2d 382 (La. App. 1996).

[18] *Flynn v. Sandahl*, 58 F.3d 83 (7th Cir. 1995).

[19] *Redmond v. City of Overland Park*, 672 F. Supp. 473 (D. Kan. 1987). In a more recent case, a federal court of appeals refused to allow a suit for damages against an officer's supervisor who had allegedly attempted to convince the officer's psychotherapist to change his diagnosis of the officer. The Court commented that "it was not clearly established that [the officer] had a constitutionally-protected right to autonomy in deciding to seek psychological counseling." *Shields v. Burge*, 874 F.2d 1201 (7th Cir. 1989). The case turned on the law of damages under the federal civil rights laws, which provide that no suit for damages under those laws is possible against a public official unless it can be established that the official's actions "violated clearly established statutory or constitutional rights of which a reasonable person would have known." *Harlow v. Fitzgerald*, 457 U.S. 800 (1982).

[20] *Fraternal Order of Police v. City of Philadelphia*, 812 F.2d 105 (3d Cir. 1987).

[21] The notion that the degree of compelled disclosure of medical information which is permissible may increase if the disclosure is sought in response to a particular incident has been accepted by other courts. *See Gutierrez v. Lynch*, 826 F.2d 1534 (6th Cir. 1987)(upholds ordinance requiring law enforcement officers on sick leave for more than 30 days to release medical information about their disability prior to return to work). In addition, if the medical information involves prior drug use, there may be even a greater diminishment of the officer's privacy interests in the information. *National Treasury Employees Union v. Department of Treasury*, 25 F.3d 237 (5th Cir. 1994).

[22] *New Jersey Transit PBA, Local 304 v. New Jersey Transit Corp.*, 895 A.2d 472 (N.J. Super. A.D. 2006).

[23] *White v. City of Boston*, 7 Mass.L.Rptr. 232 (Mass. Sup. 1997); *see Brumley v. Pena*, 62 F.3d 277 (8th Cir. 1995).

[24] 42 U.S.C. §12112(d).

[25] *Roe v. Cheyenne Mountain Conference Resort, Inc.*, 124 F.3d 1221 (10th Cir. 1997).

[26] *Pennsylvania State Troopers Ass'n v. Miller*, 2008 WL 4452469 (M.D. Pa. 2008).

[27] *Henthorn v. Olsten Corp.*, 5 WH Cas.2d 539 (N.D. Ill. 1999); *Kinchelow v. Robinson Property Group, L.P.*, 4 WH Cas.2d 987 (N.D. Miss. 1998). *See generally* W. Aitchison, *The FMLA: Understanding The Family & Medical Leave Act*, 108 (LRIS, 2003).

[28] *Joseph v. McCann*, 147 P.3d 547 (Utah App. 2006). *See Hafner v. Beck*, 916 P.2d 1105 (App. 1995); *Ervin v. American Guardian Life Assurance Co.*, 545 A.2d 354 (1988); *Keene v. Wiggins*, 138 Cal.Rptr. 3 (1977); *Johnston v. Sibley*, 558 S.W.2d 135 (Tex. App.1977).

[29] *Korostynski v. State of New Jersey*, 630 A.2d 342 (A.D. 1993); *Law Offices of W.A. Pangman v. Zellmer*, 473 N.W.2d 538 (Wis. App. 1991).

[30] *White v. Fraternal Order of Police*, 909 F.2d 512 (D.C. Cir. 1990); *Coughlin v. Westinghouse Broadcasting and Cable, Inc.*, 603 F. Supp. 377 (E.D. Pa. 1985); *Jones v. Jennings*, 788 P.2d 732 (Alaska 1990); *State of Hawai'i Organization of Police Officers v. Society of Professional Journalists*, 927 P.2d 386 (Haw. 1996); *Obiajulu v. City of Rochester*, 625 N.Y.S.2d 779 (N.Y. A.D. 1995); *Early v. The Toledo Blade*, 720 N.E.2d 107 (Ohio App. 1998); *Cowles Publishing Co. v. State Patrol*, 748 P.2d 597 (1988).

[31] *Bradshaw v. City of Los Angeles*, 270 Cal.Rptr. 711 (Cal. App. 1990); *see Worden v. Provo City*, 806 F. Supp. 1512 (D. Utah 1992)(right to privacy does not prohibit disclosure of disciplinary record and events surrounding officer's resignation).

[32] *Multimedia, Inc. v. Snowden*, 647 N.E.2d 1374 (Ohio App. 1995)(discipline and personnel records); *Lorain Journal Co. v. City of Lorain*, 9 IER Cases 443 (Ohio App. 1993)(polygraph records of applicants).

[33] *Bangor Publishing Co. v. City of Bangor*, 544 A.2d 733 (Me. 1988)(names of applicants for chief's job; applicants had been promised confidentiality by employer); *Barton v. Shupe*, 525 N.E.2d 812 (Ohio 1988)(internal investigation file; employer promised not to release file to public).

[34] *Jones v. City of Wilmington*, 299 F. Supp. 2d 380 (D. Del. 2004).

[35] *In re Grand Jury Subpoenas v. United States*, 40 F.3d 1096 (10th Cir. 1994)(*Garrity* statements obtainable by federal grand jury); *Flores v. City of New York*, 615 N.Y.S.2d 400 (A.D. 1994)(civilian review board records obtainable in civil litigation).

[36] *Moore v. Dormin*, 662 N.Y.S.2d 239 (N.Y. 1997).

[37] *Fettke v. City of Wichita*, 957 P.2d 409 (Kan. 1998).

[38] *State of Hawai'i Organization of Police Officers v. Society of Professional Journalists*, 927 P.2d 386 (Haw. 1996).

[39] *United States Department of Defense v. Federal Labor Relations Authority*, 510 U.S. 487 (1994).

[40] *Herald Co., Inc. v. Kent County Sheriff's Dept.*, 680 N.W.2d 529 (Mich. App. 2004); *State ex rel. Keller v. Cox*, 707 N.E.2d 931 (Ohio 1999); *see Motley v. Parks*, 2001 WL 682791 (Cal. App. 2001); *King County v. Sheehan*, 57 P.3d 307 (Wash. App. 2002).

[41] *Henderson v. City of Chattanooga*, 133 S.W.3d 192 (Tenn. App. 2003).

[42] *Kallstrom v. City of Columbus*, 136 F.3d 1055 (6th Cir. 1998); *see State ex rel. Keller v. Cox*, 707 N.E.2d 931 (Ohio 1999).

[43] *Barber v. Overton*, 496 F.3d 449 (6th Cir. 2007).

[44] *Cohen v. Newsom*, 2008 WL 2156995 (N.D. Cal. 2008).

[45] *Nation v. State Dept. of Correction*, 158 P.3d 953 (Idaho 2007).

[46] *National Treasury Employees Union v. Von Raab*, 489 U.S. 656 (1989). *See also Skinner v. Railway Labor Executives Association*, 489 U.S. 602 (1989).

[47] *National Treasury Employees Union v. Department of Treasury*, 25 F.3d 237 (5th Cir. 1994)(random testing of Customs Service employees); *Penny v. Kennedy*, 915 F.2d 1065 (6th Cir. 1990)(random testing of police officers and firefighters); *Guiney v. Roache*, 873 F.2d 1557 (1st Cir. 1989)(approves of random drug testing of officers who carry guns and those who participate in drug interdiction); *McKenna v. City of Philadelphia*, 771 F. Supp. 124 (E.D. Pa. 1991)(approves of mandatory drug testing for Philadelphia police returning from work-related disabilities; disapproves

of body cavity searches of same officers); *Brown v. City of Detroit*, 715 F. Supp. 832 (D. Mich. 1989)(approves of random drug testing for Detroit police); *Toal v. Ward*, 4 IER Cases 1842 (N.Y. Sup. 1989)(random testing of all uniformed New York City police officers); *Seelig v. Koehler*, 4 IER Cases 1538 (N.Y. A.D. 1989)(random testing of corrections officers approved); *Gdanski v. New York City Transit Authority*, 561 N.Y.S.2d 51 (A.D. 1990)(testing of officers returning from hospitalization); *McCloskey v. Honolulu Police Department,* 799 P.2d 953 (Haw. 1990)(random testing of police officers); *City of Annapolis v. United Food and Commercial Workers*, 565 A.2d 672 (Md. App. 1989)(testing of all police officers during annual physical). *But see AFGE v. Thornburgh*, 720 F. Supp. 154 (N.D. Cal. 1989)(random testing of all employees of Federal Bureau of Prisons not constitutional). In one case, a court approved of mandatory AIDS screening for firefighters, reasoning that the risk of HIV transmission in the performance of a firefighter's duties provided a compelling governmental reason for the testing. *Anonymous Fireman v. City of Willoughby*, 779 F. Supp. 402 (N.D. Ohio 1991).

Prior to the *Von Raab* decision, the vast majority of courts considering the issue had held random testing of law enforcement officers to be unconstitutional. *Lovvorn v. City of Chattanooga, Tennessee*, 846 F.2d 1539 (6th Cir. 1988); *Guiney v. Roache*, 686 F. Supp. 956 (D. Mass. 1988); *Policemen's Benevolent Association v. Township of Washington,* 672 F. Supp. 779 (D. N.J. 1987); *Taylor v. O'Grady*, 669 F. Supp. 1422 (N.D. Ill. 1987); *Feliciano v. City of Cleveland*, 661 F. Supp. 578 (N.D. Ohio 1987); *American Federation of Government Workers v. Weinberger*, 651 F. Supp. 726 (S.D. Ga. 1986); *Bostic v. McClendon*, 650 F. Supp. 245 (N.D. Ga. 1986); *Capua v. City of Plainfield*, 643 F. Supp. 1507 (D. N.J. 1986); *Penny v. Kennedy*, 648 F. Supp. 815 (E.D. Tenn. 1986); *Turner v. Fraternal Order of Police,* 500 A.2d 1005 (D.C. App. 1985); *City of Palm Bay v. Bauman*, 475 So.2d 1322 (Fla. App. 1985); *Allen v. County of Passaic*, 530 A.2d 371 (N.J. Sup. 1986); *Fraternal Order of Police v. City of Newark,* 524 A.2d 430 (N.J. A.D. 1987); *Seelig v. Koehler*, 1988 PEB ¶35,185 (N.Y. 1988)(CCH). Courts which upheld random drug testing for law enforcement officers included the following: *McDonell v. Hunter,* 809 F.2d 1302 (8th Cir. 1987)(corrections officers); *Mack v. United States FBI*, 653 F. Supp. 70 (S.D. N.Y. 1986)(FBI agents); *Wrightsell v. City of Chicago*, 678 F. Supp. 727 (N.D. Ill. 1988)(police officers; test given in course of annual physical); *Caruso v. Ward*, 530 N.E.2d 850 (N.Y. App. 1988)(members of special volunteer elite organized crime control bureau).

[48] *National Treasury Employees Union v. Customs Service*, 27 F.3d 623 (D.C. Cir. 1994)(civilian employees); *National Treasury Employees Union v. Department of Treasury,* 25 F.3d 237 (5th Cir. 1994)(civilian employees); *AFGE v. Roberts,* 9 F.3d 1464 (9th Cir. 1993)(prison employees); *National Treasury Employees Union v. Hallett*, 776 F. Supp. 680 (E.D. N.Y. 1991)(civilian employees).

[49] *Miller v. Vanderburgh County*, 610 N.E.2d 858 (Ind. App. 1993).

[50] *Ford v. Dowd*, 931 F.2d 1286 (8th Cir. 1991); *McDonnell v. Hunter,* 809 F.2d 1302 (8th Cir. 1987).

[51] *Delaraba v. Nassau County Police*, 632 N.E.2d 1251 (N.Y. App. 1994).

[52] *Jackson v. Gates*, 975 F.2d 648 (9th Cir. 1992)(case resulted in $150,000 verdict for officer); *Ford v. Dowd*, 931 F.2d 1286 (8th Cir. 1991); *McDonell v. Hunter*, 809 F.2d 1302 (8th Cir. 1987).

[53] *Razor v. New Orleans Dept. of Police*, 926 So.2d 1 (La. App. 2006).

[54] *Felder v. Kelly*, 619 N.Y.S.2d 46 (A.D. 1994).

55 *Giammarino v. Ward*, 555 N.Y.S.2d 359 (A.D. 1990).

56 *Copeland v. Philadelphia Police Department*, 840 F.2d 1139 (3d Cir. 1988)(even though girlfriend recanted her allegation, the drug test was upheld).

57 *Kinter v. Board of Fire and Police Commissioners of Palatine*, 550 N.E.2d 1126 (Ill. App. 1990).

58 *Fulcher v. Koehler*, 552 N.Y.S.2d 31 (A.D. 1990); *Candia v. City and County of San Francisco*, 2003 WL 22373886 (Cal. App. 2003).

59 *Jeffrey v. Koehler*, 561 N.Y.S.2d 417 (A.D. 1990); *Baldini v. Ward*, 550 N.Y.S.2d 645 (A.D. 1990).

60 *Miller v. Vanderburgh County*, 610 N.E.2d 858 (Ind. App. 1993).

61 *Martinez v. Ward*, 561 N.Y.S.2d 195 (A.D. 1990).

62 *Barreras v. New Mexico Corrections Dept.*, 838 P.2d 983 (N.M. 1992).

63 *Jackson v. Gates*, 975 F.2d 648 (9th Cir. 1992).

64 *Richard v. Lafayette Fire And Police Civil Service Bd.*, 983 So.2d 195 (La. App. 2008).

65 *National Treasury Employees Union v. Yeutter*, 918 F.2d 968 (D.C. Cir. 1990); *Kennedy v. New York*, 10 IER Cases 1174 (S.D. N.Y. 1995). *But see Byrne v. Massachusetts Bay Transportation Authority*, 196 F. Supp. 2d 77 (D. Mass. 2002).

66 *Kennedy v. New York City*, 10 IER Cases 1174 (S.D. N.Y. 1995).

67 *Seelig v. Koehler*, 556 N.Y.S.2d 832 (N.Y. App. 1990). A court in a different state has reached the contrary result that an officer subject to drug testing is not entitled to representation by counsel. *Corgiat v. Police Board of Chicago*, 614 N.E.2d 1232 (1993).

68 *Guiney v. Police Commissioner of Boston*, 582 N.E.2d 523 (Mass. 1991). *But see Holmes v. Owens*, 14 IER Cases 345 (Tenn. App. 1998)(random testing permissible under Tennessee Constitution).

69 *Anchorage Police Department Employees Association v. Municipality of Anchorage*, 24 P.3d 547 (Alaska 2001)(police and fire); *Petersen v. City of Mesa*, 83 P.3d 35 (Ariz. 2004)(firefighters).

70 *Smolicz v. Borough/Town of Naugatuck*, 2006 WL 2085291 (D. Conn. 2006).

71 *Ripley v. Lake City*, 218 Fed.Appx. 948 (11th Cir. 2007)(exigent circumstances).

72 *Shields v. Burge*, 874 F.2d 1201 (7th Cir. 1989).

73 *United States v. Taketa*, 923 F.2d 665 (9th Cir. 1991).

74 *PBA Local No. 38 v. Woodbridge Police Dept.*, 832 F. Supp. 808 (D. N.J. 1993)(no reasonable expectation of privacy in Department's telephone lines which were "beeped"); *State of Hawai'i v. Bonnell*, 856 P.2d 1265 (Haw. 1993)(reasonable expectation of privacy in break room); *Speer v. Ohio Dept. of Rehabilitation and Correction*, 624 N.E.2d 251 (Ohio App. 1993)(reasonable expectation of privacy in bathroom).

75 *Los Angeles Police Protective League v. Gates*, 907 F.2d 879 (9th Cir. 1990). The search of the sergeant's garage was pursuant to an "administrative warrant" based upon probable cause. The jury initially awarded more than $2.9 million in damages against the City and its officials. Rather than face a new trial, the sergeant accepted a judgment of $1.5 million. Because of questions concerning the immunity

of some of the Department's officials from damages, the appeals court sent the case back to the trial court for a reallocation of damages.

76 *Biehunik v. Felicetta*, 441 F.2d 228 (2d Cir. 1971).

77 *Los Angeles Police Protective League v. Gates*, 579 F. Supp. 36 (C.D. Cal. 1984).

78 *Kirkpatrick v. City of Los Angeles*, 803 F.2d 485 (9th Cir. 1986). *See also Proffit v. District of Columbia*, 790 F. Supp. 304 (D. D.C. 1991)(corrections officer who was suspected of involvement with drug trafficking was lawfully strip searched based on an anonymous tip that the officer would be reporting to work with an ounce of cocaine); *McKenna v. City of Philadelphia*, 771 F. Supp. 124 (E.D. Pa. 1991)(body cavity searches of officers returning from disability not permitted); *Scoby v. Neal*, 734 F. Supp. 837 (C.D. Ill. 1990)(rule requiring strip search of all correctional officers entering an institution struck down as violative of right to privacy); *Brown v. City of Detroit*, 94 Fire & Police Reporter 87-8 (Wayne Co., Mich. 1994)(employer consented to $975,000 judgment in favor of officers who had been strip searched). *See generally Security and Law Enforcement Employees v. Carey*, 737 F.2d 187 (2d Cir. 1984).

79 *McKenna v. City of Philadelphia*, 771 F. Supp. 124 (E.D. Pa. 1991).

80 *Anderson v. Department of Public Safety and Corrections*, 985 So.2d 160 (La. App. 2008); *see Allegheny County Prison Employees Independent Union v. County of Allegheny*, 315 F. Supp. 2d 728 (W.D. Pa. 2004).

81 *Westbrook v. City of Omaha*, 231 Fed.Appx. 519 (8th Cir. 2007).

82 *Fraternal Order of Police/Department of Corrections Labor Committee v. Washington*, 394 F. Supp. 2d 7 (D. D.C. 2005).

83 *Pennington v. Metropolitan Government of Nashville and Davidson County*, 511 F.3d 647 (6th Cir. 2008); *Reyes v. Maschmeier*, 446 F.3d 1199 (11th Cir. 2006).

84 *Driebel v. City of Milwaukee*, 298 F.3d 622 (7th Cir. 2002).

85 *United States v. Mendenhall*, 446 U.S. 544 (1980).

86 *Cerrone v. Brown*, 246 F.3d 194 (2d Cir. 2001).

87 *Terry v. Ohio*, 392 U.S. 1 (1968).

88 *Aguilera v. Baca*, 510 F.3d 1161 (9th Cir. 2007).

89 *Smith v. Department of General Services of PA*, 181 Fed.Appx. 327 (3d Cir. 2006), *citing Graham v. Connor*, 490 U.S. 386 (1989).

90 *Taysom v. Lilly*, 2000 WL 33710847 (D. Utah 2000).

91 *O'Connor v. Ortega*, 480 U.S. 709 (1987).

92 *United States v. Taketa*, 923 F.2d 665 (9th Cir. 1991).

93 *See Bambrick v. City of Philadelphia*, 1994 WL 649342 (E.D. Pa. 1994); *Chicago Fire Fighters Local No. 2 v. City of Chicago*, 717 F. Supp. 1314 (N.D. Ill. 1989)(reasonable suspicion not necessary for search of firefighter's locker); *Moore v. Constantine*, 574 N.Y.S.2d 507 (A.D. 1993)(no reasonable expectation of privacy in trooper's locker where supervisors routinely obtained access to the work-related contents of the locker). In one case, a court even approved of a warrantless search of an officer's gym bag on the grounds that the bag was placed in the officer's car, which he had impliedly granted his employer consent to search. *Gamble v. State*, 552 A.2d 928 (Md. App. 1989).

94 *Moore v. Constantine*, 574 N.Y.S.2d 507 (A.D. 1993).

[95] *Fraternal Order of Police/Department of Corrections Labor Committee v. Washington*, 394 F. Supp. 2d 7 (D. D.C. 2005).

[96] Owing to an unusual statutory scheme, some federal police officers challenging blanket locker searches may be required to exhaust the grievance procedure in their collective bargaining agreements before bringing a lawsuit alleging an illegal locker search. *Fraternal Order of Police v. United States Postal Service*, 988 F. Supp. 701 (S.D. N.Y. 1997).

[97] *Lowe v. City of Macon*, 720 F. Supp. 994 (M.D. Ga. 1989).

[98] *Shields v. Burge*, 874 F.2d 1201 (7th Cir. 1989). In refusing to allow the officer to sue for damages for the search of the desk as well as a search of a closed briefcase found in his department-issued car, the Court stressed that its decision might well have been different had the case arisen in a criminal law setting.

[99] §3309, Government Code of California.

[100] *Mullican v. City of Ontario*, 2004 WL 858721 (Cal. App. 2004).

[101] *Diana v. Oliphant*, 2007 WL 3491856 (M.D. Pa. 2007).

[102] *PBA Local No. 38 v. Woodbridge Police Dep't*, 832 F. Supp. 808 (D. N.J. 1993).

[103] *Abbott v. Village of Winthrop Harbor*, 953 F. Supp. 931 (N.D. Ill. 1996); *see Jandak v. Village of Brookfield*, 520 F. Supp. 814 (N.D. Ill. 1995).

[104] *Quon v. Arch Wireless Operating Co., Inc.*, 529 F.3d 892 (9th Cir. 2008).

[105] *Haynes v. Attorney General of Kan.*, 2005 WL 2704956 (D. Kan. 2005).

[106] *Hart v. Clearfield City, Davis County*, 815 F. Supp. 1544 (D. Utah 1993).

[107] *Bernhard v. City of Ontario*, 270 Fed.Appx. 518 (9th Cir. 2008), *quoting United States v. Falls*, 34 F.3d 674 (8th Cir. 1994); *see Trujillo v. City of Ontario*, 428 F. Supp. 2d 1094 (C.D. Cal. 2006).

[108] *Kohler v. City of Wapakoneta*, 381 F. Supp. 2d 692 (N.D. Ohio 2005).

[109] *Rosario v. U.S.*, 538 F. Supp. 2d 480 (D. P.R. 2008).

[110] *United States v. Taketa*, 923 F.2d 665 (9th Cir. 1991). *But cf. Moore v. Dormin*, 662 N.Y.S.2d 239 (N.Y. 1997)(use of hidden video camera in jail office used by many employees and occasionally cleaned by inmates does not violate right to privacy).

[111] *United States v. Taketa*, 923 F.2d 665 (9th Cir. 1991). In *Thorton v. University Civil Service Merit Board*, 507 N.E.2d 1262 (Ill. App. 1987), the Court upheld the use of a video camera in a police station which was designed to record an officer's conduct as part of a disciplinary (not criminal) investigation.

[112] The seminal theoretical discussion of the "right to be let alone" can be found in Griswold, *The Right To Be Let Alone*, 55 N.W.U.L.Rev. 216 (1960).

[113] *E.g., Duckworth v. Sayad*, 670 S.W.2d 88 (Mo. App. 1984). *See also Eisenstadt v. Baird,* 405 U.S. 438 (1972). A minority view is that the right to privacy only protects marital relationships. *See Baron v. Meloni*, 556 F. Supp. 796 (W.D. N.Y. 1983).

[114] *Ravin v. State*, 537 P.2d 494 (Alaska 1975).

[115] *E.g., Marcum v. Catron*, 70 F. Supp. 2d 728 (E.D. Ky. 1999); *Duckworth v. Sayad*, 670 S.W.2d 88 (Mo. App. 1984).

[116] *Shuman v. City of Philadelphia*, 470 F. Supp. 449 (E.D. Pa. 1979).

[117] *Thorne v. City of El Segundo*, 726 F.2d 459 (9th Cir. 1983). Though the law now seems settled that adulterous conduct, standing alone without any concomitant adverse impact on an officer's job is not a sufficient reason to discipline an officer, earlier cases split on the subject. The following cases all upheld the discipline of law enforcement officers for adulterous conduct. *Wilson v. Swing*, 463 F. Supp. 555 (M.D. N.C., 1978)(adulterous affair with another officer); *Steward v. Leary*, 293 N.Y.S.2d 573 (1968)(officer must be a model to be emulated); *Corwin v. Ellenville*, 415 N.Y.S.2d 299 (1979)(six instances of adulterous conduct); *Faust v. Police Civil Service Commission of Borough of State College*, 347 A.2d 765 (Pa.Cmwlth. 1975)(sexual misconduct encouraged disorder and fostered public fear); *Borough of Darby v. Coleman,* 407 A.2d 468 (Pa.Cmwlth. 1979)(adultery falls within the definition of "conduct unbecoming"); *Wolfe v. Sanders*, 110 S.E. 808 (1920)(officer who "deliberately violated the sanctity of another's home would be a reproach to decent government"). The following earlier cases all reversed the discipline of law enforcement officers for adulterous conduct. *Smith v. Price*, 616 F.2d 1371 (5th Cir. 1980)(conduct protected by right of privacy); *Shuman v. City of Philadelphia*, 470 F. Supp. 449 (E.D. Pa. 1979)(conduct within scope of right to privacy, and protected unless adverse effect on on-the-job performance); *Saunders v. Kennedy*, 159 N.Y.S.2d 113 (1957)(needs to be a relationship between conduct and inadequate job performance); *Risner v. State Personnel Board of Review*, 381 N.E.2d 346 (Ohio App. 1978)(standards for morality same for officers as for public).

[118] *Briggs v. North Muskegon Police Department*, 563 F. Supp. 585 (W.D. Mich. 1983), *aff'd*, 746 F.2d 1475 (6th Cir. 1984).

[119] *Major v. Hampton*, 413 F. Supp. 66 (E.D. La. 1976).

[120] *Thorne v. City of El Segundo*, 726 F.2d 459 (9th Cir. 1983).

[121] *Bruns v. Pomerleau*, 319 F. Supp. 58 (D. Md. 1970).

[122] *Battle v. Mulholland,* 439 F.2d 321 (5th Cir. 1971).

[123] *Oliverson v. West Valley City,* 875 F. Supp. 1465 (D. Utah 1995); *see Seegmiller v. LaVerkin City*, 528 F.3d 762 (10th Cir. 2008).

[124] *Singleton v. Cecil*, 176 F.3d 419 (8th Cir. 1999).

[125] *City of Sherman v. Henry*, 928 S.W.2d 464 (Tex. 1996).

[126] *Shawgo v. Spradlin*, 701 F.2d 470 (5th Cir. 1983); *Kukla v. Village of Antioch*, 647 F. Supp. 799 (N.D. Ill. 1986). *See also Swope v. Bratton*, 541 F. Supp. 99 (W.D. Ark. 1982).

[127] *Smith v. Price*, 446 F. Supp. 828 (M.D. Ga. 1977)(emphasis in original).

[128] *E.g., Fout v. California State Personnel Board*, 186 Cal.Rptr. 452 (Cal. App. 1982).

[129] *Mercer v. City of Cedar Rapids*, 308 F.3d 840 (8th Cir. 2002); *Puzick v. City of Colorado Springs*, 680 P.2d 1238 (Colo. App. 1988).

[130] *Sylvester v. Fogley*, 465 F.3d 851 (8th Cir. 2006).

[131] *Wieland v. City of Arnold*, 1000 F. Supp. 2d 984 (E.D. Mo. 2000).

[132] *Shuman v. City of Philadelphia*, 470 F. Supp. 449 (E.D. Pa. 1979).

[133] *Bowers v. Hardwick*, 478 U.S. 186 (1986).

[134] *Delahoussaye v. New Iberia*, 29 GERR 1050 (5th Cir. 1991); *Fleisher v. City of Signal Hill*, 829 F.2d 1491 (9th Cir. 1987). *See generally Truesdale v. University of North Carolina*, 371 S.E.2d 503 (N.C. App. 1988).

[135] *Childers v. Dallas Police Department*, 513 F. Supp. 134 (N.D. Tex. 1981).

136 *Padula v. Webster*, 822 F.2d 97 (D.C. Cir. 1987).

137 *Walls v. City of Petersburg*, 895 F.2d 188 (4th Cir. 1990).

138 *Dawson v. State Law Enforcement Division*, 7 IER Cases 629 (D. S.C. 1992).

139 *Lawrence v. Texas*, 539 U.S. 558 (2003).

140 *Saal v. Middendorf*, 427 F. Supp. 192 (N.D. Cal. 1977); *Society for Individual Rights, Inc. v. Hampton,* 63 F.R.D. 399 (N.D. Cal. 1973); *Norton v. Macy*, 417 F.2d 1161 (D.C. Cir. 1969). The cases involving the military's "don't ask, don't tell" policy provide elliptical support for the notion that one's homosexual status, standing alone, may not be the basis for discharge from employment. *See Able v. United States*, 155 F.3d 628 (2d Cir. 1998); *Holmes v. California Army National Guard*, 124 F.3d 1126 (9th Cir. 1997).

141 *Society for Individual Rights v. Hampton*, 63 F.R.D. 359 (N.D. Cal. 1973).

142 *City of Dallas v. England*, 846 S.W.2d 957 (Tex. App. 1993).

143 *Warren v. City of Asheville*, 328 S.E.2d 859, (N.C. App. 1985).

144 *Waters v. Chaffin*, 684 F.2d 833 (11th Cir. 1982).

145 *Dale v. City of Phillipsburg*, 50 FEP Cases 1737 (D. Kan. 1989).

146 *Briggs v. North Muskegon Police Dept.*, 563 F. Supp. 585 (W.D. Mich. 1983).

147 *Fabio v. Civil Service Commission of the City of Philadelphia*, 414 A.2d 82 (Pa. 1980).

148 *Hambsch v. Department of Treasury*, 796 F.2d 430 (D.C. Cir. 1986).

149 *Voorhees v. Shull*, 686 F. Supp. 389 (E.D. N.Y. 1987); *Philadelphia Lodge No. 5 v. City of Philadelphia*, 599 F. Supp. 254 (E.D. Pa. 1984); *Loughran v. Codd*, 432 F. Supp. 259 (E.D. N.Y. 1976); *Atterberry v. Police Commissioner of Boston*, 467 N.E.2d 150 (Mass. 1984).

150 *Crain v. Board of Police Commissioners of the Metropolitan Police Dept.*, 920 F.2d 1402 (8th Cir. 1990).

151 *Uryevick v. Rozzi*, 751 F. Supp. 1064 (E.D. N.Y. 1990).

152 *Pienta v. Village of Schaumburg, Illinois*, 710 F.2d 1258 (7th Cir. 1983).

153 *Kelley v. Johnson*, 425 U.S. 238 (1976).

154 *See also Weaver v. Henderson*, 984 F.2d 11 (1st Cir. 1993)(Court sustains ban on mustaches in state police agency); *Stradley v. Andersen*, 478 F.2d 188 (8th Cir. 1973)(hair length regulations); *Dake v. Bowen*, 521 N.Y.S.2d 345 (A.D. 1987)(Court sustains ban on mustaches in county sheriff's office).

155 *Rathert v. Village of Peotone*, 903 F.2d 510 (7th Cir. 1990); *see Zalewska v. County of Sullivan, New York*, 316 F.3d 314 (2d Cir. 2003)(employer can ban skirts without violating constitutional rights).

156 *Weaver v. Henderson*, 984 F.2d 11 (1st Cir. 1993).

157 *Inturri v. City of Hartford*, 165 Fed.Appx. 66 (2d Cir. 2006).

158 *City of Boerne v. Flores*, 521 U.S. 507 (1997).

159 *Potter v. District of Columbia*, 2007 WL 2892685 (D. D.C. 2007).

160 *Fraternal Order of Police v. City of Fort Lauderdale*, PEB ¶45,389 (Florida)(CCH, 1988)(grooming); *Fraternal Order of Police and Anne Arundel County*, Case No. 08-51355 (Simmeljkaer, 2008)(tattoos); *FOP Lodge No. 123 and*

City of Oklahoma City, No. 06-552-02 (2006)(tattoos); *Laurel Baye Healthcare of Lake Lanier*, 352 NLRB No. 30 (NLRB 2008)(tattoos). *See* discussion of mandatory subjects of bargaining in Chapter 2.

[161] *City of Pana*, PEB ¶49,055 (CCH, 1986).

[162] *City of Detroit and Detroit Police Officers Association*, (Brown, 1990)(unreported decision; copies available from LRIS).

[163] *Francis v. Keane,* 888 F. Supp. 568 (S.D. N.Y. 1995).

[164] Courts from the following states have upheld regulations on off-duty employment of law enforcement officers: **Arkansas**, *Dalton v. Russellville*, 720 S.W.2d 918 (Ark. 1986); **Illinois**, *Hayes v. Civil Service Commission of the City of Chicago*, 108 N.E.2d 505 (Ill. App. 1952); **Indiana**, *Fraternal Order of Police v. City of Evansville*, 559 N.E.2d 607 (Ind. 1990); **Massachusetts**, *Wilmarth v. Town of Georgetown*, 555 N.E.2d 597 (Mass. App. 1990); **Michigan**, *Allison v. City of Southfield*, 432 N.W.2d 369 (Mich. App. 1988); **Kentucky**, *Hopwood v. Paducah*, 424 S.W.2d 134 (Ky. 1968); **New Jersey**, *Isola v. Borough of Belmar*, 112 A.2d 738 (N.J. 1955) and *Hofbauer v. Board of Police Commissioners*, 44 A.2d 80 (N.J. 1945); **New York**, *Flood v. Kennedy*, 190 N.E.2d 13 (N.Y. 1963), *Trelfa v. Centre Island,* 389 N.Y.S.2d 22 (A.D. 1976); **North Carolina**, *Edwards v. City of Goldsboro*, 981 F. Supp. 406 (E.D. N.C. 1997); **Oregon**, *Cox v. McNamara*, 493 P.2d 54 (Or. App. 1972) and *Croft v. Lambert*, 357 P.2d 513 (Or. 1960); **South Dakota**, *Willard v. Civil Service Board of Sioux Falls*, 63 N.W.2d 801 (S.D. 1954); **Texas**, *Lombardino v. Civil Service Commission, City of San Antonio*, 310 S.W.2d 651 (Tex. App. 1958); **Virginia**, *Decker v. City of Hampton*, 741 F. Supp. 1223 (D. Va. 1990). Arbitrators have reached similar results. *See Town of Wethersfield*, PEB ¶45,340 (CCH, 1980)(upholds denial of request for off-duty work as an ambulance driver). A Louisiana court has struck down a similar regulation. *City of Crowley Firemen v. Crowley*, 280 So.2d 897 (La. 1973)(regulation applied to both police and fire). Another court has implied that blanket prohibitions on outside employment may be too overreaching to be enforced. *See Roper v. Versailles*, 436 A.2d 1058 (Pa. Cmwlth. 1981).

[165] *Isola v. Borough of Belmar,* 112 A.2d 738 (N.J. Sup. 1955); *see Ammon v. City of Coatesville*, 838 F.2d 1205 (3d Cir. 1988); *Rhodes v. Smith*, 254 S.E.2d 49 (S.C. 1979).

[166] *Bowman v. Township of Pennsauken*, 709 F. Supp. 1329 (N.J. 1989).

[167] *United States v. National Treasury Employees Union*, 513 U.S. 454 (1995); *Weicherding v. Riegel*, 160 F.3d 1139 (7th Cir. 1998).

[168] *Benelli v. City of New Orleans*, 478 So.2d 1370 (La. App. 1985).

[169] §1126, Government Code of California. *See Long Beach Police Officers Association v. City of Long Beach*, 759 P.2d 504 (Cal. 1988)(discusses application of off-duty employment statute to activities not specifically listed in statute).

[170] *Vaughn v. Lawrenceburg Power System*, 269 F.3d 703 (6th Cir. 2001).

[171] *Waters v. Gaston County*, 57 F.3d 422 (4th Cir. 1995); *Parks v. City of Warner Robins*, 43 F.3d 609 (11th Cir. 1995); *Brennan v. San Juan County Sheriff's Dept.*, 34 F.3d 1071 (9th Cir. 1994); *Parsons v. County of Del Norte*, 728 F.2d 1234 (9th Cir. 1984); *Collier v. Civil Service Commission*, 817 S.W.2d 404 (Tex. App. 1991). A rare case striking down an anti-nepotism rule is *State ex rel. Bloomingdale v. City of Fairborn,* 443 N.E.2d 181 (Ohio 1983), where the Court found the rule inconsistent with a civil service requirement that all job appointments be made on the basis of fitness and merit.

172 *Anderson v. City of LaVergne*, 371 F.3d 879 (6th Cir. 2004).

173 *Keeney v. Heath*, 57 F.3d 579 (7th Cir. 1995).

174 *See United States v. Guest*, 383 U.S. 745 (1966).

175 *E.g., Ahern v. Murphy*, 457 F.2d 363 (7th Cir. 1972); *Andre v. Board of Trustees of the Village of Maywood*, 561 F.2d 48 (7th Cir. 1977); *Wright v. City of Jackson, Mississippi*, 506 F.2d 900 (5th Cir. 1975); *Miller v. Krawczyk*, 414 F. Supp. 998 (E.D. Wis. 1976); *Marabuto v. Emeryville*, 183 Cal.App.2d 406 (1960); *Clinton Police Department Bargaining Unit v. City of Clinton*, 464 N.W.2d 875 (Iowa 1991)(residency within ten miles of place where officer reports for work); *Police Association of New Orleans v. New Orleans*, 649 So.2d 951 (La. 1995)(residency within city; only partial grandfathering of existing employees); *Detroit Police Officers' Association v. Detroit,* 190 N.W.2d 97 (Mich. 1971), appeal dismissed, 405 U.S. 950 (1971). *See generally* Policemen-Firemen Residency Requirements, 4 A.L.R. 4th 380 (1981).

176 *Denver v. Industrial Commission of the State of Colorado*, 666 P.2d 160 (Colo. App. 1983); *Smiley v. Winnfield Police Department*, 438 So.2d 680 (La. App. 1983); *Berg v. Minneapolis*, 143 N.W.2d 200 (Minn. 1966); *Quigley v. Blanchester*, 242 N.E.2d 589 (Ohio App. 1968); *Nevitt v. Board of Supervisors of Logan Township*, 379 A.2d 1072 (Pa.Cmwlth. 1977).

177 *McCarthy v. Philadelphia Civil Service Commission*, 424 U.S. 645 (1976). Following *McCarthy*, the following cases all upheld residency requirements for cities and counties. *Salem Blue Collar Workers Association v. City of Salem*, 33 F.3d 265 (3d Cir. 1994); *Grace v. City of Detroit*, 760 F. Supp. 646 (E.D. Mich. 1991); *Clinton Police Department Bargaining Unit v. City of Clinton*, 464 N.W.2d 875 (Iowa 1991); *Police Association of New Orleans v. City of New Orleans*, 649 So.2d 951 (La. 1995); *Seabrook Police Association v. Town of Seabrook*, 635 A.2d 1371 (N.H. 1993); *Morgan v. City of Wheeling*, 516 S.E.2d 48 (W.V. 1999).

178 *Walsh v. City and County of Honolulu*, 423 F. Supp. 2d 1094 (D. Haw. 2006)(pre-employment residency requirement); *Grace v. City of Detroit,* 760 F. Supp. 646 (E.D. Mich. 1991)(requirement that applicant be resident 60 days before filing application); *NAACP v. Town of Harrison*, 749 F. Supp. 1327 (D. N.J. 1990)(requirement that applicant be resident at time of application and appointment; 0.2% of city's residents were black); *Perez v. Personnel Board of Chicago,* 690 F. Supp. 670 (N.D. Ill. 1988); *Musto v. Redford Township*, 357 N.W.2d 791 (Mich. App. 1984).

179 *Buclary v. Borough of Northampton*, 1991 WL 133851 (E.D. Pa. 1991).

180 *Lewis v. City of Kinston*, 488 S.E.2d 274 (N.C. App. 1997).

181 *City of Ashland v. Ashland Fraternal Order of Police*, 888 S.W.2d 667 (Ky. 1994)(prohibition on city residency requirements); Revised Code of Washington §35.22.610 (prohibition on city residence requirements).

182 *County of Cook v. Illinois,* 807 N.E.2d 613 (Ill. App. 2004); *Carafano v. City of Bridgeport*, 196 Conn. 662 (1985); *Town of Lee v. LRC,* 485 N.E.2d 971 (Mass. App. 1985); *Detroit POA v. City of Detroit*, 215 N.W.2d 803 (Mich. 1974); *Murray v. City of Jennings*, 639 S.W.2d 220 (Mo. 1982); *Township of Moon v. Police Officers of Township of Moon*, 498 A.2d 1305 (Pa. 1985).

183 *Wolf v. City of Cleveland*, 2003 WL 2143779 (Ohio App. 2003).

CHAPTER 7

A LAW ENFORCEMENT OFFICER'S FREEDOM OF SPEECH RIGHTS

Public Employees And Free Speech.

For many years, it was thought to be well established that public employees, including law enforcement officers, had free speech rights roughly the same as other citizens. As the United States Supreme Court once held, a public employer may not condition public employment upon compliance with unconstitutional conditions of employment.[1] The Court observed in another case, if "the government could deny a benefit to a person because of his constitutionally protected speech...his exercise of that freedom would be penalized and inhibited."[2]

In 2006, the Supreme Court changed those well-established principles. Through the issuance of its opinion in *Garcetti v. Ceballos*, a case later termed a "revolution" in free speech law, the Supreme Court has made it clear that public employees in fact have virtually no free speech rights relating to their jobs, at least insofar as the speech is made while on duty. *Garcetti* imposed new tests for free speech cases involving public employees, and radically altered the law in the area.

The On-Duty/Off-Duty Distinction – The Threshold Question For Whether Speech Is Protected.

At issue in *Garcetti v. Ceballos* was whether the First Amendment protected a deputy district attorney who had been retaliated against for reporting to his superiors his suspicions that a deputy sheriff had falsified facts in search warrant applications. The Court began by signaling its intention to limit the scope of free speech protections for public employees by observing that the First Amendment "protects a public employee's right, in certain circumstances, to speak *as a citizen* addressing matters of public concern." If an employee is speaking "as a citizen," the Court found, the employee "must face only those speech restrictions that are necessary for their employers to operate efficiently and effectively." The Court acknowledged that there was "some possibility" that when employees speak as citizens, they will be protected by the First Amendment.

However, it is a different matter, the Court found, when public employees are speaking in the course of their jobs. In such cases, the Court concluded, "employees are not speaking as citizens for First Amendment purposes," and their speech is entirely unprotected by the First Amendment.[3] That means that, at least as far as the First Amendment is concerned, the employer is free to terminate, suspend, demote or transfer the employee because it does not like the employee's speech. Under *Garcetti*, it does not matter what the topic of the officer's speech is, or whether the speech is a matter of public concern. As one court put it, "Even if the speech is of great social importance, it is not protected by the First Amendment so long as it was made pursuant to the worker's official duties."[4]

These rules have already led law enforcement officers to seek protections for on-the-job speech in havens other than the First Amendment. Where the First Amendment might not be a bar to firing a police officer for engaging in speech the employer disfavors, the officer might well find protection in the discipline clause of a collective bargaining agreement, through a civil service system, or under a state whistleblowing statute.

Garcetti itself did not define when speech is made pursuant to official job duties. Courts have been quick to give a broad interpretation to when a law enforcement officer is speaking in the course of her duties and thus is not entitled to First Amendment protection for the speech. An officer's job description is not the end of the inquiry.[5] Instead, an officer's duties can range beyond what is written in the job description, and can include "*ad hoc* or *de facto* duties."[6] Similarly, the fact that the speech may have been made inside or outside of the workplace or that the speech concerned the employee's employment is not dispositive. Instead, whether the speech was made as an employee or as a private citizen entails an examination of the "content, form, and context" of the speech.[7]

Following these rules, courts have found that the following kinds of speech have all been made as part of an officer's job duties, and have cited *Garcetti* in holding that the speech has no First Amendment protections, and that an officer can constitutionally be disciplined for the speech:

- A report by a corrections officer to his supervisor that fellow corrections officers used excessive force on an inmate,[8] a police officer's report to his sergeant that other officers violated the law in their treatment of citizens,[9] and a police officer's report to his supervisors about the misconduct of fellow employees.[10]

- A statement by a police officer to the Police Chief that the Chief was involved in a cover-up of an underage drinking incident potentially involving the city manager.[11]

- Cooperation with an outside agency's investigation into potential corruption in the officer's own agency.[12]

- Concerns expressed by a sergeant to his commander as to whether an officer-involved shooting happened as described by the officers.[13]

- Reports by police firearms trainers through the chain of command about health and safety concerns concerning the firing range.[14]

- Statements made in the internal affairs process[15] or as part of other investigations.[16]

- A complaint by a police lieutenant that a commander and a captain had impeded a murder investigation,[17] and a report by a detective that members of a task force had tipped off suspects.[18]

- A statement by a collision investigation instructor working for the Pennsylvania State Police that a supervisor had changed the curriculum in a way that no longer complied with National Highway Transportation Safety Administration standards.[19]

- A canine officer's memoranda in opposition to cutbacks in the canine training program.[20]

- Statements made at a staff meeting,[21] or made to supervisors in the process of protesting a reorganization plan.[22]

- A tip to an officer in another unit about the location of a fugitive.[23]

- A report made through channels that the Police Chief was intoxicated during a police response.[24]

A Texas case provides a good example of the distinction between "speech as an employee" and "speech as a citizen." The case involved a police officer who posted information on a law enforcement-restricted website that gang activity might occur on specific dates in the future. The officer also complained to a district attorney that the officer's supervisors had destroyed a citation given to a politically-connected individual. A court found the former speech to be "speech as an employee," particularly since the officer was assigned to gang duties and was required to have a department-issued password to access the web page. The complaint to the district attorney, on the other hand, was speech as a citizen, and was not in the officer's official job responsibilities.[25]

A far-reaching case on what an officer's duties are for purpose of the *Garcetti* rule is *Nixon v. City of Houston*. *Nixon* involved an officer who, on his own and without instruction from his supervisors, went to the scene of an accident that followed a high-speed police chase. The officer sought, but did not obtain, permission from on-scene supervisors to speak to the press. Nonetheless, the officer spoke to reporters, said he was "embarrassed to be a police officer," and criticized his department's pursuit policy. A court found that the First Amendment did not prevent his discharge:

> "Under *Garcetti,* it is clear that Nixon's media statement at the scene of the accident is not protected by the First Amendment because it was made pursuant to his official duties and during the course of performing his job. Nixon spoke to the media while on duty, in uniform, and while working at the scene of the accident. Before he made the statement, he made an attempt to get the approval of a supervisor to do so. His statement was intended to inform the public of the circumstances of the high-speed chase, the subsequent accident, and HPD's high-speed chase policy. Quite simply, there is 'no relevant analogue to speech by citizens.' The fact that Nixon's statement was unauthorized by HPD and that speaking to the press was not part of his regular job duties is not dispositive – Nixon's statement was made while he was performing his job, and the fact that Nixon performed his job incorrectly, in an unauthorized manner, or in contravention of the wishes of his superiors does not convert his statement at the accident scene into protected citizen speech."[26]

Employers have argued that *Garcetti* should apply to speech made by union officials who also work for the employer. Courts have rejected those arguments, finding where statements are made on behalf of a law enforcement union, they are not part of the employee's job, and hence potentially have First Amendment protection.[27]

The Employee Speaking As A Citizen — Core Principles.

While employees who are speaking as citizens have, in the Supreme Court's words, "some possibility" of First Amendment protection, the Court has clearly narrowed the circumstances under which off-duty speech is constitutionally protected. The Court has made clear that public employees' off-duty free speech rights are not absolute, and that governmental employers "may impose certain restraints on the speech of their employees, restraints that would be unconstitutional if applied to the general public." [28]

In analyzing off-duty free speech cases, courts now follow a four-part test. First, courts determine whether the employee spoke about a matter of public concern.[29] If so, courts then balance the interests of the employee, as a citizen, in commenting upon matters of concern and the "interest of the State, as an employer, in promoting the efficiency of the public services it performs through its employees."[30] If the balance weighs in favor of the employee, courts then determine whether the protected speech was a "substantial or motivating factor in the adverse action against the employee."[31] Finally, if the employee establishes these factors, an employer is given the opportunity to show that it would have reached the same disciplinary decision even absent the employee's protected speech.[32]

The Supreme Court has clearly narrowed the circumstances under which even off-duty speech is constitutionally protected.

The Employee Speaking As A Citizen — When Is Speech A Matter Of Public Interest?

Speech is considered to be in the public interest if it can fairly be considered to relate to "any matter of political, social, or other concern to the community."[33] Within these broad standards, some general rules emerged to determine that if the speech concerns certain general subject matters, it is likely to be protected by the First Amendment. The following sections outline those general subject matters the rules govern.

Criticism Of The Chief Or Sheriff.

Perhaps the highest degree of protection is afforded to speech about the performance of a police chief or sheriff.[34] Particularly where the criticism is made to the governing body of the employer, the speech is likely to be protected by the

First Amendment.[35] Even where the criticism is directed to the media or is posted on a web page[36] rather than to the governing body, it is almost certain to be considered to be a matter of public interest.[37] As phrased by one court, "Speech which discloses any evidence of corruption, impropriety, or other malfeasance on the part of city officials, in terms of content, clearly concerns matters of public import."[38] Such speech, particularly where it takes the form of a vote of no confidence in the chief or sheriff, may also be protected as "concerted activity" under state or local labor laws.[39] Similarly, campaigning for a political candidate constitutes protected speech,[40] as is an announcement that a deputy intends to run against the incumbent sheriff.[41]

Speech About The Governing Body Of The Employer.

Speech which criticizes the governing body itself or the governing body's relationship with the law enforcement agency, is entitled to a high degree of protection under the First Amendment.

Speech which criticizes the governing body itself or the governing body's relationship with the law enforcement agency, even that which entails work in a campaign to recall a city council member or county commissioner, is entitled to a high degree of protection under the First Amendment.[42] Similarly, speech in which an officer encourages members of the public to attend meetings of the governing body to speak out about their law enforcement concerns is almost certainly protected under the First Amendment.[43] In one notable case, a court found that a city violated a police chief's constitutional rights by terminating him in retaliation for his public expression of concern that some candidates for city council were convicted felons.[44]

Discussion Of The Department's Budget Or Personnel Practices.

Also clearly entitled to protection is speech about the budgetary priorities of either the law enforcement agency or the entire local governmental body, at least to the extent the speech addresses broad budgetary priorities.[45] As well, speech alleging a misappropriation of public funds concerns a matter of public importance.[46] As is the case with speech about the performance of a chief or sheriff, unless an officer's comments about a budget or use of funds are completely false and result in significant disruption in the law enforcement agency, they are likely to be completely protected. Thus, courts have held that the First Amendment protects public comments on a residency ordinance [47] and comments critical of a department's affirmative action plan.[48]

Speech About Departmental Procedures.

A law enforcement officer's speech about departmental procedures, so long as the speech is made off duty and does not compromise ongoing investigations, is accorded a high level of protection. Such protected speech has included the following:

- Speech about the allocation of an agency's patrol force.[49]

- Comments on the need for or the effects of a reorganization in the department[50] or the prosecutor's office.[51]

- Discussion of alleged misconduct in the police department.[52]

- Criticism of the workings of the employee assistance program.[53]

- Protests about the imposition of a ticket quota system.[54]

- Criticism of the capabilities of a bomb squad to respond to emergencies safely and adequately.[55]

- Criticism of the deployment of personnel.[56]

- An evaluation of the department's overall capabilities.[57]

- Criticism of a proposed merger of a department's youth program with another program.[58]

A theme running through many of these cases is that statements about workplace safety in a law enforcement environment are generally thought to be about matters of public concern.[59] This theme is so strong that one court has even ruled that criticism of a police department's lax enforcement of a law forbidding smoking in the workplace was about a matter of public concern.[60]

An unusual case involved the Police Chief of Starkville, Mississippi, who, through the process of significantly modernizing his department, became embroiled in a dispute with his city council. The council hired a special investigator to reinvestigate a three-year-old unsolved homicide. When the city council later announced that the special investigation resulted in a "logical suspect being identified," the press asked the Chief for his reaction. The Chief responded by saying: "I have been denied being a part of the investigation and denied access to the investigative report. I think I was denied access to the report because it is totally inaccurate and they know I can point out inconsistencies." The council reacted by firing the Chief, who subsequently sued for violation of his free speech rights. In ordering the Chief reinstated with full back pay, a federal court commented on the public importance of certain investigative procedures:

> "The public criticisms [the chief] raised with respect to the independent investigative findings clearly spoke to a matter of public concern. If nothing else, [the council's] issuance of a press release announcing the completion of the independent investigation of the yet unsolved murder case plunged the matter into the public domain."[61]

Speech About The Justice System.

Speech about the justice system is also given a high degree of protection under the First Amendment. In one case, a court held that a deputy sheriff who wrote a pre-sentence letter to a judge on behalf of a suspect had engaged in protected speech, and upheld a judgment of $127,000 in favor of the deputy.[62] In another case, a deputy sheriff in Georgia was fired after publicly complaining that the Sheriff allowed contact visits between male and female inmates, permitted inmates with suspended licenses to drive, and allowed on-duty deputies to gather oysters for parties thrown by the Sheriff and his political supporters. The Court found that these allegations concerned matters of public interest which, if "largely true, are likely to enjoy protection."[63] In similar cases, courts have held protected statements about the lack of security in a jail,[64] pervasive sexual harassment of female officers by male inmates of a correctional facility,[65] a complaint to a district attorney about the performance of a sheriff,[66] and an officer's decision to bring a lawsuit alleging nepotism in his police department.[67]

Testimony In Court.

The post-*Garcetti* law is still evolving as to whether truthful testimony in court by a law enforcement officer is "speech as a citizen" or is speech made pursuant to the officer's job responsibilities. The majority rule seems to be that truthful testimony is "speech as a citizen" and protected by the First Amendment. In a case involving the Atlantic City Police Department, a federal appeals court reasoned:

> "It is axiomatic that every citizen owes to his society the duty of giving testimony to aid in the enforcement of the law. The Supreme Court has relied on this principle in rejecting attempts by citizens, regardless of their role in our society, to circumvent their obligation to comply with judicial process. We have acknowledged the importance of this same principle when evaluating First Amendment retaliation claims. We find persuasive a sister court's reasoning that testimony is offered in a context that is inherently of public concern. Employees either could testify truthfully and lose their jobs or could lie to the tribunal and protect their job security."[68]

In a far-reaching case, a federal appeals court sided with a Pittsburgh police officer who wanted to testify as an expert witness in excessive force cases, including one brought against his own department. The Court found that the Department's rules – which allowed it to restrict any of its employees from testifying as expert witnesses – were overbroad and too far-reaching. The Court found that "court testimony, whether compelled or voluntary, is always a matter of public concern."[69] In an analogous case, another federal appeals court ruled that instructors in a police academy had been unlawfully retaliated against in violation of the First Amendment because of their testimony as experts against police in excessive force cases.[70]

A case out of Miami is to the contrary. The officer had testified before a grand jury that SWAT team members had planted evidence at the scene of a shooting, and claimed that he was later retaliated against because of his testimony. Almost in passing, a court found the testimony unprotected by the First Amendment, commenting: "In accordance with the Police Department's regulations, and the officer's obligations as a State-certified law enforcement officer, the officer's subpoenaed grand jury testimony occurred pursuant to his official duties as a police officer for the City of Miami Police Department, and was not speech as a private citizen."[71]

Filing Lawsuits.

The activity of filing a lawsuit is given a high degree of protection under the First Amendment. The right to "petition" all branches of government, including the courts, has been described by the Supreme Court as "among the most precious of the liberties safeguarded by the Bill of Rights."[72] Only if the litigation is completely baseless is an employer likely to prevail where it has taken adverse action against the employee because the employee filed a lawsuit against it.[73]

The right to petition is not merely limited to lawsuits filed in court. In general, the petition clause protects against retaliation for "filing non-sham lawsuits, grievances, and other petitions directed at the government or its officials.[74] The right to petition even extends to cover administrative proceedings such as workers' compensation claims.[75]

Speech About Departmental Morale.

Also likely to be protected is a law enforcement officer's speech about department morale. Such speech may be more protected if it is made through the chain of command, but is entitled to considerable protection no matter how it is made.[76]

In one of the leading cases in the area, the president of the Baltimore City Police Union was suspended for 12 months for violating Police Department regulations. The basis for the suspension was the officer's public criticism of the Department in a television interview where he said there were problems in the Department's reporting and patrol procedures, that the Department's morale had "hit its lowest ebb" and that if the situation continued, "the bottom is going to fall out of the City." The Court found the officer's speech to be protected and reversed the officer's suspension. The Court noted that nothing the officer said was shown to be false and that the officer's fitness to perform his daily police duties was not impaired. The Court stressed the fact that the officer's statements were not directed towards a superior with whom he would come into daily or frequent contact and did not affect the discipline, harmony, or the general efficiency or effectiveness of the police department.[77]

Also likely to be protected is a law enforcement officer's speech about department morale, which may be more protected if it is made through the chain of command, but is entitled to considerable protection no matter how it is made.

Speech About Union Issues.

A law
enforcement
officer's
speech about
union issues is
entitled to wide
protection,
even if the
speech offends
or otherwise
disturbs the
employer.

A law enforcement officer's speech about union issues is entitled to wide protection, even if the speech offends or otherwise disturbs the employer.[78] While the fact that speech is related to union matters is no *guarantee* of First Amendment protection, "that fact does point in the direction of finding that the speech involved a matter of public concern," and weighs "heavily in the public concern calculus."[79] Such speech can also be protected under state labor laws. In one case, for example, a court found a web site criticizing the Police Chief to be protected activity under a collective bargaining law.[80]

For example, in one case a probationary police officer serving as union president was fired after publicly protesting the City's decision not to award a pay raise to officers. Even though the officer would normally be thought to have little job protection as a probationary employee in a state without mandatory collective bargaining, the Court nonetheless reversed the officer's discharge and ordered him reinstated with full back pay. The Court noted that it had "no difficulty" concluding that the officer's statements concerning the pay raise were protected speech:

> "[The officer's] speech dealt with the rate of compensation for members of the city's police force and, more generally, with the working relationship between the police union and elected city officials. First, compensation levels undoubtedly affect the ability of the city to attract and retain qualified police personnel, and the competency of the police force is surely a matter of great public concern. Second, the interrelationship between city management and its employees is closely connected with 'discipline and morale in the workplace' – factors that 'are related to an agency's efficient performance of its duties.' * * * Third, the way in which an elected official or his appointed surrogates deal with diverse and sometimes opposing viewpoints from within government is an important attribute of public service about which the members of society are entitled to know. Finally, [the officer's] speech was specifically and purposefully directed to the public both through city council meetings and a television interview."[81]

In another case, a probationary police officer was fired after he advocated that "blue flu" might be a way of exerting pressure for a wage increase for the members of the Police Department.[82] The Court ruled that the officer's statements could not be the basis for disciplinary action in the absence of concrete evidence of harm to the Police Department resulting from the statements. The Court held that vague statements by the Police Chief expressing concern about "the potential for leading to a conspiracy to engage in blue flu" was not sufficient to show actual harm to the Police Department:

> "As the Supreme Court has reaffirmed since *Pickering*, public employees do not forswear the protections of the Constitution simply by swearing to uphold the Constitution. Public employers are fully justified in protecting the integrity of their work force and

in maintaining the efficiency of individual employees; but such legitimate missions cannot be used as an excuse to rid their work force of an employee simply because he has exercised the rights guaranteed by fundamental law. In each case, reviewing courts must set what was done in the context of contemporaneous events and reasons, to make sure that a true balance is struck between the responsibilities of public employers and the rights of their employees. Applied to this case, that process clearly precludes judicial sanction of the action taken against [the officer]."[83]

Speech about union matters can be impolite, even offensive, and still be protected by the First Amendment. For example, in *Chico Police Officers' Association v. City of Chico,* the president of a police union was disciplined after a newsletter was posted on a bulletin board in the police station. The newsletter, entitled "The Centurion," referred to the "Chief and his lackeys," and commented on ongoing contract negotiations as follows:

"The Centurion reminds you that the Chief is standing between you and a contract, with his hands in your back pockets; squeezing your wallet on one side, trying to take your 4/10 on the other side, and all this while you thought you were simply getting – uh, the shaft. Resist for now the temptation to revolt."

The Court found that the statements in the newsletter concerned two matters of public importance, labor negotiations and the relationship between the Chief and his subordinates. In the absence of concrete harm resulting from the publication of the newsletter, the Court found the statements in the newsletter to be protected by the First Amendment.[84] Even if statements in union newsletters are not protected under the First Amendment, they may well be protected expression under state labor laws giving unions the right to represent employees.[85]

Mixed results exist as to whether law enforcement associations have a free speech right to solicit funds through appeals to the public. Some courts strike down such bans, finding the solicitation of funds to be an integral part of the protected activities engaged in by the law enforcement association. Other courts uphold the bans on solicitation, reasoning that "solicitation of advertisements to benefit law enforcement is inherently coercive because the persons solicited will experience pressure to purchase an advertisement, so that their support of law enforcement will become known to police or so that their failure to buy an advertisement will be noticed."[86] General restrictions on telephone solicitations, such as the statutes creating the national "Do Not Call" lists, have been upheld as constitutional.[87]

Speech About Areas Within The Employee's Expertise.

The Supreme Court has struck down a prohibition on lower-level federal employees accepting honoraria for speeches and writing articles. The Court held that the government was required to show that the interests of both potential audiences and the employees themselves were outweighed by the actual impact of the speech on the operation of government.[88] In an analogous case, a federal court of appeals ruled unconstitutional the State of Texas' ban on employees serving as expert witnesses on behalf of parties suing the State, finding that the ban inappropriately restricted speech on matters of public concern, and that the State's desire to prevent employees from acting against its interests was overridden by the free speech rights of the employees.[89] Similarly, a sergeant's efforts to conduct concealed weapons classes while off duty was held to be constitutionally protected.[90]

Speech About Alleged Discrimination.

Courts give a curious treatment to speech about alleged discrimination or harassment. If the speech is on a "macro" level – that is, if it involves claims of systemic discrimination on the part of an agency – the speech is given very high protection.[91] However, if the speech is only about harassment of an individual employee, it is much less likely to be protected.[92]

The leading case on speech about widespread discrimination is *Leonard v. City of Columbus*, which involved a series of protests by black officers alleging racial discrimination within the Columbus Police Department. The protests culminated in some of the officers picketing the Department while in uniform and off duty. During the picketing, the officers removed an American flag emblem from the sleeves of their uniforms. The Court, reversing the discharges of the officers, held that the removal of the patches constituted symbolic speech protected by the First Amendment, and noted as follows:

> "The conduct of the officers involved no violence or disorder: they peacefully removed the American flag from their uniforms. Representing as it does precepts fundamental to this nation, the American flag frequently has been the focal point of suits involving freedom of expression. Significantly, the officers in no way mutilated or defaced the flag; rather in their view they expressed their deep respect for it and the principles it represented. * * * Appellants sought to emphasize a widely-held perception of racially discriminatory practices in the City of Columbus Police force. These practices concerned not only internal police matters, but matters of interest to the community-at-large as well."[93]

In another case, a court held protected a letter prepared by a black officers' association stating that "supervisors are attempting to target, categorize, and defame black officers who exhibit any form of leadership qualities."[94] Courts have also held protected by the First Amendment complaints about racial epithets used by officers against members of the local African-American community,[95] a letter directed to the chief about increasing bigotry towards Spanish-speaking officers,[96] complaints about racial or gender-based promotional decisions,[97] testimony before a public safety committee that a police department was anti-Semitic and has systemic racism,[98] objections raised by an officer to the police chief injecting religion into work-related decisions,[99] a protest that only African-American employees were invited to a meeting,[100] the publication of racial slurs made by a police chief,[101] complaints about supervisory toleration of harassment of whistleblowers, and a pregnancy-discrimination complaint filed by a town's first woman police officer.[102]

Less free speech protection is accorded to complaints about individual harassment. Though the law is still unsettled in the area, it is still evolving in the direction that individual harassment complaints may not be protected by the First Amendment.[103] Some courts seem reluctant to follow this trend, and still find public interest inherent in, and thus First Amendment protection accorded to, complaints of harassment on the grounds that such complaints seek to expose "improper operations of the government or question the integrity of governmental officials."[104]

Speech Made In Private Or Unrelated To The Job.

The law is hugely in flux as to the degree of protection given to off-duty speech unrelated to the job. For many years, it was thought that if an officer's statements are made privately under circumstances where they could not reasonably be expected to be publicized, the statements are likely to be protected by the First Amendment regardless of their nature.[105] For example, in one case an off-duty police captain was drinking in a bar with a fellow employee he believed to be his friend. The captain described the Chief as a "son of a bitch, a bastard, and as sorry as they come and nothing but a back-stabbing son of a bitch." When the fellow employee promptly reported these comments to the Chief, the captain was disciplined. The Court, in reversing the discipline, was clearly skeptical about the Department's reasons for being interested in regulating such speech:

> "On one side, we have an off-duty police officer who was merely bellyaching about his job over drinks. On the other hand, we have a police department whose asserted interests in suppressing the speech do not fully withstand scrutiny."[106]

The law seems to have changed, though, with the Supreme Court's 2004 decision in *City of San Diego v. Roe*.[107] In *Roe*, a police officer with the City of San Diego, California, made a video of himself stripping off a police uniform and masturbating. He sold copies on eBay, under a user name of Codestud3@aol. com. The uniform was not the specific uniform worn by San Diego police officers, and Roe did not identify himself as a San Diego police officer (though he did sell "uniforms of the San Diego Police Department" along with other items of police equipment). The Supreme Court upheld the City's decision to terminate Roe, finding that Roe's activity related to his employment. The Court observed that "Roe's activities did nothing to inform the public about any aspect of the Department's functioning or operation. Roe's expression was widely broadcast, linked to his official status as a police officer, and designed to exploit his employ-

The law is hugely in flux as to the degree of protection given to off-duty speech unrelated to the job.

er's image. The speech in question was detrimental to the mission and functions of the employer."

Thus far, the application of *Roe* has been confined to somewhat similar fact situations. For example, one court upheld the discharge of an Arizona police officer who maintained a web page selling adult videos featuring both himself and, more prominently, his wife.[108] Even though the officer's web page made no reference whatsoever to the fact that he worked as a police officer, the Court reasoned that "the public expects officers to behave with a high level of propriety, and, unsurprisingly, is outraged when they do not do so. The law and their own safety demands that they be given a degree of respect, and the sleazy activities of [the officer and his wife] could not help but undermine that respect." In a similar case, a Florida court upheld the termination of deputies for participating for compensation in sexually explicit photographs and videos available for paid viewing on the Internet. The Court concluded that the deputies' "expressive conduct does not involve a matter of public concern and could affect the efficiency and reputation of the Sheriff's Office regarding the public."[109]

What this line of recent cases suggests is that governmental employers have broader latitude to regulate the off-duty, non-job-related speech than had otherwise been thought to be the case.

Whistleblowing Speech.

The *Garcetti* decision, discussed earlier in this chapter, has significant ramifications in the protection of whistleblowing speech. For many years, speech about corruption or criminal activity within the officer's law enforcement agency was very likely to be given protection by the First Amendment.[110] As one court noted:

> "It would be absurd to hold that the First Amendment generally authorizes corrupt officials to punish subordinates who blow the whistle simply because their speech somewhat 'disrupted the office.' Thus, an employee's First Amendment interest is entitled to more weight where he is acting as a whistle-blower exposing government corruption."[111]

Garcetti, however, allows an employer to retaliate against an employee's whistleblowing speech so long as the speech was made as part of an employee's job. What follows are examples of speech of a whistleblowing nature that were held to be protected by the First Amendment, but where *Garcetti* now makes it unlikely that the speech would have any constitutional protection:

- Statements made in connection with an officer's investigation of a fellow law enforcement officer's conduct of buying previously-leased employer vehicles at below market value.[112]

- A complaint about improprieties in the finances of a special investigations unit.[113]

- A complaint that fellow officers had used excessive force.[114]

- A police officer's speech voicing a speculative belief that the police chief could have stolen money from the evidence room.[115]

- A report alleging brutality by another officer.[116]

- Where sheriff's deputies disclosed to other law enforcement agencies that they believed that their supervisors knew that a co-worker was stealing narcotics for his personal use.[117]

- A statement by an internal affairs investigator that she believed an officer had been dishonest in testimony.[118]

- Complaints that officers had falsified reports.[119]

- A complaint about corruption and racism in a police department.[120]

- Where an officer complained of the behavior of a fellow officer who, while transporting a female prisoner on a train, allowed her to have the run of the train, unhandcuffed, have sex, drink, and consume drugs.[121]

- The raising through channels of other officers' receipt of illegal gifts.[122]

- Cooperation with an external corruption investigation into the officer's own department,[123] or the internal investigation of corruption.[124]

- Allegations that a supervisor used his authority to coerce employees to buy vehicles from his wife's car dealership.[125]

- The raising through channels of a complaint about sexual harassment and the falsification of time cards.[126]

In all of these situations, the employee could constitutionally be disciplined for making the speech. This is not to say that speech of this nature is entirely unprotected. *Garcetti* only interprets and applies the First Amendment. It is completely possible, if not likely, that while this sort of speech may not be constitutionally protected, it may be protected by a statute prohibiting discrimination against whistleblowers.[127] Many states have strengthened the protections granted whistleblowers by enacting statutes containing specific guarantees. States with whistleblowing statutes include Alaska, Arizona, Arkansas, California, Colorado, Connecticut, Delaware, Florida, Georgia, Hawai'i, Illinois, Indiana, Iowa, Kansas, Kentucky, Louisiana, Maine, Maryland, Massachusetts, Michigan, Minnesota, Mississippi, Missouri, Montana, Nebraska, Nevada, New Hampshire, New Jersey, New York, North Carolina, North Dakota, Ohio, Oklahoma, Pennsylvania, Rhode Island, South Carolina, South Dakota, Tennessee, Texas, Utah, Vermont, Washington, West Virginia, and Wisconsin.[128]

Though the standards vary from state to state, central to a successful claim under most whistleblower statutes is that the employee show that discipline or some other material change in working conditions[129] resulted from the employee's reporting of a violation of the law – that is, that there be an element of retaliation against the employee for publicly reporting illegal conduct. The employee need only have a "reasonable belief" that illegal conduct has occurred, and need not have absolute proof of the illegality.[130] As one court put it, to require proof that an actual violation of the law occurred before whistleblower protection existed would require "each whistleblower to become equal parts policeman, prosecutor, judge and jury. A whistleblower could never be certain that a statute has actually been violated until the perpetrator was found guilty in court."[131] Protection of whistleblowing speech is no less vigorous if the officer reports the violation of the law to an outside law enforcement agency or through channels in the officer's own department.[132]

Whistleblowing statutes do have different standards depending upon how they are written. Pennsylvania, for example, gives whistleblowing protection to employees who report not just crimes, but also "waste and wrongdoing."[133] In New Jersey, the speech must concern a "clear mandate of public policy" to be protected by the whistleblower law.[134] In some states, the officer is required to report the violation of the law to some law enforcement agency, and will not be entitled to whistleblower protection by merely holding a press conference exposing the violation,[135] where in other states internal reports of illegal conduct suffice to trigger whistleblower protections.[136] If the employee fails to raise the alleged violation of law until after discipline has been imposed, the employee will have no claim under a whistleblower statute.[137] Also, whistleblower laws typically do not protect statements about flawed departmental policies or decisions where the statements do not allege a violation of the law.[138] Additionally, in some states, whistleblowing statutes require an employee to exhaust all administrative and contractual remedies before bringing a lawsuit under the statute,[139] and may as well have very abbreviated statutes of limitations.[140]

Artistic Speech.

Regardless of its content, artistic speech is accorded a high degree of protection under the First Amendment. Such protected speech by law enforcement officers has ranged from appearing in "blackface" during a stage show[141] to the writing of poems critical of city management.[142] However, it is possible for artistic speech to be unprotected if it goes too far. For example, in one case a court upheld the discipline of an officer who drew cartoons depicting other officers as rats, and showing the rats engaged in a variety of sexual behaviors which was linked to the ability of the rats to be promoted.[143]

It is possible for artistic speech to be unprotected if it goes too far.

The Employee Speaking As A Citizen — When Do The Employer's Interests Override Those Of The Employee?

Speech Which Is Disruptive To The Organization.

The most difficult free speech cases with which the courts grapple are those where the speech is about matters of public importance, but where the speech also causes significant disruption in the law enforcement or other public agency. The courts have clearly been concerned that the "disruption" factor in the *Pickering* balancing test could be inappropriately claimed as a basis for disciplining an employee for otherwise protected speech. For example, in one case the Supreme Court dealt with the discharge of a probationary civilian employee of a sheriff's office who had expressed dismay to a co-worker that the assassination attempt on President Reagan had failed. The Court rejected the employer's argument that the comments caused disruption in the workplace, and held that the employee's free speech rights were paramount to the employer's interests.[144]

In a separate case, *Connick v. Myers*, the Supreme Court dealt with the case of an employee who was fired for circulating a questionnaire throughout her office. The Court found that the employee's speech was not entitled to protection because, in part, it disrupted the office, undermined the employee's supervisor's authority, and destroyed close working relationships.[145] The Supreme Court narrowed the "disruption" factor, however, by emphasizing that all but one of the questions on the questionnaire dealt with issues pertaining to the employee's personal grievances rather than matters of public concern, and stressing that employers would be required to make an even "stronger showing" of disruption in cases where the speech dealt more directly with issues of public concern. Most courts applying the *Connick* rationale have also given a narrow reading to the disruption factor, commenting, for example, that "real, not imagined, disruption is required," and the close working relationship exception cannot serve as a pretext for stifling legitimate speech.[146]

Some courts, though, require only a minimum of potential disruption before an employer may discipline a law enforcement officer. In one case, a police officer was disciplined for stating in the presence of a subordinate who had been caught speeding that if a high-ranking officer had been speeding, the Department would have taken no action. The Court upheld the discipline of the officer, finding that the officer's statements "planted the seed of dissension by implying that officers of varying ranks received disparate treatment." The Court was not troubled by the fact that no actual disruption of the working of the Department resulted from the officer's statements, and instead pointed to the importance of camaraderie and close working relationships in a police department in order to fulfill the depart-

Some courts require only a minimum of potential disruption before an employer may discipline a law enforcement officer.

ment's responsibilities.[147] Other cases in which courts have found disruption in the workplace resulting from speech include the following:

- Where an officer encouraged his fellow officers to surreptitiously tape record supervisors in the hopes of obtaining evidence of bargaining law violations.[148]

- Where an officer made unauthorized and inaccurate statements to the press about a shooting.[149]

- Where a watch commander wrote a letter alleging that a city's community policing was designed only to benefit minorities.[150]

- When an officer protested the failure of his department to promote him.[151]

Statements Made As An Extension Of A Personal Grievance Or Concern.

Some statements which are facially about matters of public interest may not be protected by the First Amendment if the real basis for the statements is a personal grievance between the employee and the employer which has nothing to do with matters of public interest.[152] A good example involved a detective with the Boulder, Colorado Police Department who responded to the Jon Benet Ramsey murder. While she was involved in the investigation, and continuing for some period of time following her removal from the case by the Police Chief, the detective and other officers involved in the investigation were widely criticized in the media. The detective protested the gag order prohibiting anyone in the Department from speaking to the media about the Ramsey investigation. Later, the detective retained an attorney who demanded that the detective be allowed to defend herself in the media, or that the Chief come to her defense. When the Chief declined both requests, the detective brought a free speech lawsuit against the Department.

A federal appeals court dismissed the lawsuit, finding that the issue was not a matter of public interest, but was instead a purely personal concern:

> "The detective argues that, even if the content of her speech primarily sought to restore her personal reputation, the performance and integrity of a highly visible public official necessarily is a matter of public concern. While we agree that the performance and integrity of a public official could be a matter of public concern, that is not always so. The fact that she was a police detective working on a murder investigation which had garnered tremendous media attention does not alone transform her speech designed to refute media criticisms of her personal, individual competence in that particular investigation into speech on a matter of public concern."[153]

In a similar case from an analytical standpoint, a court found unprotected by the First Amendment a police officer's complaints to the mayor about a requirement for electronic deposit of payroll checks. The officer issued probable cause affidavits against the town treasurer and a bank employee for "theft" from each of the officer's paychecks of the $5.00 fee for cashier's checks the officer requested from the bank. The Court found that the officer was the only "victim" of the electronic deposit practice, and that thus the speech was merely an extension of a personal dispute and not a matter of public interest.[154]

In recent years, relying on the Supreme Court's decision in *Connick v. Myers*, some federal courts seem to have expanded their view of what "personal disputes" are that remove constitutional protection from speech. The following types of speech have all been ruled by courts to be unprotected by the First Amendment on the theory that they are extensions of personal disputes and not expressions of public interest:

- Criticism of a policy which required all officers on sick leave to remain at their homes except to seek medical treatment. The Court rejected the officer's arguments that the speech concerned "matters of significance to his own family and all relatives of city police officers."[155]

- Complaints about a fellow officer making sexually suggestive phone calls to the first officer's wife.[156]

- Complaints about how overtime was handled in the department.[157]

- Opposition to taking a civil service promotional examination because there were other employees who had been promoted without taking an examination.[158]

- Speech disclosing a letter sent from a sheriff to an ex-convict commending the ex-convict for his work with a juvenile program. The deputies disclosing the letter did not believe the sending of the letter was inappropriate, and the sole motive in disclosing the letter was to embarrass the Sheriff politically since the ex-convict had subsequently been arrested for sexually abusing minors.[159]

- Statements made by a police toxicologist defending himself against charges of laboratory errors.[160]

- Allegations of inappropriate discipline in a police department.[161]

- The writing of a satirical memorandum that ridiculed the officer's encounter with members of a special plainclothes squad organized by the Chief of Police and which implied that the members of the squad had nothing better to do than spy on uniformed police officers. The Court cited the fact that the officer intended the memorandum to be a purely private joke between himself and a friend, and the memorandum attained public mention solely due to an unnamed third person posting it on the Police Department bulletin board.[162]

- Use of a mobile computing system to post a message that the Police Chief should attend the funerals of officers killed in the line of duty.[163]

- The filing of a lawsuit alleging that a police department retaliated against an officer for making a workplace safety complaint.[164]

- The notation of workplace activities in a private log which was later read by a supervisor,[165] and entries in an officer's private diary about the Chief.[166]

- A letter written by an officer that was critical of the performance of a colleague.[167]

- Speech about the improper uses of an inmate trust fund, where the jailer copied checks from the trust fund and showed copies to a friend who happened to be a magistrate. The jailer did not advise the media or give anyone other than her friend copies of the checks.[168]

- Testimony as a character witness for a reputed organized crime associate.[169]

- Pursuit of disorderly conduct charges against his girlfriend, also a member of the same police department.[170]

In yet another case, a court held unprotected complaints lodged by a deputy with the State Attorney's office that his Sheriff had misappropriated County property and had paid a female employee with whom he may have been romantically involved overtime and sick leave she had not earned. In upholding the deputy's termination for causing a "schism" in the Sheriff's Office, the Court made the following comment, which provides an excellent example of how far federal courts will go today in allowing discipline for speech under *Connick*:

> "It is also clear from the record that [the deputy] did not investigate or challenge potential overtime or sick leave abuses by employees other than the sheriff's alleged favorite, suggesting that personal animus toward the sheriff and the female employee was his primary purpose. * * * By confronting the sheriff and conducting an investigation of the Department, Breuer in fact threatened the authority of the sheriff to run the Department."[171]

What makes speech a matter of public interest and not merely of private concern? Courts attempting to apply *Connick* have struggled with the issue, with the results seemingly dependant upon the political predilections of the judge deciding the case. For example, courts have reached different conclusions about speech criticizing an employer's promotional process – some courts hold the speech protected, citing the public's interest in efficiency in the police department, while others find it to be of purely private concern.[172] At a minimum, the fact that the media reports the speech tends to make it a matter of public interest.[173]

Speech Which Is Knowingly False.

Where an officer's speech is knowingly false, it is not likely to be protected. For example, in one case an off-duty officer was in a nightclub when on-duty officers from his Department arrived to close down the club due to overcrowded conditions. The off-duty officer began to criticize the Department for "harassing" the owner of the club, and said that the owner "takes care of the Parkville Police and we should not hassle him." The Court sustained the officer's discharge for making these statements, noting that the officer's statements "were unsubstantiated, and were knowingly and recklessly false."[174]

Personality Conflicts.

Speech which is motivated by a personality conflict is not as likely to be protected by the First Amendment. A leading case in this area involves a lieutenant who, while conducting roll call, described his superior as a most "unreasonable, contrary, vindictive individual" whose behavior was "unreasonable, belligerent, arrogant, contrary and unpleasant." The Court held that these statements were not protected speech:

> "Certainly a prohibition against the communication of an officer's disaffection to rank-and-file members of the department during regular duty hours may be considered as a necessary adjunct to the department's substantial interest in maintaining discipline, morale and uniformity."[175]

In another case, a police officer was fired after he did the following: (1) Told the Chief and the Chief's second in command that they were incompetent; (2) referred to the city manager, with whom he had once been friendly, as a "back-stabbing son of a bitch"; (3) told the Chief that "the whole world is going to come down around you when a court of law gets this, for your siding with [the city manager]"; (4) urged the city manager to take a swing at him; (5) threatened a reporter with a lawsuit; (6) said that the officers of the Department had no respect for the Chief's leadership; and (7) posted vulgar cartoons on the Department's bulletin board. While the Court found that some of the officer's comments tangentially related to issues of public importance, it concluded that the "accusations, threats and abusive conduct toward his superiors in the Police Department and city government were made in spite and were a venting of personal frustration."[176]

Racially Or Sexually Derogatory Speech.

Racially or sexually derogatory speech is almost always not protected by the First Amendment. For example, a court has upheld the discharges of police officers who rode in a parade on a float that featured mocking stereotypes of African-Americans. The Court commented: "One does, of course, have a First Amendment right not to be terminated from public employment in retaliation for engaging in protected speech. But one's right to be a police officer or firefighter who publicly ridicules those he is commissioned to protect and serve is far from absolute. Rather, it is tempered by the reasonable judgment of his employer as to the potential disruptive effects of the employee's conduct on the public mission of the police and fire departments."[177]

Similarly, a court upheld the discharges of sheriff's deputies who engaged in a variety of Nazi mannerisms and comments while on duty.[178] In another case, a court held that the First Amendment did not protect statements by an officer who had just attended a workshop on police brutality that in St. Louis, many "Billy Bob, tobacco chewing white police officers" are recruited from "Boondocks, Missouri" and lack diversity and racial sensitivity, and that "often abusive officers were sissies in high school and grade school. But when they put on that uniform they are the man they never were before."[179] Examples of unprotected speech with racial or sexual overtones have also included the use of the word "nigger" while on the job,[180] a statement that female police applicants should interview in the nude,[181] where officers referred to a fingerprint technician as a "bitch,"[182] where an off-duty officer responded to e-mail solicitations from charitable organizations with racially and religiously derogatory comments,[183] and one instance where an officer deliberately referred to his city's Mayor Goldsmith as "Mayor Goldstein."[184]

The low tolerance courts give to speech of a racial character is shown by one case involving an off-duty officer who wore a "white power" T-shirt to a private party on Martin Luther King Day. When the newspapers published a story about the incident that listed the officer's employment, he was discharged. The Court upheld the discharge on the grounds that the speech associated with wearing the T-shirt – a matter of opinion on race relations which would seem to be entitled to constitutional protection – was not of public interest:

> "[The officer's beliefs] relating to the swastika and the strength or power of white people are purely matters of personal interest, not matters of public concern."[185]

Speech Endorsing Services Related To The Job Or Which Exploits The Job.

If an officer endorses certain services related to the job where the endorsement might undercut the agency's need to maintain neutrality about the services, the speech will likely be unprotected. Examples of such speech would be the endorsement of bail bond companies or personal injury or criminal law firms. In one case involving the endorsement by a sheriff's deputy of a certain ambulance company, the Court explained why such speech is unprotected:

"In this case the sheriff's department attempts to foster an image of impartiality in its relations with emergency services. It is without question, and I do not understand Plaintiff to argue otherwise, that an image of impartiality is an appropriate and legitimate goal of Defendants. For example, Defendants could prohibit employees from acting as advertising representatives for a home security system. This would be an appropriate prohibition, eve n though it would severely restrict employees' exercise of their First Amendment freedoms. Likewise, Defendants could prohibit their employees from endorsing a particular detective agency.

"It is not only important for the sheriff's department to maintain impartial relations with commercial enterprises delivering emergency services, but it is also important that the sheriff's department avoid any appearance of partiality in its relations with the emergency services. An otherwise innocent act, such as praising a particular emergency service's actions, could be perceived by the public as an endorsement. The sheriff's department has a legitimate concern in how the public perceives it. Thus, the sheriff has an interest in limiting deputies' opportunities to contribute to the public debate on ambulance services that is significantly greater than its interest in limiting a similar contribution by any member of the general public."[186]

In an analogous series of cases, courts have held that a law enforcement officer does not have the right to "exploit" his or her job for political purposes. The leading case involved a lieutenant in the Cincinnati Police Division who appeared at National Rifle Association rallies wearing his police badge, and who was identified by the NRA as a Cincinnati police lieutenant. When the employer ordered him to cease identifying himself as a Cincinnati police officer at the rallies, the lieutenant brought a lawsuit alleging that his free speech rights had been violated. A federal court rejected the suit, holding that the Department had the right to control both the use of its uniform as well as the use made by its officers while off duty of their status as police officers.[187]

Profanity And Name Calling.

Though the courts generally focus on the overall subject matter of the speech rather than the particular words used, it is clear that speech which is couched in profanity or name calling is likely to be accorded a lesser degree of protection under the First Amendment.[188] For example, courts have held that likening a sheriff to Adolf Hitler,[189] calling a city councilman a "dummy" [190]or labeling a police chief "vindictive"[191] does not constitute protected speech, nor does the use of "rough street language."[192]

Speech By 'Policy-Makers.'

As detailed in the chapter on the rights of officers to engage in political activities, certain high-ranking "policy-makers" have limited First Amendment rights with respect to their employment. Following this rationale, a court rejected the lawsuit of an Indianapolis police lieutenant who was turned down for promotion to major after giving a television interview in which he stated that he was not surprised that that the actions of an officer charged with murder had "slipped through the system" and that a supervisor had failed to investigate the allegations against the officer. The Court found that the First Amendment did not protect against the discipline or failure to promote a policy-making employee when that individual has engaged in speech on a matter of public concern in a manner that is critical of superiors or their policies.[193]

The Employee Speaking As A Citizen – When Is Discipline Motivated By The Employee's Speech?

Even assuming that the employee can establish that his speech as a "citizen" was about a matter of public interest, and that the interests of free speech override the employer's interests, the employee must still prove that the speech was a substantial or motivating factor behind the employer's disciplinary action.[194] In assessing this, courts evaluate such factors as the employer's stated motivation for the discipline, the timing of the speech and the discipline, and the strength of any independent reasons for disciplining the officer.[195] Even if the employer has multiple reasons independent of the officer's speech for disciplining an officer, and only one of the reasons withstands later scrutiny, the discipline will be upheld.[196]

The Employee Speaking As A Citizen – What Level Of Discipline Implicates The First Amendment?

A wide range of disciplinary and non-disciplinary actions implicate the First Amendment. Most certainly, the discharge, demotion, or suspension of an officer in retaliation for protected speech is enough of an "adverse employment action" to trigger the First Amendment.[197] The question courts consider is whether "the alleged retaliatory conduct was sufficient to deter a person of ordinary firmness from exercising his First Amendment rights."[198] Even if an officer is only improperly reprimanded,[199] transferred, suspended with pay,[200] loses the opportunity to work overtime,[201] or is the recipient of disciplinary memoranda or a disciplinary investigation for having engaged in protected speech, a cause of action for violation of the officer's First Amendment rights exists.[202] The decommissioning of a deputy sheriff, even though the issuance of a commission is completely discretionary on the part of a sheriff, is sufficient to trigger First Amendment protections.[203]

In addition, while probationary employees are generally considered to be "at-will" employees who may be discharged for any reason, they may not be discharged in retaliation for the exercise of their free speech rights.[204] In some circumstances, even the employer merely contacting the media can amount to impermissible retaliation.[205] Only extremely minor adverse administrative actions fail to trigger First Amendment analysis,[206] such as a poor performance evaluation.[207]

Occasionally, employers will have two motives in disciplining employees. One motive would be a legitimate basis for discipline based on the employee's job performance. The second motive would be an impermissible retaliation for the employee's exercise of free speech rights. The usual rule is that for discipline to be upheld in such a "mixed motive" case, the employer must prove that it would have taken the same disciplinary action against the employee on the very same day even if the employee had not engaged in protected speech.[208]

A Public Employer's Rules And Regulations Concerning Speech.

Where employer rules limiting an officer's speech are otherwise permissible, the rules still must be as clear and understandable as possible. Otherwise, if "men of common intelligence must necessarily guess at [their] meaning," the regulations may be "void for vagueness" in violation of the due process guarantees of the Fifth Amendment to the United States Constitution.[209]

In addition, regulations controlling speech must be as narrowly drawn as possible, or they may suffer from the constitutional defect of "overbreadth."[210] A governmental rule is "overbroad" and violates the First Amendment's free speech guarantees if the rule is expansive enough to prohibit both protected and unprotected speech.

In a classic case, a regulation of the New York State Police prevented officers from making any off-duty speeches to groups without first obtaining permission from the employer. A court acknowledged that while the employer could regulate some off-duty speeches which pertained to departmental matters, the attempted control over all off-duty speeches and the rule which allowed such control to turn on the content of the speech, were unconstitutionally overbroad:

> "[The department] may constitutionally regulate certain types of activities by Troopers. They may not do so, however, under regulations that give supervisory officials the power to curb speech at their own discretion * * * In the present case, supervisory officials of the Division of State Police have been given unbridled authority to determine what types of speech may or may not be regulated. Under our system of jurisprudence, such a scheme cannot stand."[211]

Regulations controlling speech must be as narrowly drawn as possible, or they may suffer from the constitutional defect of "overbreadth."

In a conceptually similar case, the Albemarle County, Virginia Police Department crafted a "return to work" plan for an officer about whom it had fitness-for-duty questions. The Plan required that the officer "refrain from any verbal or written communications to third parties, including but not limited to county employees, relating to your employment that are in any way critical or negative towards the county executive, the chief of police or other police department management or command staff, or any other county official or employee." A court quickly found serious constitutional problems with the Plan, observing that the Plan could only possibly be constitutional if limited to communications that were not in the public interest. Since the Plan's reach was so great that it would have even prevented the officer from commenting on racial issues in the Department, a topic clearly constitutionally protected, the Court found the Plan unconstitutional.[212]

Occasionally, a court will find that an "overbreadth" argument reaches too far. In one case, a Wilmington, Delaware officer contended that a department rule requiring him to be "truthful and forthright" was overbroad in the sense that it would require absolute truthfulness in every phase of an employee's life. A court rejected the officer's arguments, finding that the employer had appropriately limited the applicability of the rule to testimony in court and job-related statements.[213]

'Prior Restraints' On Speech, And Regulations Requiring Approval Before Contact With The Media.

When an employer is trying to prohibit speech before it happens, it has a significantly higher burden of proving the legitimacy of its actions than it would if simply disciplining an employee after the speech occurs.[214] Following this general approach, courts have regularly held that rules in law enforcement agencies requiring prior approval before making public statements are not only unconstitutionally overbroad, but also run afoul of the law's dislike of any prior restraints of speech.[215] Prior restraints – rules which seek to limit speech before it is made – are viewed with a great deal of suspicion because "they pose risks of self-censorship by speakers in order to avoid being denied a license to speak." In addition, prior restraints make it "more likely that an employee will be subject to sanctions after speaking [because the employer] will be more inclined to discipline an employee who has disregarded its orders."[216]

Many law enforcement agencies have rules that, if challenged, would almost certainly be struck down as impermissible prior restraints. For example, a rule prohibiting an officer from speaking to the press on any subject related to the job would not only be overbroad, but would be an impermissible prior restraint.[217] The same principles would invalidate rules prohibiting speaking with the press without first receiving approval from the officer's department,[218] rules prohibiting officers from appearing at meetings of a public body to discuss departmental matters,[219] or rules prohibiting officers from making disparaging remarks about other

> Courts have regularly held that rules in law enforcement agencies requiring prior approval before making public statements are not only unconstitutionally overbroad, but also run afoul of the law's dislike of any prior restraints of speech.

employees or regarding departmental operations.[220] Indeed, about the only types of "prior-approval media contact" rules that are permissible would be those that prohibit employees from making "formal releases" on behalf of the employer (as opposed to speaking personally) without prior approval.[221]

The Right To Refrain From Speech.

The First Amendment's free speech guarantees also prohibit a governmental employer from compelling employees to engage in political speech. In one case, an officer argued that his department had compelled him to participate in an over-time detail which involved participation in a "photo-opportunity" on the Capitol steps supporting a ban on assault weapons. Though the Court declined the claim because it disagreed with the officer's contention that he was in fact compelled to participate in the demonstration, it commented that "the First Amendment is violated when police officers are compelled to participate in an expressive activ-ity, such as the demonstration in favor of the assault weapons ban, even though they oppose the message being presented. Freedom of speech includes the right to refrain from speaking."[222]

Freedom Of Speech And The Internal Investigation Process.

Occasionally when a law enforcement officer is the subject of an internal investigation, the officer is instructed not to discuss the subject of the investigation with other individuals. The order may extend to barring discussion with all other individuals; more commonly, the order extends only to potential witnesses or other suspects in the internal investigation.

As long as the order not to discuss an internal investigation is narrowly drawn to apply only to potential witnesses or suspects so as not to jeopardize the inves-tigation, the order is permissible.[223] If the order goes further, however, it is likely not enforceable. For example, if the order attempts to forbid an individual from discussing the matter with union representatives, the order would likely run afoul of an employee's right to representation in the disciplinary process.[224] Similarly, if the order attempts to forbid an individual from discussing the matter with fam-ily members or friends who are not involved in the investigation, the order would probably violate the officer's rights to freedom of speech, freedom of association, and privacy.

As long as the order not to discuss an internal investigation is narrowly drawn to apply only to potential witnesses or suspects so as not to jeopardize the investigation, the order is permissible.

NOTES

[1] *Elrod v. Burns*, 427 U.S. 347 (1976).

[2] *Perry v. Sindermann*, 408 U.S. 593 (1972).

[3] *Garcetti v. Ceballos,* 547 U.S. 410 (2006).

[4] *Williams v. Dallas Ind. Sch. Dist.*, 480 F.3d 689 (5th Cir. 2007).

[5] *Garcetti v. Ceballos,* 547 U.S. 410 (2006).

[6] *Weisbarth v. Geauga Park Dist.*, 499 F.3d 538 (6th Cir. 2007).

[7] *Hoover v. County of Broome*, 2008 WL 1777444 (N.D. N.Y. 2008).

[8] *Hoover v. County of Broome*, 2008 WL 1777444 (N.D. N.Y. 2008).

[9] *Sillers v. City of Everman, Tex.*, 2008 WL 2222236 (N.D. Tex. 2008).

[10] *Vose v. Kliment*, 506 F.3d 565 (7th Cir. 2007).

[11] *Ewing v. City of Monmouth, Ill.*, 2008 WL 818334 (C.D. Ill. 2008).

[12] *Cheek v. City of Edwardsville, Kan.*, 2008 WL 4150029 (10th Cir. 2008).

[13] *Baranowski v. Waters*, 2008 WL 728366 (W.D. Pa. 2008).

[14] *Foraker v. Chaffinch,* 501 F.3d 231 (3d Cir. 2007).

[15] *Bradley v. James,* 479 F.3d 536 (8th Cir. 2007); *Clayton v. City of Middletown*, 564 F. Supp. 2d 105 (D. Conn. 2008); *Pottorf v. City of Liberty, Mo.*, 2007 WL 2811098 (W.D. Mo. 2007).

[16] *Bradley v. James,* 479 F.3d 536 (8th Cir. 2007); *Kasprzycki v. Dicarlo*, 584 F. Supp. 2d 470 (D. Conn. 2008).

[17] *Callahan v. Fermon*, 526 F.3d 1040 (7th Cir. 2008).

[18] *Sigsworth v. City of Aurora, Ill.*, 487 F.3d 506 (7th Cir. 2007).

[19] *Sullenberger v. Jobe,* 2008 WL 698976 (W.D. Pa. 2008).

[20] *Haynes v. City of Circleville, Ohio*, 474 F.3d 357 (6th Cir. 2007); *see Andrew v. Clark*, 472 F. Supp. 2d 659 (D. Md. 2007)(internal memoranda).

[21] *Kamholtz v. Yates County*, 2008 WL 5114964 (W.D. N.Y. 2008).

[22] *Mills v. City of Evansville, Ind.*, 452 F.3d 646 (6th Cir. 2006).

[23] *Schad v. Jones*, 415 F.3d 671 (7th Cir. 2005).

[24] *Bradley v. James*, 420 F. Supp. 2d 974 (E.D. Ark. 2006).

[25] *Turner v. Perry*, 2009 WL 179205 (Tex. App. 2009).

[26] *Nixon v. City of Houston*, 511 F.3d 494 (5th Cir. 2007).

[27] *Fuerst v. Clarke,* 454 F.3d 770 (7th Cir. 2006); *Shefcik v. Village of Calumet Park*, 532 F. Supp. 2d 965 (N.D. Ill. 2007); *Shirden v. Cordero*, 509 F. Supp. 2d 461 (D. N.J. 2007); *Mortara v. Katkocin*, 2007 WL 4105283 (D. Conn. 2007); *see Justice v. Danberg*, 571 F. Supp. 2d 602 (D. Del. 2008).

[28] *City of San Diego v. Roe*, 543 U.S. 77 (2004); *Connick v. Myers,* 461 U.S. 138 (1983).

[29] *Rankin v. McPherson*, 483 U.S. 378 (1987); *Baron v. Suffolk County Sheriff's Dept.,* 402 F.3d 225 (1st Cir. 2005).

[30] *Pickering v. Bd. of Educ.*, 391 U.S. 563 (1968).

[31] *Davignon v. Hodgson*, 524 F.3d 91 (1st Cir. 2008); *McCarthy v. City of Newburyport*, 252 Fed.Appx. 328 (1st Cir. 2007).

[32] Hubbard v. Administrator, 735 F. Supp. 435 (D. D.C. 1990).

[33] Connick v. Myers, 461 U.S. 138 (1983).

[34] Jordan v. Carter, 428 F.3d 67 (1st Cir. 2005)(criticism of chief); Bass v. Richards, 308 F.3d 1081 (10th Cir. 2002)(criticism of sheriff); Myers v. City of Highland Village, Texas, 269 F. Supp. 2d 850 (E.D. Tex. 2003); Edmundson v. Borough of Kennett Square, 881 F. Supp. 188 (E.D. Pa. 1995)(allegation that police chief had financial interest in company which built new squad room without a public bid).

[35] Clemons v. Dougherty County, Ga., 684 F.2d 1365 (5th Cir. 1982); Taylor v. Town of Freetown, 479 F. Supp. 2d 227 (D. Mass. 2007)(complaints to city council about chief); Beach v. City of Olathe, Kansas, 185 F. Supp. 2d 1229 (D. Kan. 2002)(allegations of unethical conduct on part of chief); Clary v. Irvin, 501 F. Supp. 706 (E.D. Tex. 1980); Lunsford v. Montgomery County, 2007 WL 1028531 (Tenn. Ct. App. 2007); see Johnson v. Multnomah County, Oregon, 48 F.3d 420 (9th Cir. 1995)(claim that supervisor part of "good old boy network" and violated law a matter of public interest).

[36] Shelton Police Union, Inc. v. Voccola, 125 F. Supp. 2d 604 (D. Conn. 2001).

[37] Curran v. Cousins, 509 F.3d 36 (1st Cir. 2007); O'Donnell v. Barry, 148 F.3d 1126 (D.C. Cir. 1998); Brukiewa v. Police Commissioner, 263 A.2d 210 (Md. 1970).

[38] See v. City of Elyria, 502 F.3d 484 (6th Cir. 2007); Conaway v. Smith, 853 F.2d 789 (10th Cir. 1988); Thompson v. Montgomery, 2007 WL 1875787 (E.D. Ark. 2007).

[39] City of Lawrence, 15 Mass. Labor Cases 1162 (1988)(violation of state labor laws to even investigate union official for participation in no-confidence vote).

[40] Brady v. Fort Bend County, 145 F.3d 691 (5th Cir. 1998).

[41] Swanson v. Otterloo, 993 F. Supp. 1224 (N.D. Iowa 1998).

[42] Bieluch v. Sullivan, 999 F.2d 666 (2d Cir. 1993)(state trooper's speech about operation of local town protected by First Amendment); Biggs v. Village of Dupo, 892 F.2d 1298 (7th Cir. 1990)(statements to press regarding the interference by politicians with police department protected speech about matter of public importance); Spiering v. City of Madison, 863 F. Supp. 1065 (D. S.D. 1994); Maxey v. Smith, 823 F. Supp. 1321 (N.D. Miss. 1993)(police chief's criticism of outside investigation ordered by City Council into murder/rape investigation protected by First Amendment); Fairbanks v. City of Bradenton Beach, 733 F. Supp. 1447 (M.D. Fla. 1989)(police chief who was fired for initiating investigation into city council was engaging in protected speech).

[43] Schnabel v. Tyler, 646 A.2d 152 (Conn. 1994)(upholds $370,000 jury verdict in favor of police officer against chief who disciplined him for encouraging citizen to attend city council meeting).

[44] Cragg v. City of Osawatomie, 143 F.3d 1343 (10th Cir. 1998).

[45] Pickering v. Board of Education, 391 U.S. 563 (1968); Eggleston v. Bieluch, 203 Fed.Appx. 257 (11th Cir. 2006).

[46] Wulf v. City of Wichita, 883 F.2d 842 (10th Cir. 1989); VanTassel v. Brooks, 355 F. Supp. 2d 788 (W.D. Pa. 2005); Edmundson v. Borough of Kennett Square, 881 F. Supp. 188 (E.D. Pa. 1995).

[47] Holder v. City of Allentown, 9 IER Cases 1170 (E.D. Pa. 1994).

[48] *Department of Corrections v. State Personnel Board*, 69 Cal.Rptr.2d 34 (Cal. App. 1997).

[49] *Jones v. City of Allen Park*, 167 Fed.Appx. 398 (6th Cir. 2006)(circulation of rumors about employee).

[50] *Brukiewa v. Police Commissioner*, 263 A.2d 210 (Md. 1970). *See also Moore v. Kilgore*, 877 F.2d 364 (5th Cir. 1989)(firefighter could not be discharged for protesting layoffs).

[51] *Zamboni v. Stamler*, 847 F.2d 73 (3d Cir. 1988).

[52] *Thompson v. City of Starkville*, 901 F.2d 456 (5th Cir. 1990).

[53] *Watters v. City of Philadelphia*, 55 F.3d 886 (3d Cir. 1995).

[54] *Ruhlman v. Barger*, 435 F. Supp. 447 (W.D. Pa. 1976).

[55] *Weast v. Pierce County*, 2002 WL 987315 (9th Cir. 2002).

[56] *Gustafson v. Jones*, 117 F.3d 1015 (7th Cir. 1997).

[57] *Manhattan Beach Police Association v. Manhattan Beach*, 881 F.2d 816 (9th Cir. 1989); *Brasslett v. Cota*, 761 F.2d 827 (1st Cir. 1986). To the extent that an officer has first attempted to exhaust the chain of command, the degree of protection granted to the officer's speech will likely be higher. *See Perry v. City of Kinloch*, 680 F. Supp. 1339 (E.D. Mo. 1988).

[58] *Miller v. Jones*, 444 F.3d 929 (7th Cir. 2006).

[59] *Shefcik v. Village of Calumet Park*, 532 F. Supp. 2d 965 (N.D. Ill. 2007); *Penska v. Nevada*, 2007 WL 2571987 (D. Nev. 2007); *McCullough v. City of Atlantic City,* 137 F. Supp. 2d 557 (D. N.J. 2001); *Scott v. Godwin*, 147 S.W.3d 609 (Tex. App. 2004).

[60] *Howcroft v. City of Peabody*, 747 N.E.2d 729 (Mass. App. 2001).

[61] *Maxey v. Smith*, 823 F. Supp. 1321 (N.D. Miss. 1993).

[62] *Buzek v. County of Saunders*, 972 F.2d 992 (8th Cir. 1992); *see Zicarelli v. Leake*, 767 F. Supp. 1450 (N.D. Ill. 1991)(reverses termination of corrections officer who testified as a character witness for a defendant in a bifurcated death penalty hearing).

[63] *Cooper v. Smith*, 855 F. Supp. 1276 (S.D. Ga. 1994); *see Casey v. City of Cabool*, 12 F.3d 799 (8th Cir. 1993)(complaint that a city clerk had used city resources to effect repairs at her home protected by First Amendment).

[64] *Campbell v. Arkansas Dept. of Corrections*, 155 F.3d 950 (8th Cir. 1998); *Mascetta v. Miranda*, 957 F. Supp. 1346 (S.D. N.Y. 1997).

[65] *Freitag v. Ayers*, 463 F.3d 838 (9th Cir. 2006).

[66] *Rohr v. Nehls*, 2006 WL 2927657 (E.D. Wis. 2006).

[67] *Pollock v. Ocean City*, 968 F. Supp. 187 (D. N.J. 1997).

[68] *Reilly v. City of Atlantic City*, 532 F.3d 216 (3d Cir. 2008).

[69] *Swartzwelder v. McNeilly*, 297 F.3d 228 (3d Cir. 2002).

[70] *Kinney v. Weaver*, 367 F.3d 337 (5th Cir. 2004); *see Robinson v. County of Los Angeles*, 2009 WL 118081 (9th Cir. 2009); *Johnson v. Lapeer County*, 2006 WL 2925292 (E.D. Mich. 2006); *Hoffman v. Dougher*, 2006 WL 2709703 (M.D. Pa. 2006)(testimony before EEOC).

[71] *Deprado v. City of Miami*, 446 F. Supp. 2d 1344 (S.D. Fla. 2006).

[72] *United Mine Workers, Dist. 12 v. Ill. State Bar Ass'n,* 389 U.S. 217 (1967).

[73] *Powell v. Alexander*, 391 F.3d 1 (1st Cir. 2004).

74 *San Filippo v. Bongiovanni*, 30 F.3d 424 (3d Cir. 1994).

75 *Diana v. Oliphant*, 2007 WL 3491856 (M.D. Pa. 2007).

76 *Walje v. City of Winchester*, 773 F.2d 729 (6th Cir. 1985)(radio interview); *City and Borough of Sitka v. Swanner*, 649 P.2d 940 (Alaska 1982)(letter to city council).

77 *Brukiewa v. Police Commissioner*, 263 A.2d 210 (Md. 1970). *See also Brawner v. City of Richardson, Texas*, 855 F.2d 187 (5th Cir. 1988).

78 *Wulf v. City of Wichita*, 883 F.2d 842 (10th Cir. 1989)(letter to attorney general complaining that supervisory police officer not allowed to join fraternal police organization constituted speech which is a matter of public importance); *Lajoie v. Connecticut State Board of Labor Relations*, 837 F. Supp. 34 (D. Conn. 1993)(organizational efforts for union for special deputies protected by First Amendment).

79 *Davignon v. Hodgson*, 524 F.3d 91 (1st Cir. 2008).

80 *City of Detroit v. Detroit Police Officers Ass'n*, 2007 WL 4248562 (Mich. App. 2007).

81 *McKinley v. City of Eloy*, 705 F.2d 1110 (9th Cir. 1983).

82 *Tygrett v. Barry*, 627 F.2d 1279 (D.C. Cir. 1980).

83 *Tygrett v. Barry*, 627 F.2d 1279 (D.C. Cir. 1980).

84 *Chico Police Officers Association v. City of Chico*, 283 Cal.Rptr. 610 (Cal. App. 1991).

85 *Omaha Police Union Local 101, IUPA, AFL-CIO v. City of Omaha*, 759 N.W.2d 82 (Neb. 2009).

86 *Auburn Police Union v. Carpenter*, 8 F.3d 886 (1st Cir. 1993).

87 *Fraternal Order of Police, N.D. State Lodge v. Stenehjem*, 431 F.3d 591 (8th Cir. 2005).

88 *United States v. National Treasury Employees Union*, 513 U.S. 454 (1995).

89 *Weicherding v. Riegel*, 160 F.3d 1139 (7th Cir. 1998).

90 *Edwards v. City of Goldsboro*, 178 F.3d 231 (4th Cir. 1999).

91 *See Baron v. Suffolk County Sheriff's Dept.*, 402 F.3d 225 (1st Cir. 2005)(upholds $500,000 jury verdict); *Tao v. Freeh*, 27 F.3d 635 (D.C. Cir. 1994)(speech about alleged discrimination by FBI against Chinese Americans); *Marshall v. Allen*, 984 F.2d 787 (7th Cir. 1993)(speech about sexual harassment); *Wilson v. University of Texas Health Center*, 973 F.2d 1263 (5th Cir. 1992)(speech about sexual harassment); *Wulf v. City of Wichita*, 883 F.2d 842 (10th Cir. 1989)(letter to attorney general complaining of sexual harassment by one officer constituted speech which is a matter of public importance); *Matulin v. Village of Lodi*, 862 F.2d 609 (6th Cir. 1989)(speech about alleged discrimination in police force of high public importance; discharge of probationary police officer reversed); *Baron v. Hickey*, 242 F. Supp. 2d 66 (D. Mass. 2003)(allegations of supervisory toleration of harassment); *Brown v. Scotland County*, 2003 WL 21418099 (M.D. N.C. 2003)(raising issues of discrimination during department meeting on racism); *Walton v. Safir,* 122 F. Supp. 2d 466 (S.D. N.Y. 2001)(complaints by probationary employee about discrimination in special investigations unit); *Carlisle v. Lopresti*, 47 F. Supp. 2d 973 (N.D. Ill. 1999); *Erickson v. Hunter*, 932 F. Supp. 1380 (M.D. Fla. 1996)(complaints of gender discrimination a matter of public interest); *Poulsen v. City of North Tonawanda*, 811 F. Supp. 884 (W.D. N.Y. 1993); *Cathey v. Fowler*, 57 FEP Cases 59 (N.D. Ga. 1990)(state trooper's filing of charges of race discrimination

with state equal employment agency amounted to protected speech); *Cox v. Civil Service Commission of Douglas County*, 614 N.W.2d 273 (Neb. 2000)(speech about racial discrimination in department). Only one reported case has held that a law enforcement officer's speech about alleged discrimination concerned private matters not protected by the First Amendment. *See Evans v. City of Indianola*, 778 F. Supp. 333 (N.D. Miss. 1993).

[92] *Conley v. City of Lincoln City*, 2004 WL 948427 (D. Or. 2004); *Barth v. Village of Mokena*, 2004 WL 434195 (N.D. Ill. 2004).

[93] *Leonard v. City of Columbus*, 705 F.2d 1299 (11th Cir. 1983). Numerous cases have addressed speech centering around the symbol of the American flag. *See Texas v. Johnson*, 491 U.S. 397 (1989); *Spence v. Washington*, 418 U.S. 405 (1974); *Street v. New York*, 394 U.S. 576 (1969).

[94] *Cromer v. Brown*, 88 F.3d 1315 (4th Cir. 1996).

[95] *Nance v. City of Newark*, 2008 WL 2115120 (D. N.J. 2008).

[96] *Cotarelo v. Village of Sleepy Hollow Police Dept.*, 460 F.3d 247 (2d Cir. 2006).

[97] *Deloughery v. City of Chicago*, 2002 WL 31654942 (N.D. Ill. 2002).

[98] *Mandell v. County of Suffolk*, 316 F.3d 368 (2d Cir. 2003).

[99] *Delisle v. Brimfield Township Police Department*, 94 Fed.Appx. 247 (6th Cir. 2004).

[100] *Victor v. McElveen*, 150 F.3d 451 (5th Cir. 1998).

[101] *Shelton Police Union, Inc. v. Voccola*, 125 F. Supp. 2d 604 (D. Conn. 2001).

[102] *Lehmuller v. Village of Sag Harbor*, 982 F. Supp. 132 (E.D .N.Y. 1997).

[103] *McCall v. Board of Commissioners of County of Shawnee, Kansas*, 291 F. Supp. 2d 1216 (D. Kan. 2003).

[104] *Campbell v. Galloway*, 483 F.3d 258 (4th Cir. 2007); *Ashcraft v. Beicker*, 2008 WL 538919 (D. Colo. 2008).

[105] *Bass v. Richards*, 308 F.3d 1081 (10th Cir. 2002).

[106] *Waters v. Chaffin*, 684 F.2d 833 (11th Cir. 1982); *see Bass v. Richards*, 308 F.3d 1081 (10th Cir. 2002).

[107] *City of San Diego v. Roe,* 543 U.S. 77 (2004).

[108] *Dible v. City of Chandler*, 502 F.3d 1040 (9th Cir. 2007).

[109] *Thaeter v. Palm Beach County Sheriff's Office*, 449 F.3d 1342 (11th Cir. 2006).

[110] *Tejada-Batista v. Morales*, 424 F.3d 97 (1st Cir. 2005); *Forsyth v. City of Dallas, Texas,* 91 F.3d 769 (5th Cir. 1996); *Glass v. Dachel*, 2 F.3d 733 (7th Cir. 1993); *Brawner v. City of Richardson, Texas,* 855 F.2d 187 (5th Cir. 1988); *Brockwell v. Norton*, 732 F.2d 664 (8th Cir. 1984); *Jayjohn v. City of Wellston*, 2005 WL 2416554 (S.D. Ohio 2005); *Gros v. Port Washington Police District*, 944 F. Supp. 1072 (E.D. N.Y. 1996); *McDonald v. City of Freeport*, 834 F. Supp. 921 (S.D. Tex. 1993); *Shoemaker v. Allender*, 520 F. Supp. 266 (E.D. Pa. 1981); *Solomon v. Royal Oak Township*, 656 F. Supp. 1254 (Mich. 1986).

[111] *Hughes v. Whitmer*, 714 F.2d 1407 (8th Cir. 1983).

[112] *Baldassare v. State of New Jersey,* 250 F.3d 188 (3d Cir. 2001).

[113] *Gratsch v. Hamilton County,* 2001 WL 406440 (6th Cir. 2001).

[114] *Fairley v. Andrews*, 430 F. Supp. 2d 786 (N.D. Ill. 2006).

[115] *Stanley v. City of Dalton, Georgia*, 219 F.3d 1280 (11th Cir. 2000).

[116] *Taylor v. Keith*, 338 F.3d 639 (6th Cir. 2003).

[117] *Blume v. Meneley*, 283 F. Supp. 2d 1189 (D. Kan. 2003).

[118] *Branton v. City of Dallas*, 272 F.3d 730 (5th Cir. 2001).

[119] *Barry v. New York City Police Department*, 2004 WL 758299 (S.D. N.Y. 2004).

[120] *Bennett v. City of Holyoke*, 230 F. Supp. 2d 207 (D. Mass. 2002).

[121] *Shepard v. Wapello County, Iowa*, 303 F. Supp. 2d 1004 (S.D. Iowa 2003).

[122] *Perez v. Agostini*, 37 F. Supp. 2d 103 (D. P.R. 1999).

[123] *Cooper v. Smith*, 89 F.3d 761 (11th Cir. 1996).

[124] *Cahill v. O'Donnell*, 7 F. Supp. 2d 341 (S.D. N.Y. 1998).

[125] *Mascetta v. Miranda*, 957 F. Supp. 1346 (S.D. N.Y. 1997).

[126] *Saunders v. Hunter*, 980 F. Supp. 1236 (M.D. Fla. 1997).

[127] *Walton v. City of Milford, Tex.*, 2008 WL 631240 (N.D. Tex. 2008)(speech complaining about ticket quotes not protected by First Amendment, but was potentially protected by state whistleblower statute).

[128] **Alaska**: Alaska State Section 39.90.100; **Arizona**: Section 38-531, Arizona Revised Statutes; Section 1102.5; **Arkansas**: Arkansas State Annotated 11-10-106; **California**: Labor Code, West's Annotated California Code; Section 24-50.5-107; **Colorado**: Colorado Revised Statutes (state employees only); Section 4-61dd, as amended by P.A. 85-559, L. 1985; **Connecticut**: General Statutes of Connecticut; Section 5115; **Delaware**: Title 29, Delaware Code Annotated; **Florida**: Act 267, L. 1987, Section 112.3187, Florida Statutes; **Georgia**: OCGA Section 45-1-4; **Hawai'i**: Hawai'i Revised Statutes; Chapter 127, Section 19c.1; **Illinois**: Personnel Code, Illinois Revised Statutes; Section 36-1-8-8; **Indiana**: Indiana Statutes; Section 730.3; **Iowa**: Code of Iowa; Section 75-2973; **Kansas**: General Statutes of Kansas; Section 61.102, **Kentucky**: Kentucky Revised Statutes; Section 30:1074.1; **Louisiana**: Louisiana Revised Statutes; Section 832, et seq.; **Maine**: Title 26, Revised Statutes of Maine; Article 64A, Section 12; **Maryland**: Annotated Code of Maryland; Section 181.931; **Massachusetts**: Massachusetts Annotated Laws ch. 149, Section 185; **Michigan**: Michigan State Annotated Section 17.428(2)(1981); **Minnesota**: Minnesota Statutes; H.B. 659, L. 1987; **Mississippi**: Mississippi Code Annotated, Section 25-9-171 (2003); **Missouri**: Missouri Statutes; Section 275-E:1; **Montana**: Montana Code Anno. Section 39-2-904 (2007); **Nebraska**: Nebraska Revised Statute, §81-8,254 (2003); **Nevada**: Nevada Laws 1991, Chapter 672; **New Hampshire**: New Hampshire Statutes Annotated; Section 34:19, **New Jersey**: New Jersey Statutes Annotated, Section 215; **New York**: McKinney's Consolidated Laws of New York, as amended by Chapter 744, L. 1986; **North Carolina**: North Carolina General State Section 126-84 (1989); **North Dakota**: North Dakota Cent. Code Section 34-01-20 (2003); **Ohio**: Ohio Revised Code Annotated 4113.52; **Oklahoma**: Oklahoma Statutes Annotated, Title 74 Section 840-2.5 (2002); **Oregon**: Chapter 240, Section 316(5), Oregon Revised Statutes; **Pennsylvania**: Title 43, Sections 1421 to 1429, Pennsylvania Statutes; Section 36-15; **Rhode Island**: Rhode Island General Laws; Section 8-27; **South Carolina**: Code of Laws of South Carolina; **South Dakota**: South Dakota Codified Laws Section 3-6-26, 3-6-27; **Tennessee**: Tennessee Code Annotated Section 50-1-304 (2003); **Texas**: Article 6252-16a, Vernon's Texas Statutes and Supplements; Section 67-21; **Utah**: Utah

Code Annotated; Section 42.40.070; **Vermont**: Vermont Statutes Annotated Title 18, Section 1427 (2003); **Washington**: Revised Code of Washington; Section 6C-1, as enacted by HB 4364, L. 1988; **West Virginia**: West Virginia Code; Section 230.80; **Wisconsin**: Wisconsin Statutes Annotated.

[129] *Montgomery County v. Park*, 246 S.W.3d 610 (Tex. 2007).

[130] *Lytle v. City of Haysville*, 138 F.3d 857 (10th Cir. 1998); *Frederick v. Department of Justice*, 73 F.3d 349 (4th Cir. 1996); *Texas Dept. of Criminal Justice v. McElyea*, 239 S.W.3d 842 (Tex. App. 2007).

[131] *Newberne v. Department of Crime Control and Public Safety*, 618 S.E.2d 201 (N.C. 2005); *Fox v. City of Bowling Green*, 668 N.E.2d 898 (Ohio 1996).

[132] *Schultea v. Wood*, 27 F.3d 1112 (5th Cir. 1994), *affirmed in part, reversed in part,* 47 F.3d 1427 (5th Cir. 1995).

[133] *McClain v. Munn*, 2008 WL 975059 (W.D. Pa. 2008).

[134] *Watkins v. State of New Jersey, Office of Atty. Gen.*, 2005 WL 3711182 (N.J. Super. A.D. 2006).

[135] *City of Beaumont v. Bouillion*, 896 S.W.2d 143 (Tex. 1995).

[136] *Brown v. Mayor of Detroit*, 734 N.W.2d 514 (Mich. 2007).

[137] *Mills v. Leath*, 4 IER Cases 1462 (S.C. Ct. Cm. Pl. 1989).

[138] *Harris County Precinct Four Constable Department v. Grabowski*, 922 S.W.2d 954 (Tex. 1996).

[139] *Fairbanks v. City of Bradenton Beach*, 733 F. Supp. 1447 (M.D. Fla. 1989)(police chief discharged for initiating investigation of candidates for city council).

[140] *Jakimowicz v. City of Philadelphia*, 2008 WL 383329 (E.D. Pa. 2008).

[141] *Berger v. Battaglia*, 779 F.2d 992 (4th Cir. 1985). The officer later settled the civil suit for $200,000. Fire and Police Personnel Reporter, p. 165 (November, 1991). In a later case, an officer who dressed in blackface at a private Halloween party was found to not be engaged in artistic speech. The Court distinguished the *Berger* case by commenting that "artistic expression before a public audience is quite different from a decision to wear a costume to a private Halloween party." *Tindle v. Caudell,* 10 IER Cases 1227 (8th Cir. 1995).

[142] *Eiland v. City of Montgomery*, 797 F.2d 953 (11th Cir. 1986).

[143] *Normand v. City of Baton Rouge*, 572 So.2d 1123 (La. App. 1990).

[144] *Rankin v. McPherson*, 483 U.S. 378 (1987).

[145] *Connick v. Myers*, 461 U.S. 138 (1983).

[146] *McKinley v. City of Eloy*, 705 F.2d 1110 (9th Cir. 1983). *See Biggs v. Village of Dupo*, 892 F.2d 1298 (7th Cir. 1990)(statements to press regarding the interference by politicians with police department held protected speech and not disruptive); *Darnell v. Ford*, 903 F.2d 556 (8th Cir. 1990)(reversal of demotion of state patrol troop commander for supporting the "wrong" candidate for superintendent of state police; no disruption shown); *Cochran v. City of Los Angeles*, 222 F.3d 1195 (9th Cir. 2000)(inappropriate criticism of supervisor directed towards subordinates of supervisor; disruption shown).

[147] *Prince Georges County v. Younkers*, 615 A.2d 1197 (Md. App. 1992).

[148] *Moen v. Town of Fairfield*, 713 A.2d 321 (Maine 1998).

[149] *Davidson v. City of Elkhart,* 696 N.E.2d 58 (Ind. App. 1998).

[150] *Campbell v. Towse*, 99 F.3d 820 (7th Cir. 1996).

[151] *Gros v. Port Washington Police District*, 944 F. Supp. 1072 (E.D. N.Y. 1996).

[152] *Holland v. Maryland*, 2009 WL 122575 (4th Cir. 2009); *Kirby v. City of Elizabeth City, North Carolina*, 388 F.3d 440 (4th Cir. 2004); *Beeler v. Behan*, 464 A.2d 1091 (Md. App. 1983).

[153] *Arndt v. Koby*, 309 F.3d 1247 (10th Cir. 2002).

[154] *Hensley v. Jasper Police Department*, 163 F. Supp. 2d 1006 (S.D. Ind. 2001). *See also Smith v. Fruin*, 28 F.3d 646 (7th Cir. 1994)(protests of City's lax enforcement of workplace smoking laws was a personal dispute about a matter not concerning the public interest); *Morgan v. Ford*, 6 F.3d 750 (11th Cir. 1993)(claim of sexual harassment was a personal dispute not protected by the First Amendment); *McEvoy v. Shoemaker*, 882 F.2d 463 (10th Cir. 1989)(letter to city council complaining of mismanagement in police department aired personal frustration at perceived unfairness of supervisors' promotional decisions, and did not involve matters of public interest); *Wilson v. City of Littleton*, 732 F.2d 765 (10th Cir. 1984)(failure to remove shroud placed on badge to mourn death of another officer does not concern a matter of public interest and officer can be discharged for insubordination); *Hughes v. Whitmer*, 714 F.2d 1407 (8th Cir. 1983); *Hall v. Mayor and Director of Public Safety*, 406 A.2d 317 (N.J. Sup. 1979)("personal attack" on chief).

[155] *Crain v. Board of Police Commissioners*, 920 F.2d 1402 (8th Cir. 1990).

[156] *Foxx v. Town of Fletcher*, 2008 WL 927543 (W.D. N.C. 2008).

[157] *Cherry v. Pickell*, 188 Fed.Appx. 465 (6th Cir. 2006); *Shefcik v. Village of Calumet Park*, 532 F. Supp. 2d 965 (N.D. Ill. 2007).

[158] *Garzella v. Borough of Dunmore*, 2007 WL 1140448 (M.D. Pa. 2007).

[159] *Coughlin v. Lee*, 946 F.2d 1152 (5th Cir. 1991).

[160] *Carroll v. Neumann*, 204 F. Supp. 2d 1344 (S.D. Fla. 2002).

[161] *Edmundson v. Borough of Kennett Square*, 881 F. Supp. 188 (E.D. Pa. 1995).

[162] *Angle v. Dow*, 822 F. Supp. 1530 (S.D. Ala. 1993).

[163] *Golt v. City of Los Angeles*, 214 Fed.Appx. 708 (9th cir. 2006).

[164] *Ruotolo v. City of New York*, 514 F.3d 184 (2d Cir. 2008).

[165] *Connor v. Clinton County Prison*, 963 F. Supp. 442 (M.D. Pa. 1997).

[166] *Verri v. Nanna*, 972 F. Supp. 773 (S.D. N.Y. 1997).

[167] *Myers v. Wilkes-Barre Twp.*, 204 F. Supp. 2d 821 (M.D. Pa. 2002).

[168] *Knight v. Vernon*, 23 F. Supp. 2d 634 (M.D. N.C. 1998).

[169] *Green v. Philadelphia Housing Authority*, 105 F.3d 882 (3d Cir. 1997).

[170] *Grigley v. City of Atlanta*, 136 F.3d 752 (11th Cir. 1998).

[171] *Breuer v. Hart,* 909 F.2d 1035 (7th Cir. 1990).

[172] *Compare Powell v. Basham*, 921 F.2d 165 (8th Cir. 1990)(speech criticizing "good ole boy" promotional process of public interest) with *McEvoy v. Shoemaker*, 4 IER Cases 1222 (10th Cir. 1989)(letter to city council complaining of mismanagement in police department aired personal frustration at perceived unfairness of supervisors' promotional decisions, and did not involve matters of public interest); *Gros v. Port Washington Police District*, 944 F. Supp. 1072 (E.D. N.Y. 1996)(officer's complaints that he was not promoted unprotected by First Amendment); *O'Connell v. Montgomery County, Maryland*, 923 F. Supp. 761 (D. Md. 1996)(captain's protests

about failure of chief to promote him were not of public interest, but were purely personal to the captain).

173 *Broderick v. Roache*, 767 F. Supp. 20 (D. Mass. 1991)(speech by union president).

174 *Beeler v. Beehan*, 464 A.2d 1091 (Md. App. 1983).

175 *Kannisto v. City and County of San Francisco*, 541 F.2d 841 (9th Cir. 1976).

176 *McMurphy v. City of Flushing*, 802 F.2d 191 (6th Cir. 1986).

177 *Locurto v. Giuliani*, 447 F.3d 159 (2d Cir. 2006).

178 *McMullen v. Carson*, 754 F.2d 936 (11th Cir. 1985)(active membership in Ku Klux Klan and use of media by deputy to link himself to Klan's activities); *Wright v. Glynn County*, 932 F. Supp. 1476 (S.D. Ga. 1996)(repeated use of word "nigger"); *Black v. City of Auburn, Alabama*, 857 F. Supp. 1540 (M.D. Ala. 1994)(derogatory and indecent remarks to and about women); *Boone v. Mingus*, 697 F. Supp. 1577 (S.D. Ala. 1988)(reference to black suspect as being motivated by "ignorance in an animalistic social response to the sight of the police in his neighborhood/habitat").

179 *McLin v. Board of Police Commissioners*, 2001 WL 574585 (8th Cir. 2001).

180 *Vinci v. Nebraska Dept. of Correctional Services*, 571 N.W.2d 53 (Neb. 1997).

181 *Reinhart v. City of Maryland Heights*, 930 F. Supp. 410 (E.D. Mo. 1996).

182 *Burns v. City of Detroit*, 660 N.W.2d 85 (Mich. App. 2003).

183 *Pappas v. Giuliani*, 290 F.3d 143 (2d Cir. 2002).

184 *City of Indianapolis v. Heath*, 686 N.E.2d 940 (Ind. App. 1997); *see Eaton v. Harsha*, 505 F. Supp. 2d 948 (D. Kan. 2007).

185 *Lawrenz v. James*, 852 F. Supp. 986 (M.D. Fla. 1994). *See Lumpkin v. Brown*, 73 FEP Cases 895 (9th Cir. 1997)(upholds discharge of human rights commissioner who made public statements condemning homosexuality as sinful).

186 *Zook v. Brown*, 575 F. Supp. 72 (C.D. Ill. 1983), *reversed on other grounds*, 748 F.2d 1161 (7th Cir. 1984).

187 *Thomas v. Whalen*, 51 F.3d 1285 (6th Cir. 1995); *Harper v. Crockett*, 868 F. Supp. 1557 (E.D. Ark. 1994)(officer who said "just wait until the next time they're getting robbed and I'm the first one in getting shot at" when frustrated by long wait in line at bank was not engaged in protected speech). *See Detroit Fire Fighters Ass'n, Local 334 v. City of Detroit*, 508 F. Supp. 172 (E.D. Mich. 1981).

188 *Germann v. Kansas City*, 776 F.2d 761 (8th Cir. 1985)(calling the chief "chicken shit"); *Kannisto v. City and County of San Francisco*, 541 F.2d 841 (9th Cir. 1976)(calling a supervisor "vindictive and unpleasant"); *Morris v. Crow*, 117 F.3d 449 (11th Cir. 1997)(use of profane language to chew out supervisor in view of coworkers); *Marshall v. City of Atlanta*, 614 F. Supp. 581 (D. Ga. 1984)(profanity towards supervisors); *Dumez v. Houma Municipal Fire and Police Civil Service Board*, 408 So.2d 403 (La. App. 1981)(saying "f___ you" to a lieutenant); *Sims v. Baer*, 732 S.W.2d 916 (Mo. 1987)(use of obscenity).

189 *Curran v. Cousins*, 509 F.3d 36 (1st Cir. 2007).

190 *Hasenstab v. Board of Police Commissioners*, 389 N.E.2d 588 (Ill. 1979).

191 *Kokkinis v. Ivkovich*, 10 F. Supp. 2d 995 (N.D. Ill. 1998).

192 *Hansen v. Soldenwagner*, 19 F.3d 573 (11th Cir. 1994)(use of word "shit" when testifying not protected speech); *Black v. City of Auburn*, 857 F. Supp. 1540

(M.D. Ala. 1994)(use of "bitch" and "whore" not protected speech); *United States v. Caver*, 41 M.J. 556 (N.M. Ct. Crim. App. 1994)(calling a fellow employee a "slut bitch" not protected speech); *Jacocks v. Montgomery County*, 472 A.2d 485 (Md. App. 1985) (telling a lieutenant that "he could take his job and stick it up his ass" not protected speech).

[193] *Nanavaty v. City of Indianapolis*, 202 WL 1926158 (7th Cir. 2002).

[194] *Coszalter v. City of Salem,* 320 F.3d 968 (9th Cir. 2003); *Ulrich v. City and County of San Francisco,* 308 F.3d 968 (9th Cir. 2002).

[195] *Mory v. City of Chula Vista*, 2008 WL 360071 (S.D. Cal. 2008).

[196] *Douglas v. DeKalb County, Ga.*, 2007 WL 4373970 (N.D. Ga. 2007).

[197] *Delisle v. Brimfield Township Police Department*, 94 Fed.Appx. 247 (6th Cir. 2004)(suspension).

[198] *McKee v. Hart,* 436 F.3d 165, (3d Cir. 2006).

[199] *Bates v. Mackay*, 321 F. Supp. 2d 173 (D. Mass. 2004).

[200] *Butczynski v. Luzerne County*, 2007 WL 295420 (M.D. Pa. 2007)(suspension with pay); *Maimone v. City of Atlantic City*, 903 A.2d 1055 (N.J. 2006)(transfer).

[201] *Jones v. City of Allen Park*, 167 Fed.Appx. 398 (6th Cir. 2006).

[202] *Dill v. City of Edmond, Oklahoma*, 155 F.3d 1193 (10th Cir. 1998)(transfer from detective to patrol officer); *Forsyth v. City of Dallas, Texas*, 91 F.3d 769 (5th Cir. 1996)(transfer from undercover to patrol duties); *Hughes v. Whitmer*, 714 F.2d 1407 (8th Cir. 1983); *Swilley v. Alexander*, 629 F.2d 1018 (5th Cir. 1980)(letter of reprimand); *Albert v. City of Hartford*, 529 F. Supp. 2d 311 (D. Conn. 2007)(disciplinary investigation); *Barry v. New York City Police Department*, 2004 WL 758299 (S.D. N.Y. 2004)(transfer to patrol duties); *Knight v. City of New York*, 303 F. Supp. 2d 485 (S.D. N.Y. 2004)(receipt of disciplinary memoranda); *Yoggerst v. Stewart*, 623 F.2d 35 (7th Cir. 1980)(verbal reprimand); *Simpson v. Weeks*, 570 F.2d 240 (8th Cir. 1978)(transfer to jail assignment); *McNamara v. Chicago*, 700 F. Supp. 917 (N.D. Ill 1988)(transfer without loss of pay); *Carlisle v. Lopresti*, 47 F. Supp. 2d 973 (N.D. Ill. 1999)(transfer to different station); *Arenal v. City of Punta Gorda*, 932 F. Supp. 1406 (M.D. Fla. 1996). *But see Wallace v. Suffolk County Police Dept.*, 396 F. Supp. 2d 251 (E.D. N.Y. 2005)(initiation of disciplinary investigation not sufficient to trigger First Amendment).

[203] *Bergeron v. Cabral*, 535 F. Supp. 2d 204 (D. Mass. 2008).

[204] *Sangendorf-Teal v. Rensselaer County*, 100 F.3d 270 (2d Cir. 1996).

[205] *Angelella v. Pittston Township*, 2007 WL 2688724 (M.D. Pa. 2007).

[206] *Quantz v. Edwards*, 264 Fed.Appx. 625 (9th Cir. 2008)(launching of investigation into officer); *Sharp v. City of Palatka*, 529 F. Supp. 2d 1371 (M.D. Fla. 2008)(omission of officer's name from press release).

[207] *Hughes v. Stottlemyre*, 454 F.3d 791 (8th Cir. 2006).

[208] *Sangendorf-Teal v. Rensselaer County*, 100 F.3d 270 (2d Cir. 1996).

[209] *Broadrick v. Oklahoma*, 413 U.S. 601 (1973).

[210] *Grayned v. City of Rockford*, 408 U.S. 104 (1972).

[211] *Micilcavage v. Connelie*, 570 F. Supp. 975 (N.D. N.Y. 1995); *Firefighters Association of D.C. v. Barry*, 742 F. Supp. 1182 (D. D.C. 1990).

[212] *Mansoor v. Trank*, 319 F.3d 133 (4th Cir. 2003).

[213] *Gibson v. Mayor and Council of the City of Wilmington*, 176 F. Supp. 2d 248 (D. Del. 2001).

[214] *Mansoor v. Trank*, 319 F.3d 133 (4th Cir. 2003).

[215] *E.g., Wernsing v. Thompson*, 286 F. Supp. 2d 983 (C.D. Ill. 2003).

[216] *Latino Officers Association v. Safir,* 13 IER Cases 199 (S.D. N.Y. 1997), *vacated on other grounds,* 170 F.3d 167 (2d Cir. 1999); *Harman v. City of New York,* 945 F. Supp. 750 (S.D. N.Y. 1996).

[217] *Muller v. Conlisk*, 429 F.2d 901 (7th Cir. 1970).

[218] *Kessler v. City of Providence*, 167 F. Supp. 2d 482 (D. R.I. 2001); *Wolf v. City of Aberdeen*, 758 F. Supp. 551 (D. S.D. 1991)(strikes down ban on speaking to press without prior departmental approval); *Holland v. Dillon*, 531 N.Y.S.2d 467 (N.Y. Sup. 1988)(reversal of five-day suspension for speaking to press about overcrowded conditions in jail).

[219] *Pesek v. City of Brunswick*, 794 F. Supp. 768 (N.D. Ohio 1992)(strikes down ordinance forbidding employees from speaking during public meetings on departmental matters).

[220] *Wolf v. City of Aberdeen*, 758 F. Supp. 551 (D. S.D. 1991)(strikes down rule forbidding employees from commenting on internal business decisions or departmental rules); *Salerno v. O'Rourke*, 555 F. Supp. 750 (D. N.J. 1983)(discipline for speaking with press reversed).

[221] *Shelton Police Union, Inc. v. Voccola*, 125 F. Supp. 2d 604 (D. Conn. 2001); *Belch v. Jefferson County*, 108 F. Supp. 2d 143 (N.D. N.Y. 2000).

[222] *Donaggio v. Arlington County, Virginia*, 880 F. Supp. 446 (E.D. Va. 1995).

[223] *See Los Angeles Police Protective League v. Gates*, 579 F. Supp. 36 (C.D. Cal. 1984).

[224] *See National Labor Relations Board v. J. Weingarten, Inc.*, 420 U.S. 251 (1975).

CHAPTER 8

A LAW ENFORCEMENT OFFICER'S FREEDOM OF ASSOCIATION RIGHTS

The Roots Of The Freedom Of Association.

Though the United States Constitution nowhere mentions the phrase "freedom of association," the Supreme Court has inferred such a right into the freedoms of speech and assembly found in the First Amendment. There are two types of freedom of association protected by the Constitution.[1] The first type of freedom of association covers the right to associate for the purpose of those activities that are otherwise protected by the First Amendment – activities such as speech, the exercise of religion, and engaging in politics.[2] This area is often referred to as the freedom of "expressive association,"[3] and is subject to the same legal tests as questions about speech. Accordingly, one finds courts questioning whether an officer's associations are made as part of the job and balancing the officer's interests against the employer's interests in regulating the association.[4]

The second type of freedom of association involves choices to enter into and maintain certain intimate relationships, choices that are protected by the Constitution as a basic safeguard of individual freedom.[5] This area is often referred to as freedom of "intimate association," and quite often involves an overlap with the constitutional right to privacy.

Freedom Of Expressive Association And Law Enforcement Labor Organizations.

The freedom of expressive association has been applied in several contexts in cases involving law enforcement officers. Perhaps most prominently, the freedom of association gives a blanket protection to any law enforcement officer who wishes to join a labor organization.[6] Although most forms of speech usually have to be about a matter of public concern to be protected, union membership is on a higher plane and does not require a matter of public concern for constitutional protection.[7] The freedom of association is so strong that even a police chief, who is an at-will employee and can be fired for almost any reason without recourse, cannot be disciplined for joining a labor organization. The freedom of association also prohibits an employer from deliberately attempting to destroy an association of law enforcement officers for the purpose of preventing the exercise of First Amendment rights.[8]

The right to join a labor organization does not, in and of itself, carry with it any right to compel an employer to bargain collectively[9] or to facilitate the collection of dues through a payroll deduction system.[10] As described in Chapter 2, collective bargaining rights are controlled by state law.[11] Nor does the freedom of association require the employer to give any particular benefit such as time off to employees to facilitate their union activities.[12] However, simple membership by an officer in a labor organization, or even active participation in the activities of a labor organization, cannot be prohibited by an employer.[13] Damages for violation of freedom of association can be significant; one case in 2008 resulted in a jury

The freedom of association gives a blanket protection to any law enforcement officer who wishes to join a labor organization.

award of $165,000 in favor of a police officer who had been targeted by a police chief after the officer assumed a leadership position in the local labor organization.[14]

An officer claiming that an employer has violated his free association rights with respect to a labor organization must prove that the discipline imposed on him was for membership in or activities with the organization, and not for other conduct. For example, in one case a deputy sheriff for DeKalb County, Georgia, who was the president of a local union belonging to the International Brotherhood of Police Officers, organized a "ticket slow-down" in an effort to disrupt the County's revenue stream from tickets and enhance the union's bargaining leverage. The deputy also surreptitiously tape recorded a conversation with the police chief in violation of the County's policies and was involved in three domestic disturbances that resulted in 911 calls. Upholding the officer's discharge, a court commented that an employee may not use union activities as a "cloak of immunity" for conduct unbecoming an officer.[15]

The freedom of association also bars an employer from inquiring into the off-duty legal activities of a police union. For example, in one case an employer compelled officers to answer questions in an internal affairs investigation about the off-duty statements of other officers – union leaders – about whether the police chief should be replaced. A court found the employer's questions to violate the free association rights of officers, finding that the internal affairs investigators "intruded into quintessentially protected associational activity."[16]

The application of freedom of association to the activities of labor organizations often creates protections that overlap with those found in the relevant collective bargaining law. Most collective bargaining statutes prohibit an employer from "interfering" with the activities of a labor organization.[17] Conduct that rises to being a violation of the constitutional freedom of association will almost certainly amount to a violation of a union's right to be free from inappropriate employer interference with its internal activities.

Freedom Of Expressive Association And Membership In Organizations With Divergent Political Views.

The First Amendment's guarantee of freedom of association also protects membership in political or quasi-political organizations, so long as those organizations are (1) organized, (2) take positions on public questions; and (3) engage in activities protected by the First Amendment, such as speech. Even membership in organizations with tenets that may include violation of the law may be protected by the First Amendment, so long as the employee does not participate in organized activities which violate law and there is no impact on the employee's job performance or demonstrable effect on the law enforcement agency. In other words, there is a distinction drawn between "mere membership in an organization" and a person's active participation in advocacy of the illegal conduct of the organization.[18]

The need for a provable impact on the job is demonstrated by two cases involving the Ku Klux Klan. In one case, *McMullen v. Carson*, the termination of a sheriff's office employee for membership in the Ku Klux Klan was upheld where the employee appeared on television and identified himself as a Klansman and a sheriff's employee. The Court stressed the fact that the employee himself drew the link between himself and the Sheriff's Office, and commented as follows:

> "The unrebutted evidence establishes that had [the sheriff] not acted promptly in discharging plaintiff, the credibility of the Sheriff's Office within the Jacksonville community at large, and particularly within the Jacksonville minority community, would be devastatingly and catastrophically impaired because the Klan is widely perceived as an organization dedicated to racism, criminality, and violence. Relations between the Sheriff's Office and the Jacksonville minority community, already fragile as of February 1982, would have deteriorated even further had Sheriff Carson not discharged the plaintiff. In addition, enforcing the law on the streets would have been more difficult, in light of the already existing lack of cooperation by black citizens with white police officers and the frequently expressed reaction in the black community that arrests would have been resisted more often if plaintiff remained an employee in the Sheriff's Office."[19]

Contrasted with the *McMullen* case is *Murray v. Jamison*, where the Court reversed a termination of an employee for membership in the Ku Klux Klan. Critical in the Court's decision was the fact that the employee was terminated for simple membership in the group and that the employer had made no showing of adverse impact on the employee's job.[20]

Freedom Of Association And Membership In Groups That Do Not Engage In 'Expressive' Behavior.

If the group with which an officer is associating is non-religious and does not engage in any political or labor activities, an employer has much more latitude under the First Amendment to forbid membership in the group. A case involving four corrections officers who were disciplined for being members of the Outlaws motorcycle club is a good example of the leeway courts give to employers in this area. The Court hearing the case held that the Outlaws themselves did not engage in "expressive behavior," but were a form of social club. The Court concluded that one of the four officers, who joined the club simply to ride motorcycles, did not himself engage in "expression" by joining the club. The Court did find that the other three officers joined the Outlaws to express support for the organization and the conduct was potentially protected by the First Amendment:

"We think it plain that by repeatedly consorting with the Outlaws and wearing Outlaws colors and apparel in public – even at such times as they were not members of the Outlaws, the three officers engaged in expressive activity approving of the nature of the Connecticut chapter of the Outlaws, of the national Outlaws organization, and of other Outlaws chapters. The fact that law enforcement agencies believe the Outlaws and many of its chapters engage in criminal activity is sufficient in itself to make the nature of those entities a matter of public concern."

However, the Court found that because of the nature of the Outlaws, the officers' approval "of the nature and character of the Outlaws had the potential in several ways to disrupt and reflect negatively on DOC's operations, and that DOC's interest in maintaining the efficiency, security, and integrity of its operations outweighed the associational interests of those plaintiffs."[21]

Freedom Of Expressive Association And The Right To Privacy In One's Membership In Organizations.

The right to freedom of association includes not only the freedom to associate with others, or with groups, but also includes the right to privacy in one's associations.[22] As put by one court, "The right of association protects confidentiality in one's private, civic, and political associations, particularly where government intrusion may result in a chilling effect on collective action."[23] Thus, in an early case involving freedom of association, the Supreme Court struck down a requirement that public school teachers disclose the names of organizations to which they belonged, noting:

> "It is not disputed that to compel a teacher to disclose his every associational tie is to impair that teacher's right of free association, a right closely allied to freedom of speech and a right which, like free speech, lies at the foundation of a free society. * * * Such interference with personal freedom is conspicuously accented when the teacher serves at the absolute will of those to whom the disclosure must be made – those who any year can terminate the teacher's employment without bringing charges, without notice, without a hearing, without affording an opportunity to explain."[24]

The compelled disclosure of organizational memberships has been struck down when applied to law enforcement officers, even when the officers in question held sensitive positions in the police agencies. For example, in *Fraternal Order of Police v. Philadelphia*, a city sought to compel officers applying for transfer to an anti-corruption unit to disclose the names of all organizations to which they belonged. The Court rejected the compelled disclosure, holding that the disclosure "seriously" violated the officers' rights to privacy.[25]

The right to freedom of association includes not only the freedom to associate with others, or with groups, but also includes the right to privacy in one's associations.

Freedom Of Association And 'No Contact' Orders.

Many jurisdictions use "no contact" orders as part of the internal investigations process. A typical "no contact" order forbids the employee from discussing the investigation with others while the investigation is pending. To the extent that a "no-contact" order does not forbid the employee from discussing the matter with individuals in a privileged relationship – the employee's spouse, attorney, minister, union representative, and the like – the order is likely to be enforceable. In one case, a court even upheld an order forbidding a female officer from having *any* off-duty contact with a male officer, citing the fact that the female officer had previously complained that the male officer was harassing her.[26]

Freedom Of Intimate Association And Personal Relationships.

Choices to enter into and maintain certain intimate human relationships must be secured against undue intrusion by the State because of the role of such relationships in safeguarding the individual freedom that is central to our constitutional scheme.

A law enforcement officer's right to freedom of association protects the officer's freedom to engage in personal relationships in much the same manner as the right to privacy. As the Supreme Court has noted, "choices to enter into and maintain certain intimate human relationships must be secured against undue intrusion by the State because of the role of such relationships in safeguarding the individual freedom that is central to our constitutional scheme."[27] If a governmental employer intentionally interferes with a protected personal relationship, the officer may have a claim against the employer.[28]

Not all associations with others are constitutionally protected. Instead, the Supreme Court has observed that protected associations "are distinguished by such attributes as relative smallness, a high degree of selectivity in decisions to begin and maintain affiliation, and seclusion from others in critical aspects of the relationship."[29] As such, there is a continuum of human relationships potentially protected by the freedom of intimate association. Extremely close relationships, such as family relationships and marriage, are generally afforded greater protection from government interference than are merely social ones.[30]

The law is still evolving whether the freedom of intimate association applies to an unmarried couple living together. The emerging trend seems to be that freedom of association does protect such relationships. As one court commented, such relationships, "which for some are the natural precursor or alternative to marriage, deserve just as much protection. It would defeat the aim of protecting marital relations if protection was denied to serious intimate relations that often lead to marriage."[31] Taking a more conservative viewpoint on a related issue, a court has held that the freedom of intimate relationships does not protect an officer's adulterous relationship.[32]

There is a good deal of conceptual overlap between the freedom of intimate association and the right to privacy. The right to privacy extends to personal decisions about marriage, procreation, contraception, family relationships, child rearing and education, and abortion.[33] As discussed in Chapter 6, in some circumstances, the right to privacy in connection with relationships has been extended to matters implicating individual autonomy, whether or not the individuals in the relationship are married.[34] As with the freedom of intimate association, a continuum of protection exists with the right to privacy, in that the more traditionally familial in nature the relationship is, the more likely it is that the relationship will be protected.

These principles were well illustrated in a case involving a lieutenant who was threatened with discipline for maintaining an off-duty relationship with a woman on probation for the felony of receiving stolen property. A court stated that it was "uncomfortable announcing a new, general rule that all dating relationships are constitutionally protected, especially when that rule is advocated by a government employee who works in the sensitive area of law enforcement." The Court acknowledged that a "sanctioned marital relationship" between the lieutenant and the probationer would be protected, but "doubted that the amorphous social relationship between the two, although apparently intimate to some degree, is entitled to the full scope of constitutional protection." Finding that the relationship had the potential for disruption in the workplace, the Court found the relationship unprotected by the Constitution.[35]

Occasionally, law enforcement officers will raise freedom of association claims based upon their relationships with individuals with whom they are unrelated and with whom they are not involved in a romantic relationship. Such relationships are generally not protected by the freedom of intimate association.[36]

Freedom Of Association And 'Association With Criminals' Regulations.

Virtually all law enforcement agencies have regulations prohibiting employees from associating with individuals who either have been convicted of crimes or who are being prosecuted. Occasionally, the regulations go so far as to prohibit associations with those who merely have criminal reputations.

For many years, such regulations were regularly upheld by the courts.[37] However, in 1985, the decision in *Dunn v. McKinney* made it clear that such "association" regulations had to be clear and meet certain minimum standards.[38] *Dunn* involved the lawsuit of a deputy sheriff who was forced to resign for violating a rule prohibiting deputies from "voluntarily maintaining or establishing associations or dealing with known criminals except in the line of duty and with the knowledge of the Sheriff." The Court first quoted with approval language indicating that the freedom of association extended to protect more than purely political associations, holding:

> "It is too late in the day to doubt that this freedom of association extends only to political or conventional associations and not to the social or unorthodox."[39]

Virtually all law enforcement agencies have regulations prohibiting employees from associating with individuals who either have been convicted of crimes or who are being prosecuted.

The Court next recognized that a rule narrowly drawn to prohibit "close relationships with felons" by law enforcement officers would stand on a different footing from the regulation it was considering. However, for several reasons the Court found the regulation used to compel the resignation of the deputy unconstitutionally vague and overbroad and in violation of the freedom of association.

First, the Court found that by attempting to bar relationships with known "criminals," the regulation used a term that was vague and might, by its terms, be construed to bar relationships with known traffic violators (who meet the dictionary definition of "criminal" by virtue of having broken the law). Second, the Court found the word "known" to be impermissibly vague, and in the following passage indicated that even the Sheriff had a difficult time interpreting his own rule:

> "The Sheriff also could not define the word 'known'; he wavered between whether it means a convicted criminal, a convicted criminal who the community knows was convicted, or just an 'unsavory type individual' with a bad reputation. The Sheriff also had trouble defining just what types of 'associations' or 'dealings' were prohibited by the rule, and stated several unwritten exceptions and qualifications to the rule. This Court has held that '[m]en of common intelligence are not required to guess at the meaning of an ordinance.' Because even Sheriff McKinney could only guess at the meaning of his own rule, the Court must conclude that it is unconstitutionally vague."

Finally, the Court found that by using the vague term "criminals," the regulation reached too far, and attempted to regulate associations protected by the First Amendment:

> "If a deputy's spouse received a traffic ticket, the Sheriff could order the deputy to stop associating with the criminal spouse. There is no end to the types of 'associations or dealings' the Sheriff could prohibit under a literal interpretation of his rule. The Court agrees with Sheriff McKinney's own statement that the rule 'is pretty broad,' and concludes that, on its face, the anti-association rule must be struck down as unconstitutionally overbroad."

As time has passed since *Dunn*, courts have seemed to adopt a sliding-scale approach to "association with criminals" regulations. The more family-based a relationship is, the more the department must prove a need to regulate the relationship.[40] In cases where the relationship is especially close (i.e., spouse, "significant other" or blood relative), an employer will likely have to prove a demonstrable effect on job performance in order to validly apply its regulations to prohibit the relationship.[41] However, where the relationship is purely social in nature, a department will have great latitude in prohibiting or controlling the relationship.[42] In addition, the more clear it is that the person the officer associates with is a "criminal," the easier it will be for the department to regulate the relationship. For example, if the object of the officer's attention is an inmate who is currently on active probation or in custody, the employer will be given greater latitude to forbid the association.[43] And, to the extent that the employer completely forbids the relationship upon pain of discharge as opposed to imposing lesser burdens on the relationship, the employer's decision will receive higher scrutiny.[44]

An important case dealt not with the specific application of an "association with criminals" rule to a particular employee, but instead with a broad-based challenge to the entire rule. In the case, the Michigan Department of Corrections had a rule that prohibited employees from all non-work contact with prisoners, parolees, probationers, and their relatives and visitors unless the Department granted an exception to the rule. In a 2-1 decision, a federal appeals court upheld the rule as not violating the free association rights of employees. On the issue of whether the rule prohibited familial relationships such as marriage, the Court applied a test looking at whether the rule had a substantial impact on the collective marriage rights of corrections officers:

> "The rule does not prevent a large portion of employees from forming intimate associations; all employees continue to enjoy the ability to form intimate associations – just not with offenders. Nor are those affected by the Rule absolutely or largely prevented from forming intimate associations with a large portion of the otherwise eligible population. While the plaintiffs stress the large offender population in Michigan, it is only a little over 1% of the state's population. Even if the number of visitors and family members should exceed the number of offenders ten-fold, surely a generous estimate, employees would only be barred from intimate association with about 10% of the state's population (whereof 9% are subject to routinely-granted exemption under the current Rule). This is far from the absolute bar against marrying a majority of the jurisdiction's population said to be a direct and substantial interference. Moreover, the simple expedient of transferring to another part of the state government or taking employment in the private sector is available to employees here."[45]

In all "association with criminals" cases, a central feature is the specificity of the employer's rules. The narrower and clearer the rules, the more likely they will be upheld.[46]

How Freedom Of Association Cases Are Handled By The Courts.

The courts handle freedom of association cases in much the same way they do free speech lawsuits. First, an officer must prove that he was engaging in associative activity not in the course of his employment, but rather "as a citizen."[47] Once an officer has met his burden on this threshold legal issue, a court must determine (1) whether the officer's interest in engaging in associative activity outweighs the employer's interest in discouraging the activity in order to ensure the efficient operation of government services, and (2) whether the officer's conduct played

An officer must prove that he was engaging in associative activity not in the course of his employment, but rather as a citizen.

a substantial part in the decision to demote or discharge the employee.[48] If the employer meets this burden, the burden shifts back to the employee to show that the employer's actions were a pretext for illegal retaliation.[49]

NOTES

[1] *McKane v. Soldenwagner*, 1991 WL 236507 (S.D. Fla. 1991). *See generally Griswold v. Connecticut*, 381 U.S. 479 (1965).

[2] *See N.A.A.C.P. v. Alabama*, 357 U.S. 449 (1958).

[3] *Piscottano v. Murphy*, 511 F.3d 247 (2d Cir. 2007).

[4] *D'Angelo v. Sch. Bd. Of Polk County*, 497 F.3d 1203 (11th Cir. 2007); *VanCamp v. McNesby*, 2008 WL 2557539 (N.D. Fla. 2008).

[5] *Roberts v. United States Jaycees*, 468 U.S. 609 (1984).

[6] *Smith v. Arkansas State Highway Employees*, 441 U.S. 463 (1979); *Thomas v. Collins,* 323 U.S. 516 (1945); *Guarnieri v. Duryea Borough*, 2007 WL 4085563 (M.D. Pa. 2007).

[7] *Guarnieri v. Duryea Borough*, 2007 WL 4085563 (M.D. Pa. 2007); *Zerman v. City of Strongsville, Ohio*, 180 L.R.R.M. 2859 (N.D. Ohio 2006).

[8] *Mortara v. Katkocin*, 2007 WL 4105283 (D. Conn. 2007)("core union activity" is protected by the First Amendment); *Healy v. Town of Pembroke Park*, 643 F. Supp. 1208 (S.D. Fla. 1986)(City illegally disbanded police department and contracted out work after officers had joined a labor organization).

[9] *Griffith v. Lanier*, 521 F.3d 398 (D.C. Cir. 2008).

[10] *Laredo Fraternal Order of Police v. City of Laredo, Tex.*, 2008 WL 678698 (S.D. Tex. 2008).

[11] *Alaniz v. City of San Antonio*, 82 L.R.R.M. 2983 (W.D. Tex. 1971); *Atkins v. City of Charlotte*, 296 F. Supp. 1068 (W.D. N.C. 1969).

[12] *Fraternal Order of Police v. County of Douglas*, 699 N.W.2d 820 (Neb. 2005).

[13] *Police Officers' Guild v. Washington*, 369 F. Supp. 543 (D. D.C. 1973); *Melton v. City of Atlanta, Georgia*, 324 F. Supp. 315 (D. Ga. 1971).

[14] *Shrum v. City of Coweta, Okla.*, 2008 WL 920343 (E.D. Okla. 2008).

[15] *Douglas v. DeKalb County, Georgia*, 2007 WL 4373970 (N.D. Ga. 2007); *see Tuskowski v. Griffin*, 359 F. Supp. 2d 225 (D. Conn. 2005)(no freedom of association right to refer to supervisor as "idiot").

[16] *Local 491, International Broth. of Police Officers v. Gwinnett County, Georgia*, 510 F. Supp. 2d 1271 (N.D. Ga. 2007).

[17] *E.g.*, 5 ILCS 315 (10)(Illinois statute prohibiting interference).

[18] *Davis v. Phenix City, Alabama*, 183 L.R.R.M. 2881 (M.D. Ala. 2008).

[19] *McMullen v. Carson*, 754 F.2d 936 (11th Cir. 1985).

[20] *Murray v. Jamison*, 333 F. Supp. 1379 (W.D. N.C. 1971).

[21] *Piscottano v. Murphy*, 511 F.3d 247 (2d Cir. 2007).

[22] *N.A.A.C.P. v. Alabama*, 357 U.S. 449 (1958).

[23] *Local 491, International Broth. of Police Officers v. Gwinnett County, Georgia*, 510 F. Supp. 2d 1271 (N.D. Ga. 2007).

[24] *Shelton v. Tucker*, 364 U.S. 479 (1960). *See also N.A.A.C.P. v. Alabama*, 357 U.S. 449 (1958)(compelled disclosure of an organization's membership list infringes upon members' First Amendment rights).

[25] *Fraternal Order of Police, Lodge #5 v. City of Philadelphia*, 812 F.2d 105 (3d Cir. 1987).

[26] *Driggers v. City of Owensboro, Kentucky*, 110 Fed.Appx. 499 (6th Cir. 2004).

[27] *Roberts v. United States Jaycees*, 468 U.S. 609 (1984). *See generally* Karst, "The Freedom of Intimate Association," 89 Yale L.J. 624 (1980).

[28] *Ashcraft v. Beicker*, 2008 WL 538919 (D. Colo. 2008).

[29] *Roberts v. United States Jaycees*, 468 U.S. 609 (1984); *see Martin v. City of Dothan*, 2008 WL 541289 (M.D. Ala. 2008).

[30] *Driggers v. City of Owensboro, Kentucky*, 110 Fed.Appx. 499 (6th Cir. 2004); *Swanson v. City of Bruce, Miss.*, 105 Fed.Appx. 540 (5th Cir. 2004); *Cameron v. Grainger County, Tennessee*, 2007 WL 1306522 (E.D. Tenn. 2007); *Wieland v. City of Arnold*, 100 F. Supp. 2d 984 (E.D. Mo. 2000).

[31] *Poleo-Keefe v. Bergeron*, 2008 WL 3992636 (D. Vt. 2008); *Anderson v. City of LaVergne*, 371 F.3d 879 (6th Cir. 2004)(for summary judgment purposes, a dating relationship between a police officer and an administrative assistant for the police department qualified as an intimate association because the two were monogamous, had lived together, and were romantically and sexually involved); *Akers v. McGinnis*, 352 F.3d 1030 (6th Cir. 2003)(personal friendship is protected as an intimate association).

[32] *Beecham v. Henderson County, Tennessee*, 422 F.3d 372 (6th Cir. 2005).

[33] *See Carey v. Population Servs. Int'l*, 431 U.S. 678 (1977).

[34] *See, e.g., Eisenstadt v. Baird*, 405 U.S. 438 (1972).

[35] *Wieland v. City of Arnold*, 100 F. Supp. 2d 984 (E.D. Mo. 2000).

[36] *Miller v. Maddox*, 51 F. Supp. 2d 1176 (D. Kan. 1999); *see Weinberger v. Navarro*, 957 F. Supp. 220 (S.D. Fla. 1997)(no constitutional right to associate with Muhammed Ali).

[37] *Baron v. Meloni*, 556 F. Supp. 796 (W.D. N.Y. 1983)(freedom of association does not protect officer having relationship with wife of crime figure); *Sponick v. City of Detroit,* 211 N.W.2d 674 (Mich. App. 1973)(upholds similar rule); *De Grazio v. Civil Service Commission*, 202 N.E.2d 522 (Ill. 1964)(upholds similar rule).

[38] *Dunn v. McKinney*, 622 F. Supp. 259 (D. Wyo. 1985).

[39] *Dunn v. McKinney*, 622 F. Supp. 259 (D. Wyo. 1985), *quoting Burns v. Pomerleau,* 319 F. Supp. 58 (D. Md. 1970)(police department cannot bar employment simply because applicant is a nudist).

[40] *See Wilson v. Taylor*, 733 F.2d 1539 (11th Cir. 1984)(police officer has protected constitutional interest in off-duty dating of known felon's daughter).

[41] *Reuter v. Skipper*, 4 F.3d 716 (9th Cir. 1993)(Court strikes down ban on corrections officer sharing living quarters with an ex-felon); *Clark v. Alston*, 442 F. Supp. 2d 395 (E.D. Mich. 2006)("the mere fact that an employer uses an individual's marital relationship in an employment decision will not always constitute an undue or impermissible intrusion into the marital relationship").

[42] *Vieira v. Presley*, 988 F.2d 850 (8th Cir. 1993)(freedom of association does not protect relationship between officer and friends who were the target of a criminal investigation); *Fagan v. City of Marco Island*, 2005 WL 1667662 (M.D. Fla. 2005)(freedom of association does not protect relationship between officer and former boss, a convicted felon).

[43] *Ross v. Clayton County, Ga,* 173 F.3d 1305 (11th Cir. 1999)(Court upholds demotion of officer for living with his brother, an active probationer); *Keeney v. Heath,* 57 F.3d 579 (7th Cir. 1995)(Court upholds ban on social relationships between corrections officers and inmates).

[44] *Montgomery v. Stefaniak,* 410 F.3d 933 (7th Cir. 2005).

[45] *Akers v. McGinnis,* 352 F.3d 1030 (6th Cir. 2003).

[46] *Williams v. Miami-Dade County, Florida,* 969 So.2d 389 (Fla. App. 2007).

[47] *Douglas v. DeKalb County, Georgia,* 2007 WL 4373970 (N.D. Ga. 2007).

[48] *Olson v. State of New York,* 2007 WL 1029021 (E.D. N.Y. 2007); *Day v. Borough of Carlisle,* 180 L.R.R.M. 2022 (M.D. Pa. 2006).

[49] *Morris v. City of Chillocothe,* 512 F.3d 1013 (8th Cir. 2008).

CHAPTER 9

THE RIGHT TO ENGAGE IN POLITICAL ACTIVITIES

The Right To Engage In Political Activities.

One of the most difficult areas of First Amendment law affecting law enforcement officers concerns the involvement of law enforcement officers in the political process. It is not at all surprising that law enforcement officers are often interested in the political process since governmental function is inherently political in nature, and law enforcement services usually are the most visible of governmental functions. Since the wages, benefits and other working conditions of law enforcement officers are frequently affected by the decisions of elected officials, law enforcement officers often wish to become involved in the political process as a means of gaining greater control over their work lives. Also, law enforcement officers are no more immune from the "political bug" than any other class of individuals, and seek elective office themselves with some regularity.

Law enforcement officers often wish to become involved in the political process as a means of gaining greater control over their work lives.

Over the years, many employers have attempted to limit political activities on the part of their law enforcement officers. Such limitations run the range from bans on running for elected office to complete prohibitions against engaging in any political activity except for the limited act of voting. At the other end of the scale, some law enforcement agencies insist that their law enforcement officers become involved in the political process by supporting particular candidates for office. For example, court decisions are issued with some regularity involving cases where a sheriff has fired some or all of his deputies who supported the "wrong" candidate for sheriff in the previous election.

The biggest complicating factor in the area of the political rights of law enforcement officers is the inconsistent manner in which courts have approached the issue. On seemingly indistinguishable facts, courts located in different areas of the country have rendered completely contrary decisions on whether a law enforcement officer may engage in a certain type of political activity. Even different courts in the same court system – the federal courts of appeal – often sharply disagree with each other on fundamental questions affecting the First Amendment political rights of law enforcement officers.

Cases involving the political activity of law enforcement officers fall into four categories:

- Cases where law enforcement officers are seeking elective office;

- Cases where law enforcement officers, or the organizations to which they belong, are seeking to make political contributions or otherwise become involved in partisan or non-partisan political contests;

- Cases where law enforcement officers have been disciplined for their political beliefs or activities; and

- Political patronage cases.

Since the United States Supreme Court has spoken only infrequently on such issues, many of these conflicts exist today, with no indication that they will be resolved in the foreseeable future.

Law Enforcement Officers As Political Candidates.

The starting point for any discussion of the political rights of law enforcement officers must begin with the notion that the right to engage in political activities and join a particular political party, though fundamental rights protected by the First Amendment to the United States Constitution, may nonetheless be restricted under appropriate circumstances in the public employer/employee environment.[1] However, restrictions on the political activities of law enforcement officers are constitutionally permissible only if such restrictions are "justified by a reasonable necessity * * * to achieve a compelling public objective."[2]

State and local governmental bodies have occasionally taken actions that tend to deter public employees from seeking elective office. Such actions have taken one of three forms: (1) Statutes or rules prohibiting public employees from running for office, so-called "resign to run" rules; (2) statutes or rules requiring that public employees seeking elective office, or those who have been successful in obtaining office, take a leave of absence; and (3) in the absence of controlling rules or regulations, taking of disciplinary action against public employees who have run for elective office. As long as the controlling statutes or regulations are narrowly drawn, actions falling into categories (1) and (2) are likely to be upheld as not violative of the First Amendment rights of employees. Actions falling into the third category, however, are much more suspect and are not only likely to be struck down, but also will likely form the basis for substantial money-damage verdicts against the employer.

The Supreme Court's decision in *Clement v. Fashing* validates the legitimacy of resign to run rules as long as they serve a compelling public interest, or "rationale predicate." *Fashing* upheld Texas statutes that require an officeholder who becomes a candidate for the state legislature to resign his present post in the event the terms of the two offices overlap. Although the Circuit Court struck these provisions down because the broad scope posed equal protection and First Amendment challenges, the Supreme Court declared that the public policy served by the legislation is "sufficient to warrant the *de minimis* interference with appellees' interests in candidacy." Thus, the Court chose to favor candidates' responsibility to their present office over what they saw was lesser a restriction on their ability to participate in the political process.[3]

Fashing focused on three policy considerations to justify the existence of the resign to run rule: (1) To prevent a candidate already holding an office from neglecting his present duties during his bid for election; (2) to discourage a judicial officer seeking election from making politically motivated decisions to further his candidacy; and (3) to limit the difficulties that accompany interim elections and appointments. Thus, as long as a resign to run rule is tailored to serve a

The right to engage in political activities and join a particular political party, though fundamental rights protected by the First Amendment, may nonetheless be restricted under appropriate circumstances in the public employer/ employee environment.

broad public or state interest, it should overcome its inherent restriction on First Amendment or equal protection rights.

A similar regulation in a city police department was upheld in a separate case. In that case, the Court reasoned that the Department's regulation was permissible because the regulation concerned attracting qualified persons for the job of police officer through guaranteeing job security free from the political arena and because it ensured the impartial execution of the laws.[4]

If a law enforcement agency may constitutionally forbid employees from running for political office while remaining a member of the department, it may on the same grounds refuse to allow a leave of absence to an employee to serve in political office.[5] Similarly, a law enforcement agency may require an employee who is seeking political office, or who has been elected to political office, to take a leave of absence for the duration of the campaign or term of office.[6] However, simply because an employer can forbid an officer from running for office altogether, it may not allow the officer to run and then discipline the officer because it dislikes the officer's political platform.[7]

Where there are no preexisting rules or regulations barring political candidacy and a law enforcement agency restricts such activities on a case-by-case basis through the disciplinary process, its actions are extremely suspect and can expose the employer to significant liability.[8] This potential for liability exists even in a sheriff's office where a deputy has announced the intention to run against the incumbent sheriff.[9] For example, in one case a deputy sheriff was demoted to "turnkey status" after he circulated nominating petitions to run for sheriff. The demotion was issued by the incumbent sheriff allegedly because the deputy took his daughter home from school early in violation of a city ordinance and did not respond to an emergency call. Two months later, the deputy was suspended for five days without pay for allegedly allowing a prisoner to escape. The Sheriff then relayed the two sets of charges to a local newspaper, which subsequently printed the charges. A jury found that the deputy was clearly being punished by the Sheriff for his decision to run for elective office and that the deputy's actions were completely protected by the First Amendment. On appeal, the Court upheld an award of $750,000 in favor of the deputy.[10]

In a similar case, a deputy had received positive performance ratings from his sheriff prior to when the deputy declared his candidacy for sheriff. After declaring his candidacy, the deputy was suspended for five days for leaving a proof of service card to be picked up by another deputy, a routine practice in the Department. Two months later, the deputy was fired for allegedly failing to respond to an "unusual noises" call in a prompt manner. An appellate court upheld a jury verdict of $81,466 in favor of the deputy. The appellate court's comments in upholding the punitive damage award describe the tenor of the case:

> "The evidence shows that the Sheriff suspended [the deputy] for five days without conducting any hearing, disciplined him for minor infractions, pressured a statement from [a local marshal], threatened [the deputy's] job and offered to forget the charges – all with the intent

to force [the deputy] out of the sheriff's race or, if that failed, punish him for the effort. From all of this evidence a jury could reasonably find that [the sheriff] acted with malicious intent."[11]

There is a dissenting viewpoint, albeit one that has garnered only mixed reviews in the courts. In a 1997 case, the federal Sixth Circuit Court of Appeals upheld the right of an elected official to fire an employee who announced her candidacy against the elected official. As the Court put it, "the First Amendment does not require that an official in an employer's situation nourish a viper in the nest."[12] Though the majority rule throughout the country would prohibit such a termination, and though even the Sixth Circuit clearly has misgivings about its 1997 decision, it continues to adhere to it and apply it to deputy sheriffs who are fired after they become candidates for sheriff. A dissenting judge has even described the 1997 decision in the following terms:

> "Still, like a stray cat that hangs around the door and infests the house with fleas, this decision continues to plague this Court's jurisprudence."[13]

Political Contributions And Other Campaign Activities By Law Enforcement Officers.

Perhaps nowhere is the law with respect to the free speech rights of law enforcement officers as confused as with respect to the right to make political contributions and to engage in other campaign activities. As the previous discussion indicates, the First Amendment rights of law enforcement officers to run for elective office can be regulated by narrowly drawn and applied rules. The question in this area is whether the right to make political contributions and to engage in other political campaign activity – both of which are less politically involved activities than actually running for office – can be similarly regulated.

As a general concept, it has long been accepted that the making of political contributions constitutes speech protected by the First Amendment.[14] However, as discussed in Chapter 7, the First Amendment freedom of speech rights of public employees can be regulated if an overriding governmental interest exists for the regulation. The difficulty has been in drawing the line as to how extensive the regulation of such activity may be before it violates the First Amendment. Exemplifying this difficulty, the leading cases in the area follow two seemingly contradictory theories as to the extent of permissible regulation.

The 'Relationship To Job Performance' Theory.

The first of the two theories is that the regulation of political contributions and campaign activity is permissible only when it solely regulates conduct that the employer has an overriding reason to regulate because of the nature of the employee's job. The case of *Phillips v. City of Flint*,[15] which involved provisions in a city charter that prohibited employees from contributing to political campaigns or from becoming involved in any fashion in city council elections, is an early decision advocating this first theory. The Court in *Phillips* began by recognizing the City's "interest in insulating its civil servants from political pressures and, conversely, in preventing its employees from developing enough influence to elect the public officials with whom they will be bargaining over conditions of employment."[16] However, the Court found that the city charter was unconstitutionally overbroad in that it appeared to forbid all political activities by city employees, including such activities as supporting or opposing special assessment measures, zoning ordinances, school budgets, annexations, and the like. In short, the Court found, there must be a relationship between the employee's job and the type of controls sought by the employer over the employee's political activities:

> "Where the political activities of a public employee are unrelated to his job responsibilities, he must be treated for purposes of adjudicating his First Amendment rights as a member of the 'general public.'"[17]

These theories were strictly applied in the case of *Perez v. Cucci*. In *Perez*, the Court held that the right to associate with political parties of an officer's own choice and to support its platforms and candidates is an integral part of the First Amendment's protection of freedom of association. In the case, the officer was demoted from detective to patrolman because he openly espoused the candidacy of a mayoral incumbent who was defeated for reelection. In a lengthy opinion, the Court reinforced the concept that an employer must convincingly prove a relationship between an officer's political activities and the job in order to regulate those activities. Finding that the City had failed to establish such proof, the Court awarded the officer damages equivalent to four years' differential between patrol and detective pay and $25,000 in punitive damages.[18]

A similar result was reached in *McNea v. Garey*, where the Court considered the constitutionality of rules of the Cleveland Police Department that prohibited officers from discussing political matters while on duty and from having "direct or indirect connection" with political organizations.[19] The Court found both rules unconstitutionally overbroad and in violation of the First Amendment. As was the case in *Phillips*, the Court recognized that the City had an interest in regulating the political activities of its police officers in pursuit of the goal of a politically impartial police force, and commented that "total impartiality is essential to effective law enforcement." Nonetheless, the Court found an insufficient relationship between the sweeping ban on political activity found in the rules and the goal of a non-political police force. As put by the Court, the City failed to show (1) "that allowing the police of the City of Cleveland to freely express their political opinions creates an imminent threat to the safety of the citizens of Cleveland," or (2) that the City had a "substantial interest in restricting non-partisan political activity, and the indirect or non-active political connections" described in the rules.[20]

A similar approach of looking for a relationship between regulations governing political activity and job performance was taken by the court in *Oregon State Police Officers Association v. State of Oregon.*[21] The case involved a state statute providing that "no member of the state police shall in any way be active or participate in any political contest of any general or special election, except to cast the ballot of the member of the state police."[22] The Court found the statute to be unconstitutionally overbroad and in violation of the freedom of speech rights of the state troopers covered by the statute. The Court found that in order to be constitutional, the regulation of the political activities of law enforcement officers must be narrowly tailored to those activities which are "incompatible with an individual's public duties."[23] Following similar theories, courts have struck down a ban on using union leave time for political purposes[24] and a state statute forbidding public employees from making political contributions through voluntary payroll deduction.[25]

The 'Unpoliticized Police Department' Theory.

The specific relationship between restrictions on a law enforcement officer's political activities and the officer's "public duties" found so critically necessary in the *Phillips*, *McNea*, and *Oregon State Police Officers Association* cases has, at least implicitly, found not to be necessary in the other major cases in the area. In two of the cases, the Court upheld the same regulation of the Kansas City Police Department, which forbade any political contributions by police officers.[26] The courts in both cases upheld the regulation, holding that the public's interest in an unpoliticized police department outweighed the First Amendment rights of employees to make political contributions.[27]

A similar result was reached in a Texas case, where the Court upheld a regulation which prohibited the following: (1) The making of financial contributions by police or fire employees or their organizations to city council candidates; (2) the public endorsement of city council candidates by police or fire employees or their organizations; (3) the circulation of endorsement petitions for city council candidates by police or fire employees; (4) the soliciting and/or receiving of campaign funds on behalf of city council candidates, or for any partisan political campaigns; and (5) the managing of partisan political campaigns. The Court's lengthy discussion of the justifications for such regulations in the public policy of an unpoliticized police force bears repeating:

> "At least four * * * societal interests may be identified: The interest in an efficient government; that in a government which enjoys public confidence; that in the rights of individual citizens to be free of governmental discrimination based on their political activities or connections; and that in the right of governmental employees to be free of employer pressure in their personal political decisions. The potential conditions which would be harmful or injurious to these important societal interests include the following three. First, the

condition could exist in which 'employment and advancement in Government service' is made to 'depend on political performance' rather than on 'official effort' or 'meritorious performance.' This not only impairs the efficiency of government directly by depriving it of the services of the more capable for the positions so affected, but also indirectly, by its adverse effects on employee morale. This condition is also injurious to the governmental employees' rights to be free of employer pressure to affiliate with a candidate they may personally abhor or 'to perform political chores in order to curry favor with their superiors rather than to act out their own beliefs.' Moreover, this condition obviously tends to undermine public confidence in government. A second harmful condition is that of governmental employees 'practicing political justice,' or exercising 'political influence * * * on others,' or channeling 'governmental favor through political connections.' Such a condition is seriously injurious to the rights of individual citizens to be free of governmental discrimination based on their political activities or connections. * * * Third, the condition may occur under which the 'political influence of federal employees' is brought to bear without restraint 'on the electoral process,' or the governmental work is employed to build a powerful 'political machine.' This condition undermines public confidence in government both because it tends to cast government in the light of master rather than servant to the people, and because it involves use of governmental power for purposes other than those for which the government was instituted."[28]

Along the same lines, *Horstkoetter v. Department of Public Safety* involved a regulation of the Oklahoma Department of Public Safety which prohibited troopers from displaying political yard signs. In rejecting a constitutional challenge to the regulation, a court held that the regulation "promotes efficiency and harmony among law enforcement personnel. In some cases, public endorsement of candidates by police officers has stirred great controversy within police departments and has detracted from the efficiency and the quality of the services provided by law enforcement." While the Court also held that the regulation could not be applied to require the removal of political yard signs posted by the troopers' spouses on jointly-owned property, it ruled that the regulation, at least as applied to the troopers themselves, served to "assure persons aspiring to careers in law enforcement that they are not obliged to make public display of political affiliation."[29]

The difficulty with this latter line of cases may be that the decisions reach too far. The approach taken by the *Phillips*, *McNea*, and *Oregon State Police Officers Association* cases – that laws restricting the First Amendment rights of public employees must be narrowly drawn to meet specific and articulable governmental needs tailored to the particular employee's job function – is a fairly standard form of analysis applied by courts in First Amendment cases.[30] The broader approach taken by *Pollard*, *Reeder*, *Wachsman* and *Horstkoetter* in sustaining sweeping regulations covering political activity is fairly atypical in First Amendment cases. Given this conflict in the current case law, however, a good deal of uncertainty exists concerning the constitutionality of the regulation of the making of political contributions and engaging in political campaign activity by law enforcement officers.

The Discipline Of Law Enforcement Officers For Their Political Beliefs.

While the regulations of a law enforcement agency may control the political activities of law enforcement officers to a lesser or greater extent depending upon the circumstances, the discipline of officers for their political beliefs is not constitutionally permissible.[31] It is only when the political beliefs of the law enforcement officer are carried out into actual and substantial political activity that any form of discipline or regulation of the officer becomes at all permissible.[32] In the absence of a regulation prohibiting such activities altogether, in order for a law enforcement officer to be constitutionally disciplined on the basis of political activities, there must be a demonstrable relationship between the political activities and the officer's on-duty performance.

An employee claiming that discipline has been imposed because of the employee's political beliefs has the burden of showing that the employer actually knew of the employee's beliefs and acted on that basis.[33] While it is possible to show by inference that the employer's decision was based on the employee's political beliefs, the best evidence consists of statements made by the employer establishing the impermissible basis for discipline.[34]

One of the most significant cases in this area is *Matherne v. Wilson*.[35] In *Matherne,* a deputy supported an opponent of the incumbent sheriff. The only evidence of political activity on the part of the deputy was that he had served as a cook at a meeting of potential supporters of the Sheriff's opponent while off duty and out of uniform, although there was some evidence that he had parked the Sheriff's Department car nearby where it was visible to passersby. Later, at the local Catfish Festival, the deputy's wife and son wore assorted hats, shirts and buttons supporting the Sheriff's opponent. The Court ruled that the discharge of the deputy under these circumstances was violative of the First Amendment, and rejected the Sheriff's arguments that the deputy's political beliefs impaired his working relationships with his superiors and created strife within the Sheriff's Office.[36]

Along the same lines, a court upheld the right of a reserve deputy to privately support a candidate for sheriff. The Court found that the deputy's statements that he preferred the non-incumbent's political philosophy to involve a matter of public concern, and that the deputy's speech related "to his assessment of the viability of a potential candidate's campaign and his belief about the relative merits of two potential candidates for public office. Such political speech is at the core of protected speech."[37]

It is only when the political beliefs of the law enforcement officer are carried out into actual and substantial political activity that any form of discipline or regulation of the officer becomes at all permissible.

In a similar case, *Cerjan v. Fasula*, a deputy went to the station to pick up his paycheck while on vacation and off duty. The deputy was wearing a jacket with an inscription on the back supporting the candidacy of the Sheriff's opponent. The deputy remained in the facility no more than five minutes and never entered the public area of the station. The Court reversed the deputy's discipline, noting that the employer failed to bring forward convincing proof that the deputy was not satisfactorily performing his duties, or that his support of the Sheriff's opponent interfered in any way with the discharge of his duties.[38] In a later case, a jury awarded a sheriff's deputy $117,600 when her job was downgraded in retaliation for her support of the Sheriff's opponent in an election.[39]

Finally, the law is clear that a law enforcement officer has a right not to engage in political activity. A good case on point is *Sykes v. McDowell*, which involved the discharge of a sheriff's road deputy who was fired after he refused to become involved in an election for sheriff.[40] Over a six-month period of time, the incumbent sheriff of Etowah County, Alabama had spoken to the deputy about the deputy's lack of political support for the Sheriff. When the deputy protested that he merely wanted to be a deputy and to be left out of politics, the Sheriff told the deputy that he "did not have any constitutional rights" while he worked for the Sheriff. After a series of similar confrontations and the deputy's refusal to sign a newspaper advertisement for the Sheriff, the deputy was transferred to the jail, an assignment all concerned viewed as punitive. In upholding an award requiring the deputy's reinstatement and assessing damages of $114,054 against the Sheriff, the Court explicitly found that the deputy's steadfast refusal to become involved in politics was protected by the First Amendment:

> "The record reveals that [the deputy] was firm in avowing his right not to speak in the county about political affairs. He asserted his 'constitutional right' not to be coerced into 'becoming on [the sheriff's] side.' He told Major Tinsley, in response to an accusation that his friends were running for sheriff, that he hoped he was friends with men he had worked with for eight hours a day. He refused to sign a newspaper ad supporting [the sheriff]. This he did in the face of explicit threats of retaliation. * * * A public employee who positively asserts the right not to speak when ordered to support his employer is within the protection of the First Amendment."

In a similar case, a police chief stayed uninvolved during the campaign for the Whitehall Township, Pennsylvania executive (the equivalent of mayor). Once the new executive took office, she promptly fired the Chief and nominated as his successor an individual who made yard signs for her during her campaign and obtained a limousine for her use during her inauguration. When the executive's choice for chief failed the civil service examination, she disbanded the civil service commission. Under these circumstances, the Court had little difficulty concluding that replacing the Chief with a "political crony" who was "unqualified for the position, both in terms of experience and performance," violated the Chief's First Amendment rights.[41]

Political Patronage Cases.

In general, a governmental employer seeking to discharge an employee because of the employee's political affiliation must show that the employee is a high-level employee, that "there is room for principled disagreement in the decisions reached by the employee and his superiors," and that the employee "has meaningful direct or indirect input into the decision-making process." In other words, the employer must show that the employee falls within what has come to be known as the political loyalty/policymaker rule.[42] Even if an employee is found to be a policymaker, the employee's status is only one factor to be taken into account in the traditional free-speech balancing test assessing whether an employer's disciplinary action violates free speech rights, and does not automatically provide an employer with complete immunity from liability.[43]

In applying the policymaker test, courts look to the following factors:

- The nature and responsibilities of the employee's office;

- Whether responsibilities of the office are not well defined or are of broad scope;

- Whether the responsibilities of the employee include acting as an advisor or formulating or implementing policies or goals;

- Whether the office includes control of a budget and employees, and, if so, how large a budget and how many employees;

- Whether the office calls for close work with highly-ranked governmental officials, making personal or political loyalty a necessity; and

- The salary received by the employee, especially compared to other employees.[44]

One court holding that a lieutenant in a sheriff's office was not a policymaker was careful to note that rank alone does not dispose of the issue of whether an individual is a policymaker:

"While non-policymaking individuals usually have limited responsibility, that is not to say that one with a number of responsibilities is necessarily in a policymaking position. The nature of the responsibilities is critical. Employee supervisors, for example, may have many responsibilities, but those responsibilities may have only limited and well-defined objectives. An employee with responsibilities that are not well-defined or are of broad scope more likely functions in a policymaking position. * * * Even this formula is not all encompassing. '[T]he ultimate inquiry' * * * is not whether the label 'policymaker' or 'confidential' fits a particular position; rather, the question is whether the hiring authority can demonstrate that party affiliation is an appropriate requirement for the effective performance of the public office involved.'"[45]

Because the political loyalty/policymaker rule is so narrowly construed, it is rare to find political patronage discharges sustained today. In limited cases involving chiefs of police,[46] other high echelon employees,[47] or personal secretaries to elected police chiefs,[48] political patronage discharges are still allowable, but the vast majority of law enforcement employees are now insulated from such disciplinary action.[49] The ban on patronage even applies where a high-ranking member of a state police agency has been retaliated against for supporting one individual's candidacy for promotion to superintendent of state police.[50]

Cases still occasionally arise where a newly-elected sheriff decides to fire or demote all or some of the previous sheriff's deputies, or where a newly-elected mayor fires the incumbent police chief, and does so either as an outright gesture of political patronage or as an ostensible "housecleaning" measure.[51] Usually, such firings violate the free association rights of employees.[52] However, there are three limited exceptions allowing such political patronage.

First, in some states where deputy sheriffs are at-will employees, an incoming sheriff would likely be allowed to replace policymaking or upper echelon employees under the political loyalty/policymaker rule.[53] Second, also in at-will employment states, if the terms of office of pre-existing deputies expired with the term of office for the previous sheriff, there would be no obligation on the part of the incoming sheriff to reappoint the prior deputies.[54] As one court commented, there is still "considerable uncertainty" in the law in this area, with "judicial confusion and inconsistency."[55] Some courts have found at-will deputies to be policymakers unprotected by the First Amendment;[56] a majority of courts reject the notion that a rank-and-file deputy sheriff or corrections officer is a policymaker who can be discharged for political reasons.[57] Lastly, if an at-will deputy persists in associating with a recently unelected sheriff and disruption results in the workplace as a result, the First Amendment will offer the deputy no protections.[58]

State Statutes And Political Activities Of Law Enforcement Officers.

Several states have enacted laws that specifically preserve the rights of law enforcement officers to engage in a broad range of partisan and non-partisan political activity. Maryland has a good example of such a statute:

> "Participation in politics or political campaigns and the free expression of political opinions by employees of this State or of any county, municipal corporation, city, political subdivision, public authority, body political or board of education shall not be prohibited, and each employee shall retain all rights and obligations of citizenship provided in the Constitution and laws of the State of Maryland, and in the Constitution and laws of the United States of America;

however, no such employee shall: (1) Engage in political activity while on the job during working hours; (2) Advocate the overthrow of the government by unconstitutional and violent means; or (3) Be obligated to contribute or render political service."[59]

Another example of such a law can be found in Delaware, which has enacted a statute providing that a law enforcement officer "has the same rights to engage in political activity as are afforded to any other person," provided that the officer not engage in such activity while in uniform, while acting in an official capacity, or while on duty.[60] California has a law providing that except when on duty or in uniform, "no public safety officer shall be prohibited from engaging, or be coerced or required to engage, in political activity," and specifically recognizes the right of a law enforcement officer to run for election to a school board.[61]

Political Activity And Collective Bargaining Agreements.

Provisions in law enforcement collective bargaining agreements also can guarantee the rights of law enforcement officers to engage in political activity. For example, the collective bargaining agreement covering Chicago's police officers allows officers to engage in virtually any form of political activity, restraining officers only from engaging in political activity on duty or in their patrol districts (unless they happen to live in the district), and requiring officers seeking elective office to seek a leave of absence:

> "The Employer shall not prohibit a police officer from or discriminate against his engaging in political activities or campaigning while off duty, provided that the officer does not: Wear a uniform or any part thereof which would identify the individual as a police officer, or use property (including documents or records) of the Police Department; Display or otherwise lead others to believe he is carrying a badge, baton or gun; Hold himself out as a police officer, except that a truthful response to a legitimate question shall not be a violation of this section; Engage in such activities in a District(s) where he is assigned, unless the officer lives in the District, except that the Employer shall not transfer an officer into a District for the purpose of preventing him from engaging in such activities. Any officer who runs for political office shall take a leave of absence upon the filing of the petition for office pursuant to the Employer's regular leave of absence policy."[62]

NOTES

[1] *Coughlin v. Lee*, 946 F.2d 1152 (5th Cir. 1991).

[2] *Morial v. Judiciary Commission of Louisiana*, 565 F.2d 295 (5th Cir. 1977). *See also United States Civil Service Commission v. National Association of Letter Carriers*, 413 U.S. 548 (1973).

[3] *Clements v. Fashing*, 457 U.S. 957 (1982); *see also Morial v. Judiciary Commission of Louisiana*, 565 F.2d 295 (5th Cir. 1977).

[4] *Otten v. Schicker*, 655 F.2d 142 (8th Cir. 1981). *See also Wilbur v. Mahan*, 3 F.3d 214 (7th Cir. 1993)(upholds order requiring deputy sheriff running for sheriff to take unpaid leave of absence); *Krisher v. Sharpe*, 763 F. Supp. 1313 (E.D. Pa. 1991)(upholds 90-day suspension for state trooper who ran for county supervisor job; regulation required employee to resign prior to running for office); *Fernandez v. State Personnel Board*, 852 P.2d 1223 (Ariz. App. 1992)(upholds resign-to-run rule in state employment); *Asher v. Lombardi*, 877 S.W.2d 628 (Mo. 1994)(upholds resign-to-run rule in sheriff's office); *Harkleroad v. New Mexico State Police Board*, 705 P.2d 676 (N.M. 1985)(upholds resign-to-run rule in state police agency); *Lecci v. Looney*, 307 N.Y.S.2d 594 (N.Y. A.D. 1970)(upholds departmental rule that no member could be a delegate or representative to a convention for the nomination of any political candidate).

[5] *Rogers v. Village of Tinley Park*, 451 N.E.2d 1324 (Ill. App. 1984)(police officer who was denied a leave of absence after elected to city council must forfeit job on grounds of "incompatibility of offices"); *see also Schloer v. Moran*, 475 N.E.2d 1193 (Ind. App. 1985)(same).

[6] *Boston Police Patrolmen's Association v. City of Boston*, 326 N.E.2d 314 (Mass. 1975).

[7] *Sharp v. City of Palatka*, 529 F. Supp. 2d 1354 (M.D. Fla. 2007).

[8] *Jordan v. Ector County*, 516 F.3d 290 (5th Cir. 2008).

[9] *Swanson v. Van Otterloo*, 993 F. Supp. 1224 (N.D. Iowa 1998).

[10] *Young v. Langley*, 793 F.2d 792 (6th Cir. 1986).

[11] *Perry v. Larson*, 794 F.2d 279 (7th Cir. 1986).

[12] *Carver v. Dennis*, 104 F.3d 847 (6th Cir. 1997).

[13] *Greenwell v. Parsley*, 541 F.3d 401 (6th Cir. 2008).

[14] *Buckley v. Valeo*, 424 U.S. 1 (1976).

[15] *Phillips v. City of Flint*, 225 N.W.2d 780 (Mich. App. 1975).

[16] *Phillips v. City of Flint*, 225 N.W.2d 780 (Mich. App. 1975); *see Cincinnati v. Ohio Council 8, AFSCME*, 638 N.E.2d 94 (Ohio App. 1994).

[17] *Phillips v. City of Flint*, 225 N.W.2d 780 (Mich. App. 1975). *See also American Federation of State, County and Municipal Employees v. Michigan Civil Service Commission*, 274 N.W.2d 804 (Mich. App. 1978).

[18] *Perez v. Cucci*, 725 F. Supp. 209 (D. N.J. 1989).

[19] *McNea v. Garey*, 434 F. Supp. 95 (N.D. Ohio 1976).

[20] *See also Martin v. State Board of Education*, 381 A.2d 234 (R.I. 1977).

[21] *Oregon State Police Officers Association v. State of Oregon*, 766 P.2d 408 (Or. App. 1988), *affirmed* 783 P.2d 7 (1989).

[22] §181.400(2), Oregon Revised Statutes.

23 The *Oregon State Police Officers Association* case was decided under a state constitutional provision virtually identical to the First Amendment. *See* Article I, Section 8, Oregon Constitution.

24 *Michigan State AFL-CIO v. Michigan Civil Service Com'n*, 566 N.W.2d 258 (Mich. 1997).

25 *United Auto Workers v. Philomena*, 15 OPER ¶1291 (Ohio App. 1998).

26 *Reeder v. Kansas City Board of Police Commissioners*, 733 F.2d 543 (8th Cir. 1984); *Pollard v. Board of Police Commissioners*, 665 S.W.2d 333 (Mo. 1984).

27 *Horstkoetter v. Department of Public Safety*, 159 F.3d 1265 (10th Cir. 1998); *Wachsman v. City of Dallas*, 704 F.2d 160 (5th Cir. 1983).

28 *Wachsman v. City of Dallas*, 704 F.2d 160 (5th Cir. 1983), quoting extensively from *United States Civil Service Commission v. National Association of Letter Carriers*, 413 U.S. 548 (1973). *See also Perry v. Pierre*, 518 F.2d 184 (2d Cir. 1975)(upholds ban on officers attempting to "influence any voter"); *Ruff v. City of Leavenworth, Kansas*, 858 F. Supp. 1546 (D. Kan. 1994)(upholds ban on police officers endorsing city council candidates). *See also Lecci v. Looney*, 307 N.Y.S.2d 594 (A.D. 1970).

29 *Horstkoetter v. Department of Public Safety*, 159 F.3d 1265 (10th Cir. 1998).

30 *See Grayned v. City of Rockford*, 408 U.S. 104 (1972); *Fort v. Civil Service Commission of the County of Alameda*, 392 P.2d 385 (Cal. 1964); *Allen v. Board of Education of Jefferson County*, 584 S.W.2d 408 (Ky. App. 1979).

31 *McCormick v. Edwards*, 646 F.2d 173 (5th Cir. 1981); *Murphy v. Butler*, 512 F. Supp. 2d 975 (S.D. Tex. 2007).

32 *Rogenski v. City of Moline*, 285 N.E.2d 230 (Ill. App. 1972)(holds unconstitutional discipline of officer for discussing politics with citizen while on the job).

33 *Graning v. Sherburne County*, 172 F.3d 611 (8th Cir. 1999).

34 *Bueno v. City of Donna*, 714 F.2d 484 (Tex. 1983).

35 *Matherne v. Wilson*, 851 F.2d 752 (5th Cir. 1988).

36 *See also Barrett v. Thomas*, 649 F.2d 1193 (5th Cir. 1981)(reinstatement of deputy who worked for opponent of sheriff's campaign).

37 *Bass v. Richards*, 308 F.3d 1081 (10th Cir. 2002).

38 *Cerjan v. Fasula*, 539 F. Supp. 1226 (N.D. Ohio 1981).

39 *Morris v. Crow*, 33 G.E.R.R. 980 (M.D. Fla. 1995).

40 *Sykes v. McDowell*, 786 F.2d 1098 (11th Cir. 1986).

41 *Conjour v. Whitehall Township*, 850 F. Supp. 309 (E.D. Pa. 1994).

42 *Tomczak v. City of Chicago*, 765 F.2d 633 (7th Cir. 1985).

43 *McEvoy v. Spencer*, 124 F.3d 92 (2d Cir. 1997); *Bates v. Hunt*, 3 F.3d 374 (11th Cir. 1993).

44 *Elrod v. Burns*, 427 U.S. 347 (1976); *Shakman v. Democratic Organization of Cook County*, 722 F.2d 1307 (7th Cir. 1983).

45 *Thomas v. Carpenter*, 881 F.2d 828 (9th Cir. 1989).

46 *Rodez v. Village of Maywood*, 641 F. Supp. 331 (N.D. Ill. 1986); *Mele v. Fahy*, 579 F. Supp. 1576 (D. N.J. 1984). *But see Kuhlmann v. Bloomfield*, 521 F. Supp. 1242 (E.D. Wis. 1981)(police chief not policymaker).

47 *See Hadfield v. McDonough*, 407 F.3d 11 (1st Cir. 2005)(assistant superintendent); *Rose v. Stephens*, 291 F.3d 917 (6th Cir. 2002)(police commissioner); *Fazio v. City and County of San Francisco*, 125 F.3d 1328 (9th Cir. 1997)(assistant district attorney). In its most recent pronouncement on the issue, the United States Supreme Court suggested that the "policymaker" exception applied only to "high level" employees. *Rutan v. Republican Party of Illinois*, 497 U.S. 1050 (1990).

48 *Soderstrum v. Town of Grand Isle*, 925 F.2d 135 (5th Cir. 1991); *see Steele v. City of Bluffton*, 31 F. Supp. 2d 1084 (N.D. Ind. 1998)(secretary to mayor).

49 *Zorzi v. County of Putnam*, 30 F.3d 885 (7th Cir. 1994); *Click v. Copeland*, 970 F.2d 106 (5th Cir. 1992)(deputy sheriffs); *Barrett v. Thomas*, 649 F.2d 1193 (5th Cir. 1981)(deputy sheriffs); *Francia v. White*, 594 F.2d 778 (10th Cir. 1979)(deputy sheriffs); *Tedeschi v. Reardon*, 5 F. Supp. 2d 40 (D. Mass. 1998)(deputy sheriffs); *Mysinger v. Foley*, 651 F. Supp. 328 (W.D. Ark. 1987)(deputy sheriffs); *Grysen v. Dykstra*, 591 F. Supp. 282 (W.D. Mich. 1984)(deputy sheriffs); *Biddle v. City of Ft. Wayne*, 591 F. Supp. 72 (N.D. Ind. 1984)(police lieutenant); *Kuhlmann v. Bloomfield Township*, 521 F. Supp. 1242 (E.D. Wis. 1981); *Hollifield v. McMahan*, 438 F. Supp. 591 (E.D. Tenn. 1977)(deputy sheriffs). *See Pharris v. Looper*, 6 F. Supp. 2d 720 (M.D. Tenn. 1998)(while deputy tax assessor policymaker, field technician was not).

50 *Duckworth v. Ford*, 995 F.2d 858 (8th Cir. 1993); *Darnell v. Ford*, 903 F.2d 556 (8th Cir. 1990).

51 *McBee v. Jim Hogg County, Texas*, 730 F.2d 1009 (5th Cir. 1984). The failure to rehire a deputy sheriff is considered tantamount to a discharge from employment. *Adkins v. Miller*, 421 S.E.2d 682 (W.Va. 1992).

52 *Heggen v. Lee*, 284 F.3d 675 (6th Cir. 2002).

53 *Silva v. Bieluch*, 351 F.3d 1045 (11th Cir. 2003); *Heideman v. Wirsing*, 7 F.3d 659 (7th Cir. 1993)(upholds firing of probationary officer who became involved in barroom political discussion); *Dimmig v. Wahl*, 983 F.2d 86 (7th Cir. 1993)(upholds firing of probationary deputy who refused to actively participate in sheriff's reelection campaign); *Upton v. Thompson*, 930 F.2d 1209 (7th Cir. 1991)(upholds discharge of deputies who supported candidate who opposed the sheriff); *Terry v. Cook*, 866 F.2d 373 (11th Cir. 1989)(newly-elected sheriff's refusal to rehire or reappoint predecessor's employees upheld because in Alabama, deputy is by law the alter ego of the sheriff and therefore political considerations are not prohibited in employment decisions); *Maschmeier v. Scott*, 508 F. Supp. 2d 1180 (M.D. Fla. 2007); *Wallikas v. Harder*, 118 F. Supp. 2d 303 (N.D. N.Y. 2000)(captain in sheriff's office could be a policymaker depending upon authority and relationship with sheriff); *Mills v. Meadows*, 1 F. Supp. 2d 548 (D. Md. 1998)(upholds firing of captain in sheriff's office who supported newly-elected sheriff's opponent). *See generally Branti v. Finkel*, 445 U.S. 507 (1980).

54 *Whited v. Fields*, 581 F. Supp. 1444 (W.D. Va. 1984); *Dove v. Fletcher*, 574 F. Supp. 600 (W.D. La. 1983), *vacated without opinion*, 744 F.2d 92 (5th Cir. 1983).

55 *Flenner v. Sheahan*, 107 F.3d 459 (7th Cir. 1997).

56 *Jenkins v. Medford*, 119 F.3d 1156 (4th Cir. 1997); *Cutcliffe v. Cochran*, 117 F.3d 1353 (11th Cir. 1997); *Dimmig v. Wahl*, 983 F.2d 86 (7th Cir. 1993); *Upton v. Bausman*, 930 F.2d 1209 (7th Cir. 1991); *Terry v. Cook*, 866 F.2d 373 (11th Cir. 1989); *Knight v. Vernon*, 23 F. Supp. 2d 634 (M.D. N.C. 1998).

57 *Heggen v. Lee*, 284 F.3d 675 (6th Cir. 2002); *Brady v. Fort Bend County*, 145 F.3d 691 (5th Cir. 1998); *Hall v. Tollett*, 128 F.3d 418 (6th Cir. 1997); *Flenner*

v. *Sheahan*, 107 F.3d 459 (7th Cir. 1997); *Zorzi v. County of Putnam,* 30 F.3d 885 (7th Cir. 1994); *Wallace v. Benware*, 67 F.3d 655 (7th Cir. 1995); *Burns v. County of Cambria, Pennsylvania*, 971 F.2d 1015 (3d Cir. 1992); *Jones v. Dodson*, 727 F.2d 1329 (4th Cir. 1984); *Tedeschi v. Reardon*, 5 F. Supp. 2d 40 (D. Mass. 1998); *Swanson v. Van Otterloo*, 993 F. Supp. 1224 (N.D. Iowa 1998); *Hollifield v. McMahan*, 438 F. Supp. 591 (D. Tenn. 1977).

[58] *Busey v. Board of County Commissioners of the County of Shawnee, Kansas*, 277 F. Supp. 2d 1095 (D. Kan. 2003).

[59] Article 33, §28-1, Annotated Code of Maryland.

[60] Title 19, §9200, Delaware Code Annotated.

[61] Gov't Code of Calif. §3302. *See Fort v. Civil Service Comm'n of the County of Alameda*, 38 Cal.Rptr. 625 (Cal. 1964).

[62] *Quoted in Model Law Enforcement Contract*, 1999 Edition (Labor Relations Information System, Portland, OR).

CHAPTER 10

RELIGION AND THE LAW ENFORCEMENT WORKPLACE

For many years, lawsuits involving religion and the law enforcement workplace were few and far between. Recent years have seen a marked increase in the lawsuits, with an almost astonishingly broad range of issues arising, ranging from grooming codes to accommodating modified work schedules to dealing with an employee's Sabbath to disciplinary cases involving officers refusing to enforce laws they believe to be inconsistent with their religious beliefs.

Sources Of The Law On Religious Discrimination.

The sources of prohibitions against religious discrimination in the workplace are both constitutional and statutory. The First Amendment to the Constitution provides that "Congress shall make no law respecting an establishment of religion, or prohibiting the free exercise thereof…" These two aspects of the First Amendment are commonly referred to as the "Establishment Clause" and the "Free Exercise Clause" respectively. The overriding principle behind both clauses is that of governmental neutrality towards religion: The Establishment Clause prevents government from endorsing religion, and the Free Exercise Clause prohibits government from restraining or burdening individuals in the exercise of their religious beliefs.[1]

In addition to the federal constitution, each state constitution has at least some clauses that provide religious freedoms. Some state constitutions roughly parrot the First Amendment. Others provide even greater protections, particularly in the area of the establishment of religion.

The federal statutes prohibiting religious discrimination are collected in Title VII of the Civil Rights Act of 1964. Title VII prohibits discrimination "against any individual with respect to his compensation, terms, conditions, or privileges of employment, because of such individual's…religion."[2] Under Title VII, the term "religion" includes "all aspects of religious observance and practice, as well as belief." An employer must accommodate an employee's religious observance unless the employer demonstrates that undue hardship would result.[3] Statutes forbidding religious discrimination also exist at the state level, and often at the local level in the form of ordinances.

The 'Establishment' Of Religion In The Workplace.

The mandate of the First Amendment's Establishment Clause is that of neutrality – neutrality between different religions, and between religious beliefs and non-religious beliefs.[4] Cases involving the Establishment Clause ask three questions about governmental action: (1) Is the actual purpose of the action entirely religious in nature; (2) is the primary effect of the action the promotion or inhibition of religion; and (3) does the action create excessive administrative entanglement between religion and government.[5] If a governmental employer violates any of the three prongs of this test, its actions will violate the Establishment Clause.

As might be imagined, there are few Establishment Clause cases arising out of a law enforcement environment. The cases do arise, though, and have been arising with greater frequency. For example, in 2006, members of Elmbrook Church, an evangelical Christian church in Wisconsin, formed an organization of law enforcement officers called the Fellowship of Christian Centurions. Milwaukee County Sheriff David Clarke invited the Centurions to make a presentation at a Sheriff's Department leadership conference, which all deputies with the rank of sergeant or above were required to attend. At the conference, Clarke first explained to the deputies the criteria that he would use in deciding who he would promote to captain. Clarke also distributed written material, which included a quotation from the Bible and an instruction to deputies to build an inner circle of advisors, which included people who among other things were "people of faith." Subsequently, one of the Centurions addressed the assembly, quoting from the Bible and distributing written materials promoting the Elmbrook Church. At Clarke's request, Centurions made similar presentations at roll calls.

A federal court reversed the County's and Clarke's arguments that the Centurions were not a religious group and that their message was not religious, citing the fact that the Centurions' speeches invoked the Bible and the Centurions were an avowedly Christian organization. The Court found the County's actions "particularly troubling" because they promoted religion through the "coercive power of government. The Court explained that "the present case involves coercion because the County required deputies to attend the leadership conference and/or roll calls and did not advise them that they could skip the Centurions' presentations or offer them an opportunity to comfortably dissent. Clarke and the County invited representatives of a Christian organization to present a proselytizing Christian message to deputies at meetings held at the workplace during working hours, which deputies were required to attend, and conveyed a message of endorsement of the presentations. The effect of this was to promote religion and to do so coercively."[6]

A somewhat similar case arose in the Delphi, Indiana Police Department. A discharged dispatcher sued the Department, contending that, from the first days of her employment, the Police Chief had embarked on an effort to convert her to Christianity. She alleged that she was repeatedly subjected to workplace lectures by the Chief on his views of appropriate Christian behavior, to admonitions that she needed to be "saved" and faced damnation, and to rather intimate inquiries into her social and religious life. A federal appeals court held that a jury could find that by requiring the dispatcher to submit to these religious dialogues by means of intimidation, the Chief engaged in the kind of coercion proscribed by the Establishment Clause – even if he ultimately terminated her for lawful reasons.[7]

From time to time, the legitimacy of chaplaincy programs in law enforcement agencies has been challenged on Establishment Clause grounds. The results indicate that a carefully constructed chaplaincy program may be constitutionally acceptable. For example, in *Malyon v. Pierce County*, a court rejected an Establishment Clause challenge to a chaplaincy program, noting that no public funds were used to pay the volunteer chaplains and that the chaplains were selected through a bidding process open to all regardless of denomination.[8] However, in *Voswinkel v. City of Charlotte*, a court cited the Establishment Clause in striking down a police chaplaincy program where the employer contracted with a particular church to provide a chaplain and paid half the chaplain's salary.[9]

The 'Free Exercise' Of Religion In the Workplace, And Religious Discrimination.

As a starting proposition, a governmental employer has no right to interfere with or attempt to influence the religious *beliefs* of its employees. As stated by the Supreme Court, "the Free Exercise Clause categorically forbids government from regulating, prohibiting, or rewarding religious beliefs as such."[10] That prohibition, however, does not prohibit an employer from enforcing workplace rules that are neutral on the basis of religion and which either regulate *conduct* that may be religious in nature or have an impact on religious behavior. Where such a rule exists, courts examine the motivation behind the rule, the need for the rule, the alternatives to the rule that would address the same interests of the employer, and whether any reasonable accommodation can be made for the employee.

> A governmental employer has no right to interfere with or attempt to influence the religious beliefs of its employees.

How Religious Discrimination Lawsuits Proceed.

In religious discrimination cases, courts use a modified version of the shifting burden of proof tests commonly used in other types of discrimination cases. First, the employee has the burden to establish a *prima facie* case of religious discrimination. A *prima facie* case of religious discrimination is established if (1) the employee has a bona fide religious belief, the practice of which conflicts with an employment duty; (2) the employee informs the employer of the belief and the conflict with the employee's duties; and (3) the employer threatens or subjects the employee to discriminatory treatment because of the employee's inability to fulfill the job requirements.[11] If the employee has proven a *prima facie* case, then the employer has the burden to show either that it attempted to reasonably accommodate the employee's religious beliefs or that any accommodation of the employee's needs would result in undue hardship.[12]

An often important component to religious discrimination cases is proof that an employer was motivated by the employee's religion in making an employment decision that adversely impacts the employee.[13] Proof of an employer's religious motivation can either be through direct evidence or by inference. Proof by inference is generally accomplished through showing a combination of a religiously-hostile workplace and adverse employment action against an employee, or by showing that similarly-situated employees without overt religious beliefs were treated differently.[14] For example, in one case involving the Suffolk County, New

> An often important component to religious discrimination cases is proof that an employer was motivated by the employee's religion in making an employment decision that adversely impacts the employee.

York Police Department, a Jewish inspector filed a religious discrimination lawsuit when he was repeatedly passed over for promotion. A court allowed the lawsuit to proceed, citing among other things, pro-Catholic statements made by the Police Commissioner, repeated anti-Jewish epithets aimed at the inspector, and the consistent promotion of Catholic officers over the inspector.[15]

An often debated issue is how far proof of religious epithets in the workplace gets an employee towards showing an inference of discrimination. The emerging rule appears to be that if the epithets are uttered by other than those with decision-making authority over the particular action claimed to be discriminatory, proof of the epithets does not establish the requisite inference of discrimination.[16] Thus, a court found that disparaging remarks towards Muslims made by sergeants in the Philadelphia Housing Authority Police Department did not establish an inference of discrimination, as the sergeants were entirely uninvolved in the termination of a Muslim officer.[17]

At times, an employer's actions may not have been motivated by hostility to an employee's religion, but are rather intended to "burden" the employee's exercise of his religion as a means of punishing the employee. In *Shrum v. City of Coweta, Oklahoma*, the Police Chief rearranged the schedule of an officer so that the officer would have to work during the day on Sunday, a conflict with the officer's off-duty responsibilities as a minister, and a conflict which the Chief anticipated would result in the officer resigning. The Chief refused to accommodate the officer's request for a change in shift, a refusal motivated by the officer's prominent role in the labor organization representing officers in the department. A federal appeals court found that the burden the shift imposed on the officer's religion could amount to a Free Exercise Clause violation, a conclusion reinforced when a jury later issued verdict of $224,242 in damages against the City.[18]

The Need For Adverse Employment Action.

As with other forms of discrimination, an employee must show a sufficiently severe "adverse employment action" to establish a claim for religious discrimination. Usually, this means that the employee must prove he was discharged, demoted, transferred or suspended due to his religious beliefs or practices.

Occasionally, employees who voluntarily resign from employment will contend that they were "constructively discharged." A constructive discharge occurs when a person quits his or her job under circumstances in which a reasonable person would feel that the conditions of employment have become intolerable.[19] An employee resigning under such circumstances will be allowed to maintain a discrimination lawsuit just as if he or she were in fact discharged.

These principles were prominently tested in a case involving a Jehovah's Witness who was a recruit for the Washington State Patrol. The recruit claimed he was constructively discharged because he refused to participate in "flag formation" and salute the flag with a hand salute. Under the tenets of the Jehovah's Witness religion, any form of pledge of allegiance or flag salute shows a disrespect for God.

An employee must show a sufficiently severe "adverse employment action" to establish a claim for religious discrimination.

The recruit contended that his notification to the Patrol of the conflict between his duties and his religious beliefs coupled with the failure of the Patrol to make any attempt to talk him out of his decision to resign was the equivalent of a constructive discharge. A court was unimpressed, citing the fact that "cadets voluntarily quit the Academy for a variety of personal reasons throughout the rigorous six-month training regimen. Indeed, the trooper offered as one of his reasons for wanting to resign the fact that he was forced to be away from his family more than he wished. That the Academy staff did not make extraordinary efforts to talk him out of leaving does not give rise to a legal conclusion that he was constructively discharged."[20]

Facially Neutral Employment Practices.

A "facially neutral" employment practice that has an impact on religion is much more likely to be upheld than one that is specifically directed at religion.[21] For example, if an employer requires that hair be neatly groomed and cut short, the employment practice is facially neutral in that it does not specifically target a religion. If such an employment practice is based on legitimate operational reasons, it will likely withstand challenge even if it adversely impacts those with particular religious beliefs. Thus, a uniformly-enforced grooming code calling for trimmed hair can legally be applied to a Rastafarian law enforcement officer who desires to wear dreadlocks in conformance with his religious beliefs.[22]

An employer is at risk if it allows exemptions from a facially-neutral employment policy for non-religious reasons, but refuses to do so for employees requesting exemptions from the policy because of their religious beliefs. For example, the City of Newark, New Jersey Police Department enacted a regulation prohibiting its uniformed officers from wearing beards and other facial hair, but allowed exemptions for some purposes, such as medical conditions. Two Sunni Muslim police officers, who followed the obligation of their religion to grow beards and faced disciplinary proceedings because of it, challenged the no-beards policy as interfering with their religious freedoms. A court agreed with the officers, concluding that the decision to exempt beards worn for medical reasons, but not for religious reasons, amounted to discrimination because the employer made a categorical value judgment in favor of secular exemptions and hostile to religious exemptions. The Court found significant that the Department could not offer any important reasons for its discrimination against the free exercise of religion and its no-beards policy.[23]

Reasonable Accommodation.

An employer has an obligation to reasonably accommodate an employee's religious beliefs, so long as the accommodation can be accomplished without undue hardship. An accommodation results in undue hardship when there is more than a *de minimis* cost to the employer. Such costs can be in the form of lost efficiency or higher wages.[24] Undue hardship may also be present when an accommodation would cause more than a *de minimis* impact on coworkers, such as causing coworkers to shoulder the employee's share of potentially hazardous work.[25]

A good example of a reasonable accommodation case involved a Baptist minister who worked as a Jefferson County, Kentucky, deputy sheriff. The deputy requested a transfer to the employer's criminal unit, and then sued the employer when it refused to grant him a schedule with Sunday as a day off. A court observed that "Title VII requires only reasonable accommodation, not satisfaction of an employee's every desire." Since the employee's former job – the job from which he requested the transfer – allowed him Sunday as a day off, the Court found that the employer had already reasonably accommodated the employee before the transfer request, and need not have done anything more.[26]

Another case involved a police officer who desired to wear a gold cross on his uniform as a symbol of his evangelical Christianity. When the officer refused to comply with an order that he remove the pin pursuant to a department rule prohibiting the wearing of buttons or pins on the uniform, he was terminated for insubordination. A federal appeals court upheld his discharge in the face of a challenge that the employer failed to reasonably accommodate his religious beliefs by allowing him to wear the pin. The Court found that "the no-pins policy does not target religion but only incidentally affects Daniels' individual religious practice, and thus is acceptable. A police department cannot be forced to let individual officers add religious symbols to their official uniforms."[27]

Along the same lines, a court rejected the arguments of a Muslim police officer in Philadelphia that she should be allowed to wear a khimar, or head covering, while on duty. The Court found that the Department's directive concerning religious attire "has a compelling public purpose. It recognizes that the Police Department, to be most effective, must subordinate individuality to its paramount group mission of protecting the lives and property of the people living, working, and visiting in the City of Philadelphia. The Directive's detailed standards with no accommodation for religious symbols and attire not only promote the need for uniformity, but also enhance cohesiveness, cooperation, and the *esprit de corps* of the police force. Prohibiting religious symbols and attire helps to prevent any divisiveness on the basis of religion both within the force itself and when it encounters the diverse population of Philadelphia."[28]

Seniority Systems.

With some regularity, cases arise concerning employees whose religious beliefs require the observation of a particular day as a Sabbath, but who do not have the seniority to select days off that include their Sabbath. When Congress drafted Title VII, it was careful to give a good deal of protection to seniority systems, whether established by a collective bargaining agreement or employment practice:

"Notwithstanding any other provision of this subchapter, it shall not be an unlawful employment practice for an employer to apply different standards of compensation, or different terms, conditions, or privileges of employment pursuant to a bona fide seniority or merit system, * * * provided that such differences are not the result of an intention to discriminate because of race, color, religion, sex or national origin."[29]

Thus, seniority systems are not, in and of themselves, illegal employment practices, even if they provide different levels of job security, compensation and privileges to employees. As the United States Supreme Court has observed, "neither a collective bargaining contract nor a seniority system may be employed to violate [Title VII], but we do not believe that the duty to accommodate requires an employer to take steps inconsistent with the otherwise valid agreement."[30]

The mere existence of a seniority clause does not completely end the analysis in seniority-Sabbath cases. While employers are not required to breach their seniority systems to make accommodations for employees' Sabbaths, they must still attempt accommodations that are consistent with their seniority systems and that impose no more than a *de minimis* cost.[31] In a case involving a Carson City, Nevada corrections officer, a court found that establishing a system of shift trading that would allow an employee to permanently not work her Sabbath would constitute an undue hardship. However, the Court found that requiring the employer to create a shift with split days off might not create an undue hardship, provided that all employees were allowed to bid on the newly-created shift under the employer's collectively bargained seniority system.[32] In a case involving a small North Carolina police department, a court found that allowing an officer to not work on his Sabbath would have impaired the ability of the department to provide an acceptable level of law enforcement services, and was an accommodation that was unreasonable.[33]

Officers Refusing To Enforce Particular Laws Because Of Their Religion.

An increasing number of cases have involved law enforcement employers that have refused to accommodate requests made by their employees for alternate assignments in order to avoid a conflict with their religious beliefs. Thus far, employers have prevailed in all such cases.

For example, in one case a state trooper requested that his employer not assign him to investigate crimes at a casino. The trooper believed that the assignment would involve his facilitation of gambling, and would thus violate his religious beliefs. When the employer refused to accommodate the trooper's request and discharged him for refusing to work the casino detail, the trooper brought a religious discrimination suit.

A court upheld the trooper's discharge. As the following passage indicates, the Court was clearly concerned about any influence religion might have on the enforcement of the law:

> "Many officers have religious scruples about particular activities: To give just a few examples, Baptists oppose liquor as well as gambling, Roman Catholics oppose abortion, Jews and Muslims oppose the consumption of pork, and a few faiths include hallucinogenic drugs in their worship and thus oppose legal prohibitions of those drugs. If Endres is right, all of these faiths, and more, must be accommodated by assigning believers to duties compatible with their principles. Does the law require the State Police to assign Unitarians to guard the abortion clinic, Catholics to prevent thefts from liquor stores, and Baptists to investigate claims that supermarkets mis-weigh bacon and shellfish? Must prostitutes be left exposed to slavery or murder at the hands of pimps because protecting them from crime would encourage them to ply their trade and thus offend almost every religious faith?"[34]

Following this general approach, another court held that the law offered no protection for a Roman Catholic FBI agent who claimed a right on religious grounds to be free of any assignment concerning nonviolent opposition to military activities.[35] In a similar case, another court found that Title VII did not protect a Roman Catholic Chicago police officer who refused to protect abortion clinics and their clients. The concurring opinion in the case stated the issue more powerfully than the Court's majority opinion:

> "Public protectors such as police and firefighters must be neutral in providing their services. The public knows that its protectors have a private agenda; everyone does. But it would like to think that they leave that agenda at home when they are on duty – that Jewish policemen protect neo-Nazi demonstrators, that Roman Catholic policemen protect abortion clinics, that Black Muslim policemen protect Christians and Jews, that fundamentalist Christian policemen protect noisy atheists and white-hating Rastafarians, that Mormon policemen protect Scientologists, and that Greek-Orthodox policemen of Serbian ethnicity protect Roman Catholic Croats. We judges certainly want to think that U.S. Marshals protect us from assaults and threats without regard to whether, for example, we vote for or against the pro-life position in abortion cases."[36]

Religious Harassment.

Just as Title VII prohibits racial and sexual harassment, it also prohibits religious harassment in the workplace. The same general rules concerning an employer's obligations, discussed in Chapter 13, apply with all forms of harassment prohibited by Title VII. Thus, the alleged harassment must be so severe and pervasive that it alters the conditions of employment. Consistent with the emerging law concerning sexual harassment, one-time or even occasional religious epithets directed at a law enforcement officer by co-employees will generally not be enough to establish a claim for religious harassment,[37] nor will religious epithets that are too remote in time.[38]

A case from Decatur, Georgia illustrates how difficult it may be for a police officer to successfully claim religious harassment. In the case, a Muslim officer was subjected to the following:

- That other officers frequently referred to him by the nickname "Taliban" or "Al Queada";

- That other officers insulted Muslim dietary restrictions by asking him if he was going to have "the pork sandwich or the hot dog" for lunch;

- That a supervisor, when he encountered women in traditional Muslim dress while riding in the patrol car with the Muslim officer, asked the officer if the women were "his wife" or "his mother";

- On one occasion, while the officer was undergoing "pepper spray" training, another supervisor yelled, "That's what you get for bombing us, you damn Taliban!"; and

- On another occasion, a lieutenant superimposed the officer's face onto an FBI "Seeking Information" poster to depict plaintiff as an Islamic terrorist suspected of being associated with the September 11, 2001 hijackers.

In dismissing the officer's religious harassment claim, a court commented that the officer's "allegations consist almost entirely of offensive statements. A hostile work environment generally does not arise from the mere utterance of an epithet which engenders offensive feelings in an employee. To create a hostile work environment, racial slurs must be so commonplace, overt and denigrating that they create an atmosphere charged with racial hostility. Assuming that the fellow officers made the statements attributed to them, the statements do not indicate an atmosphere charged with racial hostility."[39]

NOTES

[1] *Rosenberger v. Rector and Visitors of the Univ. of Virginia*, 515 U.S. 819 (1995).

[2] 42 U.S.C. §2000e-2(a)(1).

[3] 42 U.S.C. §2000e(j).

[4] *McCreary Co. v. Am. Civil Liberties Union*, 545 U.S. 844 (2005).

[5] *Lemon v. Kurtzman*, 403 U.S. 602 (1971).

[6] *Milwaukee Deputy Sheriffs Ass'n v. Clarke*, 513 F. Supp. 2d 1014 (E.D. Wis. 2007).

[7] *Venters v. City of Delphi*, 123 F.3d 956 (7th Cir. 1997).

[8] *Malyon v. Pierce County*, 935 P.2d 1272 (Wash. 1997).

[9] *Voswinkel v. City of Charlotte*, 495 F. Supp. 588 (W.D. N.C. 1980).

[10] *McDaniel v. Paty*, 435 U.S. 618 (1978).

[11] *Richardson v. Dougherty County, Ga.*, 185 Fed.Appx. 785 (11th Cir. 2006); *Balint v. Carson City, Nevada*, 180 F.3d 1047 (9th Cir. 1999).

[12] *Tiano v. Dillard Dep't Stores, Inc.*, 139 F.3d 679 (9th Cir. 1998).

[13] *Kosereis v. State of Rhode Island*, 331 F.3d 207 (1st Cir. 2003).

[14] See *Jones v. New York City Department of Corrections*, 2001 WL 262844 (S.D. N.Y. 2001); *Beck v. City of Durham*, 129 F. Supp. 2d 844 (M.D. N.C. 2000).

[15] *Mandell v. County of Suffolk*, 316 F.3d 368 (2d Cir. 2003).

[16] *E.g., Gomez v. Allegheny Health Serv., Inc.*, 71 F.3d 1079 (3d Cir. 1995).

[17] *Morrison v. Philadelphia Housing Authority*, 2002 WL 538983 (E.D. Pa. 2002).

[18] *Shrum v. City of Coweta, Okla.*, 449 F.3d 1132 (10th Cir. 2006).

[19] *Draper v. Coeur Rochester, Inc.*, 147 F.3d 1104 (9th Cir. 1998).

[20] *Lawson v. State of Washington*, 296 F.3d 799 (9th Cir. 2002).

[21] *Saabirah El v. City of New York*, 2002 WL 1482785 (S.D. N.Y. 2002); *Kelly v. City of New York*, 2002 WL 1482795 (S.D. N.Y. 2002).

[22] See *Booth v. State of Maryland*, 327 F.3d 377 (4th Cir. 2003).

[23] *FOP v. City of Newark*, 170 F.3d 359 (3d Cir. 1999).

[24] *Opuku-Boateng v. California*, 95 F.3d 1461 (9th Cir. 1996).

[25] *Bhatia v. Chevron U.S.A., Inc.*, 734 F.2d 1382 (9th Cir. 1984).

[26] *Irvin v. Aubrey*, 92 S.W.3d 87 (Ky. App. 2001).

[27] *Daniels v. City of Arlington, Texas*, 246 F.3d 500 (5th Cir. 2001).

[28] *Webb v. City of Philadelphia*, 2007 WL 1866763 (E.D. Pa. 2007).

[29] 42 U.S.C. §2000e-2(h).

[30] *Trans World Airlines v. Hardison*, 432 U.S. 63 (1977).

[31] *Leonce v. Callahan*, 2008 WL 58892 (N.D. Tex. 2008).

[32] *Balint v. Carson City, Nevada*, 180 F.3d 1047 (9th Cir. 1999).

[33] *Perkins v. Town of Princeville*, 2006 WL 4694727 (E.D. N.C. 2006).

[34] *Endres v. Indiana State Police*, 334 F.3d 618 (7th Cir. 2003).

[35] *Ryan v. Department of Justice*, 950 F.2d 458 (7th Cir.1991).

[36] *Rodriguez v. Chicago*, 156 F.3d 771 (7th Cir. 1998).

[37] *Ekerman v. City of Chicago*, 2003 WL 1193262 (N.D. Ill. 2003); *Winnie v. City of Buffalo*, 2003 WL 251951 (W.D. N.Y. 2003); *Cutler v. Dorn*, 955 A.2d 917 (N.J. 2008).

[38] *Reilly v. Nevada*, 2007 WL 983848 (D. Nev. 2007)(six years from religious epithets to alleged discrimination).

[39] *Hyath v. City of Decatur*, 2006 WL 825779 (N.D. Ga. 2006).

CHAPTER 11

THE RIGHTS OF LAW ENFORCEMENT OFFICERS TO BRING CIVIL LAWSUITS

The Expansion Of 'Police Officer Plaintiff' Lawsuits.

There has been a significant increase in the number of civil lawsuits brought by law enforcement officers against those who injure or otherwise damage them in the course of the officers' jobs. Once, the risk of such injuries were thought to "go with the territory" of a law enforcement officer's job, with the officer possibly filing only a workers' compensation claim for the injury and without the officer even considering filing a lawsuit as a plaintiff in civil court.

Today, the traditional reluctance of law enforcement officers to bring civil lawsuits has largely disappeared. A primary cause of this development has been an increasing perception held by law enforcement officers that the sanctions provided by the criminal justice system are inadequate to deter the type of activity that results in injuries to officers. Officers view civil lawsuits capable of producing awards of hundreds of thousands of dollars, which are usually enforceable for up to 20 years and are difficult to discharge in bankruptcy, as providing just such a deterrent.[1]

In addition, law enforcement employers have begun to appreciate that they too benefit from such lawsuits. If a law enforcement officer is successful in many types of personal injury lawsuits, the employer will recoup workers' compensation benefits, health insurance costs, and other payments the employer made to the officer resulting from the officer's injury.

Finally, there is a growing belief that workers' compensation benefits may be inadequate to compensate for the harm done through an on-the-job injury. Substantial awards[2] provide a financial incentive for officers to pursue remedies outside of workers' compensation or pension benefits.

> *There is a growing belief that workers' compensation benefits may be inadequate to compensate for the harm done through an on-the-job injury.*

Law enforcement officer-plaintiff lawsuits are covered by tort law. A tort is a civil wrong based on other than breach of contract.[3] Tort lawsuits fall into three general categories. The first type of suit, known as a claim for an intentional tort, alleges that the defendant has engaged in **intentional** conduct that produced injury to the officer. The second type of suit alleges that the officer's injuries were caused by the **negligent** conduct of the defendant, essentially alleging that the defendant unreasonably breached the standard of care owed to the officer.[4] The last category includes suits that do not neatly fall into either of the first two categories, including claims for **defamation of character** and **products liability**.

The right of a law enforcement officer to bring a civil lawsuit, even against the officer's employer, is protected by the First Amendment's "petition" clause. This protection means that an employer cannot retaliate against the officer because the officer has participated in a lawsuit.[5]

Intentional Torts.

Many of the torts committed on law enforcement officers are intentional torts. As noted in a leading treatise on torts, the intent necessary to establish an intentional tort need not even be the intent to actually cause harm to another person:

> "The intent with which tort liability is concerned is not necessarily a hostile intent, or a desire to do any harm. Rather it is an intent to bring about a result which will invade the interests of another in a way that the law forbids. The defendant may be liable although intending nothing more than a good-natured practical joke."[6]

The four intentional torts most commonly alleged by law enforcement officers are assault and battery, malicious prosecution or abuse of process, intentional infliction of emotional distress, and intentional interference with contract.

The intent necessary to establish an intentional tort need not even be the intent to actually cause harm to another person.

Assault And Battery.

The torts of assault and battery have to be distinguished from the crimes of assault and battery, which usually have a very different meaning. The tort of battery is defined as any act where one person touches another in an offensive or harmful way without permission.[7] Batteries of law enforcement officers occur in a wide variety of settings. A battery occurs every time a law enforcement officer is shot, slugged, slapped, bit, spit upon, kicked, struck by a thrown rock, or wrestled to the ground, or in any other instance where another individual engages in intentional conduct which causes offensive or harmful physical contact with the officer. Even shoving an officer amounts to a battery.[8] Actions which are tort batteries are similar to the crime of assault. The tort of assault, on the other hand, is defined as an attempted battery which places an individual in fear that a battery will occur.[9] The crime of menacing is usually similar to the tort of assault.

Malicious Prosecution And Abuse Of Process.

One of the most vexing concerns in a law enforcement officer's work life is that he or she may be subject to lawsuits for astronomical sums of money. Although the lawsuit may have absolutely no basis in fact, it still causes considerable stress for the officer, subjects the officer and the officer's family to financial insecurity while the lawsuit is pending, and may affect the officer's credit rating. An officer may also occasionally be the target of wrongfully initiated criminal proceedings solely because of actions performed in the course of the officer's duty.

One approach law enforcement officers have used to counter baseless legal proceedings against them has been to sue the person initiating the proceedings. Such lawsuits, involving the torts of "malicious prosecution" or "abuse of process," seek to recover damages for the inappropriate legal proceedings.

The torts of malicious prosecution and abuse of process are very similar. The tort of malicious prosecution exists whenever an individual wrongfully initiates

<u>criminal</u> proceedings against another. The tort of abuse of process exists whenever the wrongfully initiated proceedings are <u>civil</u> in nature instead of criminal.

The elements of a malicious prosecution or abuse of process lawsuit are as follows:

- Judicial proceedings must have been initiated without probable cause. For malicious prosecution to exist, an actual criminal prosecution in court must be initiated.[10] The arrest of the officer without the later filing of a criminal complaint is not enough.[11]

- The judicial proceedings were initiated with malice; that is, with knowledge that the underlying basis for the proceedings was false, or in reckless disregard of the truth or falsity of the basis for the proceedings.

- The judicial proceedings were finally and completely resolved against the defendant.[12]

If there have been criminal proceedings against the officer, and in the process of the criminal case a ruling was made that there was probable cause to initiate the investigation, no malicious prosecution lawsuit can subsequently be filed even if the criminal charges are resolved in the officer's favor.[13] If a grand jury indicted an officer, there is an extremely heavy burden to overcoming the presumption that there was probable cause for the initiation of the proceedings.[14] The only exceptions to this rule are where there is evidence that the criminal prosecution was induced by fraud, corruption, perjury, fabricated evidence, or bad faith, or that the officer chose not to fully contest the issue of probable cause in the criminal case for "tactical reasons." [15]

The courts are split on whether an abuse of process suit may be filed against an individual who wrongfully initiates an internal complaint against a law enforcement officer. Some courts hold that if the entity conducting the internal investigation has powers and procedures that are equivalent to those of an administrative agency or other quasi-judicial body, the filing of a false internal complaint with the department may be the basis for an abuse of process suit.[16] Other courts reject this reasoning, holding instead that all citizens are absolutely privileged to file complaints with governmental bodies, even if the complaints are false.[17]

From time to time, law enforcement officers bring lawsuits against prosecutors, alleging either malicious prosecution in the decision to bring criminal charges against the officer, or some other claim such as defamation. The usual rule is that where prosecutors have absolute immunity and cannot be sued for prosecutorial decisions such as the decision to bring charges, they can be sued when acting outside of their formal prosecutorial role. Thus, in one case a court held a prosecutor immune from lawsuit when the prosecutor refused to prosecute any cases brought by an officer because of concerns about the officer's veracity, but not immune from liability for writing letters to the police department and the mayor expressing his views of the officer's credibility.[18]

Intentional Infliction Of Emotional Distress – The Tort of 'Outrage.'

The third type of intentional tort lawsuit which is regularly brought by law enforcement officers is known as intentional infliction of emotional distress, often called the tort of "outrage." Because the standard of proof for the tort of emotional distress is so difficult to meet, virtually all of these suits have been unsuccessful.[19]

In order to prove intentional infliction of emotional distress, the officer must establish that the defendant engaged in conduct intending to inflict emotional distress upon the officer. The conduct must either be extreme or clearly outrageous and must "go beyond all possible bounds of decency and be regarded as atrocious and utterly intolerable in a civilized community."[20] Examples of conduct which courts have held fail to meet the standard for outrageousness include the following:

For a claim of intentional infliction of emotional distress to exist, the conduct must "go beyond all possible bounds of decency and be regarded as atrocious and utterly intolerable in a civilized community."

- Sexual harassment in the workplace (even where the harassment is patently offensive).[21]

- Racial discrimination.[22]

- A sergeant calling an officer a "fucking bitch" with "a brain the size of a pea."[23]

- Terminating an officer after falsely accusing him of crimes, all in response to the officer's whistleblowing activity.[24]

- Swearing at an officer, extending his probation, and chastising him for drinking soft drinks in a patrol car.[25]

- Writing a letter on department stationery to the chief criticizing an officer and stating that the officer was unqualified.[26]

- Commenting to a whistleblowing officer that his "ass was grass."[27]

- Denying an officer backup, failing to remedy complaints of not receiving backup, interrupting radio transmissions, ostracizing her, and subjecting her to unwarranted criticisms.[28]

- A statement that a white officer would "never get anywhere" in the department as long as she maintained a relationship with an African-American man.[29]

- Where an employer based a discharge decision on the unreliable results of a drug test, and refused to notify the officer of the name and address of the laboratory performing the test.[30]

Occasionally, a court will find that an officer has stated a claim for intentional infliction of emotional distress. As might be expected from the strict standard of proof in such cases, the level of the employer's conduct must be truly extreme before a court will let such a suit proceed. Example of "outrage" claims which have been allowed to proceed include the following:

- Where, after an officer's suicide attempt, a police chief rebuffed the efforts of the officer's wife and others to have the officer released from incarceration so the officer could be treated for mental illness.[31]

- Where a restaurant worker spat in a state trooper's food, seeking some measure of revenge for what he perceived as harassment by the police for his skateboarding.[32]

Intentional Interference With Contract.

A fourth type of intentional tort often asserted by law enforcement officers is that an individual has intentionally interfered with the employment contract the officer has with his employer. To prove an "interference with contract" claim, an officer must show four things: (1) The existence of a contract with a third party; (2) the occurrence of an act of interference that was willful and intentional; (3) that the act was a proximate cause of the damage;` and (4) that actual damage or loss occurred.[33] Theoretically, even a supervisor could be liable for interfering with an officer's employment contract with the employer; however, to establish liability in such cases, the officer would be required to show that the supervisor was acting so contrary to the employer's interests that the supervisor's actions could only be motivated by personal interests.[34] In normal cases, since interference with contract requires that the officer have a contract with a *third party*, it is impossible for the employer to wrongfully interfere with its own contract with the employee.[35] Since these standards are so difficult to meet, it is rare to find a case in which an employee has successfully established the wrongful interference with a contract.[36]

Negligence Cases And The Firefighter's Rule.

A law enforcement officer's right to bring a lawsuit against a third party whose negligence has resulted in an on-the-job injury to the officer is considerably more limited than the right to bring a lawsuit for an intentional tort. In general, a law enforcement officer bringing a negligence lawsuit must show:

- That the officer suffered injuries resulting from actions or inaction on the part of a third party;

- That the third party showed a lack of the degree of care which a reasonable person would have shown under the circumstances.

An officer who brings a successful claim in negligence is generally entitled to recover the following kinds of damages: (1) Lost wages; (2) medical expenses; (3) compensatory damages for any permanent or temporary loss of function in any part of the body; (4) repair or replacement costs of property damaged in the incident; (5) payments for pain and suffering; and (6) punitive damages, usually only in cases where the defendant has acted wantonly or willfully. Out of a damage award or settlement, the officer generally must repay his employer for any workers' compensation benefits or medical costs the employer has paid arising out of the incident.[37]

What limits the rights of law enforcement officers to bring negligence suits is the so-called "Firefighter's Rule." The Michigan case of *Kreski v. Modern Wholesale Electric Supply Co.* serves as a model for the rationale behind the Firefighter's Rule.[38] In that case, an officer responded to a breaking and entering call at a lounge. The inside of the lounge was dark, and the officer was seriously injured when she fell approximately ten feet to the basement through an open trap door immediately behind some swinging doors. The officer sued the lounge for negligence for allowing the dangerous condition to exist. The Court rejected the officer's suit, holding in essence that the officer assumed the risks of such injuries by taking the job of a law enforcement officer:

> "It is beyond peradventure that the maintenance of organized society requires the presence and protection of firefighters and police officers. The fact is that situations requiring their presence are as inevitable as anything in life can be. It is apparent that these officers are employed for the benefit of society in general, and for people involved in circumstances requiring their presence in particular. * * * The public hires, trains, and compensates firefighters and police officers to deal with dangerous, but inevitable situations. Usually, especially with fires, negligence causes the occasion for the safety officer's presence. * * * The very nature of police work and fire fighting is to confront danger. The purpose of these professions is to protect the public. It is this relationship between police officers, firefighters, and society which distinguishes safety officers from other employees."

The Court advanced a second theory for the Firefighter's Rule, one specifically related to the obligations of landowners or occupiers to third parties entering on their land. The Court believed that it would be unreasonable to impose on landowners the obligation to keep their premises in a condition where no injuries could occur to a firefighter or a law enforcement officer arriving at an unusual time of the day:

> "Firefighters and police officers often arrive at unpredictable times and may enter portions of the premises not open to the public. Thus it is an unreasonable burden on landowners to require them to prepare their premises for the arrival of police officers or firefighters."

The last rationale advanced for the Firefighter's Rule was that law enforcement officers and firefighters can receive some measure of compensation for their injuries suffered on the job through a workers' compensation or disability system. In the words of the Court, the existence of workers' compensation benefits "fairly spreads the cost of those injuries to the public as a whole rather than individual property owners."

What limits the rights of law enforcement officers to bring negligence suits is the so-called "Firefighter's Rule."

In other words, the Firefighter's Rule bars lawsuits by law enforcement officers and firefighters for injuries sustained as a result of negligence which created the need for their presence at a particular scene.[39] While the Firefighter's Rule was initially limited just to lawsuits brought by firefighters and law enforcement officers against the owners or occupiers of land, it has been expanded in recent years, at least in some states, to all negligence lawsuits brought by law enforcement officers and firefighters where the injuries suffered were caused by negligence which was the reason for the presence of the officer or firefighter.[40] A few courts go even farther, and extend the Firefighter's Rule even to cases where the negligence which harmed the officer or firefighter was not the conduct that " required the assistance" of the officer or firefighter.[41]

There has been considerable debate over the years about the fairness and underlying theoretical basis of the Firefighter's Rule. As the Michigan Supreme Court held in *Kreski*, the rule itself rests on the assumption that law enforcement officers and firefighters are "different" from other types of employees:

> "In sum, firefighters and police officers are different than other employees whose occupations may peripherally involve hazards. Safety officers are employed, specially trained, and paid to confront dangerous situations for the protection of society. They enter their professions with the certain knowledge that their personal safety is at risk while on duty. Property owners and occupiers cannot reasonably predict visits by safety officers or control their activities while on the premises. Finally, injuries suffered by safety officers while in the course of their employment are compensable by workers' compensation, thereby spreading the cost and risk to the public. Thus, as a matter of public policy, we hold that firefighters or police officers may not recover for injuries occasioned by the negligence which caused their presence on the premises in their professional capacities."[42]

The debate about the Firefighter's Rule notwithstanding, the majority of states have adopted and still apply the Firefighter's Rule.[43] Courts have upheld the Firefighter's Rule even in the face of equal protection challenges arguing that applying the rule to police officers and firefighters but not other classes of employees violates the principles of equal protection of the laws.[44]

There is clearly growing discontent with the Firefighter's Rule. The Oregon Supreme Court squarely rejected the Firefighter's Rule in 1984, holding that it is inappropriate to assume that law enforcement officers and firefighters legally assume any risks in the course of their jobs. Other courts, including those in Colorado, Pennsylvania, and South Carolina, have rejected the Firefighter's Rule on similar grounds,[45] while courts in other states have narrowed the rule considerably.[46] Some states limit the Firefighter's Rule only to lawsuits against landowners or lessees, refusing to extend the Rule beyond the confines of what is known as "premises liability."[47] The growing trend against the Firefighter's Rule has continued slowly but steadily, the New Jersey, New York, Minnesota, Nevada, Alaska,

Michigan, and Florida state legislatures enacting statutes that have either modified the Rule or completely repealed it.[48]

Negligence Cases Which Are Not Barred By The Firefighter's Rule.

The Firefighter's Rule has numerous exceptions, and does not bar suits by law enforcement officers and firefighters for the following negligent acts:

• Negligence Which is Independent of the Reason the Officer was Called to the Scene.

In most states, the Firefighter's Rule only bars negligence suits where the injuries which are the basis of the suit were suffered as a result of negligence which caused the officer to respond to a particular scene in the first place. Suits for negligence where the negligence is independent of the reason an officer was called to a scene are not barred by the Firefighter's Rule.

Examples of such independent negligence are numerous enough that it almost appears that the courts have expanded this exclusion from the Firefighter's Rule because of discomfort with the underlying basis for the Firefighter's Rule itself. Under the "independent investigation" exception, courts have allowed the following lawsuits to proceed:

- A lawsuit by an officer who was struck by a vehicle while giving a motorist a ticket.[49]

- A lawsuit by an officer who was injured while working off duty in uniform at a construction site when a truck ran into a telephone wire which subsequently struck the officer.[50]

- A highway patrol officer's negligence action against a truck driver after the officer was injured as a result of collision with the driver during high-speed response to a domestic disturbance.[51]

- A lawsuit brought by an officer against the driver of a truck which struck him while he was directing traffic around an unrelated accident.[52]

- A lawsuit brought by an officer who was injured when the panes of a revolving door collapsed on her while she was performing a building search.[53]

- A lawsuit against a city that maintained streets by an officer who was injured when, in pursuit of a stolen vehicle, his car slid on a road covered with ice and snow.[54]

- A lawsuit by an officer against his employer when his patrol car was struck by a fellow officer's car during a pursuit.[55]

- A lawsuit brought by an officer who supervised the evacuation of the scene of a train wreck, and was injured by exposure to methyl chloride when, during an attempt to stabilize a derailed train car, the car fell to the ground and released the gas.[56]

- A lawsuit for injuries suffered when a motorcycle officer was struck by a car while responding to a call for service.[57]

• Higher Than Simple Negligence.

The Firefighter's Rule does not bar negligence lawsuits where the defendant has actively engaged in more than simple negligence, and has acted in either an intentional, willful or wanton manner, or has failed to take appropriate precautions in an extremely hazardous situation.[58] For example, in *Chinigo v. Geismar Marine, Inc.*, a deputy responded to a call that a tank truck was leaking a clear liquid.[59] After chasing the truck with lights and siren on for a mile, the deputy succeeded in stopping the truck, which had no markings indicating what it was carrying. Only after the deputy had finished questioning the driver for some time about the paperwork for the cargo did the driver inform the deputy to stay away from the truck, which contained styrene monomer, a dangerous chemical. After suffering from a variety of symptoms, the deputy sued the tank truck owner for negligence, and recovered $121,000. An appellate court affirmed the judgment, finding that the failure to place warning signs on the truck and the failure of the driver to warn the deputy constituted negligence. The Court rejected the application of the Firefighter's Rule by holding that the wanton manner in which the defendant handled the ultra-hazardous chemical constituted more than the ordinary negligence which is contemplated by the Firefighter's Rule.

• Repeated Calls to the Same Location.

One of the underpinnings of the Firefighter's Rule is that a landowner or occupier should not be required to take special precautions for the only occasional visit to the property by an officer or firefighter. The protections of the Firefighter's Rule can be lost, however, if the calls for service to a particular location become frequent.

The case of *Adelsperger v. Riverboat, Inc.* illustrates this principle. The lawsuit was filed by a sheriff's deputy who sustained severe injuries when trying to arrest an intoxicated suspect at a lounge. The deputy alleged that the lounge owner was negligent in allowing repeated excessive alcohol consumption on its premises and in not providing even rudimentary security measures. The Court rejected the lounge's attempt to shield itself from liability by using the Firefighter's Rule:

> "The Rule is frequently justified by a belief that the owners and occupiers of real property should not be discouraged from making an occasional call to the police or fire department out of fear that the officers who respond may sustain injuries on the property in the course of their dangerous jobs. In this case, it appears that the occasional calls had become almost a nightly event. If the allegations are true, the

Riverboat Inn had essentially retained the Sheriff's deputies as unpaid security guards to whom no workers' compensation or other benefits were provided. Moreover, the deputies were being asked to quell violence which was not discouraged, and even affirmatively promoted, by the policies and practices of the Riverboat Inn."[60]

• Failure of Products.

The Firefighter's Rule does not bar lawsuits for injuries resulting from the failure of products used by the law enforcement officer or firefighter. As stated by one court, the assumption of risk underpinnings of the Firefighter's Rule do not extend to the risks that equipment will fail:

> "Certainly the danger that safety equipment may be defective is not an inherent part of the job and is not a risk knowingly and voluntarily assumed."[61]

• Resisting Arrest.

When an officer is bringing a lawsuit, there is often a strategic advantage to filing a lawsuit in negligence, since insurance policies generally cover damages for negligence but do not cover damages for intentional torts. For this reason, officers bringing lawsuits when they have been injured by suspects they have arrested will often claim that they were injured due to the negligence of the individual who resisted arrest. In such cases, courts have rejected attempts by defendants to shield themselves with the Firefighter's Rule, finding that there is no public policy reason to apply the Firefighter's Rule in resisting arrest cases.[62]

• Serving Alcohol to an Intoxicated Person – "Dram Shop" Act Violations.

The Firefighter's Rule also does not prevent lawsuits based upon "dram shop" acts – statutes which prevent the serving of alcohol to visibly intoxicated persons. In one case, an officer suffered severe injuries in a high-speed chase of a motorist who had recently purchased, while in an already intoxicated condition, two 12-packs of beer from the same convenience store in one evening. The officer brought a lawsuit against the convenience store, alleging that the store's violation of the dram shop act by selling alcohol to the intoxicated driver constituted negligence which led to the officer's injuries. The Supreme Court of Iowa affirmed a judgment of $1,151,000 to the officer. The Court rejected the argument that the Firefighter's Rule barred the officer's lawsuit, holding that the Firefighter's Rule only denies the right to bring a lawsuit when the lawsuit is based on the same conduct which initially caused the need for the officer's presence in the first place.[63]

• Driving While Intoxicated.

If a law enforcement officer is injured by an intoxicated driver, it is likely that the officer's claim will not be barred by the Firefighter's Rule. An important case is *McCarthy v. Ehrens*, where a New Jersey State trooper was struck by a car and killed while crossing a freeway on foot to try to apprehend a drunken driver who,

When an officer is bringing a lawsuit, there is often a strategic advantage to filing a lawsuit in negligence, since insurance policies generally cover damages for negligence but do not cover damages for intentional torts.

after disobeying the trooper's instructions to pull over, had crashed his car into the median.[64] The Court rejected the driver's attempt to have the trooper's estate's lawsuit against him dismissed because of the Firefighter's Rule. The Court squarely carved out an intoxicated driver exception to the Firefighter's Rule:

> "As long as conduct is willful and wanton, there is no immunity under the 'Firefighter's Rule' as the public policy underlying the basis of the rule would not be served. When an individual drives upon the highway in an intoxicated condition conscious that injury is likely to result from his conduct and displays reckless indifference to the injurious consequences of his behavior, willful and wanton misconduct may serve as a basis for liability."

• Suits Against Other Than Landowners or Renters.

In those states that base the Firefighter's Rule exclusively on theories of "premises liability" – a complicated set of rules dealing with the obligations of land owners and renters to members of the public – the Firefighter's Rule does not bar a lawsuit by a police officer against the individual who injured him if the defendant was not a landowner or renter. For example, in a Connecticut case, a court upheld a judgment in favor of an officer injured while pursuing a suspect on private property. The Court refused to extend the Firefighter's Rule to protect other than landowners and renters, reasoning "because the Firefighter's Rule is an exception to the general rule of tort liability that, as between an innocent party and a negligent party, any loss should be borne by the negligent party, the burden of persuasion is on the party who seeks to extend the exception beyond its traditional boundaries. The history of and rationales for the Rule persuade us, however, that it should be confined to claims of premises liability."[65]

Law Enforcement Officers As Plaintiffs In Defamation Lawsuits.

Another civil lawsuit frequently brought and rarely won by law enforcement officers is that of defamation of character. The tort of defamation occurs whenever an individual makes a false statement about another to a third party, and the making of the statement causes damages to the defamed party.[66] Written defamation is generally called "libel," while oral defamation is termed "slander."[67] While there was once a significant distinction in the proof necessary in libel and slander cases, that distinction has all but disappeared today, with libel and slander considered simply variations of the same tort of defamation.

The act of making the defamatory statement, whether the statement is written or oral, is called the "publication" of the statement. A statement is considered published when it is made to any third party.[68] A defamatory statement is published, for example, when a newspaper prints an article about an officer, when an individual tells friends a story about the officer, or even when a drug laboratory sends an incorrect analysis of a drug screening to an employer.[69] If the statement is false, and if it is directed at a specific person, it is defamatory.[70]

The 'Malice' Standard In Defamation Cases.

At the root of the lack of success in bringing defamation lawsuits is the so-called "public official" rule applied in defamation cases brought by law enforcement officers. This rule requires that a statement about a "public official" be made with "malice." Law enforcement officers have regularly been held to be public officials for the purposes of defamation cases.[71] The malice standard has even been applied to comments about an officer's role as president of a police union.[72]

As defined by the Supreme Court, "malice" means that the defendant made the statements either knowing that they were false, or with reckless disregard of the truth or falsity of the statements.[73] As explained by one court:

> "The concept of actual malice in defamation cases involving public officials is separate and distinct from the traditionally defined common-law standard of malice or actual malice. Actual malice in the context of defamation may not be inferred from evidence of personal spite, ill will, or deliberate intention to injure, as the defendant's motives for publishing are irrelevant. A defamation plaintiff who is required to show actual malice must demonstrate, with convincing clarity, that the defendant published the defamatory statement either with actual knowledge that the statement was false, or with a high degree of awareness of its probable falsity."[74]

What makes defamation cases difficult to win under the "malice" standard is that, as with any standard of proof involving a subjective state of mind, proof of actual intent or recklessness is difficult, if not impossible, to obtain. It would be a rare and, to say the least, incautious publisher of defamatory material who would admit to having acted intentionally or recklessly in publishing defamatory matter. Because of this, even in cases where extremely serious false statements have been made about law enforcement officers, recovery under the "malice" standard has been all but impossible.

An excellent case in point arose in Oregon, where the publisher of the largest newspaper in the state devoted an entire article to one law enforcement officer, whom it termed a "racial bigot" inclined to use excessive force against blacks. The article went on to say that the officer used racially demeaning language and was heavy handed in his use of force. In reaching its decision, the Court accepted the following as accurate: (1) That all of the statements in the article were false; (2) that the newspaper had information which it failed to publish which established that the officer it was accusing was innocent of the charges the paper was making; (3) that the newspaper relied on sources who used the officer's name, but who gave physical descriptions of a person who could not have been the officer; (4) that many of the sources provided information which was more than ten years old; (5) that the newspaper had no pressing deadlines which would have prevented a more complete investigation; and (6) that the newspaper had no first-hand information about the plaintiff. In spite of all this evidence, the Court still ruled that there was absolutely no evidence of either recklessness or intentional conduct sufficient to meet the "malice" standard.[75]

In a similar case, Daniel Schorr, a commentator for National Public Radio, was contemplating doing a story on "the way in which the media trample on the privacy of people." In preparing the story, Schorr recalled that an individual who deflected the assassin's gun in an attempt on President Ford's life in 1975 was later identified as a homosexual, and instructed his assistant to locate the name of the individual. The assistant produced the name of the FBI agent who grabbed the gun from Lynette "Squeaky" Fromme when she tried to assassinate President Ford. Neither Schorr nor his assistant recalled that there were two attempts on President Ford's life and that the incident they were recalling involved an individual who saved President Ford during the attempt on his life by Sara Jane Moore. Schorr broadcast the name of the FBI agent in his story, identifying him as a homosexual. In spite of Schorr's admitted error, the FBI agent lost his defamation lawsuit. The Court found that while Schorr and NPR "could have been more diligent in their research," since there was no evidence that Schorr entertained any serious doubts as to the truth of his statement, he did not act with the requisite degree of malice.[76]

Other cases in which law enforcement officers have been unsuccessful in defamation cases abound. Examples of such cases are as follows:

- A newspaper which claimed that an officer struck and kicked one of its reporters lost a $150,000 defamation verdict to the officer at trial. An appeals court overturned the award, finding that even though the paper did not adequately check the information provided by its one source, the story told by that source was not "inherently improbable."[77]

- A court rejected a judgment in favor of two police officers falsely accused by a newspaper of having falsified evidence in a murder case, even though the newspaper failed to interview a critical witness.[78]

- A newspaper that falsely accused an officer of being involved in "reported break-ins by policemen" was found to have not acted with actual malice, with the Court imposing on the officer the high burden of proving actual malice by clear and convincing evidence, rather than by the lower standard of a preponderance of the evidence.[79]

- A court criticized a newspaper for "slipshod journalism" when a reporter failed to check sources or to even completely read a court file, the contents of which he misstated in a story, but nonetheless held that the officer had not established that the newspaper acted with actual malice.[80]

This is not to say that law enforcement officers have been uniformly unsuccessful in bringing defamation lawsuits under the malice standard. Individuals are not free to make false statements about or publish unsubstantiated rumors concerning police officers if they "in fact entertained serious doubts as to their truth."[81] From time to time, an officer will be able to prove with such clarity that the defendant made statements knowing they were false that a court will uphold a defamation judgment in the officer's favor.[82] One such case involved a Washington State Patrol trooper who issued a speeding ticket to a doctor. The doctor became so incensed over the ticket that he returned to the area where the trooper was working minutes later and began interfering in a second traffic stop the trooper was making. After a verbal exchange with the trooper, the doctor left the scene. Six months later, and long after he had been convicted in a contested trial on the speeding ticket, the doctor claimed that the trooper assaulted him and threatened to kill him when asking him to leave the scene of the second stop. The trooper won his defamation suit against the doctor, in large part because the two individuals in the car involved in the second traffic stop contradicted the doctor's testimony and because the doctor testified that he made his claims in an attempt to get the trooper both fired and criminally prosecuted.[83]

The 'Opinion' Rule In Defamation Cases.

Even if a law enforcement officer can show that the defendant acted with malice in making certain statements, the officer may still not win a defamation lawsuit. The next burden the officer must meet is to show that the statements were allegations of fact, not expressions of opinion. Most courts hold that expressions of opinion "having no provable factual connotations" are protected by the First Amendment, and may not be the basis for a defamation lawsuit.[84] As one court stated:

> "An assertion that cannot be proved false cannot be held libelous. A writer cannot be sued for simply expressing his opinion of another person, however unreasonable the opinion or vituperous the expressing of it may be."[85]

The real debate under the opinion rule is whether certain statements are declarations of fact or expressions of opinion. Since there are no hard-and-fast rules existing which apply in this area, the decisions of courts are predictably divergent. If there is a tendency, it is to find that statements are those of opinion and not fact.[86] For example, the following statements have been held to be protected statements of opinion, even though they appear at first blush to either be outright statements of fact or have factual components:

- An allegation that an officer engaged in "police brutality."[87]

- Stating that an investigator was "ripping off the system" while receiving a salary for serving as an investigator while also receiving a disability pension from another employer.[88]

Individuals are not free to make false statements about or publish unsubstantiated rumors concerning police officers if they "in fact entertained serious doubts as to their truth."

- Calling a police chief a "fat ass."[89]

- A statement that an officer engaged in "killing, raping, and planting false evidence."[90]

- A statement by singer George Michael that the officer who arrested him for "performing a lewd act" in a park's men's room "entrapped" him was ruled to be a protected statement of opinion; however, Michael's statement that the officer first exposed himself and masturbated in order to entice Michael into his conduct was ruled to be a statement of fact that could support a defamation lawsuit.[91]

Statements Made By An Employer.

There exists a separate privilege which protects statements made by an employer in the normal course of business.

There exists a separate privilege which protects statements made by an employer in the normal course of business. Under this privilege, statements made to a prospective employer during a reference check are protected unless they are made with malice – that is, with knowledge that the statements were false or with reckless disregard of the falsity of the statements.[92] If an employee has consented to the reference check – usually the case in the hiring process – then the statements are all the more likely to be privileged.[93] The more generalized the comment made by the former employer, the more likely it is that the comment will be constitutionally protected. For example, a court held that a statement that an officer did not "meet up" with departmental standards was too vague to constitutionally support a defamation verdict.[94]

A similar privilege also exists with respect to communications by a current employer about an employee.[95] Thus, a court found privileged statements made by a police captain about an officer's threats against other officers because the captain's statements were made in the normal course of business to individuals such as the captain's supervisors and an examining doctor.[96] In addition, if an officer who is applying for another job signs a release authorizing the former employer to disclose information about the officer's employment, the former employer cannot be sued for statements made during a reference check, even if the statements were made with malice.[97]

The 'Absolute Privilege' Bar To Some Defamation Actions Brought By Law Enforcement Officers.

Even if the law enforcement officer can show that the defendant acted with malice in making false factual statements about the officer, the officer still may not recover in a defamation action. Some states have, by the decisions of the courts, adopted an "absolute privilege" bar to defamation actions brought by law enforcement officers and other public servants. Under this theory, any citizen is granted an absolute privilege to make statements about the on-the-job conduct of a public servant to the employee's supervisor. Even if the citizen knows that the statements were false at the time they are made, the statements are considered privileged, and the employee is barred from bringing a suit based upon the statements.[98] In some states the absolute privilege doctrine goes even further, and shields public officials who make statements within the scope of their duties.[99] In these states, even statements made by a supervisor about an employee are absolutely privileged.

The "absolute privilege" rule applies in another context. If the false statements about the officer are made in the course of testimony in court, the statements cannot be the basis for a defamation lawsuit.[100] The "absolute privilege" rule may even bar defamation lawsuits against an officer's employer if the allegedly defamatory statements are made in the course of quasi-judicial proceedings such as unemployment or workers' compensation hearings,[101] city council meetings,[102] or arbitration hearings.[103]

Even if the citizen knows that the statements were false at the time they are made, the statements are considered privileged, and the employee is barred from bringing a suit based upon the statements.

'Anti-SLAPP' Statutes.

Out of the perception that law enforcement officers and other employees have been filing too many defamation lawsuits, some states have enacted so-called "Anti-SLAPP" statutes. In the eyes of those legislatures, law enforcement officers have filed Strategic Lawsuits Against Public Participation (hence "SLAPP"), lawsuits filed not for their merits, but simply to harass and economically harm those who legitimately criticize an officer's performance. Anti-SLAPP statutes usually allow for the dismissal of claims early in the litigation process, with the officer bringing the lawsuit potentially liable for the litigation costs of the defendant.[104]

Section 425.16 of the California Code of Civil Procedure is a fairly typical anti-SLAPP statute:

> "A cause of action against a person arising from any act of that person in furtherance of the person's right of petition or free speech under the United States or California Constitution in connection with a public issue shall be subject to a special motion to strike, unless the court determines that the plaintiff has established that there is a probability that the plaintiff will prevail on the claim."[105]

Without question, anti-SLAPP statutes are designed to inhibit law enforcement officers and other public employees from filing defamation lawsuits.[106] Since anti-SLAPP lawsuits only result in the dismissal of meritless defamation claims, courts have held that they do not violate the free speech, due process, or equal protection rights of public employees.[107]

Damages In Defamation Cases.

If a law enforcement officer can clear all of these hurdles and prevail in a defamation case, damages can be substantial. A successful plaintiff in a defamation case is entitled to recover for damage to the plaintiff's reputation and for the effect of the defamation on the plaintiff's promotional and advancement opportunities within the law enforcement agency employing the plaintiff, on the plaintiff's home life, and on the plaintiff's emotional condition. In many cases, if the allegations against the plaintiff are serious enough, courts may assume that damages have resulted to the plaintiff rather than requiring specific proof of damages.[108] Under this rule, known as defamation *per se*, damages are presumed if the false statements are significant, such as statements that an officer committed a crime or was in an adulterous relationship.[109]

Product Liability Lawsuits.

The purpose behind the laws establishing product liability is to ensure that the costs of injuries resulting from the use of a defective product are borne by the manufacturer who places the defective product on the market, rather than by the person injured by the product's failure.

Law enforcement officers use a variety of equipment in their jobs, ranging from vehicles to firearms to specialty items such as tear gas. The failure of any of this equipment can cause the injury or death of the officer. As with other areas of "police plaintiff" cases, law enforcement officers have only recently begun to bring lawsuits against the manufacturer or distributor of products which have failed and caused injury to an officer.[110]

The purpose behind the laws establishing product liability is to ensure that the costs of injuries resulting from the use of a defective product are borne by the manufacturer who places the defective product on the market, rather than by the person injured by the product's failure.[111] Liability for selling or reselling a defective product can rest on the seller's negligence, upon breach of an expressed or implied warranty that the product will not fail, or upon a theory of strict liability. Strict liability exists where an individual sells a product in a defective condition which is unreasonably dangerous to the user or consumer of the product.[112]

The Employer's Right To A Share Of An Officer's Recovery.

If an officer has received workers' compensation benefits for an injury and later is successful in a civil lawsuit against a third party and collects damages for the same injury, the employer likely has a right under state law to "contribution" from the officer. In other words, the employer is entitled to recoup some portion or perhaps all of its workers' compensation payments from the recovery made in the lawsuit provided the employer complies with whatever procedures are required in its state to obtain "contribution."[113] "Contribution" rules are a creature of state laws, and the extent of "contribution" requirements and the procedures an employer must follow vary significantly from state to state.

Lawsuits Against One's Employer.

With some exceptions, law enforcement employers operate under the protection of a "workers' compensation bar." Under such a bar, which is usually created by state statute, the exclusive remedy an injured law enforcement officer has against the employer is that remedy which is provided by applicable workers' compensation or pension laws.[114] In other words, employees are completely barred from bringing negligence or many other lawsuits against their employers, no matter how inadequate or insufficient the workers' compensation remedy might be.[115] A workers' compensation bar prevents not just lawsuits against an officer's department, but all agencies run by the same employer.[116] However, workers' compensation bars typically do not prohibit lawsuits against an officer's employer under rights granted by statutes such as anti-discrimination or anti-harassment laws,[117] nor do they prevent lawsuits for injuries which have been intentionally committed.[118] Also, workers' compensation bars only apply to injuries covered by workers' compensation laws; if, for example, psychological injuries are not covered by workers' compensation laws, then employees can sue their employers alleging those injuries without running afoul of a workers' compensation bar.[119]

There is some conflict in the law as to whether workers' compensation bars apply when an officer is given a temporary assignment to work for a different employer. In two cases, courts have found that workers' compensation bars prohibited lawsuits even against another law enforcement agency to which the officer was temporarily assigned as part of a joint task force.[120] In a separate case, a court found that a workers' compensation bar did not prohibit a lawsuit by an officer who had been struck by lightning while assigned to work at a training academy run by a different agency. [121]

One notable exception to workers' compensation bars is that they do not prevent lawsuits against an officer's employer under the federal Civil Rights Act. For example, a federal court let a lawsuit proceed which was filed by the widow of an officer killed by his sergeant in a SERT training exercise. The Court found that the officer had the right under the Fourth Amendment to be free from unreasonable "seizures," which under the law includes the right to be free from assaults, and that the officer's Fourth Amendment right was protected under the Civil Rights Act.[122]

Occasionally, a state will enact a statute that partially or completely eliminates the workers' compensation bar, allowing at least some forms of lawsuits to be filed by an officer against her employer. In New York, for example, the state legislature passed a statute providing that a public safety officer has the right to file a lawsuit against an employee who negligently injures the officer if the defendant failed "to comply with the requirements of any of the statutes, ordinances, rules, orders and requirements of the federal, state, county, village, town or city governments."[123] Thus, if an employer fails to provide a safe workplace and violates a state safety statute akin to OSHA, and if an officer is injured as a result of the safety violation, the officer may be allowed to sue the employer.[124]

With some exceptions, the exclusive remedy an injured law enforcement officer has against the employer is that remedy which is provided by applicable workers' compensation or pension laws.

Except in unusual circumstances, workers' compensation bars also prohibit lawsuits against fellow employees for injuries caused by them. In order for the workers' compensation bar to apply, the employer must establish that both employees were on duty and were acting in the course and scope of employment when the injuries occurred. For example, in one case a police officer responded to a domestic disturbance call at the house of a fellow officer. When the first officer tried to stop the second officer from beating his wife, the second officer threw the first officer onto a cement sidewalk casing, causing multiple fractures. The Court rejected the City's claim that the workers' compensation bar prohibited the lawsuit, reasoning that the second officer was off duty and not acting in the course and scope of employment at the time of the injury.[125] In addition, in some states the workers' compensation bar does not restrict lawsuits against the employer for the intentional injurious conduct of a fellow employee.[126]

Occasionally, officers have attempted to sue their employers for negligently handling internal affairs investigations. Courts have uniformly rejected these lawsuits. If an employer has a contract governing employees which requires that certain procedures be used in investigating a case, then the employer may be liable for breaching that contract if it does not follow those procedures. The remedy for such a contract violation is obtained through the grievance procedure under a collective bargaining agreement. However, the employer will not also be civilly liable for negligence in following improper procedures during the internal affairs investigation.[127]

Another type of lawsuit against one's employer which is not barred by workers' compensation laws can arise out of the hiring process. In one case, a civil service board inaccurately scored an entrance test for the position of deputy sheriff, resulting in an applicant receiving a higher score than she should have. The Sheriff hired the applicant, who quit her former job to hire on with the Sheriff's Department. When the improper test scoring was subsequently discovered, the Sheriff fired the deputy, who in turn sued the civil service board for negligence in the way it scored her test. A court refused to dismiss the lawsuit, holding that the civil service board owed a duty to applicants to score a test correctly, and that it could have foreseen that if it negligently scored a test that applicants could be harmed by the negligence.[129]

Where no workers' compensation bar exists – as with most police officers in Washington, for example – one sees a wide array of negligence lawsuits filed by public safety officers against their employers. For example, in the absence of workers' compensation bars public safety officers have brought successful lawsuits against their employers for failure to properly design an emergency driving training course,[129] for failing to properly supervise a training exercise,[130] and even for wrongful termination.[131]

NOTES

[1] The right of law enforcement officers to bring civil suits has been upheld under a state constitutional provision allowing all citizens the right to access to the courts. *See State of Ohio ex rel. Christian v. Barry*, 175 N.E. 855 (1931). Additionally, the right of law enforcement officers to bring such suits has been upheld under the general theory that a law enforcement employer cannot validly issue a rule barring employees the right to access to the courts. *See Hawkins v. Kercheval*, 10 Tenn. 535 (1882).

[2] *USAA Cas. Ins. Co. v. McDermott*, 929 So.2d 1114 (Fla. App. 2006)($681,303 verdict for deputy who suffered a back injury in an on-the-job collision).

[3] The law generally defines a "tort" as a civil wrong which is not based upon a breach of contract. 1 Wigmore, *Select Cases on the Law of Torts* vii (1912).

[4] *Borders v. Daniel*, 2007 WL 4465790 (La. App. 2007).

[5] *Hill v. City of Scranton,* 411 F.3d 118 (3d Cir. 2005); *McGovern v. City of Jersey City*, 2008 WL 58820 (D. N.J. 2008).

[6] W. Keeton, *Prosser and Keeton on Torts* 36 (5th Ed. 1984).

[7] *Garcia v. Illinois State Police*, 545 F. Supp. 2d 823 (C.D. Ill. 2008).

[8] *Feeney v. Powell*, 2008 WL 2478385 (D. N.J. 2008).

[9] §24, Second Restatement of Torts. *See Rozenboom v. Proper*, 441 N.W.2d 11 (Mich. App. 1989)(discusses tort of assault in context of case where officer shot by a suspect).

[10] *Rhodes v. Prince*, 273 Fed.Appx. 328 (5th Cir. 2008); *Smith v. Department of General Services of PA,* 181 Fed.Appx. 327 (3d Cir. 2006).

[11] *Almerico v. Dale*, 927 So.2d 586 (La. App. 2006).

[12] *Pronger v. O'Dell*, 379 N.W.2d 330 (Wis. 1985).

[13] *Dias v. Elique*, 276 Fed.Appx. 596 (9th Cir. 2008).

[14] *Deoma v. City of Shaker Heights*, 587 N.E.2d 425 (Ohio App. 1990).

[15] *Awabdy v. City of Adelanto,* 368 F.3d 1062 (9th Cir. 2004).

[16] *Lewis v. Allen*, 698 S.W.2d 58 (Tenn. 1985).

[17] *Miner v. Novotny*, 498 A.2d 269 (Md. 1985); *Magnus v. Anpatiellos*, 516 N.Y.S.2d 31 (A.D. 1987).

[18] *Beck v. Phillips*, 685 N.W.2d 637 (Iowa 2004); *see Botello v. Gammick*, 413 F.3d 971 (9th Cir. 2005).

[19] Officers are even more unlikely to succeed in court on a separate tort known as the negligent infliction of emotional distress. In most states, negligent infliction of emotional distress only exists if the officer is injured as a result of negligence committed in his presence which, though it causes no physical injury to the officer, causes emotional distress on the officer's part. *Does I-VI v. KTNV-Channel 13*, 863 F. Supp. 1259 (D. Nev. 1994).

[20] *Clark v. Township of Falls*, 890 F.2d 611 (3d Cir. 1990); *Angle v. Dow*, 822 F. Supp. 1530 (S.D. Ala. 1993).

[21] *Andrews v. City of Philadelphia*, 895 F.2d 1469 (3d Cir. 1990); *Efird v. Riley*, 342 F. Supp. 2d 413 (M.D. N.C. 2004).

[22] *Hargraves v. City of Philadelphia*, 2007 WL 1276937 (E.D. Pa. 2007).

23 *Penhollow v. Board of Commissioners for Cecil County*, 695 A.2d 1268 (Md. App. 1997).

24 *McClain v. Munn,* 2008 WL 975059 (W.D. Pa. 2008).

25 *City of Green Forest v. Morse*, 9 IER Cases 625 (Ark. 1994).

26 *Stabler v. City of Mobile*, 844 So.2d 555 (Ala. 2002); *see Shipman v. California Dept. of Corrections and Rehabilitation*, 2008 WL 44350 (Cal. App. 2008).

27 *Thomas v. Douglas*, 877 F.2d 1428 (9th Cir. 1989).

28 *Kramarski v. Village of Orland Park*, 2002 WL 1827637 (N.D. Ill. 2002).

29 *Williams v. Perry*, 960 F. Supp. 534 (D. Conn. 1996).

30 *Landrum v. Board of Commissioners*, 685 So.2d 382 (La. App. 1996).

31 *Houck v. City of Prairie Village, Kansas*, 912 F. Supp. 1428 (D. Kan. 1996).

32 *Phillips v. Restaurant Management of Carolina, L.P.*, 552 S.E.2d 686 (N.C. App. 2001).

33 *Holloway v. Skinner*, 898 S.W.2d 793 (Tex. 1995).

34 *O'Bryant v. City of Midland*, 949 S.W.2d 406 (Tex. App. 1997).

35 *Batchelder v. Andover Police Dept.*, 2008 WL 1759104 (Mass. App. Ct. 2008).

36 *See Dill v. City of Edmond, Oklahoma*, 155 F.3d 1193 (10th Cir. 1998).

37 *Gurliacci v. Mayer*, 590 A.2d 914 (Conn. 1991)(officer who recovered judgment against deputy chief whose car struck hers while he was driving while intoxicated obligated to repay City for costs of workers' compensation benefits).

38 *Kreski v. Modern Wholesale Electric Supply Co.*, 415 N.W.2d 178 (Mich. 1987).

39 *Wadler v. City of New York*, 869 N.Y.S.2d 444 (A.D. 2008). *See also Santangelo v. State of New York*, 494 N.Y.S.2d 49 (Ct. Cl. 1985).

40 *Gibson v. Leonard*, 32 N.E. 182 (Ill. 1892)(probable origination of Firefighter's Rule).

41 *White v. State*, 2008 WL 3915357 (Ariz. App. 2008); *White v. State*, 963 A.2d 222 (Md. App. 2008).

42 *Kreski v. Modern Wholesale Electric Supply Co.*, 415 N.W.2d 178 (Mich. 1987).

43 **Arizona**: *Garcia v. South Tucson*, 640 P.2d 1117 (Ariz. 1982); **California**: *Walters v. Sloan*, 571 P.2d 609 (Cal. 1977); **Connecticut**: *Roberts v. Rosenblatt*, 148 A.2d 142 (1959); **Hawai'i**: *Thomas v. Pang*, 811 P.2d 821 (Haw. 1991); **Idaho**: *Winn v. Frasher*, 777 P.2d 722 (Idaho 1989); **Illinois**: *Jackson v. Urban Inv. Property Services*, 839 N.E.2d 650 (Ill. App. 2005); **Iowa**: *Pottebaum v. Hinds*, 347 N.W.2d 642 (Iowa 1984); **Kansas**: *Calvert v. Garvey Elevators, Inc.*, 694 P.2d 433 (Kan. 1985); **Kentucky**: *Buren v. Midwest Industries, Inc.*, 380 S.W.2d 96 (Ky. 1964); **Maryland**: *Flowers v. Rock Creek Terrace*, 520 A.2d 361 (Md. 1987); **Missouri**: *Phillips v. Hallmark Cards*, 722 S.W.2d 86 (Mo. 1986); **Nebraska**: *Lave v. Neumann*, 317 N.W.2d 779 (Neb. 1982); **New York:** *Marsillo v. City of New York*, 844 N.Y.S.2d 673 (N.Y. Sup. 2007); **Nevada**: *Steelman v. Lind,* 634 P.2d 666 (Nev. 1981); **New Hampshire**: *England v. Tasker*, 529 A.2d 938 (N.H. 1987); **Rhode Island**: *Sobanski v. Donahue*, 792 A.2d 57 (R.I. 2002); **Washington**: *Sutton v. Shufelberger*, 643 P.2d 920 (Wash. App. 1982).

44 *Randich v. Pirtano Construction Company, Inc.*, 804 N.E.2d 581 (Ill. App. 2004).

45 *Banyai v. Arruda*, 799 P.2d 441 (Colo. App. 1990); *Christensen v. Murphy*, 678 P.2d 1210 (Or. 1984); *Breen v. Eagle Valley Homes Inc.*, 2002 WL 31730849 (Pa. Com. Pl. 2002); *Trousdell v. Cannon*, 572 S.E.2d 264 (S.C. 2002).

46 *DeLaire v. Kaskel*, 842 A.2d 1052 (R.I. 2004)(refuses to apply Firefighter's Rule to animal control officers); *Wright v. Coleman*, 436 N.W.2d 864 (Wis. 1989)(significant limitation of the Firefighter's Rule to only some cases where a landowner or occupier of land acts negligently); *Cole v. Hubanks*, 2001 WL 34077547 (Wis. App. 2003)(avoids question of whether Firefighter's Rule applies to law enforcement officers).

47 *Levandoski v. Cone*, 841 A.2d 208 (Conn. 2004); *Hollister v. Thomas*, 955 A.2d 1212 (Conn. App. 2008).

48 *See* §112.182, Fla. Stat. (Supp. 1990); N.J. Stat. Ann. §2A:62A-21. *See generally Wiley v. Redd*, 885 P.2d 592 (Nev. 1994)(discusses Nevada law narrowing Firefighter's Rule); *Roma v. United States*, 344 F.3d 352 (3d Cir. 2003)(interpreting New Jersey Law). Minnesota adopted the Firefighter's Rule in *Hannah v. Jensen*, 298 N.W.2d 52 (Minn. 1980), only to have the Minnesota legislature statutorily abolish the Rule shortly thereafter. *See Lang v. Glusica*, 393 N.W.2d 181 (Minn. 1986). New York's legislature has virtually eliminated the Firefighter's Rule, at least for police officers. *See Giuffrida v. Citibank Corp.*, 760 N.Y.S.2d 397 (N.Y. App. 2003); *Brown v. Ellis*, 548 N.Y.S.2d 841 (N.Y. City Civ. Ct. 1989). Even Michigan, the courts of which have strongly endorsed the Firefighter's Rule, has statutorily created some exceptions to the Rule. MCL 600.2967.

49 *Armstrong v. LeBlanc*, 216 N.W.2d 79 (Mich. App. 1974), *reversed on other grounds*, 236 N.W.2d 419 (Mich. 1975).

50 *Gould v. George Brox, Inc.*, 623 A.2d 1325 (N.H. 1993).

51 *Terry v. Garcia*, 134 Cal.Rptr.2d 565 (Cal. App. 2003).

52 *Gibbons v. Caraway*, 565 N.W.2d 663 (Mich. 1997); *Sharkey v. Mitchell's Newspaper Delivery, Inc.*, 560 N.Y.S.2d 140 (A.D. 1990); *Aetna Casualty & Surety Co. v. Vierra*, 619 A.2d 436 (R.I. 1993).

53 *Winston v. BMA Corporation*, 857 N.Y.S.2d 140 (App. Div. 1990).

54 *Woods v. City of Warren*, 455 N.W.2d 382 (Mich. App. 1990).

55 *Beaupre v. Pierce County*, 166 P.3d 712 (Wash. 2007).

56 *Guadagno v. Baltimore & Ohio Railroad Co.*, 548 N.Y.S.2d 966 (N.Y. A.D. 1989).

57 *Johnson v. Teal*, 769 F. Supp. 947 (E.D. Va. 1991); *Stehlik v. Johnson*, 514 N.W.2d 508 (Mich. App. 1994).

58 *State Farm Mutual Automobile Insurance Company v. Hill*, 775 A.2d 476 (Md. App. 2001)(Firefighter's Rule does not apply to intentional conduct); *Ruotolo v. State*, 574 N.Y.S.2d 904 (A.D. 1991)(Firefighter's Rule does not bar reckless driving claims); *Goodwin v. Hare*, 436 S.E.2d 605 (Va. 1993)(Firefighter's Rule does not bar lawsuits for intentional conduct).

59 *Chinigo v. Geismar Marine Inc.*, 512 So.2d 487 (La. App. 1987).

60 *Adelsperger v. Riverboat, Inc.*, 573 So.2d 80 (Fla. App. 1990).

61 *Court v. Gizelinski*, 379 N.E.2d 281 (Ill. App. 1978); *Price v. Tempo, Inc.*, 603 F. Supp. 1359 (E.D. Pa. 1985); *Hauboldt v. Union Carbide Corp.*, 467 N.W.2d 508 (Wis. 1991). A minority of courts will apply the Firefighter's Rule if the product's

defect was open and apparent to the officer or firefighter. *Flowers v. Rock Creek Terrace Ltd. Partnership*, 520 A.2d 361 (Md. 1987).

[62] *Lanza v. Polanin*, 581 So.2d 130 (Fla. 1991); *Worley v. Winston*, 550 So.2d 694 (La. App. 1989); *McAtee v. Guthrie*, 451 N.W.2d 551 (Mich. App. 1989); *Cristiano v. Marinaccio*, 548 N.Y.S.2d 378 (Sup. Ct. 1989). The search for insurance occasionally becomes somewhat attenuated, as in *Willard v. Kelley*, 803 P.2d 1124 (Okla. 1990), where an officer who was shot by an uninsured motorist was attempting to recover under an uninsured motorist insurance policy on the theory that the shooting arose out of a car stop and thus out of the motorist's "use" of the car.

[63] *Gail v. Clark*, 410 N.W.2d 662 (Iowa 1987). *See also McAtee v. Guthrie*, 451 N.W.2d 551 (Mich. App. 1990).

[64] *McCarthy v. Ehrens*, 514 A.2d 864 (N.J. Sup. 1986).

[65] *Levandoski v. Cone*, 841 A.2d 208 (Conn. 2004); *see Pope v. Sotil*, 2002 WL 959883 (Conn. Super. 2002).

[66] *Zappola v. Hennig*, 20 F. Supp. 2d 1150 (N.D. Ohio 1998).

[67] A defamatory statement is deemed to have been "published" whenever it is made to a third person. As used in this context, "publication" need not necessarily mean the preparation of printed material.

[68] *Graning v. Sherburne County*, 172 F.3d 611 (8th Cir. 1999).

[69] *Landrum v. Board of Commissioners of Orleans Levee District*, 758 F. Supp. 387 (E.D. La. 1991).

[70] *Algarin v. Town of Wallkill*, 421 F.3d 137 (2d Cir. 2005).

[71] **Arizona**: *Olive v. City of Scottsdale*, 969 F. Supp. 564 (D. Ariz. 1996); **Arkansas**: *Karr v. Townsend*, 606 F. Supp. 1121 (W.D. Ark. 1985); **California**: *McCoy v. Hearst Corporation*, 278 Cal.Rptr. 596 (Cal. App. 1991); **Colorado**: *Willis v. Perry*, 677 P.2d 961 (Colo. 1983); **Connecticut**: *Moriarity v. Lippe*, 294 A.2d 326 (Conn. 1972), *discussed in Sevetz v. Coe*, 1990 WL 265738 (Conn. Sup. 1990); **Georgia**: *Goolsby v. Wilson*, 246 S.E.2d 371 (Ga. App. 1978); **Iowa**: *Mercer v. City of Cedar Rapids*, 308 F.3d 840 (8th Cir. 2002); **Illinois**: *Coursey v. Greater Niles Township Publishing Corp.*, 239 N.E.2d 837 (Ill. 1968); **Louisiana**: *Landrum v. Board of Commisioners*, 685 So.2d 382 (La. App. 1996); **Maine**: *Roche v. Egan*, 433 A.2d 757 (Me. 1981); **Maryland**: *Hohman v. A.S. Abell Co.*, 407 A.2d 794 (Md. App. 1979); **Mississippi**: *NAACP v. Moody*, 350 So.2d 1365 (Miss. 1977); **Missouri**: *Ramacciotti v. Zinn*, 550 S.W.2d 217 (Mo. App. 1977); **Nevada**: *Posadas v. City of Reno*, 851 P.2d 438 (Nev. 1993); **New Jersey**: *Cibenko v. Worth Publishers, Inc.*, 510 F. Supp. 761 (D. N.J. 1981); **New Mexico**: *Ammerman v. Hubbard Broadcasting, Inc.*; 572 P.2d 1258 (N.M. App. 1977); **New York**: *Gilligan v. King*, 264 N.Y.S.2d 309 (A.D. 1965); **North Carolina**: *Cline v. Brown*, 210 S.E.2d 446 (N.C. App. 1974); **Ohio**: *Kiser v. Lowe*, 236 F. Supp. 872 (S.D. Ohio 2002); *Jackson v. Columbus*, 883 N.E.2d 1060 (Ohio 2008); **Oregon**: *McNabb v. Oregonian Pub. Co.*, 685 P.2d 458 (Or. App. 1984); **Pennsylvania**: *Coughlin v. Westinghouse Broadcasting & Cable, Inc.*, 780 F.2d 340 (3d Cir. 1985); **Rhode Island**: *Hall v. Rogers*, 490 A.2d 502 (R.I. 1985); **South Carolina**: *Fleming v. Rose*, 567 S.E.2d 857 (S.C. 2002); **Texas**: *Times Herald Printing Co. v. Bessent,* 601 S.W.2d 487 (Tex. App. 1980); **Utah**: *Madsen v. United Television*, 797 P.2d 1083 (Utah 1990); **West Virginia**: *Starr v. Beckley Newspapers Corp.*, 201 S.E.2d 911 (W.Va. 1974); **Wisconsin**: *Pronger v. O'Dell*, 379 N.W.2d 330 (Wis. App. 1985). *But cf. Penland v. Long*, 922 F. Supp. 1085 (W.D. N.C. 1996)(corrections officer not a public figure).

[72] *Stuart v. Porcello*, 603 N.Y.S.2d 597 (A.D. 1993).

[73] Three of the most significant cases defining the "malice" standard are *New York Times v. Sullivan*, 376 U.S. 967 (1964); *Curtis Publishing Co. v. Butts*, 388 U.S. 130 (1967); *Herbert v. Lando*, 441 U.S. 153 (1976).

[74] *Deoma v. City of Shaker Heights*, 587 N.E.2d 425 (Ohio App. 1990); *see Smith v. Huntsville Times Company, Inc.*, 888 So.2d 492 (Ala. 2004).

[75] *McNabb v. Oregonian Publishing Company*, 685 P.2d 458 (Or. App. 1984).

[76] *Buendorf v. National Public Radio, Inc.*, 822 F. Supp. 6 (D. D.C. 1993).

[77] *Speer v. Ottaway Newspapers, Inc.*, 828 F.2d 475 (8th Cir. 1987).

[78] *McCoy v. Hearst Corporation*, 231 Cal.Rptr. 518 (Cal. 1986), *discussed in McCoy v. Hearst Corporation*, 278 Cal.Rptr. 596 (Cal. App. 1991).

[79] *Reed v. Northwestern Publishing Co.*, 512 N.E.2d 828 (Ill. App. 1987).

[80] *Costello v. Ocean County Observer*, 643 A.2d 1012 (N.J. 1994). *See also Early v. The Toledo Blade*, 720 N.E.2d 107 (Ohio App. 1998).

[81] *Jackson v. Columbus*, 883 N.E.2d 1060 (Ohio 2008), *quoting St. Amant v. Thompson*, 390 U.S. 727 (1968).

[82] *Wagner v. City of Memphis*, 971 F. Supp. 308 (W.D. Tenn. 1997).

[83] *Richmond v. Thompson*, 901 P.2d 371 (Wash. App. 1995).

[84] *Milkovich v. Lorain Journal Co.*, 497 U.S. 1 (1990); *White v. Fraternal Order of Police*, 909 F.2d 512 (D.C. Cir. 1990); *McCausland v. City Of Atlantic City*, 2006 WL 1451060 (N.J. Super. A.D. 2006). *See generally Gertz v. Robert Welch, Inc.*, 418 U.S. 323 (1974).

[85] *Hotchner v. Castillo-Puche*, 551 F.2d 910 (2d Cir. 1977).

[86] *VanCamp v. McNesby*, 2008 WL 2557539 (N.D. Fla. 2008)(statement that a sheriff had "cheated" promotional candidates by bypassing them a matter of opinion); *Taylor v. Town of Freetown*, 479 F. Supp. 2d 227 (D. Mass. 2007)(statement that officer spoke aggressively a matter of opinion).

[87] *Turner v. Devlin*, 848 P.2d 286 (Ariz. 1993).

[88] *Leddy v. Narragansett Television, L.P.*, 843 A.2d 481 (R.I. 2004).

[89] *Kirkland v. City of Peekskill*, 634 F. Supp. 950 (S.D. N.Y. 1986).

[90] *Jorg v. Cincinnati Black United Front*, 792 N.E.2d 781 (Ohio App. 2003).

[91] *Rodriguez v. Panayiotou*, 314 F.3d 979 (9th Cir. 2002).

[92] *Introini v. Richland County*, 9 IER Cases 1143 (D. S.C. 1993); *Dvorak v. O'Flynn*, 808 S.W.2d 912 (Mo. App. 1991).

[93] *Miron v. University of New Haven Police Dept.*, 931 A.2d 847 (Conn. 2007); *Kenney v. Gilmore*, 393 S.E.2d 472 (1990); *Chambers v. American Trans Air, Inc.*, 577 N.E.2d 612 (Ind. App.1991); *Holdaway Drugs, Inc. v. Braden*, 582 S.W.2d 646 (Ky. 1979); *Butler v. Folger Coffee Co.*, 524 So.2d 206 (La. App.1988); *Jacron Sales Co. v. Sindorf*, 350 A.2d 688 (1976); *Burns v. Barry*, 228 N.E.2d 728 (1967); *Dalton v. Herbruck Egg Sales Corp.*, 417 N.W.2d 496 (1987); *Stuempges v. Parke, Davis & Co.*, 297 N.W.2d 252 (Minn. 1980); *Carter v. Willert Home Products, Inc.*, 714 S.W.2d 506 (Mo. 1986); *Circus Circus Hotels, Inc. v. Witherspoon*, 657 P.2d 101 (1983); *Erickson v. Marsh & McLennan Co.*, 569 A.2d 793 (1990); *Gengler v. Phelps*, 589 P.2d 1056 (1978); *Walsh v. Consolidated Freightways, Inc.*, 563 P.2d 1205 (1977); *Swanson v. Speidel Corp.*, 293 A.2d 307 (1972); *Pioneer Concrete of Texas, Inc. v.*

Allen, 858 S.W.2d 47 (Tex. App. 1993); *Bankhead v. Tacoma,* 597 P.2d 920 (1979); *Calero v. Del Chemical Corp.,* 228 N.W.2d 737 (1975).

[94] *Mercer v. City of Cedar Rapids,* 308 F.3d 840 (8th Cir. 2002).

[95] *Leatherman v. Rangel,* 986 S.W.2d 759 (Tex. App. 1999).

[96] *Jackson v. District of Columbia,* 541 F. Supp. 2d 334 (D. D.C. 2008).

[97] *Smith v. Holley,* 827 S.W.2d 433 (Tex. App. 1992).

[98] *See Mayle v. Grant Joint Union High School District,* 2003 WL 1564677 (Cal. App. 2003)(statement made about officer in official school district proceedings); *Brown v. Department of Corrections,* 33 Cal.Rptr.3d 754 (Cal. App. 2005)(complaints made about the conduct of officers); *Chamberlain v. City of Portland,* 56 P.3d 497 (Or. App. 2002)(statement made by a police sergeant about an officer's conduct on an Explorer Scout trip); *Putter v. Anderson,* 601 S.W.2d 73 (Tex. App. 1980)(complaint made to internal affairs investigators absolutely privileged).

[99] *Cassell v. India,* 964 So.2d 190 (Fla. App. 2007).

[100] *Briscoe v. LaHue,* 460 U.S. 325 (1983).

[101] *Doss v. City of Savannah,* 660 S.E.2d 457 (Ga. App. 2008).

[102] *Schultea v. City of Patton Village,* 2006 WL 3063457 (S.D. Tex. 2006).

[103] *Rolon v. Henneman,* 517 F.3d 140 (2d Cir. 2008).

[104] *Espinoza v. City of Imperial,* 2008 WL 2397430 (S.D. Cal. 2008); *San Diego County Deputy Sheriff's Association v. Toyen,* 2003 WL 21142988 (Cal. App. 2003).

[105] §425.16, California Code of Civil Procedure.

[106] *See Lopez v. Hiddleston,* 2002 WL 393047 (Cal. App. 2002); *Davis v. Benton,* 874 So.2d 185 (La. App. 2004).

[107] *People v. Health Laboratories of North America, Inc., et. al.,* 104 Cal.Rptr.2d 618 (Cal. App. 2001); *Lee v. Pennington,* 830 So.2d 1037 (La. App. 2002).

[108] *See* 20 Am. Jur. 2d Section 419, *Libel and Slander* (1970), and cases cited therein.

[109] *Gordon v. Boyles,* 99 P.3d 75 (Colo. App. 2004).

[110] *E.g. Miniero v. City of New York,* 833 N.Y.S.2d 845 (N.Y. Sup. 2007). Damage awards in product liability cases can be substantial. In *Christofferson v. Michelin Tire Corp.,* 273 Cal.Rptr. 356 (Cal. App. 1990), a jury awarded $1,591,880 to a highway patrolman who was injured when a tire on his motorcycle failed. In the case, the Court ordered a new trial because the jury had not been informed of the nature of a settlement with the manufacturer of the motorcycle, Kawasaki, where the patrolman received a minimum of $200,000 and a maximum of $1,000,000 (depending upon the outcome of the litigation against Michelin).

[111] *See* §402A, Second Restatement of Torts.

[112] *See Fish v. Amsted Indus., Inc.,* 376 N.W.2d 820 (Wis. 1985).

[113] *Foster v. Knox,* 2008 WL 2068261 (Conn. Super. 2008).

[114] *Cerka v. Salt Lake County,* 988 F. Supp. 1420 (D. Utah 1997); *Sellers v. Akron,* 2006 WL 1686797 (Ohio App. 2006); *Kaya v. Partington,* 681 A.2d 256 (R.I. 1996); *Hawkins v. West Virginia Dept. of Public Safety,* 672 S.E.2d 389 (W.Va. App. 2008). §22-307 of the Illinois Pension Code is a typical workers' compensation bar: "Whenever any city enacts an ordinance pursuant to this Division, no common law or statutory right to recover damages against such city for injury sustained by any policeman while engaged in the line of his duty as such policeman other than the

payment of the allowances of money and of the medical care and hospital treatment provided in such ordinance, shall be available."

[115] *LaPosta v. Borough of Roseland*, 2007 WL 3125232 (D. N.J. 2007); *Cerka v. Salt Lake County,* 988 F. Supp. 1420 (D. Utah 1997). A workers' compensation bar only prevents certain types of lawsuits for personal injuries. It does not prevent lawsuits for violation of constitutional or statutory rights nor, typically, does it prevent lawsuits for personal injuries which have been intentionally caused by the employer.

[116] *Accardi v. City of Simi Valley, California*, 21 Cal.Rptr.2d 292 (Cal. App. 1993).

[117] *Santmyer v. City of Syracuse*, 654 N.Y.S.2d 547 (A.D. 1997).

[118] *Bullin v. Correctional Medical Services, Inc.*, 908 So.2d 269 (Ala. App. 2004).

[119] *Callan v. Bernini*, 141 P.3d 737 (Ariz. App. 2006); *Adams v. Collins*, 392 S.E.2d 549 (Ga. App. 1990).

[120] *Walrond v. County of Somerset*, 888 A.2d 491 (N.J. Super. App. 2006).

[121] *Kincel v. Com., Dept. of Transp.*, 867 A.2d 758 (Pa.Cmwlth. 2005).

[122] *Jensen v. City of Oxnard*, 145 F.3d 1078 (9th Cir. 1998).

[123] New York State General Municipal Law, §205-e.

[124] *See Balsamo v. City of New York*, 733 N.Y.S.2d 431 (A.D. 2001).

[125] *Carillo v. Hamling*, 556 N.E.2d 310 (Ill. App. 1990).

[126] *Bustamante v. Tuliano*, 248 N.J.Super. 492 (A.D. 1991).

[127] *Olive v. City of Scottsdale*, 10 IER Cases 1467 (D. Ariz. 1995).

[128] *Merrick v. Thomas*, 10 IER Cases 1104 (Neb. 1994).

[129] *Lascheid v. City of Kennewick*, 154 P.3d 307 (Wash. App. 2007).

[130] *Locke v. City of Seattle*, 172 P.3d 705 (Wash. 2007).

[131] *Bickford v. City of Seattle*, 17 P.3d 1240 (Wash. App. 2001).

CHAPTER 12

WORKERS' COMPENSATION AND THE RIGHT TO A SAFE WORKING ENVIRONMENT

Workers' Compensation Laws.

In exchange for employees foregoing the right to sue their employers in court for most injuries suffered on the job, employees are allowed to bring workers' compensation claims against their employers.

The workers' compensation system strikes a balance between several competing interests. In exchange for employees foregoing the right to sue their employers in court for most injuries suffered on the job, employees are allowed to bring workers' compensation claims against their employers.[1] In a workers' compensation case, the employee's fault in causing his or her own injury is not relevant, and the defenses of contributory negligence and assumption of the risk cannot be raised.[2] Instead, all that is at issue in a workers' compensation case is whether the employee was injured or became ill on the job and, if so, the extent of the injury.

In exchange for this system where their fault in causing an injury is not relevant, employees must give up the higher level of damages that could be obtained in court. Workers' compensation systems classify most injuries on a "scheduled" basis where, after the degree of injury is assessed, one merely consults a rate schedule to determine what the benefits are for the injury. Compensation for the few injuries such as back injuries that are "unscheduled" is usually measured in terms of the percentage of wage-earning capacity the employee has lost as a result of the injury. With either a scheduled or an unscheduled injury, the relative level of benefits is low compared to those obtainable in civil litigation. For example, a law enforcement officer in California who loses an eye is entitled to a lump sum of $17,714, a figure substantially lower than the damages a jury would likely award for the same injury.

If an injury is compensable, the workers' compensation system pays all reasonable medical and psychological costs incurred by the officer in treating the injury. Medical treatment is "reasonable" even if it is only designed to manage symptoms rather than provide a cure for the underlying condition.[4] If an officer subsequently receives damages in a personal injury lawsuit filed against the individual or entity which caused his injuries, the officer likely will be required to repay the workers' compensation system out of the proceeds from the lawsuit for the costs of medical treatment and lost wages.

Workers' compensation laws also have non-retaliation provisions.

Workers' compensation laws also have non-retaliation provisions. These statutes usually prohibit employers from taking an adverse employment action against an employee because the employee exercised her workers' compensation rights. In evaluating workers' compensation retaliation claims, courts use the same sort of shifting-burden-of-proof approach applied in discrimination cases.[5]

It is important to distinguish state workers' compensation systems from local pension funds that have a disability component. The law in a particular jurisdiction will dictate which applies in the officer's case.[6] On some occasions, local pension funds parallel the structure used by state workers' compensation systems. However, in the majority of cases, local pension systems are likely to be more generous to employees than the workers' compensation system – both in the level of benefits afforded and in the definition of when an employee is so injured as to be "disabled."

Injury Claims And Disease Claims.

Workers' compensation cases come in two varieties: (1) injury claims and (2) claims based on a disease. Of the two, injury claims are the easiest to establish. All that is generally at issue in an injury claim is the extent of the employee's injury, though there are rare cases where a court or workers' compensation agency is simply unconvinced by an officer's account that an injury happened on the job.[7]

Disease claims are by far the more complicated type of workers' compensation cases, since it is difficult to determine whether many diseases are caused by on-the-job activities or exposure. The courts seem to have settled on two types of theories for proving on-the-job causation in disease cases. The first theory requires some direct proof of causation, much the same as is the case in injury claim cases. The second theory, known as the "exposure" theory, requires a workers' compensation claimant to show three things in order to establish the necessary link to on-the-job causation: (1) A prolonged exposure to a condition; (2) a causal relationship between the exposure and the disease; and (3) that a hazard posed by the condition is greater than that to which the general public is exposed.[8]

Types Of Workers' Compensation Claims.

What follows is a description of some of the more frequently-occurring types of workers' compensation cases involving law enforcement officers.

Heart Disease Claims.

Some of the thorniest workers' compensation cases involving law enforcement officers are those involving heart conditions. The causation of a particular heart condition is always difficult to establish, since a variety of factors ranging from on-the-job stressors to specific strenuous events on the job[9] to lifestyle habits and genetics may all play a role in causing or aggravating the condition.[10] What is clear, though, is that law enforcement officers suffer from an abnormally high rate of heart disease.[11]

At least 27 states have addressed the high incidence of heart conditions among law enforcement officers and firefighters by passing "presumptive causation" laws, which relieve an officer or a firefighter suffering from a heart condition of all or most of the burden of showing the condition was caused by on-the-job factors.[12] The theory behind "presumptive causation" laws is not only that heart conditions are an occupational hazard for police officers and firefighters, but also that "heart condition[s] are unique conditions which generally [are] not the result of any particular incident but involve a gradual and progressive degeneration as a result of the continuous stress and strain of the job."[13] New York's statute is an example of such a presumptive causation law:

> "Notwithstanding the provisions of any general, special or local law or administrative code to the contrary, any condition of

At least 27 states have addressed the high incidence of heart conditions among law enforcement officers and firefighters by passing "presumptive causation" laws.

impairment of health caused by diseases of the heart, resulting in total or partial disability to a paid member of the uniformed force of a paid police department, where such policemen are drawn from competitive civil service lists, who successfully passed a physical examination on entry into the service, which examination failed to reveal any evidence of such condition, shall be presumptive evidence that it was incurred in the performance and discharge of duty, unless the contrary be proved by competent evidence."[14]

Where presumptive causation statutes have been enacted, they have been applied to cover a wide variety of cardiac problems suffered by law enforcement officers, including heart attacks,[15] angina,[16] arrhythmia,[17] hypertension,[18] coronary artery disease,[19] and atherosclerosis.[20] There is a split in authority on whether the heart condition of atrial fibrillation is covered by presumptive causation statutes. One line of cases holds that atrial fibrillation is outside of the presumption since there is "no activity or function in the performance of police duties which can predispose or precipitate atrial fibrillation attacks."[21] A second line of cases fully covers atrial fibrillation by the presumption.[22]

Some presumptive causation statutes, like the New York law described above, require that an officer pass a physical examination upon hire in order to later qualify for the presumption,[23] or that a pre-employment physical not show the existence of certain conditions.[24] Others impose on the employer the obligation to conduct pre-employment physicals, and if the employer fails to do so, do not allow the employer to later attack the presumption for an employee who did not have a pre-employment physical.[25] Depending upon how the relevant statutes are written, heart presumptions may only apply to city police officers, and not to deputy sheriffs.[26]

In order to overcome the effect of a presumptive causation statute, the employer bears the burden of proving by clear evidence that the heart condition is not attributable to job-related activities or stresses.[27] In this regard, the employer has both the burden of production (marshaling sufficient evidence to show that there were no job-related causes for the heart condition) and the burden of persuasion (convincing a Court that the evidence clearly shows that no job-related factors caused the heart condition). In general, this means that the employer must show that the heart disease was caused by non-work-related factors and that there was no proximate causal connection between the disease and the employment.[28] Once the presumption is rebutted, the burden shifts to the officer to show either direct medical evidence of causation or a specific job-related event that triggered the coronary condition.[29]

Occasionally, an employer will try to rebut the presumption of causation by submitting general medical evidence that there is no statistical link between public safety work and heart disease (rather than focusing on the individual officer's condition). In other words, the employer argues against the presumption itself, rather than the application of the presumption to a particular claim. Courts have been notoriously unreceptive to such arguments, finding the validity of the presumption

> In order to overcome the effect of a presumptive causation statute, the employer bears the burden of proving by clear evidence that the heart condition is not attributable to job-related activities or stresses.

to be a matter for a legislature to decide and beyond the scope of medical evidence to contradict. As phrased by one court, "what is not permitted is for an expert to deny or contradict the presumption altogether, simply because the expert does not agree with the basis for it."[30]

Where no presumptive causation statute exists, an officer seeking compensation for a heart condition must generally establish three things: (1) That the heart disease was contracted in the course of employment; (2) that the disease's impact on the officer's employment results in a hazard which distinguishes the employment from other types of jobs; and (3) that the employment creates a risk of contracting the disease in a greater degree and in a different manner than in the public generally.[31] Applying such a test, a court found that the prolonged periods of immobility sitting in a police car which contributed to a migrating blood clot which killed an officer were sufficiently unique to police work to render the officer's widow's claim compensable under the workers' compensation laws.[32]

Other 'Presumptive Causation' Conditions.

Many presumptive causation laws apply to more than just heart conditions. California law, for example, includes within its presumptive causation laws hernia, pneumonia, cancer and leukemia, tuberculosis, blood-borne infectious disease, illness or death from exposure to certain biochemical substances, meningitis, Lyme disease, and lower back impairments.[33] Under the "World Trade Center Bill," a presumption exists under New York law that any physical or mental illness that results in disability to a police officer who participated in World Trade Center rescue, recovery, or cleanup operations for a minimum of 40 hours between September 11, 2001 and September 12, 2002, is presumptively caused by the job and is the "natural and proximate result of an accident."[34]

Mental Disease, Stress, And Post-Traumatic Stress Disorder Claims.

Numerous studies have shown that the job of a law enforcement officer is more stressful than virtually every other occupation.[35] In addition, the last ten years have seen an explosion of knowledge concerning post-traumatic stress disorder (PTSD) and, in particular, how PTSD can arise out of a critical incident. These facts alone, however, do not give law enforcement officers carte blanche to file stress-related disability claims. Instead, courts have analyzed the stress claims of law enforcement officers in much the same way as they analyze questions of whether diseases were caused by on-the-job exposure.

There are currently four standards applied in various states as to what elements a law enforcement officer must establish in order to be successful in a stress-related claim. Depending upon which standard a state follows, an officer's stress claim may or may not be compensable. As with stress claims filed by other employees, there is an increasing reluctance on the part of the courts to hold compensable a law enforcement officer's mental disease or PTSD claim.

The strictest of the four standards holds that stress claims are only compensable if they are **accompanied by physical manifestations or accompany a physically traumatic event**.[36] A case from Montana illustrates the difficulty officers have in proving stress claims under this standard. In the case, an officer responded to a suicide call to find a 17-year old girl, who had shot herself in the head, cradled in the arms of her father. The officer administered cardiopulmonary resuscitation to the girl, helped an ambulance crew carry the girl to an ambulance, and escorted the ambulance to the hospital. After he learned that the girl died at the hospital, the officer began to suffer from severe stress, which eventually disabled him from working as a police officer. The Montana Supreme Court upheld the denial of workers' compensation benefits to the officer, holding that without a physical component to his condition, the officer's stress claim was not compensable.[37]

The second line of cases requires that the officer prove that the stress **"must have resulted from a situation of greater dimensions than the day-to-day emotional strain and tension which all employees performing the same type of work must experience."**[38] As paraphrased by another court, this standard requires that the law enforcement officer claiming a stress disability must prove that the disability was not a "natural incident" of police work, and that other officers have not been able to perform similar high-pressure work for years without debilitating effects.[39] The line-of-duty incident precipitating the stress need not be the sole cause of the officer's condition; it is sufficient that it is a material contributing factor to the condition.[40] As held by another court following this standard:

> "The psychologically traumatic event must be one that is generally outside the worker's usual experience and one that would evoke significant symptoms of distress in a worker in similar circumstances. We read these two criteria as further qualifying what is required in order for there to be a psychologically traumatic event. We interpret the first qualifying phrase, 'outside of a worker's usual experience,' as referring to the employment. What might constitute a psychologically traumatic event in one employment may not in another."[41]

Courts are clearly concerned that this approach might bring about inappropriate claims. For example, in New Jersey courts have ruled that emotional disabilities must result from "direct personal experience of a terrifying or horror-inducing event that involves actual or threatened death or serious injury, or a similarly serious threat to the physical integrity of the member or another person." In the view of the courts, this limitation achieves "the important assurance that the traumatic event posited as the basis for an accidental disability pension is not inconsequential but is objectively capable of causing a reasonable person in similar circumstances to suffer a disabling mental injury."[42] Echoing the same sorts of concerns, a District of Columbia court found that post traumatic stress brought about when an officer's stop of a car led to an officer-involved shooting was not an incident beyond the normal scope of what a police officer faces, and that the officer's stress claim should be denied.[43]

A good example of this approach is found in a case involving a Pittsburgh police officer who was claiming a stress disability. A court found insufficient the officer's claim that a stress disability could be based on the fact that he was assaulted four times over the course of his career, concluding:

> "Confronting violence is not an everyday part of an officer's duties, but that does not make it abnormal. Violence may never be routine to an officer, but it unfortunately is not abnormal."

However, the Court did find sufficient the idea that the stress claim could be based on the officer receiving a bona-fide death threat from a gang, a threat coupled with a $50,000 bounty payable to one who killed the officer, and death threats to the officer's child, reasoning that such threats were not in the normal range of experience for law enforcement officers.[44]

Though proving stress claims under this second standard is difficult, some examples of successful stress claims under the standard exist. In one case, a court found compensable a police captain's suicide, where the captain's stress was brought upon by his role disciplining officers involved in a prostitution sting operation and the subsequent intense media scrutiny that resulted.[45] In another case, a detective was assigned to a case involving a serial killer. During the assignment, the killer murdered more victims and terrorized the community. The detective began suffering from extreme stress and depression, and eventually shot himself. The Court upheld the workers' compensation claim of the detective's widow, ruling that the detective's stress resulted from abnormal working conditions which overrode the detective's judgment.[46] A similar result was obtained in a case where an officer's one-on-one standoff with an individual pointing a high velocity semi-automatic assault rifle at him was deemed by the Court to be an "extraordinary event" that caused the officer's post-traumatic stress injury.[47]

The third standard uses fundamentally the same test, but **compares the stress suffered by the officer to the stress of all employees, not just other law enforcement officers**.[48] Under such a standard, which from an officer's perspective is easier to prove than either of the first two standards, a court found compensable the claim of an officer who suffered panic attacks after discovering irregularities in an audit of an evidence room.[49] A similar finding of compensability was reached in a claim for workers' compensation benefits for psychological injuries resulting from the stress of a long-term undercover assignment.[50] However, courts have found non-compensable the hypertension of a police chief resulting from the stress produced by his fears concerning job security,[51] the stress claim of a state trooper attributed to low staffing levels in dispatch,[52] the claim of an officer who watched a fellow officer die from a heart attack,[53] the claim of an officer who had a severe psychological reaction to a transfer,[54] and a claim filed by an officer for stress resulting from differences in management style with his supervisors.[55]

The most lenient of the four standards questions only whether the officer suffered stress on the job and, if so, **whether the stress was a contributing factor to**

the officer's ultimate disability.[56] A decreasing number of states use this fourth standard in deciding law enforcement officer stress claims.[57]

Because the concepts of stress and stress-related injuries are still evolving, courts are frequently lenient with respect to the timeliness of the making of stress-related claims. There is no better example of this than the decision in *Henry v. Industrial Commission of Arizona*.[58] The *Henry* case involved a Phoenix police officer who, in 1960, was involved in an incident which was later described as follows:

> "On 21 March 1960, claimant and a partner stopped an automobile containing two males. * * * This being before two-way radios, claimant's partner went to call in to see if the men were wanted. After he left, a call came in over the car radio that there had been an armed robbery nearby. Believing the men to be the robbers, claimant approached the car. By that time one of the suspects had crawled into the back seat. As claimant arrived at the car, the suspect took a pistol out of a paper bag and stuck it in claimant's face. A struggle ensued. Each man had two hands on the pistol, but claimant could not prevent the barrel from being pointed at his nose. The suspect started to pull the trigger and claimant watched the cylinder begin to rotate. As he described it, 'I was going like that, struggling for the gun and I couldn't get it out of my nose and the cylinder started to turn. As the cylinder started to turn, I thought I saw an orange flash and my whole face went, but it didn't. It didn't.' The gun had apparently misfired."

After this incident, the officer's career went rapidly downhill. He became an alcoholic, and became the object of station-house jokes because of his physical reaction to loud noises. He suffered a nervous breakdown, and in 1965, was eventually forced to resign from the Department. The officer filed a workers' compensation claim in December 1984, seeking compensation for the post-traumatic stress disorder he had suffered 24 years before. The Court allowed the officer to process the claim, holding that the claim was timely in light of the fact that post-traumatic stress disorder was not diagnosed as a treatable explanation for the officer's condition until 24 years after the incident.[59] The Court noted that the workers' compensation law "does not place upon the employee the duty of knowing the nature of his disability and its relation to his employment before these things are reasonably ascertainable by the medical profession."[60]

Stress claims can also involve unusual factual situations and often present difficult issues for a court to decide. For example, in *Newlun v. Department of Retirement Systems*, a police officer sought a stress disability for his cocaine addiction. The officer was a narcotics detective who became addicted to cocaine when he used drugs as part of his undercover work. Citing evidence that the officer reported his drug use to his employer and was not told to stop using drugs, the Court approved the grant of a line-of-duty pension to the officer.[61] In another difficult case, a court found that an officer's alcoholism was not compensable, holding that there was no connection between the officer's off-duty drinking and his on-duty performance even though the officer had been hospitalized for alcoholism and had been disciplined for alcohol-related misuse of his firearm.[62] Another case was *Linnen v. Beaufort County Sheriff's Department*, where a deputy suffered injuries to his head, back, and knees when he fainted after the Sheriff told him he was firing him. The Court held the injuries compensable, since the factor causing the stress leading to the faint – being fired – arose out of the course and scope of employment.[63]

Probably the most thorough discussion of the compensability of post-traumatic stress disorder can be found in the New Jersey Supreme Court's 2003 opinion in *Brunell v. Wildwood Crest Police Department*. In the case, the Court traced the evolution of knowledge about PTSD, and how courts around the country have reacted to claims of PTSD. In the end, the Court concluded that a workers' compensation claimant could argue that PTSD fell either within the "accidental injury" model for workers' compensation claims – where the PTSD is triggered by an unintended or unexpected occurrence – or within the "occupational disease" model for workers' compensation claims, where the condition arises out of job hazards that are greater than those encountered in the normal range of occupations.[64]

On occasion, an officer who has been severely disciplined will file a workers' compensation stress claim contending that depression or some other mental disease has resulted from the officer's involvement in the disciplinary process. Though there are some exceptions, most such claims are denied, with courts finding that mental conditions arising out of the imposition of discipline are not compensable under workers' compensation laws. [65]Similarly, anxiety over poor job performance is unlikely to be the basis for a successful stress claim.[66]

Hearing Loss Claims.

Law enforcement officers are exposed to significant levels of noise on a regular basis. In addition to the city and motor vehicle noises to which they have daily exposure, they also are regularly, though more infrequently, exposed to very different kinds of noises produced by sirens and on the firing range. These types of exposure can lead to high frequency hearing loss.

Such a condition was found compensable under workers' compensation laws in *City of Miami v. Tomberlin*. The Court reviewed the evidence before it on the officer's hearing loss:

> "[An otolaryngologist] initially treated [the officer] for his hearing problems. He determined that [the officer] has a progressive high frequency hearing loss which results in his being unable to hear properly in noisy situations. He found that [the officer's] hearing loss is related to his exposure to a noisy environment. Other evidence was presented to show that, especially in his earlier years as a police officer, [the officer] was exposed to greater than acceptable levels of noise during firing range routines and that the noise level in the downtown Miami area where [the officer] works regular duty reaches greater than the acceptable level of decibels at certain times. Therefore, competent

substantial evidence in the record supports the deputy commissioner's finding that due to his on-the-job exposure to noise, [the officer] suffers a progressive hearing loss and therefore treatment for that loss is compensable."[67]

Pulmonary Disease Claims.

Another risk to which law enforcement officers, particularly those assigned to urban areas, are regularly exposed is that of pulmonary difficulties stemming from prolonged exposure to smog. In *City of Miami v. Tomberlin* (the same case discussing the type of evidence necessary to sustain a hearing loss claim), the Court found compensable a pulmonary condition based on the following evidence:

> "As to the pulmonary condition, [the officer] testified that he has noticed a shortness of breath during the last several years. Dr. Lerner, his treating physician for his lung condition, was of the opinion that, although some people who are not exposed to toxins develop the same condition from which [the officer] suffers, a great probability exists that [the officer's] prolonged exposure to a higher than normal level of air pollutants in the downtown area of Miami has affected [the officer's] lung function and caused his pulmonary condition. Other evidence showed that the downtown area of Miami has, at times, contained pollutants that were higher than EPA standards."[68]

Back Injury Claims.

As with all workers' compensation claims that involve other than "presumptive causation" conditions, it is an officer's burden to prove that a back condition is caused by the job. Almost always, this will require an officer to produce medical evidence tying the particular injury to the job.[69]

Occasionally, an officer will suffer from a congenital or degenerative back problem such as spinal stenosis or arthritis, and will have his or her back injury aggravated by an on-the-job injury. Most states will allow workers' compensation coverage for the aggravated injury; some states refuse to provide such benefits, reasoning that the workers' compensation benefits are inappropriate since the underlying condition was not incurred in the course of duty.[70]

Injuries Suffered While Traveling Or Commuting.

In general, under a doctrine known as the "going and coming" rule, injuries which are suffered while traveling to and from work are not compensable.[71] However, an exception to the general rule of non-compensability of such injuries exists if the employer benefits from the law enforcement presence of the commuting officer. The general tests for whether the employer benefits from the presence of the law enforcement officer during the commute is whether (1) an express

Under a doctrine known as the "going and coming" rule, injuries which are suffered while traveling to and from work are not compensable. However, an exception exists if the employer benefits from the law enforcement presence of the commuting officer.

policy or routine practice of commuting while on duty exists; (2) the officer may be disciplined for failing to render the services; (3) the employee was in uniform at the time of the incident; and (4) the employer provides changing facilities for employees.[72] Applying these tests, a court in a case involving the City of Detroit held compensable the injuries suffered by a motorcycle officer who took his motor-cycle home and was required to write traffic tickets on his way to and from work. Even though the officer's injury occurred outside of the city limits, the officer was required to travel the shortest route to and from home, a route that took him outside of the city limits.[73] Similarly, an injury suffered by an officer traveling to work on public transportation was held compensable in *Jasaitis v. City of Paterson*, where the Court reasoned that the officer's uniform signaled to members of the public that the officer was on duty.[74] In awarding workers' compensation benefits to an officer injured in an off-duty collision involving her take home car in anoth-er case, a court commented as follows:

> "It is undisputed that the officer was not on scheduled duty, and she was using the police car in furtherance of a personal errand – namely, transporting her grandmother to and from her mother's house. That is not to say, however, that her use of the vehicle was purely personal so as to place her without the Act. Under the unique circumstances of this case, where the Police Department assigned the cars, required officer response to certain, specified situations, and encouraged off-duty use of the vehicles – albeit within departmental guidelines – each time the officer and any other participating officer placed the vehicle in operation, a business purpose was being furthered. * * * Thus, while arguably the catalyst for the officer's use of the patrol car might have been personal in nature, once she deployed the vehicle on the streets of Montgomery County, any such personal purpose was overridden by the needs of the Department, in essence, transforming her errand into one imbued with business aspects."[75]

Injuries suffered while attending court on a day off are usually compensable under workers' compensation laws. In an Oregon case, a law enforcement officer was killed in an automobile accident which occurred while the officer was driv-ing to court to testify on a job-related case on his day off. The Court upheld the grant of widow's benefits to the officer's wife, reasoning that "but for [the officer's] court appearance, he would not have been traveling when and where he was at the time of the accident." The Court also noted that had the officer lived, he would have been compensated for a minimum of four hours work for the disruption and inconvenience associated with an officially-required court appearance on his day off.[76] A minority view finds injuries suffered in accidents while driving to court appearances during an officer's time off to be non-compensable, on the theory that testifying in court is a routine part of an officer's job.[77]

Along the same analytical lines, if an employee is injured while traveling to a training class scheduled by the employer, the injury is likely to be compensable under a workers' compensation system,[78] particularly if the employee is driving a marked police car.[79] On the other hand, if an employee is injured while driving to a restaurant during an unpaid meal period in the middle of a training session, or if the employee is driving to work in her personal car (even if in uniform),[80] or if the employee is driving to work in plainclothes in an unmarked car,[81] the employee's injuries would not be compensable.[82] Similarly, if the employee is injured while deviating from normal duties to run a personal errand, the employee is usually not considered to be in the "course of employment," making injuries suffered while running the errand not covered by workers' compensation.[83]

Injuries While On Standby Duty.

Another frequently-litigated issue is whether injuries suffered while on standby duty are compensable. A leading case in the area is *Gonzalez v. Workers' Compensation Appeals Board*. In *Gonzalez*, a sheriff's deputy was placed on on-call status, which required him to be available for contact by telephone or radio and to be in such mental and physical condition and in such proximity to his assigned vehicle as to be able to respond to a call within a reasonable time. While on standby status, the deputy was injured while playing in a softball game with his supervisor's permission. A court found the deputy's injuries compensable, reasoning that the compensation paid the deputy and the control over the deputy's time converted the standby time to on-duty status:

> "[The deputy's] obligation to be on standby periodically and to be subject to standby requirements were terms of his employment contract. Even time that normally would be considered off-duty time can be converted to on-duty time by the scope of the employer requirements the employee must satisfy." [84]

Other Off-Duty Injuries.

In general, injuries incurred while off duty are not compensable under workers' compensation or disability laws.[85] An exception to this general rule exists where the off-duty law enforcement officer was injured either while taking action to enforce the law, or where the officer's off-duty activities directly benefited his employer. For example, in one case an officer, who was required by his employer to carry his badge and identification while off duty, was shot and killed after he displayed his badge to an individual who was causing a disturbance. The Court ruled that the officer died because of a "risk peculiar to the employment" as a law enforcement officer, and that his family was entitled to survivor's benefits.[86] In a similar case, a court found compensable injuries suffered by an off-duty police officer who was shot when he and a friend were confronted by a group of men while mountain biking. The Court reasoned that "although the officer was off duty, the relevant code of conduct for his employment required him to act in an official capacity if [he] observe[d] an incident requiring police action to safeguard life, property, or prevent the escape of a felon or violent criminal. Because of that duty, he was exposed to an increased risk of being injured by gunfire if a crime or other threat to life occurred in his presence than would be faced by a similarly situated non-officer."[87]

In another case, an officer who was working off duty as a security officer for a motel was shot and killed by an individual he was questioning after a robbery victim identified the person as having recently robbed him. The Court found that when the officer undertook official police duties during the course of interviewing the criminal suspect, he was acting in the course and scope of his employment as a police officer when he was shot, and that his family was entitled to survivor's benefits. The Court reasoned that the officer's obligation to take appropriate action required the conclusion that he was acting solely as a police officer when he was killed:

> "His on-duty status began when the robbery victim yelled to him that he had been robbed by the subject being questioned. Although the deceased was performing a function of his role as an independent contractor security guard at the time he stopped the subject for questioning, that role ceased as soon as he had reason to believe a felony had been committed. At that point, he became solely an officer of the Police Department."[88]

A fourth case involving the grant of benefits arose when an off-duty officer observed a vehicle acting suspiciously in his neighborhood. When the vehicle tried to ram the officer, the officer stepped out of its way to avoid being hit, grabbing the vehicle's door as it passed and identifying himself as a police officer. During this time, he was dragged 30 feet and was thrown from the truck, resulting in injuries to his neck, back, left shoulder, right knee, and both hands. In approving the officer's claim for workers' compensation benefits, a court concluded that "when the truck passed [the officer] he grabbed onto the truck and identified himself as a State Police Officer. Thus, the officer ceased to function solely as a private citizen and began to operate, at least in part, as a State Police Officer."[89] Using similar rationale, a court awarded workers' compensation benefits to an officer who accidentally shot himself while taking off his gun at home. The Court found significant the fact that the employer did not provide a place on its premises for the storage of service revolvers.[90] Analogously, another court found compensable an intoxicated officer's fatal fall from a balcony at a hotel where a police convention was being held, concluding that the officer's consumption of alcohol at a hospitality room rendered the fall in the course and scope of employment.[91]

The cases resulting in a denial of benefits also tend to focus on whether the employer derives any benefit from the officer's off-duty activities. One case involved an off-duty sergeant who suffered an injury in an automobile accident on a causeway, with the accident resulting from an altercation with two men in a bar where the sergeant had gone for a night of social drinking. The Court found that even though one of the individuals who accosted the sergeant (and later caused the accident) happened to be a suspect, the sergeant's lack of knowledge of the wanted status of the individual negated any on-the-job nexus.[92] Other cases involving off-duty injuries which result in no award of workers' compensation benefits to officers have included:

- Where an officer was injured in an accident while driving to a meeting of his labor organization. The officer was given leave by a collective bargaining agreement to attend union meetings.[93]

- Where an officer was injured while bowling in a tournament held to acknowledge and thank public safety workers.[94]

- Where an officer injured his hand on a towel dispenser in a locker room while preparing to begin his shift.[95]

- Where an officer was injured while practicing with his service weapon at home in anticipation of his firearms qualification.[96]

If the employer temporarily suspends an employee with or without pay, and instructs the employee not to take any law enforcement action while on suspension, then injuries suffered by the officer while on suspension which otherwise would be in the course and scope of his employment are not compensable under the workers' compensation laws. In one case, a trooper for the Arkansas State Police who served on a multi-agency drug task force was suspended with pay pending a disciplinary investigation. The trooper's employer instructed the trooper not to engage in any law enforcement action while on suspension. In spite of these instructions, the trooper participated in a drug raid, during which he was shot in the chest. An appeals court rejected the trooper's compensation claim, finding that an employer has the "unqualified right…to determine what an employee shall or shall not do."[97]

Because of the benefit to the employer of the officers' actions, courts hold compensable under the workers' compensation laws injuries from accidental discharges of firearms occurring when an officer is cleaning a service weapon at home.[98] Even officers who are injured in off-duty sports events sponsored or approved by their departments may be covered by workers' compensation laws. In one case in which an officer was injured during an off-duty sports activity, the officer's department had provided release time for officers to engage in such events. Since the activities took place at local schools and were designed to benefit the youth of the community, the Court ruled that the injury was compensable under workers' compensation laws since the employer gained benefits from the athletic activities.[99] On the other hand, if the athletic injuries are suffered in off-duty programs which do not directly or indirectly benefit the employer, the injuries are not likely to be compensable,[100] even if the officer believes the athletic program is necessary to remain physically fit for the job.[101]

Injuries Suffered During Physical Agility Testing Or Training.

If an injury is suffered during a physical agility test either conducted or required by the employer, there is no question but that the injuries are compensable under the workers' compensation system. If the injury is suffered off duty while training for an employer-required physical fitness or agility examination, the injury will be compensable if the employee can show (1) that the employee subjectively believed that his or her participation in the training was expected by the employer; and (2) that the employee's belief was objectively reasonable. Applying this test, a court required the payment of workers' compensation benefits to a California Highway Patrol trooper who was injured off duty while practicing long jumping in preparation for the Patrol's mandatory annual physical fitness test.[102] Another court upheld the workers' compensation claim of a SWAT officer who was injured while engaged in physical fitness training on his vacation. The court reasoned that the officer "is a member of a special tactical unit, designed to handle high-risk problems. Members of SWAT are required to pass a physical fitness test to qualify for the unit initially, and are required to pass supplemental physical fitness tests each year. Members of SWAT engage in paid, on-duty physical fitness training each month, and have been reprimanded for not being physically fit enough to perform the job-related task of climbing a wall while on assignment. Hence, physical fitness is indisputably a requirement of membership in SWAT."[103]

Not all claims for injuries suffered in potentially job-related physical fitness activities are successful. For example, one court rejected the compensation claim of a police officer who was injured playing basketball during his lunch hour, reasoning that the officer's belief that he was expected to participate in the basketball game in order to stay in shape was not "objectively reasonable."[104] If the injuries are suffered during a pre-hire physical agility test, the fact that the injured applicant is not yet an employee precludes coverage of the injuries under the workers' compensation laws.[105]

If an injury is suffered during a physical agility test either conducted or required by the employer, the injuries are compensable under the workers' compensation system.

Total Disability And The Availability Of Light Work.

Though some exceptions exist, as a general rule a law enforcement officer is not entitled to complete disability benefits if there is work available within the law enforcement agency which the officer is capable of performing.[106] Even if the work is "light duty" in nature, the officer may have an obligation to accept the work in lieu of continuing to receive disability benefits.[107]

Accidental Disability Claims.

Some workers' compensation systems provide for increased benefits if an employee is able to show that his or her physical condition is attributable to an on-the-job "accident."[108] An "accident" is usually defined as a "sudden, fortuitous, unexpected mischance,"[109] or a traumatic event.[110] Often, such statutory schemes require the employee to show that the injury was incurred at a definite time and place, and was not merely the gradual worsening of underlying chronic problem.[111]

Accidental disability claims can be difficult to prove. One case, *Engber v. New York State Comptroller*,[112] involved a detective who fell from a telephone pole while repairing a court-ordered wire tap. A court rejected the detective's accidental disability claim, reasoning: "Although the detective maintains that an inconsistency in the positioning of a peg – akin to a rung on a ladder – on the pole led to his fall during his descent, we note that he was aware of the inconsistency. Because he had used the same peg in climbing up the pole, the inconsistency cannot be said to have been unexpected while climbing down. Inasmuch as he further testified that he had climbed 'hundreds' of similar poles during the course of his employment, the incident in question emanated from a risk inherent in his regular job duties." In a similar case, a court upheld the rejection of accidental disability benefits for an officer who injured his knee when he slipped on loose gravel and stones while responding to a call. The Court concluded that the officer was not entitled to accidental disability retirement benefits because he had been at the site numerous times before for similar calls, was familiar with the terrain, and had taken several steps away from his vehicle before he slipped.[113]

Courts have approved accidental disability claims under the following conditions:

- Where an assistant police chief tripped on a step in front of a revolving door to the municipal building. The lights over the revolving door were not working and the passage to the door was partially obstructed by bottled water and construction material.[114]

- Where a police officer was threatened by an armed suspect and watched victims burn to death.[115]

- Where an officer slipped on a pool of water in a bathroom.[116]

- Where an officer was sprayed in the face with pepper spray during on-the-job training.[117]

- Where an officer stepped in a hole during a training exercise.[118]

- Where an officer slipped on wet pavement while entering his patrol car.[119]

- An officer who lost his balance and fell while getting up from his desk.[120]

Accidental disability benefits have been denied where an officer slipped and fell while using stairs at a police department's headquarters,[121] where an officer fell on uneven pavement while searching for a prowler,[122] where the injury occurred during training,[123] where an officer claims a stress disability resulting from serving in an undercover role investigating police corruption,[124] and where an officer's hearing loss was sustained over a long period of time, caused by routine performance of his duties in controlling crowds at parades and other events.[125]

Federal Death Benefits.

The families of law enforcement officers who are killed in the line of duty are entitled to receive federal death benefits, notwithstanding any local workers' compensation laws. The Public Safety Officers' Benefits Act (PSOBA), enacted in 1968, provides that whenever a public safety officer has died as the "direct and proximate result of a personal injury sustained in the line of duty," the federal government must pay $100,000 to the family of the officer. The amount of the federal death benefit has increased over time and is now linked with the cost of living. As of January 1, 2009, it was valued at $315,746. The PSOBA program is administered by the Bureau of Justice Administration (BJA).

The PSOBA was effective on September 29, 1976, and applies only when the injuries suffered by the officer occurred after the effective date of the law.[126] The PSOBA defines a public safety officer as a person "involved in crime and juvenile delinquency control or reduction, or enforcement of the criminal laws" who works for a federal, state, or local governmental body. Even reserve officers such as members of a sheriff's "posse" are covered by the PSOBA if they have full law enforcement responsibilities, and even if those responsibilities are not often or routinely exercised.[127]

The history of the PSOBA is replete with resistance by the Department of Justice (DOJ) to a broad reading of the law, a resistance that has had to have been overcome by the courts and Congress. When the PSOBA was first being considered, the Department of Justice lobbied to limit the scope of "line of duty." As the DOJ argued before Congress: "We believe that accidental death is a hazard of many types of employment and we are aware of no rationale that would suggest Federal intervention in these situations. Providing survivor benefits for those who are killed accidentally should be the responsibility of the employer in the same manner as other employment benefits."[128] As one court commented, "the Department of Justice lost that battle."[129] Congress declined to limit the scope of the PSOBA to exclude accidental deaths, and instead required only that a public safety officer incur fatal injuries sustained in the line of duty.

Congress authorized the BJA to establish "rules, regulations, and procedures as may be necessary to carry out the purposes of the PSOBA."[130] Pursuant to that authority, the BJA then issued a regulation limiting benefits to the families of officers who were killed in the "course of controlling or reducing crime, enforcing the criminal law, or suppressing fires."[131] A court then struck down this regulation, finding that "the express intent of Congress was for the families of all law enforcement officers involved in 'enforcement of the laws,' whether criminal or civil, to be eligible for PSOBA survivor benefits, if they died enforcing those laws. Since the regulation undermines Congress' direction, it is contrary to law, as well as arbitrary and capricious, and is entitled to no deference."[132]

In emphasizing that a broad reading should be given to "line of duty" and overturning a BJA decision denying benefits to the family of an officer killed while driving home, a court emphasized that the PSOBA should be liberally construed in favor of allowing benefits:

> "The grave physical risks facing public safety officers are imminent whenever an officer is under a duty to take actions to protect the public. For officers who are under such a duty at all times, the potential for physical risk pervades their daily lives, both on and off the clock. Placing officers under such a continuous duty with its inherent risks confers a significant benefit on society. In exchange, the PSOBA rewards officers with the peace of mind that their survivors shall be provided for should the risks ever prove fatal. The PSOBA benefits also, to some extent, compensate the survivors for the loss of their spouse or parent to a line of duty death."[133]

In some states, benefits may also be available from the state government for law enforcement officers disabled in the line of duty, or for the families of officers killed in the line of duty.[134] Some states also have statutes that require employers to continue health insurance for officers who suffer certain types of compensable workers' compensation injuries.[135] Benefits such as these are also a common feature of collective bargaining agreements and/or pension systems.

State Occupational Safety Laws Applicable To Law Enforcement Officers.

OSHA requires every employer to furnish employees "employment and a place of employment which are free from recognized hazards that are causing or are likely to cause death or serious physical harm" to employees.

The federal Occupational Safety and Health Act (OSHA) requires every employer to furnish employees "employment and a place of employment which are free from recognized hazards that are causing or are likely to cause death or serious physical harm" to employees.[136] However, OSHA exempts from its coverage state governments and political subdivisions of state governments such as cities and counties.[137] Thus, in order to avail themselves of a tool to ensure a safe working environment, law enforcement officers have turned to state and local safety laws.

At least 30 states have passed statutes which are patterned after OSHA and which are applicable to state and local governments. Oregon's Safe Employment Act is typical of such laws. The Act begins by imposing on all employers the obligation to take "every" measure which is reasonably necessary to protect the life, safety, and health of employees:

> "Every employer shall furnish employment and a place of employment which are safe and healthful for employees therein, and shall furnish and use such devices and safeguards, and shall adopt and use such practices, means, methods, operations and processes as are reasonably necessary to render such employment and place

of employment safe and healthful, and shall do every other thing reasonably necessary to protect the life, safety and health of such employees."[138]

Similar to OSHA, the Oregon Safe Employment Act grants the director of the agency administering the Act broad powers to investigate all safety complaints, including the right to make surprise visits to work sites and to issue citations upon finding safety violations:

> "Whenever the director has reason to believe, after an inspection or investigation, that any employment or place of employment is unsafe or detrimental to health or that the practices, means, methods, operations or processes employed or used in connection therewith are unsafe or detrimental to health, or do not afford adequate protection to the life, safety and health of the employees therein, the director shall issue such citation and order relative thereto as may be necessary to render such employment or place of employment safe and protect the life, safety and health of employees therein."

The Oregon law also grants the director the authority to order changes, improvements, and repairs in equipment used on worksites:

> "The director may in the order direct that such additions, repairs, improvements or changes be made, and such devices and safeguards be furnished, provided and used, as are reasonably required to render such employment or place of employment safe and healthful, in the manner and within the time specified in the order."[139]

Where such safety in employment practices statutes exist, they can be a powerful tool when used by law enforcement officers seeking to improve the safety of the equipment they are provided, or of their general work site. Under the laws, an employer has an obligation to provide its employees with equipment that is safe, sound, and suitable for its intended use.[140] As early as 1973, Oakland, California's police officers used California's safety laws to convince a court to rule that the City was required to furnish a firearm to each officer at the employer's expense on the theory that a firearm is an essential piece of safety equipment.[141] Oregon's statute has been successfully used by law enforcement officers to require safer practices in the way the evidence from drug laboratories is processed by police agencies, to require that appropriate safety measures be taken in a criminal identification bureau in order to ensure that harmful chemicals and fingerprint dust were not inhaled by employees, and to require an employer to purchase portable radios and guns for employees. Washington's law, which is substantially similar to Oregon's, has been applied to require a county sheriff's office to purchase bulletproof vests for its employees and to increase staffing in the rural areas of the county to provide for greater backup. Nevada's law, also similar to Oregon's, has been applied to curtail the practice of requiring law enforcement employees attending training classes to eat food prepared by inmates at the local medium security prison.[142] Given the fact that such safety in employment laws also usually provide for a civil penalty ranging up to $10,000 for each safety violation,[143] the laws can provide a significant incentive for law enforcement employers to provide the safest possible working environments. In addition, depending upon how they are written, state safety laws can even provide the basis for a lawsuit by the employee against the employer for injuries suffered as a result of an unsafe working environment – a lawsuit that would be an exception to the usual rules of a workers' compensation bar.[144]

Laws requiring that law enforcement employers furnish safe working environments for their employees have been enacted in the following states: Alabama, Alaska, Arizona, Arkansas, California, Connecticut, Georgia, Hawai'i, Idaho, Illinois, Indiana, Iowa, Kentucky, Louisana, Maryland, Michigan, Minnesota, Montana, Nevada, New Hampshire, New Jersey, New Mexico, New York, North Carolina, Ohio, Oklahoma, Oregon, South Carolina, Tennessee, Texas, Utah, Vermont, Virginia, Washington, West Virginia, and Wyoming.[145]

Social Security Benefits.

Severely disabled officers may be entitled to Social Security disability benefits. The Social Security Act defines the term "disability" as the "inability to engage in any substantial gainful activity by reason of any medically determinable physical or mental impairment which…has lasted or can be expected to last for a continuous period of not less than 12 months." The Act also provides that an individual will be deemed disabled "only if his physical or mental impairment or impairments are of such severity that he is not only unable to do his previous work but cannot, considering his age, education, and work experience, engage in any other kind of substantial gainful work which exists in the national economy."[146] Because these standards are so difficult to meet and require such a high level of disability, it is rare to encounter a court case granting a disabled officer Social Security benefits.[147]

NOTES

[1] *Story v. Mechling*, 214 Fed.Appx. 161 (3d Cir. 2007); *Kubajak v. Lexington-Fayette Urban County Government*, 2003 WL 22462035 (Ky. App. 2003); *O'Hare v. City of New Rochelle*, 672 N.Y.S.2d 352 (A.D. 1998).

[2] The only circumstances in which the employee's fault would be relevant in a workers' compensation case would be if the employee deliberately injured himself.

[3] *Kelly v. McCall*, 688 N.Y.S.2d 812 (A.D. 1999); *State ex. rel Chime v. Board of Trustees*, 623 N.E.2d 32 (Ohio 1993). *But see Johnson v. Public Employees Retirement Board*, 968 P.2d 793 (N.M. App. 1998)(subsequent employment must be in position commensurate with that of police officer's position to be disqualifying).

[4] *See Haynes v. Workers' Compensation Appeal Board (City of Chester)*, 833 A.2d 1186 (Pa.Cmwlth. 2003).

[5] *E.g., Walker v. Massachusetts Dept. of Correction*, 23 Mass.L.Rptr. 388 (Mass. Super. 2007).

[6] Louisiana, for example, excludes deputy sheriffs from statewide workers' compensation laws. *Trahan v. Acadia Parish Sheriff's Office*, 950 So.2d 151 (La. App. 2007).

[7] *Penton v. City of Hammond Police Dept.*, 991 So.2d 91 (La. App. 2008).

[8] *City of Oelwein v. Board of Trustees*, 567 N.W.2d 237 (Iowa App. 1997)(Hepatitis C); *Festa v. Teleflex*, 382 So.2d 122 (Fla. App. 1980).

[9] *City of Clairton v. WCAB*, 506 A.2d 537 (Pa.Cmwlth. 1986)(specific incidents of lifting heavy persons and wrestling with an intoxicated individual).

[10] *Wills v. Public Safety Personnel Retirement Board*, 743 P.2d 944 (Ariz. App. 1987).

[11] J. Violanti, J. Vena & J. Marshall, *Disease Risk and Mortality Among Police Officers*, 14 J. Police Sci. & Admin. 17 (1986).

[12] An example of the difficulty in establishing the causation of heart disease is *O'Connor v. Board of Trustees of Louisiana State Police*, 429 So.2d 450 (La. App. 1983), where the Court ruled that hypertension is a continuing illness which was not compensable under a retirement plan.

[13] *Uniformed Firefighters Association v. Beekman*, 420 N.E.2d 938 (N.Y. 1981).

[14] Municipal Law, § 207-k. The presumption that heart disease is caused by the job can be overcome by a showing that other factors have caused the disease. *Vecchiarello v. Board of Trustees*, 453 N.Y.S.2d 971 (1982).

[15] *Berry v. County of Henrico*, 247 S.E.2d 389 (Va. 1978).

[16] *Brown v. Levitt*, 397 N.Y.S.2d 171 (1977).

[17] *Lemmerman v. McGuire*, 422 N.Y.S.2d 568 (1979).

[18] *Montgomery County Police Department v. Jennings*, 431 A.2d 721 (Md. App. 1981); *Butler v. Pension Board of Police Dept.*, 147 N.W.2d 27 (Iowa 1966).

[19] *Metropolitan Washington Airports Authority v. Lusby*, 585 S.E.2d 318 (Va. App. 2003).

[20] *Bussa v. Workmen's Compensation Appeals Board*, 66 Cal.Rptr. 204 (Cal. App. 1968).

21 *Callaghan v. Bratton*, 677 N.Y.S.2d 125 (A.D. 1998). *See also Booher v. City of Bristol*, 1997 WL 581104 (Tenn. 1997)(heart attack brought about by sudden exertion not covered by presumption).

22 *McCarthy v. Board of Trustees*, 760 N.Y.S.2d 326 (A.D. 2003).

23 *Prince George's County, Maryland v. Maringo*, 828 A.2d 257 (Md. App. 2003).

24 *Bledsoe v. City of Dickson-Dept. of Police*, 2006 WL 1815808 (Tenn. Workers' Comp. Panel 2006).

25 *Town of Waverly Law Enforcement v. Owens*, 657 S.E.2d 161 (Va. App. 2008).

26 *Jones v. County of Washington*, 725 A.2d 255 (Pa.Cmwlth. 1999).

27 *Punsky v. Clay County Sheriff's Office*, 2008 WL 2787559 (Fla. App. 2008); *Larberg v. Hevesi*, 793 N.Y.S.2d 645 (A.D. 2005); *Skae v. Regan*, 617 N.Y.S.2d 237 (A.D. 1994); *Buchanan v. Pennsylvania State Police*, 620 A.2d 575 (Pa.Cmwlth. 1993); *Wytheville Law Enforcement and Virginia Municipal Group Self-Insurance Association v. Wheeler*, 2003 WL 182513 (Va. App. 2003).

28 *City of Hopewell v. Tirpak*, 502 S.E.2d 161 (W.Va. App. 1998); *Butterworth v. Bratton*, 663 N.Y.S.2d 573 (A.D. 1997).

29 *Bohanan v. City of Knoxville*, 136 S.W.3d 621 (Tenn. 2004).

30 *City of Frederick v. Shankle*, 785 A.2d 749 (Md. App. 2001).

31 *Malchik v. Division of Criminal Justice*, 835 A.2d 940 (Conn. 2003).

32 *City of Bedford Heights v. France*, 616 N.E.2d 177 (Ohio 1993); *see City of Jonesboro v. Marshall*, 2003 WL 1919482 (Ark. App. 2003).

33 California Labor Code §§ 3212-3212.12 and §§ 3213-3213.2. The "blood-borne infectious disease" presumption applies only to diseases that are transmitted via contact with blood, such as Hepatitis and AIDS, not just a condition caused by any organism that can travel within the bloodstream of its host. *DuFour v. Workers' Comp. Appeals Bd.*, 2007 WL 2285900 (Cal. App. 2007).

34 *McAdams v. Kelly*, 851 N.Y.S.2d 64 (Sup. 2007).

35 *E.g.,* H. Selye, *The Stress of Police Work*, 1 Police Stress 7 (1978); http://www.heavybadge.com/efstress.htm; http://www.tearsofacop.com/police/articles/loh.html.

36 *E.g., Richard E. Jacobs Group, Inc. v. White*, 202 S.W.3d 24 (Ky. 2006); *Kubajak v. Lexington-Fayette Urban County Government*, 180 S.W.3d 454 (Ky. 2005); *Sanden v. Cincinnati*, 881 N.E.2d 919 (Ohio App. 2007).

37 *Stratemeyer v. Lincoln County*, 855 P.2d 506 (Mont. 1993); *see Kubajak v. Lexington-Fayette Urban County Government*, 2003 WL 22462035 (Ky. App. 2003); *Wood v. Ohio State Highway Patrol*, 808 N.E.2d 887 (Ohio App. 2004).

38 *Sugrue v. Contributory Retirement Appeal Board*, 694 N.E.2d 391 (Mass. App. 1998); *Harvey v. Raleigh Police Department*, 384 S.E.2d 549 (N.C. App. 1989); *Watley v. City of Murfreesboro*, 2007 WL 3010636 (Tenn. Workers' Comp. Panel 2007); *Village of Random Lake v. Labor and Industry Commission*, 415 N.W.2d 577 (Wis. App. 1987); *see Hayes v. City of Toledo*, 577 N.E.2d 379 (Ohio App. 1989)(stress resulting from accidental discharge of gun during roll call not compensable under workers' compensation laws); *Zink v. Workers' Compensation Appeal Board*, 828 A.2d 456 (Pa.Cmwlth. 2003).

39 *Dubie v. Police and Fire Disability Fund*, 530 N.E.2d 946 (Ohio App. 1989)(suicide ruled non-compensable injury as officer did not show stress was

greater than on other workers); *Osborne v. Oklahoma City Police Department*, 882 P.2d 75 (Okla. 1994); *City of Carbondale*, PEB ¶45,097 (CCH, 1978)(officer's neuroses were not a "natural incident" of police work since other officers had been able to perform high-pressure work for years with no debilitating effects, and there was no evidence that the officer's condition was caused exclusively by his employment).

[40] *Robbins v. Board of Trustees*, 670 N.E.2d 1177 (Ill. App. 1996).

[41] *Jensen v. New Mexico State Police*, 788 P.2d 382 (N.M. App. 1990).

[42] *Patterson v. Board of Trustees, State Police Retirement System*, 942 A.2d 782 (N.J. 2008).

[43] *Franchak v. District of Columbia Metropolitan Police Dept.*, 932 A.2d 1086 (D.C. 2007).

[44] *City of Pittsburgh v. Logan*, 810 A.2d 1185 (Pa. 2002); *see Tretternero v. Police Pension Fund of the City of Aurora*, 643 N.E.2d 1338 (Ill. App. 1994)(threat of discipline not an abnormal working condition for police officer); *see Borough of Beaver v. Workers' Compensation Appeal Board (Rose)*, 810 A.2d 713 (Pa.Cmwlth. 2002)(false accusations, public airing of those accusations, suspension, termination, stripping of duties and authority on reinstatement, and deliberate ostracism instigated by Police Chief, were abnormal working conditions for police officer); *North Huntingdon Township v. Workmen's Compensation Appeal Board*, 644 A.2d 227 (Pa.Cmwlth. 1994)(grand jury investigation into department not an abnormal working condition for a dispatcher); *Parson v. Springettsbury Township*, 642 A.2d 579 (Pa.Cmwlth. 1994)(incident with barricaded gunman not an abnormal working condition for a police officer); *Arbogast v. Baltimore County*, 622 A.2d 808 (Md. App. 1993)(brutality and misconduct charges not an abnormal incident for a police officer); *Squilla v. Marple Township*, 606 A.2d 539 (Pa.Cmwlth. 1991)(reprimand issued to police officer was not an abnormal working condition).

[45] *City of Loveland Police Dept. v. Industrial Claim Appeals Office of State of Colorado*, 141 P.3d 943 (Colo. App. 2006).

[46] *City of Scranton v. W.C.A.B.*, 583 A.2d 852 (Pa.Cmwlth. 1991).

[47] *City of Philadelphia v. Civil Service Commission*, 712 A.2d 350 (Pa.Cmwlth. 1998).

[48] *Wall v. Pension Board*, 533 N.E.2d 458 (Ill. App. 1988)(no proof that the stress suffered by the officer was unique to police work); *Pennsylvania Department of Corrections v. Workers' Compensation Appeal Board (Cantarella)*, 835 A.2d 860 (Pa.Cmwlth. 2003)(stress disorder produced when inmate fondled corrections officer's buttocks); *Borough of Norwood v. Workmen's Compensation Appeal Board*, 538 A.2d 143 (Pa.Cmwlth. 1988)(stress disorder resulting from shots being fired through bathroom window of officer's home compensable).

[49] *Village of Stickney v. Board of Trustees of the Police Pension Fund of the Village of Stickney*, 842 N.E.2d 180 (Ill. App. 2005).

[50] *Knight v. Village of Bartlett*, 788 N.E.2d 205 (Ill. App. 2003).

[51] *Sibley v. City of Phoenix*, 813 P.2d 69 (Or. App. 1991).

[52] *Jensen v. New Mexico State Police*, 788 P.2d 382 (N.M. App. 1990).

[53] *Ryndak v. River Grove Police Pension Board*, 618 N.E.2d 606 (Ill. App. 1993).

[54] *Clowes v. City of Pittsburgh*, 639 A.2d 944 (Pa.Cmwlth. 1994).

55 *Olson v. City of Wheaton Police Pension Board*, 505 N.E.2d 1387 (Ill. App. 1987).

56 *Heaton v. Marin County Employees Retirement Board*, 133 Cal.Rptr. 809 (Cal. App. 1976); *In re PERA Police and Fire Plan Line of Duty Disability Benefits of Brittain*, 724 N.W.2d 512 (Minn. 2006).

57 *Gurule v. Board of Pension Commissioners*, 178 Cal.Rptr. 778 (Cal. App. 1981); *Stoner v. District of Columbia*, 368 A.2d 524 (D.C. App. 1977); *Hunter v. City of Tampa*, 379 So.2d 426 (Fla. App. 1980); *Gibbons v. Retirement Board*, 106 N.E.2d 516 (Ill. 1952); *Hairford v. State Police Retirement Board*, 360 So.2d 220 (La. App. 1978); *Goode v. New York City Transit Police Dept.*, 454 N.Y.S.2d 212 (1982).

58 *Henry v. Industrial Commission of Arizona*, 754 P.2d 1342 (Ariz. 1988).

59 C. Martin, H. McKean & J. Veltkamp, *Post-Traumatic Stress Disorders in Police and Working with Victims*, 14 J. Police Sci. & Admin. 98 (1986).

60 *Henry v. Industrial Commission of Arizona*, 754 P.2d 1342 (Ariz. 1988), quoting *Mead v. American Smelting & Refining Company*, 399 P.2d 694 (Ariz. App. 1965). *See also Gibbons v. Retirement Board*, 106 N.E.2d 516 (Ill. 1952)(11-year gap between precipitating event and claim); *Flint v. Town of Bernalillo*, 878 P.2d 1014 (N.M. App. 1994)(claim for post traumatic stress need not be filed until diagnosis is made, not when officer first starts suffering from symptoms).

61 *Newlun v. Department of Retirement Systems*, 770 P.2d 1071 (Wash. App. 1989).

62 *City of Indianapolis v. Hargis*, 588 N.E.2d 496 (Ind. 1992).

63 *Linnen v. Beaufort County Sheriff's Department*, 408 S.E.2d 248 (S.C. App. 1991).

64 *Brunell v. Wildwood Crest Police Department*, 822 A.2d 576 (N.J. 2003).

65 *Jagielnik v. Board of Trustees*, 649 N.E.2d 527 (Ill. App. 1995); *Youngs v. Village of Penn Yan*, 687 N.Y.S.2d 888 (A.D. 1999); *Paparella v. Safir*, 685 N.Y.S.2d 220 (A.D. 1999); *Woldrich v. Vancouver Police Pension Board*, 928 P.2d 423 (Wash. App. 1996). *But see Calovecchi v. State of Michigan*, 566 N.W.2d 40 (Mich. App. 1996).

66 *Robbins v. Board of Trustees of Carbondale Police Pension Fund*, 687 N.E.2d 39 (Ill. 1997).

67 *City of Miami v. Tomberlin*, 492 So.2d 433 (Fla. App. 1986). *But see McDonald v. Regan*, 571 N.Y.S.2d 636 (A.D. 1991)(hearing loss resulting from alarm system going off while officer was investigating a burglary not compensable); *Hambel v. Regan*, 571 N.Y.S.2d 355 (A.D. 1991)(hearing loss resulting from exposure to siren did not arise out of an "accident" and was thus not compensable).

68 *City of Miami v. Tomberlin*, 492 So.2d 433 (Fla. App. 1986).

69 *Smith v. Board of Trustees of Peace Officers' Retirement*, 745 N.W.2d 95 (Iowa App. 2007).

70 *Haynie v. District of Columbia Police and Firefighters' Retirement and Relief Board*, 640 A.2d 188 (D.C. App. 1994)(denies compensation).

71 *Luna v. Workers' Compensation Appeals Board*, 244 Cal.Rptr. 596 (Cal. App. 1988); *Westberry v. Town of Cape Elizabeth*, 492 A.2d 888 (Maine 1985); *Rantamaki v. Conrad*, 2006 WL 532109 (Ohio App. 2006). *But see Kristiansen v. Morgan*, 708 A.2d 1173 (N.J. 1998)(estate of employee killed when struck by car while crossing four-lane roadway on bridge in order to retrieve his car and go home entitled to benefits).

[72] *Guest v. Workmen's Compensation Appeals Board*, 470 P.2d 1 (Cal. 1970); *Carillo v. Workers' Compensation Appeals Board*, 197 Cal.Rptr. 425 (Cal. App. 1983).

[73] *City of Detroit*, PEB ¶45,498 (CCH 1982). *But see Pennsylvania State Police v. Workers' Compensation Appeal Board*, 694 A.2d 1181 (Pa.Cmwlth. 1997).

[74] *Jasaitis v. City of Paterson*, 155 A.2d 260 (N.J. 1959).

[75] *Montgomery County v. Wade*, 690 A.2d 990 (Md. App. 1997). *See also Wilson v. City of Shreveport*, 682 So.2d 882 (La. App. 1996)(off-duty injury suffered in collision in department-supplied car held compensable; officer was using car to drive to psychology class which was of benefit to employer).

[76] *Pounds v. Board of Trustees*, 749 P.2d 1227 (Or. App. 1988). *See Garzoli v. Workmen's Comp. App. Bd.*, 467 P.2d 833 (Cal. 1970)(injury suffered while commuting on employer-owned motorcycle compensable); *Hanstein v. City of Ft. Lauderdale*, 569 So.2d 493 (Fla. Dist. Ct. App. 1990)("Because police officers are generally charged with a duty of law enforcement while traveling on public thoroughfares, it has long been established that injuries which such officers sustain while traveling to and from work may be compensated."); *Board of Trustees v. Christy*, 269 S.E.2d 33 (Ga. App. 1980)(injury suffered while commuting on city-owned motorcycle compensable); *City of Springfield v. Indus. Comm'n*, 614 N.E.2d 478 (Ill. 1993)(holding injuries compensable for police officer returning from lunch at home because the officer was on-call and available to respond "to any request for assistance or emergency he encountered."); *Abshire v. City of Rockland*, 388 A.2d 512 (Maine 1978)(injury suffered while traveling to court compensable); *Allen v. Board of Selectmen of Weymouth*, 448 N.E.2d 782 (Mass. App. 1983)(injury suffered while traveling to court compensable); *Tighe v. Las Vegas Metro. Police Dep't*, 877 P.2d 1032 (Nev. 1994)(finding exception to going and coming rule for on-call employees, particularly police officers who are uniquely on call at all times).

[77] *City of San Diego v. Workers' Compensation Appeals Board*, 108 Cal.Rptr.2d 510 (Cal. App. 2001).

[78] *Rash v. Workers' Comp. Appeals Bd.*, 2007 WL 1520066 (Cal. App. 2007); *Griffith v. Miamisburg*, 2008 WL 5235168 (Ohio App. 2008); *Brown v. City of Wheeling*, 569 S.E.2d 197 (W.Va. 2002).

[79] *Salt Lake City Corp. v. Labor Com'n*, 153 P.3d 179 (Utah 2007).

[80] *Mayor and Aldermen of Savannah v. Stevens*, 598 S.E.2d 456 (Ga. 2004).

[81] *Cady v. County of Oneida*, 836 N.Y.S.2d 497 (N.Y. Sup. 2006).

[82] *Tutor v. City of Norfolk Police Department*, 2001 WL 1530848 (Va. App. 2001).

[83] *Morris v. Kentucky Retirement Systems*, 2003 WL 21834980 (Ky. App. 2003); *Jumpp v. City of Ventnor*, 828 A.2d 905 (N.J. 2003).

[84] *Gonzalez v. Workers' Compensation Appeals Board*, 230 Cal.Rptr. 649 (Cal. App. 1986); *State v. Dalton*, 878 A.2d 451 (Del. Supr. 2005)(charity softball game). *But see Whitehead v. Orange County Sheriff's Dept.*, 909 So.2d 344 (Fla. App. 2005)(injuries suffered while playing softball on on-call status not compensable).

[85] *See Robinson v. Police and Fire Retirement System*, 597 N.Y.S.2d 201 (A.D. 1993)(gunshot wound incurred by officer shot by wife during lunch hour not compensable); *Banfield v. City of San Antonio*, 801 S.W.2d 134 (Tex. App. 1990)(officer shot with service revolver by her 5-year old child not entitled to workers' compensation benefits).

86 *Jordan v. St. Louis Co. Police Dept.*, 699 S.W.2d 124 (Mo. App. 1985); *see In re Tadlock,* Case No. 92-10524 (Or. WCB 1992)(deputy who was attacked after he displayed his badge in an attempt to defuse an altercation was acting in the line of duty).

87 *Lane v. Industrial Com'n of Arizona,* 178 P.3d 516 (Ariz. App. 2008).

88 *City of Phoenix v. Industrial Committee of Arizona,* 742 P.2d 825 (Ariz. App. 1987); *see Harroun v. Addison Police Pension Bd.*, 865 N.E.2d 273 (Ill. App. 2007)(off-duty officer injured while attempting to stop break-in at neighbor's house; ruled compensable because officer exercising police functions).

89 *Donnini v. Pennsylvania State Police,* 707 A.2d 591 (Pa.Cmwlth. 1998).

90 *City of Harrisburg v. Workmen's Compensation Appeal Board (Gebhart)*, 616 A.2d 1369 (1992).

91 *Van Vleet v. Montana Ass'n of Counties Workers' Compensation Trust*, 103 P.3d 544 (Mont. 2004).

92 *City of North Bay Village v. Millerick,* 721 So.2d 1230 (Fla. App. 1991).

93 *McCommons v. Pennsylvania State Police,* 645 A.2d 333 (Pa.Cmwlth. 1994).

94 *Moi v. State, Dept. of Public Safety,* 188 P.3d 753 (Haw. App. 2008).

95 *Allen v. Pennsylvania State Police,* 678 A.2d 436 (Pa.Cmwlth. 1996).

96 *Feineigle v. Pennsylvania State Police,* 680 A.2d 1220 (Pa.Cmwlth. 1996).

97 *Arkansas State Police v. Davis,* 870 S.W.2d 408 (Ark. App. 1994).

98 *Montgomery County Sheriff's Department v. Workmen's Compensation Appeal Board,* 556 A.2d 962 (Pa.Cmwlth. 1989)(not possible to clean weapon at work); *Aldan v. Workmen's Compensation Appeal Board,* 422 A.2d 733 (Pa. Cmwlth. 1980)(injuries suffered by police chief). If an officer is accidentally shot by a family member with the officer's service weapon, the officer's claim for workers' compensation is not likely to succeed. *Banfield v. City of San Antonio,* 801 S.W.2d 134 (Tex. App. 1990)(officer accidentally shot by son with her service weapon).

99 *Malan v. Town of Yorktown,* 488 N.Y.S.2d 100 (A.D. 1985).

100 *Booth v. New York State Dept. of Corrections,* 871 N.Y.S.2d 783 (N.Y.A.D. 2009).

101 *City of Stockton v. Workers' Comp. Appeals Bd.*, 38 Cal.Rptr.3d 474 (Cal App. 2006); *City of Tampa v. Jones,* 448 So.2d 1150 (Fla. App. 1984).

102 *Kidwell v. Workers' Compensation Appeals Board,* 39 Cal.Rptr.2d 540 (Cal. App. 1995); *see Wilson v. Workers' Compensation Appeals Board,* 239 Cal. Rptr. 719 (Cal. App. 1987)(injury suffered while running off duty to maintain physical condition to pass fitness tests required by employer). *But see Washoe County Sheriff's Department v. Hunt,* 858 P.2d 46 (Nev. 1993)(injury suffered while jogging in preparation for physical fitness test was incurred on employee's "own time" and not compensable under workers' compensation laws). In *Owings v. Anderson County Sheriff's Department,* 433 S.E.2d 869 (S.C. 1993), the Court gave weight to a cardiologist's testimony that running while training for a physical fitness test did not aggravate the employee's preexisting cardiac problem precluding a finding that the officer's heart condition was compensable.

103 *Tomlin v. Workers' Comp. Appeals Bd.*, 76 Cal.Rptr.3d 672 (Cal. App. 2008).

104 *Taylor v. Workers' Compensation Appeals Board,* 244 Cal.Rptr. 643 (Cal. App. 1988); *see Montgomery County v. Smith,* 799 A.2d 406 (Md. App. 2002).

105 *Younger v. City of Denver*, 796 P.2d 38 (Colo. 1990).

106 A minority of courts find that an employee is entitled to a line-of-duty pension if the employee cannot perform all duties normally related to the job. *See Pierce v. Board of Trustees*, 532 N.E.2d 1004 (Ill. App. 1988).

107 *Sullivan v. Brownlee*, 331 S.E.2d 622 (Ga. App. 1985); *Board of Trustees of the Oklahoma City Police Pension and Retirement System v. Clark*, 661 P.2d 506 (Okla. 1983).

108 Some states have other forms of enhanced public safety workers compensation benefits. Illinois, for example, grants higher workers' compensation benefits if an injury is a "line of duty" injury involving "special risk, not ordinarily assumed by a citizen in the ordinary walks of life, imposed on a policeman." 40 ILCS 5/5-113 (West 2002); *see Sarkis v. City of Des Plaines*, 882 N.E.2d 1268 (Ill. App. 2008).

109 *Paparella v. Safir,* 685 N.Y.S.2d 220 (A.D. 1999).

110 *Richardson v. Board of Trustees, Police and Firemen's Retirement System*, 927 A.2d 543 (N.J. 2007); *Muller v. Board of Trustees*, 719 A.2d 699 (N.J. Sup. 1998).

111 *Chiafos v. Municipal Fire & Police Retirement System of Iowa*, 591 N.W.2d 199 (Iowa 1999).

112 *Engber v. New York State Comptroller*, 835 N.Y.S.2d 495 (N.Y. A.D. 2007).

113 *McLaughlin v. McCall,* 677 N.Y.S.2d 406 (A.D. 1998); *see Zuckerberg v. New York State Comptroller*, 847 N.Y.S.2d 286 (A.D. 2007); *Hatchard v. McCall,* 760 N.Y.S.2d 573 (A.D. 2003); *Minchak v. McCall*, 246 A.D.2d 952 (N.Y. A.D. 1998).

114 *Rosenthal v. Board of Trustees*, 675 N.Y.S.2d 350 (A.D. 1998).

115 *City of Cedar Rapids v. Board of Trustees*, 572 N.W.2d 919 (Iowa 1998).

116 *Starnella v. Bratton*, 677 N.Y.S.2d 62 (Conn. App. 1998).

117 *Traweek v. City of West Monroe*, 713 So.2d 655 (La. App. 1998).

118 *Warner v. Wurm*, 254 S.W.3d 148 (Mo. App. 2008).

119 *McCambridge v. McGuire*, 479 N.Y.S.2d 171 (N.Y. App. 1984).

120 *McCambridge v. McGuire*, 479 N.Y.S.2d 171 (N.Y. App. 1984).

121 *McGerald v. DiNapoli*, 857 N.Y.S.2d 813 (A.D. 2008).

122 *Fischer v. New York State Comptroller*, 846 N.Y.S.2d 482 (A.D. 2007).

123 *Geraci v. Hevesi*, 829 N.Y.S.2d 736 (A.D. 2007).

124 *Baird v. Kelly*, 806 N.Y.S.2d 578 (A.D. 2006).

125 *Hoehl v. Kelly*, 772 N.Y.S.2d 65 (A.D. 2004).

126 *Dawson v. U.S.,* 75 Fed.Cl. 53 (2007).

127 *Hawkins v. U.S.,* 68 Fed.Cl. 74 (2005).

128 S.Rep. No. 94-816, at 4, *reprinted in* 1976 U.S.C.C.A.N. 2504, 2506.

129 *Hawkins v. U.S.*, 68 Fed.Cl. 74 (2005).

130 42 U.S.C. § 3796c(a); 28 C.F.R. § 32.2(c)(1).

131 28 C.F.R. § 32.2(c)(1).

132 *Hawkins v. U.S.*, 68 Fed.Cl. 74 (2005).

133 *Davis v. United States*, 50 Fed.Cl. 192 (2001); *see Demutiis v. United States*, 48 Fed.Cl. 81 (2000).

134 *E.g.*, Illinois Public Safety Employee Benefits Act, 820 ILCS 320/10 (West 2004); Minn.Stat. § 299A.465 (2006); *see Phalin v. McHenry County Sheriff's Dept.*, 886 N.E.2d 448 (Ill. App. 2008); *Senese v. Village of Buffalo Grove*, 890 N.E.2d 628 (Ill. App. 2008); *In re Jerve*, 749 N.W.2d 404 (Minn. App. 2008).

135 *In re Dahl*, 2008 WL 131948 (Minn. App. 2008); *Conaway v. St. Louis County*, 702 N.W.2d 779 (Minn. App. 2005)(post-traumatic stress disorder a compensable condition triggering health insurance coverage).

136 Title 29, §654, United States Code. There is no constitutional right to a safe workplace. *Cerka v. Salt Lake County*, 988 F. Supp. 1420 (D. Utah 1997).

137 Title 29, §652(5), United States Code.

138 §654.010, Oregon Revised Statutes.

139 §654.031, Oregon Revised Statutes.

140 *MacClave v. City of New York*, 265 N.Y.S.2d 222 (A.D. 1965).

141 *Oakland Police Officers Association v. City of Oakland*, 106 Cal.Rptr. 134 (Cal. App. 1973).

142 The two decisions referred to in the text are unreported decisions; copies of the decisions may be obtained from Labor Relations Information System, Portland, Oregon.

143 *See* §50-535, Tennessee Code Annotated.

144 *Singleton v. City of New York*, 827 N.Y.S.2d 535 (N.Y. Sup. 2006).

145 **Alabama:** Alabama Code §25-1-1; **Alaska:** Alaska Statutes §18.60.010; **Arizona:** Arizona Revised Statutes §23-401; **Arkansas:** Arkansas Code Annotated § 11-2-117; **California:** California Labor Code §§140-149 and 6300-6708; **Connecticut:** Connecticut General Statutes §31-367; **Georgia:** Official Code of Georgia Annotated § 34-2-10; **Hawai'i:** Hawai'i Revised Statutes Chapter 396; **Idaho:** Idaho Code § 72-720; **Illinois:** Illinois Comp. Statutes Annotated §820/225-3; **Indiana:** Indiana Code Title 22-8; **Iowa:** Code of Iowa Chapter 88; **Kentucky:** Kentucky Revised Statutes Chapter 338; **Louisiana:** Louisiana Revised Statutes 23:13; **Maryland:** Annotated Code of Maryland Article 89, §29; **Michigan:** Michigan Compiled Laws §408.1001; **Minnesota:** Minnesota Statutes Chapter 182; **Montana:** Montana Code Annotated §50-70-201; **Nevada:** Nevada Revised Statutes Chapter 618; **New Hampshire:** New Hampshire RSA Chapter 277; **New Jersey:** New Jersey Statutes Annotated §34:6a-26; **New Mexico:** New Mexico Statutes Annotated §50-9-1; **New York:** New York §27-a, Labor Law; **North Carolina:** North Carolina General Statutes §95-126; **Ohio:** Ohio Revised Code Annotated §4167.04; **Oklahoma:** Oklahoma Statutes Annotated Title 40 §401; **Oregon:** Oregon Revised Statutes § 654.003; **South Carolina:** Code of Laws of South Carolina §41-15-80; **Tennessee:** Tennessee Code Annotated §50-501; **Texas:** Texas Labor Code Annotated §411.103: **Utah:** Utah Code Title 35, Chapter 9; **Vermont:** Vermont Statutes Annotated Title 21; **Virginia:** Code of Virginia §40.1; **Washington:** Revised Code of Washington Title 49, Chapter 17; **West Virginia:** West Virginia Code Annotated §21-3a-5; **Wyoming:** Wyoming Statutes §27-11-101.

146 42 U.S.C. § 23(d)(1)(A).

147 *Roos v. Astrue*, 2008 WL 2309166 (S.D. N.Y. 2008); *Rodriguez v. Astrue*, 2008 WL 2073508 (S.D.N.Y. 2008).

CHAPTER 13

LAW ENFORCEMENT OFFICERS AND EMPLOYMENT DISCRIMINATION

Basic Discrimination Law Principles.

In and of itself, discrimination is not illegal. However...

In the broadest sense, a claim of "discrimination" contends that an employer has treated two otherwise similarly-situated employees, or two classes of employees, in a different manner. In and of itself, discrimination is not illegal. However, when the unequal treatment is based upon an employee's status as a member of a class of individuals protected under the law, or when the discrimination is in retaliation for the employee having engaged in "protected activity," the discrimination may violate federal or state law.

Protected Classes. Different "classes" of employees have varying levels of protection against discrimination. If employees are treated differently because of their status in a "suspect" classification, then the employer's use of the classification to make employment decisions will be sustained only if the classification is narrowly tailored to serve a compelling governmental interest.[1] Thus far, the Supreme Court has applied this extremely high "compelling interest" standard only to three classifications – race,[2] alien status,[3] and national origin.[4] If a classification is "quasi-suspect" in nature, then the employer must justify its actions on the grounds that they are substantially related to a legitimate state interest.[5] Thus far, the Supreme Court has recognized two classifications as quasi-suspect: gender,[6] and illegitimacy.[7]

If a classification is neither suspect nor quasi-suspect, the only burden an employer must meet under the Fourteenth Amendment is that of showing that there is any rational basis for the use of the classification.[8] Since some rational basis exists for virtually any law that is enacted, the categorizing of a classification as neither suspect nor quasi-suspect usually sounds the death knell for an employee's employment discrimination case. The most prevalent types of employment discrimination cases where the employer has been only held to the rational basis test involve discrimination on the basis of age,[9] disability status,[10] and residency.[11]

Protected Activities. It is almost always illegal for an employer to discriminate against an employee because an employee has engaged in activities that are protected under the law. Activities can be protected in a variety of ways. The United States Constitution, for example, provides protection for employees' free speech, religion and association rights, as well as other rights including the right to privacy and the right to due process. Similar, or even greater, protections appear in many state constitutions.

The United States Constitution, for example, provides protection for employees' free speech, religion, and association rights, as well as other rights including the right to privacy and the right to due process.

An activity can be protected by federal or state statute as well. For example, almost all non-discrimination statutes such as Title VII of the Civil Rights Act, the Americans With Disabilities Act and the Family and Medical Leave Act, provide anti-retaliation protections for employees who bring discrimination claims. Other employment-related statutes, from workers' compensation laws to wage and hour laws such as the Fair Labor Standards Act, provide protections to employees who bring claims. State collective bargaining laws also confer "protected activity" status on a variety of workplace behaviors.

'Reverse Discrimination' Cases.

A fair portion of discrimination cases today are so-called "reverse discrimination" cases, usually brought by white males claiming they have been discriminated against because of either or both of their race and gender. If an employee is the victim of discrimination because of the employee's race or gender, the employee has the same access to the protection of the law no matter what the employee's race or gender might be.[12] Thus, in "reverse discrimination" cases, courts apply precisely the same legal tests as they would in discrimination lawsuits brought by women or members of racial minority groups.[13]

Reverse-discrimination cases come in a variety of forms. A fair number of them involve either challenges to a promotional system[14] or claims by applicants for a police chief's position that the applicant was not selected because the employer had an illegal preference for a member of a protected class.[15]

Title VII And The Fourteenth Amendment.

Claims of employment discrimination usually proceed under one of two legal theories. The first theory is that the alleged discriminatory conduct violates Title VII of the federal Civil Rights Act, which provides as follows:

> "It shall be an unlawful employment practice for an employer —
>
> "(1) to fail or refuse to hire or to discharge any individual, or otherwise to discriminate against any individual with respect to his compensation, terms, conditions, or privileges of employment, because of such individual's race, color, religion, sex, or national origin; or
>
> "(2) to limit, segregate, or classify his employees or applicants for employment in any way which would deprive or tend to deprive any individual of employment opportunities or otherwise adversely affect his status as an employee, because of such individual's race, color, religion, sex, or national origin."[16]

The second theory used in employment discrimination cases is that the alleged discriminatory conduct violates the equal protection clause of the Fourteenth Amendment to the United States Constitution, which reads in part as follows:

> "No State shall make or enforce any law which shall abridge the privileges or immunities of citizens of the United States; nor shall any State deprive any person of life, liberty, or property, without due process of law; nor deny to any person within its jurisdiction the equal protection of the laws."

The courts have held that employees proceeding under the Fourteenth Amendment must show that their employer has intentionally discriminated against them, a burden of proof much higher than that in a Title VII case, which only requires a showing of a discriminatory result. For that reason, most discrimination cases brought by minority and female law enforcement officers proceed under Title VII.[17] For reasons which will be discussed below, most so-called "reverse discrimination" lawsuits – lawsuits usually brought by white males challenging affirmative action plans – proceed under the Fourteenth Amendment.

Disparate Treatment And Disparate Impact Employment Discrimination.

There are two general types of employment discrimination cases: disparate treatment and disparate impact cases.[18] **Disparate treatment** occurs when an employee is singled out and treated less favorably from others similarly situated on account of race or any other factor impermissible under Title VII or the Fourteenth Amendment.[19] **Disparate impact** focuses on employment practices which are facially neutral in their treatment of different groups but which, in fact, fall more harshly on one group than another and cannot be justified by a business necessity or a bona fide occupational qualification.[20] For example, a law enforcement agency's physical fitness standards, to the extent they adversely impact women, are reviewed under traditional disparate impact analysis.[21]

Disparate Treatment Cases.

An employee complaining of disparate treatment must establish that his or her membership in a protected class "played a role in the employer's decision-making process and had a determinative influence on the outcome of that process."[22] The employee may meet this burden with either direct or circumstantial evidence.[23] In a disparate treatment case, it is usually difficult to come by direct evidence of discrimination, since employers will rarely admit that the reason for an employment decision was discriminatory in nature.[24] Instead, the evidence of discrimination is usually circumstantial or inferential in nature.[25] In such a circumstantial evidence case, a law enforcement officer must usually prove the following in order to establish a *prima facie* case of disparate treatment discrimination:

(1) The officer is a member of a protected class,

(2) The officer was qualified for the position the officer held or sought,

(3) The officer suffered an adverse employment action, and

(4) The circumstances of the adverse employment action give rise to an inference of discrimination.[26]

The burden of proving a *prima facie* case is not a heavy one,[27] though there is an occasional stumbling block. An important part of the required proof is that the employee actually have suffered an "adverse employment action." In general, an adverse employment action is one which "well might have dissuaded a reasonable worker from making or supporting a charge of discrimination." [28] Usually, the shorthand is that discharges, suspensions, demotions, transfers, and denials of transfers are sufficiently "adverse" to trigger anti-discrimination rights.[29] The following have all qualified as adverse employment actions in lawsuits brought by law enforcement officers:

- Requirements for mandatory drug testing;[30]

- Notations in a personnel file that an officer resigned for questionable reasons;[31]

- Subjecting an officer to repeated baseless disciplinary investigations;[32]

- Negative performance evaluation;[33]

- Assignment to "gym duty" for two years following the shooting of an African-American suspect;[34]

- Ddenial of overtime opportunities;[35] and

- Denial of a reassignment to a position carrying higher prestige and greater promotional opportunities.[36]

Lesser administrative actions, such as a requirement that an officer participate in a fitness for duty evaluation,[37] where an officer is placed on administrative leave with pay,[38] was lectured to,[39] was given a delayed promotion along with retroactive pay,[40] or was given the "cold shoulder,"[41] are not thought to be sufficiently adverse to allow a discrimination lawsuit. A perceived loss of prestige felt by a deputy chief as a result of departmental reorganization does not qualify as an adverse employment action;[42] nor does the denial of a training opportunity[43] or a requirement for retraining after an officer has been involved in a critical incident.[44] As one court observed in ordering a trial on whether the absence of female-only locker rooms for supervisors in the Boston Police Department was illegal discrimination, whether a particular employment action is sufficiently adverse is often a factual determination that should be made by a jury.[45]

Where an officer alleges that he or she has been the victim of a discriminatory disciplinary decision, the officer can establish the *prima facie* case by showing that he or she engaged in conduct similar to that of a person of another race or gender, and that disciplinary measures were enforced with more severity against him.[46] Key to this is that the officer must show that he or she was treated differently than a member of a non-protected class.[47]

When an officer establishes a *prima facie* case of disparate treatment discrimination, the burden shifts to the employer to produce evidence that the officer was rejected for a legitimate, non-discriminatory reason.[48] Any of a variety of reasons can suffice to meet the employer's burden of rebutting the inference of discrimination. Courts have found the following to be sufficient reasons for treating employees differently: Factual differences in the employees' situations, including misconduct of a different nature,[49] a rule that has some business motivation and is generally applicable to all employees (even if it has differing impacts on individual employees),[50] budgetary concerns,[51] the possible loss of grant funding,[52] the need to have female correctional officers supervising female inmates,[53] and performance or behavior problems on the part of the employee.[54] An employer's business motivation does not need to be a wise or correct one, it must merely be a non-discriminatory, honestly held one.[55]

If the employer fails to rebut the officer's *prima facie* showing of disparate treatment discrimination, the employer will be held to have engaged in discriminatory conduct. If the employer succeeds in making such a showing, the burden shifts back to the officer to establish either that a discriminatory reason more likely motivated the employer, or that the employer's non-discriminatory explanation is not credible, but that it is merely a "pretext."[56] If the officer is successful, the employer will be held to have engaged in discriminatory conduct. This three-part test is commonly referred to as the *McDonnell-Douglas* test, after a Supreme Court decision involving the McDonnell-Douglas Corporation.[57]

In recent years federal courts have emphasized that the burden of proving discrimination cases is ultimately a difficult one for employees. The following passage from a Pennsylvania case is illustrative of how courts approach the issue:

> "It is not the role of the courts to second-guess the wisdom, prudence or competence of the employer's decision. An employee cannot merely show that the employer's decision was wrong or mistaken, but rather, must demonstrate that the decision was motivated by discriminatory animus. The employee's evidence must allow a reasonable fact finder to infer that each of the employer's proffered legitimate, non-discriminatory reasons was either a post hoc fabrication or otherwise did not actually motivate the employment action. In other words, the employee must demonstrate such weaknesses, implausibilities, inconsistencies, incoherencies, or contradictions in the employer's proffered legitimate reasons for its action that a reasonable fact finder could rationally find them 'unworthy of credence.'"[58]

Disparate treatment cases come down to whether other employees who have been more leniently treated by the employer are in fact "similarly situated."

Often, disparate treatment cases come down to whether other employees who have been more leniently treated by the employer are in fact "similarly situated." Since employees bring to any situation differences in work history, tenure, rank, disciplinary records, and other characteristics, it has usually proven difficult if not impossible for employees claiming discrimination to establish that other employees are "similarly situated."[59] An illustrative case involved a male police captain who had an affair with a female probationary employee. The employer fired the probationary employee for the affair, but did not discipline the captain. A federal appeals court summarily dismissed the probationer's lawsuit on the grounds that she and the captain were not similarly situated since the captain had job protection rights under a civil service system.[60] Another example along the same lines involved an African-American officer who was given a 160-hour suspension for an incident that also involved a Caucasian officer, who received only a 20-hour suspension. A court found the two officers to be not similarly situated given not only their different actions during the incident, but also because of their prior disciplinary records.[61]

If the employer's proffered reasons for disciplining an employee have shifted over time, the employee may be able to show that the reasons are a pretext for discrimination.[62] At the same time, an employer is permitted to elaborate on its reasons for making an employment decision, and minor changes in its rationale for discipline will not be sufficient evidence to prove that its decision was a pretext for discrimination.[63]

Disparate Impact Cases.

Disparate impact cases under Title VII are usually characterized by the same sort of shifting burden of proof typical in disparate treatment cases. In prosecuting a claim of disparate impact, the employee bears the initial burden of proving a *prima facie* case of discrimination. This *prima facie* case must be established by a showing that (1) specifically identifies each employment practice that is challenged and (2) shows that the challenged practice causes or creates a significant disparity for those in a protected class.[64]

If the employee is successful in establishing a *prima facie* case, then the employer bears the burden of proving that the challenged employment policy is not discriminatory in intent, and that the policy serves a valid business necessity. If the employer demonstrates that the employment policy is job-related, the employee may overcome that demonstration of job-relatedness by showing by a preponderance of the evidence that other selection criteria would serve the employer's legitimate purposes without a similar discriminatory effect.[65]

Disparate impact cases start with statistical proof, with the aggrieved employee establishing that an employment practice or particular test results in a statistically disproportionate impact on the protected classification to which the employee belongs.[66] There are various approaches to statistical analysis that have been used by courts, and no consensus has developed establishing a mathematical standard against which all cases can be measured.[67] As the Supreme Court has held, "a case-by-case approach properly reflects our recognition that statistics come in infinite variety and their usefulness depends on all the surrounding facts and circumstances."[68]

Retaliation Claims.

Title VII also forbids retaliation against an employee for complaining of prohibited employment discrimination.[69] To prove retaliation, the employee must present evidence demonstrating: (1) That she engaged in protected participation or opposition under Title VII; (2) that the employer was aware of this activity; (3) that the employer took adverse action against the plaintiff; and (4) that a causal

Title VII forbids retaliation against an employee for complaining of prohibited employment discrimination.

connection exists between the protected activity and the adverse action, i.e., that a retaliatory motive played a part in the adverse employment action.[70] Similar to the showing required for claims of discrimination, once the employee has established a *prima facie* case, the employer can rebut the inference of discrimination by showing a legitimate, independent business reason for its decision, and the employee can rebut the employer's justification by showing that it is a pretext.

The anti-retaliation provision of Title VII, unlike the substantive provisions of the statute, is not limited to discriminatory actions that affect employment terms and conditions. According to the Supreme Court, to prevail on a claim for retaliation under Title VII, "a plaintiff must show that a reasonable employee would have found the challenged action materially adverse, which in this context means it well might have dissuaded a reasonable worker from making or supporting a charge of discrimination."[71] An employee need only show that his employer took an adverse action and that a reasonable employee would find the employer's action to be adverse. For example, while the initiation of a disciplinary investigation would not amount to the "adverse employment action" necessary for a discrimination claim, it would suffice to support a retaliation claim.[72]

Retaliation claims are different from substantive discrimination claims in yet another way. In order to prevail on a claim for retaliation, the employee need not establish that the conduct initially complained of amounted to an unlawful employment practice, but need only demonstrate that she had a good faith, reasonable belief that the underlying challenged actions of the employer violated the law. Complaints through the employer's internal affairs process qualify as protected activities under anti-discrimination law.[73] While the employee must show that a causal nexus exists between her protected activity and the adverse employment action, retaliatory motive need not be the sole cause of the adverse employment action, but retaliation must be a substantial or motivating factor behind the adverse action.[74]

Employees often argue that if an adverse employment action occurs shortly after they have engaged in protected activity, it is appropriate to draw an inference of discrimination. Courts view such arguments with a bit of jaundice, finding that even a three-month gap in time – assuming there is no other evidence of discrimination – is insufficient to raise the inference that the employment action was provoked by the protected activity.[75] However, if the gap between the two events is quite close, the quick sequencing of events, standing alone, can raise the necessary inference of causation. As phrased by one court considering the termination of a female deputy sheriff, "The three-day gap between Plaintiff's protected expression and the adverse action is evidence tending to show that the two were not wholly unrelated."[76]

Sexual Or Racial Harassment.

An offshoot of discrimination claims is a claim of sexual or racial harassment. In the past few years, profound changes have occurred in the law of harassment, changes that make most such lawsuits unsuccessful. Today, it is a rarity to find a law enforcement officer prevailing in a harassment lawsuit.

To understand the changes in the law, it is important to start with the requirements of Title VII itself. In order to establish a Title VII harassment claim, an employee must show the following:

- That he or she belongs to a protected group;

- That he or she was subjected to unwelcome sexual or racial harassment;

- That the harassment was based on sex or race; and

- That the harassment affected a term, condition, or privilege of employment.[77]

Sexual harassment is verbal or physical contact of a sexual nature which either creates an intimidating, hostile or offensive working environment, or which unreasonably interferes with an individual's work performance.[78] Sexual harassment can be perpetrated by members of the same or opposite sex, no matter the sexual orientation of the harasser.[79] To the extent that an officer is a willing participant in jokes of a sexual nature or sexual banter, the officer's claim of harassment will be much harder to establish.[80]

There are two main types of harassment claims. In the first, so-called "hostile work environment" claims, the employee is contending that the workplace is inappropriately tolerant of racially or sexually offensive behavior. For the employer to be sued for a hostile work environment, it must have done something for the workplace conduct to be imputed to it.[81] An employer's obligations extend even over non-employees; for example, a corrections agency has a duty to protect female corrections officers from sexual harassment by male inmates.[82] The pervasive use of derogatory or insulting terms relating to women or minorities generally and addressed to female or minority employees personally may be evidence of a hostile work environment,[83] as can be the use or display of obscene language or sexually explicit pictures or cartoons in the workplace.[84]

The second form of sexual harassment is *"quid pro quo"* harassment, where a supervisor either states or implies to an employee that the granting of sexual favors will either enhance the employee's career or ensure that the employee retains a job.[85] In addition, if a supervisor is having an affair with a subordinate, it is possible that the affair creates a hostile work environment for co-workers if the subordinate receives benefits or opportunities denied other employees.[86]

An employer is prohibited from retaliating against employees who file a harassment claim; critical to a finding of retaliation is that the employer's actions must in fact be motivated by a desire to punish the employee for filing the complaint.[87]

Sexual harassment is verbal or physical contact of a sexual nature which either creates an intimidating, hostile or offensive working environment, or which unreasonably interferes with an individual's work performance.

The Supreme Court's Significant Changes In Harassment Law.

The law of harassment has hugely changed in the last ten years. The impetus for much of the change was a 1998 Supreme Court decision known as *Oncale v. Sundowner Offshore Services*. In the case, the Court held that Title VII "does not reach genuine but innocuous differences in the ways men and women routinely interact with members of the same sex and of the opposite sex. The prohibition of harassment on the basis of sex requires neither asexuality nor androgyny in the workplace, it forbids only behavior so objectively offensive as to alter the conditions of the victim's employment."[88]

The hundreds of cases after *Oncale* show how far the law has changed to protect any employer from liability for harassment claims. For example, in the last few years, courts have found that the following conduct does <u>not</u> constitute harassment under Title VII:

- Calling an African-American woman an "Oreo," a "bitch," and an "Uncle Tom."[89]

- A sergeant discussing sex toy shopping, the use of vulgar language and sexual gestures, and a co-worker blowing up a balloon in the shape of a phallus.[90]

- A supervisor telling a subordinate he admired her breasts, that he wanted to have sex with her, that he wanted to perform oral sex upon her, and that she could make more money working at Hooters than with the employer.[91]

- A supervisor who pulled back an employee's shirt to examine her bra.[92]

- A sergeant telling his subordinate that she "looked hot" and that her leave requests would be more favorably looked upon if she wore tighter clothes, and telling her husband that "I'm eating your wife."[93]

- Comments that "your elbows are the same color as your nipples," another comment that the employee had big thighs, touching the employee's arm, and attempts to look down her dress.[94]

- A female co-worker making unwanted advances towards a female employee, including conduct such as blowing kisses, kissing her on the cheek, grabbing the employee's face, engaging in discussions about sex, the rubbing of her buttocks, and saying "love ya."[95]

- Repeated groping of a male employee's genitals by a male co-worker.[96]

Moreover, the requirement in *Oncale* that there be discrimination in order to substantiate a sexual harassment claim has led courts to reject harassment lawsuits unless the employee can show an "adverse employment action" such as discharge, demotion, transfer, or suspension. Interpreting this requirement strictly, courts have found that the following actions by an employer do not amount to the requisite adverse employment action necessary to sustain a harassment lawsuit:

- Pending disciplinary charges.[97]

- Difference in raises.[98]

- Negative performance evaluation and diminishment of job duties.[99]

- Threats.[100]

- Completing employee conduct forms.[101]

- Reprimands.[102]

- Shift change.[103]

- Heightened scrutiny from supervisors.[104]

The Supreme Court was not through with sexual harassment law when it decided *Oncale*. In 1998, the Court decided the companion cases of *Faragher v. City of Boca Raton* and *Burlington Industries v. Ellerth*.[105] In those cases, the Court dealt with a critical issue in harassment law – when an employer is vicariously liable for hostile work environment sexual harassment. For many years, the law had been settled with respect to hostile work environment harassment perpetrated by co-workers of equal or lower rank. Under those rules, an employer was liable for a hostile environment created by a non-supervisory coworker only if it was "negligent either in discovering or remedying the harassment" or, in other words, if it "knew or should have known of the harassment and failed to implement prompt and appropriate corrective action."[106] Not surprisingly, successful hostile work environment harassment claims based on co-worker conduct have been rare. It has also long been established that, as the rank or status of the harasser increases, so too does the potential liability of the employer for the harassment.[107]

Faragher and *Ellerth* dealt with when an employer is liable for hostile work environment sexual harassment perpetrated by a supervisor. The Court announced a series of new rules in *Faragher* and *Ellerth*. Under the rules, an employer is automatically liable for hostile work environment harassment perpetrated by a supervisor if the harassment is accompanied by adverse employment action such as discharge, demotion, suspension, or transfer. These serious employment decisions are often referred to as "tangible employment actions."[108] Less substantial employment actions such as reassignments do not qualify as tangible employment actions.[109]

The vast majority of sexual harassment cases, however, do not involve such overt adverse employment action. Rather, they involve employees who are the victims of solely the harassment without any accompanying employer-imposed job actions. In such cases, the Court held, an employer is liable unless it can show that it (1) had a sexual harassment policy and made some effort to stop the harassment;

(2) that the employee unreasonably failed to make use of the policy; and (3) that had the employee used the policy to complain about the harassment, the harassment would have stopped.

Almost immediately, it became apparent that employers could easily establish all three elements of the *Faragher/Ellerth* defense, and could escape liability for hostile work environment sexual harassment. The first requirement has proven the easiest to establish, since virtually all employers of any size have sexual harassment policies and, if they receive a harassment complaint, take some minimal steps to correct the harassment.[110] An employer is not required to conduct a proceeding in the nature of a trial to investigate allegations of sexual harassment. An employer may conduct an "inquiry informally in a manner that will not unnecessarily disrupt the employer's business, and in an effort to arrive at a reasonably fair estimate of truth."[111] Federal courts have generally found corrective measures inadequate only when the alleged harasser is not disciplined and harassment is allowed to continue.[112]

The second of the *Faragher/Ellerth* requirements – whether the employee unreasonably failed to make use of the policy – has proven just as easy to meet, with courts holding that there is virtually no reasonable basis, including threats of retaliation or the fact that an employer has failed to act on prior harassment complaints, for failing to use a sexual harassment policy.[113] The third requirement may be the easiest burden for the employer to meet, since an employer sued for sexual harassment could simply offer testimony that had the employee complained of the harassment, the harassment would have stopped. In addition, the failure to timely complain about the harassment through using the employer's harassment policy almost always acts as a bar to a later lawsuit for the harassment.[114]

A constructive discharge occurs where an employer deliberately and discriminatorily creates work conditions "so intolerable that a reasonable person would have felt compelled to resign."[115] The *Faragher/Ellerth* defense is not available to the employer if the employee quits "in reasonable response to an employer-sanctioned adverse action officially changing her employment status or situation, for example, a humiliating demotion, extreme cut in pay, or transfer to a position in which she would face unbearable working conditions."[116] As the Supreme Court has described it, constructive discharge represents a "worst case" harassment scenario, "harassment ratcheted up to the breaking point."[117]

Rounding out its decisions, the Supreme Court held in *Clark County School District v. Breeden* that a single sexually-suggestive statement and chuckling about the statement was not enough to constitute sexual harassment. Referring to the offensive comment, the Court found that it was "at worst an isolated incident that cannot remotely be considered 'extremely serious,' as our cases require."[118] Cases involving law enforcement officers since *Clark County* have made clear that harassment claims cannot be based on a single offensive comment, or even a relatively small number of offensive comments.[119] Exemplifying such cases, a court found that a female corrections officer had no hostile work environment claim where a male co-worker operated a parody-type figurine of a male that had his pants pulled down and that emitted noises sounding like moans and groans when a pen was inserted into a hole in the buttocks of the figurine. The Court found that the fact that the incident was not repeated was dispositive of the question of whether legally actionable harassment had occurred.[120]

It is difficult to overstate how significant the recent Supreme Court's decisions have been in rewriting the law of racial and sexual harassment. Where once the law books were replete with examples of successful harassment lawsuits, they are now almost barren of any victories by employees. Though no formal statistics have been compiled, it is a safe statement that today employers prevail in far more than 90% of harassment lawsuits.[121]

What about harassment that is simply obnoxious conduct, but is not based on an employee's race or gender? For harassment to be recognizable under Title VII, it must be based on the victim's status in a protected class. Thus, if an employer treats men and women identically but very badly, the employer's conduct will not constitute harassment, no matter how offensive the conduct may be.[122]

Affirmative Action Programs.

A good deal of uncertainty exists as to the circumstances in which public employers can voluntarily enter into or be required to use affirmative action programs.[123] The uncertainty is directly traceable to two split decisions of the United States Supreme Court in cases involving the University of Michigan.

Both cases start with the well-established proposition that any consideration of race by the government must be justified by a "compelling" interest.[124] In *Grutter v. Bollinger*, the University's law school took race into account in a non-specified way as part of the goal of enrolling a "critical mass" of minority students. The Court found that the benefits of diversity were substantial, citing the observations of high-ranking retired officers and civilian leaders of the United States military to the effect that a "highly qualified, racially diverse officer corps is essential to the military's ability to fulfill its principal mission to provide national security." The Court concluded that the law school had a compelling interest in considering race in its admissions process, reasoning that "effective participation by members of all racial and ethnic groups in the civic life of our Nation is essential if the dream of one Nation, indivisible, is to be realized."[125]

The Court's decision on the University's undergraduate affirmative action program, *Gratz v. Bollinger*, complicated matters. The undergraduate program automatically assigned one fifth of the points needed to guarantee admission to each underrepresented minority applicant solely because of race. The Supreme Court struck down the program as illegal, concluding that the program called for illegal quotas. In the Court's view, "mechanical, predetermined diversity bonuses" are never acceptable, and if race is to be used at all, it must be in "a flexible, non-mechanical way."[126]

At their core, *Grutter* and *Gratz* stand for the proposition that an affirmative action program can take race or other protected classes into consideration if there is some compelling reason to do so, but only under limited circumstances. In the first major police case since the two decisions, one involving the Chicago Police Department's affirmative action program, a court upheld the legality of the program given the nature of the Supreme Court's comments in *Grutter*. The Court held that:

> "The reality of urban policing is that minorities are frequently mistrustful of police and are more willing than non-minorities to believe that the police engage in misconduct. Distrust and a lack of confidence in the police, in turn, reduce the willingness of some community members to cooperate with the police. On the other hand, when police officers are routinely supervised by minorities, the fears that the Police Department is hostile to the minority community will naturally abate. We have previously recognized that a visible presence of minorities in supervisory positions is critical to effective policing in a racially diverse city like Chicago because supervisors set the tone for the Department. Equally important, the presence of minority supervisors is an important means of earning the community's trust.

> "All in all, we find that, as did the University of Michigan, the Chicago Police Department had a compelling interest in diversity. Specifically, the CPD had a compelling interest in a diverse population at the rank of sergeant in order to set the proper tone in the Department and to earn the trust of the community, which in turn increases police effectiveness in protecting the city. It seems to us that there is an even more compelling need for diversity in a large metropolitan police force charged with protecting a racially and ethnically divided major American city like Chicago."[127]

To the extent that an affirmative action plan is legal at all, it must then meet the requirements of Title VII. Specifically, the plan must be "narrowly tailored" to remedy prior discrimination and extend no farther than necessary to meet this goal.[128] As these requirements have been interpreted by the courts, an affirmative action plan must conform to the following standards to be "narrowly tailored":

• The Plan Must Be Temporary.

Though in some cases, the affirmative action plan need not have a specific expiration date, in all cases the plan must be temporary rather than permanent in nature,[129] and cannot last after the vestiges of discrimination have been eliminated.[130]

• The Plan Must Only Select Qualified Candidates.

While the employees' presence in a protected class such as gender or race may be a "plus" factor in selecting between candidates, the selected candidates must still meet all of the minimum qualifications for the job.[131]

• The Plan Cannot Contain Quotas.

In order to conform with the Fourteenth Amendment and Title VII, an affirmative action plan cannot impose quotas or fixed percentages of protected classes which will be hired or otherwise affected by an employment decision.[132] If a plan sets aside no fixed number of positions for protective classes but merely establishes goals which are to be sought, the plan will not be construed as having an impermissible quota.[133]

• The Plan's Goals Should Be Set by Reference to the Labor Market.

The numeric goals set by the plan should bear a direct relationship to the relevant labor market. For example, if the relevant labor market is 50% black, an affirmative action plan should set a goal of hiring or promoting blacks until approximately 50% of the work force is black.[134]

• The Plan Cannot Create an "Absolute Bar" to Other Applicants.

While an affirmative action plan can give preferential treatment to certain protected classes, it cannot act as an absolute bar to the employment or promotion of non-members of the protected classes.[135] Use of a fixed black/white ratio in promotions does not constitute an impermissible absolute bar. As noted by the Supreme Court in a case upholding a one-for-one black/white ratio for promotions in the Alabama Department of Public Safety, the ratio:

> "* * * only postpones the promotions of qualified whites. Consequently, like a hiring goal, it imposes a diffuse burden foreclosing only one of several opportunities. Denial of a future employment opportunity is not as intrusive as loss of an existing job and plainly postponement imposes a lesser burden still."[136]

• The Plan Cannot Use "Race Norming."

The Civil Rights Act of 1991 prohibited the use of "race norming," in which test scores are adjusted according to an individual's race or gender before the final hiring or promotional list is developed. Accordingly, an affirmative action plan using race norming is illegal.

• The Plan Must Affect a Limited Type of Employment Decisions.

To the extent that an affirmative action plan impacts the employment ranks of existing employees, it is less likely to be ruled valid than a plan which merely concerns hiring practices. Similarly, an affirmative action plan which causes the layoffs of existing employees is much less likely to be upheld than a plan which simply gives preferential treatment on promotional decisions to members of protected classes. The reasons for these distinctions is that plans which adversely affect the vested rights of existing employees may disrupt seniority rights or expectations under state and local laws. As noted by the Supreme Court:

> "In cases involving valid hiring goals, the burden to be borne by innocent individuals is diffused to a considerable extent among society generally. Though hiring goals may burden some innocent individuals, they simply do not impose the same kind of injury that layoffs impose. Denial of a future employment opportunity is not as intrusive as loss

of an existing job."[137]

Pregnancy Discrimination.

One of the many laws that contributed to Title VII of the Civil Rights Act was the Pregnancy Discrimination Act of 1978.[138] Essentially, the Pregnancy Discrimination Act requires employers to treat pregnant women in the same manner as other applicants or employees with similar abilities or limitations. That means that an employer cannot automatically force pregnant officers onto leave status without first determining the officers' ability to perform the essential functions of the job, and even then cannot treat pregnant officers differently that non-pregnant officers who have medical conditions that produce limitations of the same kind as pregnancy. Thus, if the employer allows other temporarily disabled employees to perform modified job tasks or reassigns them to other positions, the employer must accord pregnant officers the same considerations. Apart from the protections provided by the Pregnancy Discrimination Act, a normal pregnancy does not amount to a disability under the Americans with Disabilities Act and related laws.[139]

The Pregnancy Discrimination Act requires employers to treat pregnant women in the same manner as other applicants or employees with similar abilities or limitations.

Age Discrimination.

Because the Supreme Court has held that age is not a "suspect classification," age discrimination cases which proceed on traditional constitutional grounds have been universally unsuccessful.[140] As a result, virtually all age discrimination cases involving law enforcement officers proceed under the federal Age Discrimination in Employment Act of 1967 (ADEA), which provides protection against age discrimination for persons older than 40 years of age.[141]

The relevant portions of the ADEA provide as follows:

"It shall be unlawful for an employer —

"(1) to fail or refuse to hire or to discharge any individual or otherwise discriminate against any individual with respect to his compensation, terms, conditions, or privileges of employment, because of such individual's age;

"(2) to limit, segregate, or classify his employees in any way which would deprive or tend to deprive any individual of employment opportunities or otherwise affect his status as an employee, because of such individual's age."[142]

To prove age discrimination under the ADEA, an officer must show either direct discrimination based upon age (usually in the form of incriminating statements made by the employer) or must follow the shifting burden of proof model common to many discrimination claims. Under this model, an officer must make a *prima facie* case of age discrimination by showing the following: (1) He was within the protected age group; (2) he was doing satisfactory work; (3) he was discharged or otherwise suffered an adverse employment action; and (4) a younger person replaced him or he received less favorable treatment than younger employees.[143] If the officer makes this initial showing, the employer has the ability to show that legitimate, non-discriminatory reasons exist for its employment decision concerning the officer. If the employer meets this burden, it successfully defeats the officer's claim unless the officer is able to show that the employer's reasons are pretextual in nature.[144] In all circumstances, the officer must eventually prove, whether directly or by implication, that the employer's actions are impermissibly based on the officer's age, and not on other factors.[145] For example, a requirement that only officers over the age of 40 would be required to participate in annual heart examinations would violate the ADEA.[146]

By prohibiting discrimination on the basis of age, the ADEA immediately brought into question the validity of mandatory retirement ages. Most early cases challenging police officer mandatory retirement ages under the ADEA were successful, with mandatory retirement ages being struck down by courts in dozens of law enforcement agencies.[147]

After indecision that lasted a number of years, Congress amended the ADEA in 1996, allowing a public employer to discharge a police officer or firefighter based on his age, subject to two principal conditions. First, the ADEA specifies that the employee must have attained either the mandatory retirement age that the employer had in place as of March 3, 1983, or if the age limit was enacted after the date the 1996 exemption took effect, the higher of the retirement age specified in the post-1996 enactment or the age of 55. Second, the ADEA requires that the retirement plan be bona fide, and not a "subterfuge" to evade the purposes of the ADEA. Thus far, no court has struck down a retirement age as being a "subterfuge," even when the avowed purpose of the retirement age is to phase out older employees.[148]

Regulations setting maximum ages upon hire have generally withstood attack, since the ADEA only protects those over the age of 40.[149] This has resulted in courts reaching the rather anomalous result that laws which forbid employment as law enforcement officers if the applicant is over the age of 30 are enforceable only against those between the ages of 30 and 40, but not against those who, because they have reached their fortieth birthday, fall within the protections of the ADEA.[150] Cases challenging maximum hiring ages under the Fourteenth Amendment to the United States Constitution have similarly been unsuccessful.[151]

As with many other forms of protected class discrimination, an employee has a right to be free from a hostile work environment based upon age.[152] As with other forms of hostile work environment harassment, the employee must prove that the impermissible conduct is severe or pervasive, and that the employer failed to have in place remedial measures that would have prevented the harassment.[153]

Discrimination On The Basis Of Citizenship.

Courts have uniformly held that it is not discriminatory for a law enforcement agency to require that its employees be citizens of the United States. As one court commented:

> "It would be as anomalous to conclude that citizens may be subjected to the broad discretionary powers of non-citizen police officers as it would be to say that judicial officers and jurors with power to judge citizens can be aliens. It is not surprising, therefore, that most States expressly confine the employment of police officers to citizens, whom the State may reasonably presume to be more familiar with and sympathetic to American traditions. Police officers very clearly fall within the category of 'important non-elective officers who participate directly in the execution of broad public policy.' In the enforcement and execution of the laws the police function is one where citizenship bears a rational relationship to the special demands of the particular position. A State may, therefore, consonant with the Constitution, confine the performance of this important public responsibility to citizens of the United States."[154]

Discrimination On The Basis Of National Origin.

Title VII directly prohibits discrimination on the basis of national origin. A good example of a national origin disparate treatment case is *Jauregui v. City of Glendale*.[155] In that case, a Hispanic officer tried unsuccessfully for promotion on seven occasions. In finding that the officer was the victim of discrimination, the Court noted the following facts: (1) All persons in the supervisory ranks at the department were white males; (2) the relevant personnel at the Department were aware of the plaintiff's ethnicity; (3) the general policy had been to promote the person certified first on the list of the three candidates placing highest in the promotional examinations; (4) although ranked number one on three of the seven occasions in which he was certified for promotion, the plaintiff was never promoted; and (5) there existed an atmosphere unconducive to inter-ethnic appreciation and respect in the Department. The Court pointed out that certain officers routinely made racially derogatory remarks, drew and posted inappropriate drawings and cartoons, and posted an official Police Department notice which portrayed members of various minority racial and ethnic groups, including Hispanics, in a derogatory and insulting light. Although supervisors were aware of such activities, and in some cases participated in them, no disciplinary action was taken against the perpetrators, and one of the perpetrators was promoted to sergeant in lieu of the plaintiff. On this record, the Court awarded the retroactive promotion of the Hispanic officer.

A similar result occurred when the City of Austin, Texas, indefinitely suspended a Hispanic homicide detective for allegedly committing perjury about whether he had coerced a murder defendant's confession. His non-Hispanic partner in the investigation received only a written reprimand for essentially the same conduct. An appeals court upheld an award of more than $300,000 to the Hispanic detective, finding he was the victim of national origin discrimination. The Court found a jury could have concluded that the City's reasons for treating the two detectives differently was pretextual, noting evidence that "discrimination against Hispanics pervaded the quality and length of homicide investigations involving Hispanic victims." One officer discussed a lieutenant's use of the term "misdemeanor murders." He testified that the lieutenant said: "This Mexican here, this is a misdemeanor murder. And we don't need no overtime on this. We'll get on it tomorrow." Similarly, the lieutenant instructed officers that they had only 24 hours to solve a minority's murder. The Hispanic officer explained: "I have observed the lieutenant not paying attention to Hispanic victims getting murdered, several times, and assigning detectives just for 24 hours and then giving them something else to do. In other words, I've heard him say that any time a Hispanic or black gets killed, it's misdemeanor murder, especially if they get killed in a bar room fight." The Court found that for these reasons, the murders of minorities often remained unsolved. The record demonstrates that there were two sides to this discrimination case. The jury heard both sides and chose to believe the Hispanic detective's view of the evidence.[156]

Discrimination On The Basis Of Sexual Orientation.

Where once there was a fair amount of litigation filed asserting that law enforcement agencies wrongfully discriminated on the basis of an employee's or applicant's sexual orientation, such cases have largely vanished from the scene, perhaps owing more to evolving social sensibilities than to the confused case law in the area. Over the years, neither Title VII nor the Fourteenth Amendment had been interpreted to provide much protection against discrimination on the basis of sexual orientation. Most courts found homosexuality not to be a "protected class" under the Fourteenth Amendment, meaning that an employer need only advance a "rational basis" in order to justify discrimination against homosexuals.[157] Courts found a variety of justifications to constitute a rational basis permitting such discrimination, justifications including a fear of blackmail, a concern about the department's morale and public image, and worries about how a homosexual would react to evidence involving a homosexual crime.[158] Leading the charge in the area was the Supreme Court's decision in *Bowers v. Hardwick*, which upheld criminal laws outlawing sodomy.[159]

Then, in 2003, the Supreme Court reversed its tracks and overruled *Bowers* in *Lawrence v. Texas*, a case in which it held unconstitutional a Texas statute criminalizing certain intimate acts by consenting individuals of the same sex.[160] The logical extension of *Lawrence* into the employment area would clearly grant higher protection based upon sexual orientation. However, because there simply are no recent cases addressing the issue in any fashion in the law enforcement context, that extension has yet to occur.

Where the legal status of discrimination on the basis of sexual orientation is still unsure, one case has definitively accorded protections to a pre-operative transsexual police officer. Quoting from the decision in another case, the Court found that "sex stereotyping based on a person's gender non-conforming behavior is impermissible discrimination, irrespective of the cause of that behavior; a label, such as 'transsexual,' is not fatal to a sex discrimination claim where the victim has suffered discrimination because of his or her gender non-conformity." [161]

Any number of local ordinances forbid discrimination on the basis of sexual orientation. For example, the District of Columbia Human Rights Act includes sexual orientation in its general ban on discrimination:

> "It shall be an unlawful discriminatory practice to do any of the following acts, wholly or partially for a discriminatory reason based upon the race, color, religion, national origin, sex, age, marital status, personal appearance, sexual orientation, family responsibilities, physical handicap, matriculation, or political affiliation, of any individual:

> "(1) To fail or refuse to hire, or to discharge, any individual; or otherwise to discriminate against any individual, with respect to his [or her] compensation, terms, conditions, or privileges of employment, including promotion; or to limit, segregate, or classify his [or her] employees in any way which would deprive or tend to deprive any individual of employment opportunities, or otherwise adversely affect his [or her] status as an employee."[162]

'Class Of One' Discrimination.

From time to time, and usually with unfavorable results, law enforcement officers brought lawsuits alleging "class of one" discrimination claims under the Fourteenth Amendment.[163] The theory behind a "class of one" lawsuit was that the officer had been intentionally treated differently from others similarly situated and that there was no rational basis for the difference in treatment.[164] In 2008, through its decision in *Engquist v. Oregon Department of Agriculture*, the United State Supreme Court abruptly changed the law in the area, holding that "class of one" claims could not be brought by public employees.[165] The *Engquist* decision will almost certainly end any litigation in the area.

Discrimination And Seniority Systems.

Seniority systems, whether contained in an employer's rules or in a collective bargaining agreement, usually grant employees with longer tenure benefits in the area of job protection and promotional opportunities. In an agency with a history of prior discrimination where minority employees have only recently been hired, seniority systems can work to adversely affect minority employees by the disproportionate effect such systems have on junior employees. Occasionally such seniority systems are attacked under Title VII on a disparate impact theory. On occasion, seniority systems have been attacked where they collide with the obligation of an employer to reasonably accommodate another employee's disability, religion, or other protected class status.

The general rule is that if a seniority system has been established for a "bona-fide" (i.e., non-discriminatory) reason, the seniority system will "trump" the rights of other employees.[166] Title VII, for example, gives broad protections to bona fide seniority systems:

> "It shall not be an unlawful employment practice for an employer to apply different standards of compensation, or different terms, conditions, or privileges of employment pursuant to a bona fide seniority system provided that such differences are not the result of an intention to discriminate because of race."[167]

In order to strike down a seniority system under Title VII, an aggrieved officer would be required to show not only that the seniority system adversely affected the members of a protected class, but also that the system was the product of a discriminatory intent or illegal purpose.[168] This is a burden which is extremely hard to meet, especially if the seniority system on its face is neutral and applies equally to all officers, regardless of race or sex.[169]

NOTES

[1] *City of Cleburne v. Cleburne Living Center*, 473 U.S. 432 (1985).

[2] *Loving v. Virginia*, 388 U.S. 1 (1967).

[3] *Graham v. Richardson*, 403 U.S. 365 (1971). *But see Ambach v. Norwick*, 441 U.S. 68 (1979).

[4] *Korematsu v. United States*, 323 U.S. 214 (1944).

[5] *Mills v. Habluetzel*, 456 U.S. 91 (1982).

[6] *Mississippi University for Women v. Hogan*, 458 U.S. 718 (1982).

[7] *Lalli v. Lalli*, 439 U.S. 259 (1978).

[8] *Bowers v. Hardwick*, 478 U.S. 186 (1986).

[9] *Meek v. Rideoutte*, 56 FEP Cases 575 (D. S.C. 1989).

[10] *Lowes v. Sayad*, 614 F. Supp. 1206 (E.D .Mo. 1985).

[11] *Morgan v. City of Wheeling*, 516 S.E.2d 48 (W.V. 1999).

[12] *Henry v. Jones*, 507 F.3d 558 (7th Cir. 2007).

[13] *DeBiasi v. Charter County of Wayne*, 537 F. Supp. 2d 903 (E.D. Mich. 2008); *Jones v. City of Springfield, Ill.*, 540 F. Supp. 2d 1023 (C.D. Ill. 2008); *Gunnings v. Borough of Woodlynne*, 102 FEP Cases 1309 (D. N.J. 2007).

[14] *Alexander v. City of Milwaukee*, 474 F.3d 437 (7th Cir. 2007)(City of Milwaukee liable for police chief's promotional practices that discriminated against white candidates).

[15] *Diaz v. City of Inkster*, 2007 WL 1424206 (E.D. Mich. 2007)(upholds jury verdict of $253,997 to white applicant for chief's job).

[16] Title 42, §2000e-2, United States Code. By its terms, Title VII applies to local governmental bodies. *See* Title 42, §2000e(h), United States Code.

[17] *Washington v. Davis*, 426 U.S. 229 (1976).

[18] *Jauregui v. City of Glendale*, 852 F.2d 1128 (9th Cir. 1988).

[19] *Dale v. City of Phillipsburg*, 50 FEP Cases 1737 (D. Kan. 1989)(no disparate treatment discrimination against female where no proof that male officers treated differently).

[20] *Thrall v. Iowa Dept. of Corrections*, 69 FEP Cases 42 (8th Cir. 1995); *Black Law Enf. Officers Assn. v. City of Akron*, 51 FEP Cases 45 (D. Ohio 1989). *See Wards Cove Packing Co, Inc. v. Antonio*, 490 U.S. 642 (1989).

[21] *U.S. v. City of Erie, PA*, 411 F. Supp. 2d 524 (W.D. Pa. 2005); *Stahl v. Board of County Com'rs of the Unified Government of Wynandotte County/Kansas City, Kan.*, 101 Fed.Appx. 316 (10th Cir. 2004).

[22] *Terrell v. City of Harrisburg Police Dept.*, 549 F. Supp. 2d 671 (M.D. Pa. 2008).

[23] *Price Waterhouse v. Hopkins,* 490 U.S. 288 (1989) (O'Connor, J., concurring); *McDonnell Douglas Corp. v. Green,* 411 U.S. 792 (1973).

[24] *Hammond v. County of Los Angeles*, 72 Cal.Rptr.3d 311 (Cal. App. 2008)(rare to find direct evidence of discriminatory intent).

[25] *Redd v. City of Phenix City*, 934 F.2d 1211 (11th Cir. 1991).

[26] *Terrell v. City of Harrisburg Police Dept.*, 549 F. Supp. 2d 671 (M.D. Pa. 2008).

[27] *Batchelder v. Andover Police Dept.*, 2008 WL 1759104 (Mass. App. 2008).

[28] *Burlington Northern and Santa Fe Ry. Co. v White*, 548 U.S. 53 (2006).

[29] *Beyer v. County of Nassau*, 524 F.3d 160 (2d Cir. 2008)(denial of transfer); *Alvarado v. Texas Rangers*, 492 F.3d 605 (5th Cir. 2007)(denial of transfer); *McInnis v. Town of Weston*, 458 F. Supp. 2d 7 (D. Conn. 2006)(suspension); *Zanone v. City of Whittier*, 75 Cal.Rptr.3d 439 (Cal. App. 2008)(upholds $1.25 million jury verdict based in part on officer's transfer from detectives to patrol). *But see Moore v. City of Chicago*, 126 Fed.Appx. 745 (7th Cir. 2005)(transfer without loss of pay not an actionable adverse employment decision).

[30] *McCray v. New York City Police Dept.*, 2008 WL 207845 (E.D. N.Y. 2008).

[31] *Jones v. Wichita State University*, 528 F. Supp. 2d 1196 (D. Kan. 2007).

[32] *Ellis v. Crawford*, 2007 WL 1624773 (N.D. Tex. 2007).

[33] *Estate of Oliva v. New Jersey*, 589 F. Supp. 2d 539 (D. N.J. 2008).

[34] *Lentz v. City of Cleveland*, 410 F. Supp. 2d 673 (N.D. Ohio 2006).

[35] *Carroll v. City of Dallas, Tex.*, 2005 WL 3543347 (N.D. Tex. 2005).

[36] *Wyckoff v. Maryland*, 522 F. Supp. 2d 730 (D. Md. 2007).

[37] *Caver v. City of Trenton*, 420 F.3d 243 (3d Cir. 2005); *Semsroth v. City of Wichita*, 548 F. Supp. 2d 1203 (D. Kan. 2008).

[38] *Nichols v. Southern Illinois University-Edwardsville*, 510 F.3d 772 (7th Cir. 2007).

[39] *Garcia v. Illinois State Police*, 545 F. Supp. 2d 823 (C.D. Ill. 2008).

[40] *Mylett v. City of Corpus Christi*, 97 Fed.Appx. 473 (5th Cir. 2004).

[41] *Jones v. Wichita State University*, 528 F. Supp. 2d 1182 (D. Kan. 2007).

[42] *Berry v. City of South Portland, Me.*, 525 F. Supp. 2d 214 (D. Me. 2007).

[43] *Smith v. Township of East Greenwich*, 519 F. Supp. 2d 493 (D. N.J. 2007); *Harvey v. City of Bradenton*, 2005 WL 3533155 (M.D. Fla. 2005).

[44] *Paloni v. City of Albuquerque Police Dept.*, 212 Fed.Appx. 716 (10th Cir. 2006).

[45] *King v. City of Boston*, 883 N.E.2d 316 (Mass. App. 2008).

[46] *Daniels v. Fowler*, 57 FEP Cases 65 (N.D. Ga. 1991)(allegedly discriminatory discharge of black state trooper); *Sorlucco v. New York City Police Department*, 703 F. Supp. 1092 (S.D. N.Y. 1989)(allegedly discriminatory discharge of female probationary New York City police officer), *rev'd on other grounds*, 971 F.2d 864 (2d Cir. 1992).

[47] *Smith v. Osceola County*, 2008 WL 2036826 (W.D. Mich. 2008); *Villegas v. Harris County*, 2007 WL 4465369 (Tex. App. 2007).

[48] *Bell v. Town of Port Royal, South Carolina*, 586 F. Supp. 2d 498 (D. S.C. 2008); *Pollard v. Montgomery County*, 66 F. Supp. 2d 1218 (M.D. Ala. 1999); *Hatcher v. Greater Cleveland Regional Transit Authority*, 746 F. Supp. 679 (N.D. Ohio 1989)(fact that black officer called another black officer a "black mother fucker" in public sufficient non-discriminatory reason for discharge of first officer); *see Texas Department of Community Affairs v. Burdine*, 450 U.S. 248 (1981).

[49] *Turner v. Federal Law Enforcement Training Center*, 527 F. Supp. 2d 63 (D. D.C. 2007); *Berry v. City of Pontiac*, 2007 WL 496452 (E.D. Mich. 2007).

[50] *McCann v. Tillman*, 526 F.3d 1370 (11th Cir. 2008).

51 *Cooper v. Dallas Police Ass'n*, 278 Fed.Appx. 318 (5th Cir. 2008).

52 *Barr v. City of Eagle Lake*, 2008 WL 717821 (M.D. Fla. 2008).

53 *Everson v. Michigan Dept. of Corrections*, 391 F.3d 737 (6th Cir. 2004); *Tipler v. Douglas County, Neb.*, 482 F.3d 1023 (8th Cir. 2007). To the contrary is *Westchester County Corrections v. County of Westchester*, 346 F. Supp. 2d 527 (S.D. N.Y. 2004).

54 *Morris v. City of Chillicothe*, 512 F.3d 1013 (8th Cir. 2008).

55 *Bell v. Town of Port Royal, S.C.*, 2008 WL 1816579 (D. S.C. 2008).

56 *Hollimon v. Shelby County Government*, 2008 WL 901490 (W.D. Tenn. 2008).

57 *McDonnell Douglas Corp. v. Green*, 411 U.S. 792 (1973).

58 *Ganaway v. City of Pittsburgh*, 2008 WL 336297 (W.D. Pa. 2008).

59 *E.g., Terrell v. City of Harrisburg Police Dept.*, 549 F. Supp. 2d 671 (M.D. Pa. 2008); *Broberg v. Illinois State Police*, 537 F. Supp. 2d 960 (N.D. Ill. 2008).

60 *Mercer v. City of Cedar Rapids*, 308 F.3d 840 (8th Cir. 2002).

61 *Berry v. City of Pontiac*, 269 Fed.Appx. 545 (6th Cir. 2008).

62 *Hayes v. City of Newnan, Ga.*, 2007 WL 2765555 (N.D. Ga. 2007).

63 *Standard v. A.B.E.L. Servs. Inc.*, 161 F.3d 1318 (11th Cir. 1998).

64 *Watson v. Fort Worth Bank & Trust*, 487 U.S. 977 (1988).

65 *Vanguard Justice Society, Inc. v. Hughes*, 471 F. Supp. 670 (D. Md. 1979).

66 *Perkins v. Connecticut*, 2008 WL 691703 (D. Conn. 2008)(applicant for position within Department of Criminal Justice failed to show a statistically significant disproportionate hiring rate impacting African-Americans); *Bradley v. City of Lynn*, 443 F. Supp. 2d 145 (D. Mass. 2006)(disparate impact caused by promotional examination); *Waisome v. Port Authority of New York and New Jersey*, 758 F. Supp. 171 (S.D. N.Y. 1991)(officers failed to show "substantial difference" between white and black selection rates on sergeant's examination); *Dwyer v. Smith*, 867 F.2d 184 (4th Cir. 1989)(officer failed to prove that shotgun qualification had a statistically disproportionate impact on women). *See Griggs v. Duke Power Co.*, 401 U.S. 424 (1971)(general discussion of use of statistics in disparate impact cases).

67 *Bridgeport Guardians v. City of Bridgeport*, 933 F.2d 1140 (2d Cir. 1991)(applies 5% rule – i.e., burden of proving *prima facie* case met if employee shows that exam results would not occur, on the average, even in one in 20 cases); *Dixon v. Margolis*, 56 FEP Cases 401 (N.D. Ill. 1991)(discusses 80% rule, which concludes that if the protected class is selected by a test at less than 80% of the rate for the non-protected class, a *prima facie* case has been established).

68 *Watson v. Fort Worth Bank & Trust*, 487 U.S. 977 (1988).

69 42 U.S.C. § 2000e-3(a).

70 *Brannum v. Missouri Dept. of Corrections*, 518 F.3d 542 (8th Cir. 2008); *Anderson v. Nassau County Dept. of Corrections*, 558 F. Supp. 2d 283 (E.D. N.Y. 2008).

71 *Burlington Northern and Santa Fe Ry. Co. v. White*, 548 U.S. 53 (2006).

72 *Heba v. New York State Div. of Parole*, 537 F. Supp. 2d 457 (E.D. N.Y. 2007).

73 *Raniola v. Bratton*, 243 F.3d 610 (2d Cir. 2001).

74 *Davison v. City of Minneapolis, Minn*, 490 F.3d 648 (8th Cir. 2007).

[75] *Rogers v. Fort Wayne Police Dept.*, 2008 WL 821693 (N.D. Ind. 2008)(collecting cases); *see Stout v. City of Wagoner*, 2008 WL 2565001 (E.D. Okla. 2008).

[76] *O'Connor v. Houston*, 2008 WL 794810 (M.D. Ga. 2008).

[77] *Henson v. City of Dundee*, 682 F.2d 897 (11th Cir. 1982).

[78] *Andrews v. City of Philadelphia*, 895 F.2d 1469 (3d Cir. 1990).

[79] *Oncale v. Sundowner Offshore Services*, 523 U.S. 75 (1998); *Nichols v. Azteca Restaurant Enterprises,* 256 F.3d 864 (9th Cir. 2001); *Doe v. City of Belleville, Illinois,* 119 F.3d 563 (7th Cir. 1997); *Cromer-Kendall v. District of Columbia,* 326 F. Supp. 2d 50 (D. D.C. 2004); *Quinn v. Nassau County Police Department,* 53 F. Supp. 2d 347 (E.D. N.Y. 1999).

[80] *Staton v. Maries County,* 868 F.2d 996 (8th Cir. 1989); *Loftin-Boggs v. City of Meridian,* 41 FEP Cases 532 (D. Miss. 1986).

[81] *Ward v. Connecticut Dept. of Public Safety,* 2009 WL 179786 (D. Conn. 2009).

[82] *Freitag v. Ayers,* 463 F.3d 838 (9th Cir. 2006).

[83] *Blakely v. City of Clarksville,* 244 Fed.Appx. 681 (6th Cir. 2007)(racial epithets about African-Americans); *Ways v. City of Lincoln,* 871 F.2d 750 (8th Cir. 1989)(racial epithets directed at American Indian); *Daniels v. Fowler,* 57 FEP Cases 65 (N.D. Ga. 1991)(racial epithets directed at African-American).

[84] *Hall v. City of Clarksville,* 276 Fed.Appx. 457 (6th Cir. 2008); *Andrews v. City of Philadelphia,* 895 F.2d 1469 (3d Cir. 1992); *Carillo v. Ward,* 56 FEP Cases 1558 (S.D. N.Y. 1991); *Arnold v. City of Seminole, Oklahoma,* 614 F. Supp. 853 (E.D. Okla. 1985); *Grievance of Deborah Butler,* No. 93-17 (Vt. LRB 1994), *affirmed* 697 A.2d 659 (Vt. 1997).

[85] *Pulse v. City of North Tonowanda,* 811 F. Supp. 884 (W.D. N.Y. 1993); *Watts v. New York City Police Department,* 54 FEP Cases 1131 (S.D. N.Y. 1989).

[86] *Miller v. Department of Corrections,* 30 Cal.Rptr.3d 797 (3d Cir. 2005); *Candelore v. Clark County,* 975 F.2d 588 (9th Cir. 1992); *see Dirksen v. City of Springfield,* 64 FEP Cases 116 (C.D. Ill. 1994)(chief had affair with co-worker to whom he subsequently showed favoritism).

[87] *Pontarelli v. Stone,* 930 F.2d 104 (1st Cir. 1991)(retaliation proven when female trooper who protested treatment of female recruits in the academy was fired); *Bedford v. South Eastern Pennsylvania Transit Authority,* 867 F. Supp. 288 (E.D. Pa. 1994).

[88] *Oncale v. Sundowner Offshore Services,* 523 U.S. 75 (1998).

[89] *Washington v. Board of Trustees,* 2001 WL 47006 (N.D. Ill. 2001); *see Dodd v. City of Greenville,* 2007 WL 30333 (D. S.C. 2007)(statements such as "you bitch, I hate you," not sexual harassment).

[90] *Bertram v. Medina County,* 2008 WL 1696940 (N.D. Ohio 2008).

[91] *Russ v. Van Scoyok Associates, Inc.,* 122 F. Supp. 2d 129 (D. D.C. 2000).

[92] *McPherson v. City of Waukegan,* 379 F.3d 430 (7th Cir. 2004).

[93] *Webb-Edwards v. Orange County Sheriff's Office,* 525 F.3d 1013 (11th Cir. 2008).

[94] *Sheperd v. Comptroller of Public Accounts,* 168 F.3d 871 (5th Cir. 1999).

[95] *Pedroza v. Cintas Corp.,* 2003 WL 828237 (W.D. Mo. 2003).

96 *Pirolli v. World Flavors, Inc.*, 81 FEP Cases 783 (D. Pa. 1999). *See also EEOC v. Herbert-Yeargin, Inc.*, 266 F.3d 498 (6th Cir. 2001); *Weston v. Commonwealth of Pennsylvania*, 2001 WL 1491132 (E.D. Pa. 2001)(female coworker in correctional institution rubbed back of unwilling male employee. When employee tore a hole in the seat of his pants while at work, in the presence of inmates, co-worker placed her finger in the hole, touching employee's buttocks. Conduct not sufficiently egregious to rise to sexual harassment); *Hampel v. Food Ingredients Specialists*, 729 N.E.2d 726 (Ohio App. 1998)(threatening descriptions of the desire to engage in homosexual relations with male co-workers is commonplace in certain circles and is not necessarily indicative of a working environment hostile to men).

97 *Williams v. NYC Department of Sanitation*, 2001 WL 1154627 (S.D. N.Y. 2001).

98 *Milligan v. Citibank, N.A.*, 2001 WL 1135943 (S.D. N.Y. 2001).

99 *Breland-Starling v. Disney Publishing Worldwide*, 166 F. Supp. 2d 826 (S.D. N.Y. 2001).

100 *Rizzo v. Sheahan*, 266 F.3d 705 (7th Cir. 2001).

101 *Johnson v. City of Elgin*, 2001 WL 1188791 (N.D. III. 2001).

102 *Dority v. City of Chicago*, 2001 WL 1155286 (N.D. III. 2001).

103 *Caples v. Media One Express of Illinois, Inc.*, 2001 WL 1188882 (N.D. III. 2001)(new shift ended at 11:00 p.m. four nights a week; old shift was day shift).

104 *NiCastro v. Runyon*, 60 F. Supp. 2d 181 (S.D. N.Y. 1999).

105 *Faragher v. City of Boca Raton*, 524 U.S. 775 (1998); *Burlington Industries v. Ellerth*, 524 U.S. 742 (1998).

106 *White v. N.H. Dep't of Corr.*, 221 F.3d 254 (1st Cir. 2000); *Walker v. City of Holyoke*, 523 F. Supp. 2d 86 (D. Mass. 2007).

107 *Steck v. Francis*, 365 F. Supp. 2d 951 (N.D. Iowa 2005).

108 *Faragher v. City of Boca Raton*, 524 U.S. 775 (1998).

109 *Jones v. District of Columbia*, 346 F. Supp. 2d 25 (D. D.C. 2004).

110 *See, e.g., Weger v. City of Ladue*, 500 F.3d 710 (8th Cir. 2007).

111 *Smith v. City of Chattanooga*, 2007 WL 4374039 (Tenn. App. 2007).

112 *See EEOC v. Harbert-Yeargin, Inc.*, 266 F.3d 498 (6th Cir. 2001); *Mota v. Univ. of Tex. Houston Health Sci. Ctr.*, 261 F.3d 512 (5th Cir. 2001).

113 *E.g., Weger v. City of Ladue*, 500 F.3d 710 (8th Cir. 2007)(fear of retaliation not a basis for failing to use employer's policy); *Lauderdale v. Texas Dept. of Criminal Justice, Institutional Div.*, 512 F.3d 157 (5th Cir. 2007)(employer's failure to act on prior harassment complaints no excuse for not using the employer's policy to complain); *Leopold v. Baccarat, Inc.*, 239 F.3d 243 (2d Cir. 2001)(employee's belief that employer did not take seriously a co-worker's complaint of sexual harassment no excuse for not using the employer's harassment policy); *Shaw v. Autozone, Inc.*, 180 F.3d 806 (7th Cir. 1999); *Masters v. Town of Monterey, Tennessee*, 2008 WL 586563 (M.D. Tenn. 2008)(fear that reporting harassment would be futile no excuse for not following policy); *Dedner v. State of Oklahoma*, 42 F. Supp. 2d 1254 (E.D. Okla. 1999)(reporting harassment five days after the last incident occurred, but three months after the first incident occurred is unreasonable because the employer is not afforded an opportunity to investigate the first incidents); *Bishop v. National Railroad Passenger Corp.*, 66 F. Supp. 2d 650 (E.D. Pa. 1999); *Montero v. AGCO Corp.*, 19 F. Supp. 2d 1143 (E.D. Cal. 1998); *Fierro v. Saks Fifth Avenue*, 13 F. Supp. 2d 481

(S.D. N.Y. 1998)(an employee's fear of retaliation for reporting harassment does not alleviate his duty to use the employer's complaint policy); *Adler v. Wal-Mart Stores, Inc.*, 144 F.3d 664 (10th Cir. 1998)(a victim may have to suffer repeated harassment while an employer progressively disciplines the perpetrator because excessive discipline would subject employers to claims of wrongful termination); *Perry v. Harris Chernin, Inc.*, 126 F.3d 1010 (7th Cir. 1997), *cited in Hailemariam v. Neomedica, Inc.*, 1999 WL 495136 (N.D. Ill. 1999)(an employee must remain at her job while seeking redress through company policy, unless confronted with an aggravating situation beyond ordinary harassment).

[114] *Beverly v. Kaupas*, 2008 WL 624045 (N.D. Ill. 2008); *King v. Village of Gilberts*, 2002 WL 1559629 (N.D. Ill. 2002).

[115] *Barbusin v. Eastern Connecticut State University*, 576 F. Supp. 2d 285 (D. Conn. 2008).

[116] *Pennsylvania State Police v. Suders*, 542 U.S. 129 (2004); *Hernandez-Payero v. Puerto Rico*, 493 F. Supp. 2d 215 (D. P.R. 2007).

[117] *Pennsylvania State Police v. Suders*, 542 U.S. 129 (2004).

[118] *Clark County School District v. Breeden*, 532 U.S. 268 (2001).

[119] *Singletary v. Missouri Dept. of Corrections*, 423 F.3d 886 (8th Cir. 2005)(use of the term "nigger" not enough to establish harassment); *Lum v. Kauai County Council*, 2007 WL 3408003 (D. Haw. 2007)(reference to Chinese police chief as "Hop Sing" not enough of a foundation for a race discrimination lawsuit).

[120] *Hudson v. Fischer*, 2008 WL 5110974 (N.D. N.Y. 2008).

[121] A number of recent studies suggest that employees prevail in only 15% of all discrimination cases, including harassment cases. *Employment Discrimination Plaintiffs in Federal Court: From Bad To Worse*, 3 Harvard Law & Policy Review 1 (2009).

[122] *Richardson v. City of Albuquerque*, 857 F.2d 727 (10th Cir. 1988)(no harassment where all recruits treated equally offensively); *Halasi-Schmick v. City of Shawnee*, 759 F. Supp. 747 (D. Kan. 1991).

[123] In *United Steel Workers v. Weber*, 443 U.S. 193 (1979), the Supreme Court approved voluntary affirmative action programs undertaken by a private employer. The *Weber* case did not address the question of whether a public employer could, consistent with Title VII, voluntarily adopt an affirmative action program. *See generally* Kreiling and Mercurio, *Beyond Weber: The Broadening Scope of Judicial Approval of Affirmative Action*, 88 Dick. L. Rev. 46 (1983).

[124] *Adarand Constructors, Inc. v. Pena*, 515 U.S. 200 (1995).

[125] *Grutter v. Bollinger*, 539 U.S. 306 (2003).

[126] *Gratz v. Bollinger*, 539 U.S. 244 (2003).

[127] *Petit v. City of Chicago*, 352 F.3d 1111 (7th Cir. 2003). Courts have declined to follow the same analysis in fire departments. In *Lomack v. City of Newark*, 463 F.3d 303 (3d Cir. 2006), the Court interpreted *Grutter* to establish that educational benefits are compelling in a law school context, but not in a firefighting context.

[128] *Rutherford v. City of Cleveland*, 179 Fed.Appx. 366 (6th Cir. 2006); *Brackett v. Civil Service Com'n*, 850 N.E.2d 533 (Mass. 2006).

[129] *Youngblood v. Dalzell*, 925 F.2d 954 (6th Cir. 1994); *Bratton v. City of Detroit*, 704 F.2d 878 (6th Cir. 1983). *See generally United Steel Workers v. Weber*, 443 U.S. 193 (1979).

130 *Martinez v. City of St. Louis*, 539 F.3d 857 (8th Cir. 2008); *Detroit Police Officers Association v. Young*, 989 F.2d 225 (6th Cir. 1993); *Hammon v. Berry*, 826 F.2d 73 (D.C. Cir. 1987); *U.S. v. State*, 2007 WL 951880 (E.D. Ark. 2007); *North State Law Enforcement Officers Association v. Charlotte-Mecklenberg*, 862 F. Supp. 1445 (W.D. N.C. 1994).

131 *Maryland Troopers Association v. Evans*, 993 F.2d 1072 (4th Cir. 1993); *see Regents of the University of California v. Bakke*, 438 U.S. 265 (1978).

132 *Dietz v. Baker*, 523 F. Supp. 2d 407 (D. Del. 2007).

133 *Johnson v. Transportation Agency, Santa Clara County, California*, 480 U.S. 616 (1987); *Bullen v. Chaffinch*, 336 F. Supp. 2d 342 (D. Del. 2004).

134 *Detroit Police Officers Association v. Young*, 56 FEP Cases 261 (E.D. Mich. 1991).

135 *United Steel Workers v. Weber*, 443 U.S. 193 (1979).

136 *United States v. Paradise*, 480 U.S. 149 (1987).

137 *Wygant v. Jackson Board of Education*, 476 U.S. 267 (1986).

138 42 U.S.C. §2000e; *see Dimino v. New York City Transit Authority*, 64 F. Supp. 2d 136 (E.D. N.Y. 1999); *Lunsford v. Leis*, 686 F. Supp. 181 (S.D. Ohio 1988).

139 *Larsen v. Township of Branchburg*, 2007 WL 135706 (N.J. Super. A.D. 2007).

140 *Gregory v. Ashcroft*, 501 U.S. 452 (1991); *Massachusetts Board of Retirement v. Murgia*, 427 U.S. 307 (1976); *see Bash v. City of Galena, Kansas*, 42 F. Supp. 2d 1171 (D. Kan. 1999); *McCann v. City of Chicago*, 968 F.2d 635 (7th Cir. 1992)(different retirement ages for sergeants and patrol officers upheld under "rational basis" test of Fourteenth Amendment).

141 29 U.S.C. §§621-634.

142 Title 29, §623(a), United States Code.

143 *City of Hollywood v. Hogan*, 986 So.2d 634 (Fla. App. 2008); *Manna v. Township of Fairfield*, 2007 WL 3231894 (D. N.J. 2007); *Bash v. City of Galena, Kansas*, 42 F. Supp. 2d 1171 (D. Kan. 1999).

144 *Aldridge v. City of Memphis*, 2007 WL 4370707 (W.D. Tenn. 2007); *Sotolongo v. New York City Transit Authority*, 63 F. Supp. 2d 353 (S.D. N.Y. 1999).

145 *Kentucky Retirement Systems v. E.E.O.C.*, 128 S.Ct. 2361 (2008).

146 *Rodock v. Town of Greenwich*, 2008 WL 4633125 (Conn. Super. 2008).

147 *Whitfield v. City of Knoxville*, 567 F. Supp. 1344 (E.D. Tenn. 1983); *Hahoney v. Trabusco*, 574 F. Supp. 955 (D. Mass. 1983); *EEOC v. Tennessee Wildlife Resources Agency*, 859 F.2d 24 (6th Cir. 1988); *Heiar v. Crawford County*, 746 F.2d 1190 (7th Cir. 1985); *EEOC v. Kentucky State Police*, 860 F.2d 665 (6th Cir. 1988); *Gately v. Commonwealth of Massachusetts*, 811 F. Supp. 26 (D. Mass. 1992); *EEOC v. City of Bowling Green*, 607 F. Supp. 524 (W.D. Ky. 1985); *EEOC v. Missouri State Highway Patrol*, 47 FEP Cases 382 (5th Cir. 1988); *EEOC v. Commonwealth of Pennsylvania*, 829 F.2d 392 (3d Cir. 1987); *EEOC v. Mississippi State Tax Commission*, 837 F.2d 1398 (5th Cir. 1988); *EEOC v. State of Florida*, 660 F. Supp. 1104 (N.D. Fla. 1986); *Coleman v. City of Omaha*, 714 F.2d 804 (8th Cir. 1983); *Police Benevolent Ass'n of The N.Y. State Troopers, Inc. v. Bennett*, 477 F. Supp. 2d 534 (N.D. N.Y. 2007); *EEOC v. City of Minneapolis*, 537 F. Supp. 750 (D. Minn. 1982); *Dillon v. City of Chicago*, 30 ATLA L.Rep. 118 (N.D. Ill. 1988).

148 *Feldman v. Nassau County*, 434 F.3d 177 (2d Cir. 2006); *Minch v. City of Chicago*, 363 F.3d 615 (7th Cir. 2004); *Kannady v. City of Kiowa*, 2006 WL 3452552 (E.D. Okla. 2006). In the 1996 legislation, Congress directed the Secretary of Health and Human Services to report to Congress within three years on the feasibility of testing the ability of police officers and firefighters to complete public safety tasks. Within four years, the Secretary was to issue advisory guidelines for the use and administration of tests designed to gauge the mental and physical competence of police and firefighting personnel. After those guidelines were issued, the Secretary was directed to issue regulations identifying appropriate tests that a state or local government could use to evaluate the fitness of police officers and firefighters who had reached the mandatory retirement age specified by that government. Once those regulations were in place, state and local governments would be compelled to give their public safety personnel the opportunity to demonstrate their continued fitness for duty once they reached retirement age. P.L. 104-208 § 119(2), 110 Stat. at 3009-24-3009-25. To date, however, no such guidelines or regulations have been issued.

149 29 U.S.C. §§623 and 631.

150 *See Hahn v. City of Buffalo*, 596 F. Supp. 940 (W.D. N.Y. 1984); *Colon v. City of New York*, 535 F. Supp. 1108 (S.D. N.Y. 1982); *Sobieralski v. City of South Bend*, 479 N.E.2d 98 (Ind. App. 1985). *See also EEOC v. University of Texas*, 710 F.2d 1091 (5th Cir. 1983).

151 *Doyle v. Suffolk County*, 786 F.2d 523 (2d Cir. 1986).

152 *Sebold v. City of Middletown*, 2007 WL 2782527 (D. Conn. 2007).

153 *Kassner v. 2nd Ave. Delicatessen Inc.*, 496 F.3d. 229 (2d Cir. 2007).

154 *Foley v. Connelie*, 435 U.S. 291 (1978).

155 *Jauregui v. City of Glendale*, 47 FEP Cases 1860 (9th Cir. 1988). National origin discrimination includes discrimination against Native Americans. *Wilkinson v. Hill Co. Sheriff's Office*, 1995 FEP Summary 29 (Mont. HRC 1994).

156 *Polanco v. City of Austin, Texas*, 78 F.3d 968 (5th Cir. 1996).

157 *Padula v. Webster*, 822 F.2d 97 (D.C. Cir. 1987). *Contra Watkins v. U.S. Army*, 837 F.2d 1428 (9th Cir. 1988), *opinion withdrawn on unrelated grounds*, 875 F.2d 699 (9th Cir. 1989).

158 *Padula v. Webster*, 822 F.2d 97 (D.C. Cir. 1987); *Childers v. Dallas Police Dept.*, 513 F. Supp. 134 (N.D. Tex. 1981).

159 *Bowers v. Hardwick*, 478 U.S. 186 (1986).

160 *Lawrence v. Texas*, 539 U.S. 558 (2003).

161 *Barnes v. City of Cincinnati*, 401 F.3d 729 (6th Cir. 2005).

162 D.C. Code § 2-1402.11 (2009). *See generally Newman v. District of Columbia*, 518 A.2d 698 (D.C. App. 1986).

163 *Hayden v. Coppage*, 533 F. Supp. 2d 1186 (M.D. Ala. 2008); *Albert v. City of Hartford*, 529 F. Supp. 2d 311 (D. Conn. 2007).

164 *Village of Willowbrook v. Olech*, 528 U.S. 562 (2000).

165 *Engquist v. Oregon Department of Agriculture*, 128 S.Ct. 2146 (U.S. 2008).

166 *U.S. Airways, Inc. v. Barnett*, 535 U.S. 391 (2002)(disability); *Balint v. Carson City, Nev.*, 180 F.3d 1047 (9th Cir. 1999)(religion).

167 Title 42, §2000e-2(h), United States Code.

168 *Detroit Branch, NAACP v. Detroit Police Officers Association*, 821 F.2d 328 (6th Cir. 1987). *See generally International Brotherhood of Teamsters v. United States*, 431 U.S. 324 (1977).

169 *Black Law Enforcement Officers Association v. City of Akron*, 824 F.2d 475 (6th Cir. 1987).

CHAPTER 14

THE EMPLOYMENT RIGHTS OF DISABLED OFFICERS

Disability Discrimination Laws.

For many years, few job protections were granted to disabled police officers. In the absence of a statute protecting against disability discrimination, disabled officers seeking to remain with their departments, or disabled applicants seeking employment with a law enforcement agency, were regularly turned away by the courts.

In 1973, Congress passed the Federal Rehabilitation Act, which forbade disability discrimination by any employer receiving federal funds. Most state legislatures followed suit by adding disability discrimination to the list of employment practices prohibited by state law. In 1990, Congress passed the Americans With Disabilities Act (ADA). Title I of the ADA, which prohibits discrimination in employment-related matters on the basis of disability, began applying to public sector employers in January 1992.[1]

Initially, it appeared as though the combination of these laws, and particularly the ADA, would bring about fundamental changes in a wide variety of law enforcement personnel practices ranging from hiring practices to light-duty assignments. Reinforcing this view, in the preface to the ADA Congress expressed the thought that 36 million Americans would be covered by the law. However, the conservative approach taken by the United States Supreme Court and other federal courts towards disability cases almost completely eroded the protections of at least the federal laws concerning disability discrimination. In 2002, for example, the American Bar Association released a survey indicating that employees had lost 94.5% of ADA cases in federal court.

In 2008, Congress again intervened, passing the ADA Amendments Act of 2008. The ADAAA, as it is known, reverses many of the decisions of the United States Supreme Court that had pared back the ADA's protections. The ADAAA is sure to usher in a new wave of litigation involving disability claims by law enforcement officers.

The Americans With Disabilities Act.

The ADA prohibits discrimination in employment-related matters against qualified individuals with a disability because of the disability.

The ADA prohibits discrimination in employment-related matters against qualified individuals with a disability because of the disability.[2] The ADA defines a disability as a physical or mental impairment that substantially limits one or more of the major life activities of the individual. Individuals are protected by the ADA if they suffer from such an impairment, have a history of such an impairment,[3] or are regarded by the employer as having such an impairment.[4] Under this definition, a person need not actually be disabled in order to qualify for the ADA's protections – it is enough that others, including the employer, believe that the employee is disabled.[5]

It is not necessary for a physical or psychological disorder to be specifically listed in the ADA for the disorder to be covered by the protections of the law.[6] The ADA only applies to permanent medical or psychological conditions, not temporary, non-chronic ones.[7] Moreover, by its terms, the ADA only applies to an "employer" of qualified individuals with a disability. Individual governmental employees, including police chiefs, are not "employers" under the law and thus are not subject to suit under the ADA.[8] A pension fund may meet the definition of "employer" if it has the responsibility for determining who qualifies for admission into the pension plan, and thus has the power to significantly impact the access of a law enforcement officer to employment benefits.[9]

Substantial Limitation Of A Major Life Activity.

In order to qualify as a disabled individual under the ADA, the individual's impairment must "substantially limit" one or more major life activities of the individual.[10] The ADAAA adds to the ADA a non-exhaustive list of major life activities, including:

- Caring for one's self
- Walking
- Hearing
- Breathing
- Working
- Bending
- Standing
- Communicating

- Performing Manual Tasks
- Seeing
- Speaking
- Learning
- Reading
- Thinking
- Lifting
- Concentrating[11]

Many ADA claims were lost by employees because of the inability to prove that their condition substantially limited a major life activity. In the seminal case of *Sutton v. United Airlines, Inc.*, the Supreme Court held that the "substantially limits" assessment must be made in light of the employee's corrected condition.[12] Thus, the "substantially limits" assessment of an individual with high blood pressure should be made when the individual is taking blood pressure medication, and the assessment of an individual with vision difficulties should be made when the individual is wearing corrective lenses. Obviously, under such an approach virtually all individuals with treatable impairments will not be considered to be covered by the ADA. In a separate case, *Toyota Motor Mfg., Kentucky, Inc. v. Williams*, the Supreme Court held that "major life activities" are "those activities that are of central importance to daily life," and that "to be substantially limited...an individual must have an impairment that prevents or severely restricts the individual from doing activities that are of central importance to most people's daily lives. The impairment's impact must also be permanent or long term."[13]

Following *Sutton* and *Williams*, federal courts routinely dismissed disability claims where individuals have either been fired or not hired because of their physical or emotional impairments, but where the courts view the impairments as not substantially limiting a major life activity. Since *Sutton*, courts have rejected ADA claims for the following impairments:

- Amblyopia, or "Lazy Eye"[14]

- Asthma[15]

- Attention Deficit Hyperactivity Disorder[16]

- Bipolar Disorder[17]

- Blood Clotting Condition[18]

- Cancer, if in remission[19]

- Claustrophobia[20]

- Condomalacia patella condition[21]

- Depression[22]

- Diabetes[23]

- Drug dependency and chronic pain[24]

- Epilepsy[25]

- Hypertension[26]

- Morbid obesity[27]

- Multiple sclerosis, early onset[28]

- Panic attacks[29]

- Partial hearing loss[30]

- Partial limb amputation[31]

- Pulmonary embolism[32]

- Vision loss in one eye[33]

A person whose condition is controlled by medication, medical supplies or equipment, hearing aids, prosthetics, or other assistive technology can no longer be excluded from the definition of disabled because of these mitigating measures.

The ADAAA entirely changes these standards. The ADAAA explicitly rejects both *Sutton* and *Williams* as resulting in interpretations that were contrary to Congress' intent in passing the ADA. Contrary to *Sutton*, the ADAAA provides that mitigating measures cannot be considered in determining whether an employee is disabled. Thus, a person whose condition is controlled by medication, medical supplies or equipment, hearing aids, prosthetics, or other assistive technology can no longer be excluded from the definition of disabled because of these mitigating measures. The only notable exception is that poor vision that is correctable with lenses is not considered an impairment. However, the ADAAA prohibits any employment test or qualification standard that tests applicants based on their uncorrected vision, unless a certain level of uncorrected vision is consistent with business necessity. Contrary to *Williams*, the ADAAA's new definition of "major life activities" requires only that an impairment substantially limit one major life activity to qualify as a disability, and not just those of "central" or primary importance to individuals' lives.

Some employees have attempted to claim that their physical or psychological condition substantially limits them in the major life activity of working. After all, employees argue, they are being discharged by the employer because of their condition – that alone must establish they are substantially limited in the major life activity of working. Most of these arguments have been unsuccessful, with the Supreme Court taking the lead in holding that the major life activity of "working" means the ability to engage in a broad range of jobs, not just a single occupation.[34] Thus, a police officer who has been fired because he cannot perform the full range of duties of a patrol officer is not substantially limited in the major life activity of working if there is a broad range of other non-police related jobs he can perform.[35]

Qualified Individuals With A Disability – The Need For An Employee To Be Able To Perform The Essential Functions Of The Job, And An Employer's Obligation To Reasonably Accommodate The Employee's Disability.

Like most disability discrimination laws, the ADA does not broadly prohibit employment-related discrimination against all individuals with a disability. Rather, the law protects only "qualified individuals with a disability" when the employer's decisions have been based on the individual's disability.[36] The ADA defines qualified individuals with a disability as follows:

> "The term qualified individual with a 'disability' means an individual with a disability, who, with or without reasonable accommodation, can perform the essential functions of the employment position that such individual holds or desires."[37]

To be a "qualified individual with a disability," the employee must be able to perform the essential functions of the job either with or without reasonable accommodation.[38] The essential job functions are those of the officer's own law enforcement agency; that an officer can perform the essential job functions in other agencies with different standards is not relevant in an ADA case.[39] A finding through a workers' compensation or pension system that the officer is permanently and totally disabled may well preclude a conclusion that the officer is a "qualified" individual with a disability,[40] as may be a finding in a workers' compensation case that the officer is subject to certain medical restrictions while at work.[41] In addition, while the issue of light-duty assignments will be treated in greater detail later in this chapter, the clear trend in the law is to hold that an officer is not a "qualified" individual with a disability unless the officer has the ability to effectuate a forcible arrest.

This definition illustrates a key element of the ADA – that an employer has an obligation to "reasonably accommodate" a qualified individual with a disability. The ADA provides a number of examples of reasonable accommodation:

> "The term 'reasonable accommodation' may include (A) making existing facilities used by employees readily accessible to and usable by individuals with disabilities; and (B) job restructuring, part-time or modified work schedules, reassignment to a vacant position, acquisition or modification of equipment or devices, appropriate adjustment or modifications of examinations, training materials or policies, the provision of qualified readers or interpreters, and other similar accommodations for individuals with disabilities."[42]

Ordinarily, the disabled employee must request an accommodation under the ADA, beginning an interactive discussion between the employer and the employee as to potential accommodations.[43] Under the ADA, an employer is not required to modify an essential function of the job by way of an accommodation,[44] nor is the employer required to change the employee's supervisory structure.[45] Likewise, an accommodation is not "reasonable" if it imposes an undue hardship on an employer. For example, a law enforcement employer has no obligation to grant unpaid leave of indefinite length as an accommodation for a disabled employee.[46] In enacting the ADA, Congress provided illustrations of the types of inquiries courts will make in determining what constitutes undue hardship:

> "(A) In general, the term 'undue hardship' means an action requiring significant difficulty or expense, when considered in light of the factors set forth in subparagraph (B).

> "(B) In determining whether an accommodation would impose an undue hardship on a covered entity, factors to be considered include —

> "(i) the nature and cost of the accommodation needed under this Act;

> "(ii) the overall financial resources of the facility or facilities involved in the provision of the reasonable accommodation; the number of persons employed at such facility; the effect on expenses and resources, or the impact otherwise of such accommodation upon the operation of the facility;

> "(iii) the overall financial resources of the covered entity; the overall size of the business of a covered entity with respect to the number of its employees; the number, type, and location of its facilities; and

Under the ADA, an employer is not required to modify an essential function of the job by way of an accommodation, nor is the employer required to change the employee's supervisory structure.

"(iv) the type of operation or operations of the covered entity, including the composition, structure, and functions of the work force of such entity; the geographic separateness, administrative, or fiscal relationship of the facility or facilities in question to the covered entity."[47]

The obligation to reasonably accommodate disabled individuals increases with the size of the law enforcement agency. Because of the way the ADA defines an undue hardship, a larger agency might be compelled to make an accommodation that would be considered to be an undue hardship for a smaller agency. The types of possible accommodations range significantly, and can include such things as modified work schedules and even a ban on smoking in the workplace.[48]

The obligation to reasonably accommodate disabled individuals increases with the size of the law enforcement agency.

The ADA's Specific Bans On Discrimination.

The ADA prohibits discrimination in employment-related matters against qualified individuals with a disability. The ADA lists a variety of employment decisions which might constitute illegal discrimination, including discrimination in job application procedures; the hiring, advancement, or discharge of employees; employee compensation; job training; and other terms, conditions, and privileges of employment.[49] Congress also listed seven specific examples of prohibited discrimination in Section 102(b) of the ADA:

"(1) Limiting, segregating, or classifying a job applicant or employee in a way that adversely affects the opportunities or status of such applicant or employee because of the disability of such applicant or employee;

"(2) Participating in a contractual or other arrangement or relationship that has the effect of subjecting a covered entity's qualified applicant or employee with a disability to the discrimination prohibited by this title (such relationship includes a relationship with an employment or referral agency, labor union, an organization providing fringe benefits to an employee of the covered entity, or an organization providing training and apprenticeship programs);

"(3) Utilizing standards, criteria, or methods of administration (A) that have the effect of discrimination on the basis of disability; or (B) that perpetuate the discrimination of others who are subject to common administrative control;

"(4) Excluding or otherwise denying equal jobs or benefits to a qualified individual because of the known disability of an individual with whom the qualified individual is known to have a relationship or association;

"(5) (A) Not making reasonable accommodations to the known physical or mental limitations of an otherwise qualified individual with a disability who is an applicant or employee, unless such covered entity can demonstrate that the accommodation would impose an undue hardship on the operation of the business of such covered entity; or (B) denying employment opportunities to a job applicant or employee who is an otherwise qualified individual with a disability, if such denial is based on the need of such covered entity to make reasonable accommodation to the physical or mental impairments of the employee or applicant;

"(6) Using qualification standards, employment tests or other selection criteria that screen out or tend to screen out an individual with a disability or a class of individuals with disabilities unless the standard, test or other selection criteria, as used by the covered entity, is shown to be job-related for the position in question and is consistent with business necessity; and

"(7) Failing to select and administer tests concerning employment in the most effective manner to ensure that, when such test is administered to a job applicant or employee who has a disability that impairs sensory, manual, or speaking skills, such test results accurately reflect the skills, aptitude, or whatever other factor of such applicant or employee that such test purports to measure, rather than reflecting the impaired sensory, manual, or speaking skills of such employee or applicant (except where such skills are the factors that the test purports to measure)."[50]

Apart from the requirement to reasonably accommodate, several of Section 102(b)'s examples of discrimination have brought about changes in law enforcement personnel practices. For example, Section 102(b)(6) requires employers to carefully scrutinize all physical fitness and agility requirements to ensure that the requirements are both job-related and consistent with business necessity; in response, many law enforcement employers discarded physical standards which had been used for years either at the entrance level or as part of an incentive plan or continuing requirement for employment, including standards for uncorrected eyesight, aerobic capacity, blood pressure, and cardiovascular capacity.

Section 102(b)(2) requires law enforcement agencies to carefully consider their contractual or other relationships with third parties, since an agency can be liable for the discrimination carried out by a person with whom it has a contractual or other relationship. Section 102(b)(2) had at least three significant areas of impact:

- Law enforcement agencies are no longer able to blindly rely on physical fitness standards established by a statewide peace officer standards and training commission, for if those standards are discriminatory, the agency is liable if it uses the standards to make employment decisions.

- Law enforcement agencies and labor organizations have had to examine their collective bargaining agreements to ensure that the agreements do not discriminate on the basis of a disability. If a contractual provision such as a physical fitness plan or sick leave incentive program is illegally discriminatory, both the agency and the labor organization may be liable for the discrimination.

- Law enforcement agencies have had to take care that physicians and psychological professionals with whom they contract to examine employees and applicants are aware of the requirements of the ADA and comply with those requirements. If a professional violates the ADA by, for example, breaching the strict confidentiality requirements of the ADA, the law enforcement agency may be liable for the breach.

The Need For The Employer's Decision To Be Based Upon The Employee's Disability, And Not On Independent Grounds.

To violate the ADA, the employer's decision must be based upon the employee's disability, and not upon an independent ground. For example, in one case a group of police officers who had retired on a disability retirement brought an ADA lawsuit against the City of Los Angeles, contending that the City's policy of reducing pensions by the amount of workers' compensation benefits received by employees discriminated against disabled employees. A federal appeals court dismissed the lawsuit, finding that since the retirees had the option of choosing a service-based retirement that carried with it no workers' compensation reduction, the retirees had no claim: "The offset does not treat disabled officers differently or create disproportionate burdens because of the nature of their limitations or even their status as individuals with disabilities. It simply limits a type of compensation for work-related injuries that happens to be available only to individuals who are disabled."[51]

The ADA And Hiring.

One area of fundamental change in law enforcement personnel practices resulting from the ADA is in the area of hiring. Under the ADA, illegal discrimination specifically includes compelling applicants to undergo medical examinations and inquiries. The ADA also prohibits inquiring whether an applicant has a disability, or asking about the nature or extent of the applicant's disability.

Three limited exceptions to these bans exist. First, an employer can compel an employee to undergo a medical examination if it has a reason for doing so which is job-related and consistent with business necessity. Second, an employer can compel applicants to undergo medical examinations that are job-related and consistent with business necessity, but only after the employer has made an offer of employment to the applicant which is conditioned on passing the medical examination.[52] Such "conditional offers of employment" become binding contracts to hire an

Under the ADA, illegal discrimination specifically includes compelling applicants to undergo medical examinations and inquiries.

applicant if the applicant passes the tests that employment is contingent upon.[53] Third, even though an employer cannot inquire into an applicant's medical condition, it can inquire as to whether an applicant has the physical ability to perform the essential functions of the job.

These requirements gave rise to a number of changes in the personnel practices of law enforcement agencies, including the following:

- In most agencies, applicants were previously required to undergo a medical examination before an offer of employment is made. The ADA forbids this practice.

- The Equal Employment Opportunity Commission (EEOC) has indicated that it does not consider a physical agility test to be a "medical examination." Even if the EEOC's opinion on this matter is upheld by the courts, a legitimate question arises as to whether a prudent employer would want to give a physical agility test to an individual about whom it has no medical information. In response, many employers have now only required physical agility tests after they have made a conditional offer of employment to an applicant, and after they have had the opportunity to obtain the results of a medical examination of the applicant.

- The ban on inquiring about an applicant's medical condition or history required the revision of many employment application forms, which routinely sought information on such matters. Even requiring an applicant's history of workers' compensation claims would appear to violate the ADA. The ban also effectively eliminated pre-offer of employment polygraph examinations in most agencies, since virtually all polygraphers ask questions about an individual's medical condition as a prelude to the examination.

The ADA's outright ban on medical examinations exists only in the hiring process. As such, if the employer's reason for doing so is job-related and consistent with business necessity, the employer has the right to insist that employees returning from disability status submit to medical examinations as a predicate to returning to work.[54]

Remedies For Breach Of The ADA.

Employees or applicants alleging a breach of the ADA are required to file a complaint with the EEOC within 180 days of the alleged discrimination.[55] The EEOC can then either take up the case on behalf of the complainant or issue a "right to sue" letter to the complainant, authorizing the employee to bring a claim under the ADA in court. After proceeding through the EEOC, a complaint alleging discrimination under the ADA must be filed in federal court.

The ADA incorporates the remedies available under Title VII of the Civil Rights Act of 1964.[56] Title VII allows a court to award back pay as well as reinstatement. Compensatory damages and damages for pain and suffering are not recoverable under Title VII or the ADA. Under the Civil Rights Act of 1991, however, though there is a split in the law on the issue, in cases alleging retaliation against an employee who raises ADA claims, both compensatory and punitive damages may be available.[57] A court also has the authority to compel an employer to take appropriate action to remedy the discrimination, including the authority to require that specific reasonable accommodations be made for the employee's disability.

Other Laws Protecting Disabled Employees.

As noted above, protections against discrimination on the basis of a disability can be found in areas other than the ADA. First, 47 states have passed statutes forbidding such discrimination, and many have established administrative agencies with the power to enforce the laws. As described earlier in this chapter, state laws can provide greater protections for employees than the ADA. Second, many cities and counties have passed ordinances to the same effect. Third, the "non-discrimination" clauses in many law enforcement collective bargaining agreements frequently list disabled status as a protected classification.

Types Of Disability Discrimination Claims.

The most common single type of disability discrimination claim stems from an employer's blanket exclusion of employees who suffer from certain types of conditions. Since disability discrimination laws require that each employee or applicant be evaluated on a case-by-case basis, courts regularly strike down blanket exclusions from employment. Employees or applicants have successfully challenged blanket exclusions for a wide variety of conditions, including epilepsy, HIV-positive status,[58] Crohn's disease or enteritis,[59] insulin-dependent diabetes,[60] a history of cancer, missing limbs,[61] hypertension,[62] and uncorrected visual acuity.[63] When an employer makes an individualized assessment of an employee's or applicant's ability to perform the job, particularly when the employer uses job-related tests to make the assessment, the employer's decision is much less subject to attack under disability discrimination laws.

When an employer makes an individualized assessment of an employee's or applicant's ability to perform the job, the employer's decision is much less subject to attack under disability discrimination laws.

The Obligation To Make Light-Duty Work Available.

One of an employer's obligations under the ADA and other disability discrimination laws is to reasonably accommodate an employee through "job restructuring." Almost immediately after the enactment of the ADA, disabled officers began suing their employers on the theory that the obligation to reasonably accommodate includes the obligation to make light-duty work available. The courts have regularly rejected such claims under both the ADA and other disability discrimination laws. The courts have found instead that the essential function of the job of a police officer is to make forceful arrests, and that if a disabled officer cannot perform this essential function, there is no obligation to offer light-duty work to the officer.

The leading case on light-duty work remains *Simon v. St. Louis County, Mo.*, a case decided under the Federal Rehabilitation Act. *Simon's* eight-year trail of litigation began when a police officer who was rendered paraplegic as the result of a gunshot wound sustained in the line of duty was refused reinstatement to work by his employer. In the initial trial, the lower court found that the injured officer could not meet two requirements of the Department – that he be able to effect a forceful arrest, and that he be eligible to transfer among all positions within the Department.[64] The appellate court reversed the trial court's opinion denying the officer reinstatement, and specifically directed the trial court to consider the reasonableness of these two requirements, and whether the employer had uniformly required such abilities of all employees:

> "[T]he district court should consider whether the requirements of police officers of St. Louis County * * * are reasonable, legitimate, and necessary requirements for all positions within the Department. The district court should determine whether the ability to make a forceful arrest and the ability to perform all of the duties of all of the positions within the Department are in fact uniformly required of all officers."[65]

After a retrial pursuant to the appellate court's directions, the trial court found that the employer had uniformly required all employees to engage in forceful arrests and to be eligible for transfer to any assignment within the Department, and that a paraplegic employee who could not physically perform such arrests or be eligible for transfer to certain assignments could be refused employment, a decision which was later sustained on appeal.[66]

Similarly, in *Blumhagen v. Clackamas County*, a deputy who was injured on duty was initially assigned to a temporary light-duty position. The employer had a practice of not making permanent light-duty assignments even though there were several light-duty positions that were available, in order to provide slots to relieve officers who suffered from "burnout" on a temporary basis. Owing to the unavailability of permanent light-duty positions, the injured officer was eventually terminated. The Court affirmed the termination, noting that to require an employer to create permanent light-duty positions "would have a serious impact on the Department's entire rotational program."[67] Numerous other cases stand for the same proposition – that an employer need not create or make available permanent light-duty positions for officers unable to make a forceful arrest.[68]

If an employer does choose to have light-duty jobs for disabled employees, it must make sure that it does not artificially restrict the types of jobs that are offered in a way that assigns menial tasks to those officers performing them, or deprives the officers of meaningful promotional opportunities.[69] Moreover, if an employer makes light-duty jobs available for some employees with disabilities, it may have an obligation to make similar positions available to other disabled employees.[70]

NOTES

[1] The ADA was not applied retroactively. *Ethridge v. State of Alabama*, 847 F. Supp. 903 (M.D. Ala. 1993).

[2] ADA §102, 29 CFR §1630.4.

[3] *Burris v. City of Phoenix*, 875 P.2d 1340 (Ariz. 1994)(history of testicular cancer).

[4] *Knight v. Metropolitan Government of Nashville and Davidson County, Tenn.*, 136 Fed.Appx. 755 (6th Cir. 2005); *Winnett v. City of Portland*, 1993 WL 56074 (Or. App. 1993).

[5] 29 CFR §1630.2(h).

[6] *Barry v. City of Madison*, 7 A.D. Cases 160 (W.D. Wis. 1994); *Roulette v. Illinois Human Rights Commission*, 628 N.E.2d 967 (Ill. App. 1993).

[7] *Santiago v. New York City Police Dept.*, 2007 WL 4382752 (S.D. N.Y. 2007); *Ross v. City of New Brighton*, 1998 WL 764414 (Minn. App. 1998).

[8] *Alsbrook v. City of Maumelle*, 184 F.3d 999 (8th Cir. 1999).

[9] *Holmes v. City of Aurora*, 1995 WL 21606 (N.D. Ill. 1995).

[10] *Dent v. City of Chicago*, 2003 WL 21801163 (N.D. Ill. 2003)(officer's alleged allergy to pregnant women does not substantially limit one or more major life activities); *Tamayo v. City of New York*, 2003 WL 21448366 (S.D. N.Y. 2003)(detectives' "extreme respiratory discomfort" as a result of the employer's non-enforcement of smoking regulations does not substantially limit one or more major life activities).

[11] 42 U.S.C. §12102.

[12] *Sutton v. United Airlines, Inc.*, 527 U.S. 471 (1999); *see Murphy v. United Parcel Service*, 527 U.S. 516 (1999).

[13] *Toyota Motor Mfg., Kentucky, Inc. v. Williams*, 534 U.S. 184 (2002).

[14] *Knoll v. Southeastern Pennsylvania Transportation Authority*, 2002 WL 31045145 (E.D. Pa. 2002).

[15] *Weiss v. City of New York*, 2003 WL 1621403 (S.D. N.Y. 2003)(employee's asthma was not a disability where it was controllable through medication); *Boone v. Reno*, 121 F. Supp. 2d 109 (D. D.C. 2000)(applicant for position as FBI agent not protected by ADA since her asthma was controllable through medication); *Sanders v. FMAS Corp.*, 180 F. Supp. 2d 698 (D. Md. 2001)(asthma controllable through medication not a disability); *Saunders v. Baltimore County, Maryland*, 163 F. Supp. 2d 564 (D. Md. 2001)(asthma does not limit one or more major life activities); *Reeves v. City of Dallas*, 2001 WL 1609345 (N.D. Tex. 2001)(asthma controllable through medication not a disability); *Mayers v. Washington Adventist Hospital*, 22 Fed.Appx. 158 (4th Cir. 2001)(asthma controllable through medication not a disability). *See also Cebertowicz v. Motorola, Inc.*, 178 F. Supp. 2d 949 (N.D. Ill. 2001)(employer did not regard employee with asthma as disabled).

[16] *Van Compernolle v. City of Zeeland*, 2006 WL 1460035 (W.D. Mich. 2006).

[17] *Hill v. Metropolitan Government of Nashville*, 2002 WL 31863829 (6th Cir. 2002).

[18] *Dose v. Buena Vista University*, 229 F. Supp. 2d 910 (N.D. Iowa 2002).

[19] *EEOC v. Boyle*, 181 F.3d 645 (5th Cir. App. 2000); *EEOC v. RJ Gallagher Co.*, 181 F.3d 645 (5th Cir. 1994).

[20] *Rodriguez v. City of New York*, 2008 WL 420015 (E.D. N.Y. 2008); *Walker v. Town of Greenville*, 347 F. Supp. 2d 566 (E.D. Tenn. 2004).

[21] *Miller v. Wells Dairy, Inc.*, 252 F. Supp. 799 (N.D. Iowa 2003).

[22] *Zeiger v. Illinois Dept. of Corrections*, 2008 WL 695366 (C.D. Ill. 2008)(corrections officer's depression did not substantially limit any major life activity); *Williams v. Philadelphia Housing Authority*, 230 F. Supp. 2d 631 (E.D. Pa. 2002)(police officers whose depression did not substantially limit one or more major life activities); *Julia v. Janssen*, 92 F. Supp. 2d 25 (D. P.R. 2000)(employee whose depression was controllable through medication not protected by ADA); *Miron v. Minnesota Mining & Mfg. Co.*, 2001 WL 1663870 (D. Minn. 2001)(employee whose depression was controllable through medication not protected by ADA); *Heisler v. Metropolitan Council*, 2001 WL 1690052 (D. Minn. 2001)(employee whose depression was controllable through medication not protected by ADA).

[23] *Burroughs v. City of Springfield*, 163 F.3d 505 (8th Cir. 1998)(police officer's diabetes, controllable through medication, not protected under ADA); *Anyan v. Nelson*, 68 Fed.Appx. 260 (2d Cir. 2003)(same); *Epstein v. Kalvin-Miller International*, 100 F. Supp. 2d 222 (S.D. N.Y. 2000)(employee's diabetes and heart condition, both of which were potentially fatal if not medicated, could not form basis for finding of disability because they were controllable through medication); *Beaulieu v. Northrop Grumman Corp.*, 23 Fed.Appx. 811 (9th Cir. 2001)(diabetes does not substantially limit any major life activity); *Tropiano v. Pennsylvania State Police*, 2006 WL 2077013 (E.D. Pa. 2006)(trooper applicant's insulin-controlled diabetes not disability because it does not limit a major life activity); *Young v. Chicago Transit Authority*, 189 F. Supp. 2d 780 (N.D. Ill. 2002)(diabetes does not substantially limit any major life activity); *Anyan v. New York Life Ins. Co.*, 192 F. Supp. 2d 228 (S.D. N.Y. 2002)(diabetes controllable by medication does not substantially limit any major life activity); *EEOC v. Murray, Inc.*, 175 F. Supp. 2d 1053 (M.D. Tenn. 2001)(treatable diabetes does not substantially limit any major life activity); *Sepulveda v. Glickman*, 167 F. Supp. 2d 186 (D. P.R. 2001)(treatable diabetes does not substantially limit any major life activity); *Grant v. May Dept. Stores Co.*, 786 A.2d 580 (D.C. 2001); *Williams v. H.N.S. Management Co.*, 56 F. Supp. 2d 215 (D. Conn. 1999). *Contra Nawrot v. CPC Inter.*, 277 F.3d 896 (7th Cir. 2002)(diabetes is a disability under the ADA).

[24] *Bonieskie v. Mukasey*, 540 F. Supp. 2d 190 (D. D.C. 2008).

[25] *Arnold v. City of Appleton, Wisconsin*, 97 F. Supp. 2d 937 (E.D. Wis. 2000) (firefighter applicant not disabled because his epilepsy must be viewed in its treatable condition); *Nelson v. Ameritech*, 2002 WL 226845 (N.D. Ill. 2002)(epilepsy controlled by medication not disability); *Sanglap v. LaSalle Bank, FSB*, 2002 WL 47975 (N.D. Ill. 2002)(epilepsy controllable through medication not a disability); *Popko v. Pennsylvania State University*, 84 F. Supp. 2d. 589 (M.D. Pa. 2000)(idiopathic epilepsy [epilepsy-related sleep disorder] is not a disability when viewed in its corrective state of getting eight hours of sleep); *EEOC v. Sara Lee Corp.*, 237 F.3d 349 (4th Cir. 2001)(occasional seizures due to epilepsy did not substantially limit plaintiff in caring for herself).

[26] *Sheehan v. City of Gloucester*, 321 F.3d 21 (1st Cir. 2003)(police lieutenant's hypertension did not render him incapable of performing broad class of jobs, and City did not regard him as disabled even though it involuntarily retired him); *Stumbo v. Dyncorp Technology Services*, 130 F. Supp. 2d 771 (W.D. Va. 2001)(former police officer applying for security job in war zone not protected by ADA where his hypertension was controlled by medication); *see Williams v. Chicago Transit Authority*, 2001 WL 855421 (N.D. Ill. 2001)(hypertension controlled by medication

not protected by ADA); *Lee v. Chicago School Reform Bd. Of Trustees*, 2001 WL 709455 (N.D. Ill. 2001)(hypertension controlled by medication not protected by ADA); *Williams v. Stark County Bd. Of County Commissioners*, 7 Fed.Appx. 441 (6th Cir. 2001)(hypertension controlled by medication not protected by ADA).

27 *Caruso v. Camilleri*, 2008 WL 170321 (W.D. N.Y. 2008).

28 *Yudkovitz v. Bell Atlantic Corporation*, 2004 WL 178330 (E.D. Pa. 2004).

29 *Reeves v. Johnson Controls World Servs., Inc.*, 140 F.3d 144 (2d Cir.1998).

30 *Walton v. U.S. Marshals Serv.*, 492 F.3d 998 (9th Cir. 2007).

31 *Christensen v. City of Los Angeles*, 2002 WL 1154578 (Cal. App. 2002).

32 *Dose v. Buena Vista University*, 229 F. Supp. 2d 910 (N.D. Iowa 2002).

33 *Ditullio v. Village of Massena*, 81 F. Supp. 2d 397 (N.D. N.Y 2000)(police officer's complete loss of vision in one eye is not a disability that substantially limits the major life activity of seeing when viewed in light of the unconscious corrective measures that the body takes).

34 *Sutton v. United Air Lines, Inc.*, 527 U.S. 471 (1999).

35 *Sutton v. United Air Lines, Inc.*, 527 U.S. 471 (1999); *Fultz v. City of Salem*, 51 Fed.Appx. 624 (9th Cir. 2002); *McNiff v. Town of Dracut*, 433 F. Supp. 2d 145 (D. Mass. 2006); *Kramarski v. Village of Orland Park*, 2002 WL 1827637 (N.D. Ill. 2002); *Terry v. City of Greensboro*, 14 A.D. Cases 1494 (M.D. N.C. 2003); *Bumstead v. Jasper County, Texas*, 931 F. Supp. 1323 (E.D. Tex. 1996).

36 *Deckert v. City of Ulysses*, 4 A.D. Cases 1569 (D. Kan. 1995)(officer discharged for motor vehicle accident and other misconduct, not discharged because of disability of diabetes); *Hartman v. City of Petaluma*, 841 F. Supp. 946 (N.D. Cal. 1994)(applicant who lied about prior drug use during application process not rejected because of disability of drug addiction, but rather because of untruthfulness).

37 ADA §101(8).

38 *Fornes v. Osceola County Sheriff's Office*, 179 Fed.Appx. 633 (11th Cir. 2006); *Mincey v. City of Bremerton*, 38 Fed.Appx. 402 (9th Cir. 2002); *Shannon v. Sheahan*, 2003 WL 366584 (N.D. Ill. 2003); *Buchmeier v. Village of Richton Park*, 2002 WL 31817985 (N.D. Ill. 2002).

39 *Johnson v. City of Pontiac*, 2008 WL 125693 (E.D. Mich. 2008).

40 *Pyrcz v. Branford College*, 1999 WL 706882 (Mass. Sup. 1999); *Lang v. City of Maplewood*, 574 N.W.2d 451 (Minn. App. 1998).

41 *Jackson v. County of Los Angeles*, 70 Cal.Rptr.2d 96 (Cal. App. 1998).

42 ADA §101(9).

43 *Warren v. Volusia County, Florida*, 188 Fed.Appx. 859 (11th Cir. 2006); *Breitfelder v. Leis*, 151 Fed.Appx. 379 (6th Cir. 2005); *Coley v. Grant County*, 36 Fed. Appx. 242 (9th Cir. 2002); *Wilson v. County of Orange*, 87 Cal.Rptr.3d 439 (Cal. App. 2009).

44 *Hoskins v. Oakland County*, 227 F.3d 719 (6th Cir. 2000).

45 *Moon v. City of Bellevue*, 142 Wash. App. 1037 (2008).

46 *Hopkins v. City of Bothell*, 117 Wash. App. 1019 (2003).

47 ADA §101(10).

48 *Thursby v. City of Scranton*, 2006 WL 1455736 (M.D. Pa. 2006).

49 ADA §102(a).

[50] ADA §102(b)(1)-(7).

[51] *Brown v. City of Los Angeles*, 521 F.3d 1238 (9th Cir. 2008).

[52] ADA §102(c).

[53] *Ardito v. City of Providence*, 263 F. Supp. 2d 358 (D. R.I. 2003).

[54] *White v. City of Boston*, 7 Mass.L.Rptr. 232 (Mass. Sup. 1997); *see Brumley v. Pena*, 62 F.3d 277 (8th Cir. 1995).

[55] *Sotolongo v. New York City Transit Authority*, 63 F. Supp. 2d 353 (S.D. N.Y. 1999).

[56] 42 USC §2000e *et seq.*

[57] *Compare Kramer v. Banc of America Securities, LLC,* 355 F.3d 961 (7th Cir. 2004)(punitive damages not available) and *Bowles v. Carolina Cargo, Inc.,* 100 Fed.Appx. 889 (4th Cir. 2004)(same) *with Salitros v. Chrysler Corp.,* 306 F.3d 562 (8th Cir. 2002)(punitive damages are available in retaliation cases brought under the ADA); *Foster v. Time Warner Entertainment Co.,* 250 F.3d 1189 (8th Cir. 2001)(same); *EEOC v. Wal-Mart Stores, Inc.,* 187 F.3d 1241 (10th Cir. 1999)(same); *Muller v. Costello,* 187 F.3d 298 (2d Cir.1999)(same).

[58] *Doe v. City of Chicago*, 883 F. Supp. 1126 (N.D. Ill. 1994).

[59] *Antonsen v. Ward*, 571 N.E.2d 636 (A.D. N.Y. 1991); *Blanchette v. Spokane County*, 836 P.2d 858 (Wash. App. 1992).

[60] *Kapche v. City of San Antonio*, 304 F.3d 493 (5th Cir. 2002); *Bombrys v. City of Toledo*, 849 F. Supp. 1210 (N.D. Ohio 1993).

[61] *Stilwell v. Kansas City Police Department*, 872 F. Supp. 682 (W.D. Mo. 1995); *Champ v. Baltimore County*, 884 F. Supp. 991 (M.D. Md. 1995).

[62] *Jurgella v. Danielson*, 764 P.2d 27 (Ariz. App. 1988).

[63] *O'Neil v. Board on Public Safety Standards and Training*, 95 Fire & Police Rep. 78 (D. Or. 1994)(strikes down state training agency's statewide minimum certification requirement for eyesight); *City of Belleville v. Human Rights Commission*, 522 N.E.2d 268 (Ill. App. 1988).

[64] *Simon v. St. Louis County, Mo.,* 497 F. Supp. 141 (E.D. Mo. 1980).

[65] *Simon v. St. Louis County, Mo.,* 656 F.2d 316 (8th Cir. 1981).

[66] *Simon v. St. Louis County, Mo.,* 735 F.2d 1082 (8th Cir. 1984).

[67] *Blumhagen v. Clackamas County*, 756 P.2d 650 (Or. App. 1988).

[68] *Allen v. Hamm*, 226 Fed.Appx. 264 (4th Cir. 2007)(general order prohibiting light-duty assignments); *Hummel v. County of Saginaw*, 40 Fed.Appx. 965 (6th Cir. 2002)(corrections officer with lung condition); *Watson v. City of Miami Beach,* 177 F.3d 932 (11th Cir. 1999)(police officer compelled to take fitness-for-duty examination because of symptoms of stress); *Burch v. City of Nacogdoches*, 174 F.3d 615 (5th Cir. 1999)(firefighter suffered back injury when he fell through floor while attempting to rescue fellow firefighter in burning building); *Mengine v. Runyon*, 114 F.3d 415 (3d Cir. 1997)(hip problems resulting from bilateral aseptic necrosis); *Holbrook v. City of Alpharetta*, 112 F.3d 1522 (11th Cir. 1997)(detective with partial blindness in left eye and complete blindness in right eye); *Doner v. City of Rockford*, 77 Fed.Appx. 898 (N.D. Ill. 2003)(officer with MS could not make forceful arrests); *Maldonado v. City of Ponce*, 206 F. Supp. 2d 198 (D. P.R. 2002)(employer could insist on ability to make forceful arrest); *Miller v. Department of Corrections*, 916 F. Supp. 863 (C.D. Ill. 1996), aff'd 107 F.3d 483 (7th Cir. 1997)(blind corrections officer); *Fussell v. Georgia Ports Authority*, 906 F. Supp. 1561 (S.D. Ga. 1995)(police officer with benign tumors);

McDonald v. State of Kansas Dept. of Corrections, 880 F. Supp. 1416 (D. Kan. 1995)(400-lb. corrections officer); *Champ v. Baltimore County*, 884 F. Supp. 991 (D. Md. 1995)(officer lost use of upper left arm after motorcycle accident); *Matos v. City of Phoenix*, 859 P.2d 748 (Ariz. App. 1993)(disability and age discrimination); *Peden v. City of Detroit*, 680 N.W.2d 857 (Mich. 2004)(department could require all officers to make forcible arrests); *Batiste v. Cuyahoga Cty. Sheriff's Dept.*, 2005 WL 3120228 (Ohio App. 2005)(no right to insist on light-duty job). *But see Stone v. City of Mount Vernon*, 118 F.3d 92 (2d Cir. 1997)(paraplegic firefighter).

[69] *Cripe v. City of San Jose*, 261 F.3d 877 (9th Cir. 2001).

[70] *See generally Dargis v. Sheahan*, 526 F.3d 981 (7th Cir. 2008); *Johnson v. City of Pontiac*, 2007 WL 1013247 (E.D. Mich. 2007).

CHAPTER 15

THE FAIR LABOR STANDARDS ACT

Introduction

The Fair Labor Standards Act (FLSA), generally known as the "minimum wage law," was a product of the depression years following the stock market crash of 1929. Congress passed the FLSA in 1938, in one of a number of "New Deal" legislative packages proposed by the administration of President Franklin Roosevelt.

As initially enacted, the Fair Labor Standards Act applied only to private sector employers, and specifically excluded from coverage the United States Government, state governments, and political subdivisions of state governments such as cities and counties. The major element of the FLSA was the requirement that all private employers pay a specified minimum wage to employees, with the additional requirement that employers pay such employees who work beyond the specified maximum number of hours per week at the rate of time and one-half their regular rate of pay.[1]

The general intent of Congress in passing the Fair Labor Standards Act was threefold. First, Congress intended to provide an equalization of wages among the various states, which at the time of the initial passage of the FLSA had widely varying prevailing wage rates. Second, there existed a "public welfare" element of the FLSA, an element which stands even today as a national legislative declaration that the payment of wages below certain minimum levels is contrary to public policy. Third, the FLSA was designed to spread employment among different employees by placing financial pressure on employers through the overtime pay requirements of the FLSA. Congress reasoned that if employers were required to pay employees at the overtime rate for excess hours, they would be inclined to hire more straight-time employees rather than pay the overtime rate.[2] Given these intents, courts have held that the FLSA should not only be liberally construed, but that the provisions of the Act impose an absolute obligation on employers to pay overtime compensation where it is required by the Act.[3]

In 1966, Congress extended the FLSA for the first time to certain governmental entities, specifically including schools and hospitals.[4] In 1974, Congress again amended the FLSA to specifically include within the definition of "employer" a "public agency."[5] Congress defined a public agency as including not only the United States Government, but also state and local governmental bodies. Thus, for the first time the FLSA applied to state and local governments employing more than five individuals in a law enforcement agency.[6] This extension of the FLSA to state and local governments was later held to be constitutional by the Supreme Court in *Garcia v. San Antonio Metropolitan Transit Authority.*[7]

Insofar as law enforcement employees are concerned, the most significant aspect of the FLSA is the requirement that employees who work more than the specified maximum time periods under the FLSA must receive overtime pay at the rate of time and one-half their regular rate of pay. Determining overtime compensation under the FLSA is a three-step process:

> The most significant aspect of the FLSA is the requirement that employees who work more than the specified maximum time periods under the FLSA must receive overtime pay at the rate of time and one-half their regular rate of pay.

- Calculating the employee's total hours worked;

- Determining the applicable overtime threshold; and

- Calculating the regular rate of pay so that the employee's overtime rate can be established.

An Employee's 'Hours Worked' Under The FLSA.

The first step under the FLSA in assessing whether the employee is entitled to overtime compensation is to determine the hours worked by the employee. In general, "hours worked" is considered to be all time spent in physical or mental exertion, whether burdensome or not, which is controlled or required by the employer.[8] Such time includes not only work that an employee is assigned to perform, but also work that an employee is "suffered or permitted" by the employer to perform.[9] Under the FLSA, an employer has a strict obligation to exercise its control to ensure that the only work which is performed by employees is that work which the employer actually desires the employees to perform.[10]

Most of the problem areas in determining whether an employee is engaged in "hours worked" under the FLSA fall into the following categories.

"Hours worked" is considered to be all time spent in physical or mental exertion, whether burdensome or not, which is controlled or required by the employer.

Shift Briefing And Roll Calls.

Prior to the *Garcia* decision, many law enforcement officers were required to attend mandatory roll calls or shift briefing without compensation. Under the FLSA, such time spent in roll calls or shift briefing must be counted as hours worked.[11]

Rest Periods.

Some collective bargaining agreements provide that rest periods or break periods are not compensable time. Under the FLSA, however, any reasonably short rest period, from five to 20 minutes in duration, must be included in "hours worked" regardless of any contrary provisions in a collective bargaining agreement or a memorandum of understanding.[12]

Meal Periods.

Bona fide, duty-free meal periods, unlike rest periods, are generally not included in hours worked under the FLSA.[13] In order to be excluded from the definition of "hours worked" under the FLSA, a meal period must be at least 30 minutes in duration. Law enforcement employees who are not allowed to leave their work stations in order to eat meals will have such meal time counted as "hours worked" regardless of the duration of the meal period.[14]

Two inconsistent tests are used by the courts to evaluate whether meal periods are compensable under the FLSA. Some courts hold that meal periods are only compensable if the time spent during the meal period is "primarily for the benefit of the employer."[15] Other courts rule that if the officer is not "completely relieved of duty" during the meal period, the time spent on the meal period will be counted as hours worked.[16] Usually, the test chosen by the court will dictate the result in the case. Courts using the "predominately for the benefit of the employer" test usually conclude that meal periods are not compensable under the FLSA; courts using the "completely relieved of duty" test will regularly find meal periods compensable.

Without regard to which test is used by the court, certain factors play an important role in evaluating the compensability of meal periods. For example, if an officer is required to remain on call in barracks or similar quarters during the meal period, or is engaged in extended surveillance activities, the time spent during the meal period will be counted as hours worked.[17] Additionally, if officers on meal periods are subject to duty-related interruptions, perform paper work, are required to monitor their radios, are limited in what types of activities in which they may engage, or are restricted in their geographic movements, the time spent during meal periods will more likely count as hours worked.[18]

Donning And Doffing.

In the wake of the 2005 decision of the United States Supreme Court about the compensability of donning and doffing (putting on and taking off) specialized uniforms in the meat packing industry,[19] law enforcement officers across the country have brought lawsuits contending that they too should be compensated for donning and doffing the equipment and uniforms they wear. As of the writing of this book, the decisions on whether donning and doffing is compensable have only come from the federal trial court level, and have been in conflict.[20] It will clearly require the decision of at least one federal appeals court to settle whether an employer must compensate officers for any time donning and doffing.

On-Call Status.

On occasion, law enforcement officers, particularly those assigned to the detective function, are given a pager and are required to remain within range of the pager while on off-duty status. Thus, the question frequently arises as to whether such employees are engaged in "hours worked" under the FLSA.

The general test for whether on-call time need be counted as hours worked can be found in the Code of Federal Regulations:

"Time spent at home on call may or may not be compensable depending on whether the restrictions placed on the employee preclude using the time for personal pursuits. Where, for example, a firefighter has returned home after the shift, with the understanding that he or she is expected to return to work in the event of an emergency in the night, such time is normally not compensable. On the other hand, where the conditions placed on the employee's activities are so restrictive that the employee cannot use the time effectively for personal pursuits, such time spent on call is compensable."[21]

Applying this language, courts balance the following factors: The provisions of any collective bargaining agreement,[22] the required response times,[23] whether the employee is required to remain on the premises or at any particular place during the on-call time, the degree to which the employee is able to engage in personal activities while on call,[24] the frequency of calls to service from on-call status, the ease with which on-call employees can trade on-call responsibilities,[25] whether employees are required to remain in uniform,[26] and whether the employee's availability during the on-call time is predominantly for the employer's or the employee's benefit.[27] Virtually all such cases have resulted in a finding that the on-call time is not compensable under the FLSA.[28]

For example, the court in *Allen v. United States*[29] held that federal marshals who were provided pagers and were required to remain sober and stay within radio range of the City of Baltimore were not engaged in hours worked under the FLSA.[30] If the restrictions on the employee are more stringent than those in the *Allen* case – for example, if the officer is required to remain at a specified location and to be prepared to respond to a particular event, or if the frequency of occasions when the employee is actually recalled from on-call status is high – the time spent in on-call status will be counted as hours worked.[31] If on-call time is counted as hours worked, even time spent sleeping while on call may be included as hours worked.[32]

Canine Programs.

Canine officers are typically required to perform a variety of duties at home related to the care and maintenance of the dog. Such duties may include feeding and grooming the dog, training the dog, and taking the dog to the veterinarian. Without exception, courts have ruled that such home dog care time must be counted as "hours worked" under the FLSA, since the time spent at home working with the dog is a necessary element of the employer's canine program.[33] Most courts have refused to extend the same rationale to commuting time for canine officers, finding that the actual time spent caring for the dog during the drive to and from work was so small that the commute is not compensable under the FLSA.[34]

Exercise Time.

A number of police officers assigned to SWAT teams have brought lawsuits alleging that the time spent working out to meet the minimum physical fitness requirements of the SWAT team should be compensable as hours worked. Though the results have been mixed, in general such claims have been unsuccessful, with courts reasoning that the benefit to the employer is too indefinite, and the time spent in exercise too small to make the exercise time compensable.[35]

Time Spent Traveling To Work.

Ordinarily, travel time on a regular commute between home and work is not compensable under the FLSA as hours worked. Even if the employee is required to travel to a training assignment for an extended period – even as much as an hour in each direction – the travel time would be considered normal commuting and not compensable under the FLSA.[36] However, if an employee is called to work in an emergency situation to a location which is a substantial distance from the officer's home, travel time in excess of the regular commute is counted as hours worked.[37]

Time Spent Traveling Out Of Town.

The main questions concerning travel time for law enforcement officers under the FLSA occur with respect to travel to another city on special assignment. If necessary travel takes an officer out of town, the travel time is clearly counted as "hours worked."[38] A possible exception to this rule is created by the following regulation of the Department of Labor, which implies that certain types of overnight travel may not be counted as time worked:

> "As an enforcement policy, the [Wage and Hour] Division will not consider as work time that time spent in travel away from home outside regular working hours as a passenger on an airplane, train, boat, bus, or automobile."[39]

Under this rule, if an employee is the driver of the car on an out-of-town business trip, for example, his/her time spent traveling is compensable while the employee/passenger's time is not.

Paid Leave.

The time an employee spends on paid leave during a work period or workweek is not counted as hours worked. For example, if a police officer working five eight-hour shifts per week uses one day of paid leave during the workweek, the officer will not be entitled to overtime under the FLSA until the officer has worked an additional eight hours beyond his or her normal workweek.[40]

Other 'Hours Worked' Issues.

Under the FLSA, police officers have won compensation for the time spent maintaining uniforms and guns while off duty,[41] maintaining vehicles while off duty,[42] and for the time spent at home preparing lesson plans for classes they are instructing.[43] On the other hand, while time spent in formal police academy training (whether in class or not) must be counted as "hours worked" under the FLSA, the time spent in an academy barracks sleeping and eating need not be counted towards an employee's overtime threshold.[44]

Determining The Overtime Threshold.

The second step in assessing an employee's right to overtime under the FLSA is to determine the applicable overtime threshold. For many employees, the overtime threshold is the standard 40-hour week. However, there exists a partial exemption from the wage and hour provisions of the FLSA for certain law enforcement employees. This exemption, which has become known as the "7(k)" exemption, is based upon Section 207(k) of the FLSA, which provides as follows:

"No public agency shall be deemed to have violated Subsection (a) with respect to the employment of any employee in fire protection activities or any employee in law enforcement activities (including security personnel in correction institutions) if —

"(1) In a work period of 28 consecutive days the employee receives for tours of duty which in the aggregate exceed 240 hours; (Effective January 1, 1976, 232 hours; effective January 1, 1977, 216 hours; effective January 1, 1978, 'exceed 216 hours' is changed to exceed the lesser (A) 216 hours, or (B) the average number of hours (as determined by the Secretary pursuant to Section 6 (c)(3) of the Fair Labor Standards Amendments of 1974) in tours of duty of employees engaged in such activities in work periods of 28 consecutive days in calendar year 1975 or

"(2) In the case of such an employee to whom a work period of at least seven but less than 28 days applies in his work period the employee receives for tours of duty which in the aggregate exceed a number of hours which bear the same ratio to the number of consecutive days in his work period as 240 hours (effective Jan. 1, 1976, 232 hours; effective Jan. 1, 1977, 216 hours; effective January 1, 1978, as 216 hours (or if lower, the number of hours referred to in clause (B) of paragraph (1) bears to 28 days) compensation at a rate not less than one and one-half times the regular rate at which he is employed."

Section 207(k) thus creates alternative work periods varying in length from seven to 28 days which can be used in place of the workweek as the basis of measurement of hours worked for law enforcement employees. The purpose behind the Section 207(k) exemption was described by one court as follows:

"In extending the coverage of the FLSA to employees engaged in fire protection activities or law enforcement activities, Congress was aware of the work schedules of these employees * * * and clearly recognized that some adjustment would have to be made in the usual rules for determining hours of work in their case. Thus Congress departed from the standard 'hours of work' concept and adopted an overtime standard keyed to the length of the 'tour of duty.' In addition, Congress also adopted a new work period concept which may be used instead of the usual workweek basis for determining overtime hours."[45]

Section 207(k) specifically authorized the Secretary of Labor to investigate the actual hours worked for employees in law enforcement activities, and to establish different maximum allowable hours worked than those specified in Section 207(k) based upon the findings of the investigation. In 1983, the Department of Labor issued a regulatory notice indicating that the maximum hours worked in a 28-day cycle for law enforcement officers would be 171 hours.[46] The following table lists the different alternative work periods now permissible for law enforcement employees under a Section 207(k) exemption:

SECTION 207(K) WORK PERIODS

Days In Work Period	Maximum Hours
7	43
8	49
9	55
10	61
11	67
12	73
13	79
14	86
15	92
16	98
17	104
18	110
19	116
20	122
21	128
22	134
23	141
24	147
25	153
26	159
27	165
28	171

The primary effect of establishing a Section 207(k) exemption is to allow a law enforcement employer to work its employees for longer periods of time than would be the case in a 40-hour workweek without paying the employees at time and one-half the regular rate. Since the 207(k) exemption is the fundamental equivalent of a 43-hour workweek, a law enforcement employer can maintain the traditional practice of conducting unpaid 15-minute briefing periods at the start of a work shift without paying any overtime compensation under the FLSA. In general, the employer must take some sort of affirmative action to "establish" the exemption, whether through the enactment of an ordinance, the promulgation of an employment policy, or other means.[47] It is the employer's burden to prove that it met the standards set by the Department of Labor to "establish" the Section 207(k) exemption.[48] The fact that an employer pays overtime to employees before it is legally required to do so does not deprive it of the Section 207(k) exemption.[49]

The 'Regular Rate Of Pay' Defined.

Once hours worked have been calculated and it has been determined that the officer is entitled to overtime, the last question to resolve is the officer's overtime rate. Many law enforcement employers, either through collective bargaining agreements, memoranda of understanding, or historical practices, have long considered an employee's overtime rate as being time and one-half the hourly rate assigned for the job classification in which the employee works. The FLSA, however, requires that the overtime rate be the product of time and one-half the employee's "regular rate," an amount which may be very different from the employee's hourly rate.

Under the FLSA, the first step in determining an employee's regular rate is to compute the employee's hourly rate. Where employees already work at a specified hourly rate (and the hourly rate is a true hourly rate and not a guise for salary), that wage is considered the regular rate. The hourly rate will be considered in the initial calculation of the employee's "regular rate." Most law enforcement officers, however, do not receive hourly rates of pay, but instead work on the basis of a wage that is computed on a weekly, monthly, or other basis. In such cases, the Department of Labor's FLSA regulations provide the following specific instructions as to how weekly and longer salaries are to be converted into an hourly wage:

> "If the employee is employed solely on a weekly salary basis, his regular hourly rate of pay, on which time and one-half must be paid, is computed by dividing the salary by the number of hours which the salary is intended to compensate. If an employee is hired at a salary of $182.70 for a 35-hour week, it is understood that this salary is compensation for a regular workweek of 35 hours, the employee's regular rate of pay is $182.70 divided by 35 hours, or $5.22/hour, and when he works overtime he is entitled to receive $5.22 for each of the first forty hours and $7.83 (one and one-half times $5.22) for each hour thereafter. If an employee is hired at a salary of $220.80 for a 40-hour week, his regular rate is $5.22."[50]

The FLSA does not define "regular rate" as merely the employee's salary. Rather, Section 207(e) of the FLSA specifically provides that the "regular rate" means "all remuneration for employment paid to, or on behalf of the employee." Prior to the application of the FLSA to state and local governments, many law enforcement agencies calculated the overtime rate solely on the basis of the employee's hourly rate. Certain other payments to the employee, including incentive plan payments, shift differentials, and premium pay, had traditionally been excluded from overtime calculations.

The application of the FLSA dramatically changed these practices. The following is a partial list of the types of remuneration which must be included in the regular rate for the purposes of calculating overtime rates:

- Shift differentials.

- Education incentive payments (but not tuition and book reimbursement payments).

- Payments for achieving certain levels of law enforcement certification (e.g., police officer standards and training certification).

- Longevity premiums.

- Hazardous duty pay.

- Specialty pay assignments (e.g., detective premiums).

- "Assignment" or "working out of classification" pay.[51]

While the FLSA does include in the calculation of the regular rate some items of compensation which have not historically been included by law enforcement employers and labor organizations in the calculation of an overtime rate, the FLSA also specifically excludes certain forms of remuneration from the calculation of the regular rate. The following is an abbreviated list of the exclusions from the regular rate contained in the Section 207(e) of the FLSA:

- Any gifts made by the employer to the employee, including Christmas bonuses. (However, Christmas bonuses which are "measured by or dependent on" hours worked, production, or efficiency, must be included in the calculation of "regular rate").

- Payments made for vacation time.

- Payments made for holiday time.

- Payments made to an employee when an employee is utilizing paid sick leave provided by the employer.

- Any expenses, including travel expenses "incurred by the employee in the furtherance of his employer's interests and properly reimbursable by the employer."

- Payments to retirement plans.

- Payments of health and other insurance premiums.

- Premium payments for hours worked on an overtime basis, on Saturdays, Sundays, holidays, or the employee's regular days of rest.

The FLSA And Collective Bargaining Agreements.

The FLSA merely sets the minimum requirements for overtime compensation which must be paid to employees – it does not forbid compensating employees more than the minimum levels specified in the FLSA. Accordingly, either local laws[52] or collective bargaining agreements containing provisions that are more generous to employees than the provisions of the FLSA are valid.[53] However, where a collective bargaining agreement calls for benefits which are less generous

The FLSA does not forbid compensating employees more than the minimum levels specified in the Act.

than the benefits provided by the FLSA, the collective bargaining agreement is invalid, and the provisions of the FLSA will take precedence over any such conflicting provisions in the agreement.[54]

These principles were explained at some length in *Wahl v. City of Wichita*, a case where police officers successfully claimed that they were owed compensation for unpaid meal periods. In the case, the Court rejected the employer's arguments that its negotiations with the officers' labor organization somehow immunized it from FLSA liability:

> "The defendant at several points stresses that the Memoranda of Agreement entered into by the defendant and the local branch of the Fraternal Order of Police does not mention the compensability of officers' meal periods. Moreover, the defendant emphasizes that the FOP never raised the issue of meal period compensability in the collective bargaining negotiations preceding the memoranda.

> "The defendant's argument is without merit. As the Court previously recognized in its rejection of the defendant's motion to dismiss, the rights guaranteed employees by the FLSA are not rights subject to contract. Instead, those rights are independent of, and superior to, contract arrangements between employer and employee. * * * As plaintiffs point out, if the provisions of a pay plan or collective bargaining agreement run counter to the FLSA, the provision is to be given no effect."[55]

Compensatory Time Off Under The FLSA.

When the FLSA was initially enacted, compensatory time off was not a legal form of compensation for overtime hours worked unless the compensatory time off was taken in the same pay period in which it was earned.[56] After the *Garcia* decision, both labor organizations and management representatives in the public sector petitioned Congress to amend the FLSA to allow some form of limited compensatory time off. In 1985, Congress enacted Section 207(o) of the FLSA which, for the first time, allows compensatory time off in lieu of cash compensation for overtime:

> "(1) Employees of a public agency which is a State, a political subdivision of a State, or an interstate governmental agency may receive, in accordance with this Subsection and in lieu of overtime compensation, compensatory time off at a rate not less than one and one-half hours for each hour of employment for which overtime compensation is required by this Section.

> "(2) A public agency may provide compensatory time under Paragraph (1) only —

> "(A) Pursuant to (i) applicable provisions of the collective

bargaining agreement, memorandum of understanding, or any other agreement between the public agency and representatives of such employees; or (ii) in the case of employees not covered by Subclause (i), an agreement or understanding arrived at between the employer and employee before the performance of the work; and

"(B) If the employee has not accrued compensatory time in excess of the limit applicable to the employee prescribed by Paragraph (3)."[57]

Even with Section 207(o), the FLSA remains biased in favor of cash compensation for overtime hours worked. Absent a collective bargaining agreement or local practice to the contrary, under no circumstances is an employee entitled to insist upon compensatory time off as compensation for overtime hours worked. Similarly, an employer cannot insist that an employee take compensatory time off in lieu of cash payment for overtime. Under Section 207(o)(2), the FLSA makes it quite clear that compensatory time off can be granted only pursuant either to applicable provisions of a collective bargaining agreement or other agreement between the public agency and representatives of the employees, or, where there is no representative for the employees, an agreement reached between the employer and the employee.[58]

The FLSA is similarly strict with regard to the conditions under which compensatory time off may be utilized. Under Section 207(o), an employee who has accrued compensatory time off "shall be permitted to use such time off" within a "reasonable period" after making the request. An agreement between a labor organization and an employer describing the terms under which compensatory time off is granted will likely define what a "reasonable period" of time is.[59] The employer may deny the request for compensatory time off only if to grant the time off would "unduly disrupt" the operations of the employer.

There is significant conflict in the courts as to the meaning of the phrases "reasonable period" and "unduly disrupt." One set of courts finds that the phrase "reasonable period" does not mean the advance notice an officer must give of the desire to use compensatory time off, but rather means only that an employer must allow the officer to use compensatory time off within a reasonable period of when the officer requested.[60] One court following this line of thought even held that an employer was complying with the FLSA so long as it granted the compensatory time off within one year of the date originally desired by the officer.[61] A second set of courts rejects this interpretation, and sides with the Department of Labor in finding that "reasonable period" refers to the amount of advance notice an officer must give in requesting compensatory time off.[62] These courts also agree with the Department of Labor that the fact that an employer may have to replace an employee using compensatory time off with another employee on an overtime basis is not a basis for denying the request for compensatory time off.[63] One court has upheld an employer's policy of requiring employees to use accrued compensatory time off before being allowed to take annual leave.[64]

The FLSA remains biased in favor of cash compensation for overtime hours worked.

Under Section 207(o), the maximum amount of compensatory time off which may be accrued by a law enforcement officer is 480 hours. For individuals employed in the public sector who do not qualify as law enforcement officers under the FLSA, the maximum accrual of compensatory time off is 240 hours. Upon termination of employment, an employee is entitled to receive compensation for all accrued but unused compensatory time off based upon the employee's then-current regular rate of pay.[65]

The 'Prompt Pay' Requirements Of The FLSA.

Courts have long construed the FLSA to include a requirement for the prompt payment of wages.[66] The Department of Labor has ruled that "compensation to employees under the FLSA for a particular workweek must be paid to the employee on the regular payday for the period in which such workweek ends."[67] One court has held that the FLSA's prompt payment requirement was violated when the State of California paid its employees two weeks late because of a budgetary impasse in the state legislature.[68] The FLSA's requirement for prompt payment of wages is not violated when the employer changes its payroll system, so long as the change is made for legitimate business purposes and does not result in an unreasonably long delay in payment.[69]

The Anti-Retaliation Provisions Of The FLSA.

Section 215(a)(3) of the FLSA makes it unlawful for any person "to discharge or in any other manner discriminate against any employee because such employee has filed any complaint or instituted or caused to be instituted any proceeding under or related to the FLSA."[70] Under Section 215(a)(3), an adverse employment action violates the FLSA's anti-retaliation provision if it would not have occurred "but for" the employer's retaliatory intent.[71] The employer's retaliatory intent can be proved either by direct or circumstantial evidence.[72]

Enforcement Of The FLSA.

Both individual employees and the Department of Labor have the right to bring lawsuits to enforce the FLSA. The usual statute of limitations in FLSA cases is two years; if it can be proven that the employer's violation is willful, the statute of limitations is extended to three years.

An employee who successfully brings an FLSA lawsuit is entitled to receive all overtime pay due. Unless the employer can show that it was acting both reasonably and in good faith, the employee is also entitled to receive "liquidated damages" equivalent to the amount of back pay due.[73] An employer must also pay the attorney fees of an employee who successfully brings an FLSA lawsuit.[74] Punitive damages and damages for emotional distress are not recoverable under the FLSA.[75]

NOTES

[1] 29 U.S.C. §207(a).

[2] *Walling v. Helmerich and Payne, Inc.,* 323 U.S. 37 (1944).

[3] *Walling v. Peave-Wilson Lumber Co.,* 49 F. Supp. 846 (D. La. 1943).

[4] *See* 80 Stat. 831 (1966).

[5] *See* 88 Stat. 58-60; Title 29, §203 (E)(X), United States Code.

[6] *See Miller v. Borough of Riegelsville,* 131 F.R.D. 90 (E.D. Pa. 1990)(discusses five-employee threshold).

[7] *Garcia v. San Antonio Metropolitan Transit Authority,* 469 U.S. 528 (1985). The *Garcia* decision resolved a conflict between prior Supreme Court decisions on the constitutionality of the extension of the FLSA to local governmental bodies. *See National League of Cities v. Usery,* 426 U.S. 833 (1976)(holds extension of FLSA to state and local governments unconstitutional); *Maryland v. Wirtz,* 392 U.S. 183 (1968)(holds extension of FLSA to schools and hospitals constitutional). Courts refused to apply the *Garcia* case retroactively. *E.g., Brooks v. Lincolnwood,* 620 F. Supp. 24 (N.D. Ill. 1985). Since *Garcia,* courts have repeatedly rejected arguments that Congress did not have the authority to extend the FLSA to local governmental bodies such as cities and counties. *Fraternal Order of Police, Lodge No. 3 v. Baltimore City Police Dept.,* 164 F.3d 624 (4th Cir. 1998).

[8] Title 29, §785.11, Code of Federal Regulations.

[9] Title 29, §785.11, Code of Federal Regulations. *See Bailey v. County of Georgetown,* 94 F.3d 152 (4th Cir. 1996).

[10] Title 29 §785.13, Code of Federal Regulations. *See also* Aitchison, *The FLSA – A User's Manual,* 90 (Labor Relations Information System)(4th Ed. 2004).

[11] Title 29, §553.14, Code of Federal Regulations. *See Local 889, AFSCME v. State of Louisiana,* 145 F.3d 280 (5th Cir. 1998).

[12] Title 29, §785.18, Code of Federal Regulations.

[13] Title 29, §785.19, Code of Federal Regulations. *See Marshall v. Valhalla Inn,* 590 F.2d 306 (9th Cir. 1979).

[14] Title 29, §785.19, Code of Federal Regulations.

[15] *Roy v. County of Lexington, South Carolina,* 141 F.3d 533 (4th Cir. 1998); *Leahy v. City of Chicago,* 96 F.3d 228 (7th Cir. 1996); *Houser v. North Little Rock Police Dept.,* 6 F.3d 531 (8th Cir. 1993); *Armitage v. City of Emporia,* 982 F.2d 430 (10th Cir. 1992); *Police Association of the City of Kenner v. City of Kenner, La.,* 1999 WL 212717 (E.D. La. 1999); *Arrington v. City of Macon,* 986 F. Supp. 1474 (M.D. Ga. 1997); *McGrath v. City of Philadelphia,* 864 F. Supp. 466 (E.D. Pa. 1994); *Albee v. Bartlett,* 861 F. Supp. 318 (D. Kan. 1993).

[16] *Abendschein v. Montgomery County, Md.,* 984 F. Supp. 356 (D. Md. 1997); *see* Title 29, §553.223 (b), Code of Federal Regulations.

[17] *Rushing v. Shelby County Government,* 8 F. Supp. 2d 737 (W.D. Tenn. 1997); *see* Title 29, §553.223 (b), Code of Federal Regulations. In two decisions proceeding under state wage and hour laws, courts have found that officers who were not materially relieved from duty during meal periods were entitled to compensation for the meal periods. *Madera Police Officers Assn. v. City of Madera,* 682 P.2d 1087 (Cal. 1984); *Weeks v. Chief of the Washington State Patrol,* 639 P.2d 732 (Wash. 1982). In another case, a court found that since the provisions of a collective

bargaining agreement called for unpaid meal periods, and since "reasonable restrictions as to the conduct of officers during in-shift meal periods not only enhance the respect and reputation of the Sheriff's Department as a whole but also of the individual deputies," no compensation was necessary for meal periods. *Atteberry v. Ritchie,* 756 P.2d 424 (Kan. 1988).

18 *Lamon v. City of Shawnee,* 754 F. Supp. 1518 (D. Kan. 1991); *Wahl v. City of Wichita,* 725 F. Supp. 1133 (D. Kan. 1989); *Nixon v. City of Junction City,* 707 F. Supp. 473 (D. Kan. 1988).

19 *IBP, Inc. v. Alvarez,* 546 U.S. 21 (2005).

20 *Bamonte v. City of Mesa,* 2008 WL 1746168 (D. Ariz. 2008); *Lemmon v. City of San Leandro,* 538 F. Supp. 2d 1200 (N.D. Cal. 2007); *Martin v. City of Richmond,* 504 F. Supp. 2d 766 (N.D. Cal. 2007); *Abbe v. City of San Diego,* 2007 WL 4146696 (S.D. Cal. 2007); *Maciel v. City of Los Angeles,* 542 F. Supp. 2d 1082 (C.D. Cal. 2008).

21 Title 29, §553.221(d), Code of Federal Regulations.

22 *Brock v. El Paso Nat. Gas Co.,* 826 F.2d 369 (5th Cir. 1987).

23 *Berry v. County of Sonoma,* 763 F. Supp. 1055 (N.D. Cal. 1991).

24 *Dornbos v. O'Grady,* 1990 WL 179711 (N.D. Ill. 1990).

25 *Fletcher v. City of New Orleans,* 3 WH Cases 2d 1453 (E.D. La. 1997).

26 *Ingram v. County of Bucks,* 144 F.3d 265 (3d Cir. 1998).

27 *See* Annotation, *Call or Waiting Time as Working Time Within the Minimum Wage and Overtime Provisions of the Fair Labor Standards Act,* 3 A.L.R. Fed. 675 (1970 & Supp. 1986).

28 *Paniagua v. City of Galveston,* 995 F.2d 1310 (5th Cir. 1993); *Bartholomew v. City of Burlington, Kansas,* 5 F. Supp. 2d 1161 (D. Kan. 1998); *Shepard v. City of Burlington,* 4 WH Cases 2d 1149 (D. Kan. 1998); *Ingram v. County of Bucks,* 3 WH Cases 2d 1611 (E.D. Pa. 1997); *Clay v. City of Winona,* 753 F. Supp. 624 (N.D. Miss. 1990).

29 *Allen v. United States,* 1 Cl. Ct. 649, *aff'd on other grounds,* 723 F.2d 69 (D.C. Cir. 1983).

30 *See also Moss v. United States,* 353 F.2d 746 (Ct. Cl. 1965); *Brennan v. Williams Investment Co.,* 390 F. Supp. 981 (W.D. Tenn. 1975).

31 *Renfro v. City of Emporia, Kansas,* 948 F.2d 1529 (10th Cir. 1991).

32 *Chelan County Deputy Sheriffs' Association v. Chelan County,* 745 P.2d 1 (Wash. 1987).

33 *Mayhew v. Wells,* 125 F.3d 216 (4th Cir. 1997); *Truslow v. Spotsylvania Co. Sheriff,* 1993 U.S. App. Lexis 11123 (6th Cir. 1993); *Letner v. City of Oliver Springs,* 545 F. Supp. 2d 717 (E.D. Tenn. 2008); *Baker v. Stone County, Missouri,* 41 F. Supp. 2d 965 (W.D. Mo. 1999); *Albanese v. Bergen County, New Jersey,* 991 F. Supp. 410 (D. N.J. 1997); *Thomas v. City of Hudson,* 3 WH Cases 2d 513 (N.D. N.Y. 1996); *Levering v. District of Columbia,* 869 F. Supp. 24 (D. D.C. 1994); *Nichols v. City of Chicago,* 789 F. Supp. 1438 (N.D. Ill. 1992).

34 *Bobo v. United States,* 136 F.3d 1465 (Fed. Cir. 1998); *Reich v. New York City Transit Authority,* 45 F.3d 646 (2d Cir. 1995); *Jerzak v. City of South Bend,* 996 F. Supp. 840 (N.D. 1998). A federal court in Chicago reached a contrary result, concluding that the employer benefited enough from the officers' activities during

the commute to work that the time spent commuting by canine officers should be included as hours worked under the FLSA. *Graham v. City of Chicago*, 828 F. Supp. 576 (N.D. Ill. 1993).

[35] *Dade County, Florida v. Alvarez*, 124 F.3d 1380 (11th Cir. 1997). *See* Opinion Letter of the Wage and Hour Administrator, Maria Echaveste (June 1, 1994).

[36] *Imada v. City of Hercules*, 138 F.3d 1294 (9th Cir. 1998).

[37] *See* Title 29, §785.36, Code of Federal Regulations.

[38] Title 29, §785.39, Code of Federal Regulations.

[39] Title 29, §785.39, Code of Federal Regulations.

[40] Under most collective bargaining agreements covering law enforcement officers, such paid leave is counted as hours worked in calculating overtime liability. Where a collective bargaining agreement has benefits greater than those found in the FLSA, the provisions of the collective bargaining agreement must be followed.

[41] *Albanese v. Bergen County, New Jersey*, 991 F. Supp. 410 (D. N.J. 1997); *Treece v. City of Little Rock, Arkansas*, 923 F. Supp. 1122 (E.D. Ark. 1996).

[42] *Karr v. City of Beaumont, Texas*, 950 F. Supp. 1317 (E.D. Tex. 1997).

[43] *Albanese v. Bergen County, New Jersey*, 991 F. Supp. 410 (D. N.J. 1997).

[44] *Banks v. City of Springfield*, 959 F. Supp. 972 (C.D. Ill. 1997).

[45] *Beebe v. United States,* 640 F.2d 1283 (Ct. Cl. 1981).

[46] The maximum hours allowable under the overtime thresholds created by the Section 207(k) exemption were later codified in Title 29, Section 553.230 (c), Code of Federal Regulations.

[47] *Freeman v. City of Mobile, Alabama*, 146 F.3d 1292 (11th Cir. 1998).

[48] *Adair v. City of Kirkland*, 185 F.3d 1055 (9th Cir. 1999).

[49] *Milner v. City of Hazelwood*, 165 F.3d 1222 (8th Cir. 1999); *Local 889, AFSCME v. State of Louisiana*, 145 F.3d 280 (5th Cir. 1998).

[50] §778.113 (a), Code of Federal Regulations.

[51] *Featsent v. City of Youngstown*, 70 F.3d 900 (6th Cir. 1995)(shift differential, education incentive, hazardous duty, and longevity payments must be included in the regular rate of pay); *Abbott v. United States*, 41 Fed.Cl. 553 (1998)(longevity must be included); *cf. Theisen v. City of Maple Grove*, 41 F. Supp. 2d 932 (D. Minn. 1999)(canine and longevity pay must be included; working out of classification pay need not be included).

[52] *Cranford v. City of Slidell*, 25 F. Supp. 2d 727 (E.D. La. 1998).

[53] *Walling v. Emery Wholesale Corp.*, 138 F.2d 518 (5th Cir. 1941).

[54] *Martino v. Michigan Window Cleaning Co.*, 327 U.S. 173 (1946); *Berry v. County of Sonoma,* 763 F. Supp. 1055 (N.D. Cal. 1991).

[55] *Wahl v. City of Wichita*, 725 F. Supp. 1133 (D. Kan. 1989).

[56] *Brennan v. New Jersey,* 364 F. Supp. 156 (D. N.J. 1973).

[57] Title 29, §207(o), United States Code.

[58] *Archer v. Sullivan County, Tennessee*, 129 F.3d 1263 (6th Cir. 1997).

[59] *Aiken v. City of Memphis, Tennessee*, 190 F.3d 753 (6th Cir. 1999).

[60] *Houston Police Officers' Union v. City of Houston, Tex.*, 330 F.3d 298 (5th Cir. 2003).

[61] *Mortensen v. County of Sacramento*, 368 F.3d 1082 (9th Cir. 2004).

[62] *Heitmann v. City of Chicago*, 2009 WL 764155 (7th Cir. 2009); *Beck v. City of Cleveland, Ohio*, 390 F.3d 912 (6th Cir. 2004); *DeBraska v. City of Milwaukee*, 131 F. Supp. 2d 1032 (E.D. Wis. 2000); *Canney v. Brookline*, 2000 WL 1612703 (D. Mass. 2000).

[63] Title 29, §553.25(d), Code of Federal Regulations.

[64] *Local 889, AFSCME v. State of Louisiana*, 145 F.3d 280 (5th Cir. 1998).

[65] *See* Title 29, §553.27(b), Code of Federal Regulations.

[66] *United States v. Klinghoffer Bros. Realty Corp.*, 285 F.2d 487 (2d Cir. 1960).

[67] *See* Department of Labor Opinion Letter No. 942 (Jan. 27, 1969).

[68] *Biggs v. Wilson*, 1 F.3d 1537 (9th Cir. 1993).

[69] *Rogers v. City of Troy, New York*, 148 F.3d 52 (2d Cir. 1998).

[70] 29 U.S.C. §215(a)(3).

[71] *Knickerbocker v. City of Stockton*, 81 F.3d 907 (9th Cir. 1996).

[72] *Hackney v. Arlington County Police Department,* 145 F.3d 1324 (4th Cir. 1998).

[73] *Joiner v. City of Macon*, 814 F.2d 1537 (11th Cir. 1987); *Lockwood v. Prince George's County, Maryland*, 58 F. Supp. 2d 651 (D. Md. 1999); *Braddock v. Madison County, Indiana,* 34 F. Supp. 2d 1098 (S.D. Ind. 1998); *Burgess v. Catawba County,* 805 F. Supp. 341 (W.D. N.C. 1992). Even if the employer was acting in good faith, the Court still retains the discretion to award liquidated damages. *Hayes v. McIntosh*, 604 F. Supp. 10 (N.D. Ind. 1994).

[74] *Treece v. City of Little Rock*, 141 F.3d 1170 (8th Cir. 1998).

[75] *Bolick v. Brevard County Sheriff's Department*, 937 F. Supp. 1560 (M.D. Fla. 1996).

CHAPTER 16

THE ENFORCEMENT OF OFFICERS' RIGHTS

The Choice Of Forums — Where Lawsuits Are Brought.

There are a variety of forums available to an officer whose rights have been violated. The officer could potentially file suit and pursue his case in state court, in federal court, or before an administrative agency. The choice of forum will generally depend upon the nature of the right which was violated.

If the right which was violated arises under state collective bargaining laws, one avenue for enforcement of the right may be through the state agency responsible for administering the collective bargaining law. In some states, courts hold that the exclusive jurisdiction over state collective bargaining law issues exists before such administrative agencies, and bar lawsuits in court on the same issues. In other states, the existence of a state agency administering collective bargaining laws does not preclude lawsuits in court on collective bargaining issues.

If the right that was violated arises under a collective bargaining agreement, usually the only avenue open to seek redress of the right is through the grievance procedure in a collective bargaining agreement. Grievance procedures, particularly those which end with binding arbitration, are usually considered a final and binding process, leaving no right to challenge in court the decision reached in the grievance procedure unless the decision is illegal or was fraudulently obtained.

If the right which was violated was established by civil service rules, the exclusive forum for the redress of the right is usually the civil service commission or board which established the rules. Similarly, if the underlying right was established by state statute or administrative rule, the law or rule giving rise to the right will usually dictate where a challenge to an employer's decision can be filed.

The choice of forums becomes more complicated when an officer is alleging a violation of a federal statute or a provision of the United States Constitution. At a minimum, the officer has the option to proceed in such claims in federal court, though in some discrimination cases the officer may be required to exhaust administrative remedies through the Equal Employment Opportunity Commission.[1] Claims that a state, city, or county agency has violated a federal constitutional right usually can also proceed in state court; whereas claims that the federal government has violated a constitutional right can only proceed in federal court.

One significant development in the last five years has been a shift in where federal constitutional claims against local law enforcement agencies have been litigated by police officers. As the federal courts have grown more and more conservative, officers are no longer as likely to consider federal court as the first forum of choice for vindication of a violated constitutional right. Many more cases challenging the violation of federal constitutional rights are being filed in state court than ever before, particularly in states where the courts are considered to be more liberal in their interpretation of the Constitution than the federal courts.

As federal courts have grown more and more conservative, officers are no longer as likely to consider federal court as the first forum of choice for vindication of a violated constitutional right.

Lawsuits For Violation Of Federal Constitutional Rights.

Lawsuits for money damages for violation of an officer's federal constitutional rights are controlled by a complicated set of rules. One set of rules deals with the immunity of public officials from damage lawsuits. The other set concerns whether an employer can be held liable for damages for the conduct of its officers.

Lawsuits Against Government Officials And Public Agencies; Qualified And Absolute Immunity.

Government officials who are performing discretionary functions are cloaked with a "qualified immunity" from liability, so long as their actions "could reasonably have been thought consistent with the rights they are alleged to have violated."[2] Whether a public official is protected by qualified immunity generally turns on the "objective legal reasonableness" of the official's actions viewed in light of the legal rules that were "clearly established" at the time the actions were taken.[3] Only if the public official acts in a fashion which violates clearly established legal rules will the official lose the qualified immunity from damages. As put by one court, "This standard shields all government officials except those who are either plainly incompetent or who knowingly violate the law."[4] Public officials are only potentially individually liable for illegal actions in which they personally participated.[5]

Certain public officials have an even greater amount of immunity from lawsuits. If a public official acts in a "quasi-judicial" role – acting as a disciplinary board member or in presenting the employer's case to a disciplinary board – the official has absolute immunity from any lawsuits arising out of his conduct before the board.[6]

Public agencies, on the other hand, are not entitled to qualified immunity.[7] However, public agencies can only be held liable for money damages for the violation of the federal constitutional rights of their officers if the violation is a result of an official policy or custom.[8] The employer's policy or custom "must be the moving force of the constitutional violation in order to establish the liability of a governmental body under Section 1983."[9] To show that an employer had a policy or custom which resulted in the violation of constitutional rights, an officer may rely on the actions or decisions of the supervisor who had the final decision-making authority on the issue in question.[10]

Often, it is difficult to determine who the final policymaker is for purposes of a particular employment decision. In one case, a terminated deputy sheriff sued the County that formerly employed him, contending that the sheriff acted as a policymaker when he discharged the deputy. A court disagreed, finding the existence of a civil service board that could reverse the sheriff's decision meant the sheriff was not a policymaker. Though the deputy argued that the civil service

> Government officials who are performing discretionary functions are cloaked with a "qualified immunity" from liability, so long as their actions "could reasonably have been thought consistent with the rights they are alleged to have violated."

system provided only a "sham remedy" in that the board had only overturned a sheriff's termination decision once in 15 years, the Court held that it could not "conclude that this low reversal rate renders the Board's review meaningless."[11] Other cases stand for the same proposition that civil service boards or police commissioners as well as city councils, if vested with final decision-making authority, are the policymakers for disciplinary purposes, and not police chiefs and sheriffs.[12]

A single decision by the final decision-maker may be sufficient to establish that the public employer has a policy that infringes on the employee's constitutional rights.[13] Additionally, if the decision which violates an officer's rights is not made by the final decision-maker but is later ratified by the employer, the necessary "policy or custom" may exist.[14] Also, if the final decision-maker has knowledge that there is a policy or custom of rights deprivation in the agency and permits the policy or custom to continue, the agency may be liable for monetary damages.[15]

A suit against the public agency must be brought against the employer itself, not an individual division of the employer. For example, where a suit against a city would be proper, a suit against the city's police department would ordinarily not be allowed.[16]

Tying these immunity principles together, it is possible for an employer to have violated the constitutional rights of an officer, and yet for the officer to be unable to recover against anyone. For example, a court concluded that the Philadelphia Housing Authority's suspension of an officer violated his rights to procedural due process. However, the Court found a lack of any "policy or custom" that would impose liability on the Authority, and also concluded that the supervisors who violated the officer's due process rights did not "unreasonably" believe that their actions violated the Constitution.[17]

Deferral To Arbitration.

There are occasions where the officer is seeking to enforce an underlying right that arises under not only a federal or state statute or constitutional provision, but also under the terms of a collective bargaining agreement. If that is the case, an employer will often argue that the employee is required to proceed under the contract either before or perhaps in lieu of a lawsuit. A recent Supreme Court decision has thrown a good deal of uncertainty into the area.

Previously, it had been widely thought that an employee could not be compelled to arbitrate claims for violation of federal statutory or constitutional rights. However, in *14 Penn Plaza, L.L.C. v. Pyett,* the Supreme Court held that a labor contract could compel employees to arbitrate claimed violations of the Age Discrimination In Employment Act, provided the underlying contract explicitly contained such a requirement. While it can be safely predicted that the *14 Penn Plaza* decision will apply to claims under Title VII of the Civil Rights Act, it is an open question on whether it will apply to remedial statutes such as the FLSA or to constitutional rights.[18] At present, the law is that the right to bring a lawsuit under the Fair Labor Standards Act simply cannot be waived by a labor contract.[19]

Where an employee is claiming in court that the employer's disciplinary procedures do not comport with due process, the employee must show that he tried to use whatever procedures were in fact available under the employer's system unless those procedures were obviously inadequate.[20]

Damages In Federal Civil Rights Cases.

Officers who have suffered a loss of wages owing to the violation of their constitutional or civil rights are usually entitled to back pay; if discharged from employment, they are usually entitled to reinstatement as well.[21] As phrased by one court in a freedom of speech case, the goal of a court is "to restore the plaintiff, as nearly as possible, to the economic position he would have been in, absent the prohibited discrimination."[22] The right to back pay is so strong that it even survives the wrongly-terminated officer's death and is payable to the officer's estate.[23] While most courts are in agreement on these basic principles, they are deeply divided over how to apply the principles to particular cases.

The goal of a court is "to restore the plaintiff, as nearly as possible, to the economic position he would have been in, absent the prohibited discrimination."

For example, courts are split over the issue of whether back wages should be offset by any interim earnings received by the officer during the period of time the officer was discharged. Many courts believe that to allow such an offset is tantamount to giving partial approval to the employer's violation of the officer's rights.[24] Other courts have ruled that an offset for interim earnings is necessary lest the officer receive a "windfall" from the litigation.[25] Though the matter is not free from controversy, most courts rule that an officer is not entitled to recover for lost overtime opportunities.[26] Furthermore, the right to recover either pre-judgment and/or post-judgment interest in addition to other amounts owed may depend upon the wording of the statute giving rise to the lawsuit.[27]

An unusual feature of some constitutional rights damage awards is "front pay," designed to compensate an officer for the loss of future earnings.[28] In cases where the officer is not being reinstated to employment, a court has the discretion to award front pay representing potential wages lost for a period of time extending as far as the officer's probable retirement date.[29] To adjust for the fact that there is always uncertainty as to whether the individual would have remained an officer in the future, courts take into account the discharged officer's life expectancy as well as the duty to mitigate damages by finding other work.[30]

Even where damages are awarded to compensate an officer for the loss of wages, damages for violations of constitutional rights are generally not subject to federal income tax.[31] The tax-free nature of the award is often taken into account in the assessment of the level of damages to be awarded.

In cases where an employer has violated an officer's procedural due process rights by not granting the officer a pre-termination hearing, courts will customarily award back pay up until the time when the new "curative" due process hearing is given.[32] Officers who successfully claim violations of procedural due process, and perhaps other constitutional rights, are entitled at least to nominal damages, which usually do not exceed $1.00. The grant of $1.00 in damages obviously is not intended to punish the violator or compensate the wronged officer. Instead, an award of nominal damages establishes the prevailing party for purposes of appeal and the amount of attorney fees. Such officers may recover compensatory damages as well if they are able to prove actual mental and emotional distress caused by the denial of procedural due process.[33]

Injunctions And Equitable Relief In Federal Civil Rights Cases.

In addition to the award of damages, courts have the authority to impose "equitable relief" in civil rights cases. Equitable relief often involves the use of the power of the court to order a governmental agency to do or not to do a particular act. The scope of the equitable relief granted by a court should be no wider than necessary to remedy the constitutional violation.[34]

The most common form of equitable relief is an injunction. In cases where an officer is seeking an injunction prohibiting the employer from violating the officer's constitutional rights in the future, the officer must show: (1) That the employer has violated the officer's constitutional rights in the past; (2) that it is likely that the officer will have encounters with the employer again; and (3) that, in the future encounters, the employer will again violate the constitutional rights of the officer.[35] In cases where the officer is alleging that the employer has violated First Amendment freedom of speech rights, the officer has a lesser burden of proving that the employer will violate his or her constitutional rights in the future.

Simply because an employer promises that it will not engage in the prohibited conduct in the future is not a basis to deny a request for an injunction. As noted by one court in a case where a union president was seeking an injunction against the Sheriff of Cook County, Illinois, "protestations or repentance and reform timed to anticipate or blunt the force of a lawsuit offer insufficient assurance that the practice sought to be enjoined will not be repeated."[36]

An injunction is not the only form of equitable relief available to an officer whose constitutional rights have been violated. In appropriate cases, a court can order that an officer be reinstated to his former position, hired, or promoted,[37] or that certain materials be removed from the officer's personnel files.[38]

The amount of hours expended by the attorney as well as the attorney's hourly rate must be appropriate under the circumstances of the case.

Attorney Fees In Federal Civil Rights Cases.

A successful plaintiff in a civil rights case is entitled to recover reasonable attorney fees.[39] The amount of hours expended by the attorney as well as the attorney's hourly rate must be appropriate under the circumstances of the case. Once the amount of attorney fees is established, the amount becomes known as the "lodestar," which can be increased in the court's discretion by a "multiplier." Factors which can persuade a court to increase the lodestar amount include the difficulty of the case, the financial risk to the attorney in taking the case, and whether the officer would have faced substantial difficulties in finding another attorney to handle the case.[40] Conversely, if a federal civil rights action so clearly lacks merit that a court deems the suit frivolous, the officer bringing the suit may be liable to pay the employer's attorney fees.[41]

Claims Under State Laws.

Increasingly, law enforcement officers have turned to state rather than federal courts, and to state statutes and constitutional provisions rather than their federal analogues, to assert their rights. While state litigation proceeds in much the same manner as federal lawsuits, most state claims are subject to the requirements of state governmental claims laws. These laws may require employees to give notice of the intent to sue within a relatively short period of time – often six months after the complained-of conduct. A failure to comply with a state governmental claims notice requirement will typically result in the dismissal of the lawsuit.[42]

Res Judicata And Collateral Estoppel – When Claims Have Already Been Litigated Somewhere Else.

Two related legal doctrines bar the re-litigation of claims that have already been fully litigated in another forum. The principle of *res judicata*, or as it is often called "claim preclusion," means that the entire legal claim of the employee has previously been litigated.[43] The principle of collateral estoppel, or as it is often called "issue preclusion," means that certain facts have previously been litigated.[44] If either doctrine applies, the earlier judgment will be given what is called "preclusive effect," meaning it will either entirely prevent or substantially limit the subsequent litigation. The purpose behind the doctrines is to shield parties from the burden of re-litigating claims with the same parties and to protect the courts from inefficiency and confusion that re-litigation fosters.[45] For either doctrine to apply, the earlier legal proceedings must be "final," a term that usually means that all possibility of appeals have been exhausted.[46]

Under these principles, a federal court must give to a state court judgment the same preclusive effect as would be given that judgment under the law of the state in which the judgment was rendered.[47] And, though there are some exceptions, the usual rule is that a federal court need not give preclusive effect to arbitrations conducted under collective bargaining agreements,[48] though state courts are more inclined to do so.[49]

> The principle of *res judicata* means that the entire legal claim of the employee has previously been litigated. The principle of collateral estoppel means that certain facts have previously been litigated.

NOTES

[1] *Bennett v. Chatham County Sheriff's Dept.*, 2008 WL 628908 (S.D. Ga. 2008); *Semsroth v. City of Wichita*, 2007 WL 1246223 (D. Kan. 2007). There is no requirement that an officer exhaust the employer's internal grievance procedures prior to filing a civil rights lawsuit. *Wilbur v. Harris*, 53 F.3d 542 (2d Cir. 1995).

[2] *Anderson v. Creighton*, 483 U.S. 635 (1987).

[3] *Harlow v. Fitzgerald*, 457 U.S. 800 (1982).

[4] *Scruggs v. Josephine County Sheriff's Dept.*, 2008 WL 608581 (D. Or. 2008).

[5] *Higgins v. City of Johnstown, New York*, 20 F. Supp. 2d 422 (N.D. N.Y. 1998).

[6] *Balcerzak v. City of Milwaukee*, 980 F. Supp. 983 (E.D. Wis. 1997).

[7] *Kentucky Bureau of State Police v. Graham*, 473 U.S. 159 (1985).

[8] *Monell v. Department of Social Services of the City of New York*, 436 U.S. 658 (1978); *Graning v. Sherburne County*, 172 F.3d 611 (8th Cir. 1999).

[9] *Monell v. Department of Social Servs. of City of New York*, 436 U.S. 658 (1978); *see Porter v. City of Columbus*, 2008 WL 202891 (S.D. Ohio 2008).

[10] *City of St. Louis v. Praprotnik*, 485 U.S. 112 (1988).

[11] *Maschmeier v. Scott*, 269 Fed.Appx. 941 (11th Cir. 2008).

[12] *Dempsey v. City of Baldwin*, 143 Fed.Appx. 976 (10th Cir. 2005); *Leath v. Hansell*, 2008 WL 151869 (M.D. Fla. 2008); *Dempsey v. City of Baldwin City, Kan.*, 333 F. Supp. 2d 1055 (D. Kan. 2004).

[13] *Pembauer v. City of Cincinnati*, 475 U.S. 469 (1986).

[14] *City of St. Louis v. Praprotnik*, 485 U.S. 112 (1988).

[15] *Los Angeles Police Protective League v. Gates*, 907 F.2d 879 (9th Cir. 1990).

[16] *Meek v. Springfield Police Department*, 990 F. Supp. 598 (C.D. Ill. 1998).

[17] *Solomon v. Philadelphia Housing Authority*, 143 Fed.Appx. 447 (3d Cir. 2005).

[18] *14 Penn Plaza, L.L.C. v. Pyett*, 129 S.Ct. 1456 (2009).

[19] *Barrentine v. Arkansas-Best Freight Sys.*, 450 U.S. 728 (1981); *Falzo v. County of Essex*, 2008 WL 2064811 (D. N.J. 2008).

[20] *Garzella v. Borough of Dunmore*, 280 Fed.Appx. 169 (3d Cir. 2008); *Barrows v. City of Fort Smith, Ark.*, 2008 WL 2026088 (W.D. Ark. 2008); *Staveley v. City of Lowell*, 882 N.E.2d 362 (Mass. App. 2008).

[21] *Arrington v. City of Macon*, 986 F. Supp. 1474 (M.D. Ga. 1997).

[22] *Hubbard v. Administrator, Environmental Protection Agency*, 735 F. Supp. 435 (D. D.C. 1990).

[23] *Jones v. Board of Fire and Police Commissioners of the Village of Mundelein*, 562 N.E.2d 1175 (Ill. App. 1990).

[24] *Della Vecchia v. Town of North Hempstead*, 616 N.Y.S.2d 55 (A.D. 1994).

[25] *Walck v. City of Albuquerque*, 875 P.2d 407 (N.M. App. 1994). In courts allowing an interim earnings offset, the employer must prove that the employee could have been working during the period of time the employee was discharged. *State ex rel. Butterbaugh v. Ross County Board of Commissioners*, 608 N.E.2d 778 (Ohio App. 1992).

[26] *Kraft v. Police Commissioner of Boston*, 629 N.E.2d 995 (Mass. 1994);

Trotman v. Brown, 593 N.Y.S.2d 788 (A.D. 1993); *Kaminsky v. Board of Fire and Police Commissioners of Wheeling*, 559 N.E.2d 87 (Ill. App. 1990).

[27] *Todino v. Town of Wellfleet*, 845 N.E.2d 1178 (Mass. App. 2006); *Kaminsky v. Board of Fire and Police Commissioners of Wheeling*, 559 N.E.2d 87 (Ill. App. 1990).

[28] *Wulf v. City of Wichita*, 883 F.2d 842 (10th Cir. 1989).

[29] *Luca v. County of Nassau*, 2008 WL 2435569 (E.D. N.Y. 2008).

[30] *Haskins v. City of Boaz*, 822 F.2d 1014 (11th Cir. 1987). *See generally EEOC v. Prudential Fed. Sav. and Loan Association*, 763 F.2d 1166 (10th Cir. 1985).

[31] *Bent v. Commissioner of Internal Revenue*, 835 F.2d 67 (3d Cir. 1987).

[32] *Storrs v. Municipality of Anchorage*, 721 P.2d 1146 (Alaska 1986).

[33] *Carey v. Piphus*, 435 U.S. 247 (1978).

[34] *Spagnola v. Mathis*, 859 F.2d 223 (D.C. Cir. 1988).

[35] *City of Los Angeles v. Lyons*, 461 U.S. 95 (1983).

[36] *Flood v. O'Grady*, 748 F. Supp. 595 (N.D. Ill. 1990).

[37] *O'Sullivan v. City of Chicago*, 540 F. Supp. 2d 981 (N.D. Ill. 2008)(promotion to captain ordered in discrimination case).

[38] *Chastain v. Kelley*, 510 F.2d 1232 (D.C. Cir. 1975).

[39] *County of Dallas v. Wiland*, 124 S.W.3d 390 (Tex. App. 2003).

[40] *Wulf v. City of Wichita*, 883 F.2d 842 (10th Cir. 1989)(discussion of general principles of increasing lodestar amount in freedom of speech cases); *Fahdl v. City and County of San Francisco*, 859 F.2d 649 (9th Cir. 1988)(case rejected by 30 lawyers; multiplier of 2.0 applied to attorney fees). *See generally Hensley v. Eckerhart*, 461 U.S. 424 (1983).

[41] *Kennedy v. McCarty*, 803 F. Supp. 1470 (S.D. Ind. 1992)(award of $17,629.50 in attorney fees against officer who unsuccessfully challenged termination).

[42] *Moore v. Hudson County Correctional Facility*, 2008 WL 877961 (D. N.J. 2008); *Clanton v. DeSoto County Sheriff's Dept.*, 963 So.2d 560 (Miss. App. 2007).

[43] *Blonder Tongue Laboratories v. Univ. of Ill. Found.*, 402 U.S. 313 (1971).

[44] *Ashe v. Swenson*, 397 U.S. 436 (1970).

[45] *Hillgartner v. Port Authority of Allegheny County*, 936 A.2d 131(Pa.Cmwlth. 2007).

[46] *Sosa v. DirecTV*, 437 F.3d 923 (9th Cir. 2006).

[47] *Migra v. Warren City School Dist. Bd. of Ed.*, 465 U.S. 75 (1984).

[48] *McDonald v. City of West Branch*, 466 U.S. 284 (1984); *Giglio v. Derman*, 560 F. Supp. 2d 163 (D. Conn. 2008).

[49] *Wilson v. City of Tulsa*, 91 P.3d 673 (Okla. App. 2004).

INDEX

Symbols

G

H

I

P